FEMINISM CONFRONTS HOMO ECONOMICUS

FEMINISM CONFRONTS HOMO ECONOMICUS

Gender, Law, and Society

EDITED BY

Martha Albertson Fineman
and Terence Dougherty

CORNELL UNIVERSITY PRESS   ITHACA AND LONDON

Cornell University Press gratefully acknowledges receipt of a subvention from the
School of Law, Emory University, which helped in the publication of this book.

First published 2005 by Cornell University Press
First printing, Cornell Paperbacks, 2005

Printed in the United States of America

Library of Congress Cataloging-in-Publication Data

Feminism confronts homo economicus : gender, law, and society / edited by Martha
  Albertson Fineman and Terence Dougherty.
       p. cm.
   Includes bibliographical references and index.
   ISBN 0-8014-4311-3 (cloth : alk. paper) -- ISBN 0-8014-8941-5 (pbk. : alk. paper)
   1. Feminist jurisprudence.   2. Sociological jurisprudence.   3. Law and economics.
4. Economic man.   5. Feminist economics.   6. Neoclassical school of economics.
I. Fineman, Martha.   II. Dougherty, Terence.
   K349.F453 2005
   340'.11--dc22

                                                              2004023905

Cloth printing   10 9 8 7 6 5 4 3 2 1

Paperback printing   10 9 8 7 6 5 4 3 2 1

CONTENTS

FEMINISM CONFRONTS HOMO ECONOMICUS

Introduction

Feminism Confronts *Homo Economicus*

Since the late 1960s and with ever-increasing momentum, law has come under the influence of economic theory and methodology. Although considered a specific school of thought within American legal jurisprudence, Law and Economics and the neoclassical economic model on which it is based have permeated legal analysis in a wide range of areas considered useful in the development of rules of universal application for law and policy making.

In response to the increasingly accepted notion that economic principles are and should be the primary lens through which legal and policy decisions are made, this volume was conceived to bring together essays that are critical of the Law and Economics school of thought as well as of the neoclassical economic model more generally. The essays collected in this volume present a variety of legal and nonlegal perspectives, from a variety of disciplines. All the authors are generally concerned with the implications of the wholesale incorporation of an economic model into law and policymaking. Although there are many avenues through which one can form a critique of Law and Economics and neoclassical economics, the essays in this volume primarily bring feminist perspectives to bear on *homo economicus,* the "economic man" who is the subject of neoclassical economics, either rejecting economic analysis within the law altogether or, alternatively, using economic analysis in a manner that challenges the gendered power dynamic within the law.

The interaction between feminism and economics within the legal academy over the past several decades is an interesting historical phenomenon. Like feminism, economics is a relatively new academic discipline. Economics has had a much more formal recognition and acceptance in law, however. It has become a framework for legal analysis to be used not just to provide supplementary perspectives on areas of legal inquiry but also to completely rethink core legal subjects. Tort law, contract law, and administrative law are taught today in some law schools or by some law professors exclusively through the lens of economics.

The essays in this volume confront the inroads that economics has made into the legal academy and further address the broader social and political context in which the Law and Economics school of thought has developed. In the same way that legal feminism is a constitutive part of a broader academic, social, and political movement, Law and Economics is also fundamentally formed by and formative of a broader political agenda. But unlike legal feminism, which seeks to draw attention to and suggest alternate visions for articulating power within society, Law and Economics uses principles of neoclassical economics to develop laws and social policies that maintain if not bolster current allocations of power. The essays in this volume are thus concerned with the place of economic analysis within a broader political context that seeks to use economic principles and rhetoric—in addition to law—to further and to justify certain conservative political ends.

This introduction seeks to provide a broad framework for the essays collected in this volume. After providing a description of feminism methodology and analysis as it has developed within the legal academy, we describe Law and Economics and the neoclassical economic tradition of which it is a part.

Feminist Legal Theory

Feminism as a political theory and an academic discipline has flourished to the extent that the term *feminism* has become overdetermined. There are so many different approaches, emphases, and objectives within feminism that it is difficult to speak of it as a single theory or methodology. Even describing women's and men's experiences and desires one runs the risk of being labeled an essentialist. Nonetheless, it is possible to make some generalizations about what feminism is as a mode of inquiry. As an intellectual mode of inquiry, feminism articulates a theory that individuals lead gendered lives and challenges assertions and assumptions of gender neutrality and objectivity within academic disciplines.

One important characteristic of feminist inroads into the academy is that feminism foregrounds the integration of practice and theory. As noted historian Linda Gordon has stated, feminism is "an analysis of women's subordination for the purpose of figuring out how to change it."[1] As a result of this focus within feminist theory on the practical aspects of dismantling societal subordination, many feminists have gravitated toward law and law reform as a primary focus of study and action. Feminism has had many successes in its engagement with the law and, along with other twentieth-century methodologies such as psychology, has had a definite impact on law over the past several decades. This impact is apparent not only in legal scholarship but also in doctrine employed by courts and developed by legislative bodies. The fundamental principles of discrimination and criminal law, for example, have been scrutinized and occasionally revised in light of feminist insights and arguments.

Many of the women who were part of the initial influx of women into law schools in the 1970s were explicitly interested in a feminist political agenda.

They came to law schools with the mantra that "the personal is the political" ringing resolutely in their ears.[2] They were interested in reform and the role of law in the project of engineering a society that fostered greater equality between men and women. These early feminists were optimistic about using law to attain equality with men.

In determining how best to achieve such a goal, the majority of early feminist legal theorists adopted a discrimination model for looking at the issue of gender. Their objective was to use the law to challenge biased treatment and develop laws that allowed women equal opportunities with men. Because of their determined focus on equality between men and women, these women believed that any recognition of difference between men and women within the law and any argument for "special treatment" for women within the law would operate to the disadvantage of women. These feminists focused their attention on challenging discriminatory laws that denied women full participation in public institutions, such as the jury system (in which they were successful) and the military (in which they were unsuccessful). They challenged financial and market institutions' different treatment of women and men, as in, for example, the insurance industry's differential treatment, and litigated under Title 7 of the Civil Rights Act of 1964 to enforce equal treatment for men and women in employment. Many of the early cases brought by these lawyers were strategically brought on behalf of men who had been excluded from women's institutions or who complained about favored treatment for women. The legal challenges of these "equality feminists" have had a profound impact on the participation of women in many formerly all male arenas within society.

Other feminist scholars, by contrast, have sought to develop and build on the concept of gender difference. Although these feminists differ in their articulation of the nature of such difference (be it, for example, cultural, biological, or resulting from gendered structures of power), "difference feminists" have taken the notion that women and men are fundamentally different as a basis for demanding that the law be understood as having been developed by and for institutional male dominance; as such, it should be expanded in part and reconstructed in part in order to reflect and sustain women's specific experiences. Unlike the discrimination or equality model, difference feminism is uninterested in using the law to aid women in participating in "male" institutions and structures as currently constructed.

The difference model of legal feminism has been effective in transforming the way we think about many areas of the law. For example, in the area of divorce law, by pointing out the valuable role that women as homemakers and mothers have played in the family economy, difference feminists have successfully challenged in many states the rules governing the division of property upon the dissolution of marriage. Further, the focus of difference feminists on the subordination of women led to the development of new legal paradigms within criminal and tort law, including concepts such as sexual harassment and the battered woman syndrome. In these two developments, courts began to recognize that a woman's reactions to certain kinds of flirtation in the workplace or to repeated threats and acts of violence at home might not be the same as those of the "reasonable man," which, before the efforts of difference feminists, was the primary standard through which tort and criminal legal actions were judged.

Both equality feminism and difference feminism have had a significant impact on the law. Yet it is interesting to consider in which specific areas of the law each has had its impact. As difference and equality feminists argued their causes on all fronts, each feminist paradigm was finding its successes on different sides of the public–private divide that has characterized legal jurisprudence in the United States. For example, sexuality, "domestic" violence, and family law are areas that historically and stereotypically have been considered to be of special concern to women. Although rape and sexual harassment are "public" events in that they are the focus of legal regulation and policy, the law's evident unease in dealing with these two crimes is the result of the fact that we view them as intrinsically related to activities commonly understood to be "private" activities, such as consensual sex and flirtatious seduction. It is in these areas that difference feminism has had its greatest successes within the law. By contrast, in legal arenas outside the private sphere of home, family, and sexuality, equality feminism has had its greatest successes. For feminists, the problem with this split dynamic is twofold. First, the focus on gender subordination solely within private spheres gives women a legal presence solely within such a sphere, thus casting women exclusively within a traditional role and not as public citizens. Further, such a role is one that is defined within the law in the context of victimhood. Second, although aiding women in attaining positions of power in the public sphere (the process on which equality feminists have focused their attention) is important, such efforts do not obviate a need for an analysis of structures of power and structural subordination, both gendered and otherwise, within this public sphere.

The deconstruction of the traditional public–private divide in the law is a significant area of analysis within legal feminism today because the classification of the world into such spheres contains significant paradoxes. For example, although the family traditionally has been viewed as a private sphere, it is highly regulated and controlled by the state. Law defines who may marry whom and what formalities must be observed. Law defines the consequences of marriage and parenthood during on-going relationships and imposes significant policy directives in the context of divorce and child rearing.[3] Law also defines the responsibilities of family and the role of the family within the larger society.[4]

Further, although the state is designated the quintessential public and the family the quintessential private institution, the market is distinctively chameleonlike. Markets are constructed as public (and therefore under a different, competitive set of norms) when contrasted with the family, but as private (and therefore not easily susceptible to public regulation) when paired with the state. Law and Economics decidedly views the market as a private realm and the intervention of the public government into market activities in the form of governmental regulation as suspect. Further, recent policy debates concerning privatization that are grounded in neoclassical economic rhetoric operate along the public–private divide. Proponents of privatization hold up the private market as the solution to many currently "problematic" public societal institutions, such as welfare, education, and the prison system. It is on this terrain that feminist methodology can provide a pointed critique of Law and Economics and neoclassical economics. Feminism has extensively considered the wisdom of viewing society through the public–private binary and brought to light the extent to which the private realms—in particular, the family and the market—are in fact created or at least regulated by the state. Further, feminism has brought to light the manner in which the status quo within the quintessentially private realm, the family, affects women's participation in the market. Finally, feminists have grappled with both the benefits and the burdens of public regulation of private institutions. As such, feminist methodology is particularly well adapted to providing a broad-based analysis of Law and Economics and political policy and rhetoric similarly grounded in neoclassical economics.

Law and Economics

The law has always been engaged with economic issues, and law clearly has an effect on the economic lives of individuals in society. Only within the last several decades, however, have economic theory and concepts been explicitly applied to general theoretical interpretations of the law. As a result of this application, the Law and Economics school has flourished within legal academia, in many instances eclipsing other methods of theoretical inquiry. Additionally, through the establishment of institutes and training programs for judges, law professors, and lawyers, the methodology, concepts, and rhetoric of Law and Economics have spread beyond the academy, taking root in professional and policymaking circles.

Although there are many instances in which the law and legal practice engage economics, Law and Economics as an academic discipline incorporates principles almost exclusively from neoclassical economic theory, a social science discipline grounded in political liberalism and rooted in Adam Smith's writings on the individual economic actor in the market. This actor, *homo economicus,* is a completely rational actor who enters into transactions solely to maximize his economic well-being. He is unconstrained by noneconomic impulses and desires, and he transacts with similarly situated economic men who are all presumed to be initially on equal footing to his own. The outcome of transactions entered into by *homo economicus* is considered to be "efficient" for purposes of neoclassical economic analysis if, given a limited set of resources, at least one party to the transaction is better off having entered into the transaction than would be the case had the transaction not taken place, and neither party is worse off.

Out of this theoretical framework, Law and Economics incorporates the efficiency standard of neoclassical economics into the analysis of the law. Within the law, the standard generally requires that legal actors seek to identify legal solutions to legal issues that are most "efficient" for the parties involved, thereby also resulting in an outcome that is of maximum benefit to society overall.

An underlying theme in the efficiency analysis with respect to the law—and one that has elicited a certain amount of controversy—is that there are many areas in which legal rules only serve to hinder economic and societal efficiency. According to this notion, individuals typically will bargain to efficient results in the absence of legal rules, and therefore delegalization or privatization tends to provide maximum benefit overall. This theme is in part based on the writings of neoclassical economist Ronald Coase, who demonstrated that in a vacuum, the bargaining between two parties would generally result in identical overall costs to the economy, regardless of the legal rules that initially allocate rights and responsibilities with respect to such parties. Law and Economics has taken this principle as a scientific truth and used it to normatively argue that legal rules and governmental regulation tend to hinder the efficient outcomes that would otherwise occur in the "naturally functioning" market, thus obviating the need for laws that redistribute rights and resources in an egalitarian manner. Such conclusions of Law and Economics, which are said to be supported by "scientific" economic theory, generally coincide neatly with the conservative political ideology that bemoans efforts on the part of government to include conceptions of fairness in the legal analysis of private institutions such as the market.

Although Law and Economics has made its most significant inroads into those areas of the law, such as tort law, that seek to monitor individual actors within the market, the reach of Law and Economics is far broader. Certain Law and Economics writers have argued that the efficiency standard should be a guiding principal within a general conception of justice. Richard Epstein, for example, searches for a theory of fairness that can be *reconciled* with the conclusions of economic theory.[5] Richard Posner, however, who is considered by many to be the foremost Law and Economics theorist, goes much further and actually *equates* economics with justice.[6] As Posner has asserted, what is labeled as unjust in society is in reality those actions and practices by governmental and individual actors that waste resources. As such, Law and Economics has been extensively applied to areas of the law not traditionally thought of in terms of value. For example, intimate interactions, aspects of identity such as sexuality, and intimate legal relationships such as adoption, marriage, and divorce have been theorized by Law and Economics writers in economic terms, and legal rules or regulations have been proposed (or opposed) based on principles of efficiency.

Law and Economics and the neoclassical economic model on which it is based have had a significant impact on the development of law and policy. In part because it is presented as a scientific and objective method of analysis, it has been very influential in practice and politics. Judges, legislators, and other legal policymakers now routinely use the concepts and language of Law and Economics to fashion rules having not only economic and material but also normative and ideological implications for American society. For example, much of the rhetoric and theory behind various calls for welfare reform and for the privatization of formerly publicly run societal institutions (e.g., prisons, shelters, hospitals, and so forth) are a direct outgrowth of Law and Economics.

Critics of Law and Economics come from a variety of disciplines and venues, including economics departments. Some critics question the basic premises of neoclassical economics and Law and Economics, finding the methodology to be of limited use and scope either in an abstract theoretical sense or in specific substantive areas of legal analysis. Some critics have questioned or at least revealed the political and ideological underpinnings of the claim that economics is a "science." Others have focused on the specific areas of the law that Law and Economics has scrutinized, frequently making the point that there are societal values and concerns beyond that of efficiency. This is particularly an issue of concern to critics of Law and Economics as it has been applied to relationships as complex and varied as those involving sexual and emotional intimacy. Finally, it has been pointed out by numerous critics of Law and Economics that one of the basic premises of Law and Economics—that bargaining without legal rules frequently leads to the most efficient outcomes—in many cases veils a preference for maintenance of the status quo.

Organization of This Volume

There is no single unified vision among the essays in the five parts of this volume. The authors represent a wide variety of perspectives and methodologies, although they certainly share a general orientation toward egalitarian and pluralistic ends. Readers will find disagreement about the nature of the problem, about the merits of specific proposals and approaches, and about the value and wisdom of using economic analysis. Feminists have long recognized that it is through disagreement and struggle with others who share the common goal of antisubordination and social equality that real progress in our collective thinking can be made.

The first part of the volume, "Law and Economics and Neoclassical Economic Theory," presents an overview of the theoretical issues at play in neoclassical theory and Law and Economics. The authors of these essays focus directly on the ideological and historical assumptions and biases of neoclassical theory and Law and Economics as well as on specific theorists within these traditions. These essays show Law and Economics to be part of a specific political tradition, one that engages with economic rhetoric about the state and the market in order to further certain political ends.

Part II of the volume, "Feminism Confronts Neoclassical Economic Theory and Law and Economics," presents feminist responses to neoclassical economics and Law and Economics. The writers of the essays in this part come to differing conclusions with respect to the usefulness of economic theory for feminist and critical theory. On the one hand, there is the argument that economic concepts and rhetoric can be used toward feminist ends in order to divert the current antifeminist and inegalitarian direction of law and economics policymaking. The countervailing argument is that the gendered biases inherent in neoclassical economics and the location of Law and Economics within such male-centered political tradition make untenable the notion that such economic analysis can be used toward feminist ends.

Part III of the volume, "The Costs of the Free Market: Theories of Collective Responsibility and the Withering Away of Public Goods," focuses on specific applications of economic theory as it relates to the structuring of privilege through governmental action. The essays in this part view the obsessive focus on efficiency, individualism, and utility in both Law and Economics and in our contemporary political arena as having pushed aside any concern for values such as collective responsibility, altruism, and empathy. These essays also address the impact of such a dynamic on the nature of our political democracy.

By broadening and challenging contemporary approaches to issues concerning entitlements and existing allocation of wealth, these essays engage fully and honestly with important and current issues in which economic implications are important and necessary components of public policy. A particular focus of the essays in this part is the role the U.S. federal government plays in wealth distribution through the welfare state in addition to the role of economic rhetoric in attempts to "reform" welfare programs.

Part IV of the volume, "Feminism, Economics and Labor," discusses the interplay between the performance of labor and one's access or lack of access to economic power in contemporary society. It focuses on the nature of paid versus unpaid labor in society and the gendered nature of such dichotomy. Of primary concern to feminists who engage with economics is the danger that the implementation of economic methodology to the feminist analysis of work could lead to an overemphasis on the economic value of such work and a lack of interest in values that cannot be quantified in economic terms. This debate plays out in the feminist effort to quantify unpaid caretaking work within the family (undertaken primarily by women) and the effects of such work on women's ability to participate in the paid labor force.

The final part of the volume, "Economics and Intimacy: Gendered Economic Roles and the Regulation of Intimate Relationships," focuses on the institution of the family. On a mythic level, this institution is considered to be essentially separate from public legal and market concerns. Yet it is in fact a highly regulated institution that is both affected by and productive of economic relations. The essays in this part focus on these relationships. Economic theory has recently reshaped arguments about appropriate policies governing marriage, divorce, and children. The family is increasingly reduced to an economic institution, marriage seen as another example of a bargained-for relationship, and children seen as producing costs and provoking strategies on the part of their parents. A model of the family shaped by economic concepts and ideas has both dangers and promise for feminists interested in addressing the inequalities inherent in the traditional institution of marriage in which women historically had no bargaining power.

Notes

1. Linda Gordon, *The Struggle for Reproductive Freedom: Three Stages of Feminism* in *Capitalist Patriarchy and the Case for Socialist Feminism* 107. (Z. Eisenstein ed., Longman 1979).

2. The recognition of a political agenda may help explain why some scholars who (mistakenly) view their work as apolitical and objective dismiss feminism.

3. *See, e.g.,* Uniform Marital Property Act § 4, 9A U.L.A. 109 (1998) (Classification of Property of Spouses).

4. *See* Martha Albertson Fineman, *Our Sacred Institution: The Ideal of the Family in American Law and Society,* 1993 Utah L. Rev. 387, 400 (1993) (discussing the construction of family function in society and the distribution of roles within the family to meet those assigned functions).

5. Richard Epstein, *A Theory of Strict Liability,* 2 J. Legal Stud. 151–204, 152 (1973).

6. Richard A. Posner, *The Economics of Justice* 84 (Harvard U. Press 1983).

PART I

LAW AND ECONOMICS AND NEOCLASSICAL ECONOMIC THEORY

L aw and Economics is an outgrowth of contemporary mainstream economics and, as such, is grounded in the neoclassical tradition, which has roots that reach back to the writings of Adam Smith and Jeremy Bentham. Neoclassical economics is an intellectual and ideological tradition, some of the core concepts of which have been integrated into day-to-day debate and become familiar to people in the United States. For example, Adam Smith's discussion of the "invisible hand" regulating the market is not only a standard part of United States educational curricula but is also used as a rhetorical trope in contemporary discussions of the negative effects of governmental regulation of the economy wherein the claim is made that any such regulation impedes the "natural" efficiency of the market.

Law and Economics has become a developed part of academic law. Like its neoclassic generator, it also has become a vital part of larger public debates about the appropriateness of certain governmental rules and the manner of their enforcement. Of the many questions one might ask when considering the role of Law and Economics, how coherent the method is as a rhetorical and conceptual matter might be primary among them. Is Law and Economics a rigorous formal approach for answering the many policy questions presented by the law or merely an aggregation of polemics produced by largely economically self-taught legal academics manipulating neoclassical metaphors to achieve ideologically motivated (and conservative) ends?

The essays in part I discuss the contours of both Law and Economics and neoclassical economics. Terence Dougherty's essay, "Economic Rhetoric, Economic Individualism, and the Law and Economics School," gives a broad overview of some of Law and Economics' fundamental areas of inquiry, touching on some of its methodology. Dougherty focuses on the manner in which Law and Economics has posited itself as a "scientific method" and questions the ideologically motivated consequences of viewing Law and Economics as a form of science. Further, Dougherty brings his attention to the writings of Richard Posner, one of the most prolific and widely read Law and Economics writers, discussing Posner's development of *homo economicus* from a rational actor within the economic market to a fully realized political and legal subject.

Deirdre McCloskey's essay, "The Demoralization of Economics: Can We Recover from Bentham and Return to Smith?" looks at neoclassical economics as an intellectual tradition that is said to derive from the writings of Adam Smith. McCloskey focuses on the obsessive concern within neoclassical economics with the notion of "profit regardless," the idea that rational actors act in all situations to achieve the maximal economic outcome.

McCloskey implies that this notion is an outgrowth of utilitarianism, as articulated by Jeremy Bentham, and is not an outgrowth of Smith. Although attention to "profit regardless" may be found in Smith, it is not supported by a full reading of his work. Smith, McCloskey writes, was concerned with developing "an ethical system for the middle class." "Prudence," the analog for utility within the traditional virtues, was of considerable import to Smith. It was, however, only one virtue among many. To not see prudence (or utility) within a system of virtues, as did Smith, removes any consideration for ethics from economics and thus leaves economics on a shaky foundation. McCloskey's suggestion is that the very philosophical heritage claimed by neoclassical economics—as based in Smith's espousal of a desire for an economic system focused on "profit regardless"—may in fact be a misreading of Smith's work.

Finally, Paula England's "Separative and Soluble Selves: Dichotomous Thinking in Economics" critiques neoclassical economics from a feminist perspective. England demonstrates that three basic premises of this economic model, (1) interpersonal utility comparisons are impossible; (2) tastes are exogenous to economic models and are unchanging; and (3) actors are selfish in markets, imply that humans are autonomous actors in markets and make choices unguided by empathy. England further demonstrates that, in contrast to this "separative" self acting in the market, neoclassical economists posit completely "soluble" selves within the family, who act with empathy and have no independent will or interest. England critiques the separative/soluble dichotomy, considering recent work in economics and caregiving that impact this critique.

CHAPTER I

Economic Rhetoric, Economic Individualism, and the Law and Economics School

Terence Dougherty

Before the establishment of Law and Economics as a specific movement within the legal academy, the application of economic principles and methodology to the law was limited to specific areas that lend themselves directly to economic analysis, such as antitrust law. By contrast, the Law and Economics school has been unusual in the breadth of its reach and its willingness to take on and recast in economic terms areas of the law that would appear to have a more attenuated connection to economic analysis. Law and Economics adherents have systematically applied its principles to traditional, core areas of legal study, including tort, contract, and criminal law, and have also made forays into family law and jurisprudence.

Law and Economics is a field of study that is heavily associated with individuals and institutions and with a significant body of dedicated journals, including the *Journal of Law and Economics* and the *Journal of Legal Studies*. The University of Chicago Law School is or has been home to some of the most noted Law and Economics scholars, most significantly Richard Posner, who is now a judge on the Seventh Circuit Court of Appeals.[1] In addition to being a particularly prolific and influential writer who has brought his analysis to bear on a wide range of substantive areas, Posner also has been central in the development of Law and Economics as a generalized jurisprudential theory that purports to explain the law as a system susceptible to the logic of economics.

Certain basic positions of the Chicago school of Law and Economics are closely aligned with and mutually inform numerous current political debates, which are played out in courtrooms, lawmaking institutions, and the media. Central to these debates is the notion that there is a cost intrinsic to governmental regulation. Governmental regulation hinders the potential for an efficient outcome when individuals transact in the marketplace. If free of governmental regulations, the argument goes, a willing buyer and a willing seller of a good or service will be more likely to set a price that is by definition the value of the good or service. This is said to be an efficient transaction. Put another way, given two possible outcomes to a transaction involving the allocation of resources, the most efficient outcome is the one that results in at least one person to the transaction being better off under such allocation than he or she would be under the alternate outcome, and additionally, no one is worse off.[2] The argument about efficiency is part of a long debate in American politics about the appropriate role of governmental institutions in regard to regulation of the market. This debate reaches back to Adam Smith's notion that individuals, focused on their own economic gain, will be led by the "invisible hand" of an unregulated market, ultimately promoting the overall public interest through an efficient allocation of societal resources.[3]

This chapter provides an overview of varying aspects of the Law and Economics movement. It focuses on the assertion by Law and Economics scholars that their theories are supported by the unassailable logic of science and thus serve as justification for legal interventions that have significant political consequences. This is a focus on the "economics" side of the Law and Economics movement. This section is complemented by a discussion of the legal subject, constructed within Law and Economics discourse, which brings into focus the "law" dimension of the movement. Finally, I consider a number of substantive areas of the law to which Law and Economics has turned its attention.

Economic Rhetoric and Economic Value:
Normative versus Positive Analysis

Debates about the use of economic principles as a justification for lessening governmental intervention are clearly normative in nature. They use the economic notion of efficiency to justify nonintervention as a political matter. Law and Economics, however, presents itself as a largely positivist methodology. A great deal of the Law and Economics literature foregrounds its positivist perspective.[4] By presenting itself in this way, Law and Economics, it can be argued, is a theoretical and scientifically based field that is above the fray of day-to-day political debates. As Posner has described it, economic analysis of the law is "the attempt to explain legal rules and outcomes as they are rather than to change them to make them better."[5]

Posner's assertions aside, it is bedeviling to try to grasp the difference between what is labeled positive and what is clearly normative in much of Law and Economics literature. Most of its positive arguments in fact are based on fundamental assumptions that clearly involve normative choices and political judgments.

This can be illustrated by an examination of the manner in which basic defining principles of Law and Economics are constructed. In his seminal work *Economic Analysis of Law,* Posner discusses the "background" economic principles identified as fundamental to Law and Economics. Efficiency, for example, is defined via its relationship to the allocation of resources. Posner instructs: "[w]hen resources are being used where their value is highest, or equivalently when no relocation would increase their value, we say they are being employed efficiently."[6] This may be a merely definitional stance, but he also states as a given that resources "tend to gravitate toward their most valued uses if voluntary exchange—a market—is permitted" without a third party (i.e., the government) determining, through the application of a conception of rights, the appropriate allocation of resources.[7] Governmental "permission" is understood as an abdication that sets the stage for transactions that ensure resources go to the highest bidder.

This is a difficult set of assumptions to accept. First, the number of beliefs folded into the preference for a governmental vacuum is staggering. Second, this position ignores the possibility of variations in bargaining power among participants to a transaction. Third, Posner would reduce the meaning of the term *value* to reflect a mere monetary measuring.[8] One could make the argument that the continual assertion that there is such a distinction between normative and positive analysis of economic issues is a rhetorical mechanism through which Law and Economics can provide "scientific" justification for political ends.

The scientific inevitability of the positivist efficiency principle is justified not only on the basis of abstract scientific reasoning, however. It is also claimed to be historically justified by the law itself. Posner tells us that "[i]t would not be surprising to find that many legal doctrines rest on inarticulate gropings toward efficiency."[9] He contextualizes this assertion, noting that the roots of common law legal doctrines lie in nineteenth-century laissez-faire ideology. However, beyond that initial reference to history, efficiency is valorized in a most unhistorical manner as the underlying internal, scientific logic of the law. "The common law," Posner states, "is best (not perfectly) explained as a system for maximizing the wealth of society."[10] Common law (the doctrinal manifestation of the invisible hand) constitutes movement toward efficiency. To Posner, the common law's competition—statutory and constitutional law (governmental law)—is motivated by more normative, less logical goals.

Viewing the assertions made in *Economic Analysis of Law* as rhetoric is a helpful way of positioning the Law and Economics movement within the American legal tradition. In scholar Arthur Allen Leff's early critique of *Economic Analysis of Law,* he described Posner's work as a "grand narrative novel" of the *Tom Jones* variety.[11] In this type of narrative, the protagonist imposes his particular vision on all the situations he encounters. It is through this story that he defines what constitutes problems and what are acceptable solutions as he makes his way through his society. To its adherents, Law and Economics is an ontological framework through which they can both understand and explain the world to others.

Leff saw the narrative effort of the Law and Economics movement as being consistent with the historical development of American law. He argues that our story was once that of "legal formalism," in which the law was viewed as an internally and logically consistent body of rules and principles. Formalism was eventually supplanted by "legal realism," which focused not on a concept of internal logic in law but on the empirical manner in which the law functioned in day-to-day society.

According to Leff, the transition from formalism to realism created a legal world that was "a universe normatively empty and empirically overflowing." Law and Economics eventually came to fill this void. However, rather than defining the world in terms of what "ought" be the result in a given situation and arguing from policy and perspective, Law and Economics presented itself in scientific and empirical terms. It pronounced the common law to be grounded in efficiency; it rationalized existing allocations of societal resources by suggesting that they were the result of individual choice, which was defined as constituting the most efficient and economically beneficial manner of allocation.

Leff's explanation is useful because it helps to explain the acceptance on the part of many of the dictates of Law and Economics. It provided predictability and certainty—an internal logic to the law in the wake of the uncertainty introduced by legal realism's assertions that all was context, nothing was absolute, even in the law.

There was another unsettling aspect to legal realism. Unlike either formalism or Law and Economics, legal realism specifically foregrounded the question of power interests in its view of the law. Rather than viewing the law as primarily based on a coherent set of internal governing principles, realists viewed the law as primarily motivated by external powerful interests that manipulated law in order to sustain their power. By contrast, Law and Economics decidedly avoids any analysis of power, hiding that troublesome concept under its veil of positivism. The problem with adopting the Law and Economics proponents' view that the law consists of an internal logic defined by concepts of efficiency and choice and that the operation of this logic is only hindered by governmental remediation, is that there is little need for an analysis of external and corrupting reservoirs of power. In this analysis, the distorting influence of power is not revealed by looking at those individuals or groups who have control over societal wealth; instead, it is found in the attempts of the government to redistribute such wealth in the name of "rights" or social policy.

As such, Law and Economics methodically provides its description of the internal logic of the law by providing a positivist description of how this logic can be found within all areas of the law. By analyzing merely "the way things are," without foregrounding a concern for "the way things perhaps ought be," or for what initial allocations of wealth and/or power are secured by the way things are, Law and Economics provides a very powerful justification for maintenance of the current status quo. In such respects, it seems likely that rather than being a mere application of a logical scientific method to the law, Law and Economics could be seen as part of a normative approach to the law and to politics.

In addition to the fact that under the guise of positivist description, Law and Economics takes normative positions that coincide with late twentieth-century conservative politics, it is important to note that Law and Economics is not a mere normative bastardization of neoclassical economics. The neoclassical school of economics itself in fact can also be viewed as a rhetorical model imbued with specific values. As economist Deirdre McCloskey has argued, modern economics is a particular conflation of "metaphysics, morals and personal conviction."[12] Such conflation, according to McCloskey, is merely *named* as scientific methodology by its practitioners. Further, McCloskey has shown neoclassical roots of modern economics as having been developed within a particular ethical and political framework.[13]

Economist Robert H. Nelson has taken this argument one step further. In addition to challenging the notion that economics as it is currently practiced is a value-free enterprise, Nelson has argued that modern economics is in fact a theological model, "a means of access to genuine knowledge about the world."[14] Consistent with the Judeo-Christian notion of progress, modern economics provides an ethical framework within which self-interested economic progress and advancement are prioritized as the basic ethical virtue. In a post-Enlightenment secular age, economists fill the social role of "preachers of a religion with the special character that it acts to uphold the normative foundation required for a rapidly growing modern economy."[15] As described by Nelson, "the full expression of self-interest within the setting of the market is therefore blessed by a religious cause. The religious purpose of the market is to ensure maximal efficiency in the use of material resources in society, and thus rapid movement of American society along a route of economics progress in this world."[16]

It is this religio-political impetus that perhaps explains the need within Law and Economics to bring its analysis to every area of the law, or more aptly, to bring every area of the law to fit within the model. Nelson describes as an act of faith the fervent efforts on the part of Chicago economists—the school from which Law and Economics emerged and is a part—to make descriptive inroads into virtually all areas of societal and legal analysis. According to Nelson, "[i]f something cannot be explained today in a narrowly individualistic framework of economic analysis, it is the belief of the 'Chicago Project' that in the future there will be a smarter graduate student, a more insightful theory, a better statistical method that will permit us to show the full workings of the forces of self-interest in more and more areas of life."[17]

Nelson's view of economics as a modern theology fits nicely within explanations of the development of Law and Economics within legal institutions. As described earlier, Law and Economics can be understood historically as emerging during a period when the prevailing view of the law described the law as if it were devoid of a coherent set of governing principles that constitute its internal logic. The view that self-interest and economic progress are truths within the ethical framework of society provides justification for an efficiency-based legal framework and fills a need within the law for principled explanations for the law's operation. The inevitability and the coherence of a predetermined market that provides an arena within which self-interested individuals may facilitate economic progress are part of the natural law that legal institutions serve to protect.

This view of economics as a religion—or at the very least as reflective of a set of values and preferences—complicates the view of Law and Economics as a mere form of political rhetoric because it indicates the extent to which such political rhetoric derives from beliefs deeply held by a number of members of society. Law and Economics writers are not necessarily calculating when they design theories that justify a conservative political agenda. Nor are they all necessarily aware of the normative nature of their work. For if they truly see individual self-interested behavior within free markets as furthering economic and ethical progress, then it becomes more plausible that they would truly view their work as merely descriptive or positivist in nature. In addition, such a view of economics helps explain the manner in which the Law and Economics' standpoint that the market should, at most, be subject to minimal governmental regulation resonates deeply with individuals who either actually or merely aspire to benefit from nonintervention.

Economic Individualism: Efficiency, Utility, and Autonomy

As a comprehensive theory of the law, Law and Economics has developed a conception of the legal subject that is particularly adaptable to an efficiency-based model of the market. This individual subject is to an extent at odds with late twentieth-century liberal views of the individual legal subject, in particular in that it is a legal subject for whom freedom is emphasized over rights. The positivist nature of Law and Economics would present such a subjectivity as an inevitability within the efficiency-based market model. From a normative perspective, however, this emphasis on freedom may be a reaction to the late twentieth-century liberal notion that individuals have certain inalienable rights and entitlements (including economics rights and entitlements) that a government should serve to protect in light of encroachments by other self-interested individuals. To Law and Economics, by contrast, the government and the law's role should not be the protection of such rights, but rather should be the protection of individual freedom, and particularly freedom from the government in its attempt to constrain the free market via the reallocation of wealth. Individual agency is described as individual decision making within the marketplace, undisturbed by governmental interference.

The efficiency model used within Law and Economics, beyond being merely descriptive, posits an economic actor who has a certain amount of agency in that such actor, when entering into a transaction, determines whether efficiency results. Individual actors, not governmental regulation or standards, ensure efficient results. But this leaves open two questions. First, how do we know that individuals performed an analysis of whether net positive economic gain will result from a transaction? And second, how can we be assured that such a result is in fact desired by the parties to the transaction?

The answer to the first question is the notion of individual consent—the fact that the participants to the transaction actually did enter into such transaction shows that they a priori implicitly consented thereto. This implied consent of individuals within the market to transactions free of governmental regulation is a particular aspect of the construction of the legal subject within Law and Economics. Although it echoes other modern conceptions of the legal subject in that it views such subject as a rational, individual actor, unconstrained by family or communal ties, it differs in its focus. Implied consent in Law and Economics involves consent to free market activities. It contrasts quite starkly with descriptions of individual consent and autonomy in contemporary liberal conceptions of the subject. For example, in the Kantian tradition, as elaborated by John Rawls, individual consent legitimizes governmental action in that just governmental actors judge the rightfulness of laws as if all citizens could have consented thereto had they been in a position to give their consent.[18] In other words, the liberal tradition views the individual consent of the political subject as a person who consents to actions of the government; the consent provides legitimacy to governmental action and is the basis of the hypothetical original contract between the state and its citizens.[19] By contrast, consent in the Law and Economics version of the legal subject is consent to self-interested market transactions that are free from any action whatsoever by the government. Freedom from governmental action in this market is in furtherance of the interests of all individuals because such freedom is efficient.

But the answer to this first question begs the second question: assuming parties to a transaction did so evidence their consent by virtue of the transaction having taken place, how do we know that such consent was given based on a determination that net positive gain would result; how do we know that economic, efficiency-based considerations were the sought-after goal?

This question has been answered within Law and Economics literature via certain assumptions regarding the preferences of the individual legal subject. Individuals, the argument goes, have a complete, fixed set of preferences, which are unchanging over time and which are consistent across all individuals. The core of such preferences is the maximization of economic utility. As rational actors, individuals seek to maximize wealth and, as such, will rank any number of available options and elect to pursue the option that will result in the greatest economic benefit. Law and Economics in fact aspires to a complete explanation for individual behavior as fundamentally rooted in self-interest. As described by Richard Nelson, "any claim that, say, 40 percent of human behavior in some realm is irreducibly noneconomic, would be virtually to say that science is in principle restricted in its scope—that in some domains of life perhaps, god has simply reserved them for his understanding alone. . . . Clearly, there can be no such 'stopping points' within the value system."[20] As such, the very notion of human desire is grounded in pursuing maximum economic utility. Such grounding ensures consistent desired goals and stable eventual outcomes across all participants in an economic market.

In part, such distinction is based in Law and Economics' roots in utilitarianism. Utilitarianism essentially turns on the self-interested behavior of individuals, positing an optimal societal state in which the "sum of pleasures minus pains"—also described as happiness—is maximized.[21] Utilitarianism suggests that human choice involves a series of calculations of whether positive results—happiness—are greater than negative results—pain. This is similar to the dynamic in Law and Economics in which individuals make determinations as to whether a transaction is efficient. However, the Law and Economics view that wealth maximization is at the core of individual preferences is a considerably constrained version of utilitarianism, which does not limit the scope of happiness to wealth.

In fact, utilitarianism was a political theory that was most expansively articulated by eighteenth-century political theorist Jeremy Bentham as a response to rights- and equality-based political theories being promoted during the time of the American and French revolutions. As it became increasingly less possible in a post-Enlightenment era to challenge such rights- and equality-based theories by the use of a conception of divine right, utilitarianism—the individual pursuit of happiness—was posited as an alternative political theory.[22] The ability to pursue this happiness was considered essential to freedom. Although it is true that such pursuit can take on many forms (in fact Kant linked the concept of freedom under the law with the freedom to seek happiness in whatever way one saw fit),[23] Law and Economics limits happiness to the realm of wealth maximization. Posner has commented that foregrounding wealth maximization in a political theory of justice "involves a greater *respect* for individual choice than in classical utilitarianism."[24]

This is the legal subject constructed out of efficiency-based jurisprudence. Although it is true that liberalism takes great leaps in assuming that individuals consent to governmental action, it is at least as much of a stretch to locate individual consent within the marketplace. On the one hand, such a view ignores differing levels of bargaining power within the market. Additionally, it assumes the inevitability of a capitalist market that precedes the state, rather than one that is constituted, at least in part, by that state. By viewing consent to market activity as essential to individual freedom, Law and Economics makes profound assumptions regarding individual preferences with very little explanation of the reasoning behind these assumptions.

Law and Economics

Law and Economics has set its focus on numerous substantive areas of the law. Whether this is due to the desire of Law and Economics to discern an underlying logic to the law or out of a theologically driven faith in self-interest and economic progress, Law and Economics has described through the lens of efficiency virtually every substantive area of the law on which it has commented. This section focuses on four substantive areas of the law—the common law, torts, contract law, and criminal law—to demonstrate the application of the Law and Economics model. Although these four areas of the law are by no means exhaustive of Law and Economics' range of inquiry, they demonstrate common threads of efficiency, governmental non-intervention, and individual rational wealth maximization.

Common Law

The common law is a jurisprudential theory of the law with long-standing roots in the American legal tradition. The theory is that a legal tradition is fundamentally comprised of principles that develop on a case-by-case basis over time. Legal principles, rather than being rooted in the will of the king or divine right, are developed by judges in increments, each of whom reflects on principles discerned from earlier cases, resulting over time in a set of principles that are comprised of the values of, or in fact represent the custom and tradition of, the society that is governed by such law.

In common law jurisprudence, there is a notion that the common law, as developed over time, has an inherent logic. To Law and Economics scholars, this logic is in fact economics, and the movement of the common law as it has developed over time is toward economic efficiency.[25] As Posner has described it, "the common law is best explained as an effort, however inarticulate, to promote efficiency."[26]

One simple explanation for the position that efficiency is the logic of the common law is that judges prefer efficient results. More complex explanations are grounded in the very nature of the operation of the common law process. To wit: if a particular legal question can result in several different allocations of rights or entitlements, the more inefficient of those results will entail greater social costs, and thus will be more likely to be challenged. By contrast, it is not worth it to incur the costs of litigation to challenge efficient rules. In this way, over time, in a process akin to natural selection, resultant legal principles that are efficient will grow to comprise the overall principles of the common law.[27]

The economic analysis of the common law is an important insertion into the "grand narrative" of efficiency. Posner's version of individual economic autonomy and wealth maximization posits an ideally free market with individual actors entering into transactions unrestrained by governmental interference.

But at some point the operation of the law itself must be addressed. The efficiency view of the common law coheres neatly with the concept of an unregulated market because it shows the market itself as powerful enough to be constitutive of the law, rather than the other way around.

The critique of the view that the logic of the common law is efficiency comes on several grounds. For example, there is a certain incongruity between the notion that judges are either motivated by efficiency or more likely to be presented with challenges to inefficient rules when judicial language is so often couched in the language of ethics and morality. Additionally, if a non-efficiency-based principle, for example, morality, has guided the result of a particular legal controversy over a considerable period of time, it is not clear that it would in fact be efficient to incur the costs of challenging such legal rule, notwithstanding the fact that an argument could be made that the rule does not result in wealth maximization.

Writers have also noted that a rule that produces efficient outcomes in a particular case will not necessarily so result in all cases.[28] This is particularly the case in that economic circumstances change over time. Further, the view that efficiency is the logic of the common law ignores both the biases of judges toward maintaining certain allocations of power, rights, and entitlements and the additional costs to parties of challenging those initial allocations of powers, rights, and entitlements—costs that do not burden those who benefit from the status quo.

Tort Law

The economic analysis of tort law begins early in Law and Economics. In many ways, it is rooted in the 1960 article by economist Ronald Coase, "The Problems of Social Cost."[29] Coase developed the argument that in a world of (1) perfect competition, (2) perfect access to information, and (3) zero transaction costs, the allocation of resources in the economy will be efficient and will be unaffected by legal rules that allocate rights and entitlements.

In many ways, the Coase theorem, and the uses to which it has been put by Law and Economics scholars, epitomizes the use of economics within the Law and Economics school. For Coase is an economist and not a lawyer, and his theory is based on several assumptions that in many respects make questionable the applicability of such a theorem to legal analysis: perfect competition, perfect access to information, and zero transaction costs.[30] Coase foregrounds these assumptions, but many Law and Economics writers who attempt to use the Coase theorem to argue for minimal governmental intervention in the legal arena do not in fact do so. Rather than, for example, viewing perfect competition as an unattainable abstraction that is nonetheless necessary to make an abstract economic point, Law and Economics writers describe the market as a state of perfect competition that is only hindered by governmental rules. This omits an analysis of how the government itself is constitutive of the market.[31] Further, by not focusing on the unequal bargaining power among difference classes of individuals, Law and Economics obfuscates the impact of legal rules on actual individuals and groups.

Law and Economics writers have described the development of tort law as a movement toward an efficient allocation of the economic and social costs of tortious conduct, including the costs of accident losses, the administrative costs of the tort disputation system, and also the costs of precaution.[32] Richard Posner and William Landes have stated that these efficient rules positively affect individual behavior by inducing such individuals to determine the various legal and financial costs of their conduct. Rational economic actors will minimize their potential for causing harm to others when the costs to them of having caused such harm outweigh their potential gain from acting without a view to accident prevention.[33] To do otherwise would not be efficient. Although there is a certain logic to this theory, a number of writers have questioned whether tort law really does in fact affect individual behavior, pointing out the many noneconomic factors that influence individual behavior, including concerns for safety for self and ethical concerns for others.[34]

Posner and Landes's arguments about the influence of tort law on individual behavior as a result of the primary individual concern for efficiency are decidedly positivist. They are merely descriptive of their view of the way tort law has developed. Other Law and Economic writers, by contrast, have foregrounded their use of economic analysis for the specific purposes of making suggestions about appropriate standards for determining responsibility for tortious behavior. For example, in determining whether tortious behavior should be judged by the use of a negligence or a strict liability standard, Guido Calebresi and Jon Hirschoff have written favorably of the lower costs in applying strict liability.[35] A negligence standard, they argue, requires an "outside governmental institution (a judge or jury)" to perform a cost–benefit analysis as to whether the costs of accident prevention to the injurer exceed the cost–benefits from the accident being prevented.[36] The strict liability standard, by contrast, requires an inquiry solely into which of the injurer or the injured is the least cost avoider; that is, which party "was in the best position both to judge whether avoidance costs would exceed foreseeable accident costs and to act on that judgment."[37]

Contract Law

Law and Economics has touched broadly on the law governing contracts. The economic analysis of contract law has two primary focuses. First, it brings its efficiency analysis to the question of what are the appropriate default contractual rules and argues for default rules that are considered to be most efficient because they are said to lower the internal and external costs involved in contracting. Second, Law and Economics analysis looks at governmental involvement in private, contractual transactions—primarily through the judiciary—that serve to limit an individual's ability to form contractual arrangements on his or her own terms. Law and Economics writers view policy-related and non-efficiency-based theories of contractual interpretation as attacks on "the principle of freedom of contract."[38]

The first version of Law and Economics' analysis can be a useful focus of analysis. For example, contract law has identified several possible remedies for contract breach, including monetary remedies such as restitution and reliance, which seek, respectively, to pay damages to the harmed party so that s/he is restored to the same position s/he would have been in had the contract not been breached, or to pay damages to reimburse the breach party for costs incurred. The primary nonmonetary contractual remedy is specific performance, pursuant to which the party that breaches is required to perform his or her duties under the contract. Different Law and Economics writers express different views as to which theory is most efficient as a default rule. For example, Thomas S. Ulen has argued that in the absence of stipulated remedies within a contract, specific performance is less likely than monetary damages to achieve efficiency in that, among other things, it involves less transaction costs in resolving disputes, results in lower pre-formation costs, and so forth.[39] By contrast, Richard Posner has asserted that unless the breaching party is acting opportunistically, s/he should be able to breach and pay damages to the harmed party if s/he finds a better enough deal that, after paying damages to the harmed party, s/he is economically better off.[40] This is known as "efficient breach."

Regardless of where people come out on these arguments, many theorists of contract law agree that default rules can lower overall transaction costs in that they provide more certainty to parties entering into a transaction and prevent people from having to reinvent the wheel every time they enter into a contract. Further, commentators have argued that default rules free the parties to expend their energy negotiating terms that deviate from the default rules, hopefully winding up with a contract that better reflects the meeting of the parties' minds.[41] Although this may be true, default rules tend to favor the status quo and are generally drafted by, and are more favorable to, those parties with more bargaining power.

The second area of Law and Economics' inquiry into contract law is more controversial and is exemplary of the tendency of Law and Economics to go beyond a mere analysis of the economic effects of a transaction to a more normative reconstruction of the private nature of contract law. Under this view, contract law is, and perhaps historically always has been, an area of individual freedom: the freedom to contract. This freedom, the story goes, has come under attack by modern legal theories that justify governmental intervention into contract law.

Richard Epstein has made this argument in reviewing the doctrine of un-conscionability in contract law, under which a court may overturn a contract or a provision thereof on the theory that it is unduly harsh, unconscionable, or unjust.[42] Unconscionability has been applied to a number of substantive areas of contract law, such as add-on clauses and waiver-of-defense clauses. An add-on clause is a clause that grants the installment-sale seller of property a security interest in all property sold to the buyer, even property sold at later dates, such that if the buyer defaults on any payment to the seller, the seller may take back all of the property sold, regardless of the size of the remaining payments on the earlier-sold property.[43]

A waiver-of-defense clause arises in connection with property purchased with financing. In situations where sellers that provide financing to a purchaser of property and subsequently sell the financing contract to a finance company, the seller may on behalf of the finance company include a waiver-of-defense claim such that the purchaser of the property cannot withhold payments to the seller even if the seller has breached its warranty.

Richard Epstein has argued that these two contractual provisions should not be set aside on the grounds that they are unconscionable, because to do so would hinder individuals' ability to contract freely. Unconscionability, Epstein argues, should be limited to situations where fraud, duress, or undue influence is involved, or where one of the parties to the contract is of unequal bargaining power by virtue of being incompetent. Anything beyond that is an unfair policy-motivated infringement on contractual freedom that will constrain the free market.

Add-on clauses, Epstein argues, are acceptable in contracts in that they are the only means a seller of property may have to be made whole on a defaulted contract when selling goods to people without other assets. Further, lower transaction costs are incurred when the means of repayment on default is specified than would be the case if the seller were to have to go after other assets of the purchaser (if the purchaser has any other assets).

Waiver-of-defense clauses also should not be set aside as unconscionable, Epstein has argued, because such clauses put the purchaser in the same position s/he would be in had s/he purchased the property with cash; that is, a purchaser for cash hasn't the ability to hold back money from the seller if the warranty is breached. Seller-financing situations should lead to no different result. Finally, if waiver-of-defense claims were considered unconscionable terms, seller-financing would be harder to come by.

Epstein is not swayed by the argument that the unconscionability doctrine should be available with respect to add-on and waiver-of-defense clauses in light of the fact that these clauses frequently are used in contracts between parties of vastly unequal bargaining power and often where the purchaser is poor. Epstein counters that allowing contract provisions to be set aside on such grounds will constrain the market in that sellers won't want to transact with the poor due to the costliness of potential defaults. Further, Epstein says that such an argument is patronizing and would wind up creating incentives and opportunities for poor people to game the system.

Criminal Law

In contrast to the broad claims of Law and Economics to the very logic of the common law, the economic approach to criminal law seems more parochial. The application of economic methodologies to the study of criminal law was first developed by Gary Becker.[44] Becker has suggested that it is useful to view crime as an economically important activity, a societal industry, given the considerable public and private expenditures on both preventing and engaging in illegal activity.

However, Becker also posits people who commit or are about to commit crimes as rational economic actors making a priori determinations within the economic marketplace. An individual, the argument goes, will commit a given crime if the expected utility to such individual exceeds the utility that could be achieved by using time and other resources toward other activities. It is this cost–benefit analysis that is determinative of whether a person commits a crime. Consequently, to Becker, fines are the most appropriate form of punishment for all crimes other than the most serious ones, because a fine can be set so as to cause individuals to factor in the potential economic setback if caught when deciding whether to commit a crime. If the fine is set at the right level, it will persuade potential criminals that there is higher utility in performing noncriminal activities.

Such an analysis seems parochial in that it, first, ignores the myriad psychosocial factors involved in criminal activity. Further, by assuming a static set of crimes and then further assuming that individuals make a priori determinations in light of that set of crimes, the analysis ignores the manner in which what is determined to be criminal activity changes both statutorily and judicially, and often does so in light of a society's desires to regulate the activities of certain classes of people. But foremost, as an example of the economic approach to the law generally, this approach brings to light by example the very absurdity of the notion of economic rationality in its assertion that individuals, either consciously or no, make decisions regarding whether to engage in criminal activity based on calculations of utility.

Conclusion

Thirty-six years after the publication of his article, "The Problem of Social Cost," Ronald Coase explained his near-complete silence within the field of

Law and Economics. Coase said, "I have never attempted to contribute to it. . . . But my unwillingness to take part in the discussions of this subject is a result of . . . my lack of knowledge of the detailed working of the legal system and my very superficial knowledge of the legal literature."[45]

It would seem that many legal academics have not been so cautious. Many Law and Economics writers have taken some basic propositions of neoclassical economics, particularly the efficiency principle, and raised them mantralike, asserting them to be at the core of not only the legal system but also logic and individual freedom, choice and desire. These economic factors have come to eclipse all other standpoints and methodologies for these interpreters of the law. Law and Economics writers strongly assert that the core principles behind their methodology have a scientific logic, and the conclusions they arrive at based on this logic are therefore merely descriptive or positivist in nature.

On a very basic level, however, Law and Economics falls clearly within the growing political concern over governmental regulation and spending and provides a legal justification for governmental nonintervention. This justification is based on an antiquated view of society as comprised of distinct public (government) and private (market) realms. According to Law and Economics, the public realm only serves to hinder the operation of the private realm, leading to unfortunate social costs to all members of society. The view of these distinct public and private realms within Law and Economics is a weak foundation for a science. Apparently, however, it is a strong foundation for a normative philosophical approach to the law and the role of governmental institutions in regulating social interactions.

Notes

1. Although Posner is singled out here for his prominence within the legal academy, his position as an appellate judge is not unique among Law and Economics theorists. Guido Calebresi, another prominent writer in this field, holds a judgeship on another very influential circuit court (Posner sits on the Seventh and Calebresi sits on the Second Circuit). Their respective and seminal work within the Law and Economics field is noteworthy. Additionally, there are many other well-known figures within the field, e.g., Richard Epstein, a professor at the University of Chicago Law School who has written scores of influential books and articles within the field. *See, e.g.,* Richard Epstein, *Bargaining with the State* (Princeton U. Press 1993).

2. This dynamic derives from the neoclassical economic efficiency principal known as Pareto optimality. It has been further elaborated under neoclassical economics to consider the effects of the transaction in question on, and the potential need to compensate, third parties under the Kaldor-Hicks model.

3. *See generally* Adam Smith, *The Wealth of Nations* (Modern Library 1937).

4. *See, e.g.,* Milton Friedman, *The Methodology of Positive Economics,* in *Essays in Positive Economics* (U. of Chicago Press 1953).

5. Richard A. Posner, *Economic Analysis of Law* (6th ed., Aspen Publishers 2003) [hereinafter Posner, *Economic Analysis*].

6. *Id.* at 10.

7. *Id.* at 9.

8. The question of whether it is worthwhile to methodologically isolate the analysis of whether societal interactions are efficient from an analysis of justice and fairness is, of course, a relevant question as well, even assuming efficiency were a positivist methodological tool.

9. Posner, *Economic Analysis, supra* note 5, at 25.

10. *Id.*

11. *See* Arthur Allen Leff, *Economic Analysis of Law: Some Realism about Nominalism,* 60 Va. L. Rev. 451 (1974).

12. *See* Donald N. McCloskey, *The Rhetoric of Economics* 16 (U. of Wisconsin Press 1985).

13. *See, e.g.,* Deirdre McCloskey's essay in ch. 2 of this volume.

14. Robert H. Nelson, *Economics as Religion* xx (Pennsylvania State U. Press 2001).

15. *Id.* at 8.

16. *Id.* at 9.

17. *Id.* at 168.

18. John Rawls, *Political Liberalism* (Columbia U. Press 1993).

19. *See* Immanuel Kant, *Political Writings* 73 (Hans Reiss ed., H. B. Nisbet trans., Cambridge U. Press 1970).

20. Nelson, *supra* note 13, at 170.

21. Serge-Christophe Kolm, *Modern Theories of Justice* 16 (MIT Press 1983).

22. *Id.* at 16–17.

23. Kant, *supra* note 18, at 74.

24. Richard A. Posner, *The Economics of Justice* 66 (Harvard U. Press 1981) (emphasis added).

25. *See* William H. Landes & Richard A. Posner, *Adjudication as a Private Good,* 8 J. Legal Stud. 234 (1975).

26. Richard A. Posner, *The Ethical and Political Basis of the Efficiency Norm in Common Law Adjudication,* 8 Hofstra L. Rev. 487 (1980).

27. *See* Paul H. Rubin, *Why Is the Common Law Efficient?* J. Legal Stud. 51 (Jan. 1977).

28. *See* Gillian Hadfield, *Bias in the Evolution of Legal Rules,* 80 Geo. L.J. 583 (1992).

29. 3 J.L. & Econ. 1 (1960).

30. There are many writers who question Coase's results from the perspective of economics alone. *See, e.g.,* Neil Buchanan, ch. 4, this volume.

31. *See, e.g.,* Martha T. McCluskey, ch. 8, this volume.

32. *See, e.g.,* William Landes & Richard A. Posner, *The Economic Structure of Tort Law* (Harvard U. Press 1987).

33. *Id.*

34. *See* Gary T. Schwartz, *Reality in the Economic Analysis of Tort Law: Does Tort Law Really Deter?* 42 UCLA L. Rev. 377 (1994) (surveying the literature on the deterrent effects of tort law).

35. *See* Guido Calebresi & Jon T. Hirschoff, *Toward a Test for Strict Liability in Torts,* 81 Yale L.J. 1005 (1972).

36. *Id.* at 1012.

37. *Id.* at 1013.

38. Richard Epstein, *Unconscionability: A Critical Reappraisal,* 18 J.L. & Econ. 293 (1975).

39. Thomas S. Ulen, *The Efficiency of Specific Performance: Toward a Unified Theory of Contract Remedies,* 83 Mich. L. Rev. 341 (1984).

40. Posner, *Economic Analysis, supra* note 5, at 120. For a critique of this notion from within economics, *see* Neil Buchanan, ch. 4, this vol.

41. *See, e.g.,* Ian Ayres & Robert Gertner, *Filling Gaps in Incomplete Contracts: An Economic Theory of Default Rules,* 99 Yale L.J. (1989).

42. Epstein, *supra* note 37, at 293.

43. A famous contracts case on this issue is *Williams v. Walker-Thomas Furniture Co.* 350 F.2d 445 (D.C. Cir. 1965). In this case, the plaintiffs had purchased numerous items over a five-

year period from Walker Thomas, a retail store in a poor neighborhood of Washington, D.C. The purchase price for each item was apportioned across the prices of all prior purchases so that the purchaser would in effect continually owe money on even the earliest purchases. When a customer defaulted on a single monthly payment, the store sought to enforce the purchase-contract terms, allowing it to take back all of the property, even though, in the case of one of the plaintiffs, only twenty-five cents was owed on the earliest purchased property.

44. *See Crime and Punishment: An Economic Approach,* 76 J. Pol. Econ. (1968).

45. Ronald H. Coase, *Law and Economics and A. W. Brian Simpson,* 25 J. Legal Stud. 103 (1996).

CHAPTER 2

The Demoralization of Economics

Can We Recover from Bentham and Return to Smith?

Deirdre McCloskey

Adam Smith's intentions were to create an ethical system for the middle class. He was in effect following the precept of his friend David Hume, that "[r]eaders as are plac'd in the Middle Station . . . for the most numerous Rank of Men, that can be suppos'd susceptible of Philosophy, and therefore all Discourses of Morality ought principally to be address'd to them."[1]

The intentions of an author are notoriously difficult to discern and for many purposes are anyway beside the point. A poet may intend to write The Great Epic of the Dutch Nation, but if he in fact writes a long and silly poem it is the fact that matters, not his intentions. In her brilliant book, *Adam Smith's Discourse,* Vivienne Brown has observed that the Intentional Fallacy, as it is named in the Department of English, pervades the literature on Smith. According to Brown, all intentionality is to be banished, and the text is to stand alone on its discoverable effects, not on its author's own undiscoverable intentions. One can agree with her feeling that Smith's intentions are not a decisive argument yet still think that Brown raises the fallacy to a shibboleth, as the New Criticism in literary studies did. As the New Historicists have noted, a life is also a text, and a life as methodical as Smith's often reveals illuminating intentions.

Of course the effects of Smith's writings, regardless of intent, we to some degree experience as I claim he intended. Smith has been read often as the theorist of the bourgeoisie. One need only notice the Adam Smith neckties the men of Wall Street wear to know this. Certainly *The Wealth of Nations* is a holy text of classical liberalism, even if not studied carefully or critically—this, after all, is often the fate of holy texts.

And intentions are not in this case impossible to discern. There are many signs that Smith wanted to modernize the virtues to suit the society he admired, and at any rate lived in. Smith's ethical engagement with a commercial age can better be shown than told. His very first appearance in print, so far as we know, is an anonymous encomium to a bourgeois friend, in 1758.

To the memory of Mr. William Crauford
Merchant of Glasgow

Who to that exact frugality, that downright probity and plainness of manners so suitable to his profession, joined a love of learning . . . , an openness of hand and a generosity of heart, . . . and a magnanimity that could support . . . the most torturing pains of body with an unalterable cheerfulness of temper, and without once interrupting, even at his last hour, the most manly and the most vigorous activity in a vast variety of business. . . . Candid and penetrating, circumspect and sincere.[2]

This is not an encomium to Profit Regardless, a perspective that has been ascribed to Smith. Rather, it praises a bourgeois virtue.

An ethic for the bourgeoisie is not the same thing as an apology for greed. Smith was hostile to the reduction of ethics to greedy interest, which Bentham finally achieved and which Epicurus, Hobbes, and Mandeville (whom Smith discussed explicitly and at length) had earlier recommended. Mandeville's system, wrote Smith, "seems to take away altogether the distinction between vice and virtue" by the simple device of noting that people get pleasure from being thought to be good.[3] "It is by means of this sophistry, that he establishes his favourite conclusion, argument, which has not been accepted by modern economists in that private vices [and in particular the vice of Vanity] are public benefits."[4]

Bentham makes the same argument as did Mandeville, and it emerges in modern economics as the principle that every action is guided by Utility. The fallacy in its grip was first noted by David Hume and later followed by Smith: "It is the greatest fallacy of Dr. Mandeville's book to present every passion as wholly vicious [that is, self-interested, a matter of vanity], which is to any degree and in any direction."[5] Thus, if I get a little utility from love, it "follows" (say Epicurus, Mandeville, Bentham, and Gary Becker) that love is reducible to utility, and we can abandon any account of separate virtues and vices. But I get utility because I love, not the other way around. It does not follow that I love entirely because of utility. I may have gotten some amusement from my children, but I did not have them and love them down to this bitter day entirely or even largely because they were amusing. And it is therefore not true that virtues such as faith, justice, courage, and so forth can be reduced without remainder to utility.

Smith by no means approved of every activity of the bourgeoisie. He was suspicious of the rent seeking of merchants, noting that in contrast to the landlords and workers, the interests of the bourgeoisie are "always in some respects different from, and even opposite to, that of the publick."[6] Smith was read this way at the time. Hugh Blair wrote to him on April 3, 1776, commending him: "You have done great Service to the World by overturning all the interested Sophistry of Merchants, with which they have Confounded the whole Subject of Commerce."[7] As scholars on the Left have repeatedly noted, Smith was not a Thatcherite.

Neither, however, was he hostile to the values of a commercial society. Unlike European intellectuals since the great conversion of the mid-nineteenth century, Smith wanted to make a commercial society work, not to sit outside it sneering. He wished to clothe it with an ethical system. In its nakedness it was mere interest. With Thomas Paine he would say that commerce is "a pacific system, operating to cordialise mankind. . . . The invention of commerce is the greatest approach towards universal civilization that has yet been made by any means not immediately following from moral principles."[8]

Vivienne Brown disagrees. She and I agree, against the tide of opinion, that Smith is first and last a moral philosopher, that he is read badly if read as a confused precursor of Walras and Edgeworth and Debreu, and that reading Smith is a task for students of rhetoric, that his work is not to be reduced to logic or intentions alone. But Brown would reject my claim that Smith was making an ethics for a commercial society, the Middle Station in life. For example, she notes that both of Smith's books "contain instances . . . where concern is expressed over the impoverishing effects of commercial society in eroding standards of public decency as well as private morality."[9]

This is correct, but such concern is merely what one would expect from a serious discussion of bourgeois virtue. After all, Smith's writings contain considerably more instances in which delight is expressed over the enriching effects of commercial society in raising ethical standards or public decency. True, Smith was not Ronald Reagan in knee britches. But if we are not to appeal to some social democratic intention to be read into Smith and are to stick to the texts, neither is he Tony Benn in a wig.

Brown herself argues that Smith and the other Scots were busy showing how "a society may cohere and its people may live decently, in spite of the moral failure [by the highest stoic standards] of mankind at large."[10] Such a program was characteristic of the Scottish Enlightenment as against that of the French. It was not utopian, not governed by Hope. Brown does not acknowledge how very bourgeois the program is. Her main conclusion runs against the evidence of the texts: "It is a mistake, therefore, to think that in commending prudence as a lower-order virtue, *The Theory of Moral Sentiments* is praising either economic activity in general or the economic activities associated with what later became knowing as the middle class."[11] Her glancing suggestion here is that the very idea of a middle class is anachronistic and therefore plays no part in Smith's thought—not a very good argument, as one can see from the quotation from Hume with which I began the chapter. And Brown's suggestion is historicist rather than text based, being by her own method irrelevant. Indeed she offers no argument against Smith as an ethicist for a commercial society. She does not tell why the inventor of economics cannot be read in all his works as praising economic activity as a subspecies of Prudence—with reservations, as a moralist for the age, and above all within a system of other virtues, but nonetheless praising it in a way that would have been impossible only in a few other times and places outside the Scottish Enlightenment.

The "ethical system" of Smith was, in modern parlance, an ethic of the virtues. That is, it was not a search for a general precept of ethics, such as Kant was at the same time busily pursuing in his walks from home to the office in faraway East Prussia. Rules such as Kant's categorical imperative (well expressed by any bureaucrat denying you an exception: Suppose I allowed everyone to do that?) or the golden rule or the master instance of utilitarianism are not what Smith sought, or found. He sought and found a collection of virtues. In this he was heavily influenced, as he makes clear in his survey of ethical systems in *The Theory of Moral Sentiments,* by classical stoicism, Epictetus the slave, and Marcus Aurelius the emperor. An ethic of the virtues has been exposited in recent decades by Philippa Foot, Elizabeth Anscombe, Iris Murdoch, Susan Wolf, Rosalind Hursthouse, Annette Baier, Alasdair MacIntyre, John Casey, Bernard Williams, and Martha Nussbaum. (This is the only field of modern philosophy in which women's voices predominate.) But it is as old as Aristotle's *Nicomachean Ethics* and is to be set against Plato's (and Kant's and Bentham's) search for the one Good. Just as ethics is not to be reduced to Utility, neither is it to be reduced to Reason.

In her book *Moral Boundaries: A Political Argument for an Ethic of Care,* Joan Tronto argues that "what is now called 'women's morality' bears a striking similarity to the moral thinking of the Scottish Enlightenment."[12] "Men were viewed as capable of morally delicate feelings that relied upon particular social conditions for their creation."[13]

Smith's *Theory of Moral Sentiments*—which of course it is natural to see as the thing it claims to be, an exploration of virtues and vices—can be read as treating the four "pagan" or aristocratic virtues and the three "theological" or peasant virtues. The analysis of all virtues into these seven was begun in classical times and completed by Aquinas. The weight of tradition is not a knockdown argument for thinking that the seven contain all the virtues one needs to consider. Especially in view of my theme, readers won't be surprised that I believe Smith may have been mistaken to adhere to these only—it may be that a bourgeois virtue is hard to discuss in classical or Christian terms. But my thesis here is textual. I claim anyway that the whole of *The Theory of Moral Sentiments* can be divided into discussions of the various seven traditional virtues. The Pagan four are Courage, Temperance, Prudence (of Wisdom), and Justice. The Christian three are Faith, Hope, and Love.

Or rather, Smith discussed five of the seven. He left off Faith and Hope. I would argue that he did so in the belief that these "theological" virtues were inappropriate to a bourgeois society. Eighteenth-century thinkers—and politicians—were haunted by the religious wars of the previous century, an excess of Faith. In Britain, especially after the Gordon Riots of 1780, they were obsessed too by fear of Hope. Faith you can view as backward looking: one can see it, for example, in nostalgia for the Highland clan, a feature of (British) nation building in (very) late eighteenth-century Scotland. Hope is forward looking, utopian in just the way a saint is utopian. The Hope I see, with Edmund, is embodied in the French Revolution.[14]

The rest of the seven are arranged in effect along a spectrum, thus:

Courage   Temperance   Prudence   Justice   Love

The point I am making is that Smith definitely and clearly put Courage and Love on the edges. Not *off* the edge, like Hope and Faith, but away from the central virtues of a bourgeois society. Brown again would disagree. She views Smith as a neo-stoic and argues that Prudence is, in Smith, a "lower-order" virtue, useful as regulating the mass of mankind but nothing like an adequate ethic for an ethical aristocrat. I agree with her in resisting the Benthamite notion of reducing Smith to the virtue of Prudence alone. But I disagree that his texts are mainly or centrally concerned with ethical heroes and saints, aristocrats or peasants, as against the Middle Station. The evidence for Smith's placement of the virtues is thick in his writing. Consider his well-known remark that it is not from the benevolence of the butcher and baker that we expect our supper (that is, not from Love) but from their self-regard (that is, Prudence). (Other feminists have pointed out sardonically that someone had to cook the dinner, Mr. Smith [it was Mrs. Smith, his Mom], and that it *is* a matter of Love.) Or consider this less well-known fact, emphasized in Brown, that Smith was indifferent, even hostile, to commercial courage, the virtue of enterprise. He recommended prudential investing, preferably in agriculture. He was not enthusiastic for the thrusting, risk-taking entrepreneurs that, say, Marx and Engels praised so. Smith was not a romantic about capitalism, as some modern defenders of it are (Ayn Rand, for example). I repeat: Smith regarded Love and Courage as dangerous emotions, more passions than interests, as Albert Hirschman has said. It is little wonder that a Scot witnessing the benefits of secularism and peace in a country riven so recently by Love and Courage would take such a line. But in doing so he distanced himself decisively from the aristocratic virtues (above all Courage) and the Christian virtues (above all Love).

The virtue of Prudence in a commercial person is overpraised in Smith: "the prudent man is always both supported and rewarded by the entire approbation of the impartial spectator."[15] Smith here is imagining a rather spiritless Impartial Spectator, who has no taste for novelty or risk. Prudence fits his ideas of economic growth, which were that the Highlands could in time become as prosperous as Holland was in 1776, not that the national income would rise as it did by a factor of twelve or more in two centuries.

Yet Prudence is not an ethical nullity. Since the middle of the nineteenth century, Western intellectuals and artists have scorned such a bourgeois character and have believed that bourgeois life is merely the vice of greed. Prudence is simply dropped from most thinking about ethics that does not start with concrete virtues, as Smith does, and does not ask how they work in the world. John Casey notes, "[p]hilosophers here reflect common opinion: to call a judgment 'prudential' [or 'pragmatic' or 'bourgeois'] is taken by many people as meaning that it is not 'moral.' " But on the contrary, Casey observes, "[w]e can think of the man of practical wisdom as having moral imagination."[16] My late sister in 1995 objected to my change of gender, and out of love (she believed I was mad) had me twice seized by the police (after a night of terror each time, I was freed for lack of evidence of madness, I am glad to report). She exhibited the virtue of Love. But she had none of Prudence, and her moral imagination concerning the actual and possible outcomes of her intervention was defective. (Justice and Temperance were not much in evidence either.) Saint Paul in his first letter to the Corinthians says famously that you may talk with the voices of men and angels, but if you have not love you are as sounding brass and tinkling cymbals. The bourgeois answers that you may express Love abiding in all your actions, but if you have not Prudence you are as a runaway truck or an exploding steam engine.

The virtues seen as instruments for other purposes might coexist happily, each useful in its own sphere. Olaf Velthius puts it this way: "McCloskey herself states that 'the virtues of the bourgeoisie are those necessary for town life, for commerce and self-government'; just as Christian virtues are the virtues necessary to go to heaven, and aristocratic virtues to lead a good life. There seems to be no problem."[17]

The spectrum of virtues in Smith serves to put Prudence at the center, with Temperance on one side and Justice on the other. He wrote *The Wealth of Nations* as a treatise on Prudence. His then unpublished *Lectures on Jurisprudence* constitutes the germ of a treatise on Justice.[18] *The Theory of Moral Sentiments*, of course, in its first edition predates *The Wealth of Nations*. (Although he worked on *Theory of Moral Sentiments* again before his death, in a sixth edition he did not repudiate any of it and continued in spirit to be what he had always been, a professor of moral philosophy.) It can be viewed, as I have said, as a discussion of the entire system of virtues, but also as a treatise on Temperance. The Impartial Spectator of that book is the regulator of the other virtues, just as Temperance is.

Prudence was at the center, with Temperance on one side and Justice on the other. Those were Smith's three, on two of which he wrote long books and on the other of which, Justice, he could have (the student notes constituting *Lectures on Jurisprudence* are 554 printed pages long in the Glasgow edition). Temperance and Justice are themselves notably bourgeois in his writing. In any event, Temperance, Justice, and Prudence, these are the three. But the greatest is Prudence.

But something happened between Smith and now. Somehow a view of Economic Man that placed him in a system of virtues got mislaid. The mislaying was in part an episode in the general decline of ethical philosophy, down to what Mark Johnson has called "the nadir of moral reasoning in this century."[19] As expressed in A. J. Ayers's emotivism, it is the notion that ethical opinions are merely opinions:

> Ethical concepts are unanalysable, inasmuch as there is no criterion by which one can test the validity of the judgments in which they occur. . . . They are mere pseudo-concepts. . . . If I say to someone, "You acted wrongly in stealing that money" . . . it is as if I had said, "You stole that money," in a peculiar tone of horror.[20]

Thus we hear the undergraduate saying, "That's just a matter of opinion. It's a free country. Everything's relative." There is an earlier and specifically economic version of ethical nihilism, traceable I think to Bentham. The revealingly brief entry for "Morality" in Palgrave's *Dictionary of Political Economy* declares that the economists' "business is to explain, not to exhort. It is therefore beside the mark to speak of economists, as such, preaching a low morality or rejecting morality altogether."[21] George Stigler could not have put it better.

The villain I am claiming is Jeremy Bentham. My evidence for this as a doctrinal assertion is, I admit, slender. Bentham is looked on as a hero by ethical nihilists such as Stigler, Becker, or Judge Richard Posner, but perhaps some other strand of nineteenth-century thinking explains the divorce of economics from ethics. Doubtless. It would take something more forceful than a man who compared poetry to pushpins and advocated single-sex prisons and a Suez canal to turn the mind of economics away from any virtue but Prudence.

Yet the textual evidence in Bentham is plain enough. His *Principles of Morals and Legislation* calls Prudence by his word, "utility," and claims to prove that "the only right ground of action, that can possibly subsist, is, after all, the consideration of utility."[22] The way he proved this was to reduce each virtue to Prudence. How? Simple. Since, say, Love produces happiness, it must be motivated by happiness. *Q.E.D.* I have already noted Hume's—and my own—refutation of this absurdity. Bentham was unknown to Smith, but Smith does discuss in chapter 2 of part 7 of *The Theory of Moral Sentiments* "those Systems which make Virtue consist in Prudence," in particular, Epicurean ethics. It indulged "a propensity, which is natural to all men, but which philosophers in particular are apt to cultivate with a peculiar fondness, as the great means of displaying their ingenuity, the propensity to account for all appearances from as few principles as possible."[23] The propensity dominates modern economics. The philosopher Michael Oakeshott once called Bentham's work "a chaos of precise ideas"—a good description of the modern utilitarianism of Stigler, Becker, and Posner.

A demoralized economics is one without what the Dutch economist of culture Arjo Klamer calls "character." The neoclassical "agent" is a Man Without Qualities. Oddly, law-giving ethical systems depend on a denatured agent. The Good-Willed person is without "accidents" in Aquinas's sense, and so taken away from the world of context and luck and fate, away from actual stories. As John Casey puts it, "[t]he concept of a person [in Protestant Christianity, Kant, and economics after Bentham] ideally coincides with that of a rational agent."[24] By contrast, "[i]n valuing others for possessing the traditional virtues, one implicitly recognizes and values their personhood."[25] "We all inherit from Christianity, and from Kant, the assumption that there must be some set of principles of conduct which apply to all men, simply as men."[26]

What Joan Tronto said about the care ignored in most economic thought one could also say about the economic activity ignored in most moral thought: "our account of moral life should provide us with a way to respect and deal justly with others. In order to do so, we must honor what most people spend their lives doing."[27] But the separation of the spheres around 1800 put an end to Smith's project of fully ethical although bourgeois human beings. Citing Barbara Welter's class description of the Cult of True Womanhood, Tronto draws attention to the nineteenth-century notion that woman are better morally precisely because they are outside the marketplace and notes that morality is also supposed to be corrupted by an association with politics.[28] The result is realpolitik on the one hand and Sunday-morning moralizing on the other: "to view politics and morality as two separate realms of life will make it extremely difficult for moral arguments ever to have much political power. Jane Addams lost her moral authority when her pacifist leanings [in World War I] seemed a naïve type of 'morality first' politics."[29]

Tronto is not without flaws. With many others, she supposes that the male realm of long-distance trade was without morality, arguing that it is merely a matter of "unlimited economic acquisition," as though greed were peculiar to modern capitalism.[30] In fact, trade always requires morality. It often turns out that the writer is depending on Karl Polanyi's account of economic history (the only citation to him, I admit).[31] Tronto relies on Habermas for historical proof of the same assertion, that the public became more public in the eighteenth century; Habermas, like Polanyi, knew very little history.[32] I don't think Polanyi's mistake is necessary for Tronto's own argument. It is not necessary for eighteenth-century long-distance trade to represent a qualitative break with earlier forms of economy. It can still be true, as Tronto argues persuasively, that at the level of ethical theory, the late eighteenth century saw a breaking up of a unified view in which the virtues of the household and the marketplace were the same.

But what of it? What does economics lose by being demoralized? I answer from inside economics as a science. My claim is that economics makes grave errors of positive science when it ignores the system of virtues and specializes all ethics to Prudence. Economics since Bentham has been the science of Prudence, and a wonderfully successful one. I am a Chicago school economist and a great enthusiast for this intellectual program. I once wrote an entire, long book devoted to showing how Prudence can explain much.[33] But I have realized gradually that it is a scientific mistake to set the other virtues aside even when you wish to deal chiefly with Prudential consequences. It is not always impossible to "economize on love," as an economist once expressed the Mandevillean/Benthamite and anti-Smithian program of modern economics. But in many important cases it is.

A good example is what is known in economics as the Voting Paradox. It is "paradoxical," notes the economist, that people bother to vote at all in large elections, because Prudence would keep them at home. No one vote will affect the outcome—unless the election is otherwise an exact tie, a vanishingly improbable event in most large elections. A Prudent man would therefore never vote, if voting had (as it does) the tiniest inconvenience.

Yet people do vote. Oh, oh. Hmm. Some other motive than Prudence must be explaining this very important piece of behavior. Love, perhaps. Or Justice.

George Stigler and I once fell into a quarrel about this at lunch. I said: "Your theory that when people get into the voting booth they vote their pocketbooks [Prudence in my present vocabulary] must be wrong. In order to get into the booth in the first place, they have to be irrational." He became angry and contemptuous, as was his practice when faced with an argument he could not answer seriously. "It's an empirical matter," said he; "one can only know whether it works by running regressions of voting on pocketbook Prudence." He was forgetting that the existence of voters is empirical too, an empirical fact that annihilates his theory of politics before one does the regressions.

Another and more important example is the so-called Prisoner's Dilemma. Prudence, argued Thomas Hobbes, would lead men in a state of nature to defect from social arrangements. The Hobbes Problem has misled most serious thinkers about society since he posed it. The problem is this: Will a mass of unsocialized brutes form spontaneously a civil society? Hobbes's answer was no, not without a leviathan state; otherwise one can expect society to be a war of all against all and the life of man solitary, poor, nasty, brutish, and short.

But the Hobbes Problem, when you think of it, is very peculiar. Why would it be interesting to know about the behavior of a mass of unsocialized brutes when every human being is in fact already socialized? The question does not occur to most men. Women know that humans, for example, are raised in families and therefore are already socialized. But men have been fixated on the Hobbes Problem, without making the slightest progress in solving it, for three centuries now. As Annette Baier puts it, "preoccupation with prisoners and prisoners' dilemmas is a big boys' game and a pretty silly one too."[34] Or Carol Rose: "The lapse of community may occur only infrequently in our everyday lives, but this world of estrangement has had a robust life in the *talk* about politics and economics since the seventeenth century."[35]

Even quite sensible men find fascinating the mental experiment of imagining a human being who could never be. I have even found Adam Smith acceding to its charms: "In order to confute so odious a doctrine [that is, Hobbes's], it was necessary to prove, that antecedent to all law or positive institution, the mind was naturally endowed with a faculty, by which it distinguished in certain actions and affections, the qualities of right, laudable, and virtuous."[36] This is to accept Hobbes's absurd mental experiment as the frame for answering. For it is not true that something true of Hobbes's world is true or relevant or the slightest bit interesting for a world in which people are already some mother's children, or French, or economists. And like the Voting Paradox, the Hobbes Problem is contradicted by the most evident facts. People do not always cooperate, but neither do they always defect. In actual experiments they cooperate far above the level predicted by the Solely Prudence model. A bizarre feature of the experiments is that the only people who do not cooperate at such levels and who do approach the Benthamite economist's level of defection are, well, economists.

What is wrong with ignoring the system of virtues can be put econometrically. Suppose we propose to reduce all behavior, B, to a function of Prudence, P, which stands for all the variables that economists since Bentham have specialized in loving: Prudence, but profit, price, payment, property, preferences, punishment, the Profane. Being sensible, we generously admit that, well, yes, there might be other springs of conduct working at the same time—in cases such as voting or the Prisoner's Dilemma or the raising of children, the S variables of Solidarity, society, sociology, sensibility, stories, speech, sanctions, shame, the Sacred. That is, econometrically speaking, we might specify B as a linear function of P and S, with an error term ε:

$$B = \alpha + \beta P + \gamma S + \varepsilon$$

Very nice, dear. An economist caught in the Benthamite program is going to add, "Not to worry: you see, even without inquiry into S—I leave that to those idiots over in the Department of Sociology or the College of Law—I can estimate the coefficient on Prudence alone, β. I can take $\gamma S + \varepsilon$ to be a quasi-error term. Isn't that clever! And you know how quickly I can move to assume it has classical properties! I'm not in the business of explaining all behavior. Give me a break: I propose merely to explain some portion, and in many cases a large portion."

But the economist is making an econometric mistake. The estimation of the coefficients is unbiased only if the error term ε is uncorrelated with the included variable, P. But unless God (blessed by Her holy name) has arranged the world's experiment such that P and S are independent, orthogonal, unrelated in a statistical sense, the quasi-error term $\gamma S + \varepsilon$ will most definitely be correlated with the included variable, *P*. There is every reason to believe, however, that in many important cases—the Voting Paradox and the Prisoner's Dilemma, to take two, but others also, such as welfare payments, child raising, parent caring, household specialization, consumer behavior, education, technological investment, financial innovation—the virtues buried in the error term will be correlated with Prudence positively or negatively. If the correlation is substantively large (forget about its merely statistical significance, which is scientifically irrelevant), then the attempt to get insight from the Prudence variables will be substantively ruined. The experiment will not be properly controlled. If people who are rich (have high *P*'s standing for, say, Property) also by accident, or by the intervention of a latent variable, desire lots of education on nonprudential grounds (have high *S*'s standing for, say, Schooling), then a Benthamite model of why people invest in education will give wrong results. The coefficient β on Prudence will be biased. (In this case it will be biased upward, and the estimate will not even be consistent, statistically speaking: large sample sizes will not make any difference, except to render the economist, by the stupidity of statistical significance, unreasonably confident that he has the explanation in *P*.)

Albert Hirschman, who has been making this point for some decades, puts it this way:

> What is needed is for economists to incorporate into their analysis, whenever it is pertinent, such basic traits and emotions as the desire for power or sacrifice, the fear of boredom, pleasure in both commitment and unpredictability, the search for meaning and community, and so on. . . . When one has been groomed as a "scientist" it just takes a great deal of wrestling with oneself before one will admit that moral considerations of human solidarity can effectively interfere with those hieratic, impersonal forces of supply and demand.[37]

Smith's project was an ethical one. Bentham derailed it and brought economists to think only of *P*, Prudence. If economics is going to get serious about being a "positive" science, like geology or history, and not amount merely to a chaos of precise ideas, it needs to be back to Smith's project of seeing Prudence within a system of virtues, and vices, for a commercial society.

Notes

1. David Hume, *Essays* 546 (1741–42).

2. Adam Smith, *Essays on Philosophical Subjects* 262 (W. P. D. Wightman and J. J. Bryce eds., Oxford U. Press 1980).

3. Adam Smith, *The Theory of Moral Sentiments* sec. VII.ii.4.6, at 308 (D. D. Raphael and A. L. Macfie eds., Oxford U. Press 1976) [hereinafter Smith, *Moral Sentiments*].

4. *Id.* at 312–13.

5. *Id.* at 312.

6. Adam Smith, *The Wealth of Nations* book 1, ch. 10, sec. 8, para. 10, at 267 (R. H. Campbell and A. S. Skinner eds., Oxford U. Press 1976).

7. Adam Smith, *Correspondence of Adam Smith* 188 (E. C. Mossner and I. S. Ross eds., Oxford U. Press 1977).

8. Albert O. Hirschman, *The political economy of Latin American development: Seven exercises in retrospection* 108 (Center for U.S.–Mexican Studies, University of California, San Diego 1986).

9. Vivienne Brown, *Adam Smith's Discourse* 212 (Routledge 1994).

10. *Id.* at 208.

11. *Id.* at 93–94.

12. Joan C. Tronto, *Moral Boundaries: A Political Argument for an Ethic of Care* 20 (Routledge 1993).

13. *Id.* at 25.

14. If you can stand any more of this sort of intellectual history in which ideas strut around like actors on a stage, I see too a revival of Faith and Hope as political ideas in the nineteenth century. An astonishing development in Britain, the United States, and Protestant Germany in the early nineteenth century was Evangelicalism among the intelligentsia—something that would have been wholly unexpected by urbane deists such as Smith, or atheists such as Hume or Gibbon, or even the traditionally Anglican Dr. Johnson. The theological virtue of Hope reemerged in projects of moral reform by the evangelicals (such as the abolition of slavery). Eventually both merged in a secular version of Christianity by the name of socialism or a secular version of paganism called nationalism. And all our woe.

15. Smith, *Moral Sentiments, supra* note 3, at secs. VI.1.6, VI.i.11.

16. John Casey, *Pagan Virtue: An Essay in Ethics* 145, 146 (Clarendon Press 1990).

17. Olaf Velthius, The Instrumental and the Intrinsic, Kunsten Cultuurwetenschapen, Erasmus University of Rotterdam, 5 (unpublished).

18. Adam Smith, *Lectures on Jurisprudence* 1762–63, 1766 (R. L. Meek, D. D. Raphael, and P. G. Stein eds., Oxford U. Press 1978).

19. Mark Johnson, *Moral Imagination: Implication of Cognitive Science for Ethics* (U. of Chicago Press 1993).

20. A. J. Ayer (1936), *quoted* id. at 137.

21. F. C. Montague, *Morality,* in *Dictionary of Political Economy* vol. 2, at 812 (R. H. I. Palgrave ed., Macmillan 1900).

22. Jeremy Bentham, *A Fragment on Government, with an Introduction to the Principles of Morals and Legislation* 146 (W. Harrison ed., Clarendon Press 1789).

23. Smith, *Moral Sentiments, supra* note 3, at 294–300, 299.

24. Casey, *supra* note 16, at 6.

25. *Id.* at vii.

26. *Id.* at 9.

27. Tronto, *supra* note 12, at x.

28. *Id.* at 1, 3.

29. *Id.* at 8–9.

30. *Id.* at 27.

31. *See, e.g., id.* at 32.

32. *Id.* at 33.

33. D. N. McCloskey, *The Applied Theory of Price* (2d ed., Macmillan 1985).

34. Annette Baier, *What Do Women Want with a Moral Theory,* in *Virtue Ethics* 264 (R. Crisp and M. Slote eds., Oxford U. Press 1997).

35. *Id.* at 225.

36. Smith, *Moral Sentiments, supra* note 3, at 318.

37. Albert O. Hirschman, *Against Parsimony: Three Easy Ways of Complicating Some Categories of Economic Discourse,* 74 Am. Econ. Rev. 90 (1984).

CHAPTER 3

Separative and Soluble Selves

Dichotomous Thinking in Economics

Paula England

Hidden assumptions related to gender have affected the deep theoretical structure of neoclassical economics.[1] Economists have had one notion of the self for market behavior: individuals are atomized and self-interested, and have preferences that no one can change. But the self has a very different image when viewed in relation to the family, albeit an image as often tacit as explicit. The family is seen to form our preferences when we are young, and family members are seen to share money and care for each other, with little regard to narrow self-interest. Economists dichotomize the two spheres, with analysis of the market taking an extreme "separative" view of the self and analysis of the family an extreme "soluble" view.

In this essay, I review feminist theorizing that criticizes the separative/soluble dichotomy that permeates thinking about the self in Western thought. I then apply these insights to a criticism of neoclassical economics.[2]

I call one notion of the self "separative" because it presumes that humans are autonomous, impermeable to social influences, and lack sufficient emotional connection to each other to feel any empathy. I argue that three of the most basic assumptions in neoclassical economic theory—that interpersonal utility comparisons are impossible, that tastes are exogenous to economic models and are unchanging, and that actors are selfish (that is, they have independent utilities)—imply a separative notion of the self. Although each assumption is occasionally challenged, most mainstream economists accept them without much consideration. I argue that they are grounded in a general tendency in Western thought to posit and valorize the separative self. Because this model of the self ignores the inexorable interdependency of human life and the importance for human well-being of connection, feminists have criticized it as inaccurate and unworthy as a moral ideal.

When economists talk about the family, however, they seem to have an image of selves so soluble that members have no independent will or interest. It is all for one and one for all. This image is explicit in Becker's 1991 work *A Treatise on the Family*, usually credited as starting the "new home economics."[3] He posits selfishness in markets but altruism in the family, with family members acting as if they are maximizing a single family utility function.

Conflicts of interest between family members and self-interested maneuvering for advantage are ignored, or at least downplayed. Drawing on the feminist critique of the "soluble" pole of the separative/soluble dichotomy, I apply it to economic work on the family, arguing that economists exaggerate the connective empathy and altruism within families.

I then consider recent developments in economics that provide a partial corrective to this dichotomous notion of the self. I discuss bargaining models of the family that acknowledge conflicts of interest and self-interested maneuvering within the family. I also consider efforts by mainstream economists to relax the assumption that preferences are exogenous and unchanging. I argue that both are useful correctives to overly dichotomized thinking in that the theory of endogenous tastes assumes a less impermeable self, while bargaining theories bring in some degree of separation between family members. I also argue, however, that if we really want to eschew dichotomies, the unmet challenge is a model of behavior across family and market spheres that captures both the individuated and connective aspects of life.

Finally, I consider how recent work on caregiving (parenting, paid child care, teaching, nursing, counseling, and so forth) by feminist economists has tried to meet this challenge. Work on caregiving represents an attempt, still in progress, to eschew the separative/soluble dichotomy and theorize work performed in both families and markets as involving both altruistic and narrowly self-interested motives.

Feminist Critiques of the Separative/Soluble Dichotomy in Conceptions of the Self

Before applying a feminist critique to economic theory, I must first clarify what I mean by feminist theory. One result of the entry of women, often feminists, into the academy in the last thirty years has been the allegation that theories in every discipline have been affected by gender bias. Over time, feminist thought has become increasingly diverse and today contains much healthy controversy. Common to virtually all feminist views, however, is the belief that women are subordinated to men to a degree that is morally wrong and unnecessary. Beyond this, views differ as to the sources of women's disadvantage and the proper remedy.

Two major, although not mutually exclusive, emphases within feminist thinking can be discerned. One body of thought emphasizes the exclusion of women from traditionally male activities and institutions. For example, laws, cultural beliefs, and other discriminatory practices have excluded most women from political office, religious leadership, military positions, and traditionally male crafts and professions within paid employment. These exclusions are significant for women because activities traditionally regarded as male include those associated with the largest rewards of honor, power, and money. The mechanisms of exclusion are sometimes so effective that most women do not choose to enter "male" domains, although a minority have always attempted to do so. Here feminists see the corrective as allowing women to participate in these spheres on an equal basis with men. This goal is especially emphasized by liberal feminists but is shared by almost all feminists.[4] These "masculine" domains have been seen as allowing and even requiring autonomy and self-interested striving; the sense in which the men in these roles have actually been dependent on and connected to women and other men has been repressed. But because the domains have been at least rhetorically associated with the separative self, the part of feminism that insists on women's equal right to enter these roles can be seen to encourage the development of a more separated, autonomous self in women.

A second body of feminist thought emphasizes the devaluation of and low material rewards accorded to activities and traits that traditionally have been deemed appropriate for women. The sexism here is in failing to see how traditionally female activities or dispositions contribute to the economy, society, or polity. Examples include failing to see how much child rearing, household work, and volunteer work contribute to "the wealth of nations." Another example is failing to see the extent to which work by those in predominantly female occupations contributes to firms' profits, the issue raised by the movement for "comparable worth" in wage setting (England 1992; Steinberg 2001). Feminists who emphasize this sort of sexism see the remedy to include changing values that deprecate traditionally female activities as well as allocating higher rewards to such activities. This position is sometimes called cultural feminism (Warren 2001), and some socialist feminists argue for this revalorization as well.[5] Because many of women's traditional caretaking activities are embedded in familial relationships and are motivated, at least in part, by altruism or obligation, one can see this strain of feminism as valorizing connection as an ideal.

Sometimes these two feminist positions are thought to be in conflict: the first is seen as advocating that women enter traditionally male activities, whereas the second is seen as advocating women's continued attention to traditionally female activities. Of course it is entirely possible to believe that we should acknowledge the value of traditionally female activities and reward them accordingly without believing that women should continue to do a disproportionate share of these activities. Indeed, a culture that valorizes traditionally female activities would be expected to encourage men as well as women to acquire these skills and values. Therefore, the two feminist positions can be seen as compatible, because together they would agree that activities traditionally associated with either men or women should be open to both men and women, while simultaneously encouraging more equal valuation of and rewards for both kinds of activities. But there is a tension between the positions in that the first valorizes separation more and the second valorizes connection more.

Could we valorize both connection and autonomy? Could we imagine male and female selves that were both connective and yet somewhat individuated? Implicitly or explicitly, the weight of Western thought answers both questions with a no. The terms *separative* and *soluble* were coined by theologian Catherine Keller (1986), who discussed their link to pervasive gender dichotomies in Western thought. In the simplest (sexist) formulations, men are seen as naturally separative, individuated, autonomous, and dominating, whereas women are seen as naturally soluble, yielding, connected, and dominated.

In such dichotomous thinking, the only choices are to be either thoroughly masculine and separative, or thoroughly feminine and soluble. Separation and connection are seen as representing opposite poles that war with each other. To the extent that one is separate, one is not soluble, and vice versa. To the extent that one is feminine, one is less masculine (as in the pre-androgyny conception of gender), and vice versa.

In this view, to valorize one pole implies less value for the other. Historically, only men were considered fully human, because women seem to give up most of what is seen as valuably human in order to bear the burden of connection. No wonder then that liberal feminists thought the only corrective was to seek separation and autonomy for women, and no wonder that men saw only fearful loss in pursuing connection. This way of looking at things was undoubtedly influenced by the hierarchical organization of actual gender relations, such that men had authority over women and devised systems of thought that valorized their own activities.

This dichotomous thinking about the self does not allow recognition of the ways in which some degree of individuation may enhance intimacy, or of the ways that empathy may actually be enhanced by being in touch with the desires underlying one's own self-interested striving. The feminist position that I draw on here argues for delinking separation/connection from gender in prescriptions, and for seeing that individuation and connection are not necessarily at war with each other. The nondichotomous position can be called "individuals-in-relation" (Nelson 2003) or "relational autonomy" (Mackenzie and Stoljar 2000).

Because separation had been so glorified in Western thought, at least for men, and had been held out as the only fully human model of the self, the feminist critique had to start with an attack on the valorization of the separative self and of its descriptive accuracy for men or women, and particularly for women. This feminist critique of the separative-self model was first applied in a number of disciplines other than economics. Seyla Benhabib (1987) traces the ideal of separative autonomy through liberalism in political philosophy. This tradition (whether the version of Hobbes, Locke, Rousseau, Kant, or Rawls) discusses moving from a "state of nature" to the metaphorical "contract" to set up the state. Although the contract is seen to increase civility and justice, men are seen as separative and autonomous both before and after the contract. Authors failed to recognize that men are *not* entirely autonomous—that no man would have survived to adulthood but for the nurturing of a woman. Women's nurturing work was taken for granted and excluded from political theory; women and family bonds were seen as "part of nature" within a metaphysic that denigrated nature. Women's activities did not count as "moral"; only exercising "autonomy" in the public sphere did. Thus the separative self was valued, while nurturant connection was ignored or deprecated.

Psychologists have pointed out a similar emphasis on separation in developmental psychology (Chodorow 1978; Gilligan 1982). Carol Gilligan points out that Freud, Jung, Erikson, Piaget, and Kohlberg, despite their differences, all viewed individuation as synonymous with maturation and viewed connection to others as developmentally regressive. They did not acknowledge learning the capacity for intimacy and nurturance as part of maturation.

The separative self is glorified in the philosophy of science as well. Evelyn Fox Keller (1983, 1985) argues that objectivity has been defined in terms of the separation of the subject (the scientist) from the object of study. Emotional connections with one's subject matter are seen as contaminating knowledge. Keller insists, however, that some of our deepest scientific insights come from the ability to empathize with those whose behavior we study.

Some feminists applauded "connection-valorizing" authors such as Chodorow (1978), Gilligan (1982), Keller (1985), Ruddick (1989), and Held (1993) for their insistence that social scientists include in their theories the parts of human experience traditionally assigned to women. Others thought it perverse to romanticize traditionally female characteristics such as caring, yielding, altruism, and selflessness, arguing that these are understandable but self-defeating adaptations to men's domination of women (Hoagland 1988). Another objection was to the tendency of those valorizing connection to exaggerate gender differences on this dimension. This objection was paired with a fear that exaggerations of gender differences—even if seen as environmentally created rather than innate—could be used to keep women out of powerful positions (Epstein 1988; Aries 1996).

Since the early critiques of the "separative self," feminists have also become increasingly suspicious of any "universal" notion of womanhood. Poststructuralists have argued against any universal notion of human, female, or male nature (Fraser and Nicholson 1990; Nicholson 1990). Feminist theorists of color (such as Brah 2001; Collins 1990) have argued that it is often the experiences of relatively privileged white women that have been described as "the feminine" to be either rejected or valorized. For example, when one considers how insensitive white women have often been to the suffering of less privileged women they hired to clean or look after their children, one has to question whether either women's nature or social role results in empathy and caring. Just as families look less unified when men's violence toward women is recognized, women look less universally empathic when the participation of privileged white women in class, race, and national privileges is recognized.

It is something of a mantra among feminists that we should resist false dichotomies patterned on false ideas of sex differences. Julie Nelson (1992, 1996, 2003) has suggested one way that we can reject the negative connotations of both separation and connection, while embracing the positive of each. She points out that traditionally female "connective" and traditionally male "separative" qualities each have both positive and negative aspects, but argues that there is a strong tendency in Western thought to see only the positive aspect of characteristics encouraged in men and only the negative aspects of those encouraged in women.

Consider, for example, the terms *hard* and *soft*, often metaphorically associated with men and women, respectively. At least in intellectual or business life, *hard* is seen as positive and *soft* as negative. But Nelson points out that it is more accurate to see *hard* as having a positive aspect, strength, and a negative aspect, rigidity, while *soft* has a negative aspect, weakness, as well as a positive aspect, flexibility. The tendency to see the hard–soft distinction as a matter of strong versus weak and to ignore the fact that it is also a matter of flexible versus rigid is an instance of androcentric bias that keeps us seeing the good but not the bad side of male characteristics and the bad but not the good side of female characteristics. She urges a move toward nondichotomous thinking that examines how the positive characteristics associated with traditionally male and female roles can be combined because they are not really opposed to each other (Nelson 1992, 1996). Something can be strong and flexible—like a tree in the wind. Strength and flexibility are valuable in both markets and families.

In my 1993 essay (England 1993), I emphasized the need to criticize the "separative" view. I now see the important feminist project to be formulating a view that is critical of both the separative self and its often tacit and subordinated companion, the soluble self. We need to reject the false dichotomy of individual *versus* relationship. In its place, we need empirical study of how individuation and connection combine in all spheres and ethical theories that show the value of each. A feminist view of individuals-in-relation or relational autonomy sees merit in recognizing and reducing the extent to which women's autonomy is constrained by men's dominance, as liberal and radical feminists have emphasized. It also recognizes that complete independence and autonomy are neither possible nor desirable, and that intimacy, relationships, care, and connections are the source of much of what is valuable in human life, as communitarians and cultural feminists have emphasized. In a similar vein, Folbre (2001) gropes for a politics that combines the socialist feminist critique of class, race, national, and gender hierarchies and the liberal emphasis on self-governance with the traditionally feminine concern for nurture, care, and community, and calls it social feminism.

Applying the Feminist Critique
of Separative-Self Assumptions to Economics

Applying the feminist critique of the separative side of the separative/soluble dichotomy to economics, I show how three basic assumptions presume separative selves.

Interpersonal Utility Comparisons

Neoclassical economists assume that interpersonal utility comparisons are impossible. Since the 1930s, utility has been conceived as the satisfaction of an individual's subjective desires; this concept lacks any dimension of objective, measurable welfare that might form the basis for interpersonal comparison (Cooter and Rappoport 1984). As a result, neoclassical theory tells us that we cannot know which of two persons gained more from a given exchange, because the relevant "currency" in which gain or advantage is measured is utility, and utility is conceived as being radically subjective. Eschewing the possibility of interpersonal utility assumptions is also the consequence of seeing an individual's utility measured on an ordinal rather than "cardinal" scale (with equal intervals and a nonarbitrary zero point), because cardinal measurement would allow comparisons between people. This is so basic an assumption that some form of it is mentioned in most undergraduate microeconomic textbooks (Hirshleifer 1984, 476; Varian 1999, 57–58).

Using Pareto optimality as the criterion of efficiency derives at least in part from the assumption that interpersonal utility comparisons are impossible. A distributional change is defined as Pareto-superior if at least one party gains utility and no one loses any. For example, voluntary exchange between self-interested individuals produces a Pareto-superior distribution. Each party must have felt that s/he would be better off by making the exchange than by forgoing it or s/he would not have made it. When no more Pareto-superior changes can be made through exchange, the distribution is said to be Pareto-optimal. Thus, redistribution requiring some affluent persons to lose utility for the sake of a gain by the poor cannot be Pareto-superior by definition.

How does the feminist critique of separation/connection relate to interpersonal utility comparisons? The assumption that interpersonal utility comparisons are impossible flows from assuming a separative self. To see how this is true, imagine that we started by assuming the sort of emotional connection that encourages empathy. Such empathy would facilitate making interpersonal utility comparisons, because being able to imagine how someone else feels in a given situation implies the possibility of translating between one's own and another person's metric for utility. Assuming that interpersonal utility comparisons are impossible amounts to assuming a separative self and denying the possibility of an empathic, emotionally connected self. But if we assume instead that individuals *can* make interpersonal utility comparisons, then surely we would conclude that as scholars, we too are capable of making such comparisons. These comparisons would provide information about which of the individuals under study are likely to suffer more (i.e., have lower utility) than others. We then would view such comparisons between individuals' utility levels as practical measurement problems that we should try to surmount rather than consider them impossible a priori.

As long as we accept that utility comparisons between individuals are impossible, we find that the same principle applies to comparisons between groups. To answer questions about groups requires not only measuring utility but also averaging utilities across persons. Although some applied economists study inequalities in wealth or income between groups and discuss their findings in language that (often only tacitly) implies something about unequal utility between the groups, such interpretations are in fundamental conflict with the theoretical core of neoclassical economics. Hence, generalizations such as the one that women in a particular society are disadvantaged relative to men are either not made by economists or not taken to imply that social arrangements make women's average utility less than men's.

The tendency to eschew interpersonal utility comparisons is part of why positive neoclassical theories harmonize so well with conservative normative positions on distributional issues. The paradigm denies one the possibility of recognizing that those at the bottom of hierarchies average less utility than others, which would provide a basis for questioning the justice of initial unequal distribution of endowments and its consequences. The paradigm also implies that virtually all collectivistic redistribution is non-Pareto-optimal. In sum, it permits no assessments of unequal utility that otherwise might serve as grounds for advocating egalitarian redistribution; rather, it criticizes such a redistribution as inefficient (in the sense of violating Pareto optimality). For example, this assumption leads one to question the merit of assistance to the large proportion of female-headed families who live in poverty. More generally, it denies us a theoretical basis for saying existing arrangements benefit some groups more than others or, specifically, men more than women.

Tastes: Exogenous and Unchanging

What the utility maximizer of economic theory will do is often indeterminate unless one knows the individual's tastes. Tastes (also called preferences) determine the amount of utility provided by different combinations of goods,

services, leisure, working conditions, children, and so forth. They are an input
to economic models. Economists generally do not attempt to explain the origin of these tastes. In a famous article, "De Gustabus Non Est Disputandum"
(roughly translated, "there is no accounting for tastes"), George Stigler and
Gary Becker (1977) argued that there is little variation in tastes between individuals and that tastes change little over time, so most behavior can be explained by prices and endowments. Some economists see a role for disciplines
such as sociology and psychology in explaining variations in tastes. But
whether or not they believe that individuals differ in their tastes, economists
typically see tastes as exogenous to their models. This implies that they will
not change in response to interactions in markets.

There is no doubt that assuming fixed and exogenous rather than changing
and endogenous preferences radically simplifies neoclassical models. But is the
assumption reasonable? There is good reason to believe that it is not. The following questions illustrate the point: Are most individuals really so impervious to their surroundings that they can hold a job for years without their
preferences being affected by the routines they get used to in this job? Are preferences never influenced by interactions with coworkers? If they are, then
events in the labor market do affect tastes. Are consumer tastes never altered
by interactions with neighbors? If they are, then events in the housing market
(which determine the identity of ones neighbors) affect tastes. One needs to assume an unrealistic degree of emotional separation and atomism to deny the
possibility of these effects of market exchanges on tastes. A model that does
not help to elucidate how tastes change through such interactions leaves out
much of human experience. Further, as economists enlarge the scope of their
discipline, the implausibility of the assumption becomes ever clearer. Does
anyone really believe that the choice of a spouse in the "marriage market" has
no effect on later tastes?

One additional problem with ignoring the endogeneity of tastes is that it
obscures some of the processes through which gender inequality is perpetuated. In some of these processes, economic outcomes affect tastes. For example, according to common psychological theories of learning, also accepted by
some sociologists, adults encourage gender-traditional behavior of children by
explicit reinforcement and by their own behavior, which children model (Maccoby and Jacklin 1974; Kohlberg 1966). Imagine, then, that adult roles result
in part from gender discrimination in the market. This then affects the inputs
to children's socialization because they imitate the behavior of the adults
around them. Indeed, Kohlberg argues that children watch what adults of their
own sex do, leap over what philosophers call the is–ought gap, and form preferences to be like adults of their own sex. In this way, at the societal level, an
economic process, market discrimination, affects the distribution of tastes of
the next generation even if tastes are exogenous to market participation at the
individual level. Or, to take an example from later in the life cycle, if schools

or employers discriminate against women who start out wanting to enter "male" fields, women may not only adjust their choices but actually change their tastes to be consistent with the available options. In this example, tastes are endogenous to economic processes even at the individual level, in ways that perpetuate gender inequality. In an analogous fashion, given economic processes such as racial discrimination or inequality of opportunity by class background, economic processes may lead to race or class differences in tastes; but such differences too are endogenous to economic processes.

Selfishness in Markets

Neoclassical theory assumes self-interested actors. Because it says nothing explicit about what gives people satisfaction, it is not inconsistent with neoclassical assumptions that some individuals derive satisfaction from being altruistic. That is, self-interest need not imply selfishness in the sense of failing to care for others (Friedman and Diem 1990). Nonetheless, in practice most economists *do* assume selfishness *in markets*, as both Frank (1988, 2000), who is critical of the assumption, and Becker (1991, 277–306), an advocate, have pointed out. Sometimes auxiliary assumptions preclude altruism. An example is the assumption that utilities are independent. Because economists generally define A's altruism toward B as a situation in which B's utility contributes to A's utility, altruism is precluded by the assumption that actors' utilities are independent.

The assumption that individuals are selfish is related to the separative model of the self. Emotional connection often creates empathy, altruism, and a subjective sense of social solidarity. For example, the experience of attending to the needs of a child or of mentoring a student tends to make us care more about others' well-being; that is, nurturant behavior makes us more nurturing. (Note that this is also an example of changing tastes.) Separative selves would have no basis for developing the necessary empathy to practice altruism.[6]

Most labor economists assume the selfishness of employers toward employees and vice versa. If employers were altruistic toward some or all of their employees, they might pay them above-market wages, forgoing some profit. Of course, the *strategic* payment of above-market wages in "shirking" models of efficiency wages (Bulow and Summers 1986; Katz 1986) does not violate the assumption of selfishness. In these models, employers are profit maximizers and pay above-market wages only when such wages increase the productivity of workers, and thus revenue, enough to more than compensate for the costs of the higher wage.[7]

Assuming selfishness in markets fails to account for men's altruism toward other men in market behavior, altruism that may work to the disadvantage of women. When people engage in collective action, a kind of selective altruism may be at work (Elster 1979; Sen 1987). For example, when male employees collude in order to try to keep women out of "their" jobs, they are exhibiting within-sex altruism.

Sometimes selective within-sex altruism also exists between male employers and employees, so that employers are willing to pay male workers more than the contribution of the marginal worker to revenue product. This may be termed "pro-male altruistic discrimination," as opposed to the more common form of antifemale discrimination that occurs when women are paid less than the market-clearing wage for men. Matthew Goldberg (1982) has argued that competitive market forces do not erode this pro-male altruistic discrimination in the way that they erode antifemale discrimination.[8] The essence of his argument is that a nondiscriminator cannot buy out an altruistic discriminator for a price consistent with the present value of the business to the nondiscriminator. This is because the nonpecuniary utility that the pro-male discriminator is getting from indulging his taste for altruism toward male workers makes the business worth more to the discriminator than to the nondiscriminator. By contrast, a nondiscriminator's offer to buy out an antifemale discriminator (who is hiring men for more than the wage he would have to pay women) will be compelling because the nondiscriminator can make more money than the antifemale discriminator with no sacrifice of nonpecuniary utility. If we assume the absence of altruism in markets, then we cannot recognize the possibility that this selective altruism is a source of sex discrimination that can endure in competitive markets. Discrimination in favor of members of one's own racial, ethnic, or national-origin group may work similarly. Thus, recognizing selective altruism would raise questions about neoclassical economists' usual assumption that discrimination cannot endure in competitive markets.

Applying the Feminist Critique of the Soluble Self to the Economics of the Family

Even the rugged "autonomous" individuals valorized in liberal economic and political theory would seem to require a selfless altruist to take care of their dependency needs when they are very young, very old, sick, or disabled. But the broad benefits of this work, done largely by women, have remained invisible in economic and political theory until recently. It was just tacitly assumed by most economists—neoclassical, Marxist, and institutionalist—that women would provide loving care for their families and support men in their market endeavors. Of course, it was also assumed that men would, in their role as "head" of families, treat women and children with love, albeit of a paternalistic variety.

Much of this remained implicit, seldom discussed, until Gary Becker's "new home economics" became a mainstream staple. Becker (1991) explicitly assumed a single family utility function in which the "head" is an altruist. From a feminist perspective, Becker's acknowledgment that production goes on in the household and that therefore the household should be seen as part of "the economy" deserves our applause. However, Becker's assumptions about altruism and family solidarity are in need of a feminist critique. (These same criticisms apply to the more recent 1991 version of Becker's *Treatise on the Family* as well as the 1981 edition.)

From a feminist point of view, the overarching problem with Becker's work is that he fails to consider seriously that men are often *not* altruistic toward their wives and children. Becker is explicit about his belief that self-interest is the correct assumption for the market, whereas altruism is more prevalent in the family (1991, 277–306). His well-known "rotten kid" theorem posits an altruistic family head who takes the utility functions of family members as arguments of "his" own utility function. Becker does not say that the head gives no weight to his own narrow self-interest but rather that his utility function includes these preferences but also gives at least some weight to other family members' preferences (Pollak 2003). Becker argues that if the head is somewhat altruistic in this sense, then even a selfish "rotten" spouse or child will be induced to "behave" because of incentives the head sets up by redistributing away from the "rotten" family member. Commentators have pointed out, however, that the "rotten kid" theorem implicitly assumes that the family member whose altruism induces altruism in others *also* controls the resources to be distributed (Ben-Porath 1982; Pollak 1985, 2003). Otherwise the theorem does not hold; it is control over the resources that allows the head of the family to redistribute against the selfish "rotten kid" unless s/he alters behavior to be more consistent with collective family interest. Thus, the "altruist" also must be a dictator of sorts to get the result Becker wants—the ability to model the family, assuming it behaves, so as to maximize a single utility function, the utility function of the somewhat altruistic head.

Becker appears not to think that who earns the most money will affect distribution or consumption within the family. But what if the head earns most of the money needed to obtain the resources and is not so altruistic? Becker does not discuss this possibility. He does, however, discuss why he thinks men have higher earnings than women. He explains the typical (although changing) division of labor in which men specialize in market and women in household and child-rearing work in terms of its efficiency. One can certainly criticize this explanation on the grounds that it ignores the role of tradition and market discrimination. But it is also important to look at how Becker's assumption of altruistic behavior by the person who distributes resources in the family blinds him to seeing the power men can gain over women by the access to resources that earnings provide and thus the disadvantages for a woman of being a homemaker (Folbre 1994; Woolley 1996; England and Budig 1998; Kabeer 2001). To the extent that both spouses are completely altruistic, who controls distribution would not matter. But it is only on the unreasonable assumption that one or both have a completely soluble self that dissolves into the will of the other that we can imagine no conflicts of interest.

Oddly enough, the altruism of women in traditional caretaking roles does not figure much in Becker's theory. Women's altruism, at least toward children, is usually assumed by economists, but not emphasized. Indeed, the inherent dependence of the human condition is rarely discussed. As previously noted, we all need care in childhood and old age, and most of us have some periods of disability and illness during which we are dependent even during our "prime age." Even at our peak, we all benefit from love and nurturance. Where does the altruism and caring behavior that ensures this care come from? What is striking is that neither Becker nor other economists discuss this explicitly; they just seem to assume there will be enough altruism in the family to provide for dependents.

By being more explicit than other economists about altruism, Becker reveals that he actually credits the real altruism to men, despite the fact that women are socially assigned to roles such as mothering in which complete selflessness is encouraged![9] A cynic might say that Becker's notion of the altruism of the head (i.e., that the head's preferences give considerable weight to other family members' preferences) deflects our attention from the fact that the model is really very similar to traditional notions that assign the role of head to the man, allow him to be a dictator, and don't worry about whether this is really better for women and children or only for him. The fact that the altruist also needs to have control over distribution for his model of the family to work should alert us to the fact that it is not a model consistent with mutual altruism combined with mutuality in decision making in which, in the face of differences in preference, each spouse sometimes gets his or her way and sometimes yields to the wish of the other. A model that has such mutuality as one theoretical possibility seems to require rejection of the separative/soluble dichotomy.

Even if we believed that Becker was positing real mutual altruism among all family members, however, there is still an unacceptable level of dichotomous thinking in this model. I have no problem with the notion that, on average, people are more altruistic toward family members than toward strangers. I do, however, have a problem with the extreme bifurcation of the view of the way humans behave in the market and in the family. If economic man or woman is so altruistic in the family, might not some altruism be present in market behavior as well? Doesn't this altruism imply an ability to empathize with others that might permit us to make at least rough interpersonal utility comparisons? Doesn't the susceptibility of an altruist to being influenced by another's joy or pain suggest that s/he also might modify certain tastes through the process of interaction with others? If the answers to these questions are yes, as may well be the case, then the altruism assumed as the behavioral norm for the family is inconsistent with the separative self assumed for market behavior. It is simply not plausible that the altruist who displays an emotionally connective self in the family is the same person who marches out into the market selfish, entirely unable to empathize with those outside the family.

Recent Developments in Economics:
A Corrective to Separative/Soluble Dichotomies?

Bargaining Models of Marriage

Suppose that economists used their usual "separative" assumptions to model behavior among spouses and between parents and children. How would a selfish individual with unchanging tastes behave within the family? When economists analyze a situation that lacks the large number of potential buyers and sellers that characterize markets, they turn to game theory, which has become increasingly popular in economics. Formal game theory models of family bargaining and distribution have been offered in recent decades (Manser and Brown 1980; McElroy and Horney 1981; McElroy 1985, 1990; Chiappori 1992; Lundberg and Pollak 1993, 1994, 1996). Many of these models were not developed as part of a program of gender scholarship but lead to some of the same insights developed in less formal but more substantive terms by gender scholars (England and Farkas 1986, ch. 3; Sen 1990; England and Kilbourne 1990; Folbre 1994, 1997; Woolley 1996; Agarwal 1997; England 2000a, 2000b; Kabeer 2001; England and Folbre 2002b). Both groups often characterize their contributions as inconsistent with Becker's work.

Whereas, in a Beckerian world, the family has a single utility function and cooperates to allocate resources and each member's time efficiently in the service of this unitary utility function, in a bargaining world, resources affect whose interests prevail in decision making within the family and that affects each person's utility. The idea is that if you have more resources, you can get your way more often in terms of who does housework, how money is spent, and other issues on which spouses may disagree. Why might bringing money or other resources into the household give a spouse bargaining power? The game theory models that economists have applied to family bargaining answer this with the concept of threat points (see Lundberg and Pollak 1996 for an overview). Divorce threat point (also called external threat point) models emphasize that bargaining within marriage is conducted in the shadow of the possibility of divorce. An individual's threat point is what s/he has to fall back on if the marriage dissolves. This is presumably influenced by one's own earnings, one's position in the market for a new partner, and the life skills and preferences that affect how much one enjoys being single. Utility outside marriage is also influenced by how much gender discrimination there is in the labor market, the amount of child support payments the state makes absent parents pay and how strongly this is enforced, as well as state payments to single individuals or parents. McElroy (1990) calls these factors "extrahousehold environmental parameters," and Folbre (1997) calls them "gender-specific environmental parameters." Optimizing individuals will choose whether to stay in the marriage or leave by comparing the utility they experience in the marriage to what they anticipate if they leave the marriage.

Consider a couple, A and B. The better off A would be if the marriage dissolved, the better the deal B has to provide A in the marriage to make it worthwhile for A to stay in the marriage. Individuals make concessions to their partners to keep their marriages intact if they would be worse off without the spouse than in the marriage, even after having made the necessary concessions. If both spouses act this way, it follows that the better A's alternatives outside (relative to inside) the marriage, or the worse B's alternatives outside, the better bargain A (and worse B) can strike in the marriage. Resources that one could withdraw from one's partner and/or retain for oneself if the marriage dissolved are those that increase bargaining power.

Lundberg and Pollak (1993, 1996) also discuss internal threat point models. Here the issue is what one spouse can withhold from the other without departing the marriage, and what that leaves the other to fall back on within the marriage. In such models, money that comes into the household through partner A gives A power because s/he could possibly fail to share some or all of the income, even without divorce or separation. Here too earnings should lead to some power, because they are a resource one shares or could withhold. But in this model the relevance of earnings to bargaining power does not hinge on their portability if one leaves the relationship, as it does in the divorce threat model.[10]

Economists offer some evidence to support the bargaining view of marriage. Recent studies show that where women have more access to and control over economic resources (relative to men), more is spent on children (Thomas 1990; Alderman et al. 1995; Lundberg, Pollak, and Wales 1997).[11] This evidence is inconsistent with a view that altruism is so pervasive in the family that who controls the resources does not affect whose wishes prevail.

Bargaining theories allow one to see the possible disadvantages for women of a division of labor in which men specialize in market and women in household work. Such theories imply that to the extent men are not entirely altruistic, the result for women will be less decision-making power and a smaller share of resources going to them. Becker emphasizes that because of its efficiency, the pie is bigger with specialization, but even if this is true, there may be a trade-off for women between a bigger pie and a bigger share of a smaller pie. From a feminist point of view, it is important to have a theory that does not obscure this disadvantage to women of traditional arrangements.

Thus, although economic theory has downplayed connection and solidarity in market behavior, models of the household that use separative-self assumptions are a useful corrective for understanding the household precisely because perfect altruism does not prevail. On the other hand, they miss the considerable altruism and solidarity in the household that exists, although it was previously exaggerated. What is difficult is to devise models that recognize a role for both altruism and self-interested bargaining and still generate clear predictions.

Models of Endogenous Tastes

As discussed earlier, economists generally assume that tastes (preferences) are unchanging and determined exogenously. If tastes are assumed to be stable, then changes in what we choose must be the result of changes in our income or the relative prices of various choices. As discussed earlier, this is consistent with a separative self; in this view, the self is so impervious to social influences that preferences remain uninfluenced by social networks, life experiences, and so on. Robert Pollak, a persistent mainstream critic of Becker, had earlier argued for models that included endogenous preferences (Pollak 1970, 1978). (Neoclassical economists Stark and Falk [1998] also discussed empathy as an endogenous taste.) Interestingly, Becker's 1996 book, *Accounting for Tastes,* although it reprints the previously mentioned 1977 paper written with Stigler, elsewhere announces a change in position on this issue. Becker now argues that preferences for "specific commodities" (examples would be pears, listening to rap music, or having an intimate relationship with a particular person) can change over time in response to an individual's experiences; they are neither exogenous nor unchanging. Indeed, they may change because of one's social connections, an acknowledgment of the role of "social capital." For example, having parents or friends who play classical music may teach you to appreciate such music. Also, many things may be habit forming. Addictions are the extreme example of this, when, for example, today's choice to consume a drug affects the degree to which one prefers the drug to other goods in the future. In these ways, Becker now recognizes the existence of endogenous, changing preferences.

What Becker still sees as exogenous and unchanging is an "extended utility function," which specifies, for each individual, the way in which social connections and past consumption experiences determine how much utility will be gained from various combinations of specific commodities. This extended utility function is different from the standard economists' notion of a utility function that simply consists of one's preferences for commodities and rankings of all possible combinations and sequences thereof (see, e.g., Varian 1999, ch. 4). It is more like a production function for utility functions. Simply put, in the new Becker, it is no longer what you like that is seen to be unchanging but rather the process by which preferences are determined. There are still elements of the "separative self" concept apparent in making the utility production function impervious to social and economic influences. Yet I am not inclined to criticize him on this point because virtually every answer to the profound question of how we come to want what we want takes some portion of "human nature" as unchanging and asks how, given this, conditions affect our preferences. Becker examines questions such as how we can see all the decisions leading up to drug addiction as rational. A feminist cannot help but think of a parallel. If we put endogenous tastes together with a bargaining model (eschewed by Becker), we could hypothesize that being in a subordinate position leads to deferential behavior, which in turn is habit forming, further reducing women's ability to "drive a hard bargain," even when their threat point improves. This would get us close to feminist notions of internalized oppression. Although Becker does not use the model of endogenous tastes in this way, it could be usefully developed to study internalized oppression.

The New Feminist Economics of Care

A third area of recent economic work I consider is from feminists within economics and related social sciences. The study of care work—tending children, nursing, doctoring, counseling, therapy, and so forth—is an excellent example of a topic that challenges all the usual dichotomies—male/female, separative/connected, selfish/altruistic, family/market. This work is increasingly done in the market, although much care is still provided in the home. It often combines altruistic motivations with working for pay. Contrary to many critiques of commodification, feminist and Marxist, the fact that care work is done in the family does not ensure that it is done entirely out of altruism, nor should we assume that moving it into the market or paying well for it takes all the real caring out of care work (Nelson 1999; Folbre and Nelson 2000; Nelson and England 2002).

How do we know whether there will be an optimal amount of genuine care, motivated by altruism, to create a good society and a productive economy (Folbre and Weisskopf 1998)? As women have better economic alternatives outside the home and in the market other than paid care work, and because few men are attracted to care work, the question of whether in the future we will have "enough" teachers, nurses, and child-care workers comes to the fore. Care work pays less than other work requiring the same amount of skill, effort, and risk (England and Folbre 1999a; England, Budig, and Folbre 2002). We should not, however, assume that this is explained by the fact that altruism is its own reward and that the low pay for this work can be explained entirely in terms of the theory of compensating differentials. It may be that the low pay results in part from the difficulties of getting all the indirect beneficiaries of this work to pay the care workers, because care work creates positive externalities and public goods (see England and Folbre 1999a, 1999b, 2000a, 2000b, 2002a, 2003). That is, by increasing the capabilities of recipients, care makes its recipients into better spouses, parents, workers, and neighbors, and the benefits of this care diffuse to many who never pay the care worker.

We are a long way from an adequate theory of care, but it seems clear that the supply of and reward for care are affected by social norms encouraging altruism. We also see self-interested distributional struggles over how much care work men and the state will take on to reduce women's traditional responsibility for care, as well as similar struggles over whose care is paid for by the state and how much state support for care work there is (O'Connor, Orloff, and Shaver 1999). Models that see all family behavior as altruistic or that deny the possibility that care workers may be motivated both by real caring *and* pecuniary motives falsely dichotomize. We need to see the self-interested agency as well as selective empathy and connection in all spheres. What is promising is that authors are explicitly trying to avoid both sides of the dichotomy in this work; what is frustrating is how hard it is to do this and still come up with a coherent model.

Conclusion

I have argued that economists should learn from interdisciplinary feminist theory that offers models of individuals-in-relation as a corrective to traditional dichotomies of separative/soluble selves. On the basis of these feminist ideas, I have criticized economists' assumptions that in the market, interpersonal utility comparisons are impossible, tastes are exogenous and unchanging, and individuals are selfish (i.e., utilities are independent), but that in the family altruism is the rule. The first three of these assumptions of neoclassical theory contain the "separative-self" bias that fails to recognize selective altruism, endogenous tastes, and empathy in market behavior. Economists' usual assumptions about the family go to the other extreme, seeing some actors as almost entirely altruistic or soluble. Taken together, this view glorifies and exaggerates men's autonomy outside the family while giving them credit for too much altruism within the family. This view also results in an inability to see how conventional arrangements perpetuate women's subordination to men in markets and the family.

I examined recent work in mainstream and feminist economics to see how successfully either provides a corrective to the overly "separative" view of actors in markets or the overly "soluble" view of family members. Bargaining theories of marriage bring some individual self-interest back into the family, and models of endogenous tastes could, if broadly applied, show us social influences on actors in the market as well as the family, some of which perpetuate disadvantage by gender, class, and race. These contributions from mainstream economics are hopeful signs, attacking problematic assumptions one at a time. They do not, however, meet the real challenge of providing a model that includes altruism, connection, and self-interested maneuvering in both markets and families. Feminist work on the economics of care is promising in its challenge of the separative/soluble dichotomy, considering work done in families as well as markets for both love and money. Nelson (2003) extends this challenge of the separative/soluble dichotomy to the theory of firms. But we do not yet have a coherent alternative theory.

Modeling behavior when selfishness and empathy are variable and when preferences can change in response to the environment is a continuing challenge for feminist economists and other social scientists. Giving up the strong assumptions common in mainstream economic theory severely blunts the predictive power of models, even if a strong rationality assumption is retained.[12] For example, when it comes to wages and discrimination, it is harder to predict what a rational, selectively altruistic employer will do than to predict what a rational, profit-maximizing employer will do. Similarly, it is harder to predict how a rational husband who earns more than his wife will behave in a model of marriage that sees both altruism and self-interest to be present than in a model that assumes only one or the other.

Some feminists conclude that we simply need to describe reality richly, that any theorizing does violence to reality. Others believe that it takes a theory to replace a theory. My own view is that we should not give up stretching toward a comprehensive theory of human behavior and well-being even while giving up false dichotomies that have kept models simpler but also distorted them. These new models will show us both the dangers and the value in connections and in separation. They will help us understand a world in which both self-interested and other-regarding motives permeate markets and families. They will help us understand the sources of inequalities and the determinants of the happiness or misery of nations, firms, and families. In my view, this is the challenge for the coming decades of work in feminist economics.

References

Agarwal, Bina. 1997. "Bargaining" and gender relations: Within and beyond the household. *Feminist Economics* 3: 1–50.

Akerlof, George A. 1982. Labor contracts as partial gift exchange. *Quarterly Journal of Economics* 47: 543–69.

———. 1984. Gift exchange and efficiency-wage theory: Four views. *American Economic Review* 74: 19–83.

Alderman, H., P. A. Chiappori, L. Haddad, J. Hoddinott, and R. Kanbur. 1995. Unitary versus collective models of the household: Is it time to shift the burden of proof? *World Bank Research Observer* 10: 1–19.

Aries, Elizabeth. 1996. *Men and women in interaction: Reconsidering the differences.* New York: Oxford University Press.

Becker, Gary S. 1991. *A treatise on the family.* Enlarged ed. Cambridge: Harvard University Press.

———. 1996. *Accounting for tastes.* Cambridge: Harvard University Press.

Benhabib, Seyla. 1987. The generalized and the concrete other: The Kohlberg–Gilligan controversy and feminist theory. In *Feminism as critique: On the politics of gender*, ed. Seyla Benhabib and Drucilla Cornell, 77–95. Minneapolis: University of Minnesota Press.

Ben-Ner, Avner, and Louis Putterman. 1998. *Economics, values, and organization*. Cambridge: Cambridge University Press.

Ben-Porath, Yoram. 1982. Economics and the family—Match or mismatch? A review of Becker's *A treatise on the family. Journal of Economic Literature* 20: 52–64.

Bordo, Susan. 1986. The Cartesian masculinization of thought? *Signs* 11: 439–56.

Brah, A. 2001. Feminist theory and women of color. In *International encyclopedia of the social and behavioral sciences*, ed. Neil J. Smelser and Paul B. Bakes, 8:5491–95. London: Elsevier.

Bulow, Jeremy I., and Lawrence H. Summers. 1986. A theory of dual labor markets with application to industrial policy, discrimination, and Keynesian unemployment. *Journal of Labor Economics* 4: 376–414.

Chiappori, Pierre-Andre. 1992. Collective labor supply and welfare. *Journal of Political Economy* 100: 437–67.

Chodorow, Nancy. 1978. *The reproduction of mothering*. Berkeley: University of California Press.

Collins, Patricia Hill. 1990. *Black feminist thought: Knowledge, consciousness, and the politics of empowerment*. Boston: Unwin Hyman.

Cook, Karen, ed. 1987. *Social exchange theory*. Newbury Park, Calif.: Sage.

Cooter, Robert, and Peter Rappoport. 1984. Were the ordinalists wrong about welfare economics? *Journal of Economic Literature* 22: 507–30.

Eckel, Catherine C., and Philip Grossman. 1996a. Are women less selfish than men? Evidence from dictator experiments. Manuscript, Department of Economics, Virginia Polytechnic Institute and State University.

———. 1996b. The relative price of fairness: Gender differences in a punishment game. Manuscript, Department of Economics, Virginia Polytechnic Institute and State University.

Elster, Jon. 1979. *Ulysses and the sirens: Studies in rationality and irrationality*. Cambridge: Cambridge University Press.

England, Paula. 1992. *Comparable worth: Theory and evidence*. New York: Aldine de Gruyter.

———. 1993. The separative self: Androcentric bias in neoclassical assumptions. In *Beyond economic man: Feminist theory and economics*, ed. Marianne A. Ferber and Julie A. Nelson, 37–53. Chicago: University of Chicago Press.

———. 2000a. Conceptualizing women's empowerment in countries of the north. In *Women's empowerment and demographic processes: Moving beyond Cairo*, ed. Harriet B. Presser and Gita Sen, 15–36. Oxford: Oxford University Press.

———. 2000b. Marriage, the costs of children, and gender inequality. In *The ties that bind: Perspectives on marriage and cohabitation*, ed. L. Waite, C. Bachrach, M., Hindin, E. Thomson, and A. Thornton, 320–42. New York: Aldine de Gruyter.

———. 2003. Separative and soluble selves: Dichotomous thinking in economics. In *Feminist economics today*, ed. Marianne Ferber and Julie Nelson, 33–59. Chicago: University of Chicago Press.

England, Paula, and Michelle Budig. 1998. Gary Becker on the family: His genius, impact, and blind spots. In *Required reading: Sociology's most influential books*, ed. Dan Clawson. Amherst: University of Massachusetts Press.

England, Paula, Michelle Budig, and Nancy Folbre. 2002. The wages of virtue: The relative pay of care work. *Social Problems* 49, 4: 455–73.

England, Paula, and George Farkas. 1986. *Households, employment, and gender: A social, economic, and demographic view*. New York: Aldine de Gruyter.

England, Paula, and Nancy Folbre. 1999a. The cost of caring. In *Emotional labor in the service economy*, ed. Ronnie J. Steinberg and Deborah M. Figart, 39–51. Annals of the American Academy of Political and Social Science 561. Thousand Oaks, Calif.: Sage.

———. 1999b. Who should pay for the kids? In *The silent crisis in U.S. child care*, ed. Suzanne W. Helburn, 194–209. Annals of the American Academy of Political and Social Science 563. Thousand Oaks, Calif.: Sage.

———. 2000a. Capitalism and the erosion of care. In *Unconventional wisdom: Alternative perspective on the new economy,* ed. Jeff Madrick, 29–48. New York: Century Foundation.

———. 2000b. Reconceptualizing human capital. In *The management of durable relations,* ed. Werner Raub and Jeroen Weesie, 126–28. Amsterdam: Thela Thesis Publishers.

———. 2002a. Care, inequality, and policy. In *Child care and inequality: Re-thinking carework for children and youth,* ed. E. Cancian, D. Kurz, S. London, R. Reviere, and M. Tuominen, 133–44. New York: Routledge.

———. 2002b. Involving dads: Parental bargaining and family well-being. In *Handbook of father involvement: Multidisciplinary perspectives,* ed. Catherine S. Tamis-LeMonda and Natasha Cabrera, 387–408. Mahwah, N.J.: Erlbaum Associates.

———. 2003. Contracting for care. In *Feminist economics today,* ed. Marianne Ferber and Julie Nelson, 61–80. Chicago: University of Chicago Press.

England, Paula, and Barbara Stanek Kilbourne. 1990. Markets, marriages, and other mates: The problem of power. In *Beyond the marketplace: Rethinking economy and society,* ed. Roger Friedland and A. F. Robertson, 163–88. New York: Aldine de Gruyter.

Epstein, Cynthia Fuchs. 1988. *Deceptive distinctions: Sex, gender, and the social order.* New Haven: Yale University Press.

Ferber, Marianne A., and Julie A. Nelson, eds. 1993. *Beyond economic man: Feminist theory and economics.* Chicago: University of Chicago Press.

Folbre, Nancy. 1994. *Who pays for the kids? Gender and the structures of constraint.* New York: Routledge.

———. 1997. Gender coalitions: Extrafamily influences on intrafamily inequality. In *Intrahousehold resource allocation in developing countries: Models, methods, and policy,* ed. Lawrence Haddad, John Hoddinott, and Harold Alderman, 263–74. Baltimore: Johns Hopkins University Press.

———. 2001. *The invisible heart: Economics and family values.* New York: New Press.

Folbre, Nancy, and Heidi Hartmann. 1988. The rhetoric of self-interest: Ideology and gender in economic theory. In *The consequences of economic rhetoric,* ed. Arjo Klamer, Donald N. McCloskey, and Robert M. Solow, 184–203. New York: Cambridge University Press.

Folbre, Nancy, and Julie Nelson. 2000. For love or money—Or both? *Journal of Economic Perspectives* 14: 123–40.

Folbre, Nancy, and Thomas E. Weisskopf. 1998. Did father know best: Families, markets, and the supply of caring labor. In *Economics, values, and organisation,* ed. Avner Ben-Ner and Louis Putterman, 171–205. Cambridge: Cambridge University Press.

Frank, Robert. 1988. *Passions within reason: The strategic role of the emotions.* New York: Norton.

———. 2000. *Microeconomics and behavior.* New York: McGraw-Hill.

Fraser, Nancy, and Linda J, Nicholson. 1990. Social criticism without philosophy: An encounter between feminism and postmodernism. In *Feminism/postmodernism,* ed. Linda J. Nicholson, 19–38. New York: Routledge.

Friedman, Debra, and Carol Diem. 1990. Comments on England and Kilbourne. *Rationality and Society* 2: 517–21.

Gilligan, Carol. 1982. *In a different voice: Psychological theory and women's development.* Cambridge: Harvard University Press.

Goldberg, Matthew S. 1982. Discrimination, nepotism, and long-run wage differentials. *Quarterly Journal of Economics* 97: 308–19.

Granovetter, Mark. 1985. Economic action and social structure: The problem of embeddedness. *American Journal of Sociology* 91: 481–510.

———. 1988. The sociological and economic approaches to labor market analysis: A social structural view. In *Industries, firms, and jobs: Sociological and economic approaches,* ed. George Farkas and Paula England, 187–216. New York: Plenum.

Hahnel, Robin, and Michael Albert. 1990. *Quiet revolution in welfare economics.* Princeton: Princeton University Press.

Hausman, Daniel M., and Michael S. McPherson. 1993. Taking ethics seriously: Economics and contemporary moral philosophy. *Journal of Economic Literature* 31: 671–731.

Held, Virginia. 1993. *Feminist morality: Transforming culture, society, and politics.* Chicago: University of Chicago Press.

Hirshleifer, Jack. 1984. *Price theory and applications.* 3d ed. Englewood Cliffs, N.J.: Prentice-Hall.

Hoagland, Sarah. 1988. *Lesbian ethics: Toward new value.* Palo Alto, Calif.: Institute of Lesbian Studies.

Hogarth, Robin M., and Melvin W. Reder, eds. 1987. *Rational choice: The contrast between economics and psychology.* Chicago: University of Chicago Press.

Jaggar, Allison. 1983. *Feminist politics and human nature.* Totowa, N.J.: Rowan and Allanheld.

Kabeer, Naila. 2001. Family bargaining. In *International encyclopedia of the social and behavioral sciences,* ed. Neil J. Smelser and Paul B. Baltes, 8:5315–19. London: Elsevier.

Katz, Lawrence. 1986. Efficiency wage theories: A partial evaluation. In *Macroeconomic annual.* Cambridge, Mass.: National Bureau of Economic Research.

Keller, Catherine. 1986. *From a broken web: Separation, sexism, and self.* Boston: Beacon Press.

Keller, Evelyn Fox. 1983. *A feeling for the organism: The life and work of Barbara McClintock.* New York: Freeman.

———. 1985. *Reflections on gender and science.* New Haven: Yale University Press.

Kohlberg, Lawrence. 1966. A cognitive developmental analysis of children's sex-role concepts and attitudes. In *The development of sex differences,* ed. E. E. Maccoby, 82–173. Stanford: Stanford University Press.

Lloyd, Genevieve. 1984. *The man of reason: "Male" and "female" in Western philosophy.* Minneapolis: University of Minnesota Press.

Lundberg, Shelly, and Robert A. Pollak. 1993. Separate spheres, bargaining, and the marriage market. *Journal of Political Economy* 101: 988–1010.

———. 1994. Noncooperative bargaining models of marriage. *American Economic Review* 84: 132–37.

———. 1996. Bargaining and distribution in marriage. *Journal of Economic Perspectives* 10: 139–58.

Lundberg, Shelly J., Robert A. Pollak, and Terence J. Wales. 1997. Do husbands and wives pool their resources? Evidence from the U.K. child benefit. *Journal of Human Resources* 32: 463–80.

Maccoby, Eleanor Emmons, and Carol Hagy Jacklin. 1974. *The psychology of sex differences.* Stanford: Stanford University Press.

Mackenzie, Catriona, and Natalie Stoljar, eds. 2000. *Relational autonomy: Feminist perspectives on autonomy, agency, and the social self.* New York: Oxford University Press.

Mansbridge, Jane, ed. 1990. *Beyond self-interest.* Chicago: University of Chicago Press.

Manser, Marilyn, and Murray Brown. 1980. Marriage and household decision-making: A bargaining analysis. *International Economic Review* 21: 31–44,

McElroy, Marjorie B. 1985. The joint determination of household membership and market work: The case of young men. *Journal of Labor Economics* 3: 293–316.

———. 1990. The empirical content of Nash-bargained household behavior. *Journal of Human Resources* 25: 559–83.

McElroy, Marjorie B., and Mary J. Horney. 1981. Nash-bargained household decisions: Toward a generalization of the theory of demand. *International Economic Review* 22: 333–49.

Molm, Linda, and Karen Cook. 1995. Social exchange and exchange networks. In *Sociological perspectives on social psychology,* ed. Karen Cook, Gary Fine, and James House, 209–35. Needham Heights, Mass.: Allyn and Bacon.

Nelson, Julie A. 1992. Gender, metaphor, and the definition of economics. *Economics and Philosophy* 8: 103–25.

———. 1995. Feminism and economics. *Journal of Economic Perspectives* 9, 2: 31–48.

———. 1996. *Feminism, objectivity, and economics.* New York: Routledge.

——. 1997. Feminism, ecology, and the philosophy of economics. *Ecological Economics* 20: 155–62.

——. 1999. Of markets and martyrs: Is it OK to pay well for care? *Feminist Economics* 5, 3: 43–59.

——. 2003. Separate and soluble firms: Androcentric bias in business ethics. In *Feminist economics today,* ed. Marianne Ferber and Julie Nelson, 81–99. Chicago: University of Chicago Press.

Nelson, Julie A., and Paula England. 2002. Feminist philosophies of love and work. *Hypatia* (special issue: Feminist Philosophies of Love and Work) 17, 2: 1–18.

Nicholson, Linda, ed. 1990. *Feminism/postmodernism.* New York: Routledge.

Nussbaum, Martha. 1995. *Introduction, to women, culture, and development: A study of human capabilities,* ed. Martha Nussbaum and Jonathan Glover, 1–15. Oxford: Oxford University Press.

O'Connor, Julia S., Ann Shola Orloff, and Sheila Shaver. 1999. *States, markets, families: Gender, liberalism, and social policy in Australia, Canada, Great Britain, and the United States.* London: Cambridge University Press.

Pollak, Robert A. 1970. Habit formation and dynamic demand functions. *Journal of Political Economy* 78: 745–63.

——. 1976. Interdependent preferences. *American Economic Review* 66: 309–20.

——. 1978. Endogenous tastes in demand and welfare analysis. *American Economic Review* 68: 374–79.

——. 1985. A transaction cost approach to families and households. *Journal of Economic Literature* 23: 581–608.

——. 1988. Tied transfers and paternalistic preferences. *American Economic Review* 78: 240–44.

——. 2003. Gary Becker's contributions to family and household economics. *Review of Economics of the Household* 1: 111–41.

Pollak, Robert A., and Susan Cotts Watkins. 1993. Cultural and economic approaches to fertility: Proper marriage or mésalliance? *Population and Development Review* 19: 467–96.

Reid, Margaret. 1934. *Economics of household production.* New York: Wiley.

Ruddick, Sara. 1989. *Maternal thinking: Towards a politics of peace.* Boston: Beacon Press.

Schott, Robin May. 1988. *Cognition and eros: A critique of the Kantian paradigm.* Boston: Beacon Press.

Sen, Amartya. 1970. *Collective choice and social welfare.* San Francisco: Holden-Day.

——. 1982. *Choice, welfare, and measurement.* Cambridge: MIT Press.

——. 1987. *On ethics and economics.* New York: Basil Blackwell.

——. 1990. Gender and cooperative conflicts. In *Persistent inequalities: Women and world development,* ed. Irene Tinker. New York: Oxford University Press.

Sober, Elliott, and David Sloan Wilson. 1998. *Unto others: The evolution and psychology of unselfish behavior.* Cambridge: Harvard University Press.

Stark, Oded, and Ita Falk. 1998. Transfers, empathy formation, and reverse transfers. *American Economic Review* 88: 271–76.

Steinberg, Ronnie. 2001. Comparable worth in gender studies. In *International encyclopedia of the social and behavioral sciences,* ed. Neil J. Smelser and Paul B. Baltes, 4:2293–397. London: Elsevier.

Stigler, George, and Gary Becker. 1977. De gustibus non est disputandum. *American Economic Review* 67: 76–90.

Thomas, Duncan. 1990. Intra-household resource allocation: An inferential approach. *Journal of Human Resources* 25: 635–54.

Varian, Hal R. 1999. *Intermediate microeconomics: A modern approach.* 5th ed. New York: Norton.

Warren, Karen J. 2001. Feminist theory: Ecofeminist and cultural feminist. In *International encyclopedia of the social and behavioral sciences,* ed. Neil J. Smelser and Paul B. Bakes, 8:5495–99. London: Elsevier.

Woolley, Frances. 1996. Getting the better of Becker. *Feminist Economics* 2: 114–20.
Yi, Yun-Ae. 1996. Margaret G. Reid: Life and achievements. *Feminist Economics* 2: 17–36.

Notes

1. This essay reprints England 2003 with minor revisions, with the permission of The University of Chicago Press (© 2003 by The University of Chicago).

2. For valuable criticisms of neoclassical assumptions that do not draw on feminist theory, see Pollak 1970, 1976, 1978, 1988; Sen 1970, 1982, 1987; Elster 1979; Akerlof 1982, 1984; Granovetter 1985, 1988; Hogarth and Reder 1987; Frank 1988, 2000, chs. 7–8; Hahnel and Albert 1990; Mansbridge 1990; Hausman and McPherson 1993; Pollak and Watkins 1993; Ben-Ner and Putterman 1998; and Sober and Wilson 1998. There are now too many feminist critiques and reconstructions to mention them all, but some that I find especially valuable are Folbre and Hartmann 1988; Sen 1990; Nelson 1992, 1995, 1997, 1999; Ferber and Nelson 1993; Folbre 1994; and Nussbaum 1995.

3. There is a case to be made that Margaret Reid (1934) should receive credit for starting the "new home economics," but the credit is usually given to Becker. See the special fall 1996 issue of *Feminist Economics* on Reid, especially Yi 1996.

4. Jaggar 1983 contains an excellent, although critical, discussion of liberal feminism.

5. Although cultural feminists criticize Western thought for failing to see connection and interdependence between people, a related school of ecofeminism points out the analogous failure to see our interdependence with the natural environment and the fact that our instrumentalism toward our environment now threatens the planet and human life (Nelson 1997; Warren 2001).

6. Empathy usually encourages altruism; we are more apt to be kind to others if we "feel their pain." Empathy can be used selfishly, however, although I believe this is the unusual case. The person who knows you best is the one most capable of exploiting you. If A understands B's utility function well, A is more likely able to bargain with B in a way that concedes no more than is necessary; this is the truth behind adages about the advantages of a good poker face that reveals little about one's feelings and preferences. For a discussion by neoclassical economists of empathy or altruism as an endogenous taste, see Stark and Falk 1998.

7. By contrast, Akerlof's (1982, 1984) "gift exchange" model of efficiency wages presumes a sort of altruism on the part of workers and/or employers. In this sense, it is a radical departure from the usual neoclassical assumption of selfishness in markets.

8. For a nontechnical elaboration of Goldberg's argument and explanation of why economists believe market competition erodes discrimination, see England 1992, ch. 2. I have taken some liberties translating Goldberg's technical argument; his discussion is about race rather than gender discrimination, and he uses the term *nepotism* rather than *altruism*. However, he has stated in a personal communication that he considers my elaboration consistent with his argument. I refer to discrimination as altruistic (toward its beneficiaries) when employers pay a group more than marginal revenue product; if employers pay more than the going rate but less than marginal revenue product, I do not consider it altruistic.

9. In fact, an interesting body of recent experimental work suggests that women act more altruistically than men (Eckel and Grossman 1996a, 1996b). This does not necessarily imply innate sex differences but may be a socially constructed preference—an endogenous taste.

10. Threat point models have a similar logic to sociological exchange theory. For an overview of exchange theory, see Molm and Cook 1995 and Cook 1987. For applications to marital power, see Molm and Cook 1995, 220; England and Farkas 1986.

11. Some have challenged this conclusion, fearing it is a spurious correlation; factors in a woman's background that correlate with her resources may be correlated with how good she is as a mother. Alderman et al. (1995) concede that this is possible but argue that enough evidence has

accumulated about the relationship between women's resources and children's well-being to merit shifting the burden of proof to those who claim a single family utility function.

12. I have not challenged this most "sacred" neoclassical assumption of all, the rationality assumption. Some feminist philosophers argue that the concept of rationality in Western thought has been constructed to be inconsistent with anything related to traits and activities presumed to be "feminine"—nature, the body, passion, emotion—and that this has distorted the concept of rationality (Lloyd 1984; Bordo 1986; Schott 1988). Yet rationality has a fairly limited meaning in neoclassical theory. The rational actor has preferences that are both transitive (if I prefer A to B and B to C, I will prefer A to C) and complete (any two outcomes can be compared), and s/he acts on the basis of correct calculations about the means that best maximize utility, given these preferences (Sen 1987; Varian 1999). It is beyond my scope here to consider whether this neoclassical concept of rationality is relatively free from gender bias, particularly in the sense of assuming separative or soluble selves. However, even if we retain the rationality postulate, the neoclassical model needs substantial revision to make its other assumptions consistent with challenges to the separative/soluble dichotomy.

PART II

FEMINISM CONFRONTS NEOCLASSICAL ECONOMIC THEORY AND LAW AND ECONOMICS

A s the title to this book indicates, it is appropriate to talk about feminist engagement with the concepts of economics in both its neoclassic and Law and Economics versions as "confrontation." Initially, feminists who use neoclassical economic paradigms and methodologies for feminist ends, as well as those who critique or reject such paradigms and methodologies, must confront the economists' considerable lack of interest in gender issues.

On the one hand, this lack of interest can be seen as rooted in the positivist pretensions of both neoclassical economists and Law and Economics. By positing an abstract individual actor who operates within the market and is the subject of legal rules, these two overlapping disciplines can aspire to a universal description of the way humans and markets operate that is applicable regardless of gender or of any host of other individual-defining characteristics.

On the other hand, it is not a difficult analytic leap to argue that the very aspiration toward universality intrinsic to neoclassical economics and Law and Economics reflects an unwillingness to view inequalities between individuals as part of a system in which power is allocated by and through societal institutions, including law. Within those institutions, gender, race, sexuality, and class operate to disadvantage certain individuals. If the actor who is posited as the universal subject of the neoclassical economic model and of Law and Economics is in fact revealed to be white, heterosexual, elite, and male, power relationships across gender and other relevant perspectives must be addressed. It becomes apparent once *homo economicus* emerges in all of his positionality that economic rationales are often merely a way to preserve the patriarchal status quo.

Feminist theory in recent years has taken the idea of different perspectives quite seriously. While for the most part rejecting an essentialist approach to gender, race, and ethnicity, feminist scholars nonetheless have been exploring the differences among women. This has become as important a part of the work as looking at the differences in position and perspective between women and men in society and its institutions. In this volume, however, the authors use a more abstract approach—an approach that reflects the level on which we engage economics and its categories.

The essays in this part of the volume are all examples of the confrontations between feminism on the one hand and neoclassical economics and Law and Economics on the other. The first two essays directly engage with this debate, showing a divergence of opinions on the use of economics in general, and neoclassical economics in particular, within feminism. In "Playing with Fire: Feminist Legal Theorists and the Tools of Economics," Neil Buchanan passionately argues that although economic issues are of great importance to feminist legal theorists, such theorists should avoid the tools of economics. Feminist legal theory has frequently come under attack by Law and Economics writers for not being supported by "rigorous" analysis. Buchanan, however, argues that economics itself, far from being rigorous, is comprised of empty methodological tools and misused statistical analysis; moreover, it is a value-laden enterprise whose principles are at odds with the ethical principles of feminism. Further, Buchanan warns that by engaging with neoclassical economics, feminists run the risk of being adversely influenced by some of these very principles.

Douglas Kysar's essay, "Feminism and Eutrophic Methodologies," is a response to Buchanan's essay. Although Kysar agrees with much of Buchanan's analysis of the contradictions and inconsistencies within neoclassical economics, he sees no danger in feminists taking up and addressing directly economic analysis. Further, Kysar offers a description of numerous other economic methodologies, some of which are rooted, at least in part, in the neoclassical economic tradition but have much to offer feminist analysis.

These two essays are followed by Elizabeth Mayes's "Private Property, the Private Subject, and Women: Can Women Truly Be Owners of Capital?" Mayes uses the categories of gender to focus our attention on neoclassical economics broadly, exploring the liberal individual subject that is in the background of neoclassical economics and thus that is the legal subject of Law and Economics. This subject, *homo economicus,* is intrinsically connected to a liberal political and legal tradition that posits a universal (read male) actor in the political scene and who is the subject of legal rules. According to Mayes, such a subject derives from a political tradition that originates with John Locke and is defined by reference to property ownership. In fact, such a subject can be said to be constituted by virtue of what the subject owns. Mayes notes the historical tradition whereby such an individual is presumptively a male subject—and one who in fact holds women as part of his property. Mayes argues that such tradition bears on contemporary legal notions of property rights in a manner that continues to undermine women's economic position in society. Finally Mayes discusses the extent to which property rights have become increasingly abstract and fractionated as a result of increasing globalization and the continual emergence of new intangible forms of property and speculates on whether such newer forms may be employed by feminists in order to view gender and property differently.

Regina Austin's essay, "Nest Eggs and Stormy Weather: Law, Culture, and Black Women's Lack of Wealth," explicitly brings race into consideration, discussing the economic position of black women in American society. Austin focuses not on income, the allocation of which is often at the center of efforts to create economic parity, but instead on wealth. For it is wealth distribution, Austin argues, that considerably impacts individuals' control over their welfare, their stake in and connection to the future, and their peace of mind. Austin's approach and focus on the specific concerns of black women in terms of their control and access to wealth show starkly the limits of positing a universal economic actor as the focus of neoclassical economic theory and Law and Economics. Further, in viewing both the real, practical hurdles faced by black women in their efforts to accumulate wealth and the cultural and psychological factors that hinder wealth accumulation, one can also see the absurdity of viewing all individual action as motivated solely by economic agency.

This part of the volume concludes with Martha McCluskey's "Deconstructing the State–Market Divide: The Rhetoric of Regulation from Workers' Compensation to the World Trade Organization." In her essay, McCluskey brings class and capitalism to the fore and uses feminist and deconstructive methodology to examine the juxtaposition between the state and the market in current political economic rhetoric. McCluskey notes the manner in which discussions about the state and the market frequently view the market as a private nongovernmental realm that functions to economically beneficial ends. The state, by contrast, is viewed as interfering with the operation of the market when it promotes social welfare. McCluskey provides an alternative view of the market as being in fact dependent on and constituted by the state. By examining both workers' compensation law reform and recent resistance to the WTO, McCluskey demonstrates the political implications of viewing efforts to further workers' compensation benefits and regulate trade as state intervention into an otherwise economically efficient market.

CHAPTER 4

Playing with Fire

Feminist Legal Theorists and the Tools of Economics

Neil H. Buchanan

[Author's note: From 1995 through 1998, Prof. Martha Fineman led a group of feminist legal scholars and other interested social scientists through a series of workshops. These workshops were devoted in large part to a discussion of how feminist legal theorists should respond to the so-called Law and Economics movement (and its theoretical basis, neoclassical economic theory), which had become an important force in so many other areas of legal scholarship. This essay, first drafted in 1998, is based on my presentation at one of those workshops. Although I have subsequently earned a law degree, I have chosen here to preserve the outsider's viewpoint of the original draft and thus not to alter the essay extensively based on my studies in law school and afterward. While I have added some updated references and cited several sources that are likely to be familiar to legal scholars, the arguments that follow are those of a "dissenting economist" who was engaged in his first scholarly interaction with feminist legal theorists.]

Legal theorists obviously cannot and should not ignore economics.[1] Economic issues—which have long been recognized as central to certain areas of legal analysis, especially tax and antitrust law—are increasingly implicated in virtually every area of legal analysis, from labor law to contracts to property theory. The question for legal scholars is often not whether to discuss economic issues, but how.

During the discussions at Prof. Fineman's recent feminist legal theory workshops, several participants argued that feminists should use the "tools" of mainstream economics to build a more rigorous foundation for their analyses. Feminist legal theorists, it was argued, had their hearts in the right place, but their arguments lacked sufficient intellectual ("hard-headed") rigor to carry the day. Based on this view, the best strategy would be to use economic tools (which, these participants argued, are value neutral) to build a rigorous, logical foundation on which feminist legal theorists could confidently stand.

If the claim is simply that emotion alone cannot win a debate, or that feminists would be well served by availing themselves of logical constructs that they are supposedly ignoring, then there certainly is no argument. However, feminists are not guilty of the charges implicit in such an assertion. Feminist theorists in all fields have long used pointed and brilliant logic in building their arguments, employing all manner of formal analytical methods. To suggest otherwise is nothing less than an insult that legitimizes the most retrograde gender stereotyping.

The problem—which applies to all areas of legal analysis, not just feminist legal theory—is that the use of so-called economic tools is almost certain to lead to the unintentional importation of hidden assumptions that permeate mainstream economics. Yet the lure is always there. *Why not* use a model that assumes rational choice by rational actors? *Why not* use the neoclassical toolbox to measure costs and benefits, to show that a particular policy is or is not viable? *Why not* use neoclassical models, change an assumption or two, and show that a different result can be derived? Why not, indeed?

This essay presents two reasons why not. First, the supposed intellectual rigor of neoclassical economic theory is—to a surprising degree—a mirage.[2] These tools, far from being as powerful as their advocates suggest, are actually miscalibrated and easily misused. Therefore, mutating legal theory (indeed, mutating *any* theory) to conform to the methodological preferences of neoclassical economists is a mistake. Second, at least some of the hidden assumptions of neoclassical economics are fundamentally reactionary and incompatible with the goals of most feminist legal scholarship—indeed, with socially progressive scholarship in general. Using neoclassical economic analysis (even, or perhaps especially, when "turning it on its head") is the slipperiest of slopes, inviting even the careful analyst to commit lapses of reasoning and to reinforce moral and logical presumptions that should be exposed and opposed.

This slope is slippery in another way as well. Those fields that have started down the road of adopting "some" mainstream economic methods have almost uniformly found that the previously established methodologies have come to be replaced by the neoclassical approach. Because it is not obvious, a priori, that mainstream economic methods leave so little room for alternative approaches, we must all learn from the hard experiences of others who once believed that economics could provide a neutral set of tools.

This is not to say that legal theorists should leave "economic subjects" off of their agenda. It should go without saying (but, based on the discussions in the workshops, it apparently does not) that feminist legal theorists should—emphatically should!—analyze economic issues. In doing so, however, they must make sure that the methods they adopt to pursue such analyses do not reinforce the hidden prejudices of neoclassical economics. Thus, although the motivation for this essay was found in discussions among feminist legal theorists, the arguments are important to scholars in every field of social inquiry who might wish to integrate economic issues into their research.[3]

In this essay, I first describe what neoclassical economics is. I then attempt to explain why neoclassical economics is intellectually unsatisfactory, exposing what purports to be its greatest strength (logical coherence) as its principal weakness. I then proceed to explain why neoclassical economics should be morally troubling to feminist legal theorists (and others), emphasizing the prescriptive conclusions that the assumptions of neoclassical economics lead one to make. Finally, I conclude by suggesting that feminist legal theorists should be mindful of the experiences of other academic disciplines in which scholars have made the mistake of believing that they can put the genie back in the bottle.

Defining Neoclassical Economics

What is neoclassical economics? While an attempt at an exhaustive answer to that question appears below, it might be helpful to offer here a simple yet suggestive comment attuned to this essay's presumed audience of legal theorists: neoclassical economics is the theory behind the *Lochner* decision.[4] Although much of what follows is of an abstract technical nature, therefore, the legally trained reader might profitably use *Lochner* as a touchstone for understanding what is ultimately at stake.

Contrary to what many economists are taught, the moral principles underlying an economic theory *are* what define a school of thought. Neoclassical economics is, at its core, a theory of value. That is, all analyses flow from an assumption about how we should determine the value of goods and services.

This assertion itself is foreign to neoclassical economists, who typically imagine that they are involved in a "value-neutral" enterprise. Almost every introductory economics course goes to great lengths to assure its teenaged students that there is a difference between "positive economics" and "normative economics." The former is the very essence of "science," in which only propositions of logic are entertained, while the latter involves moral judgments, about which economic *scientists* are appropriately mute. "We will discuss 'if–then' statements, not 'should' statements," the students are soothingly assured. "Just learn the science, and you can then use it for whatever moral purposes you like."

Despite these claims, normative language is nearly irresistible when using neoclassical analyses. Even in an essay such as this, it is tempting to describe the results of a standard neoclassical analysis with statements such as "Thus, a subsidy would make things worse, not better," rather than the more neutral, "A subsidy moves the market away from a particular type of efficiency." The progression from fully descriptive language with all assumptions noted (such as the definitional paragraphs later in this section), to largely descriptive language with the assumptions and peculiar definitions unspoken (for example, "Perfectly competitive markets are efficient"), to normatively laden shorthand ("Eliminating the subsidy would make things better") is obvious when one stops to think about it; but it is precisely because people so frequently do not stop to think about it that it happens.

The problem, however, is not simply rhetorical. Neoclassical economics does not merely *sound* normative *some* of the time. It *is* normative *all* the time.

It starts, as noted earlier, with a definition of value. (How much more normative could one be than to make a judgment about what things are worth?) The
criterion for measuring value, according to neoclassical theory, is the willingness-to-pay principle. This says simply that things are worth what buyers are
willing to spend for them.

An especially vivid example should illuminate the concept. In 1998, Prof.
Deirdre McCloskey gave a guest lecture to the economics department of a
Ph.D.-granting university. She argued, among other things, that economists
should become more interdisciplinary, using appropriate methods currently
employed in the fields of medicine, engineering, and history. During the ques-
tion-and-answer period, the first person to speak was the chairman of the host
economics department. A committed neoclassical economist, he announced: "I
do not want any of our graduate students to believe that they should leave the
economics department and join the history department. You should be aware
that new economics Ph.D.'s are paid twice what new history Ph.D.'s are paid.
So that settles the question of value!" McCloskey, of course, had never suggested anything of the kind. Even so, the idea that economists might debase
themselves by studying history so incensed the chair that he was refreshingly
blunt about what really counts. (He could not, however, explain why his graduate students should not go to law school, where they could guarantee themselves markedly higher salaries than economics professors will ever earn.)

What are the alternatives to this criterion for measuring value? In economic
literature, to the extent that this issue is discussed at all, the discussion is usually limited to a single alternative: the labor theory of value. If goods are not
worth what people are willing to pay for them, perhaps they are worth the
total labor effort expended in making them. The dividing line between classical and neoclassical analysis, in fact, is usually drawn at the point at which
economists stopped arguing about theories of value. Neoclassicism emerged as
the dominant force over one hundred years ago, when a critical mass of economists concluded that the willingness-to-pay principle had "won" the war of
value theory. They then proceeded to build what we now call neoclassical economics on that base.

For the purposes of social and legal analysis, however, many alternative theories of value are available. All one needs is an answer to the question "What
determines what something is worth?" One might answer, "Things are valuable according to their biological necessity for humans," or "Things are valued according to their contribution to justice," or "Things are as valuable as
God says they are." People can and do easily hold any combination of these
theories of value, even when they sometimes provide inconsistent answers to
the question.

Therefore, although most economists believe that there are only two available choices (willingness to pay or the labor theory of value), legal theorists
are clearly familiar with the notion that value can be measured in different

ways. This is good, and legal theorists should not willingly limit themselves to the peculiar way that neoclassical economics defines a concept as fundamental as value.

Pareto Efficiency and Deadweight Loss

The familiar demand and supply curves from introductory neoclassical economics courses are nothing more than a graphical representation of the willingness-to-pay principle (and hence the neoclassical theory of value). Demand curves are defined as the set of prices that people *would be willing to pay* for various quantities of a single good, given the values of relevant variables such as income, tastes, and so forth. Supply curves are correspondingly defined as the set of prices that firms *would be willing to accept* in order to provide various quantities of the good, given the firms' technologies, cost of inputs, and so forth. (Strictly speaking, then, this should be called a "willingness-to-*be*-paid principle.")

The next step in neoclassical analysis, after that of defining how the values of all items should be determined, is to determine the *optimal* quantities in which items *should* be produced. (Note again the use—by supposedly neutral scientists—of such values-laden terminology.) This is done by drawing the inference that a unit of a good should be produced if the demander values it more than the seller does, whereas a good should not be produced if the producer would require a higher price to produce it than a demander would be willing to pay.

The seductive logic of free markets, of course, is based on the idea that self-interested individuals will never trade goods for which such a mutually beneficial bargain does not exist—and will always trade goods for which such a bargain does exist. After all, why would any noncoerced parties engage in a trade in which the supplier requires a price that is higher than the demander is willing to offer? Similarly, why would they *not* trade when the consumer is willing to pay more than the seller requires? The only thing left to do in the latter situation is to pick a price, which is what the Invisible Hand of the free market supposedly does for them.

This is where the concept of market equilibrium, or "market clearing," takes center stage. A market is said to be in equilibrium if the total number of units offered for sale at the going price is equal to the total number of units that buyers wish to purchase. This simply aggregates the intuition discussed above, saying that an entire market is in equilibrium if every trade that occurred in the market benefited both sides and if every such trade that is possible has actually been consummated. Again, this relies on the idea that the only reason that any goods would not be sold is that the seller is requiring a price that is higher than a noncoerced buyer would pay. The analogy to the physical notion of equilibrium is simply that there is nothing that would change the price and quantity in such a market except a disturbance from outside the system—a change in the determinants of supply and demand.

General Equilibrium

Under sufficiently stringent assumptions, there is a unique market-clearing output for every item at every point in time. Conceptually, it would be possible to compile a list of every good and service in the economy and then to figure out the market-clearing output in each market—*assuming that all other markets have also produced their market-clearing outputs.* Proceeding in such a manner, we might conclude that the market for Granny Smith apples would clear with 48,000 bushels being produced at the same time that the market for no. 2 pencils would clear with 2.745 million being produced, and so on for every good and service.

This set of outputs is achieved under the condition of "general equilibrium," which is defined as the point at which prices have been set simultaneously in every market such that all markets will clear. The concept is both powerful and subtle. At any point in time, a general equilibrium exists if the price for each good in the economy (both inputs, such as computer programming, and outputs, such as Twinkies) is such that *every* market is simultaneously in equilibrium.

When all markets have cleared in this way, the result is said to exhibit Pareto efficiency—but in a nonsynonymous switch, some economists revealingly insist on referring to this as Pareto optimality.[5] In other words, systemwide market clearing and Pareto efficiency go together: when all acceptable trades have been made, the market has achieved the neoclassical economist's ideal of efficiency.

General equilibrium recognizes that markets are interrelated, for example, that changes in the market for gasoline affect supply and demand in the market for cars (as well as the markets for natural gas, lawnmowers, subway tokens, and so on). Therefore, if there is a change in the demand for gasoline (due to, for example, news of a previously unknown environmental harm caused by oil refining), the change in the price of gasoline will affect the markets for related goods. The changes in those markets will then affect still more markets, until the ripple effect has potentially affected every market in the economy.

Many readers might recall the equilibrium price as the one that is easily seen where the supply and demand curves intersect on the standard diagram in Economics 101. Surprisingly, however, the price depicted on that ubiquitous graph is *not necessarily*—indeed, is almost certainly not—the general equilibrium price. Rather, it is the *partial* equilibrium price, which is merely the price that would clear a particular market, given the existing conditions (equilibrium or not) in all other markets. It does not require that all markets have cleared simultaneously. For example, if the market for gasoline is out of equilibrium in such a way that demanders are buying fewer gallons of gasoline than they might otherwise buy, they are likely to take the money that they would have spent on gasoline and spend it on something else (raising their demand for, say, video rentals). Similarly, because all prices will be different under this situation than under general equilibrium conditions, demanders (and suppliers) will be responding to a completely different set of prices, which will cause them to buy and sell different quantities than those that would be bought and sold in a Pareto-efficient system.

The brilliance of general equilibrium theory is its recognition that there might not be a way to set prices such that all markets are in equilibrium simultaneously. As discussed later in the chapter, the general conclusion reached by general equilibrium theorists is that one must make some rather strong assumptions in order to believe that a general equilibrium can even exist. Even then, moreover, that equilibrium can only be relevant for a given starting point of endowments of wealth, talent, social position, and so forth.

When a market or set of markets is not currently operating at its general equilibrium quantities, there are "deadweight losses." Deadweight loss is simply the dollar value of the difference between what a consumer would have been willing to pay and the amount that producers would have insisted upon receiving in order to produce the good, summed up for all units of underproduction or overproduction.[6] For example, if production of DVD players is exactly one unit less than the Pareto-efficient output, and person A would have been willing to pay as much as $1,000 for that player while producer X would have sold it for as little as $200, deadweight loss equals $800. On supply–demand diagrams, deadweight losses are usually shown as triangular areas; so deadweight loss measurements are often casually described as deadweight loss triangles.

The $800 deadweight loss is independent of the price that would have been charged, because a price of $1,000 would have implied $800 of surplus (a.k.a. profit) to the producer and none to the consumer, whereas a price of $200 would have implied a surplus of $800 to the consumer and none to the producer, with any price in between implying surpluses that add up to $800. However, to say that the economy has "lost" $800 is a bit misleading because this is not necessarily money that anyone ever would have seen. If all of the surplus would have gone to the consumer, for example, the surplus simply tells us how much of a "deal" she feels she received; it does not describe anything tangible in her bank account. Therefore, the dollar values of deadweight loss calculations are often hypothetical.

For all the technical detail, deadweight loss is actually a simple idea. It merely claims to measure the aggregate *value* of any mutually acceptable transactions that outside forces have prevented from occurring. In the standard analysis, these outside forces are typically taxes, subsidies, and outright prohibitions and are called distortions (another favorite—and revealing—word of neoclassicists).

The term typically applied to the analysis of deadweight losses is *welfare economics,* a misleading term but one that is (again) extremely revealing of the normative presumptions present in this supposedly positive analysis. The unacknowledged claim is that the general welfare of a society can be accurately measured by calculating the gains and losses that add up to deadweight losses. As a leading textbook in Law and Economics puts it: "General equilibrium is such a desirable outcome that it would be helpful to know the conditions under which it would hold."[7] "Welfare gains" to society are nothing more than reductions in deadweight losses.

Applied Work versus Cutting-Edge Theory

A further clarification is in order. Economic theorists who are currently developing the newest twists on market-based theories would largely consider the description above to be outdated and even pedestrian. As discussed later in the chapter, the current hot theoretical topics are largely in game theory and related areas. However, because this essay is dedicated to discussing how economic theory is being applied, by nontheorists and especially by noneconomists, it is important to describe not the cutting edge of new theory but the methods that are being used by the disciples and the recent converts.

In virtually every applied field (within economics and other social sciences, and in virtually every area of legal analysis), general equilibrium is still the accepted approach. Even macroeconomics has become, for the mainstream of the profession, applied general equilibrium theory. Papers with titles such as "General Equilibrium, Markets, Macroeconomics, and Money in a Laboratory Experimental Environment" and "Congestion, Land Use, and Job Dispersion: A General Equilibrium Model" are being churned out daily.[8]

This continued reliance on general equilibrium analysis is sometimes defended as being merely a necessary simplification of reality. For example, Elmendorf and Mankiw argue: "Mathematicians study Euclidean geometry (even though we now know that we live in a non-Euclidean world); physicists study frictionless planes (even though all real planes exhibit some friction); and economists study . . . general-equilibrium models with complete and perfectly competitive markets (even though markets in actual economies are neither complete nor perfectly competitive)."[9]

Note that Mankiw and Elmendorf do not say that general equilibrium is contingent on the distribution of endowments and the simultaneous clearing of markets. They simply state that the model is an ideal against which we can compare messy reality. It is not the laws of mechanics that are in question but merely the amount of friction in the plane. Clearly that analogy only makes sense if one assumes that the economy would act the way the neoclassical model says it would if only there were no imperfections. This is why the theory is called "general." Any apparent exception can be called a special case of the theory. Except in that tautological sense (that any behavior can be explained by constructing, post facto, a set of preferences that might have led to that behavior), there is no reason to believe that the neoclassical approach represents the true underlying model of economic behavior. Given its fundamental flaws (which I attempt to demonstrate below), the general equilibrium model should not be elevated in this way, as the perfect starting point from which all "exceptions" are modeled.

For most areas to which neoclassical economics has been applied, the agenda might simply be described as follows: find the deadweight loss triangle and eliminate it. Everything from discrimination to Social Security reform is fair game for the Pareto efficiency test.[10] The Law and Economics movement appears to be based in large part on the assertion that legal analysis should be dedicated to designing a legal framework that guarantees that Pareto-efficient outcomes will be achieved in every market. This either involves removing legal structures that inhibit market clearing or, in the case of the so-called Coase theorem (see below), building legal structures (property rights) so that markets can achieve Pareto-efficient general equilibrium.

Therefore, it is important to understand what is hiding behind deadweight losses, both logically and morally. The next section is devoted to describing—through an entirely "positive" analysis—just how weak are the intellectual underpinnings of neoclassical theory.

Mainstream Economics Is Not Logically Rigorous

Before proceeding, let me clarify the terms *neoclassical economics* and *mainstream economics*. The labels are somewhat arbitrary and are used loosely in the literature. For example, most economists who spend their time working on game theory still usually call themselves neoclassical economists because their work is typically merely an extension of neoclassical theory in different form. Moreover, they do not reject neoclassical doctrine—especially Pareto efficiency—but simply have chosen to analyze some issues through a different lens. The analysis in the rest of this essay, therefore, goes beyond a critique of strict neoclassical theory as defined above, extending to a more general analysis of the approaches embraced by most modern economists—even those who do not explicitly use general equilibrium theory in all of their studies.

The title of this section is probably the more surprising of the two central claims in this essay. Although many—but certainly not all—feminists are accustomed to thinking that there is something fundamentally troubling about the morality behind neoclassical economics, a surprisingly common belief appears to be that feminist legal theorists need to embrace some form of mainstream economics simply because it is so intellectually formidable. One can almost hear people saying to themselves, "Sure, I don't like the conclusions that the practitioners of neoclassical economics reach; but I have to force myself to think with my head and not with my heart. What they say is unfortunate, but it's just so darned *logical*." (This was certainly the tone of several presentations at Prof. Fineman's workshops.)

Neoclassical economics undoubtedly has the veneer of science. A Nobel Prize was created for economic "science" but not for any of the other academic social disciplines (although there has long been a Nobel Prize for literature).[11] Acceptance into virtually all Ph.D. programs in economics is now more a function of an applicant's training in math than economics (to the detriment of undergraduates' learning experiences everywhere). Although some textbooks admit that economics is not a pure science, the desire to achieve greater stature by calling economics a science is manifest.[12]

Nevertheless, the logical underpinnings of mainstream economic methods are inadequate to justify the regard in which its practitioners would like to be held. Literally scores of articles and books have been written on every aspect of these shortcomings. Moreover, even those parts of what currently constitutes mainstream economics that are not explicitly wedded to neoclassical theory—in particular, game theory—are nowhere near as logically and mathematically consistent as many people seem to think. What follows is but a brief summary of some of the most serious (and often overlooked) problems with the logical constructs of mainstream economics, starting with general equilibrium theory and moving on to theoretical and empirical methods currently in vogue.

False Trading

Much has been made (and rightly so) of the highly questionable assumptions that must be accepted to justify standard economic models. I turn to those later in the essay. More fundamental than any of those assumptions, however, is the assumption that there is no "false trading." This is an assumption necessary to make even the most simple supply-and-demand analysis valid. If one removes this assumption alone, the logical structure of neoclassical theory is seriously undermined (if not irretrievably compromised).

False trading is any transaction that occurs when one or more prices are not at their general equilibrium values.[13] For example, if there is a change in the economy (such as a change in tastes) that raises the general equilibrium price in a market from $8 to $10, it is highly likely that some transactions will be consummated out of equilibrium, at prices of $8, $9, or even $15, before the new equilibrium can be reached. (This process of finding the equilibrium price is called *tâtonnement*, which is the French word for "groping.") Because people do not know what the equilibrium price is, they simply transact at the prices that exist at a given moment. Frequently, people later regret their purchases or sales (when the price later falls or rises, respectively), but that is the nature of market transactions in the real world.

Recognizing that time actually passes while prices change might not appear to be a serious challenge to the efficiency of markets. After all, if the process of groping eventually leads to the clearing of a market, what is the problem? In fact, however, because of false trading—even allowing all of the other standard neoclassical assumptions to hold—the Pareto-efficient result occurs only with vanishingly small probability. The noted economic theorist Franklin Fisher summarizes the situation: "We have no rigorous basis for believing that equilibria can be achieved or maintained if disturbed. Unless one robs words of their meaning and defines every state of the world as an 'equilibrium' in the sense that agents do what they do instead of doing something else, there is no disguising the fact that this is a major lacuna in economic analysis."[14]

The likelihood of reaching general equilibrium is so remote, in fact, that neoclassical theorists often resort to invoking the so-called Walrasian auctioneer to justify using general equilibrium theory. This deus ex machina (named after Léon Walras, a neoclassical pioneer who did not actually invent the fictional character that bears his name) is simply assumed to set prices perfectly, as though through a huge auction, such that all markets clear instantaneously.

Nor are these problems somehow trivial or unimportant in their implications for neoclassical economic theory. Fisher goes on: "Tâtonnement stability requires extremely strong special assumptions. This has extremely important implications. Indeed it is not too strong to say that *the entire theory of value is at stake.*"[15]

In one sense, therefore, this result is "well known." That is, there is a literature that has shown that the conclusions typically drawn from supply-and-demand analysis (in particular, that "perfect" markets will reach Pareto-efficient outcomes) lack sound logical underpinnings. However, that is not the same thing as being "well known by *most* economists." Most graduate students in economics, to say nothing of undergraduates, are never taught such inelegant and inconvenient results. (Those who are, it seems, are often taught to then ignore those results.) The Law and Economics area is particularly problematic, because so many of those experimenting in this area have not undergone graduate training in economics, further increasing the likelihood that they have not come across the issues highlighted here.

General Equilibrium

As noted earlier in the chapter, mainstream economists typically consider general equilibrium to be the ideal to which markets should be allowed (or forced) to move. Indeed, Law and Economics is often explicitly concerned with setting up the legal system such that markets can achieve general equilibrium results.

Beyond the problems of false trading just noted, though, given current policies in the United States and other mixed capitalist countries, general equilibrium is not achievable. Even if one looks solely at the usual suspects—minimum wage laws, unions, environmental regulations, or any other "distortions" that one might wish to name—the conclusion must be that the economy does not and cannot move to general equilibrium unless *all* such distortions are discontinued.

Therefore, even if one conceded (the completely incorrect argument) that the economy would achieve general equilibrium if only the government would completely butt out, that simply does not mean that we can actually achieve Pareto efficiency now if we proceed on a case-by-case basis. No individual market's output is likely ever to coincide with the output that that market would produce if the whole economy were in general equilibrium.

As emphasized earlier, it is of course true that a single market could clear (that is, all of the output currently produced by sellers could actually be purchased by buyers) when other markets do not. This post-*tâtonnement* partial equilibrium is what we are almost certainly observing when we actually come across a market without surpluses or shortages. In other situations, it is unlikely that the market is clearing at all, in either a partial or a general sense, because we so often see shortages and surpluses.

To illustrate again, we might estimate that the market for a particular type of computer would be in partial equilibrium when one million units per year are sold. If, however, all markets were in general equilibrium, the equilibrium output of laptops might be two million, or one *thousand,* or any other number completely unrelated to one million. Because Pareto efficiency is defined by those general equilibrium quantities, not partial equilibrium quantities, attempts to allow (or force) the laptop market to sell one million units are not merely completely arbitrary but actually inappropriate by their own standards.

Indeed, we could not even be sure that any particular change from a partial disequilibrium to a partial equilibrium would be a movement in the right *direction,* much less to the Pareto-efficient output. To continue the example above, it is entirely possible for the general equilibrium output of computers to be 2 million, for the partial equilibrium output to be 1 million, and for the current (disequilibrium) output to be 1.5 million. Enacting policies designed to move the market to its partial equilibrium output would be *inefficient,* by Pareto standards.

One might argue that at least a partial equilibrium is *something,* that it anchors the idea that the legal system should allow and encourage people to make mutually beneficial transactions. The point of general equilibrium, though, is that a transaction that is mutually beneficial in one situation might not be—indeed, is unlikely to be—in another. If the markets for hot dogs and steak are both in partial equilibrium but the market for low-wage workers is not (because of some market imperfection that results in unemployment), then the outputs in *all three* markets are unlikely to be Pareto-efficient. That is, if a person is willing to buy three pounds of hot dogs per month and no steak, *both* quantities are likely to change if the person is suddenly able to find a job because the labor market clears. Even the primacy of mutually agreeable transactions is, therefore, undermined by the reality that the market system is almost certainly never in general equilibrium.[16]

POLICY ANALYSIS AND EFFICIENT BREACH

A central claim of mainstream economics is that it is exceptionally well suited to assist us in comparing policy choices. Indeed, its more aggressive adherents would claim that *only* neoclassical economics is able to provide such guidance.[17] Even in a more modest form, however, the point seems to be that economic analysis allows us to make important comparisons: "Legal rule A is more efficient than legal rule B." "Policy X results in less deadweight loss than policy Y." The underlying definition of efficiency is, however, dependent on too many contingencies to be meaningful. This problem is, moreover, not empirically testable. It is a matter of fundamental unknowability. If every Pareto-efficient output can only be meaningfully measured if we know what general equilibrium would look like, then we should not use misleading proxies for Pareto efficiency as criteria to differentiate among actual policy choices.

Even at the least aggregated level—the individual cause of action in law—this problem erodes the credibility of neoclassical analysis. In contract theory, so-called efficient breach describes the conditions in which a party should be allowed (and perhaps even encouraged) to breach a contract. The reasoning is merely a single-case version of Pareto efficiency: let party A breach if her gains from breaching are greater than party B's losses, with A compensating B by paying B's expectation damages. Whatever one might think about that prescription as a policy matter, it cannot be justified by true Pareto efficiency because there is no consideration of whether A's gains and B's losses will change when other variables change. Furthermore, if we encourage A to breach today, based on variables that have changed since yesterday (and might well change tomorrow), then we have no basis to call this "efficient" unless one simply conflates efficiency with expediency.

ENDOWMENTS AND GENERAL EQUILIBRIUM

A final point remains, perhaps the most important of all. Even if one were willing to stipulate that general equilibrium could be achieved, one must remember that Pareto efficiency is based on the shapes and positions of all of the demand and supply curves, which in turn are based on the endowments of wealth, property, talents, and so forth, possessed by members of the economy when trading begins.

Therefore, there must be a different Pareto-efficient general equilibrium for every set of endowments. That is, if we could bring the Walrasian auctioneer to life and learn the quantities that would prevail if the economy were to reach general equilibrium, those quantities would all change if people possessed different amounts of wealth, skills, and so on. Indeed, there is potentially a unique general equilibrium for each and every possible set of endowments. To say that a quantity of output is Pareto-efficient thus requires one to specify which set of endowments one is using to generate supplies and demands.

The particular set of endowments with which most neoclassicists concern themselves is, perhaps not surprisingly, the one corresponding to the status quo. If the current set of endowments defines the general equilibrium outputs against which deadweight losses are measured, then any attempt to *change* people's endowments is, by definition, inefficient. If an economy has a highly unequal distribution of endowments, therefore, redistributive policies will always make someone worse off (even after compensation) than they would be in the general equilibrium that is based on those endowments.

Pareto efficiency as a general concept thus need not preclude the redistribution of endowments; when coupled with the assumption that the current distribution of endowments defines efficiency, however, it must obviously preclude any such redistribution—and it does so tautologically. The moral implications of this are discussed in detail later in the chapter. In addition, if Pareto efficiency is not moored to some set of endowments, the entire notion loses its meaning and usefulness. Every policy change is both efficient and inefficient, depending on the starting point.

To summarize, neoclassical economic theory rests on three pillars: willingness to pay as a standard of value, general equilibrium as the (desired?) outcome of market interactions, and an arbitrary specification of the endowments (usually the current endowments) that determine individuals' market supplies and demands. Each of these is, at best, highly contentious. More importantly, and more dangerously, they distort our views of both the real and the possible.

Those Assumptions

Suppose that there were no false trades and that one could meaningfully define and achieve general equilibrium. There are still profound reasons why neoclassical welfare results are highly unlikely to occur. The standard assumptions taught in a comprehensive undergraduate introduction to microeconomics are (1) there are no monopolistic buyers or sellers; (2) there is free entry and exit from markets; (3) goods are homogeneous; (4) there are no effects of economic choices which are external to the decision maker ("no externalities"); and (5) perfect information exists in all markets. Although all of these assumptions are unrealistic, and all have been found to compromise the claim that economic markets are Pareto-efficient, only the fifth assumption is emphasized below.

This is not because the others are uninteresting but simply that there are even more profound gaps in the neoclassical argument that arise from other, hidden assumptions.

Beyond these five assumptions, a number of more fundamental and subtle issues are too often unexplored. Some are entirely technical, such as the assumption of gross substitutability of goods (that is, that no good is totally unique in its ability to satisfy preferences), yet are still highly questionable. Others are more practically and philosophically interesting.

The building blocks of supply and demand curves are technology and preferences. Supply and demand curves are constructed on the assumption that the technology of production (defined broadly to include the organization and methods of the production process) and people's preferences (for work versus leisure, for present versus future consumption, as well as for all types of goods) are fixed. Neoclassicists refer to technology and preferences as "deep parameters."[18]

If either technology or preferences change, however, the curves shift, and there is a new general equilibrium.[19] Of course neoclassicists spend a great deal of time discussing the results of these shifts, using both static and dynamic modeling strategies. However, this implies that the entire structure on which a particular general equilibrium result is built can be changed by nothing more substantial than whims and moods.

Therefore, the general equilibrium that defines a Pareto-efficient outcome can change while the economy is adjusting toward it. One way to avoid this inconvenient fact is to invoke the assumption of no false trading, discussed above, with each moment in time defined by its own general equilibrium prices and quantities. This is known as intertemporal equilibrium.[20]

Even if false trading is assumed away, however, the problem is not obviated, because the design of policies to replicate Pareto-efficient outcomes can only be based on old information about the economy (and, indirectly, about the underlying preferences and technology). For example, if one has concluded that there is an inefficient amount of saving in the economy, the standard proposition is to enact yet another law to encourage people to save. During that process, however, there is nothing preventing the underlying preferences for current versus future consumption to change such that the economy could suddenly be oversaving. The subsidy to saving would make the world less Pareto-efficient, not more so.

In addition to these practical considerations of the timing and structure of policies, there is the question of the nature of preferences themselves. The standard neoclassical analysis requires the exclusion of "subjective value preferences by members of a society,"[21] which in practical terms means that people mind their own business. If a reallocation of goods between two people makes both better off, this is supposed to be the end of the story. There has been a Pareto-efficient increase in trade, and the world is happier for it.

If, however, a third person has a preference for, say, the original allocation of goods between the two traders (for example, a parent who does not want his fruit-loving daughter to trade with his vegetable-loving son, lest their diets become unbalanced), then the trade does not move the world toward Pareto efficiency. In fact, a limitless number of such inconvenient types of preferences make the standard results impossible. Although neoclassicists generally refer to such preferences as unusual, this remains unproven, to say the least.

Information Economics

Of the five assumptions that underlie the claim that free markets will always result in Pareto-efficient outcomes, I now turn to the fifth assumption—that there is perfect information in economic markets.

The perfect information assumption means that all buyers and sellers have full knowledge of each other's existence, of the prices for which all goods can be traded, and of the qualities of the products that are for sale. For example, in neoclassical theory as applied to labor markets, one must assume that workers (that is, suppliers of labor) as well as firms (demanders of labor) know with equal certainty just how hard the workers will work if they are hired. Similarly, in the used car market, buyers of used cars must be assumed to know exactly as much about the quality of the car as the seller does.

One important body of work, known as information economics, analyzes from a variety of perspectives the implications of abandoning the assumption of perfect information. One of the breakthrough essays was, indeed, an analysis of the used car market by Akerlof.[22] The market for "lemons," that is, used cars, is hampered by an insurmountable information problem. Sellers of used cars know much more about their cars' quality than do potential buyers, but sellers of high-quality used cars cannot credibly convey this information to buyers because both sides recognize that self-interest may induce a seller to lie about her car's attributes. Akerlof showed, using accepted mathematical techniques, that if one takes into account this asymmetry of information, then this market cannot reach the Pareto-efficient equilibrium—or even a partial equilibrium. Buyers will hedge against the likelihood of buying a lemon by offering artificially low prices for *all* cars. Rational sellers of all but the lowest quality cars will be led to choose not to sell their cars at all, because the low price offered would make it better to continue to drive the cars rather than sell them.

Because the problem of informational asymmetries is endemic to all economic markets, the insights gained from Akerlof's work were readily extended to other goods. Lenders cannot possibly know with certainty whether a borrower intends to repay the loan or to default; insurers cannot know with complete accuracy if applicants for life insurance policies are already dying or if they intend to depart sooner than expected; lawyers do not know if their potential clients are likely to sue for malpractice (nor does the client know if the lawyer is likely to commit malpractice); employees do not know if bosses are really going to give them the raises and promotions that they promised, and so forth.

Obviously, the possibilities are endless, and the resulting literature has been large and impressive. Summarizing the broad conclusions of the field that he largely helped to create, Stiglitz concluded that "the field of information economics has established that: (1) in general, markets are not . . . Pareto efficient; (2) markets may not clear."[23] The implication is clear: altering even one assumption of the standard neoclassical model opens up a universe of non-Pareto-efficient equilibria.

On one level, of course, even the most devoted neoclassical economist will admit that information is imperfect. The only question is whether the imperfections are large or pervasive enough to matter. In that sense, therefore, information economics can be seen as a generalization of neoclassical economics—with the usual neoclassical conclusions constituting the baseline from which deviations due to information problems are measured. Indeed, information economics still accepts the conclusion that markets will reach Pareto-efficient outcomes in the rare (or, more likely, impossible) case where there is perfect information.

Moreover, information economics does not challenge the idea that Pareto-efficient outcomes would be desirable if they could be achieved. The theory of value is still the willingness-to-pay principle, and welfare outcomes are expressed in terms of deadweight loss. The innovation of information economics is its recognition of additional barriers to markets reaching Pareto-efficient equilibria, but it does not pose a challenge to the foundation underlying the Pareto efficiency concept.

EFFICIENCY WAGES

The debate over the theory of efficiency wages is illustrative. This theory recognizes that bosses do not go into the labor market because they want to hire an hour of a worker's time. Instead, they wish to purchase actual productive effort. Because bosses obviously cannot read potential employees' minds, however, workers know more about how hard they intend to work (as well as how capable they are of doing the kind of work for which they are being hired) than their bosses do. If workers must be paid by the hour (rather than at piece rates), this creates an inherent conflict in the workplace.

Efficiency wage theory predicts that bosses will offer an artificially high wage (artificial in the sense that it is not the market-clearing wage) in the hope that this will allow them to hire the most diligent workers.[24] Although the bosses realize that the resulting applicant pool will necessarily include a mixture of both good and bad workers, their fundamental lack of information leaves no alternative. Offering a high wage at least increases the number of high-quality applicants in the pool, which increases the odds of hiring *some* good workers.

This high wage, however, creates involuntary unemployment precisely because it is designed to provide bosses a larger pool of workers than they would have found in equilibrium. Crucially, therefore, the wage does not decline in the face of a surplus, and the involuntary unemployment does not disappear. This is impossible in the neoclassical view of labor markets, where rational maximizers methodically and relentlessly bring disequilibrium prices and wages into line.

The neoclassical response? Rational workers and employers will realize that the problem arises from the lack of a mechanism to guarantee predictable levels of effort and productivity. Therefore, profit-maximizing firms will "bond" workers, that is, they will require that workers post as collateral an efficient sum of money against their possible laziness.[25] If a worker is less productive than she promises to be, the boss will receive the bond. This process allows firms to hire workers for the equilibrium wage, because they do not have to pay a premium to find the best workers. Instead, the best workers reveal themselves by being willing to post bonds.

This, of course, leads to further replies by information economists about the feasibility of bonding.[26] For example, many (most?) workers do not have money on hand that they can tie up in a bond. Even if they did, they could be forgiven if they imagined that bosses would have an incentive to make false claims of employee shirking in order to confiscate the bonds. The practical problems with any bonding scheme are too numerous to list here. The theoretical point is that bonding simply replaces one type of information problem (Which workers will shirk?) with others (Which bosses will lie? Which bonding companies will embezzle funds?).

Even so, these practical arguments merely bring forth further claims that markets will come into existence to *make* bonding feasible (for example, bonding the bonding companies). Any practical or theoretical attack on the neoclassical orthodoxy can always be met with the claim that rational maximizers will make the problem go away.

WHAT IS THE "MONEY" ON THE TABLE?

The discussion of efficiency wages highlights another revealing synonym for deadweight loss: "money left on the table." This phrase invokes a precisely *incorrect* image, that markets are so efficient that no rational actor would pass up the opportunity to grab money that is there for the taking. Every profitable trade will be made. In response to a claim that, for example, "workers obviously do not take out performance bonds," the response is, "Why wouldn't they? Not to do so leaves money on the table." If there is money left on the table, therefore, it must be because of some inappropriate intervention.

This example highlights just how illusory the concept of loss really is here. If there is a deadweight loss, that merely means that there are people who might have made trades with other people, but they did not. That is not a loss in the immediate sense of a decrease in one's bank balance but rather a hypothetical loss against an imaginary baseline. If, because of false trading or other so-called imperfections, people are unaware of the existence of unsatisfied trades, nothing automatically forces the trades to occur.

Deconstructing Property Rights

A prominent area in which mainstream economics purports to provide logical rigor to the law is in the analysis of property rights. Although property is a central concern for both legal theory and economics, mainstream economists favor a highly misleading approach to property theory that is based on an artificial distinction between "market" and "nonmarket" actions—between what is internal to a market and what is external. The result is a built-in bias against anything that can be described as nonmarket action (which is usually, of course, governmental action).

One of the assumptions of perfectly competitive markets, noted above, is that there are no externalities. Externalities are defined as any effects of an economic decision that are not directly experienced by the economic agent making the decision. The classic example is, of course, pollution. It is elementary to demonstrate, on a standard supply-and-demand graph, that the presence of an externality will cause even a market without false trading and with a Walrasian auctioneer to deviate from Pareto efficiency. This type of market failure is widely viewed as a situation that calls for nonmarket intervention by governments.

In perhaps the most well-known convergence of neoclassical economic theory and legal analysis, however, advocates of the so-called Coase theorem claim that the real problem with externalities is that property rights have not been properly articulated, assigned, and enforced. Supposedly all one needs to do is give someone (anyone!) the ownership rights to an external good, and the new owners will internalize the externality automatically and efficiently. "Missing markets" are the problem, so the solution is to allow the necessary markets to come into existence. (And they *will* come into existence, because otherwise there will be money on the table.) The government does have a role, but only in the maintenance of a system of property and contract law.

The potency of this theorem cannot be underestimated. Indeed, when listing the five assumptions of perfect competition, some economists go so far as to replace the statement "No externalities" with "Property rights are well defined." The policy implication is obvious: no market interventions of any kind are justifiable. Pollution should not be combated with effluent fees (taxes on pollution) or direct regulation, but rather by giving someone ownership of the item being polluted.

The surprising corollary of this theorem is that it does not matter to whom a property right is assigned. If a polluter is given ownership of the river that it is polluting, people who care about the river can "buy off" the company to reduce or eliminate its pollution. If, on the other hand, another group is given the property right, the polluter can pay them for the right to pollute.

This symmetry is not merely incidental but simply must be true for the theory to work. Because there is only one Pareto-efficient general equilibrium set of outputs, the market must move to that single equilibrium—no matter who owns the property.

It is beyond the scope of the current investigation to critique the Coase theorem and all of its applications to economics, law, and other social inquiry. The point here is limited to this final corollary of the Coase analysis. For all of its supposed potency, the Coase theorem rests on a very special assumption about preferences, even if one accepts the rest of the assumptions necessary to drive the analysis. One must assume that there are no income effects resulting from the granting of the rights.[27] This means that if a person notices that she now possesses new property and is thus wealthier, she nevertheless will not change her relative desire for one good more than others. That is, knowing that you now own a lake and all of the land around it, you increase your demands of all goods in equal proportion rather than buying relatively more Rolls Royce limousines than you used to buy.

Clearly this is unlikely in the extreme, and awarding property rights to more than one person only complicates matters. Thus, even if it actually were possible to figure out which property rights are undefined, to define them, and to award them, the market is highly unlikely to generate Pareto-efficient results.

One possible response to this difficulty would be to return to the approach mentioned earlier, that is, that the best way to deal with market failure is to intervene in the market directly, through taxes or subsidies calibrated to achieve Pareto-efficient outcomes. However, this approach would again elevate the Pareto criterion above all others as the sole arbiter of right and wrong. This is neither good science nor good policy.

THE RHETORIC OF MARKETS

The Coase analysis provides an ideal vantage point from which to describe a fundamental philosophical critique of the neoclassical approach. McCluskey brings together a feminist critique of market ideology and the tools of literary deconstruction to expose the central rhetorical maneuver that is typically accepted by both defenders and attackers of the neoclassical approach: the definition of "action within the market" versus "action that interferes with the market."[28]

As McCluskey demonstrates, and as is implicit in the Coase analysis, the market is inherently defined by the government. Even so, arguments in favor of having the government define and protect certain rights (such as workplace safety rules) are attacked for creating deadweight losses. These rules could easily be cloaked in the rhetoric of protecting property rights: just as the law prevents a person from stealing from a company, it could prevent the company from stealing from its workers. What is being stolen is property, which (the Coase analysis recognizes) only exists if the government says it does.

Instead, both "conservatives" and "liberals" accept the classic efficiency–equity trade-off, which says that the market will inevitably be diminished by inefficient meddling by government. Liberals are liberal precisely because they often argue that the trade-off of efficiency for equity is worth it, whereas conservatives typically consider efficiency to be the primary (or only) goal. "Unless the market/non-market dichotomy itself is undone, choosing to value the state over the market—social goals over economic goals—means choosing tails instead of heads in a game of 'heads I win, tails you lose.' "[29]

The Math Paradox

A particular source of logical difficulty in mainstream economics relates, oddly enough, to the well-known trend among modern economists to express all arguments in mathematical form. It is certainly plausible to imagine that this de facto requirement will act as a filter to force everyone to make their assumptions known, to confront logical inconsistencies more readily than might be possible when arguments are in verbal form, and to allow for easy comparison of the results of one study with those of another.

To some degree, of course, this happens. The use of mathematical symbols often reminds us to specify whether we are talking about, for example, static values versus rates of growth (for example, price levels versus inflation rates). Unfortunately, the broader hope that mathematical expression would lead to greater clarity has been dashed, as the use of increasingly specialized mathematical techniques seems to have become the raison d'être of much published research (and virtually all graduate training).

Most disturbingly, the proliferation of mathematics in economics has coincided with (and has arguably been a significant cause of) the intellectual crisis of modern economics. The time spent developing and honing the mathematical techniques to make one's points distracts economists from the more important discussions. What will workers and firms do in a world with limited information and conflicting motives, for example? Trying to express arguments in a form that looks scientific paradoxically can make the theory less so.

THEORIES AND PROOFS

The problem goes deeper, however, than simply the preferred method of expression. Fundamental beliefs in economics have become effectively nonfalsifiable, even though the models used to support those beliefs are regularly overturned. The ultimate game in economic theory has become playing with the assumptions of a model in order to reverse its results. For example, if one paper has "proven" (through the rigorous application of mathematical techniques to a set of assumptions) that affirmative action lowers average economic growth, it is great sport to take that model and reverse its results by changing one seemingly innocuous assumption. The new model, proving that affirmative action increases growth, will then face the same fate.

McCloskey argues forcefully that working through the logic of alternative assumptions in this manner is inherently unscientific.[30] She refers to this as "blackboard economics," performed by economists to convince themselves that they belong in the mathematics department and not the social sciences division.

Parodying this style, she offers a "Metatheorem on Theorems: The A-Prime, C-Prime Theorem": "For each and every set of assumptions A implying a conclusion C, and for each alternative conclusion C' arbitrarily far from C—(for example, disjoint with C), there exists an alternative set of assumptions A' arbitrarily close to the original assumption A, such that A' implies C'." Or, to put it more simply: it is possible to change the conclusions as much as one needs by changing the assumptions as *little* as one likes. That is not science, no matter how much math one uses.

There is abundant evidence that neoclassical economists can and will respond to any "proof" of market inefficiency by inventing yet another reason why markets really are efficient. As a skeptical feminist economist once quipped: "Neoclassical economics is *relentless.*" The answer to every situation is to eliminate deadweight loss by allowing markets to clear. In short, the government should do nothing—and if it is already doing something, it should stop.

An exchange in a recent issue of the *Stanford Law Review* provides a telling example of the struggle for the mantle of science. The exchange essentially replicates the arguments between neoclassical traditionalists and those who would make adjustments around the edges of that approach, such as information economists.

Jolls, Sunstein, and Thaler argue in favor of an approach to Law and Economics now known as Behavioral Law and Economics.[31] They take issue with various assumptions favored by the proponents of the traditional Law and Economics approach, especially the rationality assumption. In doing so, they "prove" that under their arguably better assumptions, the results derived by their opponents are reversed.

In the same issue of the journal, Posner responds to this attack, claiming (among other things) that the rationality assumption is not central to his preferred Law and Economics analysis.[32] He then claims that the Jolls et al. approach is nonscientific, whereas his approach is the very standard of good science. In a rebuttal, Jolls et al. then claim that, yes, they really are scientific.[33]

In a dissent consistent with that offered here, Kelman chastises both sides, arguing that they "are bound together in a form of rhetorical duet or ritualized dance."[34] This is exactly right. Both sides of the argument are claiming to be scientific, and at least one side is accusing the other of being unscientific, when in fact both sides are simply arguing their beliefs in a way that they think will be forceful. One must certainly decide which side makes a more compelling argument, but not by trying to decide who are the "true" scientists.

STATISTICS AND SIGNIFICANCE

Because science, according to the standard description, possesses the great virtue of falsifiability, the answer to the blackboard economics problem would seem to lie in the use of advanced statistics and econometrics, which test theories against data. Again, however, the promise is not matched by reality. The two most severe problems spring from what is known as specification searching and a desire to report only "statistically significant" results.

As described again by McCloskey, modern econometrics is involved in its own kind of wasteful game.[35] Statistical significance, far from demonstrating a "true" cause-and-effect relationship between two variables, is entirely a function of sample size. Find a large-enough data set and it is always possible to compute a statistically significant result. For example, if one is testing whether a key parameter is equal to zero (which is the typical null hypothesis), it is always possible to prove that it is not, given a large-enough sample. After all, even 0.0001 is not zero.[36]

Such an approach is ultimately unsatisfying in both a scientific and a practical sense. The goal should be to find suggestive evidence that something important is happening, not that a parameter differs from zero at a certain level of statistical confidence. To make matters worse, the desire to report statistically significant estimates leads researchers to look for and report only the statistical tests that do just that.[37] The truth of the underlying theories is not definitively tested by these exercises, nor can it be.

Even more fundamentally important is Leamer's demonstration that the validity of all econometric tests is profoundly sensitive to the choices made by the investigator.[38] Error in econometric estimation derives from two sources: insufficient sample size and misspecification of the relationship between the variables.[39] These specification problems arise from choosing which "explanatory" variables to include and exclude, the functional form (linear, log-linear, polynomial, etc.), the number and distribution of lags for each variable, and on and on. Leamer shows that in general the misspecification error is of unknown size *and* sign. Therefore, even if one has solved the sample size problem, the true sign of a statistically significant parameter (which tells us whether an increase in variable x causes variable y to go up or down) literally cannot be known.

Because the uncertainty about the *form* of the model cannot be reduced by increasing the *sample size,* misspecification uncertainty always remains, even if sampling uncertainty has been substantially reduced by the fortuitous availability of a large data set.[40] Even with an enormous data set, estimates that are highly statistically significant can be simply wrong. Therefore, finding that a correlation between variables is statistically significant—or not—cannot be the end of the story. Only careful analysis of all of the available data, studied from a variety of perspectives, can lead to scientific insight. Statistical significance is not a substitute for reasoned judgment.

Leamer's point, therefore, is not that econometrics is a waste of time. Rather, he shows that the moral predisposition of the econometrician can determine the results of the statistical analysis. He gives as an example the question of whether the death penalty is a deterrent to murder. Using different sets of moral principles to guide his choices of specification, he reports (using real data) the range of possible effects on the murder rate from the imposition of capital punishment.

Those whose moral codes make them most likely to advocate the death penalty might specify the equation in a number of ways. Among these possibilities, Leamer's results show that the range of estimated "lives saved per execution" lies roughly between one and twenty-three. On the other hand, a different analyst using different assumptions can find estimates showing that each execution causes as many as twelve *more* murders, again within a wide numerical range. Leamer also points out that he limited his specifications to linear equations and that he consciously ignored the question of direction of causality.

This is not simply a proof of the old adages "There are lies, damned lies, and statistics" and "Figures lie, and liars figure." The implication is much larger. Anyone undertaking statistical analysis brings to the table their own morals and opinions. It cannot be otherwise. Statistics and econometrics are not, and cannot be, value neutral.

Hence, the paradox: the more mathematics we use, the less scientific we might become. The great irony is that those who would apply to their own fields of analysis the methods championed by neoclassical economists—specifically to avoid the accusation of being soft or mushy-headed—are imposing on themselves and their colleagues the necessity of learning an obscure set of skills that does not guarantee scientific purity.

Neoclassical Economics Is Morally Troubling

For many readers who have reached this point, the rest of the story may seem obvious. Neoclassical economics has been used to justify everything from pollution to discrimination against women to "efficient" suicide. What more needs to be said about its morally troubling nature? Actually, there are two paths to take in describing the moral difficulties of neoclassical economics. The first directly confronts the neoclassical theory of value to expose the moral implications of believing that everything can be bought and sold. The second indirectly exposes neoclassical immorality by showing that the model is inherently wedded to a defense of the status quo.

The More Obviously Troubling Moral Implications

The willingness-to-pay criterion defines everything as having a value measurable in dollars. Everything has a price, including the unthinkable. One former student, who was truly enamored of this theory of value (and who is now a professor at the Harvard Business School), insisted on asking all of his friends in college how much they would have to be paid to drive a nail through a live squirrel's head. People who said that they simply would not do so were quickly offered exorbitant sums and told that they could use the money to help the poor, or squirrels, or whatever.

Lest one think that this was merely the excesses of youth, a middle-aged neoclassical economist remarked to a group of colleagues that he could not understand why a house he had just walked past had a "for sale" sign on the lawn. After all, he noted, everything is for sale. A listener muttered under his breath: "How much for your daughter?"

The point is that we should not feel guilty about creating deadweight losses, because they merely represent unconsummated trades. There are, of course, many transactions that people might make in the hypothesized neoclassical state of nature that are prohibited in modern societies, such as selling one's child into slavery. Indeed, by the lights of the most pure form of neoclassical theory, why not let people make the choice to sell their children or to become slaves themselves, since we can easily define those property rights and enforce them? It is a sad commentary that this question, for many neoclassicists, is not rhetorical.

The power of the neoclassical model to excuse and rationalize the status quo is also well established. Poverty is nothing to worry about—or at least nothing to do something about. Unequal distributions of income are easily justified by neoclassical theory as "returns" to different talents and attributes. If it is not obvious just what the talent or attribute is that made a person rich, one need only look a bit harder for it. Perhaps it is entrepreneurship, which is wonderfully impossible to define. Whatever it is, though, it simply must be there or a rational maximizer would not have paid for it.

Similarly, discrimination cannot exist in a free market, except when the discriminators are willing to pay the price for the privilege of discriminating.[41] If we have difficulty discerning the rationality of people's decisions (for example, discrimination that is apparently costly to the discriminators), the problem again is that we are not looking hard enough. The market guarantees that only efficient decisions will be made.

In a recent article in the popular press, Barro makes this point quite bluntly.[42] (Barro, a macroeconomist at Harvard, is one of the founders of a fundamentalist strain of neoclassicism called New Classical Economics.) Arguing against laws that prevent employers from using physical appearance as a standard in hiring and promotion, Barro simply assumes that anything that employers do is guided by profit motivation and must, therefore, lead to Pareto efficiency.

> An interference with the market's valuation of physical appearance is justified only if the benefits from the redistribution of resources from more attractive to less attractive people are greater than the losses in overall product. Thus, it makes no sense to say that basing employment and wages on physical appearance is a form of discrimination, whereas basing them on intelligence is not. The two cases are fundamentally the same.

If one removes the words *physical appearance* and *attractive* and replaces them with *race* and *white,* Barro's statement is so outrageous as to be politically incendiary.

> An interference with the market's valuation of *race* is justified only if the benefits from the redistribution of resources from more *white* to less *white* people are greater than the losses in overall product. Thus, it makes no sense to say that basing employment and wages on *race* is a form of discrimination, whereas basing them on intelligence is not. The two cases are fundamentally the same.

Of course, very few neoclassicists would make that statement about race (in public, anyway), because the current morals of society strongly endorse the notion that racial equality is a basic right. This is precisely as it should be. Certain rights are inalienable. Therefore, they are not the same as preferences, to be bargained away for a price. Our approach to issues of human equality should be the model for our approach to all public policy issues: specify our values first, and pursue the best route to affirming those values.

COMPENSATION—REAL AND HYPOTHETICAL

Even for those who are willing to join Dr. Pangloss in believing that the world is already perfect, there are still many pitfalls of neoclassical reasoning. When faced with a deadweight loss, for example, there are two established methods of dealing with it. One is simply to remove the impediment to Pareto efficiency, such as eliminating the minimum wage. However, how can it be the case that this is a way to "make some better off without making others worse off," when clearly some workers will be hurt by a decline in their wages? The answer is the "compensation criterion," which notes that the elimination of deadweight loss always implies that the gains are larger than the losses, so that it *would be possible* for the winners to compensate the losers and still have money left over. If the compensation is not actually made, however, then this is obviously just a logic game to justify taking from some people and giving to others.[43]

Moreover, it is daunting in the extreme to imagine how to implement a plan in which, for example, those who gain from eliminating a rent control law actually pay off those who lose. Because gains and losses are often entirely psychological (and are measured by the willingness to pay), it is not possible to elicit honest answers to the question "How much have you gained or lost due to this change?"

As Crawford discusses, the point of the compensation criterion was to separate efficiency from distribution.[44] Arrow pointed out, however, that this separation is simply not possible.[45] Claiming to be more efficient requires a standard of measurement that *depends* on the distribution of endowments, as noted in a discussion earlier in the chapter.[46]

The second, and more limited, response to the discovery of deadweight loss is to enact a policy only if one can be found that does not require compensation to losers. As one workshop participant put it: "Why *not* make everyone better off, if you can do it without making anyone else worse off?"

Claiming to have found a policy that makes everyone better off without making anyone worse off, though, requires a definition of the terms *better off* and *worse off*. If one uses the willingness-to-pay criterion, the result is to accept the moral primacy of this theory of value. At the very least, those who propose such policies should be forced to admit that this is their moral standard.

More profoundly, once we agree that an appropriate goal of policy is to eliminate deadweight losses, we lose a clear reason to oppose uncompensated losses. After all, if we are willing to believe that deadweight loss is bad enough to go to the trouble of enacting a policy that hurts no one, what is so wrong with eliminating deadweight loss by only hurting a few people? (Especially if those people are politically powerless?) How many is too many to hurt? By how much can they be hurt before we start to worry?

The neoclassical theory of value leads to results that are morally troubling for those of us who are concerned with poverty, discrimination, and that elusive concept called justice. Agreeing to measure social outcomes by the neoclassical standard might well lead us to endorse policies that we would—and should—otherwise reject.

Some Subtle Moral Issues

In a famous attack on the immorality of neoclassicism and Pareto efficiency, Sen argued: "An economy can be optimal in this sense even when some people are rolling in luxury and others are near starvation as long as the starvers cannot be made better off without cutting into the pleasures of the rich. . . . In short, a society or an economy can be Pareto-optimal and still be perfectly disgusting."[47]

The neoclassical response to Sen's argument is that there is more than one situation that is Pareto-efficient. As noted earlier, the initial endowments of the actors in an economy determine a unique general equilibrium. One can construct any original set of endowments, and a general equilibrium model will generate the Pareto-efficient market prices and quantities. Therefore, one might argue, there is no morality or immorality behind Pareto efficiency because any situation can be the Pareto-efficient general equilibrium from *some* hypothetical initial set of endowments.

This is true but unsatisfying. Imagine that we were willing to measure value by the neoclassical standard but that we insisted on redistributing endowments in a way that would make the Pareto-efficient general equilibrium results morally tolerable. This method could rightly be attacked as Pareto-*inefficient* because taking endowments away from one person and giving them to another is a nonmarket act. In other words, taking away endowments from one party is Pareto-inefficient by the current standard, even while its very purpose is to create a different Pareto-efficient general equilibrium.

This contradiction puts into sharp focus the ultimate import of neoclassical economics: Any attempt to alter the status quo is inefficient by the standard of the current endowments. These endowments are privileged in the analysis simply because they exist.

CHASING OUR TAILS

Anyone who tries to choose the policies that will *minimize* deadweight losses will encounter this problem in a different form. For example, those who advocate minimum wages will learn from a standard textbook that deadweight losses are smaller if we simply subsidize incomes rather than "interfering" in the employment relationship. Similarly, any use of legal rules (such as antitrust enforcement) to redistribute income is ill-advised because the legal system should promote efficiency, "leaving distribution to the tax system."[48]

Subsidies themselves are Pareto-inefficient, however, because they too involve government interference in the marketplace. Using taxes—whether to pay for the subsidies or as redistributive tools in their own right—is also, of course, doomed by the same reasoning. Should we, nevertheless, choose the type of tax that creates the *least* deadweight loss? In a return of the blackboard economics problem discussed above, some tax analysts argue that estate taxes create less deadweight loss than any other type of tax, whereas others purport to prove that estate taxes are the most offensive taxes of all.[49]

We are pushed, therefore, from one policy to the next, with each move justified by its lesser amount of deadweight loss. Ultimately, by that logic, the only acceptable policy is to do nothing at all—or simply to choose to live with an arbitrary level of deadweight loss. Because the promise of adopting a scientific method was that it would be nonarbitrary, however, what have we gained?

The logic underlying neoclassical economics is particularly well suited to justifying the current distribution of wealth and power. To adopt neoclassical analysis is to risk predetermining our conclusions.

Old Vinegar in New Bottles

As noted earlier, many pure economic theorists have moved past the neoclassical general equilibrium approach. Some argue that the entire concept of markets and social welfare should be dropped, preferring game theory to analyze behavior of all types. Both the virtue and the pitfall of this argument are that game theory, in its purest form, makes no claims to any type of morality. One can specify any set of assumptions about how people react to stimuli, define the rules of the game, and predict a result. The result is neither good nor bad. It just is.

If such an amoral alternative exists, economists who continue to use the value-laden prescriptions of neoclassical economics apparently do not find those prescriptions sufficiently troubling to look for an alternative. However, the moral bases of neoclassical economics can operate more subtly as well. Some (if not most) game theory seems to be little more than repackaged neoclassicism. Most importantly, efficiency in game theory models is still typically measured by the standard of Pareto efficiency.

Claiming to present a "rigorous" analysis of the marriage market, for example, Wax simply imported a sexist assumption into a rational choice model—that women want to marry men more than men want to marry women.[50] The model then *proved* that women have a harder time in the marriage market—because men are less inclined to marry than are women! This circular result is simply the "equilibrium" that results from the assumed gender-based differences in preferences.

Changing the analytical tools does not change the implications of neoclassical assumptions, nor does it obviate the logical certainty that the typical neoclassical conclusions will be reached. The important thing is not merely to avoid concerning ourselves with deadweight losses but to make sure that the assumptions and—more to the point—the standards of judgment that we use are not rigged against us.

There is no good reason for noneconomists (or for non-neoclassical economists) to believe that the neoclassical approach is logically or scientifically compelling. Also, because the moral precepts of the approach are troubling, it is both unwarranted and self-defeating for feminist legal theorists and other progressive scholars to adopt its methods.

Concluding Thoughts

The arguments in this essay add up to the claim that it is dangerous to adapt neoclassical economic methods to feminist legal analysis—and, more generally, to all progressive social research agendas. The result of such adaptation is an unacceptable mutation—if not an outright repudiation—of the underlying concept of justice that motivates most feminist analysis, a concept that at least contemplates the possibility of fundamental social change. This is why the argument that we have to use neoclassical methods in order to be listened to is ultimately unpersuasive. Even if such an assertion were true, there would be precious little point in being listened to if we have nothing meaningful to say.

The danger, however, is not merely that using neoclassical methods will damage legal analysis piecemeal in those situations in which we try to apply it. The potential danger is much more sweeping: if we adopt some neoclassical methods, we are likely eventually to find ourselves adopting the entire neoclassical approach (both methods and values). This is a warning, not a prediction. However, we actually have plenty of evidence that this not only might happen but that it almost certainly will happen if we start down that road. Neoclassical economics acts as an imperialist force, imposing its methods and its presumptions on every field that it touches.[51]

For example, thirty-five years ago, some macroeconomists argued that their analysis would be improved by explicitly describing the behavioral assumptions underlying their models. Today, the leading journals in the field almost exclusively publish papers whose models are based on general equilibrium frameworks, on the basis of the assumption that all actors have rational expectations.

Similarly, tax analysis in the mainstream of the profession is almost completely dominated by the neoclassical approach. Finance was routed long ago. A sizable group of labor economists continues to resist an intense assault. As for the disciplines outside of economics that have flirted with neoclassicism (evolutionary biology, sociology, history, political science, as well as several areas of legal analysis), either they have lost the battles to maintain some of their non-neoclassical methods or they have found the fight to be long and protracted.

Feminist legal analysis, like all fields of social analysis, should certainly use whatever sound analytical principles are available. Far from being an argument in favor of adopting neoclassical principles, however, this statement is actually an emphatic reason to reject mainstream economics. The law should continue to be about justice and morality. It is essential that we consciously choose our moral principles rather than having them surreptitiously thrust upon us.

Notes

1. I thank Benjamin L. Alpers, Michael C. Dorf, Terence Dougherty, Lucinda M. Finley, Nicole C. Palasz, and an anonymous referee for their helpful comments. Douglas A. Kysar's comment following this chapter is extremely insightful and suggests many promising directions for future research. I also acknowledge the helpful input of the participants in the Feminism and Legal Theory workshops at Columbia and Cornell Law Schools and the participants in a panel at the 1999 Law and Society meetings. Finally, I owe a debt of gratitude to Martha A. Fineman, who not only supported and encouraged this project but also convinced me that I was not too old to go to law school.

2. *Rigorous* is one of the favorite words of proponents of neoclassical economics. Another is *scientific*. Some of the undesirable adjectives are *soft, squishy, anecdotal*, and *sociological*.

3. There are, of course, legal theorists whose personal morals would not be offended by the political agenda that neoclassical economics supports. While it is unlikely that many of them would identify themselves as feminists, even they would be wise to lay out their principles explicitly, rather than importing them wholesale from a paradigm that includes many hidden (potentially less appealing) assumptions. Therefore, while some of the discussion that follows will resonate most readily with political progressives, the message applies to everyone who might consider using neoclassical economics to analyze social issues.

4. *Lochner v. New York*, 198 U.S. 45 (1905).

5. Another common description of Pareto efficiency is the following: "A situation is Pareto-efficient when it is not possible to make someone better off without making someone else worse off." This description is discussed in detail later in the chapter.

6. Overproduction is not analyzed as frequently as is underproduction. For the remainder of this discussion, for the sake of clarity, only the implications of underproduction are described.

7. Robert Cooter & Thomas Ulen, *Law and Economics* 40 (3d ed., Addison-Wesley 2000).

8. Peng Lian & Charles Plott, *General Equilibrium, Markets, Macroeconomics, and Money in a Laboratory Experiment Environment*, 12 Econ. Theory 1 (1998). Alex Anas & Rong Xu, *Congestion, Land Use, and Job Dispersion: A General Equilibrium Model*, J. Urban Econ. (1999).

9. Douglas W. Elmendorf & N. Gregory Mankiw, *Government Debt* 32, Finance and Economics Discussion Series 1998–99 (Federal Reserve Board 1998).

10. Among countless examples, see Georg Hirte & Reinhard Weber, *Pareto Improving Transition from a Pay-as-You-Go to a Fully Funded System—Is It Politically Feasible?* 54 FinanzArchiv 3 (1997).

11. Actually, this is somewhat misleading. The official Nobel web site distinguishes very clearly between the actual Nobel Prizes and the economics prize: "Announcement for the 1998 Nobel Prizes and the Sveriges Riksbank (Bank of Sweden) Prize in Economic Sciences in Memory of Alfred Nobel."

12. "To be sure, macroeconomics is a young and imperfect science." N. Gregory Mankiw, *Macroeconomics* 3 (4th ed. 2000).

13. For a demonstration and discussion of false trading, see Neil H. Buchanan, A Simple Demonstration of False Trading and Its Implications for Market Equilibrium (unpublished) (available on request from the author).

14. Franklin M. Fisher, *Adjustment Processes and Stability*, in *The New Palgrave: A Dictionary of Modern Economics*, vol. 1, at 26 (John Eatwell, Murray Milgate, & Peter Newman eds., Macmillan 1987).

15. *Id.* at 27 (emphasis added).

16. This is a general equilibrium version of the Theory of Second Best, first described in a partial equilibrium context in R. G. Lipsey & Kelvin Lancaster, *The General Theory of Second Best,* 24 Rev. Econ. Stud. 1, 11–32 (1956–57). *See also* Richard S. Markovits, *Symposium on Second-Best Theory and Law and Economics: An Introduction,* 73 Chi.-Kent L. Rev. 3 (1998), and the symposium introduced thereby.

17. This belief must be at the root of attempts to expand the reach of neoclassical economic analysis into areas that were previously untouched by such thinking. Judge Posner's insistence on applying economic analysis to sex—although a spectacular failure—is certainly the most infamous such attempt. *See* Richard A. Posner, *Sex and Reason* (Harvard U. Press 1992).

18. For a good critique of this concept, *see* Lawrence Summers, *The Scientific Illusion in Empirical Macroeconomics,* 95 Scan. J. Econ. 2, 129–48 (1991).

19. This is distinct from the earlier discussion about changes in endowments. Even under a given set of endowments, curves can shift because of changes in tastes and technology.

20. *See* John Eatwell & Murray Milgate, *Introduction,* in *Keynes's Economics and the Theories of Value and Distribution* (John Eatwell & Murray Milgate eds., Oxford U. Press 1983) (exposing the fallacy of this notion of equilibrium).

21. Patrick B. Crawford, *The Utility of the Efficiency/Equity Dichotomy in Tax Policy Analysis,* 16 Va. Tax Rev. 517 (1997).

22. George Akerlof, *The Market for Lemons: Quality Uncertainty and the Market Mechanism,* 84 Q.J. Econ. 488 (1970).

23. Joseph E. Stiglitz, *Post Walrasian and Post Marxian Economics,* 7 J. Econ. Persp. 109 (1993).

24. There are at least four different efficiency wage models. The model described here is known as the adverse selection model.

25. *See* Lorne Carmichael, *Can Unemployment Be Involuntary?: Comment,* 75 Am. Econ. Rev. 1213–14 (1985).

26. *See* Carl A. Shapiro & Joseph E. Stiglitz, *Can Unemployment Be Involuntary?: Reply,* 75 Am. Econ. Rev. 1215–17 (1985).

27. *See* Hal R. Varian, *Intermediate Microeconomics: A Modern Approach,* 562–63 (4th ed., Norton 1996).

28. *See* Martha McCluskey, Telling Stories about the State and the Market: The Rhetorical Construction of Efficiency, presented at Feminism and Legal Theory Workshop: Feminism Confronts Legal Theory, Columbia Law School (February 1995).

29. *See* McCluskey, chapter 8, this volume.

30. *See* Deirdre N. McCloskey, Two Vices: Proof and Significance, presented at the annual meetings of the American Economic Association, Chicago, Ill. (Jan. 3, 1998); Deirdre N. McCloskey, *The Vices of Economists and the Virtues of the Bourgeoisie* (U. of Michigan Press 1998).

31. Christine Jolls, Cass R. Sunstein, & Richard Thaler, *A Behavioral Approach to Law and Economics,* 50 Stan. L. Rev. 1471 (1998).

32. Richard A. Posner, *Rational Choice, Behavioral Economics, and the Law,* 50 Stan. L. Rev. 1551 (1998).

33. Christine Jolls, Cass R. Sunstein, & Richard Thaler, *Theories and Tropes: A Reply to Posner and Kelman,* 50 Stan. L. Rev. 1593 (1998).

34. Mark Kelman, *Behavioral Economics as Part of a Rhetorical Duet: A Response to Jolls, Sunstein, and Thaler,* 50 Stan. L. Rev. 1577 (1998).

35. *See supra* note 30.

36. *See* Deirdre N. McCloskey & Stephen Ziliak, *The Standard Error of Regressions,* 34 J. Econ. Lit. 1, 97–114 (1996).

37. *See* J. Bradford De Long & Kevin Lang, *Are All Economic Hypotheses False?* 100 J. Pol. Econ. 1257–72 (1992).

38. Edward E. Leamer, *Let's Take the Con out of Econometrics,* 73 Am. Econ. Rev. 1, 31–43 (1983).

39. *Id.* at 32.

40. *Id.*

41. Probably the most frank statement of this is in Milton Friedman, *Capitalism and Freedom* (U. of Chicago Press 1962).

42. Robert Barro, *So You Want to Hire the Beautiful. Well, Why Not?* Business Week 18 (Mar. 16, 1998).

43. Those readers who are familiar with Kaldor-Hicks efficiency will notice that it too relies on the set of general equilibrium outputs as its reference point. Its only difference is in allowing policy actions to be enacted without compensation, so long as the losers *could have been* compensated as we move from a less Pareto-efficient set of outputs toward a more Pareto-efficient set.

44. *See* Crawford, *supra* note 21, at 517.

45. Kenneth J. Arrow, *Social Choice and Individual Values* (2d ed., Yale U. Press 1970).

46. In addition, in his summary of the findings of information economics, Stiglitz goes on to say that "[t]he distribution of income does matter. The neat dichotomy between efficiency and distribution is not, in general, valid." Stiglitz, *supra* note 23, at 109.

47. Amartya Sen, *Collective Choice and Social Welfare* (Holden-Day 1970).

48. Philip Areeda & Louis Kaplow, *Antitrust Analysis: Problems, Text, Cases* 25 (5th ed., Aspen 1997), citing L. Kaplow & S. Shavell, *Why the Legal System Is Less Efficient Than the Income Tax in Redistributing Income,* 23 J. Legal Stud. 667 (1994).

49. *See* Joseph A. Pechman, *The Rich, the Poor, and the Taxes They Pay* (Westview 1986); and Bill Beach, *The Case for Repealing the Estate Tax* (Heritage Found. 1996).

50. Amy Wax, Is There a Future for Egalitarian Marriage? presented at Feminism and Legal Theory Workshop: Economic Discourse and the Family, Columbia Law School (March 1998).

51. For an unapologetic endorsement of the spread of neoclassical economics into other fields, *see* Edward P. Lazear, *Economic Imperialism,* 115 Q.J. Econ. 99 (2000). Among many highly quotable claims, Lazear states approvingly that "economics has been imperialistic and . . . economic imperialism has been successful." *Id.* at 103.

CHAPTER 5

Feminism and Eutrophic Methodologies

Douglas A. Kysar

Economics is an eutrophic methodology. Rich in analytical and mathematical nutrients, the discipline stimulates rapid and comprehensive growth—hence the pervasive spread of economics throughout the academic world, including especially North American law schools. Its vaunted growth, however, remains of a particular sort: low-grade proliferation of reductionist thought exercises, which ultimately saps the dissolved oxygen content of the invaded discipline, killing off its more complex inhabitants.

This is the cautionary story told by Neil Buchanan in the preceding chapter. Having seen countless other academic ponds choked by the introduction of this particular foreign species, Buchanan warns feminist legal theorists to avoid even the most timid dalliance with neoclassical economics. In this response, I take issue with the lesson of Buchanan's tale. Although his critique of economics is compelling, and although I share his fear that the discipline is capable of colonizing even the most diverse and robust intellectual spheres, Buchanan's conclusion should be rejected nevertheless.[1]

Buchanan's chapter consists of two essential elements: an exposé of the theoretical shortcomings of neoclassical economics (many familiar but some that will be eye-opening to even seasoned critics of Law and Economics), and a strident call to feminists to avoid use of the legal economic methodology, lest they invite into their camp a most deceptive and most destructive Trojan Horse. With respect to the former aspect of Buchanan's project, I am largely in agreement (although I will point out an additional shortcoming of orthodox economics that did not make his short list). I disagree, however, with Buchanan's suggestion, at the end of his essay, that feminist scholars risk "having [moral principles] surreptitiously thrust upon [them]" if they dare court the dismal science of economics. Indeed, I suspect that if any academic constituency is sufficiently equipped to play with the powerful "fire" of economics without getting burned, it is plainly the feminist scholars who for decades have been unmasking the subtle moralisms and power dynamics that lurk within dominant discourses of *all* dialects. In that sense, I would encourage feminists to explore Law and Economics precisely so that they may know their enemy (if it really is an enemy) and so that we all may benefit from the resulting dialogue.

Buchanan is probably correct that ignoring an eutrophic methodology such as neoclassical economics would help maintain conceptual clarity within feminist legal theory. It would do so, however, at the risk of ceding relevance outside the discipline, if neoclassical economics continues to occupy ever-broader academic and political territory.

In more constructive fashion, I describe three alternative economic methodologies that may be worth inspection, not simply for the defensive purposes of knowing one's enemy and maintaining relevance but for the affirmative reason that they may bring fresh analytical and rhetorical methods to the feminist project. These methodologies differ in varying degrees from the neoclassical economics that incurs Buchanan's scorn. Behavioral economics (which has spread so rapidly through the legal literature as to mark *it* as possibly eutrophic) retains the essential structure of neoclassical economics but offers a far more compelling vision of human motivation and cognition. Social economics, which attempts to revive the centuries-old thought of Swiss economist Simonde de Sismondi, rejects the neoclassical notion that the common good does not exist beyond an aggregation of individualist consumers and, instead, treats persons as citizens who stand in contextual interdependence. Finally, ecological economics, a fledgling discipline being advanced by a band of economists, biologists, political scientists, and others, offers the potential to bust the neoclassical worldview wide open, reinvigorating debates over distributive equity, resource allocation, and the very notion of a life well lived. Each of these subdisciplines offers promise both in retaining the powerful analytical methods of economics and in attempting to reform its arguably problematic moral foundation.

Of course, these disciplines are not sufficiently "standard" to constitute reasons for rejecting Buchanan's warning about economics more generally; that is, promoting these rebel offshoots of economics is not the same as saying that feminist legal theorists should embrace Law and Economics qua Law and Economics. Indeed, if the rebel offshoots of economics were instead the mainstream of the profession, one suspects that there would be little need for the conversation that Buchanan and I are having. Nevertheless, I offer these alternative economic visions as a reminder of the old adage about babies and bath water: one must be careful disposing of any bath water, no matter how squalid it may appear.

Buchanan's Critique

Since the inception of Law and Economics, legal scholars have been quick to point out that the neoclassical paradigm is riddled with subtle but significant normative implications.[2] Buchanan offers a useful taxonomy of many of these implications, along with some less familiar critiques of the supposed intellectual rigor of economics. Although he touches on the somewhat notorious behavioral foundations of microeconomics (which he wryly describes as "those assumptions"), Buchanan focuses most of his attack on three fundamental but often unexamined features of the neoclassical methodology: the equation of value with willingness to pay, the attempt to separate efficiency and distributive functions of the market, and the assumption that all markets not presently being studied exist in a state of general equilibrium.

First, standard economic analysis presumes that the value of an item or outcome is determined by the amount that someone is willing to pay for it. This willingness-to-pay criterion is flawed as a measure of value in many respects. Most notably, it is not immediately clear that domestic labor, public education, mental health, adopted children, endangered species, workplace safety, and a whole range of other traditionally nonmarket goods and services should be subjected to the narrowing expression of worth in mere dollars and cents. Requiring such a calculus seems to ensure that the items under inspection will be chronically undervalued, or indeed radically redefined, by the process of monetization. The problem is compounded by the refusal of economics practitioners to engage in interpersonal comparisons of utility. That is, preferences (expressed as monetary bids) are treated as exogenously given such that theorists neither examine the manner in which a person's preferences are formed nor question their validity and social value. Additionally, even on its own terms, the willingness-to-pay criterion is problematic. As an empirical matter, people exhibit significantly different valuations, depending on whether they are or are not initially endowed with the item or outcome being valued,[3] thereby undermining the faith one may place in willingness to pay as a basis for determinative judgment. And of course one's ability to express a valuation in terms of willingness to pay is necessarily limited by the income she has available to trade. Even in hypothetical surveys designed to avoid such budget constraints, a person's monetary modulus is likely to be influenced by her economic reality.

Second, any Pareto-efficient allocation of resources is entirely contingent on the distribution among society members of income, property, technology, education, health, legal rights, and all other factors relevant to the construction of supply and demand curves. Put differently, an entire range of general equilibriums exists that corresponds to an entire range of wealth distributions, many of which could be described as grossly inequitable. For that reason, economists often speak of maximizing efficiency and achieving distributive justice as separate policy goals necessitating separate policy instruments. The problem, as Buchanan points out, is that the *current* distribution of wealth is subtly preferenced by such a conception. That is, by extricating distributive justice from the efficiency equation, one is left with a state of affairs in which any redistribution of wealth appears to violate the Pareto principle. According to Buchanan, "[i]f the current set of endowments defines the general equilibrium outputs against which deadweight losses are measured, then any attempt to *change* people's endowments is, by definition, inefficient."

Third, efforts to enhance the allocative efficiency of any discrete market are dependent on an assumption of general equilibrium that is almost certainly never fulfilled. The term *general equilibrium* refers to a state in which all markets for all products have cleared and no changes can be made in the allocation of resources to increase social wealth. Law and Economics scholars generally seek, in piecemeal fashion, the eradication of barriers to Pareto efficiency within isolated market or legal contexts.[4] Such a move, according to Buchanan, is simply not known to be welfare enhancing because it depends on the unlikely presumption that all other contexts are currently Pareto-efficient themselves. Inevitable "false trading" and other practical realities ensure that such a state of general equilibrium exists only in textbooks, leaving the efficiency-minded scholar in the uncomfortable position of advocating for legal rules with no sound theoretical basis for believing that they actually are efficient. As Duncan Kennedy put it, "[t]here is no reason to believe that summing a series of valid partial equilibrium exercises will yield a valid general equilibrium solution."[5]

In addition to the foregoing critiques, Buchanan could also have argued that economics' fidelity to methodological individualism produces a sort of theoretical framing effect that carries significant normative implications. Specifically, because economics takes freely bargaining individuals as the appropriate unit of analysis, a variety of vital social issues are placed at risk of being incidentally excluded from consideration. To the extent that such issues are considered under the neoclassical methodology, they are often treated as mere exceptions to the ordinary rule that atomistic behavior serves the collective good. Thus, no matter how frequently they arise, commons dilemmas, public goods problems, and negative externalities are all deemed aberrational settings in which the government must simply "get the incentives right" in order to correct the aberration. To give just one example, the threat of global climate change, which confronts not just communities or nations but the entire human species, is seen as an externality in the standard microeconomic model. To many economists, the problem simply stems from the fact that no one is forced to "pay" when the turn of the ignition key contributes to global warming. But when undeniably global problems are forced into the rubric of individualistic microcontrols, when the very fate of humanity is conceived of as being "external" to the focus of the model, the time may be long past for reconceiving one's analytic tools.[6]

In sum, Buchanan reveals economics as a value-laden and somewhat imprecise discipline. The primacy of willingness to pay as a measure of worth unwisely discounts (or ignores) the value of that which cannot easily be monetized or, indeed, that which should not be monetized. This problem is compounded by the agnosticism that most economics scholars display toward interpersonal comparisons of utility: on the standard account, a crust of bread should go to the highest bidder, even if it is merely used to feed birds in the park while the homeless starve nearby. Reliance on the current distributive equilibrium as an efficiency benchmark creates a conceptual frame in which attempted changes in the distribution of wealth are stigmatized as Pareto-inefficient policy moves. Moreover, the preferred state of wealth under such a conception involves not merely pecuniary resources but technology, education, political powers, and all other components of social well-being.

As Buchanan also notes, the supposed intellectual exactitude of neoclassical economics is stymied by the frequently overlooked fact that conditions of general equilibrium—which are necessary in order to make logically rigorous conclusions about the welfare effects of alternative legal regimes—do not hold for the real-world contexts in which economics so often serves as the primary mode of policy analysis. Finally, neoclassical economics is wedded to a vision of atomistic, individual behavior that systematically excludes, or at best trivializes, human dilemmas and desiderata that are defined by their social, collective nature.

Buchanan's Warning

In light of the foregoing normative presuppositions and logical shortcomings, Buchanan counsels feminist legal theorists to avoid use of the neoclassical methodology altogether. In his view, any employment of the methodology risks falling victim to its subtle, hypnotic affirmation of values that are "fundamentally reactionary and incompatible with the goals of most feminist legal scholarship." For instance, accepting the willingness-to-pay criterion as a measure of value reinforces notions of commodifiability and commensurability that may be directly at odds with rights-based critiques of market practices. Likewise, constantly measuring policy proposals against the general equilibrium that results from the current distribution of endowments may foster a built-in bias against altering that equilibrium to produce more meaningful social change. Because the willingness-to-pay criterion and the current general equilibrium yardstick are central features of the neoclassical paradigm, Buchanan concludes that feminist legal scholars who adopt the paradigm do so at their peril: "Using neoclassical economic analysis (even, or perhaps especially, when 'turning it on its head') is the slipperiest of slopes, inviting even the careful analyst to commit lapses of reasoning and to reinforce moral and logical criteria that should be exposed and opposed."

At this point Buchanan and I part company because his conclusion, to my mind, provides too strong a pesticide for the eutrophic weed of economics. An obvious, defensive reason to reject Buchanan's warning is simply to know one's enemy. If, as Buchanan argues, the normative subtext of neoclassical economics really is fundamentally at odds with the goals of feminist scholarship, then feminist scholars should become proficient in the neoclassical methodology precisely in order to excavate the embedded value judgments that appear in economically tinged discourses. Failure to do so will only help ensure that economics retains its veneer of objectivity and precision. Hidden ideologies will remain unchallenged and unexposed, even as the economic methodology is employed within policy spheres in which its concealed norms might be highly controversial. Rather than permit such subterfuge, feminist scholars should both study and confront the neoclassical methodology.

This is a brazenly strategic argument, but it is one with contemporary significance. Economics has long since oozed from its disciplinary boundaries to cover much of the substrate of academic, political, and popular thought. As Allan Hutchinson has noted, "the increasing domination of *homo economicus* is evidenced by the fact that public discourse has become hostage to economics and has begun to dance to, instead of call, the economic tune: it is thoroughly infiltrated by the economic mindset and attuned to its interests."[7] In other words, feminist legal theorists must not only contend with the normative underpinnings of neoclassical economic theory, but they also must situate their scholarship and their policy recommendations within a culture of virtual economic idolatry. Failure to do so, no matter how persuasive one's views, may result in their simply being drowned out by a chorus of costs and benefits, risks and returns, Paretos, Kaldors, and Hicks.

Thus, as a practical matter, one seeking desirable improvements in legal and cultural governance may want to at least alternatively frame her arguments in the economic vernacular simply so that policymakers can comprehend (or will acknowledge) them. Buchanan's fear, however, is that knowing one's enemy in the manner I have just described may allow the enemy "surreptitiously" to "colonize" the field of feminist theory. The argument here is urgent. In Buchanan's view, speaking in the economic tongue necessarily corrupts the speaker. It is not simply that being conversant in neoclassical discourse reinforces the primacy of that discourse for the external audience but that the internal audience becomes convinced as well. Like so many disciplinary casualties before them, feminist scholars would risk falling prey to the siren song of Friedman, Becker, Coase, and Posner, even if they employ the neoclassical methodology only for the limited purposes I have described.

This sounds much more patronizing than it is. Buchanan is right: the study of economics appears to alter the very behavior of the student. For instance, experimental research suggests that economists are more likely to engage in noncooperative behavior and less likely to contribute to public goods than noneconomists.[8] Likewise, students of economics seem to become less cooperative and less honest over the course of their study.[9] Employing the economic methodology within a previously unacquainted field also seems to lead quite naturally to the domination of that field by economics. The study of tort jurisprudence represents a powerful illustration. Where once George Fletcher spoke eloquently of tort law as "a unique repository of intuitions of corrective justice" in which socially contextualized issues of fairness and reciprocity dominate,[10] now George Priest confidently announces that "there are . . . no articles of importance within the last five years written about modern tort law that have not addressed . . . the functional economic analysis [of tort law]."[11] This shift from fairness to efficiency as the primary mode of analysis within tort law was a quick and radical transformation. Describing the loss of life and limb in the stark terms of monetary cost and benefit does not come easily to the unprejudiced mind. Nevertheless, in just a little over three decades, we have come to the point where such concepts apparently must be spoken about exclusively in the language of B, P, and L to make a contribution of "importance" to torts scholarship.

As these examples demonstrate, the threat of normative and conceptual creep that Buchanan describes is not insubstantial. Indeed, there may be good reason to suppose that it is significant. Perhaps then, rather than risk relinquishing their intellectual autonomy, feminist legal scholars *should* avoid the use of economics, even if it comes at the ultimate cost of losing the theoretical and political battles that matter most to them. Perhaps it is better to maintain principle than to gain influence. Perhaps feminist thinkers should seek resigned solace in the mantra that Solzhenitsyn so memorably recited in his Nobel lecture: "Let the lie come into the world, even dominate the world, *but not through me.*"[12] Such seems to be the advice of Buchanan.

Again, however, in my view such romanticism exacts too great a cost. As I stated at the outset, one can scarcely think of an academic constituency more likely to defy the eutrophication of economics than feminists. Steeped in Marxist, postmodern, and deconstructivist theory, feminist scholars seem more than sufficiently armed to resist whatever ideological pull the neoclassical methodology may exert. Indeed, one imagines that the more feminist thinkers engage with economics, the more refined and powerful the critique of such orthodoxy will become. After all, the most significant contributions to the critical analysis of neoclassical economics are frequently made by *feminist* thinkers.[13] Indeed, readers having any doubts about that proposition should consider that many of the very critiques launched by Buchanan in the preceding chapter have already been made in one form or another by feminist academics.[14] In other words, we have every reason to believe that Buchanan's fear, at least with respect to feminist legal theorists, is overstated.

In short, feminist legal scholars should confront the neoclassical methodology on its own terms because failure to do so will allow the methodology to conquer academic and political terrain unimpeded by the critique, exposure, and improvement that feminism can provide. Moreover, if any academic group can use the economic methodology in a positive fashion without fear of being subtly indoctrinated, it would seem to be the very feminist scholars who already have been exposing the normative underpinnings of economics. To the extent, therefore, that policymakers only credit arguments couched within the discourse of economics, feminists can and should confidently engage in such argumentation without fear of intellectual colonization.

In the remaining sections of this response, I offer a hopefully less strategic, more constructive reason for choosing not to follow Buchanan's prescription. Specifically, I offer three permutations of standard neoclassical economics that address the type of critiques Buchanan has made, but without rejecting entirely the intellectual legacy of the discipline. In essence, these alternative visions of economics attempt to keep the baby but carefully drain the bath water.

Alternative Economic Visions

Behavioral Economics

Economists have traditionally relied on a simplified view of human behavior in which individuals are assumed to process available information in a manner that guarantees maximization of their utility over time. In recent years, legal scholars have begun developing a Law and Economics with far more nuanced assumptions about behavior and choice than this comparatively wooden rational actor model. The emerging literature draws from a body of research, increasingly known to legal scholars as behavioralism, that lies at the intersection of economics and psychology.[15] In this multidisciplinary field, cognitive psychologists, experimental economists, and other behavioral researchers study the decision-making processes of individuals, with an eye toward comparing actual human behavior with the predictions of rational choice theory. Not surprisingly, it turns out that individuals frequently process information and make decisions in ways that depart from the expected utility maximizer of economic models.[16]

Moreover, one important feature of these departures from rationality is that they are consistent and predictable—that is, they are "neither rational nor capricious."[17] Because they are predictable in this manner, the cognitive findings of behavioral researchers are also capable of being modeled. Thus, a growing number of legal economists are incorporating the findings of behavioralism into the familiar economic conception of the rational actor. As three leading commentators put it, "behavioral economics allows us to model and predict behavior relevant to law with the tools of traditional economic analysis, but with more accurate assumptions about human behavior."[18]

The promise of this collaborative research project is to retain the helpful analytical framework of neoclassical economics but simultaneously steer it toward greater predictive capabilities and hence greater real-world relevance. In this manner, behavioral economics offers the ability to overcome several of the failings of orthodox economics that Buchanan identifies. Most notably, the central agenda of behavioral economics is to look critically at the canonical vision of the rational actor. Thus, behavioral theorists reexamine such fundamental questions as whether individuals always behave out of self-interest, whether effective decision making is only limited by the availability of time and information, and whether one's willingness to pay for something adequately expresses the degree to which one values it. The answers that behavioral economic scholars turn up to these questions are often not surprising to even casual observers of human interaction, but their formal scientific expression provides a strong basis on which to improve the economic methodology.

For instance, as Buchanan emphasizes early in his essay, the standard willingness-to-pay formulation of value in neoclassical economics is unduly narrow for many important tasks. With that critique, there should be little disagreement. The more interesting challenge, however, lies in constructing alternative means of comparing objects and outcomes that better capture actual human beliefs and provide a basis for policymaking. Behavioral economics attempts to contribute to that project by precisely identifying ways in which the willingness-to-pay criterion is inadequate. For example, behavioral researchers have compiled voluminous evidence of the endowment effect, a cognitive heuristic that refers to the fact that "people appear to value a commodity that they own much more than an identical commodity that they do not own."[19]

As a consequence, in addition to the income and substitution effects that Buchanan identifies, the Coase theorem is also undermined by the fact that individuals display a significant gap in their offer and asking prices with respect to items of value such as legal entitlements.[20] Because one cannot separate valuation from the question of ownership, one also frequently cannot determine who between competing users values a legal entitlement more. In other words, one cannot determine the efficient outcome without defining which valuation condition counts as the "real" one—a judgment for which economics has little to contribute. The Coase theorem's reliance on the market to settle valuation questions provides no satisfactory solution because, even in the absence of transaction costs, a whole range of potentially welfare-enhancing bargains may be impeded, depending on how one defines welfare and the size of the gap between offer and asking prices.

The implications of the endowment effect for Law and Economics are both broad and dramatic. For instance, as Jeffrey Rachlinski and Forest Jourden have explained, an adequate treatment of legal remedies must account for the fact that individuals seem to ascribe meaning to ownership *in and of itself*. The well-known nuisance case of *Boomer v. Atlantic Cement Co.*,[21] in which a trial court found in favor of a group of homeowners against a neighboring cement plant but awarded them only monetary rather than injunctive relief, provides a powerful illustration of this distinction. The standard legal economic account of *Boomer* focuses on transaction costs and other familiar barriers to exchange. On this account, awarding the plaintiff homeowners damages rather than an injunction was economically appropriate to overcome holdout problems and other strategic behavior that the plaintiffs may have adopted when bargaining with the cement plant. As Rachlinski and Jourden point out, however, "[t]he trial court's novel remedy, while economically sound, was a psychological insult."[22] The homeowners felt that an essential component of the value of their property was the ability to refuse to compromise that property except on terms and conditions to which they agreed. The trial court removed that right from the plaintiffs' bundle, leaving them feeling poorer than before, irrespective of the monetary relief they were afforded.

Thus, one can see that the endowment effect—which is but one feature from a panoply of cognitive predilections that have been identified—greatly enriches the standard legal economic model of the choice between property rules and liability rules. Law journals are now brimming with articles providing similarly rich redescriptions of the received wisdom of Law and Economics. Ironically, several have come from Christine Jolls, the feminist Law and Economics scholar who Buchanan identifies as struggling within the realm of neoclassical economics to assume the mantle of scientific rigor. For instance, Jolls has demonstrated that behavioral findings bring into question the widely held tenet of Law and Economics that legal decision makers should focus only on maximizing the allocative efficiency of outcomes, to the exclusion of concerns about wealth distribution.[23] Likewise, she has provided a novel defense of the Age Discrimination in Employment Act by use of experimental economic findings regarding people's time-varying preferences.[24] Finally, Jolls was one of the authors of the article that marked the formal arrival of behavioral Law and Economics, providing a fascinating survey of possible areas of application of behavioralist insights, along with a normative account of how the new literature significantly destabilizes the antipaternalist bias of conventional Law and Economics.[25]

Buchanan is skeptical of these and other behavioral economic applications, apparently believing that incremental improvements to the neoclassical account of choice and decision making obscure the larger failings of the discipline. Yet outright dismissal of behavioralist approaches seems premature. By premising their critiques of *homo economicus* on robust empirical findings, behavioralists have helped considerably to reopen a dialogue between Law and Economics scholars and those who find the mainstream approach unsatisfactory. That dialogue could lead to a much richer and sounder basis for regulatory decision making. As Barbara Ann White has noted, feminist jurisprudence is well situated to provide important social judgments of value in those places where the Law and Economics notions of efficiency and cost–benefit analysis are incomplete.[26] Because it exposes the failings of the standard rational-actor model of choice and valuation, behavioral Law and Economics helps maximize the likelihood that policymakers will realize when in fact those social judgments are needed.

Social Economics

A second alternative formulation of the economic methodology emerges from the work of nineteenth-century Swiss economist Simonde de Sismondi.[27] Like other economists of his day, Sismondi was concerned with the expansive political economic question of how to structure a just and prosperous society. He rejected the prevailing view of his contemporaries, Thomas Malthus and David Ricardo, who saw no hope for social improvement, given the exponential growth of human populations and the fixed availability of arable soil. Simultaneously, however, he rejected the view of Adam Smith and his followers, who believed that social improvement arose as an incidental consequence of unfettered economic competition among individual agents. Instead, Sismondi developed "an economics exploring the principles on which production of goods and services can be undertaken such that human welfare in its broadest sense is maximized."[28] The alternative theoretical framework that emerged from his work is characterized by many unique elements.

Most fundamentally, social economists join relational or cultural feminists in criticizing the dominant political and economic emphasis of autonomy and individualism over interdependency and communitarianism.[29] Sismondi's 1803 work, *De la richesse commerciale*, provides an early exposition of the notion that economics should be concerned not just with the accumulation of wealth among members of society but also with the ways in which collective welfare can be enhanced by distinct policies of governance, even ones that come at the cost of individual welfare.[30] Unchecked pursuit of material wealth by atomistic economic actors, in Sismondi's view, leads ultimately to a society devoid of stability and human dignity. As fellow social economist John Ruskin would later vehemently put it, "[t]he idea that directions can be given for the gaining of wealth, irrespective of the considerations of its moral sources . . . is perhaps the most insolently futile of all that ever beguiled men through vices."[31] To Sismondi and other social economists, therefore, the goal of economics was not the maximization of opportunities for individual pursuit of happiness but rather "the management of the national fortune for the happiness of all."[32]

This vision of human social interaction and responsibility stands in stark contrast to the dominant individualistic liberalism of neoclassical economics. On the conventional economic view, the individual is reduced to a pleasure-seeking agent whose acquisitive desires are supported by a state that protects her package of private and property rights but otherwise lets the individual alone. Family, community, and other social entities only exist under this view as aggregations of their individual constituents—no accounting can or need be made of the interests of the social entity itself. Social economists reject this conception as being wholly contrary to human experience. Even the most self-interested personal preferences are formed and satisfied within undeniably collective contexts. To ignore that reality is to abstract away from the most vital and enduring feature of the human species, its social organization.

Moreover, by denying the existence of a common good, conventional economics makes an implicit normative judgment that tends to devalue any interests arising along a social dimension. Because the universe of relevant ends is taken to consist only of those that are pursued by individuals acting as individuals, economic policies only maximize the satisfaction of self-interested individual preferences. Even the supposed neutrality of the Pareto criterion of value—which holds that a change is socially desirable if it can make somebody better off in society without making anybody worse off—is limited by a host of unstated normative positions, including most notably its focus on the welfare of *individuals* to the exclusion of groups, future generations, or society as a whole. Occasionally the neoclassical practitioner recognizes that individuals pursuing self-interested goals may lead to socially undesirable results, but such situations are cabined off as exceptional anomalies that require little more than ex post corrective governmental market intervention. Systemic conditions giving rise to these supposed anomalies are rarely examined. In sharp contrast, on the social economic account, it is not permissible to treat issues of collective welfare simply as curious sideshows; they are the main event.[33]

Methodological individualism should be contrasted therefore with alternatives, such as civic republicanism, that in the eyes of social economists comport better with humanity's actual condition: "The central idea of republicanism was the notion of *citizenship,* a term implying the mutual sharing of burdens and benefits of certain aspects of social life."[34] Social economists, by developing a political economic philosophy that recognizes the common good, likewise conceive of rights as not merely negative restraints on the state but as positive obligations that imply affirmative duties on the part of fellow citizens. As John Hobson noted, such fundamental ethical issues are obscured under the standard economic account, with its "protean fallacy of individualism which feigns the existence of separate individuals by abstracting and neglecting the social relations which belong to them and make them what they are."[35]

Social economists also point out that the neoclassical notion of rationality is, at least on some widely accepted philosophical accounts, antirational. Moral philosopher Harry Frankfurt's classic paper describes the ability to reason about one's own desires as the defining characteristic of being human.[36] Such higher-order desires reflect the cognitive introspection and evaluation that is made possible by humanity's unique awareness of self. Thus, on Frankfurt's account, rationality is best described as human deliberation about the lower-order desires that an individual "wants to want." Such deliberation is, of course, precisely the field of inquiry that economics attempts to exclude from consideration. As Nobel laureate economist Herbert Simon put it, "[r]eason . . . cannot tell us where to go; at best it can tell us how to get there. It is a gun for hire that can be employed in the service of any goal we have, good or bad."[37] In other words, economics disclaims the capacity to judge between competing ends, the very capacity that, at least according to leading philosophical accounts, is the essence of rationality.

Besides being possibly antirational, treating preferences as exogenously given in this manner also ignores the endogenous effects of the economy on the lives of its participants. For instance, as Vicki Schultz has noted, one of the primary determinants of a person's character and well-being is her "life's work."[38] In other words, an individual's work experience will have a profound influence on the formation of her personal identity, including her tastes and preferences. And of course an individual's work experience is profoundly influenced by the systems of production that exist within the prevailing economic order—a fact recognized long ago by Sismondi and other social economists.[39] Increases in productive efficiency therefore cannot be analyzed independent from the corrosive effect that they may have on the character and lives of laborers. If the late E. F. Schumacher's assessment was correct, that "[v]irtually all real production has been turned into an inhuman chore which does not enrich a man but empties him," then whatever demand is satisfied by production will also be inhuman and empty.[40] Put differently, it makes no sense to pursue efficiency improvements to better satisfy consumer preferences if the means of improvement stunt the development of the very preferences sought to be satisfied.

Social economists attempt to fill this void by making positive, logically derived statements about the normative goals of social activity. Rather than maximizing the market's ability to satisfy unexamined, subjective preferences, social economists believe that society should orient the market toward fulfilling human needs, which can be given a largely objective, quantifiable, and empirical dimension. The first step in such a project is to abandon economic agnosticism with respect to preferences. As Nicholas Georgescu-Roegen put it, "[i]t can hardly be denied that it makes *objective* economic sense to help starving people by taxing those who spend their summers at luxurious resorts."[41] Furthermore, one need only make the value judgment that human life is generally worth sustaining in order to derive basic social obligations to provide for the means of subsistence and physical health. Ruskin famously expressed this sentiment with his maxim "There is no wealth but life."[42] Hobson later developed this alternative social economic standard of valuation further, arguing that governments have an obligation to provide citizens with the means of self-realization, broadly defined to include such conditions as a living wage, meaningful and secure employment, and a healthy environment. To Hobson, the goal of economic development is not the undifferentiated accumulation of wealth but rather the bolstering of human dignity: "Wealth should be distributed according to the support it renders to the whole life of recipients. It should give to each what each is capable of utilizing for a full human life."[43]

The foregoing description provides a sketch of the social economic project and its alternative formulation of welfare and human interaction. As can be seen, the discipline provides an antidote to the stark theory of value that forms the core of neoclassical economics and that attracts the criticism set forth by Buchanan. Social economics also responds to some of the more technical difficulties of neoclassical economics that Buchanan identifies. For instance, Sismondi recognized the significance of "false trading" and other market imperfections that prevent new equilibriums from arising in a quick and tidy manner. Indeed, Sismondi argued at length that the economic theories of his rivals ignore the human costs associated with the "long and cruel sufferings" of market adjustments.[44] Workers in particular are enfeebled by such adjustments. Having invested years of apprenticeship and dedication to a particular craft, the laborer is reluctant to abandon her chosen field. Because workers are at least partially immobilized in this manner by the psychological costs associated with dislocation, the owners of capital are able to extract a greater and greater share of the surplus created by their joint productive efforts. Such inertia may appear irrational to the neoclassical economist, yet it is emphatically human to the social economist.

The conventional practice of economics ignores this inconvenient psychological reality by assuming a hypothetical, omniscient auctioneer who sets all prices (including wages) in all markets perfectly and instantaneously. No matter how many people actually fit the description, the laborer who "irrationally" continues to endure economic, physical, or psychological hardship in the workplace is assumed away by an extravagant abstraction, the Walrasian auctioneer. Yet the invention's namesake, early neoclassical economist Léon Walras, may well have balked at any economic practice that ignored human suffering for theoretical expediency in this manner. In his view, economics was fundamentally a moral discipline: "If any science espouses justice as its guiding principle, surely it must be the science of the distribution of social wealth, or as we shall designate it, *social economics*."[45] To Walras, economics posed questions of the most philosophical and ethical urgency: "What mode of appropriation is compatible with justice? Which mode of appropriation subordinates the destiny of some to the destiny of others? What mode of appropriation does reason recommend as compatible with the requirements of moral personality?"[46] Ironically, the questions posed by Walras are ignored by conventional economic practice in part through the imagined device bearing his name.

Finally, social economists also share Buchanan's suspicion of the rigor and exactitude of mathematical methodologies within economic analysis. Sismondi, for instance, observed that "to apply the mathematical language to a science which is not exact is to continuously expose oneself to error. Political economy is not founded solely on numbers, it is rather an assemblage of moral observations which cannot be submitted to calculation and which continuously change the facts. The mathematician who wants to constantly make abstractions is bound to suppress haphazardly essential variables in each of his equations."[47] Indeed, on Sismondi's scathing account, practitioners of mathematically based economics are engaged in an elaborate shell game, having "thrown themselves into abstractions which make us lose from view entirely the human being to whom the wealth belongs, and who ought to enjoy it."[48] In short, faced with Hobson's question—"If we are to have a science of human costs and utilities, of true effort and satisfactions, will the method be mathematical?"[49]—social economists firmly answer "no," justice and welfare have qualitative dimensions that can never be subsumed within a numerical rubric.

Although Sismondi's work received scant attention in his day and has only very recently been translated into English, it no doubt influenced, directly or indirectly, many of the great economic theorists. For instance, Sismondi presages much of Marx in his description of the alienating impact of modern production techniques and the dangers of separating the ownership of capital from labor (he even coined the terms *class struggle* and *proletariat*). He also provides an early rendition of the view later taken by Thorstein Veblen, Fred Hirsch, Robert Frank, and other scholars who argue that consumption often takes on a competitive, socially destructive character (in Sismondi's words, consumption expenditures are often "calculated to afford relative rather than absolute enjoyment").[50] In many respects, Sismondi's analysis of early nineteenth-century British trade policies reads like a sophisticated and balanced assessment of contemporary debates over globalization. Finally, and most notably, he was the first economist to reject laissez-faire capitalism in favor of an active government.

Yet despite these intellectual achievements, Sismondi's work and the tradition of social economics it inspired arguably have not been given their proper seat within the economic hierarchy. Social economics represents a middle path between the imperialist force of neoclassically defined capitalism and the stifling bureaucracy of Marxist socialism. Sismondi advocates the just distribution of private property ownership among society members, not its nationalization; he advocates the restoration of capital control to labor, not its abolition. He fundamentally reorients the economic inquiry from a focus on the bare accumulation of wealth to its wide diffusion and enjoyment, yet he manages to do so not with a reactionary abandonment of the basic means of production but with an appeal to ethical awareness that remains timely almost two centuries later: "It is not in any way against machines, against inventions, against civilizations that I raise my objections, it is against the new organization of society which, by taking away from the working man all property except his arms, gives him no guarantee against competition, a mad auction conducted to his disadvantage, and one of which he must necessarily be the victim. . . . Today, it is not the invention that is the evil; it is the unjust division man makes of its results."[51]

In short, Sismondi and the social economists offer a promising alternative to the radical individualism of mainstream economic thought, one that might provide especially fertile ground for legal theorists interested in advancing positive rights and concern for human dignity amid a political economic climate that tends to deny their existence. As economist Mark Lutz has written, "[a]n economic philosophy that accommodates the common good leads to an economics that does not shy away from ethical considerations and distinguishes itself by focusing on persons as citizens who stand in relation to each other, instead of treating people as acquisitive consumers."[52]

Ecological Economics

A final alternative to the standard neoclassical paradigm emerged in recent decades from the visionary work of thinkers such as Garret Hardin, Kenneth Boulding, and Nicholas Georgescu-Roegen.[53] Known as ecological economics, this fledgling discipline is being developed by a group of dedicated scholars who adopt the same general methodology as the behavioral and social economists: they examine the most robust findings from disciplines outside of economics and use those findings to steer economic analysis toward what they believe is greater real-world relevance. Thus, as behavioralists instill economic analysis with the teachings of cognitive psychology and decision theory, and as social economists attempt to restore to the discipline an understanding of humanity's sociological and communitarian nature, ecological economists bring the findings of the physical sciences to economic practice. Through their efforts, a simple but dramatic shift is beginning to take shape in humanity's vision of the relationship between economic and ecological activity.

Specifically, ecological economists view the human economy as a subsystem of the environment, whereas conventional economists view the environment as a subsystem of the economy. The former vision emphasizes natural constraints on the expansion of human production, including both the scarcity of resource inputs to the economic process and the scarcity of pollution sinks to absorb waste outputs of the process. The latter vision admits of no such limits to human economic growth, given that no conceptual superstructure such as the environment exists "around" the economy to constrain it. Economic growth is limited only by the availability of human-made capital and labor, not by natural resources.

This elementary distinction in pre-analytic vision leads to surprisingly dramatic changes in policy recommendations. As leading ecological economist Herman Daly put it, "[w]hen we draw a containing boundary of the environment around the economy, we move from 'empty-world' economics to 'full world' economics. Economic logic stays the same, but the perceived pattern of scarcity changes radically and policies must be changed radically."[54] Particularly the goal of market regulation becomes far more complicated than merely seeking to maximize allocative efficiency. In addition to establishing market conditions that allow resources to be devoted to their most-valued use, governments also must manage the absolute scale of the human macroeconomy in order to ensure that its impact does not exceed the carrying capacity of the relevant ecosystem.[55] Such regulation entails the design and use of a range of policy instruments far more diverse—and often more blunt—than traditional market-corrective devices.

More importantly, ecological economics entails conscious and transparent decision making regarding the distribution of wealth, the prioritization of preferences, and the growth of populations within a given legal community. Under the ecological economic worldview, social inequities and environmental atrocities can no longer be ignored on the ground that opportunity and nature are both infinite in their bounty; such limitless visions are exposed by ecological economists as lacking a defensible scientific foundation. Thus, once one accepts the foundational principle of ecological economics—that the level of material throughput in the economy is subject to ecological constraints—the concerns of distribution and sustainability can no longer be pushed to the side in ever-intensifying pursuit of allocative efficiency.

Put differently, both standard economics and ecological economics divide the world into fixed and manipulable spheres. Standard economics treats nonmaterial factors such as preferences and income distribution as given. The economist's task becomes simply to ensure that material factors such as resources and goods are most efficiently employed to suit the given nonmaterial parameters. In practice, the adjustment of material factors almost always involves economic growth created by ever-intensifying exploitation of natural resources. That same expansion in economic output provides the basis for political assurances that wealth inequality will somehow be alleviated through the undirected "rising tide."

Ecological economists, in contrast, take the physical environment as fixed and contemplate mechanisms for adjusting nonmaterial factors to best suit the given ecological superstructure. That is, ecological economists study "how the nonphysical variables of technology, preferences, distribution, and lifestyles can be brought into feasible and just equilibrium with the complex biophysical system of which we are a part."[56] Such adjustment requires the enhancement of resource productivity and the equitable redistribution of wealth and income, all within the context of a steady-state (that is, a nonphysically expanding) economy. It also entails the deliberate assumption by governments of a role in the formation of norms, especially with respect to cultivating preferences for nonmaterial goods.

I have advocated the use of ecological economics as a tool for legal theorizing.[57] By incorporating ecological economic insights into doctrinal and policy discussions, legal scholars could essentially leapfrog mainstream economic thought to provide both the theoretical impetus for and the practical construction of policy tools that ensure long-term environmental sustainability. Given the emerging consensus of the global scientific community regarding the state of the environment, such a conceptual advancement may have immense importance in the decades to come.[58] An additional consequence of incorporating ecological economic insights into legal theory may be to reinvigorate the debate over the inclusion of distributive effects in the analysis and choice of legal rules. The conventional economic response to distributive concerns—that growth in the scale of the economy can raise everyone's absolute level of wealth—becomes untenable as a long-run solution under the ecological economic worldview. At some point, perhaps already reached, the benefits to be gained from an increase in economic output must necessarily be outweighed by the environmental, social, and other uncounted costs entailed by such an increase. Hence, under the ecological economist's vision, governments must address the problem of inequitable wealth distribution directly and openly rather than merely hoping for the alleviation of disparities through continual economic expansion.

In this manner, one can see that ecological economics offers the potential to overcome two of Buchanan's most reviled features of neoclassical economics. First, ecological economics provides at least a partial answer to Buchanan's concern that neoclassical economics premises its efficiency predictions on partial equilibrium analysis when in fact general equilibrium analysis is required to make logically sound predictions. By making sustainable scale a primary regulatory goal, ecological economics forces decision making with respect to many of society's most vital resources from a *macroeconomic* perspective. That is, ecological economics forces the determination of absolute levels of material throughput and resource intensity in the entire economy such that basic ecosystem goods and services are not depleted or taxed beyond their ability to regenerate. Such judgments require systemic thinking across multiple markets, with input from both economic and noneconomic experts. They are, in essence, analyses of the general equilibrium that should result from sustainable use of the economy's primary material resources. Such thinking provides a marked improvement over the partial equilibrium analysis that Buchanan finds so unappealing.

Second, by forcing explicit social judgments regarding the just distribution of wealth and rights within a community, ecological economists reject the view that the distributive outcomes of markets are desirable solely by virtue of their existence. Neoclassical economics' conceptual separation of allocative efficiency and just distribution indirectly preferences the current distribution of endowments in a society simply because any changes from that distribution will appear inefficient on the allocation criterion. Ecological economics avoids this subtle conservative bias by treating distributive judgments as market-determining, not market-determined. That is, under ecological economics, social decisions regarding the distribution of wealth and entitlements must occur separate from and prior to the reallocation of resources through the market. Thus, on this account the practitioners of neoclassical economics must be content with practicing their bread and butter of maximizing the market's allocative efficiency, but only *after* both the optimal scale and distributive foundation of that market have been determined by social consensus.

Conclusion

Prominent Law and Economics theorists Robert Cooter and Thomas Ulen also have described the spread of the neoclassical economic methodology throughout law journals by evoking the image of biological invasion: "Like the rabbit in Australia, economics found a vacant niche in the 'intellectual ecology' of the law and rapidly filled it."[59] Their example is worth exploring.[60] In the early 1800s, homesick British settlers in Australia formed a social club known as the Acclimatisation Society, whose stated purpose was transforming the native ecology of the world's oldest continent into that of Mother England. Toward that end, twenty-four wild rabbits were imported to the Australian continent in the 1850s by a wealthy estate owner pining for his days of hunting in the English countryside. Within a few decades, the Australian Outback was covered by a gray blanket of several million rabbits, all ravaging native grasses, brushes, and tree sprouts and turning grassland and farmland into a dusty desert. The resulting decrease in food, brush hiding places, and burrows left native marsupials such as the wallaby, the bilby, and the bandicoot teetering on the brink of extinction.

Over the years conservationists have banded together with farmers (who suffer an estimated $A600 million of crop damage each year) to demand costly government control efforts, including the erection of a two-thousand-mile-long fence that was, alas, quickly breached. In the 1950s, the government released a virus that causes myxomatosis and that appeared to be a magic bullet, killing 90 percent of the rabbits it infected, until the population developed a resistance and began to spread again, stronger than before. Currently, with an estimated one billion rabbits hopping blissfully across the Outback, the government is grappling with the effects of calicivirus, a rabbit-hemorrhaging disease imported from China, which was inadvertently released from an experimental laboratory off the continent's southernmost shore. The saga seems primed to continue in this tragicomical fashion until either the Australian rabbit or the human population is completely eradicated.

Obviously, one suspects that Cooter and Ulen did not intend to invite the full implications of their analogy. Yet there is a sense, powerfully explored by Buchanan, in which the metaphor of economics as a gray blanket is quite apt. In his essay, Buchanan provides a sharp and revealing critique of the claim that neoclassical economic analysis is both a rigorous and a valueless science. In other words, he takes head-on the popular tale that economics is an objective and innocuous methodology, a jolly sporting opportunity occasioned by fluffy, harmless visitors from the homeland. Instead, Buchanan shows us that economics poses significant threats to our most important native species, the norms and values that inform our scholarship and our lives. And worse, Buchanan shows us that the foreign invader seems capable of rapid multiplication, evading all manner of defensive countermaneuvers and inevitably conquering our "intellectual ecology." For Buchanan, therefore, using the economic methodology is a gamble simply not worth taking.

Although not entirely unsympathetic to Buchanan's conclusion, I recommend rejecting it for two reasons. First, if economics really is an invasive force on a par with the Australian rabbit epidemic, then Buchanan's advice could only ever lead to a Pyrrhic victory: feminist legal scholars would remain free from invasion, but they would be forced onto an isolated research station with nothing but Antarctica to the south and a billion chattering bunnies to the north. Indeed, if Buchanan's characterization of economics is accurate, then some magic bullet may be needed for all of our benefit—and feminist legal theory seems to provide a likely candidate. Second, in light of various promising permutations of economic theory such as behavioral, social, and ecological economics, it may well be that we risk losing valuable, desirable subspecies in a desperate effort to rid ourselves of the primary pest. Calicivirus, after all, is suspected of killing both rabbits and native animal species, a primary reason why the Australian government did not intend to use it as a wholesale measure against the rabbit epidemic.

The quibble between Buchanan and me may seem small, but it is significant. If Buchanan's characterization of neoclassical economics is accurate, feminist legal theorists inevitably at some point will face an important choice regarding whether or not to take up the economic toolbox. Given the nature of exponential growth, this day of reckoning may arrive sooner than anyone expects. Even as we read these pages, the rabbits are out there, and they are busy breeding.

Notes

1. I am grateful to Terence Dougherty, Cynthia Farina, and Martha Fineman for helpful comments, advice, and encouragement. I also thank Neil Buchanan for stimulating discussion and exchanges.

2. *See, e.g.,* Donald H. Regan, *The Problem of Social Cost Revisited,* 15 J.L. & Econ. 427 (1972); Arthur Allen Leff, *Economic Analysis of Law: Some Realism about Nominalism,* 60 Va. L. Rev. 451 (1974); Mark Kelman, *Choice and Utility,* 1979 Wis. L. Rev. 769 (1979); Mark Kelman, *Consumption Theory, Production Theory, and Ideology in the Coase Theorem,* 52 S. Cal. L. Rev. 669 (1979); Duncan Kennedy & Frank Michelman, *Are Property and Contract Efficient?* 8 Hofstra L. Rev. 711 (1980); Ronald Dworkin, *Is Wealth a Value?* 9 J. Legal Stud. 1191 (1980); Duncan Kennedy, *Cost–Benefit Analysis of Entitlement Problems: A Critique,* 33 Stan. L. Rev.

387 (1981); Mark Kelman, *Misunderstanding Social Life: A Critique of the Core Premises of Law and Economics*, 33 J. Legal Educ. 274 (1983); Richard H. Pildes & Elizabeth S. Anderson, *Slinging Arrows at Democracy: Social Choice Theory, Value Pluralism, and Democratic Politics*, 90 Colum. L. Rev. 2121 (1990).

3. *See, e.g.*, Elizabeth Hoffman & Matthew L. Spitzer, *Willingness to Pay vs. Willingness to Accept: Legal and Economic Implications*, 71 Wash. U. L.Q. 59 (1993).

4. To be sure, many economists, and some legal economists, analyze policy questions using a general equilibrium approach that attempts to both correct for inefficiencies in the primary market and control for feedback effects resulting from other markets. *See, e.g.*, Richard S. Markovits, *Monopoly and the Allocative Inefficiency of First-Best-Allocatively-Efficient Tort Law in Our Worse-Than-Second-Best World: The Whys and Some Therefores*, 46 Case W. Res. L. Rev. 313 (1996). Such models, however, tend to be evanescent in their temporal relevance, woefully complex to construct, and, in any event, almost unavoidably incomplete. *See* Duncan Kennedy, *The Role of Law in Economic Thought: Essays on the Fetishism of Commodities*, 34 Am. U. L. Rev. 939, 963 (1985).

5. Kennedy, *supra* note 4, at 963.

6. *See* Douglas A. Kysar, *Sustainability, Distribution, and the Macroeconomic Analysis of Law*, 43 B.C. L. Rev. 1 (2001) [hereinafter Kysar, *Sustainability*]; Douglas A. Kysar, *Law, Environment, and Vision*, 97 Nw. U. L. Rev. 675 (2003).

7. Allan C. Hutchinson, *Life after Shopping: From Consumers to Citizens in Consumer Law* in *The Global Economy*, 25 (Iain Ramsay ed., 1995).

8. *See* Robert H. Frank, Thomas Gilovich, & Dennis T. Regan, *Does Studying Economics Inhibit Cooperation?* 7 J. Econ. Persp. 159 (1993) (reviewing studies and providing new evidence).

9. *See id.*

10. George P. Fletcher, *Fairness and Utility in Tort Theory*, 85 Harv. L. Rev. 537, 538 (1972).

11. George L. Priest, *The Inevitability of Tort Reform*, 26 Val. U. L. Rev. 701, 704–5 (1992). Priest may have overlooked Leslie Bender's memorable work, *Feminist Re(Torts): Thoughts on the Liability Crisis, Mass Torts, Power, and Responsibilities*, Duke L.J. 848 (1990).

12. Quoted in Jonathan Glover, *It Makes No Difference Whether or Not I Do It*, in *Applied Ethics* 138 (P. Singer ed., 1986) (emphasis added).

13. *See, e.g.*, Elizabeth Anderson, *Values in Ethics and Economics* (1996); Julie A. Nelson, *Feminism, Objectivity and Economics* (1996); *Beyond Economic Man: Feminist Theory and Economics* (Marianne A. Ferber & Julie A. Nelson eds., 1993).

14. *See, e.g.*, Julie A. Nelson, *Feminism and Economics*, 9 J. Econ. Persp. 131 (1995) (critiquing, from a feminist perspective, such standard neoclassical trappings as the assumption of rational self-interest, the reliance on econometric and mathematical techniques, and the focus on the individual as the primary unit of analysis); Barbara Ann White, *Risk-Utility Analysis and the Learned Hand Formula: A Hand That Helps or a Hand That Hides?* 32 Ariz. L. Rev. 77 (1990) (cataloging ways in which economic tools of valuation and cost-benefit analysis depend on obscured normative judgments); Barbara Ann White, *Coase and the Courts: Economics for the Common Man*, 72 Iowa L. Rev. 577 (1987) (providing an extended discussion of the multiplicity of efficiency equilibria and the significance of the initial distribution of rights in determining market outcomes).

15. *See Behavioral Law and Economics* (Cass R. Sunstein ed., 2000).

16. *See generally* Cass R. Sunstein, *Behavioral Analysis of Law*, 64 U. Chi. L. Rev. 1175 (1997); Christine Jolls, Cass R. Sunstein, & Richard H. Thaler, *A Behavioral Approach to Law and Economics*, 50 Stan. L. Rev. 1471 (1998); Jon D. Hanson & Douglas A. Kysar, *Taking Behavioralism Seriously: The Problem of Market Manipulation*, 74 N.Y.U. L. Rev. 632 (1999); Russell B. Korobkin & Thomas S. Ulen, *Law and Behavioral Science: Removing the Rationality Assumption from Law and Economics*, 88 Cal. L. Rev. 1051 (2000); Jeffrey J. Rachlinski, *The "New" Law and Psychology: A Reply to Critics, Skeptics, and Cautious Supporters*, 85 Cornell L. Rev. 739 (2000).

17. Amos Tversky & Daniel Kahneman, *Advances in Prospect Theory: Cumulative Representation of Uncertainty,* 5 J. Risk & Uncertainty 297 (1992).

18. Jolls, Sunstein, & Thaler, *supra* note 16, at 1474. Recent work by Anne Dailey using psychoanalytic research offers the even more dramatic possibility of bringing unconscious elements of motivation, personality, and social interaction into the economic analysis of human behavior. *See* Anne C. Dailey, *The Hidden Economy of the Unconscious,* 74 Chi.-Kent L. Rev. 1599 (2000); Anne C. Dailey, *Striving for Rationality,* 86 Va. L. Rev. 349 (2000).

19. Jeffrey J. Rachlinski & Forest Jourden, *Remedies and the Psychology of Ownership,* 51 Vand. L. Rev. 1541, 1551 (1998).

20. *See id.* at 1553–56.

21. 257 N.E. 2d 870 (1970).

22. Rachlinski & Jourden, *supra note 19,* at 1576.

23. *See* Christine Jolls, *Behavioral Economic Analysis of Redistributive Legal Rules,* 51 Vand. L. Rev. 1653 (1998).

24. *See* Christine Jolls, *Hands-Tying and the Age Discrimination in Employment Act,* 74 Tex. L. Rev. 1813 (1996); *see also* Christine Jolls, *Contracts as Bilateral Commitments: A New Perspective on Contract Modification,* 26 J. Legal Stud. 203 (1997).

25. *See* Jolls, Sunstein, & Thaler, *supra* note 16.

26. *See* Barbara Ann White, *Feminist Foundations for the Law of Business: One Law and Economics Scholar's Survey and (Re)View,* 10 UCLA Women's L.J. 39 (1999).

27. *See* Mark A. Lutz, *Economics for the Common Good: Two Centuries of Social Economic Thought in the Humanistic Tradition* 21 (1999).

28. *Id.* at 2.

29. *See, e.g.,* Martha Albertson Fineman, *Cracking the Foundational Myths: Independence, Autonomy, and Self-Sufficiency,* ch. 9, this vol.; Martha Albertson Fineman, *The Neutered Mother, the Sexual Family and Other Twentieth Century Tragedies* (1995); Martha Minow, *Making All the Difference* (1990); Robin West, *Jurisprudence and Gender,* 55 U. Chi. L. Rev. 1 (1988).

30. J. C. L. Simonde de Sismondi, *De la richesse commerciale* (1803).

31. John Ruskin, *Unto This Last* 58 (U. of Nebraska Press, 1967).

32. J. C. L. Simonde de Sismondi, *New Principles of Political Economy* 27 (R. Hyse 1991).

33. This social economic reconceptualization can be thought of as somewhat parallel to the feminist critique of the public–private distinction. *See, e.g.,* Ruth Gavison, *Feminism and the Public/Private Distinction,* 45 Stan. L. Rev. 1 (1992); Martha Minow, *Words and the Door to the Land of Change: Law, Language, and Family Violence,* 43 Vand. L. Rev. 1665 (1990); Frances Olsen, *The Family and the Market: A Study of Ideology and Legal Reform,* 96 Harv. L. Rev. 1497 (1983). Just as "[t]he private is public for those for whom the personal is political," Catharine A. MacKinnon, *Toward a Feminist Theory of the State* 191 (1989), the private is also public for those who suffer the social and environmental "spillover" effects of private ordering.

34. Lutz, *supra* note 27, at 3. In similar fashion, contemporary feminist thinkers have developed an ethic of care that "connotes responding to the needs of other persons with whom one is in a web of relationships, as well as alleviating the suffering of the world." Linda C. McClain, *"Atomistic Man" Revisited: Liberalism, Connection, and Feminist Jurisprudence,* 65 S. Cal. L. Rev. 1171, 1184 (1992); *see generally* Carol Gilligan, *In a Different Voice* (Harvard U. Press 1982).

35. John A. Hobson, *The Social Problem* 67 (Thoemmes Press 1996).

36. Harry G. Frankfurt, *Freedom of the Will and the Concept of a Person,* 68 J. Phil. 5 (1971).

37. Herbert A. Simon, *Reason in Human Affairs* 7–8 (1983).

38. Vicki Schultz, *Life's Work,* 100 Colum. L. Rev. 1881 (2000).

39. *See, e.g.,* Sismondi, *supra* note 32, at 555 ("When every hour is a struggle for life, all passions are concentrated in selfishness; each forgets the pain of others in what he himself suffers; the sentiments of nature are blunted; a constant, obstinate, uniform labour, debases all the faculties. One blushes for the human species, to see how low on a scale of degradation it can descend; how

much beneath the condition of animals it can voluntarily submit to maintain life."); Hobson, *supra* note 35, at 43 (questioning increases in economic productivity because they may mean "simply that we are making greater drudges of ourselves, toiling harder than before after commercial goods under conditions of work which disabled us from making a more pleasant or more profitable use of our increased possessions than our forefathers made of their smaller stock").

40. E. F. Schumacher, *Small Is Beautiful: Economics as if People Mattered* 124 (Hartley & Marks 1999).

41. Nicholas Georgescu-Roegen, *Energy and Economic Myths* 318 (1976).

42. Ruskin, *supra* note 31, at 156.

43. John A. Hobson, *Wealth and Life: A Study in Values* 230 (Allen 1929).

44. *Quoted in* Lutz, *supra* note 27, at 35.

45. Léon Walras, *Elements of Pure Economics* 79 (Augustus Kelley 1977) (emphasis added).

46. *Id.* at 77–78.

47. *Quoted in* Lutz, *supra* note 27, at 24.

48. Sismondi, *supra* note 32, at 54.

49. Hobson, *supra* note 35, at 70.

50. Sismondi, *supra* note 32, at 162.

51. *Id.* at 628.

52. Lutz, *supra* note 27, at 6.

53. *See* Kysar, *Sustainability*, *supra* note 6.

54. Herman E. Daly, *Ecological Economics and the Ecology of Economics* 51 (1999).

55. "Scale" refers to the material impact of the economy in relation to the natural environment. More precisely, it is a measure of "the physical volume of the throughput, the flow of matter-energy from the environment as low-entropy raw materials and back to the environment as high-entropy wastes." Robert Costanza, John Cumberland, Herman Daly, Robert Goodland, and Richard Norgaard, *An Introduction to Ecological Economics* 80 (1997).

56. Daly, *supra* note 54, at 4.

57. *See* Kysar, *Sustainability*, *supra* note 6.

58. In 1997, 1,586 scientists from 63 countries, including 104 of the 178 living Nobel Prize winners in the sciences, signed the World Scientists' Call for Action at the Kyoto Climate Summit, which stated that "the scientific community ha[s] reached a consensus that grave threats imperil the future of humanity and the global environment." Union of Concerned Scientists, *World Scientists' Call for Action at the Kyoto Climate Summit* (1997).

59. Robert Cooter & Thomas Ulen, *Law and Economics* 3 (2d ed. 1997).

60. *See generally* Eric Rolls, *Running Wild* (1973).

CHAPTER 6

Private Property, the Private Subject, and Women

Can Women Truly Be Owners of Capital?

Elizabeth Mayes

Private property is perhaps the key element in a liberal political ideology, a concept of wealth and resource distribution that informs as well theories of rights, privacy, and political subjecthood. Its popularity as an explanatory concept for methods of resource management and distribution is again at a high in this post-Communist era of economic globalization. This essay explores whether private property, as constructed in the liberal tradition, and as actually deployed in the globalizing economy of the contemporary United States, has an inherent gender bias that may impede women's accession to ownership parity.

The first section examines how liberal constructions of property presume a male-gendered subject as the owner of property. The second section explores how traditional property rights have fared in the post–World War II era, and how they have been evoked both to enhance and undermine women's economic position. Finally, I speculate on what the death of property, that is, its transformation into increasingly abstract, fractionated, numerous, and complex forms, may mean for women.

But first, consider: what is property? Most people conceive of property as things owned by persons. The legal or economic specialist, however, largely treats property rights in a way that obviates any necessary connection between such rights and things. Instead, the most common contemporary means of conceptualizing and adjudicating ownership is as a "bundle of rights." In other words, ownership consists of a number of rights of usage, including the rights not to use or to withhold from use by others. Some such rights can be sold off, whereas others are retained—for example, mining rights, timber harvesting rights, recreational usage, easements, rights to yields, and so forth. This perspective could lead to a sort of Zeno's paradox; when an individual owner continues to sell off various rights pertaining to a given property, at what point does she or he cease to be the "owner"?

Rights associated with ownership may be split, lost, or rendered wholly abstract. For example, governmental regulation may prohibit the owner of a tract of land containing a wetland from developing it. Or an entity may be subdivided into fractional ownership rights distributed among many people.

Think of mutual funds, pensions plans, shareholder corporations, or co-ops. Ownership rights can also be made to disappear, as when one establishes a trust, and rights are then split between trustee and beneficiary, with neither empowered to the degree that the original owner had been. Consider also that most property in contemporary capitalist economies is intangible, from stocks, bonds, and bank accounts to patents, copyrights, franchises, and brand names. Not even that paycheck for which you have sweated such long hours is immune from this logic, for when you deposit it in a bank, what you are really doing is creating a claim against an abstract legal institution.

Specialists treat such a multitude of entities under the rubric of property—from real estate statutes or public law entitlements to the rights to life, bodily security, and personal liberty—that the idea that property equals rights in things is hopelessly inadequate. As legal scholar Thomas Grey writes, "[i]t seems fair to conclude from a glance at the range of current usages that the specialists who design and manipulate the legal structures of the advanced capitalist economies could easily do without using the term 'property' at all" (73).

At the height of classical liberalism, however, around the end of the eighteenth century, the simple conception of property as thing ownership dominated legal and political thought. Freedom, conceived then in terms of escape from the enwebbed relations of feudalism, was grounded in an image of a single individual controlling his—and I mean *his*—piece of the natural world. A contemporary reading of Locke's often-cited justification of private property, which has served as a touchstone for two centuries of U.S. economic and political thought, reveals that the notion of private ownership depends on a particular kind of subject construct that intrinsically, and through its historical applications, disadvantages women.

In Locke's narrative of the origin of property, God gave the world to all "men" to be held in common (secs. 25–26). But even in this primeval community, each man "has a property in his own person," which constitutes the first private property (sec. 27). Then, whatever "man" appropriates from the common for his own use, for example, grass for his horse, wood for his fire, berries to eat, and so forth, becomes his property in the moment of its appropriation for private use (sec. 28). Thus the justification for private property, that is, exclusion of others from what was commonly owned, is the privateness of the body. It follows, then, that whatever the body is mixed with through its labor becomes a possession of the body's "owner," which is the conscious will. Labor is viewed as will-directed action whereby the will uses the body as its instrument. And labor is the means whereby private property is delineated and/or created, and the source of economic value. Thus the will's ownership (read: control) of the physical body and its faculties provides the prototype for all private property ownership as well as the justification for its existence.

Locke defines liberty in civil society as "a liberty to follow my own will in all things where that rule [of law] prescribes not" (sec. 22). Control of one's

body by one's will is both the essence of liberty and the basis for appropriation of private property. Material wealth and political freedom in the liberal
society presuppose a moment in the development of each individual when will
takes possession of the body and its faculties, followed by continuous subjective governance by an indwelling will.[1] Locke believes that two factors—the
imperative to avoid spoilage by not taking any more than can be used, and the
existence of an abundance of resources so that "enough and as good" is left
for others (sec. 33)—will naturally limit personal appropriation. But this ideal
state of affairs is thrown over by the establishment of money, which allows the
spoilage limit to be superseded, and commerce, which naturally follows from
the accumulation of money. In this more realistic latter-day world, natural limits to property accumulation—and the individual will that drives it—are gone.
Thus emerges the more libertarian view of the political subject as one whose
political and economic liberty is derived from unfettered manifestation of vo-
lition, and the influence of factors deemed external to the schema, for example, the needs or wishes of other people, the collective good, and so forth, is
seen as an infringement of such liberty.

What kind of subject is this owner of private property? Singular and autonomous, to begin with, for Locke's narrative of the origin of private property imagines a pre-civil setting peopled by already will-governed adult males,
apparently without any familial ties or dependency needs. Read as an abstract
argument, as Benhabib notes, this legitimizing story completely conceals the
overwhelming reality of biological development via physical and emotional
dependency relations (Benhabib, *Generalized,* 84). And in historical terms, it
was belied in practice by the predominance of family control of enterprise in
early capitalism, and the continuance of inheritance practices that subordinated alienability of property to patrilineal objectives. In addition, women in
seventeenth-century England were treated as family property, and their procreative and caretaking labor hidden within the private realm.

Self-ownership fails to constitute an adequate basis for equality of political
subjects, for, as Perry writes, "the requirement that a citizen own property in
his own person is the crucial move . . . by which women were excluded from
their place in the polity" (452). The Lockean political subject enjoys a freedom
based on mobility, which in a negative sense means freedom from entangle-
ment in any dependency relation that might curtail the individual will's
purview. Women's relation to their childbearing bodies does not assimilate to
the model of an autonomous individual empowered to appropriate property.
First, pregnant women and mothers are not autonomous in the sense here invoked. They are engaged in an ongoing intersubjective process that cannot (or
should not) be handled in the manner of the transitory often anonymous relations of the marketplace. Second, the childbearing process is not subject to
governance by will, except insofar as will may step in to manipulate or terminate the process; rather it is a holistic phenomenon involving emotional,

physical, and mental elements. Third, the labor of childbearing and child rearing is of a different nature than labor dedicated to value creation and appropriation of property; it is invested in a "product" destined to escape its status
as property. Thus, in the terms of the marketplace, carrying out such labor is
irrational and nonproductive. Women, from such a perspective, are economically limited by their biological capacity to create dependents.

Like Locke, Hegel grounded his account of private property formation in
the relation of the subject to "his" body, although he did this in order to derive property from self-consciousness rather than from a pre-civil condition.
Hegel's depiction of willful appropriation as the basis for delineation of the
subject again shows, from a slightly different angle, how the construction of a
capitalist subject and the construction of private property are linked. Appropriation of the object by the subject is necessary for the subject to experience
its will as absolutely free in the face of worldly determinations and limitations
(sec. 34). Further, because being is realized through property ownership, the
subject can only experience individual subjectivity by considering "himself" as
his own possession, that is, as an inanimate object into which will is extended.
The first form of property, then, is rights of manipulation of one's body, which
presupposes a body devoid of subjectivity until put under control of conscious
will. Ownership in the larger sense is constructed out of the extension of that
primal right into the external world. Hegel acknowledges that the owned body
is sentient, unlike more external forms of property, but it is still subject to
ownership because vacant of will. The nature of the relation of will to the
body is one of tenancy, demonstrated through training the body in dexterity—
in other words, controlling its movements with willful intention.

Historically, women have been placed in the category of will-vacant object,
open to being appropriated and controlled by the penetrating will of a male
owner-subject. They have been associated with the body, and especially with
involuntary bodily or psychic processes, which denies them a subject status defined by willful self-control. Keller has described this complementary gendered
pair, the prototypical subject–object dyad, as composed of a singular self-pos-
sessed mover and a multiplicate movable thing. The classic male–female pair
is made up of a "separative" self and a "soluble" self, that is, a woman possessed and influenced by a man defined by his own self-possession and imper-
viousness to influence (11). As William James's often-quoted aphorism puts it,
"a man's Self is the sum total of all that he *can* call his" (291). Such identity-
conferring possessions include a wife and children, as patronymic naming
practices demonstrate.

Private property presumes a particular construction of identity as unitary,
discrete, isolate, self-motivating, and perhaps as well self-transparent, homoge-
nous, and unchanging. Exchange of private property, by contract or through
anonymous limited sale, and perdurance of property distributions require such
a subject construct. This is not the only possible way to construct social subjects

and property—far from it. Consider, for example, the Australian Pintupi. For the Pintupi, land ownership is essentially a process of creating and sharing identity (Myers, 15). The Pintupi word approximating *property* would be better translated, according to anthropologist Fred Myers, as "identification." *Holding a country,* the expression for ownership of land, which is more precisely possession or custodianship, is an on-going negotiated process between many co-owners whose claims are based on affinal exchange, residence, and kinship.

The notion of overlapping stewardship parallels a construction of identity as overlapping, that is, comprised of a conglomerate of roles and statuses appropriate to various contexts and relationships that are not mutually exclusive. Such an identity type may be characterized as relational, that is, persons are who they are depending on who they are relating to in the context of a system of interlocking kinship categories.

By contrast, in a commodity economy, subjects are owners who are defined by their lack of relation to other owners; exchange establishes a momentary relation between objects, valued through a common mediator, not subjects. The identity of an owner-subject is exclusive, immutable, and (supposedly) inalienable. If such an owner-subject meets an other who is different, that is, not an owner-subject, "he" will relate to the other by attempting either to assimilate it to self (i.e., own or possess it) or to expel it (e.g., kill or ignore it). If an owner-subject meets an other who is similarly a subject entitled to own, the two will either battle to the death or construct a peace that divides territory and things between them. They do not, cannot, coexist on the same ground. Can women (I speak here of the cultural category "women" rather than those of a particular physiological makeup), who have long been the object rather than the subject of such battles, ever hope to become owners on an equal footing in this economic and psychic battlefield?

In addition to the gendering of both property and the subject of ownership, the form of commodity value creation reflects the dynamics of male desire (because it, in turn, is culturally constructed in this male-dominant cultural environment).[2] Simmel describes value as derived from the need for sacrifice to obtain a desired object, thus implying an epic narrative of quest, battle, and victorious capture. "In general, value develops in the interval that obstacles, renunciation and sacrifice interpose between the will and its satisfaction" (90). The desire must encounter both scarcity of its object and obstacles to obtaining it in order to create (or perceive) value. Desire, here, is construed as an intense striving based on "the anticipated satisfaction of possession," coupled with its fulfillment through "acquisition" (89). Male desire is represented (and sublimated) through such a heroic quest, whether in the realm of commodities or sexuality. Thus the very nature of value creation in a commodity economy bears the mark of gender.

What all this implies is the interchangeability of constructs of ownership and identity. In the broadest sense, one may say that psychic relations, both intra- and intersubjective, are the site of the symbolic operation of property relations, and that property relations encode and manifest the form of social relations and identity. Kuhn writes, "the family is definable exactly as property relations between men and women, and the social relations of the family are those property relations in action" (53). Thus gender relations replicate property relations, and vice versa.

Recall that the description of a sexual relationship as possession of a woman by a man is a common turn of speech. Affinal relations traditionally (i.e., in the modern era, if one may so generalize) construct the woman as object to be possessed, not possessor. Descartes defined jealousy (assumed to be a male emotion) as "a kind of fear related to a desire to preserve a possession" (quoted in Davis, 176). Along these lines, Kingsley Davis has described jealousy as not a biologically determined behavior but rather a meaningful response to a situation that violates an accustomed right. The accustomed right is that of a man to have exclusive use (i.e., private ownership) of the woman's sexual body. Here behavior testifies to Engels's assertion of female monogamy as the basis of patriarchal ownership.

Irigaray writes that the object of ownership of capitalism is both woman and commodity. Woman's body is the material site for the inscription of social value. Exchange value represents the needs or desires of male subjects, and the woman-commodity is invested with the projection of these motivational powers. "The economy . . . that is in place in our societies thus requires that women lend themselves to alienation in consumption, and to exchanges in which they do not participate, and that men be exempt from being used and circulated like commodities" (172). Thus women serve as symbolic commodities, vehicles for exchange that facilitate the establishment of communicative relations between men. Their reproductive use value and constitution as exchange value underwrite the market without any economic compensation going to them. In this scenario, the most basic symbolic and material construction of the socioeconomic order defines women (again, those categorized as "women") as objects, rather than subjects, of ownership.

Such analyses reveal that kinship and economic relations are mutually constitutive. A kinship system may be seen as a mode of distributing "property" rights in people, such as rights to sexual access, genealogical status, lineage names, family privileges, fruits of reproduction, or labor. These rights of ownership are both a form of property and a basis for identity. Mauss demonstrated how the status of legal personhood in ancient Rome was linked to the right to possess both things and people. Those not accorded this status were often themselves treated as property, for example, slaves and children. Today, still, a parent's relation to his or her child may be legally treated as ownership. A California court decision refers to the parent's right to custody as "strictly a property right" (Derdeyn, 217). This right is regarded as covered by U.S. constitutional provisions for the protection of property.

Given the historical construction of "women" as property; the gender bias imbuing notions of private property, commodification, and value creation; and the structural reliance of a liberal subject construct on interaction with non-owning objectified others, can those categorized as "women"—or should such "women"—aspire to the role and privileges of owner status in a so-called free market.

I have presented evidence to suggest that the construction of property and of subjecthood in U.S. society has been gendered, and that this conceptual ideological bias somehow limits women's accession to ownership parity. (The means whereby such a philosophical bias would become manifest on the level of real-time persons and actions has not yet been clarified.) The means whereby theoretical gender bias limits flesh-and-blood individuals may be of several kinds. One may posit culturally predominant modes of identity construction that produce "female" individuals with inculcated behavioral traits that impede their ability or desire to act entrepreneurially, compete ruthlessly, invest, accumulate, or trade. Alternately, the limitation may be posited to operate through institutional and normative barriers, such as unfair practices in hiring and promotion, or a societal bias in the division of labor or in valuation of different types of labor. Or the societal and individual aspects can be combined, by saying, for example, that childbearing (biologically gendered) and child rearing (largely culturally gendered) are not accommodated by conventional work and business schedules, and this disadvantages women. Such arguments are well known.

The advance of liberalism, however, with its ideology of equality and freedom for all, has also provided a channel through which greater and greater numbers of formerly disenfranchised persons could agitate for, and win, full subject status. In other words, the regime, in some ways, has worked against propagation of the elitism on which it was founded. Might this ability of the concepts of freedom and equality to work against their limiting origins also be true of the notion of private property? A free marketplace, where interchangeable commodities are anonymously traded, where all parties must abide by contractual obligations and regulatory constraints, could be imagined (and sometimes is portrayed) as a structure wherein limiting social conventions may be overturned by economic practice. In other words, can private property be made to work for women's advancement?

The right of self-possession, which I have asserted to be the prototype for property ownership, has provided a legal and philosophical basis for protecting oppressed groups from certain kinds of exploitation and according them at least theoretical access to formerly withheld privileges. Noting the analogy between property rights and privacy rights, one may ask whether privacy rights have or have not been invoked to enhance women's status. In the abortion debate, for example, the pro-choice platform astutely used the tradition of judicial respect for privacy rights by demanding that women be deemed exclusive owners of their own bodies, a noble goal given their historical treatment as the property of husbands and fathers.

The Supreme Court first elected to protect a woman's right to abortion on the basis of the right to privacy, derived from the fourteenth amendment clause that states, in part, that "no state shall . . . deprive any person of life, liberty or property, without due process of law." The subject construct implied in this clause is essentially Lockean. This triad of possessions—life, liberty, and property—reiterates Locke's narrative justification of private property. That is, life implies the right to exclusive ownership of one's body, liberty means the right to move that body at will except where specific powers have been ceded to a civil authority, and property refers to that with which one's will-directed actions, that is, labor, have been mixed.

Women's sexual and childbearing bodies, however, do not readily assimilate to the model of an autonomous self-owning individual whose freedom is imagined as absolute sovereignty of will within a defining membrane impenetrable to alien influence. A woman who has sex is already violated, whereas a pregnant woman is truly anomalous, because her body contains, or is imbued with, multiple life forces, thus turning on its head the implied one mind/one body identity rule.

The liberal subject construct links freedom and self-sovereignty to willful control of the body. It thus is of doubtful relevance for bodily processes, or lived situations, for that matter, which are involuntary. Pregnancy is one such involuntary bodily process; it may be engendered involuntarily, and it proceeds to its conclusion without regard for will or wish. In the larger sense, irregardless of one's reproductive capacity, the realities of embodied existence dictate that much that occurs to affect us cannot be directly controlled. Hence, a doctrine of will-based self-sovereignty—essentially the rational, calculating, self-interest-maximizing agent of laissez-faire economic theory—is inadequate. Nor is this individualistic construct adequate to the two-in-oneness of pregnancy.

Privacy rights have been used to establish a judicial tradition of protecting bodily integrity against potential intrusions, even when such intrusions are benevolently motivated. For example, one cannot be forced to donate bone marrow, even to save the life of another, nor can a criminal be made to undergo surgery to remove an implanted bullet, even if that bullet would provide valuable evidence. Such applications are analogous to respect for an owner's right to exclusive unmitigated use of owned property, irregardless of impact on the collective. But as Susan Bordo and others have noted, such rights are not fully extended to pregnant women. Courts increasingly mandate forced cesareans and prioritize the treatment of comatose women to save the fetus's life. This, says Bordo, is the consequence of extension of full subject status to the fetus.

One is faced, then, with the legally unprecedented situation of according full privacy rights to two individuals who are trying to occupy the same body.

This resembles two property owners trying to claim exclusive ownership of a single piece of real estate. The system can only resolve this conflict by deciding in favor of the property rights of one of the two parties, or perhaps by dividing the bundle of rights between them. Once the child is out of the womb, applying the bundle-of-rights perspective may be more feasible, even if inhumane, for example, by according each parent in a divorce case rights to a particular fraction of the child's time. Such an accommodation is evidently impossible in the womb.

The way issues such as abortion and custody are construed, in both legal and philosophical terms, obviously has a material bearing on property ownership, in addition to any psychic confusion or disability it may impose. For example, antiabortion laws that would force women to undergo the inconvenience and potential disability of a full-term pregnancy, not to mention the financial burden of raising a child, especially when unmarried, disadvantage women in the marketplace, where property is accumulated. If, as an element of greater involvement in child rearing, women bear a larger amount of childcare costs and labor, then again their access to property ownership is limited in comparison to men. Similarly, if women cannot take maternity leave without loss of seniority or pay, then men implicitly profit economically from women's childbearing function. And if women are saddled with more household tasks than men, their ability to participate equally in the marketing of commodifiable labor is again infringed on.

One might ask what would happen if a regime of private property were imposed on a gender-neutral social system; would it still tend to favor those who cannot, or do not, bear children? (Here, the correlation between gender and sex is not exact, because the economically disadvantaged group of those who bear children is primarily confined to those with female reproductive organs but might to a certain extent include single fathers, whereas the category of those who don't includes childless women, men, and men who choose to live as women. And childless women are still subject to all the structural and attitudinal prejudices that hamper women's economic achievement.) Insofar as private property relies on an owner-actor whose economic power derives from freedom of mobility, autonomy from relational limitations, and a singular construction of responsibility, then individuals who do not bear children, and who have no possibility of bearing children, have an intrinsic advantage in the struggle to accumulate property. It would appear from this that a neoliberal polity will be forced to value justice and equality (of fact, not of opportunity) over so-called economic freedom and fully protected property rights, in some measure, if it seeks to produce a situation in which property ownership would be equally divided between those who do and don't bear children. But does the evolution of property in the post–World War II era confirm such a conclusion?

Judicial construal of property rights has ranged from the virtual elimination of property rights from the constitutional agenda in the 1950s and 1960s to a sometimes equivocal return to protection of traditional property rights in the 1970s and 1980s. The treatment of private property as immune to government or other intrusion, although always incomplete in practice, has been further mitigated in the last fifty years by expanded scope for governmental regulation—for example, by allowance of zoning to enhance the aesthetics of municipal life, or the deployment of eminent domains without a public-use requirement. In the last several decades, environmental regulation has intruded on the traditional concept of real property ownership to the extent of producing a backlash in the form of the property rights movement. Environmental laws seek to counteract or compensate the fallacy of treating shared resources according to the liberal ideal of fractionating such resources for exclusive use and enjoyment. Thus many progressive goals have required shrinkage of traditional property rights.

Yet like privacy rights, the notion of private property has also been used as part of a progressive agenda trying to secure benefits for women and other disadvantaged groups. A movement arose in the 1970s to consider governmental economic entitlements as a form of "new property." The question here was whether Social Security, welfare benefits, and public employment should be viewed as rights, or as privileges subject to being withdrawn. At first the Supreme Court edged toward such recognition, but ultimately it declined to treat entitlements as property rights. The arguments and the way the two sides line up in terms of political orientation are illustrative of the ambivalent position of property in the emerging new economic order.

Justice Brennan, a critic of extending constitutional protection to traditional property rights, was a leader in the move to recognize entitlements as forms of property. He argued that secure economic rights would enable the poor "to participate meaningfully in the life of the community" (quoted in Ely, 151). He thus used the conservative doctrine that respect for property rights secures political freedom to promote a profoundly anticonservative position. Recognizing that women constitute the majority of welfare recipients, Brennan, with this view, would have protected a form of ownership that is largely the domain of women who have no access to more traditional types of property. If welfare benefits are viewed as a form of property that nourishes many single mothers whose child-rearing roles limit their ability to participate fully in the marketplace in order to acquire property, then denial of property status serves a conservative antifeminist agenda that throws mothers back into a position of needing paternal economic protection. So here is a case in which property rights would have been adapted to further women's economic equality.

Affirmative action may be described as a means of redistributing economic benefits in the form of employment or contractual or training opportunities. Such programs essentially modify the rules of so-called free trade by which property is formed, acquired, and exchanged in the traditional view. The case against affirmative action presumes either that market mechanisms are gender and race neutral or that, even if they are not, the government must not intervene to balance preexisting inequalities in ownership. In other words, property rights are deemed an untouchable guarantor of individual liberty even where compelling evidence exists that social mores, previous judicial handicaps, and biological differences have limited the ability of certain groups to enjoy equal access to property ownership (as constructed in its particular historical and social context) and therefore equal enjoyment of freedom.

These examples suggest that private property rights must be superseded, or redefined, to further the goal of female ownership parity. However, as I stated at the beginning of this essay, private property is no longer a defining parameter of the contemporary economy. To quote Thomas Grey, "[t]he concept of property and the institution of property have disintegrated" (74). Grey considers the collapse of property to be a process internal, rather than incidental, to the development of capitalism itself; that is, it follows from the workings of a market economy. Under a regime in which owners are allowed to divide and transfer their interests as they wish, property rights are voluntarily decomposed and recombined in other forms, creating new forms of finance and control that fractionate traditional ownership. These new claims become increasingly remote from tangible objects and are thus rendered more abstract. The technical demands of legal practice then require development of a doctrine such as the bundle-of-rights formulation of property, replacing a concept of thing ownership with a system of abstract claim structures (75).

The fractionation and disembodiment of private property may be more favorable to women's equality for several reasons. First, the construal of property as a potentially unlimited number of abstract claims dissolves the conceptual tie between a tangible thing and an autonomous owner-subject, and so undermines the sacrosanct treatment of private property as the rock on which liberty, freedom, and democracy stand. Fissionable abstract claims permit negotiation because no single claim stands on historical precedent, and this creates a space in which established power and resource distributions may be contested. Second, when the notion of private property as exclusively owned things falls away, then the subject construct it entails is brought into question. If private property in the traditional liberal sense reflected a unified autonomous subject, then post-industrial property rights suggest a subject whose various constituents of being may be divided and reorganized according to variable contexts.[3] Women throughout modernity have been deprecatingly associated with multiplicity.[4] Who knows but what the emergence of new multiplicitous subject constructs and their rise to legitimacy will give women an edge over men still tied to outdated linear rationalist modes characteristic of the unitary subject.

As with the breakup of a limiting conception of private property, this seeming chaos could provide the space for new, less intolerant, and more heterogeneous identities. It could also fuel a backlash. If one analyzes symbolically the

post-Communist infatuation with privatization, it may be understood as a regressive flight from the implications of decomposition of traditional unities. In
more concrete terms, it may well represent an effort by a capital-owning elite
to hold onto the reins of power, in the face of dispersion and fragmentation of
their power base, by reinvoking the structure of private ownership, which facilitated such unequal accumulation of wealth. In the post-Communist era of
economic globalization, privatization has been touted as a strategy of economic renovation in both formerly Communist and less-developed nations.
Yet it has contributed to the too-familiar contemporary scenario in which
major industries and utilities are sold to multinationals, production is prioritized for cash export, leading to loss of self-sufficiency in food and other es-
sentials, buying power for the middle and lower classes collapses, and
domestic economies come under extensive control by world financial institutions to reassure creditors and corporate investors. It is easy to argue that such
strategies have not remedied the global crisis—not in humanitarian, economic,
or environmental terms.

It is ironic that as public space in this country has been progressively
crowded out by commercialization of any and all remaining niches, the prop-
ertied subject returns to the private space to "cocoon," a place now entirely
dependent on inputs from globally interwoven energy and information grids.
This yearning for privacy ironically trumpets a nostalgia for discrete and isolate self-sufficiency, even while the globalizing market destroys its last vestiges.
Rather than an effective attack on the dehumanization of "growth," such
responses recall the elitist functioning of private property in its earlier incar-
nations, when it served to guarantee its possessor insulation from the marketplace—and support patriarchal privilege.

One cannot forget, however, that the traditional conception of property has
provided a moral basis for capitalism. Both historically and conceptually, liberty has been grounded in the institution of private property. Private property
is the symbol and site of a sphere of autonomy and a locus of initiative, assur-
ing to its owner a modicum of rights and protection from exploitation. Given
the dismemberment of a unified concept of private property, how could liberty
be redefined so as not to foster a property distribution system that generates
vast inequality of wealth and gobbles irreplaceable resources to satisfy its
structural need for "growth"? In an environment saturated with innumerable
potential claims to resources, which values are to prevail? Will we substitute
for a neoliberal notion of freedom some version of lifeboat ethics, a distributive ideal of the greatest possible good for the greatest possible number, a shift
to submersion of the individual in a collective, or some fatalistic renunciation
of democratic ideals? The demise of a male-gendered subject construct, insulated in its exclusively owned space, may allow creation of a more woman-
friendly vision, perhaps using the image of women's potentially childbearing
bodies as a model for compassionate sharing of a single home.

Bibliography

Baechler, Jean. "Liberty, Property, and Equality." In *Property,* ed. J. Roland Pennock and John Chapman, 269–88. New York: New York University Press, 1980.

Basch, Norma. *Women, Marriage and Property in Nineteenth-Century New York.* Ithaca: Cornell University Press, 1982.

Benhabib, Seyla. *Critique, Norm, and Utopia: A Study of the Foundations of Critical Theory.* New York: Columbia University Press, 1986.

———. *The Generalized and the Concrete Other.* New York: Oxford University Press, 1997.

Berry, Christopher. "Property and Possession: Two Replies to Locke—Hume and Hegel." In *Property,* ed. J. Roland Pennock and John Chapman, 89–100. New York: New York University Press, 1980.

Bordo, Susan. "Are Mothers Persons? Reproductive Rights and the Politics of Subjectivity." In *Unbearable Weight: Feminism, Western Culture and the Body,* 71–97. Berkeley: University of California Press, 1993.

Davis, Kingsley. *Human Society.* New York: Macmillan, 1948.

Derdeyn, A. P. "Adoption and the Ownership of Children." *Child Psychiatry and Human Development* 9, 4 (1979): 215–17.

Ely, James Jr. *The Guardian of Every Other Right: A Constitutional History of Property Rights.* Cambridge: Oxford University Press, 1992.

Engels, Friedrich. *The Origin of the Family, Private Property and the State.* New York: International Publishers, 1942.

Furbotn, Eirik, and Svetozar Pejovich, eds. *The Economics of Property Rights.* Cambridge, Mass.: Ballinger Publishing, 1974.

Grey, Thomas. "The Disintegration of Property." In *Property,* ed. J. Roland Pennock and John Chapman, 69–85. New York: New York University Press, 1980.

Grunebaum, James. *Private Ownership.* London: Routledge and Kegan Paul, 1987.

Hegel, Georg Wilhelm Friedrich. *The Philosophy of Right.* Chicago: Encyclopaedia Britannica, 1952.

Hirschon, Renee, ed. *Women and Property—Women as Property.* London: Croon Helm, 1984.

Hodes, W. William. "Women and the Constitution: Some Legal History and a New Approach to the Nineteenth Amendment." In *Women, the Law, and the Constitution: Major Historical Interpretations,* ed. Kermit Hall, 26–53. New York: Garland Publishers, 1987.

Hollowell, Peter, ed. *Property and Social Relations.* London: Heinemann, 1982.

Irigaray, Luce. *This Sex Which Is Not One.* Trans. Catherine Porter. Ithaca: Cornell University Press, 1985.

James, William. *The Principles of Psychology.* Vol. 2. Cambridge: Harvard University Press, 1981.

Keller, Catherine. *From a Broken Web: Separation, Sexism, and Self.* Boston: Beacon Press, 1986.

Kuhn, Annette. "Structures of Patriarchy and Capital in the Family." In *Feminism and Materialism: Women and Modes of Production,* ed. Annette Kuhn and AnnMarie Wolpe, 42–67. London: Routledge and Kegan Paul, 1978.

Locke, John. *Of Civil Government.* 1690; reprint, London: J. M. Dent, 1924.

Macpherson, C. B. *The Political Theory of Possessive Individualism: Hobbes to Locke.* Oxford: Clarendon Press, 1962.

Mauss, Marcel. *Sociology and Psychology Essays.* Trans. Ben Brewster. 1950; reprint, London: Routledge and Kegan Paul, 1979.

Myers, Fred. "Burning the Truck and Holding the Country: Pintupi Forms of Property and Identity." In *We Are Here: Politics of Aboriginal Land Tenure,* ed. Edwin Wilmsen. Berkeley: University of California Press, 1989.

Pennock, J. Roland, and John Chapman, eds. *Property.* New York: New York University Press, 1980.

Perry, Ruth. "Mary Astell and the Feminist Critique of Possessive Individualism." *Eighteenth Century Studies* 23 (1990): 444–57.

Rubin, Gayle. "The Traffic in Women: Notes on the 'Political Economy' of Sex." In *Toward an Anthropology of Women,* ed. Rayna Reiter, 157–210. New York: Monthly Review Press, 1975.

Simmel, Georg. *The Philosophy of Money.* London: Routledge and Kegan Paul, 1978.

Wikse, John. *About Possession: The Self as Private Property.* University Park: Pennsylvania State University Press, 1977.

Notes

1. Locke states that men are God's property but that their relation to their bodies is the same as their relation to their privately owned land; i.e., they use their will-directed labor to derive the fruits of something created by God but subject to their exclusive control.

2. The question of what caused what, that is, which cultural or biological factor occasioned the others, is probably unanswerable and not necessary to know. I note only that the coexistence of such mutually reflective cultural dynamics is not accidental.

3. The phenomenon of the so-called dissolved postmodern subject and these changes in the structure of property may be seen as mutually self-reflective.

4. This association ranges from stereotypes of women as possessing a chameleonlike personality to the far greater numbers of women diagnosed with mental pathologies of multiplicity such as multiple personality.

CHAPTER 7

Nest Eggs and Stormy Weather

Law, Culture, and Black Women's Lack of Wealth

Regina Austin

Nest egg . . . money saved and held in reserve for emergencies, retirement, etc.

Random House Webster's College Dictionary (2000)

Wise men say
Keep something til a rainy day.

Nicholas Breton, *Works* (1582), reprinted in *The Home Book of Quotations* (1964)

Don't know why there's no sun up in the sky,
Stormy weather,
since my man and I ain't together,
keeps rainin' all the time.

Stormy Weather (Keeps Rainin' All the Time), lyrics by Ted Koehler and music by Harold Arlen (1933)

Nest eggs are supposed to provide protection against a rainy day, but suppose it rains all the time? I know I am mixing metaphors or whatever, but that is black women's fate in America, is it not? Are our lives not what happens when *Poor Richard's Almanac* runs up against the Blues?

There are many ways to think about black women and economic or distributive justice, but the best way to do it may be in terms of savings, asset accumulation, or simply put, wealth. Black women have been in the red, asset-wise, since our ancestors were brought here as someone else's property. Things might have improved if the freed slaves had been given the forty acres and a mule they were promised, but that never materialized.[1] Because I very much doubt that reparations of that or any other kind will be forthcoming in the near future, it behooves us to give some thought to other means of augmenting black women's wealth.

Although some attention has been focused on income inequality between black women and others, more study needs to be directed at wealth inequality across race and gender lines. "[W]ealth is one indicator of material disparity that captures the historical legacy of low wages, personal and organizational discrimination, and institutionalized racism"[2] to which black women have been subjected in this country. As a general matter, the significance of wealth to well-being in our consumption-oriented society tends to be underestimated. Moreover, exploring policies that impact on the distribution of wealth across racial and gender groups is far scarier than discussing measures for equalizing income. Yet assets, not income, assure class mobility. It is the redistribution of the wealth, not the reallocation of income, that is likely to produce changes in the class positions of black women and their children. Indeed, if the women who are now receiving public assistance are to achieve the level of self-sufficiency really required to end welfare as we know it, then we must begin to consider creating mechanisms by which they can acquire wealth to insure their futures.

My dictionary defines wealth as "a great quantity or store of money, property, or other riches."[3] When I use the term *wealth*, however, I am referring to something more modest, basically accumulated assets. Wealth is what is left over after the bills are paid. It is what a woman is able to put aside or accumulate, especially with her employer's assistance. It is what a woman *owns* less what a woman *owes*.

Economists have various ways of categorizing and measuring wealth that may be useful for my purposes.[4] Generally, wealth is the value of total assets less total debt at a fixed point in time. For the very rich, assets may consist largely of stocks, bonds, trust funds, business equity, and nonresidential real estate. For the nonwealthy, which is to say most of us, assets include residential property; automobiles; deposits held in bank accounts, money market funds, and certificates of deposit; and individually held retirement accounts. Some measures of wealth include employer-supported or controlled pension funds, the cash surrender value of life insurance policies, and durable goods. Debt typically consists of mortgages, loans, or other obligations owed to banks, mortgage companies, credit unions, or finance companies as well as the balance due on credit card, retail store, or gasoline charge accounts.

It is not easy to determine exactly how much wealth black women possess or control. Some of the crucial data are collected separately by race and by gender, with data pertaining to black women being included in both categories. The available wealth statistics, nonetheless, suggest that black women's holdings are quite limited.

First, consider household wealth by race. Keep in mind that in 2002, female-headed households constituted roughly 43 percent of all black households, compared with 13 percent for whites.[5] Moreover, black women theoretically have control over the wealth held by black married households.

In 2000, white, non-Hispanic households had a median measured net worth of $79,400, while black households had a median measured net worth of $7,500.[6] White households had a substantially higher median measured net worth than black households in every income quintile. In the highest quintile, the median net worth of whites was $208,023 and that of blacks was

$65,141.[7] In the lowest quintile, the median net worth of whites was $24,000, compared with $57 for blacks.[8] The $57 figure represented a decline from 1994, when the median net worth of black households in the lowest quintile was measured at $250.[9]

I do not have 2000 data on the net worth of families headed by black females alone; however, female-headed households in general had a net median worth of $23,028 as compared with $91,218 for married-couple households.[10]

Older, nonmarried black women are particularly poor in terms of assets. In 2000, only 20 percent of black nonmarried women sixty-five years old and older received income from assets, compared with 50 percent of their white female counterparts.[11] Still, income from assets constituted 7.5 percent of nonmarried black women's income as opposed to 9.3 percent of white women's income.[12] Only 15 percent of nonmarried black women sixty-five years old and over received income from a private pension or annuity, whereas 24 percent of nonmarried white women, 30 percent of black married couples, and 38 percent of white married couples did so.[13] In general, older nonmarried black women were more dependent on Social Security, government employee pensions, earnings, and public assistance than were white women.[14]

The bottom line, then, is that black females seem to control very little wealth. As a result, many black women do not enjoy the numerous advantages that come with owning assets. Sickness, disability, death, unemployment, other forms of job instability, childbirth, separation, or divorce can threaten the security of a black woman and her family. Material wealth provides some protection against unexpected changes in the amount and flow of income and expenditures due to such changes in a woman's life circumstances. Assets also facilitate future consumption, particularly of expensive items like a car, a house, or a college education for one's self or one's children. Wealth also provides the foundation for the risk taking and entrepreneurship that can generate greater income and increased wealth. At some point, most people's wage-earning capacity ends; wealth in the form of savings or pension benefits eases existence during retirement. Finally, wealth provides a legacy for one's children in several ways. Children whose families have assets are more likely to maintain the class standing of their parents, if not move higher in the class hierarchy than children from families who may have comparable incomes and occupational attainment but possess fewer assets.[15] If their parents or their families have assets, young people can look to those assets for assistance in pursuing higher education, establishing families of their own, purchasing a home, or starting a business.[16] Finally, inherited wealth provides the foundation for the asset base on which each succeeding generation optimizes the life chances of its offspring.

In addition to its material value, wealth has psychic, social, and political advantages. Boxer Joe Lewis is reported to have said, "I don't like money actually, but it quiets my nerves."[17] A woman who possesses wealth has greater control over her welfare and circumstances and greater cause for peace of mind.[18] Wealth increases one's ability to plan for the future. In fact, it increases one's stake in and connection to the future. Wealth can expand one's social power and influence. People with wealth may also have a greater stake in the political system and in preserving the relative status quo.

In sum, "assets improve economic stability; connect people with a viable, hopeful future; stimulate development of human and other capital; enable people to focus and specialize; provide a foundation for risk taking; yield personal, social, and political dividends; and enhance the welfare of offspring."[19] These benefits of wealth are largely missing from the lives of black women who do not have assets.

Explanations for black women's lack of wealth fall into two broad categories that differ according to the degree of control or agency that they assume black women have over their asset accumulation. One set of reasons focuses on institutional and structural impediments to black women's wealth acquisition. The second set considers individual and cultural variables that impact negatively on black women's desire or capacity to save.[20]

In my view, structural impediments to black women's wealth accumulation on the one hand, and individual and cultural factors on the other, are dialectically related. Material conditions create cultural and psychological responses that in turn take on a life of their own, impacting on, as well as adapting themselves to, the material world. Nonetheless, more research needs to be done on the cultural and psychological factors affecting black women's wealth accumulation because they are erected as a significant impediment to the adoption of reforms of the structural obstacles.

The structural or institutional hypothesis starts with the assumption that asset accumulation is not simply a matter of saving, nest egging, or striving. According to economist Michael Sherraden, "[i]n most households unstructured savings out of the ordinary income streams is insignificant compared to institutionalized asset accumulation."[21] Savings most often "enter households through various institutional arrangements [whereby] [m]oney is guided directly into asset accumulation, and subsidized in the process."[22] Thus, the bulk of the net worth of most households consists of housing equity and retirement or pension holdings. Housing equity is subsidized by federal income tax deductions for home mortgage interest[23] and real estate taxes,[24] as well as by limitations on the recognition of gains from the sale of a principal residence.[25] Taxes are deferred on contributions to pension plans,[26] tax-deferred annuities,[27] individual retirement accounts,[28] and Keogh plans.[29] Employers may deduct contributions to qualified employee pension plans.[30] Of course, the ease with which workers can participate in these forms of asset accumulation facilitates their use.

As the discussion that follows indicates, black women are not substantial beneficiaries of the principal forms of government-subsidized asset accumulation, nor of other kinds of institutional privileges that facilitate wealth accumulation, such as beneficial tax treatment of gifts and capital gains or employee-sponsored health and life insurance.[31]

"One road to wealth is long-term steady employment in the kinds of work organizations that offer job-sponsored benefits and retirement packages."[32] That is, unfortunately, one path to wealth from which black women have been foreclosed until very recently. Black women today earn roughly 64 percent of the median weekly earnings of white men.[33] The width of the contemporary gap between black female wage earners and white men reflects vast improvements in the position of black women in the labor market. Historically, the difference between black female earnings and white male earnings was much greater. This gap has had a devastating impact on black women's wealth. "[O]ver the years these earnings shortfalls have resulted in less savings, less investments, and less transfers to succeeding generations. Over time, less income can result in vast differences in asset accumulation."[34]

In addition to low wages, black women suffer from greater job insecurity, which is attributable to unemployment and to temporary or contingent employment that interrupts the flow of income and impedes the building of assets. Although I do not have exact figures to support the claim, it appears that substantial numbers of black women do not have jobs that carry with them the sort of job-related benefits that help a woman to protect her assets and lifestyle in the event of unemployment, illness, disability, or retirement. Between 1990 and 2001, only 56.5 percent of blacks were covered by private health insurance, as compared with 73.5 percent of whites.[35] In 2000, only 40.9 percent of black female wage earners were protected by pension plans of some kind, though in this regard, they were not much worse off than white or black men or white women.[36]

Entrepreneurship and business ownership are theoretically another route to wealth accumulation. For a host of reasons, blacks, in general, have not been successful in pursuing entrepreneurial endeavors, although there is evidence that the trend is changing for both men and women.[37]

In terms of expenditures, black women are more likely to be single parents and the heads of households than are white women. Raising children entails rather large expenses. Although women in general pay more than men for many goods and services, the cost of black women's consumption is also increased by the premium or "tax" that discrimination forces blacks to pay in pursuing ordinary commercial transactions.[38]

The handicaps that black women encounter in commercial transactions extend to their dealings with financial institutions. Many black neighborhoods do not have local bank branches; instead, residents must rely on check-cashing outlets that generally charge high fees and do not offer the range of financial services that banks provide.[39] In any event, most banks do not offer accounts that suit the needs of small-balance depositors or savers. Institutional support for generalized small-scale savings is limited. Moreover, the absence of neighborhood banks also restricts the availability of sources of credit for large purchases.

The discrimination blacks have faced in the mortgage market has had a particularly devastating impact on their accumulation of wealth.[40] In their book *Black Wealth/White Wealth: A New Perspective on Racial Inequality*, sociologists Melvin Oliver and Thomas Shapiro extensively analyze the impact on blacks of discrimination in both the housing and residential mortgage markets. The authors estimate that discrimination in the form of denied mortgages, higher mortgage rates, and lost housing appreciation has cost blacks $82 billion.[41]

Oliver and Shapiro do not include in their figures the value of land that blacks have lost as a result of what David H. Harris Jr. of the Land Loss Prevention Project terms "formidable forces in the law."[42] Blacks' ownership of farm land has declined drastically since the turn of the century as a result of "partition sales, tax and debt foreclosures, adverse possession, [and] eminent domain . . . [as well as] illiteracy, racism, intimidation, and political and economic powerlessness." Urban land holdings have been impacted by "[h]ome improvement schemes, gentrification, environmental racism and the economic development activities of local governmental entities" that always seem to result in whites winding up with ownership of black folks' land.[43]

In terms of policy changes at the macroeconomic level, efforts should be made to curb the institutional impediments that block black women's ability to build their wealth and to get government on the side of wealth acquisition, particularly for poor black women. The most significant reforms would be those that increase black women's returns for their participation in the labor market, particularly through the provision of benefits such as health insurance and pensions. Other reforms that would be advantageous include ending discrimination in the housing and home mortgage markets; facilitating business development by black women, including entrepreneurship in public housing communities by pubic housing residents; and either forcing existing financial institutions to service the needs of small-scale savers or subsidizing the development of new thrift institutions such as community-based or work-based credit unions that would better serve black women.[44]

Ideally, the government should do for poor black women what it has done for working-class and middle-class white men. Beyond subsidizing IDAs (Individual Development Accounts, dedicated savings accounts similar in structure to Individual Retirement Accounts), government programs targeting poor women have not been aimed at improving their asset base and thereby permanently altering their class status.[45] As William Julius Wilson stated in his book *When Work Disappears:* "targeted programs for the poor in the United States do not even begin to address inequities in the social class system. Instead of helping to integrate the recipients into the broader economic and social life of mainstream society—to 'capitalize' them into a different educational or residential stratum, as the GI bill and the postwar mortgage programs did for working- and middle-class whites—they tend to stigmatize and separate them."[46]

I doubt that there exists, at this time, the political will to capitalize poor black women's assent to higher class standing by subsidizing their asset acquisitions, especially given the cultural explanations for black women's asset poverty. Even small-scale policy reform at the structural and institutional levels is likely to be impeded by the belief that the sparsity of black women's wealth is the result of their lack of frugality and unwillingness to make present sacrifices for future gain. Despite the breath and depth of the material, structural, and institutional impediments to black women's asset accumulation, it is black women's moral and cultural fiber that gets called into question when the subject turns to black women's net worth.

Popular ideology attributes indigenous black women's lack of wealth to their profligate spending and perverse mismanagement of money.[47] Black women are constructed as undisciplined consumers who lack the financial discipline to save. Unsatisfied with delayed gratification, they spend money that is not theirs (by bamboozling it from men) or that they do not have (by running up high credit card balances). Given the financial hardships they suffer by virtue of being near the bottom of the socioeconomic ladder, they are blamed for not conforming to the model of the economically rational actor who engages in long-range, life-cycle planning by rationally allocating her resources between current desires and future needs.[48] It does not matter that the rest of society, obsessed with consumption, is not saving as much as it once did and is running up debt. Black women's lot is worse overall, and therefore black women have more of a responsibility to exercise greater self-control and to resist the temptations of rampant consumerism. According to these notions, black women's lack of wealth is a product of the moral failure and values of individual black women and their culture.[49]

Naturally, empirical data pertinent to the accusations leveled against black women regarding their spending habits are nearly impossible to locate. Little attention generally is paid to the specifics of debt accumulation or to its gendered implications.[50] The characteristics and circumstances of black female debtors is an area of research that needs to be mined extensively.

In any event, the role that economic rationality plays in anyone's savings behavior is not clear. Cultural and psychological factors probably have greater operational power.[51] Even "[t]he economic [rationality] paradigm implies that behavior depends on expectations about the future."[52] Those expectations are likely to be the product of personal experience and of psychosocial orientations.[53]

Savings behavior seems to be less the product of a rational or systematic weighing of the costs and benefits of saving and more the result of the operation of "rules of thumb . . . that . . . reflect social and cultural norms" or habits regarding the allocation or disposition of financial resources.[54] "The foundation of all wealth is land." "Money may not be everything, but it's far ahead of what's in second place." Witty little sayings and clever ditties are part of the context in which savings behavior occurs. Thus, the amount of wealth that a segment of the population controls may reflect the amount of social capital invested in promoting the group's acquisition of material capital.

Taken all together, the cultural or sociological factors that impact on black women's saving behavior are a vast unexplored area of research, especially as these factors are impacted by or respond to the law. The condemnation of black women for their habits of thrift and economy, therefore, seems a bit premature. One of the biggest unknowns is the bearing that institutional and structural impediments have on black women's orientation to the future, and its impact, in turn, on their limited wealth accumulation. The inquiry is all the more difficult because there is no essentialist core to black women's financial existence that has across-the-board explanatory power. Black women's culture is as diverse as its practitioners. It varies among subgroups differing in age, class, sexual orientation, geographical location, and national origin. The culture, or cultures, of black women varies in part because the material, structural, and institutional factors already outlined impact different subgroups of black women differently.

I join the plea made by sociologist Patricia Hill Collins for greater support and funding of research that focuses on black women and their families as accumulators and transmitters not only of culture but also of wealth.[55] However, the inquiry into the cultural and legal aspects of black women's relative lack of assets has to begin somewhere. What follows are the speculations and many unresolved questions I have regarding the influence of cultural and legal factors on the efforts of indigenous poor, working-poor, and lower-middle-class black women to acquire wealth. What follows is also, in a way, my own research agenda for issues of wealth accumulation.

In my experience, poor and working-class black women stash money away or hide it about the house in places they hope other family members or burglars are unlikely to find it. This is especially true of women who do not have bank accounts—because banks are inconvenient to use, are not to be trusted, or require minimum deposits that the women cannot satisfy. Many black women have lost their little pot of money to an untrustworthy relative who did not share their plans for the future or to burglars who seemed to know just where to look.[56] The informal nature of savings activity makes the accumulation of assets haphazard and risky, but the institutional support for doing much more simply does not exist.

Mental accounting or the allocation of funds based on their source is very important in savings behavior. Income from some sources is spent immediately, whereas income from other sources is not. Income tax refunds represent a form of savings that many black women use to finance expensive or special purchases. Other black women put the sums they make from working a second job or engaging in informal economic activity,[57] such as selling cosmetics or braiding hair in the kitchen, into a special fund for long-range consumption. We need to know more about the relationship between the underground economy, which is to a large extent the creation of legal regulation, and black women's accretions of wealth.[58]

The figures regarding the disparity between the asset holdings of married couples and female household heads suggest that singleness is an important cause of black women's asset poverty.[59] Singleness (unlike whiteness, which is also associated with greater wealth) is assumed to be a circumstance that blacks control. It is not clear why married couples acquire so much more wealth than singles do. Asset accumulation no doubt is easier when there are two wage earners rather than one. Moreover, there may be efficiencies arising from the consolidation of living expenses and the division of labor that are produced when two adults maintain a single household. It may additionally be the case that marriage increases worries and responsibilities, which, in turn, result in greater incentives to acquire assets. Whatever the explanation, it appears that the legal, cultural, and all-important economic factors that influence rates of marriage among blacks are having an impact on rates of wealth accumulation.[60] It is possible, however, that the norms and the material reality impacting on wealth accumulation are influencing black rates of marriage.

In some segments of the heterosexual black population, saving and asset accumulation are gender roles assigned to women and are sources of conflict between women and their spouses or partners. If money is the biggest source of tension in most marriages and long-term relationships, it must be especially problematic among those torn between accumulating wealth and satisfying short-term, seemingly immediate needs. Need and risk may be viewed differently by black women and men, and the tensions caused by this disparity, if it exists, might work against the formation of more formal unions.

Many of the black women I queried on the subject of black women's wealth jokingly cited men as the chief cause of black women's asset poverty. There is a widespread notion that black women forgo long-term liaisons because black males cannot play the breadwinner role or otherwise substantially contribute to the financial well-being of a family, including asset accretions. Popular belief has it that black women are, instead, choosing to do badly all by themselves, as they say; they do not need a man to make their lives worse. Some evidence indicates, however, that economic pressures are not preventing the formation of strong and stable relationships between unmarried black males and females.[61] Black women's asset accumulation would be strengthened if more social capital in the form of culture and law was invested in promoting easier asset accumulation by those living in other than the traditional nuclear family unit.

Black women's time and money may be subject to familial and communal demands that stifle wealth accumulation. Black working people bear a greater burden than their white counterparts of helping relatives who are unable to sustain themselves without financial assistance.[62] In the case of sick or infirm relatives, the obligation may entail a woman's taking time off from work or totally suspending employment. Thus, assets that might have been used for long-term improvement of a black woman's economic status might be employed instead to support and care for a needy or otherwise dependent relative. A black woman's children indeed may represent her biggest capital investment or her greatest protection against a poor and lonely old age. A parent's expectation of support may be the quid pro quo for the sacrifices she makes to increase the earning capacity of her children. Furthermore, her children's needs to amass assets for their old age may be offset by a reciprocal obligation owed to them from their own young. Broader support for long-term health care and more generous family leave provisions that are compatible with black women's cultural obligations to family would strengthen black women's position in regard to wealth.

Black women's philanthropy to the church and to other social organizations and associations may affect their individual wealth accumulation as well. Of course charitable giving, like generosity within the extended kinship network, may create collective resources or assets that can be called on in time of need. We need to test the extent to which reciprocal communal obligations (that actually deliver material benefits in sufficient amounts to the financially distressed), as opposed to private wealth, are an important element of black people's notion of the good life.

Beliefs about the protection that social welfare programs can provide in the future could affect a black woman's incentives to save. Theoretically, "[w]hen the government provides either larger retirement benefits or a more comprehensive safety net, it reduces the incentives for a private individual to save on [her] own behalf."[63] Black women have not benefited as much as others from social welfare programs, but it is not clear that black women are aware of their relative disadvantage.

Asset accumulation by black women may also be impeded by the absence of cultural mechanisms for the smooth transfer of wealth from one generation to the next. The inability to keep wealth intact as it is passed on, or to keep it in the hands of black people who could use it, reduces its value to each succeeding generation and its contribution to black people's overall wealth. I have heard the stories black folks tell about relatives fighting over a bit of land or the small sum left in a bank account by a deceased family member. The association between wealth and family dissension may act as an impediment to wealth acquisition.

The lack of access to estate planning and to related legal services and the resulting inability to negotiate the inheritance laws have operated to deprive blacks of their ancestors' wealth.[64] For example, sociologist Carol Stack has written about blacks who returned from the North to their Southern roots in rural North and South Carolina; she found that

> people who could not readily file wills at the courthouse or who feared the entanglement of legal paper were eventually beset with problems arising from inheritance of land. "Heirs property," held in common by a group of relatives, with no clear individual title, became the usual form of land ownership among black southerners, and heirs property proved notably susceptible to tax forfeiture and forced-partition sales. An heirs farm could be force-sold under a thousand and one circumstances—what if, for example, one of the family members listed on the deed applied for admission to a nursing home?[65]

In the South, nonblacks typically stand ready to take land that blacks lose. In urbanized Northern communities, the situation is somewhat different. The houses the elderly leave behind when they die are abandoned by relatives, who do not quite know what to do with them.

It is my sense that black women, particularly older ones, have acquired more wealth than they have been able to keep or to pass along to their descendants because the women have been the victims of various frauds, schemes, and scams that take advantage of their age, gender, or lack of financial and business sophistication.[66] Banks, mortgage companies, and home improvement or repair contractors come readily to mind as culprits here.[67] Also, the insurance companies whose home service agents sell black women multiple, expensive life insurance policies, which, if they have not lapsed, pay out small face amounts inadequate to bury those insured, let alone leave their descendants a legacy, are deserving of special condemnation.[68]

Crooks have been able to commit their misdeeds in part because consumer protection services have not sufficiently extended their benefits to black women. Black women have been victimized in part because their culture has not prepared them for the task of amassing and managing assets or because the financial markets that are accessible to them have not supplied them with trustworthy advisors or intermediaries.

In my view, the biggest impediment to black women's wealth accumulation is the absence of a black economic action agenda and program directed at helping black women secure long-term financial security for themselves, their families, and their communities. Historically, black women were not educated or informed about how to manage money—how to spend it, save it, invest it, negotiate with it, or give it away.[69] As popular economic commentator George Subira put it, "proper information about money management has no systematic way of entering their lives. The information is not part of their high school or college education, is not part of the Black media (except Black Enterprise), is not offered in our churches or social organizations, and is generally not discussed intelligently at the family dinner table."[70] In explaining why blacks do not manage their money better, Subira points to such factors as a false sense of security, a belief that only the rich need or can afford guidance in managing their financial well-being, a healthy suspicion of those providing the guidance, an underutilization of financial guidance by other blacks who might serve as role models, and a lack of economic guidance from black leaders.[71] This indictment should include lawyers. I like to think that this situation is changing.[72]

Much of my recent research has explored the ways in which black economic activity has come to be associated with deviance of one sort or another. The acquisition of wealth stands on a par with other forms of economically advantageous or enterprising behavior that are treated as forbidden, mysterious, or aberrant when undertaken by blacks. Blacks are belittled or impeded as they struggle to understand and conquer their economic marginalization. The label *deviant* gets applied to the black actors on both sides of a commercial transaction: buyers and sellers, clients and lawyers, investors and investment advisors. The worst thing about the deviance approach to black economic activity is that many black people, especially women, have bought into the idea and embraced it. However, black economic activity is not deviant; it is only constructed as such to make it easier to exploit black people. It is necessary for blacks to get beyond the blanket suspicions and barriers created by the labeling of black economic activity as deviant and to begin to achieve enduring economic progress.

I like to talk in terms of building and strengthening the black public sphere. The call for an invigorated black public sphere contemplates uniting political and economic arenas with the goal of building black institutions, increasing employment opportunities for blacks, and expanding the power that comes from collectively generating wealth and controlling the messages and the mechanisms for deciding how it should be used. The black public sphere approach is based on a notion that the good life for blacks can only be achieved if blacks control outlets for their cultural creativity and their economic productivity. The black public sphere approach proceeds on the assumption that blacks can compete with anyone else and can build a base of wealth like everyone else if racist institutional and structural barriers are brought down.

Society, of course, is characterized by many competing and overlapping public spheres. Most black women participate in more than one. When it comes to managing and using wealth, many white and nonblack minority women are operating under the same disabilities that impact blacks of both genders. As Sheryl Marshall put it in an essay subtitled "Getting Money and Using It," "[w]omen have not grasped the economic implications of enfranchisement, nor the intimate connection in our political/legal system among economics, politics, and the law. It is probably safe to say that the majority of women—in spite of external manifestations to the contrary—have not internalized the concept of personal, lifelong independence."[73]

Many women do not have checking accounts, have never made an investment, do not know what they are entitled to under their spouse's Social Security or pension plans, and have no financial plan of their own.[74] Marshall attributed women's lack of financial risk taking to many factors, including women's socialization, formal education, experience, support systems, and perception by the business community.[75] The next stage of the feminist movement will likely concentrate on infiltrating and changing structures of economic power.[76] Although white women start out with access to significantly more wealth than do black women, there may be points of convergence between the black and white female public spheres. Achieving changes in public policy that will make it more likely that black women will be able to build the assets needed to support a good life for themselves and their families will require that those points of convergence be strengthened and emphasized.

It will take a great deal of time and effort to develop coalitions around women's attempts to build assets. With every election, however, and through successful organizing campaigns such as that waged against the underinvestment in breast cancer research, women's political clout is growing. Women need to use their political capital to support the accumulation of material capital with which all women might assure their long-term financial security.

Increases in black women's material capital will depend, therefore, on the combined impact of their social and political capital and that of others whose concerns mirror, overlap, and coincide with their own. In that regard, let me end with the words of Oseola McCarty, the laundry woman who donated her life's savings to the University of Southern Mississippi for scholarships for needy students.[77] Ms. McCarty's lonely and isolated existence came to an end when she took her hard-earned savings and unselfishly gave them away. The social power that wealth can create is evident in Ms. McCarty's story; by so generously donating her accumulated assets, she was rewarded with honors, attention, and a bit of fame.[78] Her contribution to the University of Southern Mississippi was more than matched by those of others stimulated by her example. Ms. McCarty published a collection of her sayings titled *Simple Wisdom for Rich Living*. On the subject of savings, she said, "the secret to building a fortune is compounding interest."[79] She is right about that.

Notes

1. See generally *The Wealth of Races: The Present Value of Benefits from Past Injustices* 6 (Richard F. America ed., 1990).

2. Melvin L. Oliver & Thomas M. Shapiro, *Black Wealth/White Wealth: A New Perspective on Racial Inequality* 50 (1995).

3. *Random House Webster's College Dictionary* 1479 (2000).

4. *See generally* Edward N. Wolff, *Top Heavy: A Study of the Increasing Inequality of Wealth in America* (1995).

5. Jesse McKinnon, *The Black Population in the United States: March 2002*, in *Current Population Reports* P20-541 3 (U.S. Bureau of the Census 2003).

6. Shawna Orzechowski & Peter Sepielli, *Net Worth and Asset Ownership of Households: 1998 and 2000*, in *Current Population Reports* P70-88, May 2003, at 2, 12–13 (U.S. Bureau of the Census 2003). Hispanic households, by the way, had median measured net worth of $9,750. An analysis similar to the one undertaken here is sorely needed with regard to Latino women.

7. *See id.* at 14, table H.

8. *See id.*

9. *See* T. J. Eller & Wallace Foster, *Asset Ownership of Households, 1993*, in *Current Population Reports* P70-47, Aug. 1995, at 9 (U.S. Bureau of the Census 1995).

10. *See* Orzechowski & Sepielli, *supra* note 6, at 13.

11. *See* Susan Grad, *Income of the Population 55 or Older, 2000* 10–11, table 1.3 (Social Security Administration 2002). The figure was 44 percent for black married couples, 72 percent for white married couples, and 29 percent for nonmarried black men.

12. *See id.* at 134, table 7.4.

13. *See id.* at 10–11, table 1.3.

14. *See id.* at 134, table 7.3.

15. *See* Oliver & Shapiro, *supra* note 2, at 157–63.

16. *See id.* at 152.

17. *My Soul Looks Back, 'Less I Forget: A Collection of Quotations by People of Color* 272 (Dorothy W. Riley ed., 1991).

18. *See* Elizabeth A. Gowdy & Sue Pearlmutter, *Economic Self-Sufficiency: It's Not Just Money*, 8 Affilia: J. Women & Soc. Work 368, 379 (1993) (survey of low-income women found an association between economic self-sufficiency and autonomy and self-determination, one component of which was putting money in a savings account).

19. Michael Sherraden, *Assets and the Poor: A New American Welfare Policy* 148 (1991).

20. *See generally* John P. Caskey, *Fringe Banking: Check-Cashing Outlets, Pawnshops, and the Poor* 81–84 (1994) (exploring stereotypes about the "saving" behavior of low-income people).

21. Sherraden, *supra* note 19, at 181.

22. *Id.*

23. *See* Internal Revenue Code § 163(h)(1), (h)(2)(D).

24. *See id.* at § 164(a)(1).

25. *See id.* at § 121(a).

26. *See id.* at §§ 219, 404.

27. *See id.* at § 403(b).

28. *See id.* at §§ 219, 408.

29. *See id.* at §§ 219, 401(c).

30. *See id.* at § 404(a).

31. *See generally* Beverly I. Moran & William Whitford, *A Black Critique of the Internal Revenue Code*, 1996 Wis. L. Rev. 751, 768–91 (1996) (reporting results of a statistical assessment of the limited benefit to blacks of key provisions of the tax code pertaining to wealth accumulation).

32. Oliver & Shapiro, *supra* note 2, at 112.

33. This statistic concerning black women compares with the 74 percent that white women earn and the 75 percent that black men earn. *See generally* Am. Fed'n State, County, & Municipal Employees, AFL-CIO, AFSCME Women, *The Wage Gap Factsheet*, available at http://www.afscme.org/wrkplace/wrfaq07.htm (last visited Aug. 3, 2004).

34. Sherraden, *supra* note 19, at 131.

35. *See* U.S. Bureau of the Census, *Statistical Abstract of the U.S.: 2003* 114, table 152 (123rd ed. 2003).

36. *See id.* at 366, table 551.

37. *See generally* Regina Austin, *"A Nation of Thieves": Securing Black People's Right to Shop and to Sell in White America*, Utah L. Rev. 147, 168–70 (1994).

38. *See generally* Frances Cerra Whittelsey & Marcia Carroll, *Women Pay More (And How to Put a Stop to It)* (1995); *see generally* Austin, *supra* note 37, at 148–56.

39. *See generally* Caskey, *supra* note 20.

40. *See generally* John Yinger, *Closed Doors, Opportunities Lost: The Continuing Costs of Housing Discrimination* (1995); Oliver & Shapiro, *supra* note 2.

41. Oliver & Shapiro, *supra* note 2, at 151.

42. David H. Harris Jr., *The Battle for Black Land: Fighting Eminent Domain*, Nat'l B. Ass'n Mag. 12 (Mar./Apr. 1995).

43. *Id.*

44. *See* Caskey, *supra* note 20, at 148–49.

45. *See generally* Creola Johnson, *Welfare Reform and Asset Accumulation: First We Need a Bed and a Car*, 2000 Wis. L. Rev. 1221.

46. William Julius Wilson, *When Work Disappears: The World of the New Urban Poor* 156–57 (1996).

47. *See generally* George Subira, *Money Issues in Black Male/Female Relationships* (1994). The indictment of black women's capacity to save tends to be directed more at younger native-born black females of all classes and less at older black women and black women who are foreign-born or members of immigrant communities.

48. *See* B. Douglas Bernheim, *The Vanishing Nest Egg: Reflections on Saving in America* 67 (1991).

49. The objective data do or do not support this view.

50. There are a few notable exceptions. *See generally* Karen Gross, *Re-vision of the Bankruptcy System: New Visions of Individual Debtors*, 88 Mich. L. Rev. 1506 (1990) (reviewing Teresa A. Sullivan et al., *As We Forgive Our Debtors: Bankruptcy and Consumer Credit in America* (1989)); Zipporah Batshaw Wiseman, *Women in Bankruptcy and Beyond*, 65 Ind. L.J. 107 (1989).

51. *See* Bernheim, *supra* note 48, at 67–80.

52. *Id.* at 69.

53. *See id.*

54. *See id.* at 64, 71.

55. *See* Patricia Hill Collins, *African-American Women and Economic Justice: A Preliminary Analysis of Wealth, Family, and African-American Social Class*, 65 U. Cin. L. Rev. 825 (1997).

56. *See, e.g.*, Mitchell Duneier, *Andrea's Dream: Going It Alone*, Chi. Trib. 1 (Dec. 27, 1994) (young black mother's drug-addicted boyfriend stole money she had put aside for utility bills from the various places she had hidden it, including a shelf in the kitchen cupboard).

57. In this context, the word *informal* means "off the books."

58. *See* Regina Austin, *"The Black Community," Its Lawbreakers, and a Politics of Identification*, 65 S. Cal. L. Rev. 1769, 1803–6 (1992).

59. *See supra* note 10 and the accompanying text.

60. *See generally The Decline in Marriage among African Americans: Causes, Consequences and Policy Implications* (M. Belinda Tucker & Claudia Mitchell-Kernan eds., 1995).

61. *See* Robin L. Jarrett, *Living Poor: Family Life among Single Parent, African-American Women*, 41 Soc. Probs. 30, 42 (1994) (reporting results of focus interviews conducted in 1988).

62. *See* John Simpkins, *All in the Family*, New Republic 27 (July 1, 1996).

63. Bernheim, *supra* note 48, at 87.

64. *See* Wayne Moore, *Improving the Delivery of Legal Services for the Elderly: A Comprehensive Approach*, 41 Emory L.J. 805, 813 (1992) (an American Association of Retired Persons telephone survey found that blacks were less likely to have wills and durable powers of attorney than whites).

65. Carol Stack, *Call to Home: African Americans Reclaim the Rural South* 44 (1996).

66. *See, e.g., Hawkins v. Greenfield,* 797 F. Supp. 30 (D.D.C. 1992) (a functionally illiterate black woman claimed she was tricked into conveying title to property to a lawyer who also duped her into moving into an increasingly rundown residence, where she resided for twenty-five years). In *Hawkins,* the court denied the attorney's motion for summary judgment on plaintiff's fraud and undue influence claims because genuine issues of material fact remained concerning the time when the applicable statute of limitations began to toll. *See id.* at 33–34.

67. *See* Paulette Brown, *African American Elderly—Targets for Fraud,* NBA Nat'l B. Ass'n Mag. 1 (Jan./Feb. 1994).

68. *See generally* Jane Bryant Quinn, *Insurance That Victimizes the Poor,* Wash. Post H02 (July 30, 1995) (exploring fraud in the home service life insurance industry). *See also* Louis Sahagun, *In Wake of Gang Violence, Insurers Come Knocking,* L.A. Times A1 (Oct. 5, 1990) (home life insurance service company targets parents in a crime-plagued neighborhood); Catherine Trevison, *Agents Faked Applications, Women Lawsuits Charge,* Tennessean 1A (Sept. 16, 1996) (a charge of fraud-based agents' intentional "clean sheeting" or recording of false answers on applications leveled against company, 86 percent of whose policyholders were black). For a fictional account of the significance of burial insurance to older black women, *see* Allen Gurganus, *Blessed Assurance: A Moral Tale in White People* 192 (1991).

69. *See* Subira, *supra* note 47, at 179.

70. *Id.* at 180.

71. *See id.* at 183–84.

72. One sign of change is the appearance of books on money management and investing written by and for blacks, including one directed at black women. *See, e.g.,* Kelvin E. Boston, *Smart Money Moves for African Americans* (1996); Cheryl D. Broussard, *The Black Women's Guide to Financial Independence* (rev. ed. 1996); Brooke M. Stephens, *Talking Dollars and Making Sense: A Wealth Building Guide for African-Americans* (1997).

73. Sheryl R. Marshall, *Women and Money: Getting Money and Using It,* in *Women and Economic Empowerment* 239, 240 (New Eng. J. Pub. Pol'y special issue, Dawn-Marie Driscoll ed., 1990).

74. *See id.*

75. *See id.*

76. *See* Dawn-Marie Driscoll, *The Third Stage: An Economic Strategy,* in *Women and Economic Empowerment, supra* note 73, at 179.

77. *See* Rick Bragg, *She Opened World to Others; Her World Has Opened, Too,* N.Y. Times A1 (Nov. 12, 1996).

78. This point was raised by Hugh F. (Trey) Daly of the Legal Aid Society of Cincinnati, who commented on this article at the Agenda for the Twenty-First Century Labor Force Conference.

79. Oseola McCarty, *Simple Wisdom for Rich Living* 19 (1996).

CHAPTER 8

Deconstructing the State–Market Divide

The Rhetoric of Regulation from Workers' Compensation to the World Trade Organization

Martha T. McCluskey

The opposition between *state* and *market* plays a central role in contemporary analysis of law and policy.[1] In popular discourse, law reforms are frequently divided into market solutions grounded in economic goals and nonmarket solutions grounded in social or moral goals. Because feminist policy proposals often seek government regulation of market practices harmful to women, feminist reforms typically appear on the nonmarket side of the divide.

Neoclassical economic theory—promoted in Law and Economics scholarship—criticizes paternalistic efforts to use governmental "rights" rather than the market to allocate resources. In this theory, ideal free markets induce individual decision makers to rationally weigh the costs against the benefits of obtaining particular goods or services, thereby encouraging decisions that produce a net societal gain. The conventional economic doctrine warns that if government grants people "rights" to certain resources independent of costs—whether safety, environmental protection, health care, or family-friendly workplaces—then, in the long run, such rights may produce a net loss to society, even hurting those who are supposed to benefit from the rights.

In the standard economic analysis, any attempt to promote social values for their own sake—such as equality, democracy, social welfare, or human rights—simply masks the economic costs of the decisions being made. The basic premise of neoclassical economics is that scarce resources make cost–benefit trade-offs inevitable. Because the economic "pie" is limited, each time a government policy diverts resources toward one well-intentioned goal, it takes resources away from something else. In this view, rather than ignoring these cost–benefit trade-offs in the guise of "rights," governments should face the tough choices between competing resource demands by subjecting those demands to the rigors of the market (or at least by mimicking the market as much as possible through cost–benefit decision making in government policies). The moral of the standard economic story is that government should give up the pretense of *transcending* the economic goals of the market and should stick instead to the more humble aim of *supporting* markets.

Rather than defending government intervention in the market, this essay aims to challenge the meta-narrative that frames the debate between state and market. My argument is that the market and the state cannot be impartially distinguished.

The market is not prior to or independent from the state but depends on and is shaped by the state. This argument has a long and articulate history in legal realist scholarship of the early twentieth century and critical legal scholarship of the late twentieth century—as well as in non-neoclassical economic scholarship and in left-wing grassroots political activism.[2] Although most law and policy experts typically claim to accept the well-developed premise that markets are constituted by and interdependent on politics and law, they typically proceed to deny or diminish this premise by nonetheless framing their analysis as a division between government regulation and market freedom.[3] For this reason, this essay offers yet another illustration of how to untangle the rhetoric and politics of the state–market divide.

Feminist theory has drawn on deconstructive methods from literary theory to explore how apparently "primal" dualisms—such as the dichotomy between male and female—are neither neutral nor entirely natural but instead are socially constructed to serve political ends.[4] Descriptions of such oppositional pairs (such as male versus female) tend to incorporate a hierarchical valuation of one side of the pair over the other (such as male over female). Feminist critiques have shown that simply reversing the hierarchical value—choosing to prioritize traditionally "female" characteristics over those traditionally labeled "male," for example—risks reinforcing the disadvantageous differences attributed to the subordinate half of the pair. Furthermore, dualisms tend to create a misleading emphasis on the difference between the two "opposites," repressing the many differences *within* each side of the dualism—differences among women, for example, can be as important as differences between men and women.

Feminist legal scholars have taken this critical methodology further to challenge other dualisms that are gendered in conception or effect, or both, including the opposition between state and market.[5] I aim to build on this work by analyzing how the opposition between state and market skews contemporary debates over questions of government regulation. To explore the rhetorical use of this state–market dualism, I draw on Jacques Derrida's deconstruction of a dualistic structure that serves as an organizing ground in Western thought—the opposition between original and supplement.[6] Derrida analyzes the contradictions of this supplement–original dichotomy in the context of literary theory: literature traditionally has been theorized as the artificial supplement to natural reality (a dichotomy between representation and presence). The original–supplement dualism has often been used to promote gender hierarchy; for example, the category *male* serves as the original (Adam), the category *female* as the supplement (Eve). This traditional story constructed women as incomplete men and holds women responsible for both fulfilling and corrupting masculinity. A similar analysis can reveal the contradictions and normative assumptions inherent in the dichotomy between government regulation and the free market—a dichotomy that is not natural, objective, or internally consistent.

In this essay, I focus on two examples of contemporary political controversies involving government regulation of "the market" to show the problems of the conventional economic analysis. First, I explore the crisis of the high cost of workers' compensation insurance, which provoked controversy and reform in many states in the early to mid-1990s. Second, I examine the crisis of resistance to the 1999 World Trade Organization (WTO) ministerial meeting in Seattle. Mainstream media and scholarship typically portrayed both of these crises as conflicts over the extent to which government policy should attempt to intervene in markets for social purposes. With both of these crises, ideas from neoclassical economic theory shaped the popular discourse and formed the underpinnings of the mainstream media and political views of the problem. Because my premise is that economic ideas are a form of political strategy as much as they are a form of scientific inquiry, and because my goal is to challenge the rhetorical use of these ideas in policymaking, I focus on popular as well as scholarly versions of neoclassical economics in both debates.

Although these two examples of economic rhetoric about the state and market are not typically analyzed as feminist concerns, and although both controversies did not focus primarily on gender, both nonetheless have important implications for feminism. In both debates, demands for more protection of workers from "market" conditions were often cast in gendered terms. Critics of expanded workers' compensation benefits often blamed injuries associated disproportionately with women and with traditionally female jobs—such as carpal tunnel syndrome and psychological stress—for producing excessive costs that disrupted insurance markets.[7] In the debate over global trade policy, commentators have explained freedom from labor standards in global trade as a means of increasing jobs and opportunities especially for third-world women, who are disproportionately sought as cheap labor for multinational corporations.[8] And with both crises, the prevailing message about the triumph of market over state serves particularly to undermine feminist efforts to reshape the "market" to better meet the needs of most women.

Workers' Compensation

Workers' compensation, the oldest social insurance program in the United States, was in crisis in many states in the 1980s and early 1990s because of high costs to employers and because of collapsing markets for private workers' compensation insurance.[9] Scholarship, political debate, and popular media all tended to narrate the recent workers' compensation crisis as a classic example of the problems of state intervention in the market. The crisis was typically presented as an example of the misguided tendency of judges and legislators to try to redistribute resources as a matter of "right" to a particular group—injured workers—without sufficient regard for the economic costs of those goals.

In the early years of the twentieth century, most U.S. states established mandatory workers' compensation insurance programs covering the majority of employees. Workers' compensation was a replacement for the tort system, which was widely believed to be unpredictable, costly, and time-consuming for both workers and employers. Workers' compensation formed a legendary bargain in which workers were said to give up their right to sue for full tort damages in exchange for the right to compensation from their employers for work-related injuries regardless of fault.

In the systems established in most states, employers generally must finance workers' compensation benefits by purchasing insurance from private insurance companies. Traditionally, employers paid noncompetitive, mandatory insurance rates set in concert by an insurance industry association subject to prior approval by a state regulatory agency.[10]

The Standard Story of the Workers' Compensation Crisis

In the standard narrative, the current workers' compensation insurance cost crisis began when state legislatures expanded benefits for work-related injuries and illnesses in the 1970s and 1980s out of concern that the majority of injured workers were left below the poverty level by inadequate benefits. Most agreed that although some expansion of benefits to cover the costs of workers' compensation was necessary to fulfill the efficient bargain, at some point this trend toward benefit expansion went too far, upsetting the balance between employers and employees that the original bargain represented.

In particular, the blame for the workers' compensation crisis fell on workers seeking compensation for injuries that do not conform to the paradigm of the classic industrial machine accident. These injuries, such as occupational diseases, repetitive motion injuries, psychological stress claims, and back strains, tended to be viewed as outside the proper scope of the workers' compensation bargain—and many of these injuries also tended (in popular opinion if not in fact) to be associated disproportionately with women workers.[11]

As benefits to injured workers increased, businesses protested the rising workers compensation insurance premium rates charged to cover the expansion of benefits paid to their workers. Nonetheless, as the story goes, judges sympathetic to the plight of individual injured workers and legislators beholden to labor interests stymied efforts to restrain rising benefit costs. Caught between the conflicting demands of business and labor, state governments took advantage of the deep pockets of the insurance industry by holding down regulated insurance premium rates despite rising benefit costs.[12]

The traditional story explains, however, that government regulators cannot escape the elemental laws of economic supply and demand. Private insurance companies responded to what they claimed were inadequate insurance rates by withdrawing from the workers' compensation market in a number of states.[13] The story explains that the crisis of an impending collapse of insurance markets finally forced recalcitrant political leaders to face up to the hard choice between businesses' interest in low insurance rates and workers' interest in high benefits. State legislatures finally contained costs by enacting major new restrictions on benefits for injured workers. Even though workers and their allies had to accept sacrifices, those costs were necessary to reduce employers' and insurers' costs. By the late 1990s, average employers' costs nationwide had fallen, insurers had record-breaking profits, and insurance markets had returned to normal.

Rate Regulation as Market Supplement

This story—and the popularized version of the economic theory that informs it—structures the relationship between insurance rate regulation and the market as one of "supplement" to "original." Derrida's exploration of the contradictions of that supplement–original theme in theories of language offers insights into the contradictions underlying the dominant theory of the relationship between government regulation and the market. Derrida explains: "the supplement is *exterior*, outside of the positivity to which it is super-added, alien to that which, in order to be replaced by it, must be other than it."[14] In the story of the workers' compensation crisis, government rate regulation intervenes in the market process of supply and demand as something outside of and defined against that market.

The traditional workers' compensation story not only distinguishes regulation from the market but also establishes that distinction as hierarchical. Market prices are natural; regulated rates are imitation. In the predominant theory, the market price is the equilibrium that naturally emerges from the interaction of market supply and demand, as a neutral reflection of individuals' voluntary cost–benefit decisions.

Nonetheless, economists and legal scholars acknowledge that in the real world, the market is inevitably imperfect. Economic analysis of law often focuses on the issue of whether market barriers block individuals from making the free and rational choices that would exist in an ideal market. In the predominant theory, government regulation in some circumstances may properly intervene to remove those obstacles to free competition in order to restore proper market functioning. Electric utilities provide the classic example of government rate regulation. Before the recent period of deregulation, the conventional wisdom was that in a free market, geographically based utility monopolies will develop to avoid duplicative capital-intensive electric transmission and distribution systems. According to this view, government regulation of utility rates appropriately protected consumers from the rent seeking that would result from these natural monopoly conditions.

Regulatory intervention in insurance markets aims to protect consumers not from a lack of market competition but from its excesses. Unlike utilities, insurance tends to have relatively low entry costs and low fixed costs. In an ideal free market, vigorous competition naturally produces business failures as the market moves toward equilibrium: firms that do not provide the best product at lowest cost lose customers, and the best firms take over the market. In an insurance market, however, the very product being sold is long-term protection from economic risk—a promise to pay for the customer's losses at some point in the future. As a result, the insolvencies that normally would perfect the market instead interfere with its functioning. Solvency protection must be imposed from the outside on insurance markets "because without it the business does not work at all, does not *insure*."[15] Rate regulation of workers' compensation insurance aims to control predatory pricing and to make up for the difficulties individual customers would have in monitoring insurers' long-term financial strength. Furthermore, because workers' compensation insurance coverage is mandatory for most employers, the traditional view was that rate regulation in workers' compensation substitutes for the natural changes in demand that would normally check fluctuations in price in a completely voluntary market.

Although conventional economic theory acknowledges that regulation may appropriately supplement the market where it falls short, it warns that regulation always risks supplanting the market it is supposed to support. In this view, regulation succeeds to the extent it minimizes its role. The idea of the supplement is that the less you use the artificial addition, the more you get the real thing. In traditional doctrine, rate regulation works when it simulates the pricing that would result from a voluntary, competitive market.

Regulation as Market Distortion

Workers' compensation was in crisis in the early 1990s because of "regulation gone amok," according to a *New York Times* op-ed essay by M. R. "Hank" Greenberg, chief executive of American International Group, Inc. (AIG), one of the largest workers' compensation insurance companies.[16] As the *Times* summarizes Greenberg's comments, the problem is that "the rates insurers can charge no longer reflect reality."[17] Greenberg explains that "[i]n a market economy, the price of insurance, like that of any other product or service, must reflect the true cost of providing it."[18]

This insurance executive's public relations effort draws on and promotes the standard neoclassical economic story of regulation. Insurance economists Patricia Danzon and Scott Harrington argue that the crisis was a problem of "rate suppression," defined as regulatory constraints that forced insurers to charge prices different from "expected costs," thereby "distorting" behavior of insurers, employers, and employees.[19] In addition, they warn that regulatory constraints on "natural" decreases in insurance supply further distorted costs.[20] Similarly, insurance expert Orin Kramer and law professor Richard Briffault explain the workers' compensation crisis as a problem of regulators' unwillingness to set rates "reflecting" rising costs.[21] They contrast "artificially" low regulated prices with "natural competitive forces" and explain that such regulatory "intervention" produces an "unhealthy" insurance market.[22]

Greenberg's commentary graphically states what the scholarly accounts suggest more subtly: reality and "true costs" lie in an ideal market preceding and separate from government regulation. Regulation causes problems when it intervenes in and distorts the ideal market it is supposed to mirror. Regulated rates should faithfully imitate—not "suppress"—the prices of the prototypical competitive market.

Derrida explains, however, that the logic of the supplement is inherently contradictory: by definition, it compensates for a lack in the original—that "which ought to lack nothing at all."[23] The supplement brings what *is* closer to what *should be,* partially replacing the natural with the imaginary. Yet the supplement only works to the extent that it remains true to the original it must correct. Economic theory decrees that government regulation is "real" (not artificial or distorted) to the extent that it mimics an ideal market acknowledged to lack real existence. The delicate task of regulation is therefore to perfect the real by imitating the ideal without detracting from either.

"Amok" regulation, in the conventional economic view expressed by Greenberg's op-ed, happens when "political interests" pressure regulators to depart from a faithful representation of competitive market pricing in order to gain at the expense of others.[24] Greenberg complains that faced with rising benefit costs, government regulators have replaced those *market* values with *political* values, such as states' interest in maintaining an attractive business climate: "with states struggling to attract and retain industry, workers' compensation rates have been artificially suppressed by state governments, even in the face of these enormous cost increases."[25]

Because rate regulation necessarily must make visible the workings of market pricing in an attempt to faithfully duplicate it, rate regulation inevitably opens up the market to corruption from outside that market. As Derrida explains, the economy of the supplement necessarily frustrates because it *exposes* at the same time that it *protects.*[26] "The dangerous supplement . . . is properly *seductive;* it leads desire away from the good path, makes it err far from natural ways, guides it toward its loss or fall and therefore it is a sort of lapse or scandal."[27]

If government can only imperfectly follow the market, even governmental attempts to remove market barriers are likely to end up diverting resources from their market ends. State rate-setting proceedings simulate the market price of workers' compensation through a process in which interested parties employ numerous lawyers, actuaries, and economists to discover the "true costs" of a particular system of workers' compensation benefits. Danzon and Harrington warn that the uncertainty involved in rate regulation "creates an opportunity for politically powerful groups to intervene" to obtain prices that depart from costs.[28] In the foreword to their book on workers' compensation rate controls, the president of the American Enterprise Institute writes, "the regulation of workers' compensation insurance in many states is a perfect example of good intentions leading to bad results" because the attempt to save small businesses from escalating premiums leads to higher costs overall.[29] Similarly, Kramer and Briffault warn that the *seductive* short-term appeal" of rate suppression leads to "devastating long-term consequences."[30] In the standard regulatory story, the risk of such government failures means that the project of correcting the imperfect real market tends to be less reliable and scientifically rigorous than the project of imagining that an imperfect real market will nonetheless promote the correct ideal.

In his op-ed essay, Greenberg concludes that regulatory failures turned the workers' compensation system into "a bureaucracy-bloated political football." Greenberg traces the governmental corruption of the insurance market to an underlying adulteration of the workers' compensation bargain. In Greenberg's view, workers (encouraged by profit-seeking doctors and lawyers) violated the original no-fault, exclusive-remedy insurance plan with what he calls "fraud, pure and simple."[31] He complains that workers filed claims for "real or imagined" injuries, such as psychological stress, "that are unrelated to the workplace," and that workers and their agents were "increasingly contesting payments administered through the system" through litigation aimed at boosting their awards.[32] Similarly, Kramer and Briffault argue that "the workers' compensation social compact has been changed to include new terms" without regard to the costs of these terms.[33] They warn of "friction costs" and "over-utilization" because expanded benefits have reached more uncertain illnesses and injuries and have invited participation by attorneys and medical experts.[34] Kramer and Briffault summarize the lesson of the workers' compensation crisis as the need to accept limits on benefits,[35] emphasizing the standard free market message that resource scarcity requires tough trade-offs.

Echoing and amplifying this message, Greenberg admonishes readers that we can only renounce this "uneconomic behavior" and defy the "special interests" who profit from it through "political courage and a firm belief in our free-market system."[36] Greenberg concludes his essay: "America has been preaching to the world about the values of a market economy. Let us lead by the example we set at home."[37]

Constructing the State–Market Boundary

Greenberg's plea reveals a conundrum in the economic reasoning that grounds the traditional workers' compensation story. The key to solving the crisis was to purge the system of "uneconomic behavior" and politicized "special interests," according to Greenberg and many scholarly commentators.[38] Yet how do they distinguish these "uneconomic" costs that corrupt the market from the "true costs" that preserve the market?

Derrida explains that the original is at once similar to and different from its supplement: the identity of the first is constituted through its reflection in the other to which it appears opposed.[39] Attempts to purify the original of contamination from the artificial are bound to fail. As Derrida notes, "nothing seems more natural than the destruction of nature."[40] Similarly, attempts to expel politics from the market lead straight from the market into politics.

Greenberg, like Harrington and Danzon, presumes that insurers' demands for more profit reflect natural forces of market competition, but that workers' demands for more benefits are anticompetitive market subversions. In the prevailing economic analysis, the answer to the workers' compensation crisis was to pay (not control) the high costs that *insurers* sought to recover, but to control (not pay) the high costs that *workers* (and their lawyers and doctors) sought to recover. To make that crucial distinction, however, commentators must depart from the market values they urge us to reaffirm.

Free-market economic theory presumes that the good society follows from a market in which each individual is free to pursue her rational self-interest, according to her own best judgment. This theory generally claims to be descriptive as well as normative. If the free market is the norm and deviations from the market the exception, then individuals must normally tend to pursue their rational self-interest.

This basic tautology (what exists is in our interest because our interests determine what exists) means that traditional economic theory might have little to say if it did not also postulate that the market has borders. Problems come from outside the bounds of the free market, when actors make inefficient, immoral, irrational, or (as Greenberg puts it) "uneconomic" choices. A central point of free market theory thus becomes distinguishing between the market and its exterior.

Yet the market cannot provide a source of value for measuring its own limits. We know something is outside the market if it is an obstacle to competitive pricing, but we only know something is an obstacle to competitive pricing because it is outside the market. So, in this market theory, we must refer to some source of value beyond the market to weed out the nonmarket behavior so that we can determine the proper scope of the market—even though such nonmarket decisions are the source of the problems we seek to solve.

For example, in the traditional story of the workers' compensation crisis, when the private insurance industry withdrew from state insurance markets in the 1980s and early 1990s, the problem of decreased insurance supply was evidence of the economic soundness of the insurance industry's demands for higher costs. Greenberg explains that insurance companies have withdrawn from the market because of "woefully inadequate rates";[41] only when insurance companies are paid rates that reflect "true costs" can the supply be sufficient to meet demand. That is, we know that insurance companies were correcting market *failures,* not corrupting the market with uneconomic special interests, when they demanded higher rates from regulators because insurance companies withdrew from the market. As Harrington and Danzon explain, insurers' response to low rates was a "natural" part of competitive market supply and demand.[42] By first locating the insurance industry on the inside of the market boundary, commentators can then (not surprisingly) explain insurance companies' actions as rational competitive market behavior.

In contrast, the standard story of the crisis places workers' increased litigation of claims denials and workers' demand for expanded benefits *outside* the market boundary. Here the problem—increased benefit demand and increased supply of legal and medical experts—proves that workers' actions are barriers that disrupt competitive pricing. Although both insurance companies and workers are contesting "prices" offered them (either insurance premium rates or payments for injuries), one is explained as an economic pursuit of "true costs" that affirms the free market and the other is explained as "uneconomic" waste and abuse that undermines the free market. Similarly, the standard economic analysis of the crisis explained employers' pressure for lower insurance rates as a problem of "political" intervention in the market that regulators should resist, not a "natural" part of the market that regulators and insurers should accommodate. In the workers' compensation crisis, insurance companies, employers, and workers all made demands of government lawmakers and regulators in pursuit of their ostensible self-interest. It is only the rhetorical location in the story that makes some interests "uneconomic" "special interests" and other interests natural market forces that promote the public interest in overall economic well-being.

Those with faith in the market might still protest that workers' and employers' demands differ from insurers' demands for higher rates because workers' and employers' demands are likely to be corrupted by "moral hazard." Moral hazard occurs when protection against loss ("insurance") produces incentives that *increase* losses beyond the level that would otherwise exist.[43] If it is difficult to distinguish "real" costs from these "extra" costs, then the "insured" can take advantage of the uncertainty to gain more protection—and to produce more losses—than originally contemplated. For example, the standard economic analysis of workers' compensation explains that expanded workers' compensation protections drove up overall costs by allowing workers (and their doctors and lawyers) to bring claims for losses unrelated to work, or unrelated to real injuries, simply to "profit from the system," as Greenberg complained.[44]

In the standard economic analysis, state regulators similarly engaged in moral hazard when they took advantage of uncertainties in the rate-setting process to make insurers cover not just previously existing costs but also the costs of expansive benefits, without corresponding rate increases. In this view, the protection of regulatory rate controls allowed states to provide more generous and costly benefits than they would have otherwise because they could force insurers, rather than employers, to cover the costs.

However, this "moral hazard" explanation for distinguishing "uneconomic" or market-disrupting behavior from market-promoting self-interest maximizing again depends on partisan rhetoric rather than on neutral economic principle or empirical evidence. The term *moral hazard* describes the problem that protection, designed to cover a given set of "real" costs, ends up distorting those costs—magnifying the original problem that was supposed to be alleviated. But how do we know the increased claims filed by workers in response to increased benefit protection constitute "excessive" rather than "real" costs? Or how do we know that decreased profits suffered by insurers in response to regulatory controls reflect "excessive" rather than "real" costs of insurer risk-taking or inefficient business practices?

Workers may stay out of work longer when they receive higher disability payments: for example, they may file more claims for psychological stress when benefit laws change to more readily compensate such injuries. But these increased claims might more accurately reflect "real" injury costs if previous benefit restrictions caused workers to underreport injuries. Whether or not changes in claims costs exaggerate or correct injury costs depends on the perspective from which the previous claims levels are viewed. Similarly, when regulators institute rate controls that make insurers absorb a greater share of insurance risk, they may be correcting excessive insurer profits and encouraging insurer accountability rather than forcing excessive insurer losses. The concept of the "original," as Derrida explains, is an image inherently subject to distortion—a representation whose apparent immediacy is derived from its position in relation to its supplement. "One can no longer see disease in substitution when one sees that the substitute is substituted for a substitute."[45]

Nonetheless, in an attempt to separate the distorting effects of moral hazard from restoring accurate pricing, economic analysis distinguishes some behavior as strategic market manipulation by responsible agents and other behavior as passive reaction to market forces by innocent victims. In the standard story of the workers' compensation crisis, insurance companies' rates simply and naturally reflect the costs of workers' benefits, unless regulators intervene by rejecting insurers' rate requests. This story assumes that rising benefit costs necessarily and self-evidently produce rising insurance premiums in a free market. Similarly, this story explains that insurers withdraw from the market when rate controls squeeze their profits because of natural forces of supply and demand.

In contrast, the standard story portrays workers' increased claims filing in response to expanded benefits as an active attempt to reap opportunistic gain. In this story, workers' cost-increasing behavior is suspect because they appear to have the power (with the help of their doctors and lawyers) to take advantage of insurers' and employers' lack of knowledge about actual injuries to exaggerate claims costs. Regulators' profit-squeezing behavior is suspect because they appear to have the power to manipulate the rate-setting process to underestimate insurance costs. In contrast, insurers' cost-increasing behavior—seeking increased insurance rates—is innocent because their increasing costs appear to be a natural and unmediated result of market facts beyond insurers' control.

Nonetheless, the insurers' passive role is determined by their place in the story rather than their power in the market. The traditional analysis reserves *agency* for the state and injured workers (along with their doctors and lawyers). The range of action afforded multinational insurance corporations such as Greenberg's, with its multibillion-dollar expertise, goes no further than the process of paying out money upon demand to the state and to injured workers. In a *New York Times* article on Maine's workers' compensation crisis, another insurance executive explained that "[w]e are the messengers who deliver the bad news about what is going on in society, and oftentimes we get shot."[46] Insurance executive Greenberg begins his op-ed essay by describing his company's alleged multimillion-dollar losses in Maine as the "worst case" example of government rate suppression. He warns of workers' strategic control over their injury claims and government's strategic control of rate regulation. Yet the most rational market actor in the story—the private insurance industry—appears to make no choices about how it does business.

By bringing insurers out of the background of the narrative, we can see that the insurance costs that appear neutral and natural are instead colored by insurers' actions. For example, Maine state regulators repeatedly found that serious mismanagement by a subsidiary of Greenberg's company played a significant role in producing that state's record workers' compensation costs.[47] In 1988, this company negotiated a deal in which it received a generous no-risk, up-front fee for providing insurance services to a large portion of the state's "assigned risk pool" businesses, with no monitoring of the company's performance and no liability for the pool's losses.[48] In 1992, many business policyholders testified that the company failed to maintain accurate records of claims paid, failed to provide any loss control services (such as safety training), and was grossly incompetent in processing claims.[49]

Similarly, it is only a partial picture of the market during the workers' compensation crisis that makes the insurance industry's decrease in underwriting appear to be the natural result of falling profits. By shifting the point of view to include the dramatic growth of a new self-insurance and risk management industry during that time, we can see commercial insurers' declining market supply as the result not of external market forces but of insurers' failed internal business strategies.[50] These new "alternative" insurance providers responded to the rising benefit costs of the period not by raising rates but in part by using innovative loss prevention techniques to control benefit costs. For example, many businesses facing high insurance rates from traditional insurance companies found that by unbundling insurance services such as claims management and safety information and subcontracting these to noninsurance company experts, they could save both on up-front insurance costs and on long-term injury costs. In Maine, while insurance companies were losing money on their workers' compensation policies, many businesses joining together in group self-insurance pools developed large surpluses, despite charging comparable "insurance premium" rates to their members. This revised picture suggests that commercial insurers reduced their supply not because regulators' "uneconomic" behavior artificially suppressed rates but because insurers' "uneconomic" behavior artificially inflated rates. In this view insurers, not workers, employers, or regulators, may be the ones most responsible for (and most profiting from) using rate regulation to avoid the tough choices imposed by market realities. Indeed, a number of studies have found that deregulation of workers' compensation insurance rates leads to lower, not higher, rates.[51]

This altered frame of reference reveals that insurance costs are not necessarily the original market reality that government regulators must reflect. Instead, insurance costs can be viewed as a supplement that should duplicate the original state that government regulators and benefit claimants' reveal. In workers' compensation insurance regulation, rates must be set based on the *projected* costs of claims for medical treatment and lost wages that will actually be paid over a period that can last for decades. Those costs are not fixed and inevitable based on a given benefit system; in fact they are produced in part by insurers' actions such as claims management and promotion of safety and reemployment programs. By setting the standards and incentives that shape insurers' actions, rate making acts as a substitute that precedes and enacts the "real costs" it must represent. When insurers complain that rates do not reflect reality, they simply mean that the reality the rates reflect is not a reality insurers like.

The World Trade Organization

Mainstream media and politicians typically have explained the WTO crisis, like the workers' compensation insurance crisis, as a problem of keeping the state in its proper place in relation to the market. In the prevailing response to the Seattle protests against the WTO, society benefits more in the long run from "free trade" than from "fair trade." This view invokes conventional economic principles to explain that tough-minded adherence to the market should override soft-hearted attempts to put social concerns above the market.

The WTO describes itself as providing the "legal ground-rules for international commerce."[52] "The World Trade Organization . . . is the only international organization dealing with the global rules of trade between nations. Its main function is to ensure that trade flows as smoothly, predictably and freely as possible."[53] In neoclassical economic theory, global competition from free movement of commerce across borders maximizes aggregate resources.

Standard Story of the WTO's Seattle Crisis

The standard story of the Seattle crisis draws on neoclassical economic theory to explain that expanded global competition necessarily weeds out the noncompetitive. "The whole point of engaging in trade is to shift resources—capital and labor—to their most productive uses, a process that inevitably causes pain to those required to shift."[54] Liberalized global markets therefore impose costs on individual firms, workers, and communities whose assets cannot satisfy the increased competitive pressure for lower-cost or higher-quality products. Even though this market discipline benefits society overall in the long run, those who lose out are likely to seek political protection. In particular, this story explains that highly paid manufacturing workers in the United States have attempted to impose trade barriers to reduce competition from cheaper foreign labor. In this view, the protests in Seattle were driven by resistance to the short-term costs of global competition—as well by as the sentimental or misguided fear of progress by "flat-earth advocates."[55] The conventional view concedes that protests nonetheless boosted popular support for the ideas that trade agreements should enforce labor and environmental rights and that some decisions about health and welfare should be made not by the market but by the state.

In the standard story, the political pressure from the protests presents government officials and politicians with a hard choice. If they give in to the demands of those who lose out from liberalized global trade, they are likely to sacrifice the societal benefits of that trade—and even to impose more costs in the long run on those who are struggling from the new global competition. The standard story explains that well-intentioned restrictions on liberalized trade will be undermined by the reality of global market forces.

For example, if the government gives in to demands for protectionism by artificially supporting U.S. jobs or high wages, consumers will pay higher prices and will risk lower living standards. Other nations are likely to retaliate by restricting access to their markets, thereby reducing U.S. export jobs. In addition, if protectionism maintains U.S. jobs at the expense of foreign jobs, poor workers in developing nations may become even worse off and even more likely to accept lower wages and worse working conditions—thereby posing an even greater long-run competitive threat to better-off workers in richer nations. Without the robust growth fostered by free trade, both developing and developed nations will have a harder time establishing or maintaining high labor and environmental standards.

The moral of the standard story is that politicians should once again reject shortsighted efforts to transcend the market for social goals. The unfortunate costs to the losers must be accepted as a necessary part of the price of long-run prosperity that will ensure more winners who can share in greater gains. At most, governments should help losers in the global market make the transition to more competitive activities, or cushion their losses, without disrupting or impeding that competition.

The WTO as Free Market Supplement

In neoclassical economic ideology, trade regulation (like insurance regulation) should mimic the ideal free market. This view presents free trade as natural and government involvement in trade as artificial. A Heritage Foundation report defending the WTO explains that, in the words of nineteenth-century economist Alfred Marshall, "free trade is not a device, but the absence of any device."[56] This report explains that the strength of free trade is its "neutrality," "simplicity and naturalness," in contrast to government "manipulation" of trade.[57]

Following the original–supplement paradigm, this distinction between natural free trade and imitation trade regulation is hierarchical and normative: free trade is a beneficial and generative force; governmental trade regulation is a potentially dangerous, stifling barrier. A *Boston Globe* report on the Seattle protests explained that the mainstream view holds that "[u]nfettered trade will naturally maximize wealth by focusing each country's economy on what it does best."[58]

In the predominant economic analysis, the proper role for trade regulation, like rate regulation in the insurance context, is to support but not supplant the natural—and naturally superior—market. Trade agreements should simulate pricing that would result from the ideal free market. But once again, this idea of regulation incorporates an inherent tension: it must compensate for a lack in the original while remaining true to that original, and it must add to the original without challenging the original market as complete in itself. Trade regulation must act as an artificial device that is as natural as possible.

In the conventional economic story, government regulation of trade in general, and the WTO in particular, corrects a "market failure"—a condition in which unregulated markets fail to produce the optimal results of an ideal free

market. Without multilateral trade rules, countries might fall victim to "pro-
tectionist urges."[59] In more technical terms, without a regulatory body such as
the WTO, countries may be caught in what economists call a "prisoner's
dilemma," in which decisions that maximize self-interest on an individual
basis end up, when taken in the aggregate, producing a result harmful to those
individuals' interest. It may sometimes be in the interest of a nation acting individually to restrict trade in favor of national products. But if other nations
similarly restrict trade, then all will be worse off than they would be under an
unrestricted trade regime.[60]

In theory, the WTO corrects this market failure by facilitating cooperation
between countries so that all act in their aggregate best interests by pursuing
free trade policies. With its establishment in 1995, the WTO added an enforcement mechanism to previous multilateral agreements of the General Agreement on Tariffs and Trade (GATT) and strengthened international cooperation
toward the goal of eliminating trade barriers. *New York Times* columnist and
author Thomas L. Friedman explains that "[t]he more countries trade with
one another, the more they need an institution to set the basic rules of trade,
and that is all the W.T.O. does."[61]

In the prevailing story, then, the WTO governs trade by enhancing rather
than restraining natural market forces. Friedman asserts that "when you don't
have walls you need more rules."[62] The *Economist* magazine distinguishes
"governments," which it says are driven by political pressure to restrictively
regulate trade, from the WTO, which it calls a trade "deregulator."[63] WTO
director general Mike Moore asserted that "we are not a world government"
but simply a forum for governments to negotiate "global rules to match the
acceleration of globalization" and a system for providing a "transparent and
predictable framework for business."[64] Moore went on to explain: "We do
not lay down the law. We uphold the law . . . the alternative is the law of the
jungle."[65]

The WTO as Market Distortion

Like other attempts to supplement the market with government regulation, the
trade policies of the WTO risk distorting rather than reflecting the market. By
establishing rules for global market competition, the WTO exposes the global
market to political scrutiny and debate. When protesters disrupted the Seattle
meeting, an *Economist* magazine editorial worried that, as a "man-made device" subject to political manipulation, the WTO could become an "appara-
tus" of government regulation rather than a "de-regulator" that frees natural
market forces from constraint.[66] In response to the Seattle protests, an essay
in the *National Review* observed that "trade negotiations naturally lead to
anti-trade rhetoric" because such negotiations treat open markets as a concession to be exchanged for access to other nations' markets.[67] As a result, the

process of establishing free trade rules may help construct trade liberalization as a costly loss of market advantage rather than as a beneficial return to an originally advantageous market.

In addition, the WTO's trade negotiation process risks disrupting its free trade ideals because it must enlist and enforce international *cooperation* in order to promote its goal of unfettered international *competition*. As the *Economist* magazine commented after the Seattle crisis, the WTO's purpose of fostering collective action by diffuse interests in support of trade liberalization has instead backfired by facilitating collective action by diverse groups *opposed* to such liberalization.[68] In particular, the protests at the Seattle meeting put pressure on American politicians to divert the WTO's focus from "free trade" to "fair trade" by including labor, human rights, and environmental standards in trade agreements and WTO enforcement powers.

The prevailing economic wisdom presents such demands for "fair trade" as another example of regulation run amok. In that view, "fair trade" proposals deviate from the WTO's original economic purposes for misguided or pretextual social welfare purposes.[69] In the mainstream analysis, WTO enforcement of labor and environmental standards would not only impede the WTO's primary goal of economic growth but also would fail to promote alternative social goals. That is because attempts to improve "free trade" with "fair trade" fail to recognize the fundamental strength and comprehensiveness of the market ideal (whatever the real market's weakness and imperfection). The *Economist* magazine chided "militant dunces parad[ing] their ignorance" in the Seattle protests, explaining that demands for "fair" trade fail to understand that "free trade" is fairest because it "makes people better off, especially the poorest people."[70] Former U.S. trade representative Carla Hills testified to Congress that "open markets and rules-based trade and investment raises standards of living, and creates the wealth necessary to deal with important issues like labor and environment."[71]

In the conventional view, therefore, trade regulation that incorporates fairness goals will upset rather than enhance the market. A Heritage Foundation report warns against "artificially increasing wages" through WTO enforcement of labor standards in developing countries.[72] The report explains that cheap and docile labor constitutes developing nations' competitive advantage in the global economy. If the WTO raised labor standards—for example by enforcing trade restrictions on products made with child labor—that would undermine developing nations' natural ability to compete in the global economy. As a result, those nations would have less economic growth, fewer jobs, and more poverty.

Expressing this theme from a "liberal" perspective, the Brookings Institute's book *Globaphobia* explains that "fair trade" rules do not make sense because they "nullify the gains from trade."[73] The authors argue that trade is more beneficial the more labor and environmental standards differ among nations.[74]

They explain that by allowing unrestricted specialization according to variations in national "tastes, conditions, or incomes . . . [t]he country with lenient pollution standards will get what it wants: more output from pollution-intensive industries," and countries with tougher pollution standards get a cleaner (internal) environment and cheaper imported goods.[75] This argument assumes that "free trade" rules allow the market to reflect authentic internal differences; "fair trade" rules, in contrast, impose a contrived and coercive uniformity based on the external subjective preferences of richer nations.

Despite the asserted strength and superiority of the free market model as a model for trade regulation, the conventional analysis acknowledges that "[f]ree trade is a fragile concept."[76] First, free trade is susceptible to challenge because it is so costly to many. Fair trade rules are a seductive alternative because they appear to ameliorate the harsh sacrifices required to produce the purported gains from liberalized trade. For example, a commentary by a scholar from the conservative Hudson Institute warned that "protectionism is a permanent temptation" because politicians want to get the benefits of free trade without paying the price of displacing noncompetitive workers and industries.[77]

In the standard story, however, the temptation to soften the market out of concern for social welfare instead leads to corruption of the market's public benefits for private gain. Rather than accepting the strengthened market discipline of free trade, those at risk of losing out to new global competition use "fair trade" to seek personal protections at the expense of society as a whole. As a *Wall Street Journal* editorial explained, "[p]lainly the Seattle activists are being used as shock troops by special interests trying to protect their own privileges at the expense of workers in the rest of the world."[78] The Hudson Institute's commentary characterized proponents of trade-based labor standards as part of an "old boys network" afraid of change or as "an amalgam of special interests from rich countries determined to keep the poor out."[79] Similarly, economist and *New York Times* op-ed writer Paul Krugman argues that U.S. labor's complaints about substandard foreign wages are driven by selfish attempts to price needier foreign workers out of the job market for the benefit of richer Americans.[80] A *Wall Street Journal* editorial complained that politicians have been tricked by "fair trade" rhetoric into "allow[ing] trade to become hostage to special interests. . . . In a more sensible world, the Seattle fiasco would be understood as a last-ditch ploy by washed-up protectionists to save their own endangered skin."[81]

The WTO's free trade principles are fragile not just because of the power of external special interests resisting sacrifices needed for the greater good, but also because of the uncertainty inherent in the WTO's mission of promoting the greater good through free trade. The WTO was formed in part to extend free trade rules beyond traditional bans on tariffs and quotas to address non-tariff barriers increasingly at issue in the newly complex and expansive context of international trade in services and information technology. But the Heritage Foundation notes that the WTO's expanded support for free trade has also weakened the very concept of free trade.[82] Nontariff regulations that restrict trade are difficult to distinguish from national policy differences that form the basis for freely competitive trade.[83] The *Economist* warns that the inherent difficulties of combating nontariff barriers make the WTO's free trade goals even more vulnerable to usurpation by special interests.[84] To cure this market fragility, free trade advocates tend to call for stronger regulators capable of making "every effort" to reduce these elusive and unpopular trade barriers,[85] as well as for regulators not "afraid to stand up" to fair trade activists.[86]

Constructing the State–Market Boundary

As with workers' compensation regulation, the idea that trade regulation should reflect rather than alter the market poses a conundrum. In trade regulation as in insurance regulation, attempts to remove politics from the market require more politics. The key to successful trade regulation is to purge the system of politicized special interests that raise costs to others in the guise of higher ideals. But the higher ideal of the unadulterated market can only be achieved through increased political intervention directed at raising costs to some.

Sound regulation, in the conventional view, must make the critical and delicate distinction between true economic ideals and false political ideals. *Globaphobia* cautions that only "impersonal markets," not politicians, can be trusted to tell the difference between rules aimed at market-blocking special interests and rules aimed at market-promoting public interest.[87] Nonetheless, the authors urge that we trust the WTO's government regulators to know that demands for rules enforcing labor standards are about politics, not economics.

Again, the distinction between what is inside and what is outside the market depends not on neutral market principles or on economic facts but on rhetorical location—and political interests. For example, in the standard analysis, when workers in rich nations demand WTO enforcement of higher labor standards, they are seeking to impose political restraints that artificially inflate costs. When multinational corporations from rich nations demand WTO enforcement of higher standards for intellectual property or capital mobility, they are seeking to follow economic principles that reflect natural market costs. The *Globaphobia* authors explain how we should know that weak intellectual property standards, but not weak labor standards, count as trade barriers: "U.S. software companies will be strongly discouraged from exporting their programs to countries where they can be easily copied without penalty."[88]

This rationale presents intellectual property standards as a trade-enhancing public benefit because those standards *increase* the supply of U.S. exports. In contrast, *Globaphobia* presents international labor standards as trade-inhibiting private gain because they *decrease* the supply of foreign jobs. Whether the trade rule is liberalizing or restricting therefore depends on whose trade gets positioned at the center of the story as the normal market and whose trade constitutes a threat to that trade from outside that market.[89]

The prevailing analysis attempts to ground this rhetorical distinction in impartial economics by constructing labor or environmental standards, but not intellectual property standards, as costly moral hazard: protections that will produce incentives to raise costs in the long run. In this theory, labor standards that protect higher-waged U.S. jobs from international competition impede the "creative destruction" that makes standards of living rise.[90] Even though such standards might provide a temporary cushion against U.S. workers' losses, that cushion might lead to long-term harm by allowing workers and governments to avoid the "job skills enhancement and retraining" that will encourage those workers to adapt to the new global economy so that they will be more competitive in the long run.[91] And, as Federal Reserve chairman Alan Greenspan explains, using trade rules to protect workers or the environment will end up creating incentives for *lower* labor and environmental standards. Because protections from global competition will end up lowering standards of living in developing nations (in the conventional theory), those nations will devote fewer resources to improving labor and environmental conditions. The more that rich nations try to protect poor nations by externally raising labor and environmental standards, the more that developing nations will be unable to afford such standards—leaving those nations with even more problems of substandard labor and environmental conditions than they would have had otherwise.

In contrast, in the standard story, rules protecting gains from high intellectual property standards produce incentives that *reduce* overall losses. Why don't these standards protect less competitive U.S. businesses from cheaper foreign competitors, thereby providing incentives for continued investment in losing industries rather than adjustment to a new economic reality? Why don't these standards reduce foreign nations' standards of living, thereby creating incentives for those nations to further disregard intellectual property rules? Because, in the standard story, WTO enforcement of intellectual property standards provides incentives for *more* competition and *more* trade, leading to *greater* overall economic wealth. In the conventional answer, intellectual property protections in trade rules encourage more investment in innovative technology and prevent foreign competitors from "hitching a free ride on research-and-development spending elsewhere."[92]

This moral hazard distinction, however, depends not on objective logic or empirical evidence of costs and benefits, but on the narrative construction of some costs as "real" or original, and some as extra and abnormal. Incentives for more high-wage jobs only distort the new reality of global markets if a market dominated by below-subsistence wages is the norm to which many workers must adjust. WTO enforcement of higher labor and environmental standards will only produce poorer nations less able to maintain such standards in a market structured to make poor labor and environmental conditions a necessary precondition for competitive market growth for poor communities.

In contrast, WTO enforcement of high intellectual property standards appears to enhance competition only because of a prior assumption that increased competition is not a market reality to which wealthier nations and producers of intellectual capital must adjust but a market distortion that regulators must correct. Legal scholars John McGinnis and Mark Movsesian assert that international intellectual property standards, but not labor and environmental standards, are economically beneficial on the theory that "weak intellectual property standards decrease trade in goods because counterfeit goods decrease the demand for real ones."[93] McGinnis and Movsesian contrast international regulation of water purity as uneconomic, saying that "Indians may not be able to afford American water safety standards, just as they unfortunately may not be unable to afford many other goods that Americans can."[94]

According to this reasoning, ensuring the purity of, for instance, videotapes of Hollywood movies benefits India's impoverished citizens more than ensuring the purity of their water. That is because, in this vision, more consumer purchases of authentic videotapes (in place of, for instance, homemade entertainment less subject to uncertainties about originality) count as an objective increase in overall economic "growth," whereas more consumer demand for clean water (in place of, for instance, bottled soft drinks less subject to contamination) is a matter of personal (or national) subjective preference about economic "distribution." Even if one assumes that demand for drinking water will not be affected by its purity, unlike the demand for videotapes, it would also seem reasonable to calculate the possibility that increased drinking of safe water could have positive spillover effects such as healthier citizens capable of producing and consuming more wealth at lower cost. By locating impoverished consumers' interest in pure water (however real), but not impoverished consumers' interest in pure videotapes (however theoretical), outside the realities of the existing market, McGinnis and Movsesian can count the indirect economic effects of pure videotapes as more beneficial to the market than the indirect economic effects of pure water. In the conventional rhetoric, intellectual property standards become a necessity for impoverished nations while labor, environmental, or human rights standards become a luxury reserved for the wealthy.[95] That distinction rests on the prior and unsupported assumption that intellectual property standards are *inherent in* a growth-producing market, whereas labor, environmental, or human rights standards are *external barriers* to such a market.[96]

By focusing on which trade rules produce unnecessary costs that hinder economic growth—moral hazard—and which produce costs necessary to promote economic growth, the standard economic analysis obscures the question of what kind of economic growth, and for whom, should count as the undistorted market ideal. Trade rules, like all regulations, inevitably shape the market reality they aim to reflect. The standard story, however, presents the market as the result of neutral economic forces, not human design, and therefore as fixed and inevitable—as long as it is not distorted by political manipulation.

The standard story of trade regulation, like the standard story of the workers' compensation crisis, tends to construct the characters with the most market power and greatest personal gain under the WTO's "free trade" regime as the most passive and impartial. In this view, if developing nations rely on child labor and polluting industries to maintain their economies, that is simply the result of supply and demand and inherent national differences, not because multinational corporations and wealthy global investors have structured the global market to increase their short-term profits at others' expense. If consumers from rich countries benefit from cheap imports made possible by the sacrifice of life and health from polluting and unsafe factories in poor nations, the standard story assumes that those consumer benefits are not selfish market manipulations at the expense of others, but the result of neutral and natural market forces that promote the general welfare. If wealthy transnational corporations support strict international rules on intellectual property, but not strict labor or environmental standards, McGinnis and Movsesian imply that we can trust that those regulations will not protect wealthy capital owners at the expense of others but will simply and accurately reflect the public's economic interest in distinguishing "real" from "counterfeit" goods.[97]

In contrast, if workers from rich nations benefit from rules linking trade to labor or environmental standards, their gains are portrayed as extra or artificial benefits conferred by political intervention at others' expense: a kind of "foreign aid program funded by selectively higher prices on certain imports and lost job opportunities," as *Globaphobia* argues.[98] McGinnis and Movsesian warn that even if international labor and environmental standards might correct market failures in theory, in practice they would fall victim to untrustworthy "special interests."[99] This vision portrays organized labor or environmental activists as powerful threats naturally inclined to undermine both democracy and the global economy.[100] In contrast, it presents the wealthy transnational corporations (and perhaps even third-world despots[101]) that gain the most from the WTO's trade policies as ingenuous bystanders needing only the WTO's guidance to align their interests with the world's poorest.[102]

In the standard story, any harm from unrestrained global competition in low-paid and otherwise substandard labor is natural and beyond regulatory control, whereas harm from *restrictions* on low-paid labor is the product of unnatural and misguided regulatory intervention. For example, the standard story warns that trade rules incorporating restrictions on imports made with child labor would result in more children in misery and fewer jobs in developing nations. The villains of this story are rich nations' labor advocates, whose political intervention in the name of rescuing poor children masks self-serving greed. In contrast, when multinational corporations withdraw jobs from poor countries, or pay adult workers wages so low their children must work for survival, they are simply passive and innocent victims forced by the market to seek higher profits elsewhere. Similarly, when higher-waged adult workers are laid off because of liberalized competition from nations with lower labor standards, the problem is simply the tragic but ultimately beneficial "wheels of progress," in Alan Greenspan's words. The personal gains to wealthy capital holders from this "tragedy," or the personal and political choices that drive these "wheels," are not part of this story.

Of course, rules "liberalizing" trade are not just "wheels" that inevitably and impartially raise living standards but are hotly contested actions of self-interested political players. For example, insurance executive (and workers' compensation op-ed writer) Hank Greenberg led his multinational company AIG to contribute nearly $1 million to both Democrats and Republicans in the late 1990s, while playing a major role in negotiating WTO rules to protect and increase his company's access to Asian financial services markets.[103] Greenberg's political pressure helped produce a 1997 WTO agreement that granted international insurers such as AIG rights to own and operate financial services businesses in more than a hundred countries.[104] Yet just as in the workers' compensation crisis, the standard story positions Greenberg's political power to shape the market to his personal advantage as a part of the invisible workings of an impersonal market in which capital is destined to flow to the place of greatest profit, regardless of the costs of that profit seeking to smaller financial service industries in developing nations, for example. But just as in the workers' compensation context, those who pay the costs of Greenberg's vision of regulation lose out not because they fail to adjust to the reality of competitive market forces but because they lack the political power to make rules for market competition based on a vision of reality that promotes their interests.

Beyond the State–Market Divide

In the traditional economic story, regulators face two choices: either remain faithful to the goals of the free market by setting insurance rates or trade rules that mimic costs of "real" market competition as much as possible, or give in to competing social welfare values. Conservatives tend to swear by the first; liberals tend to confess to the second.

Feminist strategies for resistance to traditional free market economic arguments sometimes get outmaneuvered by presuming that the free market model is a matter of logical and consistent principles. The typical liberal response to market efficiency claims tends to accept the basic structure of the traditional neoclassical economics tale, but then tries to reverse the hierarchy of the values it presents. Labor advocates may argue that goals "external" to the market—such as social welfare and democracy—are worth the sacrifice in economic growth that inevitably comes from government intervention in the market. But, as Derrida suggests, the rhetorical operation of the traditional supplement–original binary tends to turn simple reversals into confirmations of the original supremacy.[105]

When liberal proposals take market rules at face value, and accept a tragic choice between the competing social and economic values those rules appear to offer, those liberal alternatives tend to appear less desirable than the free market options they reject. The dichotomy between the free market and government regulation privileges the market, while masking its dependency on (and overlapping identity with) the state. Within this framework, the ideal free market is by definition perfect—it furthers both social and economic welfare. In contrast, the state is by definition imperfect because it frustrates both the market it mimics and the social ideals toward which it aims. Unless the market–nonmarket dichotomy itself is undone, choosing to value the state over the market—social goals over economic goals—means choosing tails instead of heads in a game of "heads I win, tails you lose."

The traditional free market model typically has been a strategy for having it both ways: behavior is described as rational and public-spirited competition motivated by economics when the behavior benefits the personal interests of free market proponents (and frequently those with whom they share class, race, and gender identity). When the same kind of behavior would disadvantage the personal interests of free market advocates and those with whom they identify, it often may appear just the opposite—an immoral, irrational "special interest" outside the market.

Inconsistency and incoherence should not be mistaken for weakness, nor deconstruction for revolution. The free market theory that pervades law and public policy has power that exceeds its advocates' rhetorical skills and economic logic. Yet those who share neither the goals nor the power of free market ideologues must not limit their resistance to supplementing conventional economic analysis with alternative methods designed to close market gaps or trim market excesses. By appropriating conventional economic rhetoric and capitalizing on its inconsistencies, we may be able to maneuver the instabilities of the market–state dichotomy toward different political ends—and to work toward displacing this dichotomy with a story that better recognizes the interrelationship of politics and economics.

Notes

1. Thanks to Terence Dougherty and Carl Nightingale for comments on drafts of this essay and to Rick Swartz, whose expert and inspiring teaching gave this project its start. I am also grateful for opportunities to present earlier versions of this essay at the February 1995 Feminism and Legal Theory Workshop at Columbia Law School and at the 1994 New Economic Criticism Conference at Case Western Reserve University.

2. For an example of legal realist critiques of the state–market dichotomy, *see* Robert L. Hale, *Freedom through Law: Public Control of Private Governing Power* (Columbia U. Press 1952), discussed in Barbara H. Fried, *The Progressive Assault on Laissez Faire: Robert Hale and the First Law and Economics Movement* (Harvard U. Press 1998); for examples of critical legal scholarship, *see* Mark Kelman, *A Guide to Critical Legal Studies* 115–50 (Harvard U. Press 1987); Duncan Kennedy, *Cost–Benefit Analysis of Entitlement Problems: A Critique,* 33 Stan. L. Rev. 387 (1981); Arthur Allan Leff, *Economic Analysis of Law: Some Realism about Nominalism,* 60 Va. L. Rev. 451 (1974); Martha Albertson Fineman, *Contract and Care,* 76 Chi.-Kent L. Rev. 1403, 1425 (2001); Elizabeth M. Iglesias, *Global Markets, Racial Spaces, and the Role of Critical Race Theory in the Struggle for Community Control of Investments: An Institutional Class Analysis,* 45 Vill. L. Rev. 1037, 1072 (2000). For an example of a non-neoclassical economist's critique, *see* Warren J. Samuels, *Maximization of Wealth as Justice: An Essay on Posnerian Law and Economics as Policy Analysis,* 60 Tex. L. Rev. 147 (1981).

3. Jennifer Nedelsky makes a similar point about the "mysterious" ways in which mainstream legal scholarship maintains the division between the public and private, and between government regulation and the market, while giving lip service to legal realist critiques of these dichotomies. Nedelsky, *Private Property and the Limits of American Constitutionalism: The Madisonian Framework and Its Legacy* 255 (U. of Chicago Press 1990).

4. Elizabeth Meese & Alice Parker, *"Grins . . . without the Cat": Introductory Remarks on "The Difference Within,"* in *The Difference Within: Feminism and Critical Theory* 3 (Elizabeth Meese & Alice Parker eds., John Benjamins Publishing Company 1989).

5. See, e.g., Martha A. Fineman, *Cracking the Foundational Myths: Independence, Autonomy, and Self-Sufficiency,* ch. 9, this vol.; Fran Olsen, *The Myth of State Intervention in the Family,* 4 J.L. Reform 835 (1985).

6. *See* Jacques Derrida, *Of Grammatology* 141–64 (Gayatri Chakravorty Spivak trans., Johns Hopkins Univ. Press 1976).

7. *See* Martha T. McCluskey, *The Illusion of Efficiency in Workers' Compensation "Reform,"* 50 Rutgers L. Rev. 657, 780 (1998) [hereinafter McCluskey, *Illusion of Efficiency*].

8. *See* Valentine M. Moghadam, *Gender and the Global Economy* in *Revisioning Gender* 128, 134–47 (Myra Marx Ferree, Judith Lorber, & Beth B. Hess eds., Sage 1999) (discussing the "feminization of labor" in the recently restructured global market and how "free market" structural adjustment policies have increased female poverty).

9. For a critical analysis of this crisis and subsequent reforms, *see* McCluskey, *Illusion of Efficiency, supra* note 7, at 657.

10. *See* Martha T. McCluskey, *Insurer Moral Hazard in the Workers' Compensation Crisis: Reforming Cost Inflation, Not Rate Suppression,* 5 Employee Rts. Emp. Pol'y J. 55, 72–83 (2001) [hereinafter McCluskey, *Insurer Moral Hazard*].

11. *See* McCluskey, *Illusion of Efficiency, supra* note 7, at 780; Allard E. Dembe, *Occupation and Disease: How Social Factors Affect the Conception of Work-Related Disorders* (Yale U. Press 1996).

12. For an example of this standard story, *see* Patricia M. Danzon & Scott E. Harrington, *Rate Regulation of Workers' Compensation Insurance: How Price Controls Increase Costs* ix–xxi, 1–11 (AEI Press 1998).

13. *Id.* at 15.

14. Derrida, *supra* note 6, at 145.

15. Spencer L. Kimball, *The Purpose of Insurance Regulation: A Preliminary Inquiry in the Theory of Insurance Law*, 45 Minn. L. Rev. 471, 523 (1961).

16. M. R. Greenberg, *Why Workers' Comp Is Crippled*, N.Y. Times 11 (Aug. 16, 1992).

17. *Id.*

18. *Id.*

19. Danzon & Harrington, *supra* note 12, at 9, 108, 141.

20. Scott E. Harrington & Patricia M. Danzon, *Rate Regulation, Safety Incentives, and Loss Growth in Workers' Compensation Insurance*, 73 J. Bus. 569–70 (2000).

21. Orin Kramer & Richard Briffault, *Workers' Compensation: Strengthening the Social Compact* 49 (Insurance Information Institute Press 1991).

22. *Id.* at 11, 50, 52.

23. Derrida, *supra* note 6, at 145.

24. *See* Danzon & Harrington, *supra* note 12, at 108–9, 118; Harrington & Danzon, *supra* note 20, at 569; Kramer & Briffault, *supra* note 21, at 52.

25. Greenberg, *supra* note 16.

26. Derrida, *supra* note 6, at 155.

27. *Id.* at 151.

28. Danzon & Harrington, *supra* note 12, at 108.

29. *Id.* at ix.

30. Kramer & Briffault, *supra* note 21, at 11 (emphasis added).

31. Greenberg, *supra* note 16.

32. *Id.*

33. Kramer & Briffault, *supra* note 21, at 13.

34. *Id.* at 9.

35. *Id.* at 4.

36. Greenberg, *supra* note 16.

37. *Id.*

38. *See* Kramer & Briffault, *supra* note 21, at 11 (criticizing "politicized" rate-making process).

39. *See* Derrida, *supra* note 6, at 149.

40. *Id.* at 151.

41. Greenberg, *supra* note 16.

42. Harrington & Danzon, *supra* note 20, at 569–70.

43. *See* George Priest, *The Current Insurance Crisis and Modern Tort Law*, 96 Yale L.J. 1521, 1547 (1987).

44. Greenberg, *supra* note 16.

45. Derrida, *supra* note 6, at 314.

46. Peter Kerr, *A Showdown on Workers' Compensation in Maine*, N.Y. Times 36 (Aug. 9, 1992) (quoting Grover Czech, vice president of Maryland Insurance Group).

47. *See* McCluskey, *Insurer Moral Hazard, supra* note 10, at 106–8.

48. *See id.*; Donald M. Kreis, *The "King" of Workers' Comp*, 23 Maine Times 2 (Sept. 6, 1991).

49. McCluskey, *Insurer Moral Hazard, supra* note 10, at 108.

50. Id. at 115–31.

51. *See* Terry Thomason, Timothy P. Schmidle, & John F. Burton Jr., *Workers' Compensation: Benefits, Costs, and Safety under Alternative Insurance Arrangements* 287 (W. E. Upjohn Inst. 2001) (concluding that the change from administered pricing to comprehensive deregulation is associated with lower employer costs); *id.* at 176–77 (summarizing previous empirical studies correlating deregulation with lower insurance costs but concluding that the overall evidence from these studies is inconsistent).

52. *See* the World Trade Organization website, http://www.wto.org/english/thewto_e.

53. *Id.* at http://www.wto.org/english/thewto_e/inbrief_e.

54. Gary Burtless, Robert Z. Lawrence, Robert E. Litan, & Robert J. Shapiro, *Globaphobia: Confronting Fears about Open Trade* 9 (Brookings Inst. 1998).

55. Thomas L. Friedman, *Senseless in Seattle,* N.Y. Times A23 (Dec. 1, 1999) (describing anti-WTO protesters).

56. Brett D. Schaefer, *The Bretton Woods Institutions: History and Reform Proposals* 68 (Economic Freedom Project of the Heritage Foundation 2000). The fine print on the cover of this report, whose author is a senior staff analyst of the foundation, notes that "nothing here is to be construed as necessarily reflecting the views of The Heritage Foundation" or as lobbying, but I take this disclaimer on writings funded and distributed by the foundation more as a protection of the foundation's economic interests than as a real denial that this report represents political views it supports.

57. *Id.*

58. Scott Lehigh, *Opposing Forces Old Discontent Reached High Heat in Seattle,* Boston Globe D1 (Dec. 4, 1999).

59. Schaefer, *supra* note 56, at 71.

60. Bernard Hoekman & Michel Kostecki, *The Political Economy of the World Trading System: From GATT to WTO* 21, 57–58 (Oxford U. Press 1995). This theory applies to large countries capable of changing the terms of trade; for small countries, unilateral free trade is likely to be economically efficient, in the typical neoclassical analysis.

61. Friedman, *supra* note 55.

62. *Id.*

63. *Who Needs the WTO?* Economist (Dec. 4, 1999).

64. Michael Moore, *In Praise of the Future,* WTO website, http://www.wto.org/english/news_e/spmm_e/spmm34_e.htm.

65. *Id.*

66. *Who Needs the WTO? supra* note 63.

67. Ramesh Ponnuru, *After Seattle,* 51 National Review (Dec. 31, 1999).

68. *Who Needs the WTO? supra* note 63.

69. *See* Schaefer, *supra* note 56, at 67–68.

70. *Clueless in Seattle,* Economist (Dec. 4, 1999).

71. Testimony of Carla Hills, Senate Finance Committee (Feb. 27, 2001).

72. Schaefer, *supra* note 56, at 88.

73. Burtless et al., *supra* note 54, at 94.

74. *Id.* at 93–94.

75. *Id.* at 94.

76. Charles M. Gastle & Elizabeth Bennett-Martin, *Demonizing the World Trade Organization Isn't Helpful,* 19 Lawyers Weekly (Canada) (Dec. 17, 1999).

77. Marie-Josee Kravis, *World Leaders Failing Free Trade: Clinton, Gore Waffle While Protesters Wage Unjust War on WTO,* National Post C07 (Dec. 3, 1999).

78. *While the WTO Burns,* Wall St. J. (Dec. 2, 1999) (editorial).

79. Kravis, *supra* note 77, at C07.

80. Paul Krugman, *Workers vs. Workers,* N.Y. Times sec. 4, at 17 (May 21, 2000).

81. *While the WTO Burns, supra* note 78.

82. Schaefer, *supra* note 56, at 84.

83. *Id.* at 85.

84. *Globalisation Blues,* Economist (Sept. 30, 2000).

85. *See* Schaefer, *supra* note 56, at 90.

86. *While the WTO Burns, supra* note 78.

87. Burtless et al., *supra* note 54, at 98–99.

88. *Id.* at 122.

89. For more detailed explanation of the indeterminacy (and politics) of "free trade" principles and the underlying pseudo-scientific concept of comparative advantage, *see* Michael H. Davis

& Dana Neacsu, *Legitimacy, Globally: The Incoherence of Free Trade Practice, Global Economics, and Their Governing Principle of Political Economy,* 69 U. Mo. Kan. City L. Rev. 733, 757–90 (2001).

90. *See* Testimony of Alan Greenspan, chairman of the Federal Reserve, Senate Finance Committee (Apr. 4, 2001) (arguing against dealing with "adjustment trauma" by "thwarting competition").

91. *Id.*

92. *The Standard Question,* Economist (Jan. 15, 2000) (citing arguments of Keith Maskus but questioning the political merits of continuing to distinguish between intellectual property and labor or environmental standards).

93. John O. McGinnis & Mark L. Movsesian, *The World Trade Constitution,* 114 Harv. L. Rev. 511, 555 n. 251 (2000). They acknowledge, however, that intellectual property standards might be suspect on "sovereignty" grounds, which they distinguish from "economic" grounds. *Id.*

94. *Id.* at 553.

95. *Id.* at 555.

96. For an insightful critical analysis of neoliberal economic arguments against linking human rights standards to trade policy, *see* Elizabeth M. Iglesias, *Human Rights in International Economic Law: Locating Latinas/os in the Linkage Debate,* 28 U. Miami Inter-Am. L. Rev. 361, 383–86 (1997).

97. *See* McGinnis & Movsesian, *supra* note 93, at 555 n. 251.

98. Burtless et al., *supra* note 54, at 125.

99. *See* McGinnis & Movsesian, *supra* note 93, at 542, 566, 549, 556–58.

100. *Id.* at 556.

101. *See* John O. McGinnis, *The Political Economy of Global Multilateralism,* 1 Chi. J. Int'l. L. 381, 392 (2000).

102. McGinnis & Movsesian, *supra* note 93, at 515–16; John O. McGinnis, *World Trade Agreements: Advancing the Interests of The Poorest of Poor,* 34 Ind. L.R. 1361, 1362 (2001).

103. Bhushan Bahree & Helene Cooper, *One Firm, One Land, Peril WTO Accord,* Wall St. J. (Dec. 10, 1997) (International edition).

104. Helene Cooper & Bhushan Bahree, *WTO Reaches Accord as Asians Agree to Open Finance Industry to Foreigners,* Wall St. J. (Dec. 15, 1997).

105. *See* Derrida, *supra* note 6, at 315.

PART III

THE COSTS OF
THE FREE MARKET

*Theories of Collective Responsibility
and the Withering Away of Public Goods*

The United States is now at a significant crossroads with respect to certain basic political principles. At the forefront of policy discussions are numerous very vocal advocates arguing about whether the federal government should or can play a role in regulating the U.S. economy, and what the limits of that role might be. A related argument involves the extent to which the federal government should be responsible for subsidizing individual U.S. citizens who are poor and/or parents by providing them with social goods, referred to in the United States as "welfare." The broader question concerns the extent to which we choose to address the worst of the excesses resulting from the growing gap between the wealthy and the poor in our late capitalist society. To what extent will we take responsibility for those individuals who are mired in poverty and who, for any number of reasons, cannot earn a living wage? Beyond our accountability to individuals who are destitute, how responsible are we as a society for providing basic social services such as universal quality education and health care—benefits taken for granted in other industrialized democracies?

Although arguments for restraint and limited governmental action have consistently been offered by members of the political and intellectual elites, it is only since the Reagan revolution of the 1980s that these ideas have become increasingly foregrounded in ways that have had a real impact on our concept of public responsibility in American society. One result has been public support and acceptance of the dismantling of the federal welfare state over the past decade and a movement away from public education, as evidenced in the creation of charter schools and school voucher programs. Although it is true that the disdain for notions of collective responsibility and a public society, currently expressed in political rhetoric, cannot be directly traced to the Law and Economics movement, it is clear that a number of its main themes—in particular, efficiency and profit maximization at all costs—are echoed in conservative political rhetoric.

The essays in this part address the influence of concepts and ideas from the field of economics on policy and political discussions at the state and national levels. Martha Fineman's essay, "Cracking the Foundational Myths: Independence, Autonomy, and Self-Sufficiency," attacks head-on the myths that historically have played a role in defining how the United States constitutes itself as a political society. Fineman uses the concepts of *inevitable* and *derivative* dependency to interrogate the extent to which one can truly understand either the state or the market without examining the role of family in relation to such realms. Fineman points out that an obsessive focus on individual rights vis-à-vis the state and individual independence and efficiency vis-à-vis the market ignores the realities of dependency and the contribution of caretakers. She urges that we value notions of collective responsibility, altruism, and empathy that are often brought to light by focusing on intimacy, caretaking, and dependency within society.

Martha McCluskey's essay, "The Politics of Economics in Welfare Reform," complements the Fineman piece and explores the manner in which redistribution is set out to be incompatible with efficiency. Proponents of welfare frequently accept the view that redistribution may not be efficient, but then nonetheless they stress the *social* value of redistribution. McCluskey, however, argues that it is important to address head-on the function of efficiency-based arguments that seek to curtail governmental spending on welfare. Such arguments, McCluskey notes, are presented as scientifically rigorous but are in fact based on political choices and moral judgments and not on economic principles. McCluskey then calls for a rethinking of the distinction within political rhetoric between what is "politically correct" and what is "economically correct."

Linda McClain's essay, "Deterring 'Irresponsible' Reproduction through Welfare Reform," further illuminates the debate within society around welfare. McClain focuses on the rhetoric of incentives surrounding welfare reform. Proponents of reform argue that the availability of welfare encourages women to procreate irresponsibly at the expense of the public fisc. McClain discusses the manner in which an obsessive focus on personal responsibility within this rhetoric ignores economic realities and initial allocations of wealth. The fact that there are individuals who are not able to participate within economic society on equal terms, traditionally African Americans and women, is a function of the failure of the market, not a function of a failure in moral responsibility.

Finally, Myra Strober's essay, "Feminist Economics: Implications for Education," discusses the role of education in choosing the "characteristics of human beings it wishes to endorse and elaborate and which it wishes to change." Strober notes that "imperialist" mainstream economics has made inroads into education that ought be noted and considered in terms of its effects on our development of a public society. Strober is troubled that many view the primary role of education to be one of providing a training ground for future workers in the economy; she notes that neoclassical economic concepts such as "self-interest, scarcity, maximization, choice, efficiency, value, and competition" have influenced education to a considerable extent. Strober challenges us to view the dangers of such inroads and states that although certain economic constructs are of use within education and to educational policy, the specific neoclassical economic constructs currently in vogue in educational curricula reflect a version of human character as narrowly self-interested. This depiction does not necessarily comport with views of human character in other economic models, including those of traditional economic writers such as Adam Smith.

CHAPTER 9

Cracking the Foundational Myths

Independence, Autonomy, and Self-Sufficiency

Martha Albertson Fineman

One complaint feminist legal theorists have is that most mainstream work fails to take into account institutions of intimacy such as the family.[1] Discussions focusing on the market, for example, typically treat the family as separate, governed by an independent set of expectations and rules. The family may be viewed as a unit of consumption, even as a unit of production, but it is analytically detachable from the essential structure and functioning of the market.

Similarly, when theoretical focus is turned to the nature and actions of the state, the family (if it is considered at all) is cast as a separate autonomous institution. Of course, the state may explicitly address the family as a site of regulation or policy, but in nonfamily contexts the extent of societal reliance on the family is un- or undertheorized. There is little recognition that policy discussions about economic and social issues implicitly incorporate a certain image of the family, assuming its structure and functioning.

In the same ways, theorists who focus on the individual seem to deny the family any potential relevance or theoretical significance in their work. Jurisprudential constructions of justice or liberty, for example, consider the individual as the relevant unit of analysis. The implications of the fact that individuals exist in family or relational contexts are largely ignored. It is no surprise, therefore, that little attention has been paid to how assumptions about the family affect the theories expounded about market and state or the nature of the individual. For example, few theorists recognize how reliant are their particular visions of the world—as "just" or "efficient" or "natural" or "empirically based"—on the consensus that the family is the institution primarily responsible for dependency.

It is my contention that this reliance on what I have termed the "assumed family" distorts analysis and policy. The family assumed is a specific ideological construct with a particular population and a gendered form that allow us to privatize individual dependency, pretending that it is not a public problem. Furthermore, the gendered nature of this assumed family is essential to the maintenance and continuance of our foundational myths of individual independence, autonomy, and self-sufficiency.[2] This assumed family also masks the dependency of society and all its public institutions on the uncompensated and unrecognized dependency work assigned to caretakers within the private family.

We focus in economic and other important public policy discussions on the appropriate relationship between market and state, and the family is relegated to the "private" sphere. Discussions proceed as though the policies that are designed to affect these institutions in the public sphere had only few implications for the unexamined private family. Even more fundamental, the discussions fail to grasp the fact that the actual (as contrasted with the assumed) family might profoundly affect the possibilities of success and failure of policies created for the market and the state.

Public and Private Concepts

To point out the neglect of the family in legal and policy theory is not the same as concluding that the family has been considered an unimportant institution. In fact, the importance of the family is asserted in its very segregation from other areas of human endeavor. This separation is exemplified in the often-repeated characterization of family law as one of three *separate* pillars of civil society—the other two being property and contract. Another manifestation of this dual characterization of the family as both separate and essential is the division of the world (and law) into the realms of the "public" and the "private."[3]

Not only is the family perceived as occupying the private sphere. It is conceptualized as embodying values and norms very different from the institutions occupying the public sphere, particularly those of the market. Family relationships are cast as different in functioning and form than relationships existing in the public world. Families are altruistic institutions held together by affectional bonds. Of course, any serious consideration of the family reveals that it is a very public institution, assigned an essential public role within society.[4] The family is delegated primary responsibility for dependency.

In this essay, I want to bring the family, or more explicitly the dependency hidden within the assumed family, into view. An assessment of the appropriateness of the aspirations and expectations we have for the family should be central to the development of all policy and the consideration of all social theory, but it is crucial to one of the most compelling problems facing society at the end of the twentieth century—the increasing inequitable and unequal distribution of societal resources and the corresponding poverty of women and children.

Collective Responsibility

Perhaps the most important task for those concerned with the welfare of poor mothers and their children, as well as other vulnerable members of society, is the articulation of a theory of collective responsibility for dependency. The idea of collective responsibility must be developed as a claim of "right" or entitlement to support and accommodation on the part of caretakers. It must be grounded on an appreciation of the value of caretaking labor.[5] A further, important concern is to ensure that any theory of collective responsibility not concede the right of collective control over individual, intimate decisions such as whether and when to reproduce or how to form one's family.[6]

The rhetorical and ideological rigidity with which contemporary policy debates have been conducted makes the claim of collective responsibility a particularly difficult task at the end of the twentieth century. Core components of America's founding myths, such as the sacredness of individual independence, autonomy, and self-sufficiency, have been ossified, used as substitutes for analysis, and thus eclipse rather than illuminate the debate.[7]

I do not reject these core concepts. I do, however, insist that we have a responsibility to reexamine them in the context of both our present society and the needs and aspirations of people today. We must view these ideals with the complexity they deserve, perhaps redefining them in the process. A commitment to a process of ongoing reexamination of core concepts recognizes that even if we are absolutely confident that we know historic meaning (which we are not), the demands of justice as well as perceptions of legitimacy require that our implementation of foundational principles resonates in the current realities of our lives.

Justice requires constant mediation between articulated historic values and current realities. It is not found in abstract pronouncements. Therefore, our understanding of independence, autonomy, and self-sufficiency should be evolving as societal knowledge, realizations, aspirations, and circumstances change. Unfortunately, the political and governmental institutions that should be facilitating and encouraging debates and reconsideration are currently partisan and polarizing in the methods they use, actually impeding understanding and exploration.

Dependency and Social Debt

Independence and self-sufficiency are complementary terms in our political discourse.[8] Their dichotomous terms of dependence and subsidy are also complementary, viewed as occurring in tandem. Both dependence and subsidy have been successfully used in a simplistic and divisive manner by politicians, social conservatives, and advocates of small government in order to control and limit contemporary policy discussions.[9]

Dependence is negatively compared with the desirable status of independence, subsidy with the meritorious self-sufficiency. Independence and self-sufficiency are set up as transcendent values, attainable aspirations for all members of society. Simplified, pejorative notions of dependence and subsidy are joined, and condemnation or pity is considered an appropriate response for those unable to live up to the ideals—those who are dependent and in need of subsidy.

In fact, dependency is assumed if an individual is the recipient of certain governmental subsides. The label of dependency becomes an argument against governmental social welfare transfers. Policymakers argue that the goal should be independence, and the subsidy ended so the individual can learn to be self-sufficient and independent.

It is puzzling as well as paradoxical that the term *dependency* has such tremendous negative connotations, its very existence prompting and justifying mean-spirited and ill-conceived political responses such as the 1995 welfare "reform." Far from being pathological, avoidable, and the result of individual failings, dependency is a universal and inevitable part of the human development; it is inherent in the human condition.

All of us were dependent as children, and many of us will be dependent as we age, become ill, or suffer disabilities. In this sense, dependency is "inevitable." Note that the examples with which I have chosen to illustrate this category of "inevitable dependency" are biological or physical in nature. Biological dependencies do not exhaust the potential range of situations of dependence, however. For example, in addition to biological dependence, one may be economically, psychologically, or emotionally dependent on others.

These other forms of dependence may even tend to accompany the physical type, which I have labeled inevitable. I distinguish economic, psychological, and emotional dependency because they are not generally understood to represent universal phenomena. As a result, assertions about their inevitability in each individual's life would be controversial. It is the characteristics of universality and inevitability (which indisputably accompany biological dependence) that are central to my argument that there is a societal or collective responsibility for dependency.

In other words, the realization that biological dependency is both inevitable and universal is theoretically important. Upon this foundational realization is built a claim for justice or right—a demand for valuing and accommodating the labor done by caretakers in our society.

I argue that the caretaking work undertaken in response to inevitable dependency creates a collective or societal debt. Each and every member of society is obligated by this debt—it transcends individual circumstances. We need not be elderly or ill or any longer children to be held responsible for this debt. Nor can we satisfy or discharge our responsibility within our individual, private families. Merely being financially generous with our own mother or duly supporting our own wife will not suffice to satisfy our share of the societal debt owed to caretakers.

My argument that the caretaking debt is a collective one is based on the fact that biological dependency is inherent to the human condition, and therefore of necessity it is of collective or societal concern. Just as individual dependency needs must be met if an individual is to survive, collective dependency needs must be met if a society is to survive and perpetuate itself.

The mandate that the state (collective society) respond to dependency, therefore, is not a matter of altruism or empathy (which are individual responses often resulting in charity); instead, the mandate is primary and essential because such response is fundamentally society preserving.

If infants or ill persons are not cared for, nurtured, nourished, and perhaps loved, they will perish. We could say, therefore, that they owe an individual debt to their caretakers. The obligation, however, is not theirs alone. It should also be apparent that a broader sense of obligation is demanded, because without this type of caretaking in the aggregate there could be no society. Caretaking labor produces and reproduces society. It provides the citizens, the workers, the voters, the consumers, the students, and so on who populate our society and its institutions. The provision of this population is possible because of the uncompensated labor of caretakers. This labor is an unrecognized subsidy not only to the individuals who directly receive it but, more significantly, to the entire society.

Institutions and Dependency

Society-preserving tasks, such as dependency work, are commonly delegated. The delegation is accomplished through the establishment and maintenance of societal institutions. For example, the armed services were established to attend to the collective need for national defense. They are structured simultaneously as the responsibility of only some designated members (volunteers or draftees) and of all members of society (taxpayers and voters).

This dual and complementary responsibility is consistent with our deeply held beliefs about how rights and obligations are accrued and imposed in a just society—collective obligations have both an individual and a collective dimension. Certain members of society may be recruited, volunteer, even be drafted for service, but they have a right to be compensated for their service from collective resources. They also have a right to the necessary tools to perform their assigned tasks and to guarantee that they will be protected by rules and policies that facilitate their performance. Caretakers should have the same right to have their society-preserving labor supported and facilitated. Provision of the means for their task should be considered the responsibility of the collective society.

This is not the way society has responded to caretaking, however. The most common form of social accommodation for dependency has been its assignment to the institution of the private family. Within that family, dependency is further delegated. Privatized dependency inevitably becomes the responsibility of the family equivalent of volunteer or draftee—the person in the gendered role of mother (or grandmother or daughter or daughter-in-law or wife or sister).

Even though dependency work benefits society, the resources necessary for caretaking have not been considered the responsibility of the collective society. Instead, each individual, private family is ideally and ideologically conceived as responsible for its own members and their dependency. The need to call on collective resources, such as welfare assistance, is considered a family as well as an individual failure, deserving of condemnation and stigma.

Derivative Dependency

The assignment of responsibility for the burdens of dependency to the family in the first instance, and within the family to women, is unjust. This arrangement has significant material consequences for the caretaker. This obvious observation introduces an often overlooked form of dependency that must be explicitly distinguished and specifically considered in social policy—derivative dependency. Derivative dependency arises on the part of the person who assumes responsibility for the care of an inevitably dependent person. The term captures the simple point that those who care for others are themselves dependent on resources in order to undertake that care. Some of those needs are for monetary or material resources, whereas others are more related to institutional or structural arrangements.

A consideration of derivative dependency reveals that the caretaker may experience both economic and structural problems. Some of the economic problems stem from the fact that within families, caretaking work is unpaid.[10] It is also undervalued in the market. In addition, this unpaid labor interferes with the pursuit and development of wage labor options. Caretaking labor saps energy and efforts that might be invested in career or market activities, those things that produce economic rewards.

There are forgone opportunities and costs associated with caretaking. Even caretakers who work in the paid labor force typically have more tenuous ties to the public sphere than do noncaretakers because they must also accommodate caretaking demands in the private. These types of costs are not distributed among all beneficiaries of caretaking (institutional or individual). Unjustly, the costs associated with caretaking are typically borne by the caretaker herself.

The structural problems are rooted in the fact that caretakers must interact with other societal institutions. They must do their caretaking within contexts, and often they need accommodations to help them fulfill their caretaking responsibilities. Many caretakers today also must work. Far from structurally accommodating or facilitating caretaking, workplaces operate according to premises that are incompatible with obligations for dependency. Workplace expectations compete with the demands of caretaking, and we assume that workers are those independent and autonomous individuals free to work long and regimented hours.

Derivative dependency, although it is inevitably associated with the tasks of caretaking, is not universal (and therefore it is not inevitably a part of each individual's experience). Derivative dependency is socially defined and structured in the context of existing societal institutions. Many people in our society totally escape taking care of others; in fact, they may be freed for other pursuits as a result of the caretaking labor of others.

Derivative dependency is culturally and socially assigned in an inequitable manner according to a script rooted in ideologies, particularly those of capitalism and patriarchy. These scripts function at an unconscious (and therefore unexamined) level, channeling our beliefs and feelings about what is considered natural and what are appropriate institutional arrangements.

When individuals act according to these scripts, in ways that are consistent with prevailing ideology and institutional arrangements, we say they have chosen their path from the available options. The construction of this notion of individual choice allows us to avoid general responsibility for the inequity of caretaking and justify maintenance of the status quo.[11] We ignore the fact that individual choice occurs within the constraints of social conditions. These constraints include ideology, history, and tradition, which funnel decisions into prescribed channels, often operating in a practical and symbolic manner to limit options.[12]

As it now stands in this society, derivative dependents are expected to get both economic and structural resources from within the family. The market is unresponsive and uninvolved, and the state is perceived as a last resort for financial resources, the refuge of the failed family. A caretaker who must resort to governmental assistance may do so only if she can demonstrate, through a highly stigmatized process, that she is needy.

Subsidy

Subsidy is nothing more than the allocation of collective resources to some persons or endeavors rather than to other persons or endeavors because a social judgment has been made that those in the first category are in some way "entitled"—the subsidy is justified. Entitlement to subsidy is asserted through a variety of justifications such as the status of the persons receiving the subsidy—their past contributions to the social good or their needs. Often subsidy is justified because of the position the subsidized persons hold or the potential value of the endeavor they have undertaken to the larger society.

Typically subsidy is thought of as monetary or economic assistance. Subsidy can also be supplied in the way we organize social structures or create and enforce social and cultural expectations, however. Understood in this way, particularly in the context of the discussion of the nature of inevitable and derivative dependency, it is obvious that subsidy is also universal. The recognition of subsidy is nothing more than the recognition that we all exist in context, in social and cultural institutions that facilitate and support us and our endeavors.

In complex modern societies, no one is self-sufficient either economically or socially. We all live subsidized lives. Sometimes the benefits we receive are public and financial; for example, farmers receive funds through governmental direct transfer programs. Public subsidies can also be indirect, such as the benefits given as a result of tax policy. Private economic subsidy systems include foundations, religious institutions, and other charities.[13] But subsidy can also be nonmonetary, such as the subsidy provided by the uncompensated labor of others in caring for us and our dependency needs.

It seems clear that all of us receive one or the other or both types of subsidy throughout our lives. Therefore, the interesting question in our subsidy-shaped society has to be why only some subsidies are differentiated and stigmatized while others are hidden. In substantial part, subsidies are hidden when they are not called subsidies (or welfare, or the dole) but termed "investments," "incentives," or "earned" when they are supplied by government and "gifts," "charity," or the product of familial "love" when they are contributions of caretaking labor.

A More Responsive State

More is needed than just my attempts to complicate current notions of dependency and subsidy. In order to move beyond simplistic catch words and engage in a national debate over the vision we want to have of ourselves as a society, it is necessary to have some mechanism for generating and sustaining discussion. Although my vision is shaped by the successes of early feminist consciousness-raising techniques in changing entrenched ideas and assumptions, the forum I advocate for altering our national consciousness must be a public one, created and supported by government. A public forum comes with the responsibility that it be inclusive and, in that way, out of the control of partisan politicians.

It is important that the forum be a public responsibility, as antiquated and quaint as that idea seems at this point in our national history. In recent decades it has become apparent that the role of the state has been overtaken by the presumed inevitability of market forces. As more and more is conceded to privatization, we are rapidly losing any sense of public responsibility. Even public education is in danger of falling victim to the privatizing siege. Missing from our discourse is strong support for an active or responsive state of the kind I am trying to imagine—a public as a mediating force against private, obscured excesses and exploitation.

Although it was less successful than it might have been, President Clinton's initiative on race offers some ideas for how the government might fulfill its public responsibility to generate discussion on important national issues. A commission was created and charged with developing, encouraging, and publicizing public discussions on racial problems and issuing a report on the state of the nation in regard to race. The report suggested some on-going initiatives that might be helpful, but one tremendous benefit of the exercise was that it put people face to face in high school gymnasiums and public halls across the country and encouraged them to talk about race.

Reflecting on this process, I could not help but think that perhaps welfare reform would have taken a very different direction if the president had employed the same mechanism. I imagine that we could have generated a series of thoughtful, factually informed, and depoliticized national discussions about the nature and implications of dependency in all its complexity to counter the inaccurate and ideologically driven sloganeering that passed for political debate. We might have even begun as a nation to realize that the real measure of any welfare reform should be whether it positively improved the welfare of all our children. We might have even reached a consensus that there is a collective as well as individual parental responsibility for children. The point might have been made that in today's world, independence and self-sufficiency require a minimal amount of social resources (structural and monetary), and that the amount required increases when one has responsibility for the care of others. Dependency on resources and/or on caretakers is not a unique position in which to find oneself; it is a universal, and therefore unifying, experience.

This scenario might not have happened, of course. But at a minimum, important questions that need to be resolved and discussed in a public forum would have been raised:

- How should the need for resources for caretaking be satisfied so that caretakers can act independently, make decisions, and fulfill societal expectations in ways that best respond to their individual circumstances?
- Should caretakers be primarily dependent on the family for the resources necessary to accomplish their tasks?
- Given the tenuous status of marriage in this society (where the divorce rate continues to hover around 50 percent, and women are expected to be wage earners as well as wives and mothers), how can politicians continue to serve up a traditional model of the family as the solution to poverty?
- Shouldn't the richest country in the history of the world have a family policy that goes beyond marriage as the solution for dependency?
- Specifically, doesn't the family as it exists today require substantial assistance from other societal institutions?

• Is it fair that the market and the state (both of which are totally dependent on caretaking labor and are in no way self-sufficient or independent from caretaking) escape responsibility for dependency and continue to be freeloaders (or free riders) on the backs of caretakers and families?

• Isn't it time to redistribute some responsibility for dependency by mandating that the state and the market bear their fair share of the burden?

As a result of such discussion, the very terms *independence* and *self-sufficiency* might well be redefined and reimagined in the public mind. Independence is not the same as being unattached. Independence from subsidy and support is not attainable, nor is it desirable; we want and need the contexts that sustain us. A different understanding of independence is needed and attainable. Independence is gained when an individual has the basic resources that enable her or him to act consistent with the tasks and expectations imposed by the society. This form of independence should be every citizen's birthright, but independence in this sense can only be achieved when individual choices are relatively unconstrained by inequalities, particularly those inequalities that arise from poverty. Independence (as well as justice) requires that those who are assigned vital societal functions are also provided with the wherewithal to accomplish those tasks. This is a state or collective responsibility, and it may not be relegated to potentially exploitative private institutions.

The Active State

To move from our current situation to a more just resolution of the dilemma of caretaking and dependency, we need more than a responsive state. The state must also be an active participant in shaping and monitoring other societal institutions. One fundamental task would be monitoring and preventing the exploitation and appropriation of the labor of some citizens through institutional and ideological arrangements. This appropriation and exploitation must be prevented even when the justification given is that it is for the good of the majority. Further, this exploitation must be prevented even in contexts in which social constraints and conventions coerce consent from the laborer.

In this endeavor, the state must use its regulatory and redistributive authority to ensure that those things that are not valued or are undervalued in market or marriage are nonetheless publicly and politically recognized as socially productive and are given value. Conferral of value requires the transfer of some economic resources from the collective to caretakers, through mechanisms for taxing those who receive the benefits of caretaking and compensating those who do the caretaking. Other societies complete this transfer in a variety of ways, such as using tax revenues to provide child-care allowances and universal benefits that assist caretakers or to guarantee a basic income.

But money is not enough.[14] The active state must also structure accommodation of the needs of caretaking into society's institutions.

The fact is that today workers (at least some of them) must shoulder the burdens assigned to the family, while market institutions are relieved of such responsibility (and are even free to punish workers who have trouble combining market and domestic labor). The state must ensure that market institutions positively respond to dependency burdens. Workers cannot be assumed to be independent and unencumbered. Often they are dually responsible for economic and caretaking activities. Restructuring workplaces to reflect that reality would more equitably distribute the burdens of dependency and forge a more just relationship between family and market institutions.[15]

Conclusion

My book *The Autonomy Myth: A Theory of Dependency* contains a dystopian fantasy in which I imagine what changes would have to be made to really foster our self-proclaimed national ideals of independence, autonomy, and self-sufficiency. This exercise is not focused on the welfare mother but on the rest of us. I contend that if we seriously wanted a world in which each individual is assumed to stand alone, to rise or fall on her or his own individual merit and be beholden to no one for her or his success, we must shape our policies to facilitate that model of society. As it stands now, we give lip service to ideals in a world in which policy and law protect and perpetuate existing and historic inequality, a world in which some individuals are subsidized and supported in their "independence" while other individuals are left mired in poverty or burdened by responsibilities not equitably shared.

For example, a society that truly sought independence as an ideal for individuals would institute a 100 percent inheritance tax. It seems obvious that inherited wealth carries with it the potential to corrupt individual initiative. Not only do we risk removing incentive with inheritance, but we also distort the meritocracy. People should not be deprived of the opportunity to demonstrate their inherent merit and worth by being burdened with the wealth of their fathers.

Of course, inherited wealth is not the only distorting factor that interferes with independence and the realization of a true meritocracy. There are also existing and unequal economic and social advantages, and it is unlikely that they will ever be totally eradicated. I struggled with how to address this fact and concluded that a lottery system is the most appropriate and just way to distribute disparate social goods.[16] The lottery would not eliminate differences in social conditions, but advantages and disadvantages would be distributed by chance. This might eventually ensure a much more level playing field, but I am willing for purposes of this exercise to concede that social equality is not attainable. If that is so and we believe that each individual can demonstrate merit and ability independent of the burdens presented by social and economic contexts, we can at least democratize the process whereby benefits and burdens are disbursed.

For example, if we wanted to put each individual to the test, we might at birth assign each child a Social Security number along with a list of the professions they might legitimately pursue, appropriately grouped into categories such as "service worker" or "professional." We could also assign the schools they would be permitted to attend. If an individual was not inclined to be satisfied with her or his lot later in life, she or he would have to find a willing person with whom to bargain or trade in order to alter the luck of the draw. To further equalize contexts, perhaps each child should be compelled to spend time in a number of different neighborhoods during childhood—two or three years in Westchester would be balanced by equivalent time in Harlem, Alabama, Ohio, and California.

The point of this exercise is not to seriously suggest that this is what anyone would want but to point out that context does matter. We do not begin our lives in equal circumstances but in unequal contexts. Society's winners and losers become winners or losers in large part because of benefits and privileges or disadvantages and burdens conferred by family position and unequal distribution of social and economic goods. The approach to resolving this type of inequality is not found in simplistic and hypocritical prescriptions and ideological placebos of independence, autonomy, and self-sufficiency.

Notes

1. This essay is based on my book *The Autonomy Myth: A Theory of Dependency* (New Press 2004), in which I argue that there is a compelling need for us to reconsider the basic distribution of responsibility for dependency among societal institutions, specifically the family, the state, and the market. This essay sets forth my ideas about dependency and suggests a mechanism for increasing public discussion about the vision of society we are collectively creating in- and outside of our political institutions.

2. Expressed as ideals, these abstract characteristics are theoretically attainable by individuals only because we assume that families exist and perform their functions—producing, nurturing, and providing for their members.

3. The characterization of the market in this public–private scheme is interesting. It is cast as public vis-à-vis the family but private vis-à-vis the state, seeming to gain the advantage of each category. In this regard, it is interesting that when the comparison is one of market versus family, the "private" sphere of the family is subject to heavy public regulation, mostly because it retains aspects of status and is not governed by contract. In contrast, the "public" arena of the marketplace is governed by bodies of designated "private" law such as contract. These contrary characterizations have ideological nuances.

4. For a historian's perspective on this topic, *see* Nancy F. Cott, *Giving Character to Our Whole Civil Polity: Marriage and the Public Order in the Late Nineteenth Century*, in *U.S. History as Women's History* (L. K. Kerber, A. Kessler-Harris, & K. K. Sklar eds., Oxford Univ. Press

1995). Cott states that "one might go so far as to say the institution of marriage and the modern state have been mutually constitutive . . . one of the principal means that the state can use to prove its existence . . . is its authority over marriage." *Id* at 109.

5. I mean to expand this notion of value beyond the labor theory of value to consider as labor things not previously considered as such. The value is measured in and by social policy, not market indicators, and demands accommodation as well as monetary subsidy.

6. This last point is an important one, but this essay deals mainly with the articulation of the claim for collective responsibility. In the larger work, I use the model of Social Security to address how subsidy can be proffered without supervising the use of the subsidy by the recipients.

7. In addition, when the subject under consideration is caretaking, it is necessary to develop a rhetoric to counter the pervasiveness of market ideology that privileges the economic and confines assessments of success, progress, and worth largely in monetary terms.

8. Autonomy is related to both of these core concepts, and therefore attention to this ideal will be a by-product of the more extended consideration of independence and self-sufficiency.

9. Liberal commentators have also used the terms in this way, falling into the dominant conceptions. See Gwendolyn Mink, *The End of Welfare* (Cornell U. Press 1998).

10. Caretaking can be provided by hired help, in which case it is underpaid. I focus here on caretaking responsibilities within family roles.

11. In particular, I have been struck by two quasi-economic responses to the point that caretakers should be compensated. I refer to one as the Porsche Preference. This is the argument that if someone prefers a child, why should that choice be treated differently than any other (such as the choice to own a Porsche). Society should not subsidize either. I hope the society-preserving nature of indulgence in our preference for children helps to distinguish it from the preference of the auto enthusiast. My other argument I label the "efficiency and exploitation" model. This argument is really nothing more than the assertion that if women allow themselves to be exploited as unpaid or underpaid caretakers, then that is the most efficient resolution for the problem of caretaking and dependency and should not be disturbed. Aside from the fact that this arrangement is not working and that it results in massive poverty and other social ills, this type of argument also demonstrates how little economics has to offer to considerations of justice.

12. Using choice as justification for existing conditions also fails to recognize that often choice of one status or position carries with it consequences not anticipated or imagined at the time of the initial decision. For example, we may say that a woman "chose" to become a mother (societal and family imperatives aside), but does this choice mean she has also consented to the societal conditions attendant to that role and the many ways in which that status will negatively affect her economic prospects? Even if she did "consent" in that she knew she was taking risks or forgoing opportunities, is the ultimate situation in which she finds herself one that society can tolerate for some of its members? In other words, are some conditions just too oppressive or unfair to be imposed by society, even if an individual ostensibly agrees to or chooses them?

13. In *The Autonomy Myth* I focus on the "coercive institutions" of state, family, and market. I term these coercive because they are regulated and controlled by law. The voluntary institutions such as charity and religion are not mandated to address dependency, although they may supply a supplemental set of resources.

14. I argue for an idealized reintegration of the roles and responsibilities of the family, market, and state for dependency. Reintegration of family, market, and state should begin with the basic premise that there are certain fundamental social goods necessary for survival and for the caretaking of others. These social goods are economic or financial in nature and include housing, health care, a basic income, and other necessities that complement and strengthen the civil and political rights we have as citizens of a democracy. The government has a crucial and undelegatable responsibility to secure that these goods are delivered independent of the market value of any individual's labor. This responsibility marks a right of citizenship no less important and worthy of governmental protection than civil and political rights and can be realized in a variety of ways.

The governmental functions in this regard fall into two basic redistributive channels: some income redistribution is necessary to provide for basic social goods, and some redistribution of responsibility is necessary so that the market and its institutions respond to dependency. The initial governmental task must be to ensure a more equitable distribution of the wealth this society is producing, a recognition that the resources currently going to all too few are really the product of a more widespread system of contribution. This financial adjustment is necessary in recognition and satisfaction of the social debt to caretakers accrued by all. The mechanism may be a restructuring of the tax and subsidy systems, crediting (and ultimately taxing) market institutions and actors on the imputed benefits they receive from the uncompensated labor of others.

15. This restructuring can take multiple forms. A variety of proposals are necessary. For example, flexible work weeks, job sharing without penalty, paid family leave, and the guarantee of a living wage would contribute to a more sharing and equitable arrangement between market and family.

16. This is not the same thing as imagining a society from behind a "veil of ignorance." One significant difference is that I suggest we mandate rotation into existing, known, and socially accepted inequalities.

CHAPTER 10

The Politics of Economics in Welfare Reform

Martha T. McCluskey

The demise of Aid to Families with Dependent Children (AFDC), the federal income support program for single parents (primarily mothers) in poverty,[1] has come to symbolize the power of a broad movement to weaken the welfare state, both in the United States and around the world.[2] The Personal Responsibility and Work Opportunity Reconciliation Act of 1996[3] instituted major federal welfare reforms by replacing AFDC with the more restrictive and discretionary block grant program called Temporary Assistance for Needy Families (TANF). This reform legislation states that its purpose, in addition to assisting families with children, is to "increase the flexibility of States in operating a program designed to . . . end the dependence of needy parents on government benefits by promoting job preparation, work, and marriage; prevent and reduce the incidence of out-of-wedlock pregnancies . . . and encourage the formation and maintenance of two-parent families."[4]

Many feminists have analyzed how supporters of recent welfare reforms often have relied on ideologies of race-based and gender-based subordination and on rhetoric expressing overt hostility to welfare recipients.[5] Arguments against AFDC invoked race and gender stereotypes to demonize single mothers of color in particular, and unmarried low-income mothers in general, portraying them as undeserving and destructive members of society whose unrestrained sexuality and fatherless children threaten the public good. Neoconservative critics of welfare invoked a hierarchical moral order in which citizenship rights primarily go to white men, with women, children, and men of color deserving of public participation only when anchored firmly to white male authority.[6]

Feminists and other welfare advocates have less thoroughly analyzed another (although overlapping) strand of arguments against welfare. Neoliberal (or "free-market") criticisms of the welfare state, and of AFDC in particular, use purportedly neutral economic principles to justify cutbacks in antipoverty programs. This approach attempts to make social welfare restrictions a matter of sensible science rather than contentious politics or moral dictate.

Neoliberal ideology embraces neoclassical economics, which teaches that social needs are constrained by the inevitable reality of scarce resources.[7] The Law and Economics school of legal theory has been particularly successful at promoting neoliberal ideas as solutions to contemporary policy problems. The primary focus of neoliberal policy is economic efficiency, the principle of maximizing aggregate gain given scarce resources by weighing the total costs and benefits of decisions. Neoclassical economics distinguishes efficiency (or economic growth) from redistribution (or social equity). In theory, efficiency is the objective and impartial question of how to increase the size of the pie, whereas distribution is the subjective and partisan question of how to divide the pie.[8] AFDC is typically presented as a classic redistributive program that transfers wealth from taxpayers to help needy families.[9]

This neoclassical economic framework is ostensively indifferent to the choice between equity and efficiency. In the conventional wisdom, economic analysis can objectively evaluate whether a policy is efficient, but not whether economic efficiency rather than equitable redistribution is the preferable policy goal. Nonetheless, this framework implicitly puts those who favor equity over efficiency in a double bind: its theory of efficiency predicts that the choice of equity over efficiency will tend to fail on both equity and efficiency grounds. According to neoliberal "free market" theory, choosing redistribution over efficiency tends to produce three interrelated kinds of unintended economic consequences: externalities, transaction costs, and moral hazard. These economic effects constitute reductions in efficiency, in the conventional neoliberal view, so that the choice of equity over efficiency is not just a noneconomic choice but is also an economically harmful choice. But according to the standard "free market" analysis, these harmful effects also end up reducing equity along with efficiency. Because redistributive policies are likely to reduce overall economic growth, in the long run they will hurt those they aim to help—because those who are supposed to benefit most from equitable redistribution are the ones most likely to be particularly vulnerable to harm from a shrinking economic pie.[10]

To counter the double bind presented by these economic arguments, welfare advocates should not simply defend the social value of redistribution. Instead, they should also challenge efficiency's status as a distinct and distinctly "economic" value. In this essay, I explore how the three supposed economic harms of AFDC—externalities, transaction costs, and moral hazard—depend on political and moral ideology, not on economic principle. In welfare policy discussions, efficiency arguments serve as a strategy by which proponents of welfare cutbacks distort debate about the *fair* division of resources with a false pretense to an *economically correct* division of resources. To challenge criticisms of social welfare programs, feminists must attack efficiency not just as the *wrong* goal but as a misleading and inherently *political* goal.

From Redistribution to Efficiency

AFDC's rise and fall tracks a change in prevailing economic ideology. AFDC originated as part of the 1935 Social Security Act, under the name Aid to Dependent Children (ADC), and then expanded substantially during the federal War on Poverty launched in 1964.[11] These New Deal and Great Society periods that nurtured AFDC were times of strong (although strongly contested) political support for the idea that markets must be regulated to promote economic and social equality. A context of substantial popular and professional faith in the power of the federal government to shape a better society helped Presidents Roosevelt and Johnson expand national social welfare programs.

By the 1970s, however, this faith tended to be replaced by cynicism about government and its role in promoting social equity. Rising economic insecurity for many middle-class Americans (particularly male industrial workers) during the 1970s and 1980s contributed to resentment of government spending aimed at helping poor families, particularly women of color.[12] Free-market, or neoliberal, ideology gained prominence, with help from sophisticated think tanks, foundations, and lobbying efforts funded by organized business and wealthy individuals.[13] In this view, government intervention is the problem, not the solution: market risk, not government security, best helps the poor and society at large. The Reagan administration applied this ideology through policies aimed at de-regulating business and cutting taxes for the wealthy, explaining that increased investment in job-producing business would "trickle down" to benefit others.[14] Throughout the 1970s and 1980s, mainstream media discussions of Great Society programs became increasingly critical.[15]

By the end of the twentieth century, the idea that the market should be regulated to promote social values tended to be presented as "archaic" in mainstream commentary.[16] Neoliberal ideology particularly directed its anti-government criticism against the welfare state,[17] which in the United States is identified disproportionately with AFDC. Even though AFDC was a relatively small portion of the federal budget (1.5%),[18] and even though the Reagan administration's military spending drove the huge increase in government debt in the 1980s, critics presented social welfare spending as the primary problem of unaffordable "big government." For example, Heritage Foundation analysts promoted welfare reform through a publication titled *America's Failed $5.4 Trillion War on Poverty,* which exhorted Congress to control the "soaring welfare costs which are slowly bankrupting the nation."[19] Although these high welfare spending figures included numerous programs other than AFDC, AFDC was virtually the entire focus of the Heritage Foundation's discussion of the problems and solutions to welfare spending. Ending "welfare as we know it," as President Clinton described his proposals to reform AFDC, became to many a sign of an important step forward into a newly triumphant free-market era emphasizing personal initiative rather than government protection.[20]

Both major parties rationalized and promoted the 1996 welfare reform legislation by asserting that policies promoting market efficiency should be the primary solution to poverty. Former House Speaker Newt Gingrich—a leader of efforts to end AFDC—explained the international movement to curtail government antipoverty programs as the result of the failure of policies promoting "wealth redistribution over wealth production."[21] He concluded that "emphasizing redistribution is a dead loser in helping the poor, compared to focusing on the production of wealth. The objective, historic long-term fact is that societies that focus on getting rich bring everybody up at a dramatically faster rate than societies that focus on redistribution succeed in raising the bottom."[22] At the 1996 GOP national convention, Colin Powell insisted that "government assistance is a poor substitute for good jobs," which come "from a faster-growing economy where the free enterprise system is unleashed to create wealth."[23] He praised Republican Party policies for leading to "greater economic growth, which is the only real solution to the problems of poverty that keep too many Americans from sharing in the wealth of this nation."[24]

Speaking about the Democratic Party's strategy for political success in 1996, Democratic Leadership Council (DLC) director Al From explained that "[i]n 1980, we believed that the government drove the economy and economic redistribution was really the hallmark of our economic policy. . . . In 1996, we recognize that economic growth in the private sector is the prerequisite for opportunity."[25] News reports and commentators presented President Clinton's signing of the 1996 welfare reform law as the culmination of the Democratic Party's change in economic vision.[26] Even Democratic Party leaders and liberals who defend a role for government regulation and income protection generally have agreed that redistribution must remain secondary and subordinate to the goal of market efficiency.[27]

In the 2000 presidential campaign, both major parties took credit for welfare reform as an example of the success of market opportunity over government protection. George W. Bush boasted about his leadership in moving welfare recipients from "dependence on public assistance to independence and employment."[28] Speaking at the 2000 Democratic convention, presidential nominee Al Gore boasted that "I fought to end welfare as we then knew it. . . . Instead of handouts, we gave people training to go from welfare to work. And we have cut the welfare rolls in half and moved millions into good jobs."[29] DLC leader Al From continued to highlight welfare reform as one of the "bold innovations" of Clinton's New Democrat approach that has brought what he describes as unprecedented economic prosperity.[30] The *Wall Street Journal* cited the "stunning decline in welfare rolls," along with the overall increase in single mothers in the workforce, as evidence that "the

Republican welfare reform has done more for the poor than the Great Society ever imagined."[31]

Efficiency's Double Standard

This mainstream consensus embraces the neoliberal message that even for those who seek equity, efficiency is the best, or at least the primary, choice. Some acknowledge that the choice of efficiency will produce harsh effects on some poor families. For example, reports on the effects of welfare reforms show that many families who have left welfare nonetheless have serious problems feeding their families even with full-time jobs.[32] But in the neoliberal reasoning, such sacrifices are necessary to promote both equity and efficiency in the long run. Those who defend redistribution as a secondary goal, out of compassion for those harmed by the new emphasis on market efficiency, remain squeezed by the double bind: because of redistribution's harmful effects on economic growth, welfare programs and their recipients must be sharply constrained.

This dominant framework therefore presents impoverished single mothers and their advocates with a losing choice.[33] We can choose efficiency, which means directing resources *away from* single mothers in poverty (restricting AFDC benefits) to promote economic growth. Or we can choose redistribution, which directs resources *toward* families in poverty at the expense of others on whom their long-term well-being depends.

Feminist theory, however, offers strategies for resisting such double binds. Traditional equality theory similarly presented a supposedly neutral trade-off between equal treatment and special treatment that nonetheless offered feminists a similar set of losing choices.[34] In that theory, women could be "equal" at the cost of ignoring gender differences (social or biological) that justified women's subordination, such as the particular demands of pregnancy or family caretaking.[35] Or women could be "different," and therefore deserving of remedies for gender-specific harm, at the cost of making women's particular needs inherently deviant and dependent on special protection.[36] With either approach to equality, women remain subordinate.

Feminists challenged that double bind, however, by showing that it rested on a double standard of "equality" and "difference." Women's reproductive or caretaking needs are "different" and in need of "special" treatment only if one assumes as the norm a person without these needs.[37] It is the implicit standard of a stereotypical man that makes the choice of equal or different treatment so costly for women—and so beneficial for men.[38] Men who conform to traditional stereotypes can be both equal *and* different—getting a double benefit instead of a double bind—because "equal" treatment is defined to privilege their specific needs not as "differences" but as unstated norms.[39]

In equality doctrine, separating "equal" treatment from "special" treatment begs the question of whose differences should be considered the standard for equality. In welfare policy, separating "efficiency" from "redistribution" similarly begs the question of whose particular economic gains should be considered beneficial to the overall public and therefore the standard for efficiency. The unstated norm that distinguishes "efficiency-promoting" policies from "redistributive" policies is on closer examination a distributive vision that tends to incorporate race, gender, class, and sexual hierarchies.

Just like the double bind of equal treatment versus special treatment that skews the choices offered by equality doctrine, the double bind of efficiency versus redistribution skews the choices offered by the welfare reform debate by resting on a double standard of economic gain.[40] Those who are economically successful under current market structures can benefit from economic policies designed to promote their interests under the guise of efficiency, because neoclassical economics assumes their particular economic interests are in the public interest. The concept of efficiency disguises a distributional norm that treats government-facilitated private economic gain by some—especially white men, wealthy individuals, and corporations—as publicly beneficial independence. In contrast, the prevailing view of efficiency assumes that government-facilitated economic gain by single mothers in poverty is a matter of dependency and irresponsibility that detracts from the public interest.

This double standard means that in predominant economic ideology, single mothers in poverty are caught in a double bind, whereas some others receive a double benefit. Wealthy capital owners, for example, can get protection from the government for their particular economic interests—such as tax cuts, or an increased supply of low-wage workers—in the name of efficiency.[41] That is because policies viewed as distributing money to middle- and upper-class families and businesses, especially those headed by white men, are more likely to be viewed as "wealth-promoting." In contrast, government policies viewed as distributing money to low-income women and men, single women and their children, and women of color are typically viewed as redistributing wealth.

Feminist scholars have analyzed how social welfare programs in the United States have tended to be stratified on the basis of race and gender status, so that first-tier programs geared toward white men offer less stigmatized and more generous benefits than do programs primarily benefiting white women and people of color.[42] That stratification, however, often is rationalized through the distinction between efficiency and redistribution. For example, in the early years after the 1935 Social Security legislation that produced AFDC, federal administrators instituted a public relations campaign to promote the Old Age Insurance program by distinguishing it from AFDC as an individual contractual benefit rather than charity.[43] Old Age Insurance was a program designed to disproportionately benefit white male workers and their dependents.[44]

Similarly, workers' compensation, also a program originally identified with and designed for white male industrial workers,[45] traditionally has been contrasted to AFDC as efficiency based.[46] In the 1970s and 1980s, most states expanded their workers' compensation coverage and benefits to better compensate a broad range of workers and injuries beyond the male-dominated heavy industry paradigm. But in the 1990s, employers and insurers successfully argued that these expansions had distorted the system's original market goals and had turned it into a redistributive welfare program. In particular, they attributed this change to increased compensation of injuries and illnesses particularly associated (in popular opinion, if not fact) with women workers, such as carpal tunnel syndrome and psychological stress claims.[47] In response, many states restricted compensation for such injuries and illnesses on the ground of restoring efficiency.[48]

Unemployment Insurance, another social welfare program designed primarily to serve middle-class white men,[49] has also traditionally been distinguished on efficiency grounds from welfare programs like AFDC.[50] Even though more mothers have now entered the workforce, in recent decades most states have restricted eligibility for unemployment benefits so that it continues to exclude most unemployed women.[51] However, efforts to modify Unemployment Insurance to better recognize the particular needs of women workers have been criticized for deviating from Unemployment Insurance's economic efficiency goals. For example, many business advocates argued that the Clinton administration's proposed regulations allowing states to use unemployment compensation funds to pay for childbirth or adoption leave would transform the program from a market-oriented "true insurance system" into a welfare entitlement aimed at "social income redistribution."[52]

In sum, this critical line between efficiency and redistribution seems to fall along gendered (and racialized) lines and serves to exclude many women from government support. Just as feminists moved from defending special treatment for women to criticizing the gendered assumptions underlying the division between equality and difference, feminists can move from defending redistribution for women to criticizing the assumptions underlying the gendered division between efficiency and redistribution.

Challenging the Efficiency/Redistribution Distinction

Most discussions of law and policy assume the line between efficiency and equity is an objective (if sometimes elusive) matter of fact, not a question of value or social status.[53] On one level, this distinction rests on a determination of whether a given policy represents "the free market" or "government intervention" in that market. But because free markets depend on government structures, and real-world markets inevitably fall short of the free market ideal, determining what government policies support the goal of a "free market" and what government policies deviate from that goal requires additional criteria for determining when markets are functioning freely.

To distinguish efficiency-promoting from redistributive policies, then, analysts often look for evidence of three harmful effects of redistribution: externalities, transaction costs, or moral hazard.[54] Although each of these interrelated concepts appears to present a neutral economic measure for determining aggregate gain, each can be applied only by making value judgments about how resources should be distributed. By recognizing these concepts as contested moral judgments rather than economic facts, we can show that supposedly redistributive policies are harmful to neither efficiency nor equity but only to particular moral visions or political interests.

Externalities

First, neoclassical economic theory states that policies that reduce harmful "externalities" promote efficiency. Efficiency requires "internalizing" all costs and benefits of a decision to the individual decision maker so that her individual net costs are equivalent to societal net costs. In the ideal free market, market prices internalize costs. By fully calculating the total costs and benefits of a particular choice, a decision maker can make efficient choices—that is, choices that will maximize total net gains given scarce resources.[55] In contrast, redistribution is about changing who gets how much rather than changing total net gains. By definition, then, redistribution means a nonreciprocal exchange in which one party's gain brings a loss to another. It follows that redistributive policies are not necessarily cost-internalizing: part of the costs of one party's gain will be borne by others, and those others will not receive benefits in return for bearing those costs.

In the conventional economic view, AFDC was a classic redistributive program because it transferred some of the costs of supporting impoverished single-parent families from those families onto taxpayers: taxpayers paid the government, and the government paid income to AFDC recipients.[56] By "externalizing" rather than "internalizing" costs, to use the terms of Law and Economics scholarship, AFDC is inefficient. In this view, AFDC benefits constitute "externalities"—that is, whatever their value for social equity, they do not produce the cost-internalizing price signals that induce individuals, acting in their own self-interest, to make decisions that increase overall economic growth. Conventional Law and Economics reasoning asserts that by externalizing AFDC mothers' costs to taxpayers without requiring reciprocal benefits, AFDC was likely to decrease taxpayers' opportunities to devote their resources to transactions that would instead produce net overall gains—profitable investments in job-creating industries, for instance.[57] In this view, the 1996 federal welfare reforms reduced AFDC's inefficient externalities: by imposing time limits on welfare benefits and by requiring reciprocal contributions for work in exchange for benefits, TANF aims to reduce income transfers from taxpayers to poor mothers and to ensure that society receives more offsetting returns from the income transfers that do occur.

Despite the technical terminology, however, calling a cost an "externality" simply amounts to saying that the cost should go to someone else.[58] Cost-internalization is ultimately about who should be responsible for which costs—an inherently value-laden and controversial question of distribution that cannot be determined by objective economic calculation. The view that AFDC *externalized* the costs of caring for children from single mothers onto taxpayers rests on the assumption that the costs of supporting and caring for children are the responsibility of single mothers, not taxpayers.

Martha Fineman powerfully challenges this assumption in her work, arguing that dependency is a universal condition that demands public responsibility from the state and market, not just from the family.[59] Despite the prominence of the idea that dependent care is a private responsibility of families, many long-standing and popular government policies treat support for dependents and for caretakers of dependents as a public responsibility as well—and assume the resulting increase in caretaking is good. For example, public funding for schools eases individual families' responsibility for child care on a regular basis throughout a substantial period of childhood.

RECIPROCAL BENEFITS OF CARETAKING

If we take seriously the value to society of dependent care, and if the societal value of that caretaking is not reduced by the class, race, gender, or sexual status of the caretaker (or dependent), then government income support for non-earning single mothers instead could be viewed as *cost-internalizing*. Martha Fineman argues that public support for caretaking could help correct the current societal situation in which the public reaps gains from dependent care but externalizes the costs of that care to women in "private" families.[60] Fineman explains caretaking as an unreciprocated subsidy by many women to the public in general, rather than as a private benefit to caretakers.[61]

The view that private caretaking labor brings public benefits has a long history. For example, in 1935, the Committee on Economic Security explained its proposal for the federal income assistance program that became ADFC by describing the public benefits resulting from government support of single mothers' caretaking: it stated that such assistance is "designed to release from the wage earning role the person whose natural function is to give her children the physical and affectionate guardianship necessary not alone to keep them from falling into social misfortune but more affirmatively to rear them into citizens capable of contributing to society."[62] AFDC developed out of earlier mothers' pension programs, which many advocated as a means of recognizing the critical civic contributions of (implicitly if not explicitly white) mothers. As President Theodore Roosevelt explained, "when all is said and done it is the mother, and the mother only, who is a better citizen than even the soldier who fights for his country . . . the mother is the one supreme asset of national life."[63]

More recently, feminist economists have used neoclassical economic arguments to explain that government support for unwaged parental child care can be cost-internalizing rather than redistributive.[64] Neoclassical economics recognizes that governments may promote efficiency by correcting market "failures" that prevent the market from setting normal cost-internalizing prices. For example, economists explain that the problem of "public goods" occurs when the total societal benefits of particular goods or services are greater than the private benefits to the buyers of those goods or services—that is, where a transaction produces "positive externalities" not captured (internalized) in the normal market price.[65] According to the conventional economic theory, the "public goods" problem happens because, for some goods and services, it is hard to limit the benefits to the individuals who pay the price of the goods or services. If the individuals who pay for the goods or services do not receive the full benefits, they may be unwilling to pay the full price. As a result, private-market decision makers may refuse to buy and sell as much of those goods and services as would be socially beneficial. Government subsidies that raise the individual buyer's private benefits to levels that recognize the societal benefits can therefore help correct this inefficient positive externality that is causing an undersupply, in the standard economic view. Following this reasoning, feminists have argued that raising children into productive adults is a public good: although parents pay much of the costs of this activity (and receive many personal benefits), additional benefits inevitably spread over onto society as a whole.[66] In this theory, programs like AFDC that provide public support for parental child care partly offset private parenting costs—thereby better internalizing the benefits (positive externalities) of parenting—to ensure that society receives the efficient level of child care.

Whether expressed in terms of citizenship visions or technical economic concepts, such arguments assert that AFDC is not an unreciprocated transfer from taxpayers to impoverished mothers but a (meager) compensation for their socially valuable child-care services. The problem is that government support for dependent caretaking has tended to be viewed as providing reciprocal public benefits rather than negative externalities only when those it assists count as members of the "public," not as subordinate "others." The original version of AFDC was designed to primarily benefit white widowed mothers.[67] As AFDC became less racially discriminatory and more open to never-married and divorced mothers, mainstream discourse was less likely to view it as providing benefits to the public and more likely to view it as providing unreciprocated gain.[68] Legal scholar Dorothy Roberts shows that arguments for welfare reform build on an ideology that denies African Americans full citizenship status.[69] Legal scholar Martha Fineman describes how rhetoric criticizing AFDC draws on ideologies that construct women not attached to men as deviant threats to society.[70] The neoliberal economic view of AFDC as an efficiency-reducing externality dominated the recent public policy debate over welfare reform not because its economic logic was superior to the feminist economic view of AFDC as an efficiency-promoting correction of an externality (the public good problem). Instead, the neoliberal economic arguments prevailed because they captured and helped legitimate prevailing moral judgments that AFDC mothers' unpaid caretaking labor is not socially valuable, given their class, race, gender, and sexual status.

In an attempt to defend opposition to AFDC on grounds other than explicit racism or misogyny, legal scholar Amy Wax argues that caretaking work alone does not constitute a public contribution sufficient to merit public income support.[71] Although she concedes that impoverished non-earning single mothers engage in productive labor, she insists that this caretaking work produces "purely private benefits" to parents and children.[72] Although accepting the "public goods" argument in general, she argues that in the specific case of caretaking by impoverished single parents, collective support for caretaking is likely to produce net social costs, that is, negative externalities.[73] She distinguishes cost-externalizing caretaking by single mothers from economically efficient caretaking work performed by non-earning wives, arguing that married caretakers supported by breadwinner husbands are cost-internalizing and can even produce net social benefits.[74] She claims (without support) that "most families consisting of mothers with employed spouses do indeed pay their own way" and that, as a unit, traditional breadwinner–homemaker families "are almost always self-supporting and able to live decently without public subsidy."[75]

Wax's bare assertion that traditional breadwinner–caretaker marriages thrive without public support ignores a substantial system of taxpayer subsidies for families with non-earning or low-earning wives—subsidies that particularly benefit the wealthiest families. Economist Nancy Folbre explains that families with sufficient income to pay federal income taxes benefit from implicit (although generally inadequate) government family allowances in the form of dependent care deductions (which increase as income increases) as well as from child-care credits that benefit most those who can afford to spend the most on child care.[76] Folbre reports that in the 1990s, families in the top federal income tax brackets could take advantage of taxpayer subsidies for child care that "far exceeded" federal expenditures on AFDC combined with child-care programs aimed to serve low-income families.[77] The home mortgage income tax deduction and tax deductions for health insurance provide huge public subsidies for wage-earning families' housing and medical costs, but these benefits are skewed to provide the most benefits to the wealthiest families.

Other federal programs give special subsidies not just to high-earning families but specifically to married parents who conform to traditional breadwinner–homemaker roles. The Social Security system's old age and survivor's benefits are structured so that non-earning wives of wage-earning husbands—but not single parents or dual-income spouses—receive subsidies for unpaid domestic labor.[78] The federal income tax system's income-splitting provision for jointly filing married couples subsidizes high-earning breadwinners married to non-earning or low-earning spouses at an annual rate of $33 billion in the mid-1990s[79] (compared with $22 billion for AFDC).[80] This huge tax break provides a system of implicit public support for unpaid family caretaking (and other unpaid labor or leisure) that goes mostly to families in which women forgo substantial wage work, again with the largest subsidies targeted to the wealthiest families.[81] In contrast, the same system of joint taxation and income splitting famously imposes a "marriage penalty" on dual-earning spouses, a penalty that particularly burdens married parents who work for low or modest wages.[82] Although legislation enacted in 2001 gradually phases out this "marriage penalty" for many dual-earner families, it retains the large tax bonus for high-earning breadwinners married to non-earning or low-earning caretaker spouses.[83] By accepting AFDC's subsidies for family child care as cost-externalizing redistribution, while erasing these lavish subsidies for wealthier, married parents as normal self-sufficiency, Wax reflects and reinforces traditional ideologies in which race, gender, and class status determine whether family caretaking deserves public support.

Like many welfare critics, Wax goes on to support her claim of negative externalities from AFDC's caretaking subsidy by distinguishing impoverished single mothers as bad parents. She asserts that "single mothers, especially among the poor and poorly educated, produce a disproportionate number of dysfunctional children" who drain collective resources.[84] Although pathologizing women's (especially black women's) sexual and economic independence and demonizing children born outside of marriage have a long history steeped in patriarchal (and white supremacist) ideology,[85] Wax and others claim to rest their similar disparaging conclusions on objective evidence of actual harms.[86] Of course, disproportionate poverty among families headed by single mothers (along with race and gender discrimination) is likely to cause many of the harmful disadvantages faced by children in these families.[87] In countries that offer generous public support for caretaking and wage-working mothers (and where the generosity and stigma of family subsidies are less dependent on the race, marriage, and class status of the recipients), widespread parenting by unmarried mothers does not seem to correspond to widespread poverty or other social problems.[88] Evidence of disadvantages of single parenting in the United States probably reflects this country's particular policy of externalizing the costs of caretaking onto single mothers (especially onto single mothers of color), not that single-parent families necessarily are more likely to externalize costs onto society.

Moreover, Wax's assumption that families with middle- and upper-class married parents are economically self-sufficient obscures the distribution of caretaking costs within families. Many feminists have argued that the legal system helps to externalize caretaking costs from breadwinning husbands onto homemaking wives and their children.[89] For example, breadwinner husbands can reap unreciprocated gains because of divorce laws that fail to adequately recognize the value of their wives' caretaking,[90] and because of legal doctrines forbidding enforcement of intra-marital contracts for compensating caretaking services.[91] If we apply this feminist critique of marriage to welfare reforms aimed at restricting support for single mothers, we can understand that these reforms do not encourage cost-internalizing families. Instead, that feminist critique shows how the reforms help to replicate and protect the traditional family's systematic externalization of caretaking costs onto women and children.

Wax suggests that such systematic externalization of the costs of child care onto women through "restrictive gender customs" that "force women to sacrifice for the greater good" actually may promote economic efficiency by ensuring a supply of public caretaking benefits that solves the "public good" problem.[92] However, policies that encourage women to devote their time to unpaid (and otherwise unreciprocated) caretaking labor typically have differed by race, class, and marital status. As a result, the supply of children for whom extensive caretaking investments produce high human capital is not simply a "public" benefit but a privilege distributed by (and reinforcing of) social caste. Moreover, the question remains whether a child-care system that relies on the sacrifice of women's economic interests is an efficiency-promoting societal gain or a redistributive private gain for men at the expense of women (and often their children). In her study of the economics of motherhood in late twentieth-century United States, journalist Ann Crittenden describes how the U.S. legal and economic systems still use systematic restrictions to provide a strong (and even increasing) supply of mothers forced to sacrifice their own economic well-being to raise children.[93] Crittenden concludes that compared with European systems that better reward caretakers for their work, the U.S. system of unreciprocated maternal sacrifice encourages low-quality child care, high rates of child poverty, low-quality fathering, and reduced personal and public gains from mothers' noncaretaking activities.[94]

RECIPROCAL BENEFITS OF WAGE WORK

Supporters of welfare reform often assume the change from AFDC to TANF internalizes "externalities" not only by reducing taxpayer assistance to single mothers but also by changing the form of that assistance. In some states at some times, recent welfare reforms have been accompanied by *increases* in government support for wage earning by impoverished single mothers.[95] Advocates of welfare reform often present this change to work-based welfare assistance as cost-internalizing on the theory that wage work gives taxpayers a reciprocal benefit in return for their assistance. For example, Wax argues that regardless of any public benefits from single mothers' unpaid caretaking, the public can reasonably expect impoverished single mothers to make personal efforts to reduce the costs of their caretaking by combining care with wage work that improves their family's economic self-sufficiency.[96]

This argument, however, rests on the questionable assumption that wage work by low-earning single mothers contributes more net benefits to taxpayers than their unpaid caretaking. It is not obvious that taxpayers in general will reap greater gains from substituting a greater supply of unpaid parental caretakers with, for instance, a greater supply of telemarketers, fast-food servers, low-wage child-care workers, or cashiers—some of the jobs most likely to absorb former welfare recipients. The material gain to poor families from substituting parental caretaking for parental low-wage labor is often small, nonexistent, or temporary.[97] Although many employers and investors may gain from an increased supply of low-wage labor, these gains are not necessarily passed on to consumers or the "public." In addition, increased low-wage labor and unpaid "workfare" by welfare recipients may harm working poor or lower-middle-class families by creating downward pressure on wages that has ripple effects extending up the wage scale.[98]

An increase in the number of single mothers who perform low-wage labor may not only fail to provide positive public gains but may also impose significant public costs. One of the leading original proponents of the economic theory of externalities, British political economist A. C. Pigou, highlighted the employment of pregnant women and mothers of newborns in factories as the most shocking example of the externality principle.[99] Pigou thought it was obvious that such work caused grave harm to children's health, producing overall social costs outweighing the private benefits of the mothers' wages.[100] It is not necessary to resort to Pigou's essentialist views of mothers or women to find strong support for the theory that family well-being is improved by protecting parents from some of the stress and time demands of wage work, especially for newborn and young children. A survey of Americans' opinions about welfare, for example, shows strong support for the view that mothers of young children should be able to refrain from wage work—except when those mothers are African American.[101] The recent Family and Medical Leave Act is premised on the idea that reducing wage work to accommodate family caretaking demands is good policy, although the act's support for unpaid leave is in practice limited to relatively affluent caretakers who can afford to forgo wage income. Indeed, many supporters of TANF's work-based welfare reforms typically also supported the theory that unpaid maternal child care is generally more beneficial to society than maternal wage work—as long as those mothers are not poor, single, or African American.[102]

The idea that the public receives a reciprocal benefit from government subsidies for low-wage work rather than caretaking seems to rest less on an expectation of concrete material gain from increased wage work and more on a theory that low-wage work, not maternal caretaking, by a certain group of women (based largely on class, race, and marital status) produces moral discipline and self-esteem (or perhaps submissiveness) that will create better families and communities in the long run.[103] One problem with this argument is that it ignores evidence that most AFDC recipients already have demonstrated these capacities through extensive participation in (generally unreported) noncaretaking work necessary to their families' survival on below-subsistence welfare benefits.[104] But even if not, judgments about welfare's efficiency stray far from objective economics when they depend on faith in the intangible moral and spiritual superiority of low-wage work over parental child care. As legal scholar Dorothy Roberts explains, such beliefs about the moral virtues of diverting some women from caring for their children to supplying cheap labor for others have long been more about redistributing socioeconomic benefits along racial lines rather than about creating overall spiritual or material benefits.[105] And even if one accepts arguments about intangible public benefits from increased low-wage work, the question remains how to balance these potential positive spillover effects against the potential negative spillover effects of low-wage work by impoverished single mothers that seemed obvious to many (in the case of white widows) at the time of AFDC's beginning. Single mothers entering low-wage work may face increased risks of violence, health problems, erosion of self-esteem from abusive work environments, inadequate child care, pressure for drug and alcohol use, and inability to maintain continuous or adequate employment, all of which might bring long-term harm to their individual families as well as to society in general.

In theory, well-funded nonparental child care and other assistance to low-wage workers, such as subsidized health insurance, transportation, housing assistance, or job training, might alleviate some of the potential societal and personal costs of replacing parental child care with low-wage work and might also produce long-term economic benefits for families that exceed AFDC's paltry benefits. According to this reasoning, states that use TANF to improve subsidies for low-wage workers may "internalize" externalities of low-wage work, for instance, by correcting for "imperfections" in the market for child care.

However, even the more generous government programs for low-wage workers that were instituted or expanded under recent welfare reforms fall far short of what many low-wage workers need to maintain the long-term well-being of themselves and their families. For example, most of this work-based assistance is short term, even though many if not most low-paid single mothers formerly on welfare are unlikely to move quickly into jobs that provide wages or benefits adequate to cover their families' needs for health insurance, child care, and other living expenses.[106] Even in states that have increased child-care spending, subsidized child care falls far short of the needs of many former welfare recipients and may not be available in the future, particularly during recessions.[107]

Aside from the question of whether TANF's work-based welfare assistance can alleviate sufficiently the costs to society of single mothers performing low-wage work and in the end produce a net societal gain, the theory that work-based assistance increases efficiency is suspect from another perspective. By shifting government support from caretaking to wage-earning, TANF shifts government support from single mothers to employers. When government helps pay single mothers' costs of working, for example, by subsidizing child care or transportation, employers gain a more reliable and productive work-force (and a greater supply of workers) than they would have otherwise, and without raising wages (or other benefits).

As a result, work-based welfare assistance externalizes *employers'* costs onto taxpayers, unless we assume that employers are not responsible for paying wages adequate to make work affordable for parents. In fact, many supporters of recent welfare reforms assume that if jobs fail to pay single mothers a minimally livable wage, the responsibility falls not on the employers but on the single mothers (and perhaps their children's fathers). Conservative welfare critic Charles Murray, for example, argues that unmarried mothers unable to support their children should not get pregnant, should abort their pregnancies, or should give up their babies for adoption.[108] This view leads to the conclusion that assisting working mothers with the costs of raising families creates inefficient externalities, despite recipients' reciprocal contribution of work. Legal scholar Vicki Schultz presents a contrasting approach to increasing the public benefits from wage work by mothers: rather than demanding more "reciprocal contributions" from poor single mothers, she argues for universal, comprehensive rights to livable wages in jobs structured to support both unpaid family care and leisure.[109]

In sum, to determine whether work requirements in recent welfare reforms reduce "externalities" compared with the caretaking support of AFDC, we must decide which costs are "internal" and which are "external" to the employment relationship and to families. Furthermore, the goal of better internalizing the costs of public support for impoverished families cannot be pursued without making judgments about whose families are "external" to the public well-being and whose are integral to that public well-being.

Transaction Costs

One of the leading figures in neoclassical economic analysis of law, R. H. Coase, recognized the inherent subjectivity of the concept of externalities and instead switched the focus of efficiency analysis to the supposedly more objective concept of transaction costs.[110] In predominant Law and Economics theory, transaction costs are the costs of resource-maximizing transactions that are not included in the transaction's price,[111] such as the difficulties of gathering information related to the transaction, and negotiating, implementing, and monitoring it. By definition, transaction costs constitute a deadweight loss that depletes the resources available for the productive transactions that maximize overall wealth. Reducing transaction costs therefore promotes efficiency.

In the conventional Law and Economics (and neoliberal) view, transaction costs provide another explanation of the unintended harmful effects of redistribution. According to this theory, government redistribution typically involves administrative costs that reduce overall societal gain (decreasing efficiency). For example, because redistributive benefits, in contrast to the benefits of free market exchanges, typically do not go to only those individuals who voluntarily pursue them, the government must establish a process for screening eligible recipients and for distributing and monitoring benefits. And because those who pay for the benefits do not do so voluntarily, the government must devote resources to enforcing and collecting the revenue to be redistributed. Furthermore, according to this theory, this administrative system inevitably distributes benefits not just to the intended recipients of redistribution but to "special interests," who gain from expanded administrative jobs and who are likely to use political influence to siphon off more resources from intended recipients of redistribution for their own gain. In his classic Law and Economics textbook, Judge Richard Posner argues that federal welfare reform is supported by evidence that "of every $1 transferred by the government [for AFDC], 23 cents is dissipated, when all the social costs of the transfer are taken into account."[112]

The difference, however, between "transactions" and "transaction costs" is again a matter of perspective, not objective economics.[113] For example, is paying a lawyer to help you negotiate a contract a transaction cost or a productive wealth-maximizing transaction? That depends on whether you are the lawyer. The distinction boils down to a question of which transactions are desirable and which are not, and to whom—a normative and distributive question likely to depend on social status and political power.

TRANSACTION COSTS OF WAGE WORK

Most advocates of welfare reform in the United States have not explicitly argued that replacing AFDC with TANF is efficient because it reduces transaction costs. Nonetheless, this argument is often implicit in descriptions of TANF as a more efficiency-oriented approach to welfare than is AFDC. In this view, many single mothers in poverty who desire to engage in wage work face numerous barriers to this transaction, such as difficulties getting information about available work, searching for jobs, finding reliable transportation, and arranging child care. Rather than removing these transaction costs, AFDC's payment for non-earning caretaking accommodates them by replacing the desired wage income with welfare benefits, which then become an additional barrier to wage work. TANF, in contrast, allows states to shift welfare assistance to focus on directly minimizing the costs of wage work. In a report surveying work and welfare in the United Kingdom, the Organisation for Economic Co-operation and Development described that country's welfare-to-work program as providing assistance with the "transactions costs" of work, such as transportation costs and the expenses of job searching.[114]

In this analysis, however, caretaking and children themselves become transaction costs that get in the way of work. If raising a family were instead the desired transaction, then AFDC rather than TANF could be viewed as the approach that better reduces transaction costs. To what degree work should be the purpose of life, and to what degree a means to other goals, is a normative question—and one often applied differentially based on class, race, and gender status. Dorothy Roberts, for example, has explained how AFDC and other social welfare policies have been designed to treat black mothers' caretaking of their own children as a socially unimportant, or even harmful, activity that gets in the way of the supposedly more important societal interest of maintaining a supply of black women for cheap labor—often as caretakers of white children.[115] Political theorist Gwendolyn Mink shows that TANF's work requirements reflected a prevailing moral judgment that mothering is a hindrance to wage work for poor, single women (and especially for black women), but that wage work is a hindrance to mothering for wealthier white married women.[116]

Indeed, some supporters of TANF's reforms suggested that the costs of entering the wage labor market, such as child-care or transportation expenses, are not transaction costs external to the transaction of wage work but instead constitute part of the price internal to the transaction. In the view of many conservative advocates of welfare reform, those who lack the skills sufficient to earn wages capable of supporting a family (or who lack a spouse with such skills) should pay the price. That means those who cannot afford to combine work and family should forgo having children or should forgo raising any children they have by relinquishing them to foster care, adoption, or orphanages.[117] And if a low-wage job does not pay enough to support transportation costs, that constitutes a price signal that should encourage workers, or aspiring workers, to develop skills adequate to secure a higher-wage job. Following that reasoning, if government assistance alleviates the costs of low-wage work, it will not promote efficiency but will instead create new deadweight losses as people fail to take advantage of market opportunities that would better meet their needs. In short, the question whether efficiency will be promoted by recognizing or by reducing the costs of sustaining working families in low-wage work depends on normative judgments about who should have responsibility for recognizing or reducing these costs—employers, workers, or society in general.

TRANSACTION COSTS OF BIG GOVERNMENT

Supporters of the federal welfare reform legislation suggested that it would reduce transaction costs by devolving substantial responsibility for program design from federal to state (and sometimes local) governments. For example, 1996 presidential candidate Bob Dole argued that replacing federal entitlements with state block grants "would save $60 billion over seven years in increased efficiency and lack of federal red tape."[118] Advocates of decentralizing welfare policy to the states explained that this change would introduce competition that would deter waste and encourage innovation.[119]

In addition, reform proponents often argued that federal control of AFDC resulted in inflexible bureaucracy that failed to tailor programs to local needs or to quickly respond to changing circumstances. Some take this devolution argument a step further, arguing that privatizing welfare will reduce waste and increase flexibility even more.[120] "With government, you pay for process. . . . When you contract out, you pay for results," explains an executive of Maximus, a private company in the lead of the welfare business.[121] Following this reasoning, states have instituted welfare reforms that have opened up welfare administration to bidding by private for-profit companies and charities.

Again, whether this decentralization and privatization will reduce the costs of achieving the goals of welfare raises normative questions about what those goals are and who can be trusted to achieve them. Red tape can be unnecessary waste *or* necessary protection *against* waste, depending on one's perspective.

Reports on the effects of TANF's devolution show that states generally have not reduced the red tape from the perspective of welfare agencies or welfare recipients. Decentralization has tended to replace previously uniform administrative systems with complex and confusing variations by state, county, and agency that create ample opportunities for error by both welfare agency staff and by recipients.[122] In addition, state and local authorities have used their new freedom from federal mandates to continue to follow federal requirements while adding new requirements on top of previous procedures.[123] This new red tape may be successful in reducing caseloads and abuse of benefits, but it is also likely to increase poverty and administrative abuse.

For example, one report describes a county that requires welfare applicants to complete up to six in-person appointments with administrative staff before being approved for benefits and to produce at these appointments detailed paperwork documenting personal and financial facts, such as divorce records, birth certificates, statements from landlords proving their child's residence, financial records, and verification of termination by former employers.[124]

Once a recipient is approved for benefits, some states' requirements for continuing those benefits are similarly onerous. To maintain welfare-to-work assistance payments, a TANF participant balancing work and family may have to comply with regular office visits and cumbersome monthly re-certification procedures involving several different agencies.[125] Many eligible welfare recipients seem to be excluded from benefits as a result of the difficulty and high costs (such as transportation and child care) of satisfying these requirements.[126]

Although some states have attempted to use their increased flexibility to reduce administrative costs for taxpayers, this may be a matter of shifting the costs of welfare transactions from governments to recipients and others. Some states have reduced administrative expenses by cutting back on welfare office staff and services such as outreach and information. Reports on the effects of recent welfare reforms suggest that many potential welfare recipients are not being informed about available benefits.[127] Again, any transaction cost reduction for taxpayers may come at the expense of exacerbating poverty and administrative burdens for welfare recipients.

Moreover, states, local governments, and private welfare providers may use their new freedom from bureaucratic constraint not only to reduce the costs of welfare transactions but to redirect those transactions to benefit others. This new potential for waste and abuse in turn has increased pressure for new bureaucracies and procedural protections aimed at monitoring and controlling these potential problems. For example, some states have used their new "flexibility" to divert federal TANF funding from support for poor families to other purposes, such as funding general tax cuts.[128] In response, the federal government has begun to monitor these practices.[129]

In addition, private providers have capitalized on TANF's new opportunities for government-assisted profit. For example, welfare-to-work services are now one of defense contractor Lockheed's fastest growing lines of business.[130] Some for-profit providers have sought to increase their earnings through anti-competitive bidding practices, such as making inside deals with government officials who are then hired to run the new welfare business.[131] Some have reduced administrative expenses by replacing unionized, well-paying civil service jobs with low-wage jobs,[132] perhaps contributing to the poverty that the welfare system is supposed to alleviate. Furthermore, government contracts with private providers are subject to abuse by providers who accept up-front payments and fail to deliver adequate services, or who meet contractual goals for caseload reduction by arbitrarily diverting eligible recipients from benefits, by skimming off the cream of recipients who would have moved off welfare quickly anyway, or by churning the same recipients in and out of benefits.[133] To control this potential for private abuse, state and local governments have had to devote substantial new resources to negotiating, monitoring, and enforcing complex contractual protections.[134]

In sum, looking to transaction costs to determine whether welfare programs promote net public gain rather than private redistribution leads back to the question of whose gains from less costly transactions should count as public benefits. The 1996 welfare reforms may have reduced some administrative costs, but those savings have probably come at the price of some increased transaction costs for welfare recipients and for taxpayers—and those savings have produced *different* transactions for both taxpayers and welfare recipients (such as less welfare and more low-wage office jobs, in some examples). Once again, welfare reforms cannot be distinguished as promoting efficiency without making assumptions about what distribution of resources is beneficial.

Moral Hazard

Moral hazard, the third concept used to measure efficiency, was perhaps the most prominent economic argument used against AFDC. Moral hazard, a term derived from the insurance industry, is the problem that people tend to be less careful to minimize costs when someone else pays the bill.[135] By protecting people against market losses, redistribution risks producing the unintended consequence of moral hazard, thereby driving up overall costs.

For example, critics often argued that by giving needy families income support, AFDC made more families needy.[136] In a common refrain accompanying recent welfare reforms, AFDC's income protection reduced incentives for women in poverty to make decisions that would avoid or reduce the costs of single motherhood (such as staying in the wage labor market, avoiding pregnancy and child rearing, or marrying wage-earning men). The moral hazard argument is implicit in the claim that AFDC creates a "cycle of dependency" that discourages impoverished families from making efforts to escape their poverty.[137] As a result of these "perverse incentives," this view explains, in the long run welfare hurts both its beneficiaries and the public in general. According to this reasoning, the 1996 welfare reforms reduced this inefficient moral hazard by imposing a variety of restrictions designed to influence welfare recipients' work, marriage, and childbearing behavior.[138]

The supposed harms of moral hazard, however, are social and political constructions, not economic truths. The moral hazard problem simply explains that shifting responsibility for costs may produce incentive effects that result in behavior changes. Whether these behavior changes count as inefficient moral hazard or instead as efficient resource-maximizing depends not on objective laws of economics but on moral judgments about whether the behavior is good or bad. Deborah Stone has coined the term *moral opportunity* to explain that behavior changes produced by social welfare protections can produce societal benefits instead of harm.[139]

For example, welfare systems in which benefit amounts increase according to family size typically appear to present a problem of moral hazard. The theory is that protection from some of the economic burdens of caring for additional children encourages women to take less care to avoid having (or keeping) children whose care they otherwise could not afford. As part of recent welfare reform legislation, many states have adopted "family cap" provisions that prevent welfare recipients from receiving benefit increases if they have additional children while on welfare. According to supporters, these restrictions reduce inefficient moral hazard by correcting incentives for non-earning single mothers to engage in the costly behavior of having more children than they would without government support. Many critics of such restrictions dispute the empirical claim that welfare recipients' decisions to bear or raise children are in fact influenced by such incentives, arguing that it is doubtful that welfare benefits are sufficient to alleviate the economic burdens of additional children, or that women have control over the number of children they bear *and* would make that choice based on economic gain.[140]

Regardless of the empirical evidence, however, a more basic theoretical problem with the moral hazard rationale for family cap restrictions is that there is no neutral *economic* ground for labeling a woman's interest in having more children as inefficient "moral hazard" rather than productive self-interest maximizing. During the recent period of welfare reforms for families in poverty, governments have dramatically increased their assistance for geographically mobile businesses—often called corporate welfare.[141] If a corporation decides to hire more workers at a particular plant because of tax incentives, that decision to take advantage of the extra profit protection to increase jobs is often considered an example of productive economic development rather than unproductive moral hazard.

Even more fundamentally, the very existence of corporations arguably involves moral hazard: the grant of limited liability to business owners allows them to take risks that would be avoided if shareholders were held personally liable for the harmful results of a business.[142] But of course the corporate form is predominantly considered a cornerstone of efficient wealth maximization, not redistribution that causes moral hazard. The difference between these corporate examples and the welfare example rests not on impartial economic principle but on moral judgments to value jobs over children and investor wealth over caretaker wealth.

If we make different assumptions about whose gains constitute public benefits, we can view welfare reforms as *increasing,* not *reducing,* harmful moral hazard. For example, reform advocates have justified the shift from AFDC's caretaker subsidies to TANF's subsidies conditioned on work as a means of correcting the moral hazard problem of recipients' disincentives for wage work. However, the change to work-based assistance and work requirements risks creating new moral hazard on the part of employers. TANF's increased incentives for wage work protect employers against labor costs by increasing labor supply (thereby reducing wage pressures) and, in the case of work-based assistance, by protecting employers against some of the costs of maintaining a reliable, productive workforce.

TANF's protection against employers' labor costs, like AFDC's protection against single mothers' caretaking costs, could be criticized for producing a "cycle of dependency." If cheap and docile labor provides employers with an easy means of avoiding changes and innovations that would lower overall costs in the long run by providing better working conditions along with better profits, then that cost protection will encourage employers to choose investments and business plans that make such "high-road" production strategies even more difficult to achieve, locking them into behavior that arguably hurts society overall. Without such protection against labor costs, other things being equal, employers would have more incentives to reduce the costs of production in other ways, perhaps through lower executive salaries, lower investor returns, or more cost-effective operations, or even by forgoing certain lines of business that are unprofitable without cheap labor.

Inevitability of Efficiency's Double Standard

By challenging welfare's supposedly harmful externalities, transaction costs, and moral hazard effects as problematic value judgments, not as principles of nature or economics, feminists can escape the double bind that makes generous government support for mothers in poverty seem harmful to women and to society in general. Feminists have argued for rethinking the standard of equality to recognize women's particular needs (such as childbearing) as normal, not different. Similarly, feminists can argue for rethinking the standard of efficiency to recognize government support for the particular caretaking needs of many women as integral to public gain, not as harmful redistribution.

A fourth economic criticism of redistribution poses a more difficult challenge to feminists and welfare advocates. This argument holds that redistribution will not work because the market ultimately will swamp any government action aimed at redirecting resources to the poor. This fourth criticism seems to contradict the previous three criticisms of redistribution's harms, which assume the market is fragile and easily subject to government disruption. Instead, the fourth argument assumes the market is so strong and impermeable that government interventions will inevitably fail to produce their intended distributional changes.[143]

In this view, wealthy capital owners may be able to force others to support their private interests as necessary to the public well-being, regardless of moral legitimacy, and to impose public penalties if others seek government assistance. For instance, if governments support generous welfare policies that harm wealthy individuals or businesses by decreasing the availability of low-wage labor and by increasing taxes, then those wealthy capital owners may threaten general economic stability, and those in poverty in particular, by withdrawing their investment and tax dollars.

Such a result, however, would *not* be determined by inevitable, natural market forces, as economic criticisms of welfare spending often assert. Just like the neoliberal argument that redistribution will destroy the market, the neoliberal argument that the market will destroy redistribution wrongly assumes a market that is fixed, pre-political, and distinct from government. Instead, market "forces" are produced by government policies and laws that shape the distribution of bargaining power.

For example, the 1996 welfare reforms devolving welfare policy to the states and localities increase the bargaining power of wealthy capital owners and taxpayers by increasing their ability to threaten withdrawal from states or localities that increase welfare spending. Supporters of welfare reforms have frequently invoked the need to maintain a favorable business climate as a reason to restrict welfare.[144]

At the international level, government policies have also recently contributed to increasing the market power of wealthy capital owners who benefit from restricting welfare and from an increased supply of poverty-stricken workers. For example, the International Monetary Fund and World Bank pressure developing nations to adopt structural adjustment programs that cut welfare spending in order to increase returns to global investors.[145] As these international financial institutions make developing nations more attractive to investors, they increase competition for capital between developing nations and wealthier nations, thereby pressuring wealthier nations to hold down social spending as well. For example, even during a period of projected budget surpluses in the United States, political leaders of both major parties remained reluctant to substantially expand welfare programs.[146] If instead the focus of international trade and financial policy shifted from protecting international investment to enhancing the global bargaining power of labor, the poor, and average citizens,[147] national and local political leaders would face less pressure to reduce welfare spending.

Conclusion

The divide between redistribution and efficiency has a long history of undermining government support for women in poverty. Even during times of relatively strong political support for the idea of redistribution, that framework relegated AFDC to an inferior position in the social welfare hierarchy. Now that the predominant neoliberal ideology has discredited the idea of redistribution in mainstream discourse, those who advocate for welfare as a safety net for the newly triumphant market face even steeper challenges. Those who attempt to defend a place for welfare on egalitarian grounds separate from efficiency must confront critics who argue that such redistribution will produce secondary effects—externalities, transaction costs, and moral hazards—that will distort the efficient market and frustrate egalitarian goals in the long run. Like "special treatment" in inequality doctrine, "redistribution" in economic policy tends to remain secondary and circumscribed, subject to stigma and suspicion.

However, just as defending special treatment is not the only logical strategy for reconciling support for women's particular needs with equality, defending redistribution is not the only strategy for reconciling support for women's particular needs with overall economic well-being. Just as feminists counter the supposed problems of special treatment by redefining the underlying concept of gender equality, feminists can redefine the concepts of a normal and beneficial market. Rather than defending economic support for women as an *alternative* to market efficiency, feminists can advocate alternative visions of publicly beneficial markets that better recognize the economic benefits of women's caretaking (and of women's wage labor). In practice, that would mean considering welfare policy as intertwined with policies affecting market structures, such as labor, employment law, corporate law, financial regulation, and trade policy. For example, feminist welfare policy should advocate corporate responsibility to communities, workers, and families as central to public morality and productivity.

In the contemporary United States, politics is widely disparaged as a matter of special interests, but neoclassical economics is widely worshiped as universal truth. In response, feminists should identify and resist the moral and political judgments that inevitably permeate dominant standards of market efficiency. By recognizing that politics and economics are inevitably inseparable, we can better challenge the message that policies protecting wealthy corporate and capital interests are "economically correct," but that policies protecting impoverished women are merely "politically correct."

Notes

1. For comments on drafts of this essay, I thank Terence Dougherty, Carl Nightingale, and participants in the November 1996 Feminism and Legal Theory Workshop at Columbia Law School. In addition, this essay benefited from conversations with Frank Munger.

AFDC provided more limited support for a small number of two-parent families facing unemployment. *See* Jill Duerr Berrick, *From Mother's Duty to Personal Responsibility: The Evolution of AFDC,* 7 Hastings Women's L.J. 257 n. 1 (1996).

2. *See* Daniel Yergin & Joseph Stanislaw, *The Commanding Heights: The Battle between Government and the Marketplace That Is Remaking the Modern World* 362 (1998); Thomas J. Duesterberg, *Reforming the Welfare State,* 35 Society 44, 48 (1998).

3. Pub. L. No. 104-193, 110 Stat. 2105.

4. 42 U.S.C. § 601 (2000).

5. *See* Martha Albertson Fineman, *The Neutered Mother, the Sexual Family, and Other Twentieth Century Tragedies* 110–18 (1995) [hereinafter Fineman, *Neutered Mother*]; Dorothy E. Roberts, *Welfare and the Problem of Black Citizenship*, 105 Yale L.J. 1563, 1563–66 (1996) (book review); Lucy A. Williams, *The Ideology of Division: Behavior Modification Welfare Reform Proposals*, 102 Yale L.J. 719, 741–46 (1992) [hereinafter Williams, *Ideology of Division*].

6. *See, e.g.,* George Gilder, *The Coming Welfare Crisis*, 11 Heritage Found. Pol'y Rev. 25 (1980).

7. *See* Richard A. Posner, *Economic Analysis of Law* 3 (5th ed. 1998) [hereinafter Posner, *Economic Analysis*].

8. A. Mitchell Polinsky, *An Introduction to Law and Economics* 7 (2d ed. 1989).

9. *See, e.g.,* Anne L. Alstott, *Tax Policy and Feminism: Competing Goals and Institutional Choices*, 96 Colum. L. Rev. 2001, 2077 (1996).

10. *See, e.g.,* Gordon Tullock, *The Reality of Redistribution*, in *Poverty and Inequality: Economics of Income Redistribution* 127–31 (Jon Neill ed., 1997).

11. For historical accounts of the development and expansion of AFDC, *see* David T. Ellwood, *Poor Support: Poverty in the American Family* (1988); Michael B. Katz, *In the Shadow of the Poorhouse: A Social History of Welfare in America* (1996).

12. *See* Theodore R. Marmor, Jerry L. Mashaw, & Philip L. Harvey, *America's Misunderstood Welfare State: Persistent Myths, Enduring Realities*, 8–11 (1990); Michael Katz, *The Undeserving Poor: From the War on Poverty to the War on Welfare* 138 (1989).

13. *See* Charles Noble, *Liberalism at Work: The Rise and Fall of OSHA* 114–19 (1986); Jean Stefancic & Richard Delgado, *No Mercy: How Conservative Think Tanks and Foundations Changed America's Social Agenda* 3 (1996).

14. *See* Michael Meeropol, *Surrender: How the Clinton Administration Completed the Reagan Revolution* 4, 79–86 (1998).

15. Marmor et al., *supra* note 12, at 12.

16. Yergin & Stanislaw, *supra* note 2, at 369; Robert L. Bartley, *Archaic Liberalism: Still a Winner?* Wall St. J. (Aug. 28, 2000).

17. *See* Anthony Giddens, *The Third Way: The Renewal of Social Democracy* 13 (1998).

18. *See* Joel F. Handler & Yeheskel Hasenfeld, *We the Poor People: Work, Poverty, and Welfare* 8 (1997).

19. Robert Rector & William F. Lauber, *America's Failed $5.4 Trillion War on Poverty* 44 (1995).

20. *See* Duesterberg, *supra* note 2, at 44.

21. Newt Gingrich, *Remarks*, at Progress and Freedom Foundation Conference (Jan. 22, 1996) (Fed. News Service).

22. *Id.*

23. Colin Powell, *Powell's Speech to GOP Convention*, Investor's Business Daily A2 (Aug. 14, 1996).

24. *Id.*

25. Quoted in Marie Cocco, *Democrats Celebrating Political Skill, Not Soul*, Newsday (Aug. 22, 1996).

26. *Id.*; Al From, *The New Democratic Platform*, New Democrat (Sept.–Oct. 1996); Gil Klein, *"Reinvented" Democrats March On*, Tampa Tribune 6 (Aug. 31, 1996).

27. *See* Al From, *Clinton's Not "Republican-Lite,"* USA Today 19A (Aug. 26, 1996). For examples of scholarly defenses of redistribution as secondary to and separate from principles of market efficiency, *see* Michael J. Graetz & Jerry L. Mashaw, *True Security* (1999); Anne L. Alstott, *Work v. Freedom: A Liberal Challenge to Employment Subsidies*, 108 Yale L.J. 967 (1999).

28. Governor Bush Heralds Michigan Welfare Reform, Presidential Campaign Press Materials (June 27, 2000).

29. Larry King et al., *Democratic National Convention: Al Gore Accepts the Party's Presidential Nomination*, CNN Live Event/Special (Aug. 17, 2000), transcript 00081704V54.

30. Al From, *Democrats 2000: A Party Rejuvenated Goes on Display*, San Diego Union-Tribune G-1 (Aug. 13, 2000).

31. *Apologize to Newt*, Wall St. J. (May 8, 2000) (editorial).

32. *See* Neil deMause, *Turning the Tables: Welfare Reform Faces a Time Limit of Its Own*, In These Times 16 (June 12, 2000) (summarizing findings of studies by the Urban Institute, the Welfare and Human Rights Monitoring Project, and the Washington Welfare Reform Coalition).

33. *See* Martha T. McCluskey, *Subsidized Lives and the Ideology of Efficiency*, 8 Am. U. J. Gender Soc. Pol'y & L. 115, 124 (2000) [hereinafter McCluskey, *Subsidized Lives*].

34. *See* Catharine MacKinnon, *Toward a Feminist Theory of the State* 221 (1989).

35. *See* Martha Albertson Fineman, *The Illusion of Equality: The Rhetoric and Reality of Divorce Reform* 21–30 (1991) [hereinafter Fineman, *Illusion of Equality*]; Linda J. Krieger & Patricia N. Cooney, *The Miller Wohl Controversy: Equal Treatment, Positive Action and the Meaning of Women's Equality* 13 Golden Gate U. L. Rev. 513 (1983).

36. *See* Wendy W. Williams, *Equality's Riddle: Pregnancy and the Equal Treatment/Special Treatment Debate*, 13 N.Y.U. Rev. L. & Soc. Change 325 (1985).

37. *See* Lucinda M. Finley, *Transcending Equality Theory: A Way Out of the Maternity in the Workplace Debate*, 86 Colum. L. Rev. 1118, 1156 (1986).

38. *See* Catharine MacKinnon, *Feminism Unmodified* 34 (1987).

39. *Id.* at 39.

40. *See* McCluskey, *Subsidized Lives, supra* note 33, at 128.

41. Id. at 130–31 (discussing claims that tax cuts for the wealthy and deficit-cutting policies are efficient). *See also* Richard A. Posner, *The Economics of Justice* 81 (1981) (claiming that wealthier people promote efficiency more than others because they have "higher marginal products").

42. *See* Linda Gordon, *Pitied But Not Entitled: Single Mothers and the History of Welfare* (1994); Jill Quadagno, *The Color of Welfare: How Racism Undermined the War on Poverty* (1994); Barbara J. Nelson, *The Origins of the Two-Channel Welfare State: Workmen's Compensation and Mothers' Aid*, in *Women, the State, and Welfare* (Linda Gordon ed., 1990).

43. *See* Gordon, *supra* note 42, at 283–84.

44. *See* Jill Quadagno, *The Transformation of Old Age Security: Class and Politics in the American Welfare State* (1988); Mimi Abramovitz, *Regulating the Lives of Women: Social Welfare Policy from Colonial Times to the Present* 253 (1988).

45. Nelson, *supra* note 42, at 136; Julian Go III, *Inventing Industrial Accidents and Their Insurance: Discourse and Workers' Compensation in the United States, 1880s–1910s*, 20 Social Science History 401, 425 (1996).

46. *See* Martha T. McCluskey, *The Illusion of Efficiency in Workers' Compensation Reform*, 50 Rutgers Law Review, 657, 673 (1998) [hereinafter McCluskey, *Illusion of Efficiency*].

47. *Id.* at 780, 784, and n. 432; *see also* Allard E. Dembe, *Occupation and Disease: How Social Factors Affect the Conception of Work-Related Disorders* 49–52 (1996) (demonstrating a long history of gender and race bias in determining which injuries count as work related).

48. *See generally*, McCluskey, *Illusion of Efficiency, supra* note 46.

49. Abramovitz, *supra* note 44, at 287.

50. *See, e.g.*, Joseph M. Becker, S.J., *The Location of Financial Responsibility in Unemployment Insurance*, 59 J. Urb. L. 509, 542–43 (1982) (describing unemployment insurance as a market-oriented program in contrast to "welfare programs").

51. Lucy A. Williams, *Unemployment Insurance and Low-Wage Work*, in *Hard Labor: Women and Work in the Post-Welfare Era* 158–59 (Joel Handler & Lucie White eds., 1999).

52. *See, e.g.*, Amanda Milligan, *Fears over Family Leave: Critics Assail Government's Proposed Expansion of Act*, Crain's Chicago Business SB14 (Sept. 13, 1999) (quoting lawyer Claire Weiler as saying, "the proposal 'seems to be taking a system that is a true insurance system and then expanding it for many. . . . That looks more like a social income redistribution' "); *Proposed Payments Could Raise Payroll Taxes*, 4 Death Care Business Advisor (Jan. 31, 2000) (reporting that the U.S. Chamber of Commerce criticized this proposal as "a large new welfare entitlement");

Robyn Blumner, *New Welfare in Everything But Name,* Times Union (Albany, N.Y.) A11 (July 22, 1999) (criticizing proposal on the ground that it would "transform unemployment benefits from a program that insures against joblessness into a new form of welfare"). *See also* Gillian Lester, *Unemployment Insurance and Wealth Redistribution,* 49 U.C.L.A. L. Rev. 335 (2001) (discussing modifications to meet caretaking women's unemployment needs as problematic "redistribution" but counting the original design to satisfy some white men's unemployment needs as principled economics and actuarial science).

53. *See* McCluskey, *Illusion of Efficiency, supra* note 46, at 663–67 (explaining and criticizing this assumption); Patrick B. Crawford, *The Utility of the Efficiency/Equity Dichotomy in Tax Policy Analysis,* 16 Va. L. Rev. 501, 514 (1997) (exploring and questioning this assumption). *See generally* Martha T. McCluskey, *Efficiency and Social Citizenship: Challenging the Neoliberal Attack on the Welfare State,* 78 Ind. L.J. 783 (2003) (explaining how the efficiency–equity distinction is central to ideological efforts to discredit welfare state programs and to reinvigorate race, class, and gender hierarchy).

54. *See* McCluskey, *Illusion of Efficiency, supra* note 46, at 723–50, 918 (explaining and criticizing this evidence).

55. *See* Jon D. Hanson & Kyle D. Logue, *The First-Party Insurance Externality: An Economic Justification for Enterprise Liability,* 76 Cornell L. Rev. 129, 161 n. 138 (1990).

56. *See, e.g.,* Suzanne Elise Shanahan & Nancy Brandon Tuna, *The Sociology of Distribution and Redistribution,* in *The Handbook of Economic Sociology* 733, 734 (Neil J. Smelser & Richard Swedberg eds., Princeton U. Press 1994).

57. *See* Lee Anne Fennell, *Interdependence and Choice in Distributive Justice: The Welfare Conundrum,* 1994 Wis. L. Rev. 235, 293–94, 298 n. 274 (summarizing and partly questioning efficiency concerns about AFDC's "expropriation" of resources of those more well-off); Posner, *Economic Analysis, supra* note 7, at 500–503 (arguing generally that income transfers from the wealthier to the poorer may be inefficient because "the people who work hard to make money and succeed in making it are, on average, those who value money most, having given up other things such as leisure to get it").

58. McCluskey, *Illusion of Efficiency, supra* note 46, at 725.

59. Martha Albertson Fineman, *Cracking the Foundational Myths: Independence, Autonomy, and Self-Sufficiency,* ch. 9, this vol.

60. *Id.* (describing this "externality" as a debt owed by society to caretakers).

61. *Id.*

62. *Fiftieth Anniversary Edition of the Report of the Committee on Economic Security of 1935 and Other Basic Documents Relating to the Development of the Social Security Act* (Alan Pifer & Forrest Chisman eds., 1985).

63. Theda Skocpol, *Protecting Soldiers and Mothers* 337 (Harvard U. Press 1992) (quoting Roosevelt's address to the First International Congress in America for the Welfare of the Child, organized by the Congress of Mothers in 1908) (discussed in Linda C. McClain, *Care as a Public Value: Linking Responsibility, Resources, and Republicanism,* 76 Chi.-Kent L. Rev. 1673, 1701–2 (2001).

64. *See* Shirley P. Burggraf, *The Feminine Economy and Economic Man: Reviving the Role of Family in the Post-Industrial Age* 173–75 (Perseus Books 1999) (arguing for treating support for family caretaking as productive investment rather than charity); Nancy Folbre, *Who Pays for the Kids? Gender and the Structure of Constraint* 117–19 (Routledge 1994) (arguing that spreading the risks of family caretaking beyond individual women in families may be efficient because of the societal value of that care).

65. *See* Amy Wax, *Is There a Caring Crisis?* 16 Yale J. on Reg. 327, 340, & nn. 40–41 (book review) [hereinafter Wax, *Caring Crisis*].

66. *See* Burggraf, *supra* note 64, at 33–34, 51–66; Paula England & Nancy Folbre, *Who Should Pay for the Kids,* 563 Annals Am. Acad. Pol. & Soc. Sci. 194 (1999).

67. *See* Robert C. Lieberman, *Shifting the Color Line: Race and the American Welfare State* 118–40 (1998); Gordon, *supra* note 42, at 271–80.

68. *See* Handler & Hasenfeld, *supra* note 18, at 31–33; *see generally,* Jill Quadagno, *The Color of Welfare: How Racism Undermined the War on Poverty* (1994).

69. *See* Roberts, *supra* note 5, at 1563; *see* also Kenneth J. Neubeck & Noel A. Cazenave, *Welfare Racism: Playing the Race Card against America's Poor* (Routledge 2001).

70. Fineman, *Neutered Mother, supra* note 5, at 101–22.

71. Amy L. Wax, *Rethinking Welfare Rights: Reciprocity Norms, Reactive Attitudes, and the Political Economy of Welfare Reform,* 63 Law & Contemp. Probs. 257, 276–80 (2000) [hereinafter Wax, *Welfare Rights*] .

72. *Id.* at 278.

73. *Id.*

74. *Id.* at 276, 276 n. 61.

75. *Id.* at 276.

76. Nancy Folbre, *The Invisible Heart: Economics and Family Values* 111–18 (New Press 2001).

77. *Id.* at 118.

78. *Id.* at 98–99.

79. Congressional Budget Office, *For Better or Worse: Marriage and the Federal Income Tax* (1997); discussed in Lawrence Zelenak, *Doing Something about Marriage Penalties: A Guide for the Perplexed,* 54 Tax. L. Rev. 1 (2000).

80. Michael B. Katz, *The Price of Citizenship: Redefining the American Welfare State* 318 (Metropolitan Books 2001) (citing U.S. House of Representatives, *1996 Green Book* 447–48, table 8-15).

81. *See* Martha T. McCluskey, A Critical Analysis of the Treatment of Dependent Care and Household Expenses in Federal Income Tax Theory 55–56 (1988) (unpublished manuscript on file with author); Martha T. McCluskey, From "Affluent Husband Care" to Worker Care: Rethinking Support for Family Caretaking Labor (2004) (unpublished manuscript on file with author). Although this tax break is gender-neutral on its face and so is available to breadwinner/caretaker married couples regardless of gender division, the vast majority of the higher-earning couples who reap most of the gains from this tax break have male breadwinners and female non-earners or low earners. For example, in 1998, nearly half of upper-income marriages (with members earning $250,000 to $499,999) had just one wage earner, and 90 percent of those wage earners were men. Nancy Ann Jeffrey, *The New-Economy Family,* Wall St. J. W1 (Sept. 8, 2000), discussed in Ann Crittenden, *The Price of Motherhood: Why the Most Important Job in the World Is Still the Least Valued* 117, 291–92 n. 15 (Owl Books 2001) (citing statistics that at the very highest income levels, virtually all marriages conform to the male breadwinner/female homemaker model).

82. *See generally* Edward McCaffery, *Taxing Women* (1997) (describing in detail what he describes as tax law's secondary-earner bias, commonly, and misleadingly, called the "marriage penalty"); Amy C. Christian, *The Joint Return Rate Structure: Identifying and Addressing the Gendered Nature of the Tax Law,* 2 J.L. & Pol. 241 (1997).

83. *See* Economic Growth and Tax Relief Reconciliation Act of 2001, Pub. L. 107-16, §§ 301–3 (codified in various sections of 26 U.S.C.). Marvin J. Williams, *The Marriage Penalty Dilemma: Some Relief on the Way,* 46 Nat'l. Pub. Accountant 32 (2001).

84. Wax, *Welfare Rights, supra* note 71, at 278–79.

85. *See* Neubeck & Cazenave, *supra* note 69, at 31–35.

86. *See, e.g.,* William A. Galston, *Civil Society, Civic Virtue and Liberal Democracy,* 75 Chi.-Kent L. Rev. 603, 606–7 (2000); Wax, *Welfare Rights, supra* note 71, at 279 n. 69.

87. *See* Fineman, *Neutered Mother, supra* note 5, at 104–6; Joel F. Handler, *The Poverty of Welfare Reform* 36 (1995); *see also* Neil deMause, *Father Knows Best,* In These Times 8 (Feb. 7, 2000) (summarizing criticisms of statistics on single parenting's harms).

88. *See* Karen Christopher, *Family-Friendly Europe,* 13 Am. Prospect 59–61 (Apr. 8, 2002) (citing data showing a poverty rate—before government assistance—of 42 percent of single mothers in the United States compared with 11 percent in Sweden); Sarah Lyall, *For Europeans, Love, Yes; Marriage, Maybe,* N.Y. Times 1 (Mar. 24, 2002) (reporting that, e.g., 62 percent of births in

Iceland and 49 percent of births in Norway are to unmarried parents but that policies focus on supporting parenthood rather than marriage and that single parenthood in many European countries is not associated with stigma or poverty).

89. *See* June Carbone & Margaret Brinig, *Rethinking Marriage: Feminist Ideology, Economic Change, and Divorce Reform*, 65 Tulane L. Rev. 953 (1991) (discussing a number of feminist proposals for better accounting for the costs of caretaking at divorce); Crittenden, *supra* note 81, at 149–85 (discussing how family law makes married mothers who specialize in caretaking rather than wage earning responsible for the bulk of child-care costs without sufficient reciprocal rights to share in the wage earners' income or property).

90. *See generally* Fineman, *Illusion of Equality, supra* note 35.

91. *See* Reva B. Siegel, *The Modernization of Marital Status Law: Adjudicating Wives' Rights to Earnings, 1860–1930*, 82 Geo. L.J. 2127 (1995) (discussing laws protecting husbands' property rights in wives' family labor).

92. *See* Wax, *Caring Crisis, supra* note 65, at 342–43.

93. *See* Crittenden, *supra* note 81, at 98–103, 260–61 (discussing employment discrimination against women and parents); 219–21 (discussing labor market restrictions on the immigration of paid child-care workers); 115–18 (discussing tax laws discouraging maternal wage work); 153–61 (discussing divorce law's failure to reward maternal caretaking). For discussions of how race and sex discrimination in employment prevent women's freedom to choose rewarding wage work over family care, *see* Neubeck & Cazenave, *supra* note 69, at 193–95; Vicki Schultz, *Life's Work*, 100 Colum. L. Rev. 1881, 1898–99 (2000).

94. *See* Crittenden, *supra* note 81, at 4, 23–24, 213–14, 104, 50, 257, 125.

95. *See* Handler, *supra* note 87, at 62–75 (discussing pre-TANF state work incentive programs providing employment assistance); Handler & Hasenfeld, *supra* note 18, at 74–77 (summarizing more recent work support programs); Thomas L. Gais & Cathy M. Johnson, *Welfare Reform, Management Systems, and Their Implications for Children*, 60 Ohio St. L.J. 1327, 1344–45 (1999) (discussing states' expanded work support services following TANF).

96. Wax, *Welfare Rights, supra* note 71, at 276–77.

97. *See* Kathryn Edin & Laura Lein, *Making Ends Meet: How Single Mothers Survive Welfare and Low-Wage Labor* xix–xxi (Russell Sage Found. 1997).

98. *See* Robert M. Solow, *Guess Who Pays for Workfare*, in *Work and Welfare* 26–30 (Amy Gutman ed., Princeton U. Press 1998).

99. *See* David A. Moss, *Socializing Security: Progressive-Era Economists and the Origins of American Social Policy* 64 (1996) (citing A. C. Pigou, *Wealth and Welfare* 163 (1912)).

100. *Id.*

101. Martin Gilens, *Why Americans Hate Welfare* 186–87, and table 8.1 (1999) (giving survey data showing that most Americans are willing to exempt work requirements for welfare mothers with young children); 67–79 (showing that widespread perceptions that blacks lack a strong work ethic drive opposition to welfare programs perceived as supporting blacks).

102. *See* Gwendolyn Mink, *Welfare's End* 23–25 (Cornell U. Press 1998); Crittenden, *supra* note 81, at 251–53.

103. *See* Gais & Johnson, *supra* note 95, at 1334–35 (discussing what they call the "environment theory" that work provides poor families with psychological and social benefits).

104. *See* Edin & Lein, *supra* note 97, at 6 (reporting that interviews with nearly four hundred welfare-reliant mothers show that all but one engaged in income-producing activities).

105. *See* Dorothy Roberts, *The Value of Black Mothers' Work*, 26 Conn. L. Rev. 871–73 (1994); Dorothy Roberts, *Shattered Bonds: The Color of Child Welfare* 173–200 (Basic Books 2002) [hereinafter Roberts, *Shattered Bonds*].

106. *See* Handler & Hasenfeld, *supra* note 18, at 75–78.

107. *See* Peter Pitegoff & Lauren Breen, *Child Care Policy and the Welfare Reform Act*, 6 J. Affordable Housing & Community Dev. L. 113, 115 (1997); Jonathan Cohn, *Child's Play: Why Universal, High Quality Day Care Should Be Elementary*, 11 Am. Prospect 46–49 (June

19–July 3, 2000) (discussing problems concerning access to child care that continue despite increased funding).

108. Kevin Butler, *Charles Murray on Welfare's Woes and the Ills of Out-of-Wedlock Births*, Investor's Bus. Daily A22 (Sept. 1, 2000).

109. Schultz, *supra* note 93, at 1945–48, 1955–57. In addition, she proposes "vigorous anti-discrimination, affirmative action, and pay equity measures" to ensure equal access to fulfilling work. *Id.* at 1955–56.

110. See R. H. Coase, *The Firm, the Market, and the Law* 95–96 (1988), discussed in Pierre Schlag, *An Appreciative Comment on Coase's "The Problem of Social Cost": A View from the Left*, 1986 Wis. L. Rev. 919, 921–44 (1986); McCluskey, *Illusion of Efficiency, supra* note 46, at 726.

111. *The MIT Dictionary of Modern Economics* 432 (David W. Pearce ed., 4th ed. 1995).

112. Posner, *Economic Analysis, supra* note 7, at 509 (citing Sheldon Danziger & Robert Haveman, *How Income Transfer Programs Affect Work, Savings, and the Income Distribution: A Critical Review*, 19 J. Econ. Lit. 975, 1020 (1981)).

113. See McCluskey, *Illusion of Efficiency, supra* note 46, at 736–40; Pierre Schlag, *The Problem of Transaction Costs*, 62 S. Cal. L. Rev. 1661, 1663 (1989).

114. Organisation for Economic Co-Operation and Development, *Towards a Better Integration of Work and Welfare: UK*, in OECD *Economic Development Surveys—United Kingdom* 69 (1998).

115. Dorothy Roberts quotes a cartoon featuring a politician who explains that an AFDC recipient is a bad mother because she "hang[s] around the house taking care of the kids" and that she'll be cut off welfare if she doesn't take a job. "Doing what?" the welfare mother asks. "Taking care of someone else's kids," the politician answers. Roberts, *Shattered Bonds, supra* note 105, at 180 (quoting *Wasserman's View*, Boston Globe 10 (Sept. 25, 1995)). *See also* Mink, *supra* note 102, at 129–31 (criticizing welfare-to-work requirements for "institutionalizing [poor and single] mothers as a caste of providers for other people—of goods, services, and *care* for other people and their children").

116. Mink, *supra* note 102, at 23.

117. *See* Butler, *supra* note 108 (quoting Murray's discussion comparing the decision to bear a child "even though you have very little money, very little education and are very young" to child abuse and neglect); Galston, *supra* note 86, at 603, 608 (criticizing births by poor, single teenaged mothers on the grounds that "it is wrong to bring a child into the world if one is not adequately prepared to raise the child"); Rickie Solinger, *Beggars and Choosers: How the Politics of Choice Shapes Adoption, Abortion, and Welfare in the United States, 1998–99* (2001) (reporting on efforts to promote adoption and foster care as the solution to single mothers' poverty). For critical discussions of such arguments, *see* Linda C. McClain, *"Irresponsible" Reproduction*, ch. 11, this vol.; Christopher Jencks & Kathryn Edin, *Do Poor Women Have a Right to Bear Children?* 20 Am. Prospect 47 (1995). Dorothy Roberts shows that recent welfare reforms have worked together with changes in child welfare policy to create a system particularly aimed at breaking up black families. Roberts, *Shattered Bonds, supra* note 105, at 173–200.

118. Rich Hood, *Voters Still Want Welfare Reform*, Kan. City Star L1 (May 26, 1996).

119. Malcolm Gladwell, *Remaking Welfare: In States' Experience, A Cutting Contest*, Wash. Post A1 (Mar. 10, 1995) [hereinafter Gladwell, *Remaking Welfare*].

120. Jonathan Walters, *The Welfare Bonanza*, Governing Magazine 34 (Jan. 2000).

121. *Id.*

122. *See* Marcia K. Meyers, *How Welfare Offices Undermine Welfare Reform*, 11 Am. Prospect 41, 42–44 (June 19–July 3, 2000).

123. Gais & Johnson, *supra* note 95, at 1349–50 (citing Irene Lurie, *State Capacity Study: Implementing PRWORA at the Local Level* (May 12, 1999) (address at the 1999 Welfare Reform Evaluation Conference sponsored by the Administration for Children and Families, Office of Planning, Research, and Evaluation, U.S. Department of Health and Human Services).

124. Meyers, *supra* note 122, at 42–43.

125. *Id.* at 44.

126. *Id.* at 42–43; *see also* Ted Kleine, *The Shadow of Poverty in America: Allied Forces,* In These Time 17 (June 12, 2000) (reporting on welfare advocates' campaign that claimed "long and cumbersome processes" were contributing to denying access to welfare benefits).

127. *See* Meyers, *supra* note 122, at 43–44; Kleine, *supra* note 126.

128. *See* Joshua Green, *The Welfare Shell Game,* 11 Am. Prospect 36 (June 19–July 3, 2000) (giving example of Texas).

129. *Id.*

130. Walters, *supra* note 120, at 34.

131. *See* Christopher Cook, *Cozy Ties,* Houston Press (July 10, 1997).

132. *See* Sharon Dietrich, Maurice Emsellem, & Catharine Ruckelshaus, *Work Reform: The Other Side of Welfare Reform,* 9 Stan. L. & Pol'y Rev. 53, 60 n. 140 (1998).

133. *See* Melissa Kwaterski Scanlan, *The End of Welfare and Constitutional Protections for the Poor: A Case Study of the Wisconsin Works Project and Due Process Rights,* 13 Berkeley Women's L.J. 153, 163–64 (1998).

134. *See* Walters, *supra* note 120.

135. For thorough and excellent analyses of moral hazard, *see generally* Tom Baker, *The Genealogy of Moral Hazard,* 75 Tex. L. Rev. 237 (1996); Carol Heimer, *Reactive Risk and Rational Action: Managing Moral Hazard in Insurance Contracts* (1985).

136. Rector & Lauber, *supra* note 19, at 3.

137. *Id.; see also* Fineman, *Neutered Mother, supra* note 5, at 117 (criticizing examples of this argument).

138. *See* Katz, *supra* note 80, at 326. For a discussion of similar welfare reform measures implemented by states before the 1996 reform legislation, *see* Williams, *Ideology of Division, supra* note 5, at 719.

139. Deborah A. Stone, *Beyond Moral Hazard: Insurance as Moral Opportunity* 6 Conn. Ins. L.J., 11 (2000).

140. *See* Handler, *supra* note 87, at 106; Williams, *Ideology of Division, supra* note 5, at 739–40; McClain, *supra* note 117, at 407–8.

141. *See* McCluskey, *Subsidized Lives, supra* note 33, at 140.

142. *See* Baker, *supra* note 135, at 273 and n. 179; Reiner H. Kraakman, *Corporate Liability Strategies and the Costs of Legal Controls,* 93 Yale L.J. 857, 874 (1984).

143. *See* Frances E. Olsen, *Family and the Market: A Study of Ideology and Legal Reform,* 96 Harv. L. Rev. 1497, 1503 (1983) (making a similar point about apparently contradictory criticisms of market "intervention").

144. *See* Gladwell, *Remaking Welfare, supra* note 119, at A01.

145. *See* McCluskey, *Subsidized Lives, supra* note 33, at 133–34.

146. *See* Robert B. Reich, *Is Scrooge a Democrat Now?* 11 Am. Prospect 96 (2000); Harold Meyerson, *Bill and Al's Excellent Adventure,* L.A. Weekly 30 (Jan. 28, 2000); John B. Judis, *Embarrassment of Riches,* 11 Am. Prospect 10–11 (2000).

147. For an example of one proposal to implement such a shift by increasing transparency and democratic representation in the IMF and other international institutions, *see* U.S. Representative Bernie Sanders's Global Sustainable Development Resolution, http://www.bernie.house.gov/imf/global.asp.

CHAPTER 11

Deterring "Irresponsible" Reproduction through Welfare Reform

Linda C. McClain

In recent years, there have been countless calls for reversing the rise in irresponsibility in American society.[1] Many voices urge that law and public policy should encourage, or require, personal responsibility and should no longer tolerate, much less reward, irresponsibility. A prime target in the campaign for personal responsibility has been procreative irresponsibility, or "irresponsible" reproduction. In the rhetoric of irresponsibility, reproductive behaviors and choices deemed irresponsible serve as an indicator of moral decline, social breakdown, and pathology.[2]

This public alarm and indignation about "irresponsible" reproduction reaches a fevered pitch when such reproduction implicates the public fisc through welfare programs. In the debates of the 1990s over welfare reform, lawmakers and others made repeated appeals for legislative change that would end "illegitimacy," restore personal responsibility, and persuade people (women and adolescent females) to stop having children that they could not afford to support without public assistance. These debates culminated in Congress's passing—and President Clinton's signing into law—the Personal Responsibility and Work Opportunity Reconciliation Act of 1996 (PRWORA), major legislation that dramatically altered the social welfare state in the United States by eliminating a federal entitlement to welfare and replacing Aid to Families with Dependent Children (AFDC) with the Temporary Assistance for Needy Families program.[3] A central charge in those debates was that welfare recipients procreate at the expense of taxpayers, who, in contrast, have children only if they can afford them. Thus, proposals to combat the rates of "illegitimate" births and welfare dependency—"irresponsible" behaviors induced by welfare—advocated doing so by altering the incentives and excluding certain categories of mothers and their children from public assistance.

This essay looks back on the rhetoric of irresponsible reproduction as it figured in the congressional debates about welfare reform leading to the passage of PRWORA.[4] Those debates in turn echoed the persistent calls, from various cultural critics, pundits, and academics, for restoring personal responsibility. The essay critically evaluates how such rhetoric distinguishes responsible and irresponsible reproduction. It examines assumptions about the relationship between the incentive effects of governmental programs and human motivation, agency, and victimization. It contends that the procreation stories told in such public policy discourse are simplistic, reductive, and inadequate. They cannot serve as an adequate basis for serious public debate about reproduction and responsibility or for changing law and public policy. The models of responsible and irresponsible reproduction are flawed and reflect a problematic gender ideology and troublesome stereotypes about people in poverty. A serious public conversation about reproduction and responsibility, and especially about how law and public policy should foster responsibility, must include important dimensions that are now missing. Public responsibility for the existence of poverty and for the care and support of children is one such dimension. Moreover, feminist analysis of the concepts of responsibility and irresponsibility would enrich such a conversation by focusing on topics such as the impact of gender inequality, male irresponsibility, and violence against women on women's family choices and the extent to which single motherhood should be viewed as a "deliberate choice."[5] A continuum model of agency and responsibility offers a useful framework for thinking about such issues and developing alternative models of responsible reproduction.

At the conclusion of this essay, I turn briefly to a prominent theme in post-PRWORA rhetoric about welfare reform: promoting "responsible fatherhood." Sometimes described as the next phase of implementing the reforms begun by PRWORA, responsible fatherhood is not only the organizing concept of an influential social movement but also the object of governmental efforts at the state and federal levels.

Identifying the Problem of "Irresponsible" Reproduction

In assessing the rhetoric of "irresponsible" reproduction, threshold questions are, What activities constitute procreative irresponsibility and why? In answering these questions, it is helpful to begin with a working model of what, as gleaned from the rhetoric, constitutes responsible reproduction. "Responsible" reproduction, first and foremost, takes place within marriage, the traditional, "legitimate" family form. Such reproduction occurs when parents are self-sufficient and can meet their "private" responsibility for material support of their family without public assistance. They are adults who possess the maturity or mental and moral capacity to make responsible decisions about reproduction. In contrast, "irresponsible" reproduction takes place outside of marriage. It occurs when parents are not self-sufficient but, instead, encouraged by the incentive of welfare benefits, shift the financial costs of parenting to others (e.g., the taxpayer-supported welfare state). Or it is undertaken by teens, persons who do not possess the maturity or capacity to make morally responsible reproductive decisions, let alone serve as responsible parents. I demonstrate that these contrasting models of responsible and irresponsible reproduction are both over- and underinclusive.

The rhetoric of procreative irresponsibility suggests three primary targets of the charge: "single mothers," "welfare mothers," and "teen mothers." My initial formulation, which focuses on women and ignores men, echoes the discourse. However, each of these three paradigms could be reformulated in terms of male irresponsibility. For example, one could target as irresponsible single fathers who do not marry or remain part of the familial households of the women they impregnate, "deadbeat dads" who fail to meet their financial as well as other responsibilities to their children, and promiscuous or "predatory" males who prematurely engage in reproductive sex with teen females or who sexually exploit or abuse them. In fact, men are not wholly absent as targets of the rhetoric of procreative irresponsibility, as the increasing condemnation of the deadbeat dad suggests, and there is a growing call for responsible fatherhood. Yet there are significant differences in why mothers as opposed to fathers are deemed irresponsible and in the social opprobrium attached to each.

The single mother, the welfare mother, and the teen mother may coincide in particular women, and the rhetoric of irresponsible reproduction often erroneously conflates all single mothers into one undifferentiated stereotype. However, I separate them analytically to illustrate how they exemplify three aspects or types of irresponsibility: immorality, unaccountability, and incapacity. The single mother defies ideas of traditional sexual morality and of morally responsible choice because she is a mother outside of marriage (this is especially true if her motherhood originated in out-of-wedlock childbearing). The welfare mother's irresponsibility lies in her unaccountability. She fails to take responsibility for the consequences of her actions because she reproduces and then shifts the financial costs of rearing her children to the public. The teen mother signifies irresponsibility through incapacity or immaturity. As the phrases "children having children" and "babies having babies" suggest, she procreates and becomes a parent without having attained a threshold level of maturity and moral responsibility. But there is considerable crossover among these aspects of irresponsibility, particularly in the association of poverty not only with sexual immorality but also with the violation of moral principles of self-sufficiency. At its broadest, the rhetoric often criticizes *all* single-family households for imposing costs on society and questions the capacity of *all* single mothers to be effective parents without a man in the household.[6]

The Single Mother

The rhetoric of procreative irresponsibility is replete with references to crises concerning the rise in "illegitimacy" or "out-of-wedlock" births; the increase in "single-parent," "broken," or "nonintact" families; and the problem of "the failure of families to form."[7] For those who sound this alarm, part of the crisis is that the demographic trends cut across racial, ethnic, and class lines and that rates of nonmarital procreation among white Americans are now approaching those of African Americans of thirty years ago (when Daniel Patrick Moynihan initially issued his warning).[8] Along these lines, the proposed Personal Responsibility Act (the precursor to PRWORA) identified "the reduction of out-of-wedlock births" as an important governmental interest to be advanced by welfare reform. The act contained numerous assertions about the importance of marriage and the negative consequences of "illegitimacy," some differentiated according to race but all contributing to "the crisis in our Nation."[9] Thus, the discourse overtly uses racial terms to warn of dangerous crossovers. Such warnings also contain the offensive premise that social problems are tolerable so long as they affect only minorities but warrant society's serious attention when they spill over to mainstream (white) society.[10]

What is irresponsible about reproduction by single mothers? As former education secretary William Bennett testified before Congress, it violates "an important moral principle" that "having children out-of-wedlock is wrong," independent of any economic arguments against it.[11] Feminist legal theorist Martha Fineman ably illustrates that the single mother features as "deviant" in such public policy discourse precisely because of her "singleness" and the absence of a man in her family.[12]

Furthermore, the increasing societal acceptance of such deviant families is seen as part of the crisis.[13] Then vice president Dan Quayle's Murphy Brown speech, in which he publicly condemned the popular television series *Murphy Brown* for glorying single motherhood and "mocking the importance of fathers," was an instructive sally in this cultural war.[14] One of the feared consequences of the decline in stigma attached to out-of-wedlock births is that when adult women, especially prominent women, have children outside of marriage without any sign of shame or remorse, they serve as poor role models for adolescent females, who are said to engage in imitative behavior.[15] But unlike their wealthier adult counterparts, it is argued, these young mothers are likely to be or to become poor, to rely on the welfare system to support their children one generation after another, and to suffer numerous other social consequences. Indeed, Quayle's speech linked "intergenerational poverty" to a "poverty of values" and criticized the reliance of young single mothers on the state, instead of a husband, as a provider.[16]

Some voices within the discourse suggest that the problem is not so much a poverty as a plethora of values, but articles like "Dan Quayle Was Right" argue that we should not be equivocal about, or equally tolerant of, diverse family forms.[17] Such diversity, the argument goes, harms children and undermines society. Thus, there is tension in the discourse about whether the crisis results only from mother-headed homes caused by "illegitimacy," or from all "fatherless" households, including those created by divorce or otherwise.[18]

Although the concern about deviation from traditional mores and the absence of shame seems most publicly visible around the notion of illegitimacy, some voices also urge a return to the use of shame and even some legal restrictions to combat the increasing social acceptance of divorce.[19]

The Welfare Mother

A second aspect or type of irresponsibility found in the rhetoric of irresponsible reproduction is unaccountability, vividly illustrated by the welfare mother. In contrast with the welfare mother, responsible reproducers have children only if they can support them and do not expect the welfare state to assume the costs of their reproductive decisions. In this view, it is irresponsible to bring children into the world if one cannot or does not care (or provide care) for and financially support them.[20] Proponents of "family cap" provisions, which render a woman already on public assistance ineligible for additional welfare benefits for children born during her welfare tenure, argued that it is only fair that poor people should play by the same rules and adhere to the same value system as do working-class and middle-class families, who have to ask whether they can afford to have a child or will need to earn additional income, and who do not receive an automatic wage increase every time they have a child.[21]

In the rhetoric about the welfare mother, marriage again serves as a proxy for responsible reproduction. As Quayle put it, "[a] welfare check is not a husband. The state is not a father."[22] Murray maintains that until the welfare state tampered with "natural forces" by making single-mother families economically viable, a combination of stigma, social sanction, and legal rules about marriage kept such units, which are "a net drain on the community's resources," to a manageable number.[23] As Fineman observes, the assumption is that the only way a mother can avoid poverty for herself and her children is by being linked to a father's financial resources.[24]

If economic viability is the test for responsible reproduction and a "legitimate" family, as Murray suggests, then many families headed by mothers indeed fail the test: families consisting of a mother and her children have a higher rate of poverty than do two-parent families.[25] But the focus on illegitimacy as a cause of welfare dependency proves underinclusive. Although a significant number of single-parent families with children born outside marriage received AFDC benefits, divorce or marital separation was the most common precipitating factor leading women to seek such benefits.[26] Conversely, equating "illegitimacy" with the lack of economic viability is also overinclusive, because many nonmarital families are not in poverty, raising the question whether society has any justification for treating such families (a category that Murray downplays) as "illegitimate" and irresponsible.

Marriage proves overinclusive as a proxy for responsible reproduction because it does not guarantee self-sufficiency or the absence of poverty. First, high divorce rates and low rates of child support payment by noncustodial fathers substantially contribute to mothers' poverty and reliance on welfare.[27] Second, marriage proves a very ineffective antipoverty program for stay-at-home mothers, who, after divorce, become "displaced homemakers" whose underinvestment in their own human capital disadvantages them in the market.[28] Third, in many instances, even if women in poverty married the fathers of their children, they would still be in poverty and in need of public assistance.[29] Fourth, a growing population among the poor consists of married couples with children, families in which one or both parents participate in the paid labor market.[30] Would two-parent families below a certain income level be judged irresponsible reproducers? Finally, if the test for responsible reproduction is reproducing without expecting to shift the costs of support to others, few families would pass the test when one considers the many subsidies, tax benefits, and credits on which American families depend.[31]

The Teen Mother

The teen mother, the third target of the irresponsibility critique, illustrates the association of irresponsibility with immaturity or incapacity. The cry of "children having children" or "babies having babies" captures this aspect of irresponsibility while also warning of cultural breakdown and moral crisis. Proponents of the Personal Responsibility Act invoked the dependent welfare teen as a symbol of the cruelty of the current system, which is said to induce children to have children by holding out the prospects of an apartment and benefits.

As with the categories of single mother and welfare mother, the use of proxies in the rhetoric surrounding the teen mother leads to over- and underinclusiveness. Teen mothers induced to procreate by welfare benefits often serve as a proxy for both the single mother and, especially, the welfare mother. This proxy system yields a distorted picture: although many single women receiving AFDC became mothers during their teens, teen mothers comprise a very small percentage of mothers on AFDC, and young teens, an even smaller percentage.[32] Further, although teen mothers tend to be poorer, stay on welfare rolls somewhat longer, and may face more problems than adult women in leaving the rolls, teen mothers "do not inevitably end up as long-term welfare recipients."[33]

The popular coinage "children having children" is particularly problematic. First, the majority of births to adolescent mothers are to females aged eighteen or nineteen, generally not considered to be children.[34] Similarly, the rhetoric does not address married teen mothers who are presumably deemed capable of making responsible decisions. Indeed, a historical perspective suggests that teenage pregnancy outside of marriage has been prevalent throughout American history and that what constitutes today's "crisis" is that pregnant teens no longer resolve the "problem" by marriage or adoption.[35]

Second, the notion of children having children suggests a general moral incapacity, immaturity, and lack of moral agency among all teenage females and lends itself to reductive accounts of why such females become pregnant. Such accounts discourage careful analysis of the complex set of reasons for adolescent pregnancy, including sexual exploitation and victimization, insufficient motivation to avoid pregnancy, unrealistic judgments about the consequences of their actions, and deliberate and (from such young women's perspectives) rational choices about motherhood.[36]

Third, the specter of children having children may mask divisions of opinion about precisely what the problem of teen reproductive irresponsibility is. The term suggests that the problem is "irresponsible" sex in the sense that *children* should not be having sex at all, let alone be parents. Yet one might also view the problem as one of "irresponsible" sex in the sense that teens should be exercising responsibility if they are sexually active by avoiding unwanted or unwise consequences such as pregnancy, parenthood, and diseases.[37]

Finally, this assumption of incapacity also includes a blanket assumption that all teen mothers are incompetent parents and hinders serious discussion of why teen parenting is problematic and how, if prevention of early parenting fails, society should help teen parents be responsible.

Further Costs of Irresponsible Reproduction

In the rhetoric of irresponsible reproduction, one charge common to all three targets—single mothers, welfare mothers, and teen mothers—is that such family forms are costly for children, for society, and for men's roles as fathers. One common claim is that there is substantial evidence that children in families with only one biological parent as the result of nonmarital birth or divorce ("nonintact" or "disrupted" families) are at a disadvantage compared with children in two-parent ("intact") families, in significant part because of the poverty of such families.[38] There are staggering lists of social problems or pathologies traced back to the root cause of "broken families" and "the breakdown of intact traditional families."[39] Although some, like Murray, trace such problems directly to nonmarital families, terminology such as the "intact" family (two married, biological parents) versus the "nonintact," "broken," or "disrupted" family clearly sweeps more broadly to implicate many family forms. Indeed, scholars who study single-parent families find that families originating in nonmarital births and in divorce have many similarities, including their supposed consequences for children.[40] More typically, however, as the welfare reform debates illustrate, a more inclusive diagnosis of the supposed costs of all single-parent families gives way to a diagnosis of illegitimacy as the root problem requiring a solution.[41]

Assessing the Rhetoric of Irresponsible Reproduction

Procreation Stories Told in Welfare Discourse

In the discourse about irresponsible procreation, there are a number of assumptions about agency and responsibility. In conservative rhetoric, for example, one finds the following, at times overlapping and conflicting, models of welfare recipients: the rational actor responding to incentives; the victim of a perverse governmental system; the culpable exploiter of that system; and the deviator from natural gender roles. The first three models were prominent in legislative efforts surrounding PRWORA.[42] The fourth is a key part of some prominent conservative analyses of welfare and seems to play some role in the rhetoric of responsible fatherhood. All of these models derive from a model of responsible reproduction: that undertaken in marriage by self-sufficient adults who provide for their own children without governmental assistance.

WELFARE RECIPIENTS AS RATIONAL ACTORS, VICTIMS, AND EXPLOITERS

A recurrent theme in the discourse of welfare reform is the need to change perverse incentives supposedly created by welfare programs. In *Losing Ground*, Charles Murray argued, quite influentially, that it was not necessary to look to such explanations as the "*Zeitgeist* of the 1960s," macroeconomic conditions, cultural pathologies, or racial differences to account for increased rates of illegitimacy, welfare dependency, and unemployment of the young. Rather, the poor and the not-poor alike make rational decisions to maximize their advantage; however, what is rational at the economic level of the poor may appear irrational from the perspective of the middle class.[43]

At times, the political rhetoric surrounding PRWORA echoed Murray's claim that poor people act and respond rationally to incentives.[44] When government subsidizes behavior such as illegitimacy and procreation by people who cannot afford to support their children, it is no surprise that "what you subsidize, you get more of."[45] But the rhetoric more often sounded themes of a lack of responsible self-direction and of seduction and entrapment by a perverse incentive structure. For example, the House Republicans' *Contract with America* assumes that incentives in the welfare system lead people into a dependency trap: "The Great Society has had the unintended consequence of snaring millions of Americans into the welfare trap."[46] This trap appears to undermine people's moral capacity and produce both an economic dependency and a destructive psychological state of dependency.[47]

The imagery of welfare recipients as victims of misguided governmental policies might suggest that they should be excused from blame because of irresponsibility in the sense of incapacity. Yet these victims are found doubly irresponsible because they engage in behavior that is also irresponsible in the sense of being reckless, self-destructive, and costly for society (such as illegitimacy, family breakdown, crime, and increasing poverty itself).[48] Thus, the welfare recipient as victim gives way to the welfare recipient as culpable exploiter of the system: the images of the able-bodied idler, the welfare queen, the deadbeat dad, or the food stamp cheater all suggest evasion of responsibility by imposing costs on, or shifting them to, others.[49] Although governmental programs designed "to give a helping hand to the neediest" have "bred" such problems, it is the persons who engage in such activity who must be held accountable by the government's "requiring" them "to take personal responsibility for the decisions they make."[50]

Welfare recipients, with compromised moral capacities, must be led firmly down the path toward responsible self-government. To accomplish responsible self-government is to be held accountable to a specified set of norms about responsible conduct. These themes of the moral incapacity of the poor and the diagnosis of their need for regulation have a long history.[51]

Attention to the racial dimension of these images of irresponsibility is critical. Even when the rhetoric does not overtly use racial terms, it may aim particularly at the "dependency and irresponsible reproduction" of people of color, especially African Americans.[52] For example, many critics of welfare rhetoric observe that the stereotypical image of the welfare recipient is a black, unmarried woman.[53] Although white women in fact constituted a slightly greater percentage of all AFDC recipients at the time of the debate over PRWORA, "no one has a clear image of who or where these [white] recipients are."[54] The fact that a higher percentage of African-American women are single parents because of nonmarital births than because of divorce, and that a higher percentage of white women become single parents by divorce or separation than by nonmarital births, may also contribute to why "illegitimacy" is more readily associated with welfare dependency, pathology, and social crisis than is divorce.[55] Further, even claims of a common crisis may mask harsher and more punitive attitudes concerning the reproductive and mothering behavior of women of color.[56] Indeed, Lucy Williams argues that public perceptions of the poor as "other," that is, African Americans who have "warped values," undergird such behavior modification measures as family caps.[57]

ILLEGITIMACY, DEPENDENCY, AND WOMEN'S AGENCY

The welfare debate mirrors the over- and underinclusiveness of the broader rhetoric of reproductive irresponsibility by using the notion of illegitimacy to signify single mothers and welfare mothers, and marriage to signal responsible reproduction. With the problem of poverty and its solution defined in terms of reducing illegitimacy, it is not surprising that Congress's findings accompanying major welfare reform legislation focused on reproductive behavior and family forms rather than on factors such as macroeconomic contributors to unemployment and underemployment, the difficulty parents face finding adequate and affordable child care and medical benefits, and the causes of the disproportionate poverty of mothers (especially women of color).[58]

It is certainly reasonable to question the possible incentive effects and social consequences of governmental programs and to determine whether they are at odds with the purposes underlying such programs. However, what is striking is the lack of complexity and empirical foundation in the proposed behavioral models of how welfare accounts for women's (and men's) reproductive choices and behaviors. One reductive assumption in such models is that the availability of welfare benefits, which are below the poverty level in every state (and have declined in real value over the last two decades), provides incentives for women to procreate outside of marriage.[59] This reductive portrait of women and the causal effects of welfare on their motivations played a central role in recent welfare reform efforts, despite the substantial body of scholarship refuting the charge that the availability of welfare benefits induces nonmarital births, and despite testimony before Congress that there was no solid evidence for concluding that eliminating benefits will significantly reduce nonmarital births.[60] Nor did evidence of actual demographic patterns—that is, that the families of women on AFDC were no bigger than those of the rest of the population and, indeed, tended to be smaller—exert any countervailing effect on the imagery of the welfare recipient/rational actor procreating in response to incentives.[61]

Moreover, the initial evaluation of New Jersey's family cap measure revealed no statistically significant difference between birth rates of women subject to the cap and those who were not.[62] Therefore, one might persuasively argue (as some members of Congress did in opposition to family caps) that responsible political officials should not support a measure that may simply reduce the income of poor families with young children.[63] For some, however, the absence of empirical support for such arguments seemed to be beside the point, for even if one grants that welfare does not cause illegitimacy, it should no longer subsidize it.[64]

This reductive model of incentives assumes that, just as welfare causes illegitimacy, so reforming welfare is an effective solution to the problem. It ignores the fact that the rise in nonmarital births is not limited to women who rely on, or will likely rely on, public assistance for support, but is spread throughout the income distribution.[65] As many scholars have observed, this increase in single-parent families is primarily attributable not to welfare but to broader cultural trends concerning divorce, premarital sexuality, nonmarital pregnancy and parenting (including, to the dismay of some, the decline of stigma), decreases in married women's fertility rates, and increases in women's work force participation, as well as to certain macroeconomic trends.[66]

Another assumption inherent in these models is that women and adolescent females exercise a high degree of agency in their reproductive lives. Thus, like rational actors, they can and will respond to incentives and disincentives, that

is, to carrots and sticks, and they can and will control their male sexual partners. For example, Gary Bauer, head of the Family Research Council, stated
that he supported the benefit exclusions in the Personal Responsibility Act,
notwithstanding his organization's opposition to legal abortion, because he
hoped they would re-create "that culture where women tell men to get lost."[67]
Similarly, a central justification for the New Jersey family cap legislation was
to encourage rational and responsible decision making by AFDC recipients
about economic costs of procreation. In legal challenges to this scheme, liti-
gants questioned this assumption of agency and argued not only that women
did not make reproductive decisions on the basis of the availability of more
benefits, but also that many pregnancies of women on public assistance, like
those of many women not on public assistance, are unintended.[68] Moreover,
restrictive laws governing access to abortion (laws restricting funding and
counseling, as well as informed consent requirements) and limited access to
family planning and contraceptive services introduce further constraints on
poor women's supposed "rational" decision making about reproduction.[69] As
I elaborate later in this essay, this assumption of rational calculation and control is often problematic for women in general, and particularly for adolescent
females, who experience high rates of rape and sexual abuse.

WELFARE, GENDER IDEOLOGY, AND RESPONSIBLE FATHERHOOD

The fourth model of welfare recipients, the deviator from natural gender roles,
features in the dramatic (and problematic) gender ideology present in some
prominent conservative analyses of welfare. Moreover, traces of this ideology
are found across the broader spectrum of voices associated with the "responsible fatherhood" movement, which shares an uneasiness about women forming families without men and is often critical of the existing welfare system for
its supposed messages about and impact on fathers.[70] (As I discuss at the conclusion of this essay, the theme of encouraging responsible fatherhood is a centerpiece of discussions about the next phase of welfare reform.)

In this gender ideology, the rise in welfare rates and in single-parent families traces to the pernicious effects of the government's tampering with proper
gender roles. By facilitating women's ability to maintain a family independent
of men's financial support, welfare is harmful because it renders men unnecessary, depriving them of their cultural role of provider and leading them to seek
satisfaction in predatory, promiscuous, and irresponsible sex—including "irresponsible fathering of random progeny," children they will not support.[71]
Motherhood is largely shaped by biology or nature, but fatherhood must be
defined by culture to domesticate a masculinity that otherwise inclines in the
direction of violence, sexual aggression, and promiscuity.[72] The welfare state
has "cuckolded" men, robbing them of their role as husband and provider by
inducing women with children to depend instead on government (which may

be a better provider).[73] It is instructive to recall former vice president Quayle's objection to this substitution: "A welfare check is not a father, the state is not a husband."[74] Indeed, being a provider, some conservative commentators argue, is at the core of manhood.[75] Such accounts assume that women, in their role as gatekeepers, can and should exercise their agency by "just saying no" to sex and pregnancy outside of marriage. The "failure of families to form" reflects women's failure to engage successfully in their proper cultural task of domesticating or "taming" men into marriage, monogamous commitment, and paternal support of children.[76]

This tale of thwarted masculinity presents baffling questions about the nature of masculinity and the role of men as fathers. It is instructive to consider this theme in the context of arguments about the pathology and social disorder attributed to "fatherless" families.[77] On the one hand, men outside the fatherhood role are irresponsible, antisocial, sexually predatory, and violent. On the other hand, a woman parenting without a father's presence produces a dangerous family form, particularly dangerous for boys, who turn out to be young males who manifest the same dangerous behaviors as undomesticated men. Although this analysis supposes that men are both the problem and the solution, one might also conclude that the evidence drawn from nature warrants endorsement of the model of the single (female) parent family. That is, males are simply too unreliable and irresponsible as providers and child rearers (not to mention violent) to risk bringing them into the household.[78] In any event, given the unattractive portrait of men and marriage found in this gender ideology, one can hardly blame women if they exercise available options to avoid both.

There are tensions between women's interests and the problematic gender ideology of conservative analyses of welfare relevant to the discourse of irresponsible reproduction and welfare reform. First, in charging that governmental programs intended to solve problems of poverty are really the source of the problem, Murray, Gilder, and the proponents of responsible fatherhood ignore the fact that AFDC and its precursors came into being precisely because women and children lacked a breadwinner.[79] Moreover, this model suggests that public policy should address family poverty primarily by encouraging or requiring fathers' personal responsibility, with no guarantee that reliance on it will be adequate and no recognition of collective responsibility for the well-being of children.

Second, welfare also serves an important (even subversive) role in facilitating female independence from men and marriage by providing women with the economic resources (albeit inadequate) to leave an abusive, violent, or unsatisfactory relationship with a man.[80] Third, the gender ideology of man as provider, robbed of his role by welfare, may divert attention from structural factors impairing the ability of many men to be providers and it may treat such men as irresponsible failures, while ignoring ways to foster women's economic well-being.[81]

Fourth, some proponents of male responsibility argue that monogamous marriage is the antidote for male violence, and that when men are detached from their roles of father and husband, they are more likely to engage in violence toward women.[82] Such arguments underestimate the extent to which male violence may have led to a detachment from the home: the incidence of male violence against women within marriage is simply too high to make this defense of marriage persuasive.

Personal or Collective Responsibility

Through the lens of personal responsibility, the welfare crisis seems to stem largely from people procreating irresponsibly and parenting without the financial resources or the willingness to work and save to provide for their children. The core failing of the welfare state lies in its perverse incentive structure that encourages such procreation. Through another lens, the welfare reform rhetoric of the 1990s, in focusing on personal responsibility, obscures questions of causal and collective responsibility. It engages in scapegoating and ignores the macroeconomic and systemic reasons for poverty as well as the demands of social justice and society's collective responsibility for supporting the poor.

The rhetoric of reproductive irresponsibility accepts the status quo of economic arrangements and distribution of resources as an unproblematic baseline from which to assess both personal responsibility and fairness. It fails to inquire whether, for example, poverty and welfare dependency derive not from "bad behavior" but from economic inequality rooted in structures of sex, race, and class.[83] As Herbert Gans contends in *The War against the Poor,* "most of the time most of the poor do not violate the fundamental moral values" and indeed "want to work in secure, well-paid, and respectable jobs like everyone else"; perceptions to the contrary aid in labeling them and condemning them as "undeserving."[84] There is too little attention paid to the problem that people are unable to live consistent with their values and to designing public policies that value families and children. Instead, the problem of family poverty is reduced to a "poverty of values" charge and to failure of personal responsibility and of not playing by the rules.[85] Addressing the real economics problems that face many families in poverty, however, would require serious economic and family policies and a degree of governmental investment that is anathema in an era in which reducing governmental spending and saving taxpayers' money are primary objectives of welfare reform.

The critique of unaccountability contains the implicit assumption that everyone could have adequate resources to provide for children without reliance on governmental assistance if only they played by the rules. Christopher Jencks and Katherine Edin argue persuasively that if poor women heeded this call and deferred childbearing until they were financially prepared—which is equated with such measures as getting an education, a job, and a husband—they might never bear a child because many of those women will never be able to afford to have children without some public assistance.[86] Moreover, the burden falls disproportionately on groups such as African Americans and women who have suffered historical subordination and discrimination and whose poverty results in part from governmental policies and laws.[87] Why shouldn't the relevant inquiry be what resources an individual could expect to command in a society whose economic distribution met the requirements of fairness and justice? If the problems associated with single-parent families are significantly or even, as some feminist scholars conclude, primarily due to poverty, why not propose a programmatic commitment to addressing the causes of that poverty so that single-mother households are economically viable?[88]

There are also powerful feminist analyses that strengthen arguments for collective responsibility by focusing on the issue of dependency and its relationship to the poverty of single-mother families. Fineman argues that in a society such as our own, there inevitably will be people who are dependent on others for care, a primary example being children. In our society, women overwhelmingly provide that care. They assume the burdens of inevitable dependency, which generally disable them from being full market participants and in turn lead to their "derivative dependency" on others for resources.[89] Traditionally, the burdens of inevitable dependency have been allocated to the "private" marital family (or "natural" family), and within the family, to the mother, who was, at least in theory, provided material resources by the husband/father. The state has relied on the private family to perform these functions and has subsidized it in various ways.[90]

Fineman argues that the failure of the natural family to adequately meet these burdens accounts, in part, for the rise of single-mother families. Fineman's proposal is that we eliminate any special status afforded marriage, redefine the basic family unit as the mother–child (or caretaker–dependent) unit, and redistribute to it the social and economic subsidies now provided to the married family.[91] I do not endorse Fineman's proposal to abolish marriage,[92] but her proposed redefinition of the family valuably highlights the vital task of meeting the burdens of "inevitable dependency" as a component of social reproduction and the way in which proponents of reproductive responsibility fail to address the role of collective responsibility in meeting those burdens.

Enriching Public Discourse about Reproduction and Responsibility

A serious public conversation about reproduction and responsibility needs to take into account dimensions of the issue of responsibility as illuminated by feminist work, which serves both a critical role of pointing out flaws of current models and a constructive role of contributing to better models.

Toward Better Procreation Stories:
Missing Dimensions of Responsibility and Irresponsibility

MEN'S IRRESPONSIBILITY AND WOMEN'S LIVES

Contemporary paradigms of irresponsible reproduction focus heavily on women, but they could instead center on the irresponsibility of men. Male irresponsibility is a familiar theme in feminist work on sexuality, procreation, and the family. Feminist historian Linda Gordon observes that in the nineteenth and early twentieth centuries, feminist work on behalf of single mothers treated women as blameless victims of male irresponsibility as a way to find women harmless and render them worthy of help, not responsible or culpable for their plight.[93] Contemporary feminists identify male irresponsibility as a cause of unwanted pregnancy, abortion, single motherhood, family poverty, and family violence, often critiquing the ways that law permits or perpetuates such irresponsibility.[94] Male irresponsibility here includes both moral irresponsibility and unaccountability, acting in ways that are heedless of consequences for self and others, fleeing responsibility for those consequences, and failing to honor obligations. Some examples relating to reproduction include not taking responsibility for contraception, not accepting responsibility for pregnancy, and not meeting family responsibilities by parenting or paying child support. This location of causal responsibility is an important counter to the disproportionate focus on women's supposed irresponsibility. To some extent, this is recognized in the rhetoric of irresponsible reproduction in calls to target deadbeat dads and encourage responsible fatherhood.[95]

Studies chronicling causes of poverty in the lives of poor single mothers who have relied on welfare offer ample illustrations of the causal relationships between men's irresponsibility and women's single parenthood, poverty, and recourse to welfare.[96] These stories of women's lives find confirmation in other empirical work, revealing that "for many women, poverty is caused, exacerbated, or prolonged by an abusive relationship," with such consequences as homelessness, recourse to welfare, and job loss or impediments.[97] To the extent that women choose to leave problematic relationships with men, they, in the process, make certain choices about their family form. Yet in many cases male irresponsibility precipitated those choices, just as it constrained women's power and increased the caretaking and financial burdens of mothering.

FEMALE IRRESPONSIBILITY AND MALE DOMINANCE

What about female irresponsibility? Dominance feminism places women's subordination as a result of male domination and patriarchy at the core of an understanding of women's lives.[98] In the context of irresponsible procreation, dominance analysis suggests that the most crucial questions about responsibility implicate issues of power—namely, women's relative lack of power vis-à-vis that of men—and the impact of power on women's moral agency. Catharine MacKinnon contends that women "often do not control the conditions under which they become pregnant" and that it is "exceptional when they do," given current conditions of sex inequality (including the effects of socialization about male sexual entitlement to women's bodies).[99]

This analysis shifts the meaning of women's irresponsibility from immorality or unaccountability to incapacity, or compromised capacity, resulting from male power and sex inequality. It also leads to a questioning of the model of women as rational actors who can simply "tell men to get lost," "tame" them, and respond to financial disincentives to procreation (such as family caps). Dominance feminism may well run the risk of minimizing or denying the extent to which women do experience meaningful agency in their sexual and reproductive lives.[100] Nonetheless, it is valuable in focusing on the continuing problems that surround women's sexual experiences with men and affect their ability to exercise responsibility in the sense of agency and autonomy.[101] It would enrich the rhetoric of irresponsible reproduction to elaborate on the extent to which men's sexual aggression, abuse, and violence (often within families) features in the lives of women labeled as irresponsible reproducers.[102]

All of these issues of power and irresponsibility are especially important when looking at teenage girls and their sexual interactions with teenage boys or, in the more typical case, adult men.[103] Research on adolescent females' sexual and reproductive experience reveals that much sexual activity, particularly in the case of younger female teens, results from male sexual abuse (often by relatives), exploitation, coercion, and aggression (including battering).[104] Moreover, teenage females often have a sense of responsibility for arousing and satisfying male desire, which impairs an independent sense of their sexuality or sexual desire.[105] Feminists examining such phenomena conclude that to realize the vision of women of all ages controlling their reproductive lives, "we must break the cultural linking of masculinity with sexual dominance and femininity with sexual passivity and subordination."[106]

Among the reasons for women's unintended pregnancies are contraceptive failure and nonuse of contraception. Women's contraceptive experiences may reflect lack of access, ignorance, inattention, misplaced reliance on (mis)representations by male partners, or deliberate choice (as well as the current imperfect state of contraceptive technology).[107] An analysis of why so many pregnancies are unintended should also address the role played in such decisions by the various constraints on the choices made by adolescent females and women as they relate to men's attitudes and behaviors.[108] Obviously, in any discussion of reproductive responsibility, assertions, often made by teen females, that an unintended pregnancy "just happened" invite closer attention to the capacity and opportunity for the exercise of responsibility.[109] But such an examination should also ask these questions of men.

SINGLE MOTHERHOOD AS A DELIBERATE CHOICE

In her book *The Neutered Mother, The Sexual Family and Other Twentieth-Century Tragedies*, Martha Fineman argues: "Single motherhood as a social phenomenon should be viewed by feminists as a practice resistive to patriarchal ideology, particularly because it represents a 'deliberate choice' in a world with birth control and abortion. As such, the existence of single motherhood as an ever-expanding practice threatens the logic and hold of the dominant ideology."[110]

Thus, Fineman would argue that there is often a subversive message about a choice of female identity by a mother outside the structure of the patriarchal family. As her reference to birth control and abortion indicates, Fineman posits some degree of control by women over their reproductive lives. Dorothy Roberts suggests that feminists should consider whether "deviant" (single) mothers might offer a glimpse of "liberated motherhood" because they exist outside of patriarchal expectations of marriage and challenge assumptions about family forms and proper female dependency on men.[111]

"Deliberate choice" may seem a strong phrase to apply to women's reproductive and mothering decisions, especially if such choices flow from or are affected by male irresponsibility or dominance. Feminist analysis of motherhood suggests an interplay of deliberate choice and constraint. Fineman's stance is certainly not incompatible with recognizing constraints on choice. Indeed, to stress the ways that patriarchal ideology of motherhood shapes women's experiences, she portrays motherhood as a colonized concept.[112] Barbara Omolade, in her account of the lives of black single mothers, describes women who apparently became pregnant in a consensual relationship rather than setting out to be single mothers. But they then made a choice to leave a problematic relationship, most often because of male violence, in this sense rejecting norms of patriarchal authority.[113] There are, however, other stories of single motherhood in which women clearly signal choices not driven by male power or irresponsibility. Consider women who decide to adopt children or to bear a child outside of marriage because they do not want to miss the experience of motherhood (one prominent example is the group Single Mothers By Choice), and lesbians who form families together.[114]

One strength of Fineman's stance is that it squarely meets the rhetoric of procreative irresponsibility—in which account single motherhood and "illegitimacy" are signs of immorality—by contending that single motherhood issues a challenge to patriarchal ideology about the natural and proper family form. A feminist rebuttal would further affirm women's choices about different family forms, pointing to the strengths of such families, which may allow women and their children a more egalitarian family structure free of male domination and violence.[115]

Toward a Continuum Model of Agency and Responsibility

FEMINIST DILEMMAS: AGENCY, VICTIMHOOD, AND RESPONSIBILITY

A central dilemma in feminist work is articulating meaningful conceptions of agency and responsibility without ignoring constraints on choice or reducing selfhood to victimhood. These issues are vital to a discussion of reproduction and responsibility. Feminists in law as well as in other disciplines have also argued for models of self that acknowledge the impact of constraints on choice, yet hold to the possibility of meaningful agency.[116] Such work often takes as a point of departure the problems of patriarchy and subordination (or oppression) and the possibilities of survival and resistance.[117] An important question raised by this feminist work is how these conceptions of agency and responsibility should translate to an analysis of women's reproductive choices and to the realm of law and public policy.

A CONTINUUM MODEL OF AGENCY AND RESPONSIBILITY

Examination of women's lives suggests that rather than an undiluted image of woman as agent or victim, an adequate portrait of the reproductive lives of women requires a continuum model. Such a model would not treat the category "single mother" or "female-headed household" as a monolith, but would begin with an assumption that there is a spectrum across which women and female teenagers experience the interplay of agency, responsibility, and victimization in their sexual and reproductive lives. Factors such as age, race, ethnicity, class, sexual orientation, and cultural and religious beliefs will also likely be relevant to their location on such a spectrum. Notions of deliberate choice as well as of limited or constrained choice are important to such a continuum model.

For analytic purposes, it may be useful to distinguish several distinct occasions or opportunities for the exercise of agency and responsibility within a woman's reproductive and mothering experience: the underlying sexual activity (or recourse to assisted reproduction) leading to pregnancy (including use or nonuse of contraceptives); the resolution of the pregnancy; the relationship between the woman and her partner; and the woman's mothering role. Women may face constraints or subordination to varying degrees at each of these points. Thus, although a woman or a teenage female may experience a lack of agency or control over the sexual activity leading to pregnancy, she may experience a greater sense of agency and responsibility in her handling of the pregnancy and its outcome.[118] Or, although she may not initially intend to get pregnant, she may then deliberately choose to become a mother. Moreover, a woman may make deliberate choices concerning her relationship with the father of her child, or her partner, that affect her status, that is, whether she becomes a single mother, gets married, or gets divorced.

Studies of the lives of women in poverty suggest the usefulness of a continuum model, given the range of experiences of such women. Although there are some common themes, such as the role played by the sexually and financially irresponsible male partner, abuse by such a male partner, or the reluctance to terminate a pregnancy by abortion, there is also great diversity among the women who rely on welfare.[119] Those differences relate not only to reproductive choices and behaviors, but also to the degree of agency and responsibility such women manifest in other parts of their lives. In fashioning sensible public policy, it would be useful to consider such a continuum in determining the kind and amount of help women would need to leave poverty.[120]

A continuum model may also be helpful in thinking about the issues of adolescent pregnancy and motherhood. Such reductive phrases as "children having children," which fail to differentiate between younger teen mothers and the much more typical eighteen- or nineteen-year-old teen mother, not only lend themselves to blanket assumptions about teen females' incapacity but also, some feminists argue, may predispose public policy discourse to the characterization of teenage females as victims rather than agents.[121] Nonetheless, there is reason for concern about the lack of agency and autonomy that many adolescent females, particularly younger teens, appear to have with respect to their sexual behavior and pregnancies. This raises questions about the capacities of such adolescents to make morally responsible and fully voluntary choices. Pointing to the evidence of the extent to which such teens are victims of sexual abuse, coercion, and pressure, and to the impact of gender socialization on them, is one important response to reductive models of why teens get pregnant and the punitive proposals at the forefront of recent welfare reform efforts.

Yet feminist and other scholarship suggests that some adolescent females who get pregnant, continue their pregnancies, and keep their children may be making rational choices from the point of view of their own assessment of their circumstances.[122] Indeed, it is ironic, in light of the themes in the rhetoric of irresponsible reproduction as a falling away from "family values" and marriage, that such adolescent females often appear to be acting out a romantic dream of combining sex, pregnancy, and marriage, only to be disappointed by the abandonment by their male partners.[123] Poverty itself appears to play a causal role in such decisions, because poor teens may have insufficient motivation to avoid early parenthood and may view the opportunity cost of having a child while young as lower than young women might in more favorable economic circumstances.[124] A continuum model might approach this challenge by saying that such teens are acting pursuant to an understanding of the good life for them, and in this sense they are morally responsible agents, but that we should seriously consider whether the severe constraints they face impair their exercise of agency and lead to what may often be unwise choices.

The "personal responsibility" solution that PRWORA advocated for teen mothers in poverty was to remove the supposed incentives encouraging teens to have a baby (e.g., AFDC and government-funded housing). Feminist scholarship about adolescent pregnancy and motherhood concludes instead that the solution is to address the underlying constraints and circumstances that young women face in order to afford them the opportunity for making better choices.[125] Feminists would also aim to help young women who do have children become responsible parents and lead successful lives, by supporting the provision of public assistance to help them do so. For such young women, motherhood can provide a transformative occasion for developing and exercising "responsible agency." [126]

MOTHERING, ABORTION, AND RESPONSIBILITY

One source for formulating feminist paradigms of reproductive responsibility and irresponsibility along a continuum model is feminist work on mothering. In her influential book *Maternal Thinking*, Sara Ruddick describes mothering as a practice, "a kind of work" that someone does when she responds to the demands of children.[127] Fineman similarly speaks of what mothers do as a "specific practice of social and emotional responsibility."[128] Patricia Hill Collins stresses that the experience of mothering by women of color reveals themes of responsibility for physical and psychic survival not only of children but of racial and ethnic communities, and the interplay of agency and constraint, resistance and oppression.[129]

Such feminist work on motherhood cautions against idealizing or romanticizing motherhood. It recognizes that not all mothers accept the challenges of responsible mothering. Moreover, it notes that mothers often perform the tasks of mothering under less than optimal conditions, including poverty, racial discrimination, and societal devaluation and lack of accommodation of mothers' work.[130] Mothers struggle to balance their responsibilities to meet children's emotional, physical, and material needs. When they are in poverty, they face such added challenges as mothering on limited material resources and protecting their children in physically dangerous housing and neighborhoods.[131] Valerie Polakow's portraits of single mothers vividly suggest the material obstacles with which such mothers struggle, often as a result of welfare rules and regulations.[132] Given the many tasks single mothers must perform, it might be more accurate to conclude that the problem with single-parent families is not that mothers are irresponsible but that they bear a disproportionate amount of responsibility and receive insufficient help from fathers and society.

Another useful source in elaborating ideas of responsibility and irresponsibility in the area of reproduction is feminist analyses of women's abortion decisions. One irony in the debate over irresponsible reproduction is that the very reasons single motherhood is viewed as problematic (lack of second parent, lack of economic resources, youth of the mother, or not ready for responsibility) are reasons women frequently give for choosing to terminate pregnancies through abortion.[133] Yet those same reasons are viewed by many as morally unacceptable, according to public opinion polls about abortion.[134] This debate highlights the double binds women face about their reproductive choices. Pregnant women who decide to have abortions, and therefore not to become mothers, because they are single, young, lack economic resources, or lack an acceptable relationship with the father are condemned as immoral and irresponsible, while women with similar life circumstances who decide not to have abortions, and therefore to become mothers, are also condemned as immoral and irresponsible.[135]

To meet charges of irresponsibility and "convenience abortion," a number of feminists have used "responsibility" talk in defending legal abortion and in arguing that abortion can be a moral, responsible choice.[136] Feminist and other work on the abortion decision suggest that a morally responsible decision to choose abortion may involve a determination by a woman of her capacity to be responsible for, or assume parental responsibility for, a new human life.[137] In abortion litigation, "voices of women" amicus briefs have presented women's narratives to illustrate that women exercise their moral responsibility in making often difficult choices not to continue pregnancies.[138] Some feminists explicitly use the language of motherhood to suggest that women's abortion decisions might be seen as within a continuum of mothering decisions, that is, that a woman's assessment of her responsibilities and circumstances may lead her to conclude that she cannot be a responsible mother.[139] Accounts of women who would be mothers if they could be often point to the lack of societal accommodation of mothers and children (e.g., the work–family conflict), the negative impact of motherhood on women's equal citizenship, and failures of collective responsibility.[140] As a defense of abortion rights, this approach may have strategic risks because it implies, if not concedes, that abortion rights are contingent on current social conditions. However, it may be a useful source in constructing a model of the social preconditions for responsible reproduction.

Responsibility and the Role of Judgment and Voice

JUDGMENT IN FEMINIST INQUIRY

An attempt to provide a more adequate framework for a public conversation about reproduction and responsibility must address the issue of normative judgment. There is an important role for normative judgment and critical evaluation in feminist inquiry. Such judgment requires careful evaluation of women's lives, choices, and circumstances in order to gain understanding of

issues of agency and victimization and to formulate feminist models of responsibility and the preconditions for agency.

There has been a deep impulse in feminism, throughout its history, to
engage in judgment or critical evaluation with a view to helping women. Arguably, the role of consciousness raising as a feminist method yielding knowledge about women's lives reflects this impulse. But, as applied to other women,
a stance of judgment may suggest an us/them or self/other relationship in
which feminists attempt to interpret the experience and voices of other
women. Particularly when differentials such as race, ethnicity, and class exist,
there are risks of incomprehension and misinterpretation as well as solipsistic
use of one's own experience as a measure or norm. The consequences are exacerbated when the interpreter is in a position of power (e.g., to prescribe policy agendas or to regulate the lives of the women under interpretation).[141]

The problems of judgment and of inclusion and exclusion have led to much
attention in contemporary feminist legal discourse to listening to women's
voices and attending to difference as well as commonality.[142] In the context of
poverty discourse, some feminists have called for putting the voices and experiences of poor women at the center rather than the margin of welfare discourse.[143] Listening to the voices of single mothers, especially poor mothers,
brings out their own reactions to being labeled deviant and irresponsible. For
example, some poor single mothers who receive public assistance strongly re-
sent being used as scapegoats for such national problems as the budget deficit.
Moreover, they express the view that it is nobody's business why they made
the sexual and reproductive choices that they did, arguing that they have a
right to have children and that they and their children have a right to survive.[144] An inquiry into poor women's perspectives leads to asking such questions as why are single mothers poor, and why are women generally at greater
risk for poverty? Is the problem simply the sexual and reproductive choices
these women have made? Or is it the practical and structural problems that
women encounter in attempting to be caretakers and providers (sometimes exacerbated by the welfare system itself) in the absence of the assumption of collective responsibility? Critical evaluation of women's lives thus contributes to
an insistence on a richer vocabulary of responsibility.

Listening to women's voices in an attempt to engage in critical evaluation
of issues of responsibility is not a panacea but brings with it the challenge of
evaluating the complexity of voice and of women's choices. Thus, even in feminist circles, some voices echo the current rhetoric in criticizing women who
have children when they cannot afford them and urge that women take responsibility for their reproductive lives.[145] Similarly, some present or former
"welfare mothers" support family caps, partly on the basis of beliefs about
why other women have children.[146] One plausible interpretation of this phenomenon is the role of internalization of society's negative images of welfare
mothers.[147] But it is also important to acknowledge the strong impulse to use

the vocabulary of responsibility to inquire about women's reproductive choices and behavior and to attempt to establish feminist norms of responsible choice. My argument here is that feminist work on women's exercise of responsibility, deploying a continuum model of agency and responsibility to frame such questions, would lead to more complete answers and to better public policies than those currently promoted by the proponents of personal responsibility.

Coda: Promoting Responsible Fatherhood as Welfare Reform, Phase Two

As Congress debates the reauthorization of PRWORA, perhaps the most striking development in the ongoing discussion of government's role in encouraging personal responsibility in the areas of reproduction and family formation is the growing prominence of responsible fatherhood and marriage promotion as organizing concepts for next steps to take in implementing PRWORA and advancing welfare reform. Generally, this idea of promoting "responsible fatherhood" entails affirming the important role fathers play in children's well-being and encouraging fathers to provide financial and emotional support for their children, and to become more involved in their children's lives because of the importance of such involvement to children's well-being.[148] During the mid-1990s, around the time of the debate over PRWORA, a new social movement calling for "responsible fatherhood" was emerging. One influential text in this movement, David Blankenhorn's *Fatherless America*, diagnosed fatherlessness as the "most urgent" social problem driving an array of other social ills.[149] The voices in this movement cross racial and class lines, sounding common themes about the importance of fathers and the dire consequences for women, children, society, and indeed men when men flee paternal responsibility and fatherhood is no longer at the core of cultural definitions of manhood. Voices in this movement have been critical of welfare policy because it is said to focus too much on women, to subsidize fatherless families, and to fail in recognizing the important role of men in the family.

As early as 1995, President Clinton directed federal agencies to evaluate their programs to see how they might strengthen the role of fathers in families.[150] The Clinton/Gore administration often spoke of promoting responsible fatherhood as an important next step in welfare reform.[151] The cause of responsible fatherhood enjoys broad bipartisan support. Not only has nearly every state formed a task force or undertaken some initiatives to promote responsible fatherhood,[152] but in the last few years, Congress has considered proposed "responsible fatherhood" legislation.[153] During President George W. Bush's first term, his administration launched both "responsible fatherhood" and "healthy marriage" initiatives. And Bush's plan for welfare reauthorization, Working toward Independence, includes a much-discussed $1.5 billion to strengthen families by promoting healthy marriage and responsible fatherhood.[154]

In this essay, I must defer a full consideration of this development and highlight several comparative points about the rhetoric of deterring irresponsible reproduction, made during the debating PRWORA, and the current rhetoric of promoting marriage and responsible fatherhood. First, there is an obvious element of continuity because a key goal of PRWORA was to promote marriage and end childbearing and child rearing outside the two-parent, marital family. Likewise, proposals to promote responsible fatherhood stress the importance of marriage and the unique and irreplaceable role of the father within the family. For example, proposed federal legislation authorizes the federal government to conduct a media campaign that "promotes and encourages involved, committed, and responsible fatherhood and married fatherhood."[155] As discussed earlier, marriage is unlikely to prove a satisfactory, all-purpose antipoverty program, both because of some men's earning capacity and family violence, as well as because of changing demographic and economic realities. As feminist critics of calls for responsible fatherhood argue, "marriage is not the solution for everyone, nor is it the solution to poverty."[156] Moreover, such critics argue that these efforts fail to reckon adequately with the problem of family violence.[157] In this regard, it is notable that some of the legislative proposals to promote responsible fatherhood appear to recognize the problem of violence against women and children, because they include funding for instruction in nonviolent conflict resolution.

A second point is that a perhaps unintended positive consequence of the efforts to promote responsible fatherhood might be to bring about incremental changes in family dynamics and work–family arrangements that would advance long-standing feminist goals for reform. Earlier in this chapter I suggested that two missing dimensions of the discussion of responsibility were the problem of male irresponsibility within families and the problem of women's disproportionate responsibility for caregiving labor, undertaken without adequate societal support. For example, two central feminist themes have been that women bear a disproportionate burden within families for caregiving and household labor and that current work–family arrangements devalue caregiving and are insufficiently supportive of parents' efforts to care for their children. The responsible fatherhood movement envisions that fathers should not only support their children financially but also play an active role in their lives.[158] To that end, some proponents of responsible fatherhood have sought "father-friendly workplaces" that would allow fathers better to play a role in their children's lives.[159] Indeed, in the 2000 presidential campaign, both Bush and Al Gore extolled the role of father as the most important duty or job any man will ever have.[160] This sort of recognition of the value of parenting seems to stand in stark contrast to the rhetoric of the 1990s that urged mothers to move into the workplace away from their children so that they could have the dignity of a "real" job.

To put the point dramatically, if phase one of welfare reform was moving mothers into the paid workplace, phase two is moving fathers more into the home. That is, it is possible that promoting responsible fatherhood may encourage incremental movement away from the traditional male breadwinner–female caregiver model. But as these efforts have unfolded so far, government is not seeking radical social change, which would encourage fathers to become full-time caregivers, while mothers are full-time breadwinners. The assumption appears to be that women must now handle parenting and market responsibilities, and so fathers must learn to do the same. Similarly, it must be understood that the goal of getting fathers more involved in the home does not mean that governmental proponents of responsible fatherhood are promoting either a completely egalitarian division of household labor or an androgynous model of parenting (of the sort supported by some feminist theorists).[161] To the contrary, proponents of responsible fatherhood often speak of fathers' unique and irreplaceable contributions to children and resist any notion of androgyny, or that mothers and fathers do the same thing.[162] Moreover, some groups within the social movement (such as Promise Keepers and the Nation of Islam) adhere to norms of male authority and leadership and female submission within the home, norms sharply at odds with such important principles of political morality as sex equality and the repudiation of a family governance model premised on male domination.[163] Thus, as governmental authorities seek to use the broader social movement as a resource for promoting responsible fatherhood, it is important to be attentive to possible clashes with such public principles.

Third, if the appeal to responsible fatherhood recognizes the paramount role of father (or parent), what sort of responsibility does government have to support responsible fatherhood (and motherhood)? And what does playing by the rules mean in this context? Here there are some striking and potentially encouraging rhetorical shifts from the discourse of the 1990s. As I discussed earlier, a central premise in the rhetoric surrounding PRWORA was that welfare recipients failed to play by the rules because they—unlike working families—expected public subsidies for their families. Both the responsible fatherhood movement and the policy discourse about implementing PRWORA make it apparent that this was an inaccurate statement of the social contract. The new social contract seems to be that persons who manifest their personal responsibility by working for wages may reasonably expect governmental support of their efforts to provide for their families. Indeed, in contrast to the punitive rhetoric about illegitimacy surrounding PRWORA, legislators supporting responsible fatherhood legislation stress that their goal is not to condemn unwed fathers but to offer resources to help them.[164] Thus, while "deadbeat dads" still draw condemnation, the rhetoric of responsible fatherhood speaks of empowering "dead broke" dads and of helping to enhance their earning potential. If it were possible to push the rhetoric of responsible fatherhood in the direction of valuing caregiving by fathers *and* mothers, then perhaps attention to responsible fatherhood could engender broader efforts to foster the capacities of parents to be responsible caregivers and to help parents meet the often conflicting demands of market and household labor. This is unlikely to occur until there is a more explicit focus on the importance of caring for children as an end in itself, and not just—as is often the case in discussions about moving mothers from welfare to work—as an obstacle to successful market participation. One risk of the current rhetoric about responsible fatherhood is that it may assume that getting fathers more actively involved in their children's lives will eliminate the significant problem that many parents cannot find safe, affordable, quality substitute child care for their children so that they can participate in the workplace and provide financial support for their children.[165]

Finally, the responsible fatherhood movement often makes claims about marriage as the optimal family form, about the unique and irreplaceable contribution fathers make to children's lives, and about the serious social problems assumed to arise from a father's absence. These claims raise challenging empirical questions. As one article observed, "despite scholarly disagreement over the meaning of these concepts and the extent and consequences of father absence, these debates influence how the public, policy makers and the research community frame various questions concerning fathers and families."[166] President Clinton's 1995 initiative, which authorized federal funding for fatherhood research initiatives, has played a role in encouraging an already growing scholarly literature about fatherhood and in shaping research agendas.[167] The Bush administration's heightened emphasis on marriage promotion and responsible fatherhood will no doubt amplify such efforts. One recent survey of this literature notes a movement away from simplistic understandings of father involvement and absence. It suggests that ongoing scholarly efforts would profitably take up such challenging empirical questions as the social construction of fathers' identities, diversity and difference among fathers, and their experiences and involvement, and "whether men have gendered practices as fathers that uniquely contribute to their children's development."[168] Engaging with this ongoing scholarly project and seeking to learn from it could help the current policy discussions about responsible fatherhood avoid the kind of reductive and simplistic models that shaped the recent debate over welfare reform.

Conclusion

Responsibility talk is pervasive in public policy circles, in the academy, and among the public generally, and it is likely to be for some time to come. My conclusion is not that we should abandon the idea of personal responsibility, but that we should investigate more critically the deployment of the categories of responsibility and irresponsibility in relationship to welfare reform and reproductive freedom. If we seriously engage the idea that we as a nation and as members of diverse communities should talk about reproduction and responsibility in the context of proposals for legal reform and public policy, then we need a better basis for such a conversation. I have argued that one way to critique and enrich that discourse is to bring feminist analysis of issues of responsibility and irresponsibility in women's reproductive and mothering experiences into the conversation. Viewing the question of reproduction and responsibility through such a lens illuminates missing dimensions in the current rhetoric and its models of human agency and responsibility.

Notes

1. *MacNeil/Lehrer News Hour,* PBS television broadcast, July 10, 1995 (interviewing political analysts and public officials on why "personal responsibility" has become such a "hot political theme"). Elsewhere, I have offered a critical assessment of the role attributed to rights and "rights talk" in the decline of personal responsibility. Linda C. McClain, "Rights and Irresponsibility," *Duke Law Journal* 43 (1994): 989–1088. This essay is adapted from a longer article, Linda C. McCain, " 'Irresponsible' Reproduction," that was originally published in 47 *Hastings Law Journal* 339 (1996).

2. Gertrude Himmelfarb, *The De-Moralization of Society: From Victorian Virtues to Modern Values* (New York: Alfred A. Knopf, 1994), 222–24, 237–40; William J. Bennett, *The Index of Leading Cultural Indicators* (New York: Simon and Schuster, 1994), 72–77.

3. The Personal Responsibility Act originated in the House Republicans' *Contract with America,* as legislation to implement the contract's approach to welfare reform. *Contract with America: The Bold Plan by Rep. Newt Gingrich, Rep. Dick Armey, and the House Republicans to Change the Nation,* ed. Gillespie and Bob Schellhas (New York: Times Books, 1994). In January 1995, the Personal Responsibility Act was introduced in Congress. By the end of 1995, the House and Senate approved the compromise bill, the Personal Responsibility and Work Opportunity Act of 1995. Robert Pear, "Welfare Bill Cleared by Congress and Now Awaits Clinton's Veto," *New York Times,* Dec. 23, 1995, 1. On January 9, 1996, President Clinton vetoed the act, saying that it did " 'too little to move people from welfare to work' and made excessive cuts in welfare spending." Robert Pear, "G.O.P.'s Plan for Welfare Draws a Veto," *New York Times,* Jan. 10, 1996, C19. Congress subsequently held hearings on a version of the act endorsed by the National Governors' Association. Robert Pear, "House Democrats Assail Welfare Plan Backed by Governors," *New York Times,* Feb. 21, 1996, A16. Later in 1996, Congress passed the Personal Responsibility and Work Opportunity Reconciliation Act of 1996, which President Clinton signed into law. Public Law No. 104-193, 110 Stat. 2105 (codified as amended in various sections of 42 U.S.C.).

4. This essay also has a coda which briefly considers developments that have taken place since the publication of the original article cited in note 1.

5. Martha Albertson Fineman, *The Neutered Mother, The Sexual Family, and Other Twentieth Century Tragedies* (New York: Routledge, 1995), 125.

6. Nancy Dowd critically assesses the justifications for stigmatizing female-headed, single-parent families. These justifications consist of arguments that such families are poor, "psychologically unhealthy," and immoral. Nancy Dowd, "Stigmatizing Single Parents," *Harvard Women's Law Journal* 18 (1995): 19–82. Dowd further argues that the myths and stereotypes on which these justifications rest hide "implicit stories of race and gender that reek of oppression" (45).

7. Daniel P. Moynihan, "Defining Deviancy Down," *American Scholar* 62 (1993): 17–30; Charles Murray, "The Coming White Underclass," *Wall Street Journal,* Oct. 29, 1993, A14; William J. Bennett, written testimony, Hearings on Welfare Reform by the Subcommittee on Human Resources, House of Representatives Ways and Means Committee, Jan. 20, 1995.

8. Murray, "Coming White Underclass," A14; Bennett, written testimony, 1–2. For example, Charles Murray and William Bennett use as a benchmark Moynihan's earlier report, *The Negro Family* (1965), which cautioned that the prevalence of female-headed households in the African American community set that community apart from white America and linked that "unstable" family structure to a number of problems faced by African Americans.

9. H.R. 4, 104th Congr., 1st sess., § 100 (1995).

10. Murray, "Coming White Underclass," A14.

11. Bennett, written testimony, 3.

12. Fineman, *Neutered Mother,* 101–25.

13. William Raspberry, "Women Taming Men," *Washington Post,* Nov. 24, 1993, A10.

14. Andrew Rosenthal, "Quayle Says Riots Sprang from Lack of Family Values," *New York Times,* May 20, 1992, A1, A20.

15. William F. Buckley, remarks on *Firing Line,* PBS television broadcast, Mar. 15, 1994; Barbara Dafoe Whitehead, "Dan Quayle Was Right," *Atlantic Monthly,* Apr. 1993, 47, 52. Regina Austin describes criticism of Liz Walker, an unmarried black news anchorwoman who became pregnant, for the poor role model she set for black teenagers and critiques *Chambers v. Omaha Girls Club,* 629 F. Supp. 925 (D. Neb. 1986), which upheld the dismissal by Girls Club (predominantly staffed by African American women) of an unmarried, pregnant African American woman from employment because of the role model requirements of the club. Regina Austin, "Sapphire Bound!" *Wisconsin Law Review* (1989): 539–78.

16. Rosenthal, "Quayle Says Riots Sprang from Lack of Family Values," A26.

17. Whitehead, "Dan Quayle Was Right," 47.

18. David Blankenhorn, *Fatherless America* (New York: Basic Books, 1995); Whitehead, "Dan Quayle Was Right," 47.

19. William A. Galston, "Needed: A Not-So-Fast Divorce Law," *New York Times,* Dec. 27, 1995, A11; Whitehead, "Dan Quayle Was Right," 52.

20. Murray, "Coming White Underclass," A14. This was also a central premise of President Clinton's initial proposal for welfare reform; "The Work and Responsibility Act of 1994, Detailed Summary," n.d., 31.

21. Gov. James Florio and Assemblyman Wayne Bryant, *Changes in State Welfare Reform Programs,* Hearings before the Subcommittee of Social Security and Family Policy and Committee on Finance, 102nd Cong., 2d sess., Feb. 3, 1992, 3–16; John H. Cushman Jr., "Rivals Criticize Bill on Welfare Offered by Dole," *New York Times,* Aug. 7, 1995, A1, B6.

22. "Excerpts from Vice President's Speech on Cities and Poverty," *New York Times,* May 20, 1992, A20.

23. Murray, "Coming White Underclass," A14.

24. Fineman, *Neutered Mother,* 106.

25. Dowd, "Stigmatizing Single Parents," 19–82; "Single Women and Poverty Strongly Linked," *New York Times,* Feb. 20, 1994, A35.

26. House Committee on Ways and Means, *Overview of Entitlement Programs: Background Material and Data on Programs within the Jurisdiction of the Committee on Ways and Means, Green Book,* 103d Cong., 2d sess., 1994, 451 (hereafter *Green Book*); General Accounting Office, "Families on Welfare: Sharp Rise in Never-Married Women Reflects Societal Trend," GAO/HEHS-94-92, May 1994, 3.

27. Sara McLanahan and Gary Sandefur, *Growing up with a Single Parent: What Hurts, What Helps* (Cambridge: Harvard University Press, 1994), 24–26; Cheryl Wetzstein, " 'Deadbeat' Dads Fight Finance-Only Fatherhood: More Pay if Given Right to Play," *Washington Times,* May 13, 1994, A8.

28. Carol Rose, "Women and Property: Gaining and Losing Ground," in *Property and Persuasion* (Boulder, Colo.: Westview Press, 1994), 233.

29. Christopher Jencks and Kathryn Edin, "Do Poor Women Have a Right to Bear Children?" *American Prospect,* Winter 1995, 43–44.

30. Jason DeParle, "Sharp Increase Along the Borders of Poverty," *New York Times,* Mar. 31, 1994, A18.

31. Michael Wines, "Taxpayers Are Angry. They're Expensive, Too," *New York Times,* Nov. 20, 1994, sec. 4, p. 5.

32. *Green Book,* 401.

33. Lucy Williams, "Race, Rat Bites, and Unfit Mothers: How Media Discourse Informs Welfare Legislation Debate," *Fordham Urban Law Journal* 22 (1995): 1190.

34. Deborah L. Rhode and Annette Lawson, introduction to *The Politics of Pregnancy,* ed. Annette Lawson and Deborah L. Rhode (New Haven: Yale University Press, 1993), 1, 3.

35. Susan E. Harari and Maris A. Vinovskis, "Adolescent Sexuality, Pregnancy, and Childbearing in the Past," in Lawson and Rhode, *Politics of Pregnancy,* 23–45.

36. I discuss some of these factors in the section titled "Enriching Public Discourse about Reproduction and Responsibility."

37. Diana M. Pearce " 'Children Having Children': Teenage Pregnancy and Public Policy from the Woman's Perspective," in Lawson and Rhode, *Politics of Pregnancy,* 47.

38. McLanahan and Sandefur, *Growing up with a Single Parent.* McLanahan and Sandefur use the label "disrupted family," regardless of whether children were born outside or within marriage because *"from the child's point of view,"* the family is disrupted if the biological parents live apart, including with a step-parent (6). To measure future adult success, defined in economic terms, they look at three indicators: educational attainment, labor force attachment, and early family formation (19–22). They find that children from single-parent families have higher rates of school dropout, teen pregnancy and parenting, and disengagement from the labor market (32–40).

39. Karl Zinsmeister, "Parental Responsibility and the Future of the American Family," *Cornell Law Review* 77 (1992): 1005–11; Moynihan, "Defining Deviancy Down," 24; Murray, "Coming White Underclass," A14.

40. McLanahan and Sandefur, *Growing up with a Single Parent,* 97–98.

41. Personal Responsibility and Work Opportunity Act, 1995, § 101 ("findings").

42. The analysis that follows is based on *Contract with America* and the debates in the House and Senate over the Personal Responsibility Act (later enacted, with some modifications, as PRWORA), which are collected in the *Congressional Record.*

43. Charles Murray, *Losing Ground* (New York: Basic Books, 1984), 154–62.

44. Eloise Anderson, "A Senate Retreat on Welfare," *New York Times,* Sept. 16, 1995, 19.

45. Bennett, written testimony, 3.

46. *Contract with America,* 65.

47. For an insightful analysis of these types of associations of "dependency," see Nancy Fraser and Linda Gordon, "A Genealogy of Dependency: Tracing a Keyword of the U.S. Welfare State," *Signs* 19 (1994): 309–36.

48. *Contract with America,* 65.

49. For some examples from the debates over the Personal Responsibility Act, see the statement of Rep. Ensign, *Congressional Record* (daily ed.) Mar. 21, 1995, H3362–63, reporting resentment by a working mother with a disability that her tax dollars go to someone on welfare; statement of Rep. Holden defending punitive measures for "deadbeat parents" because "[w]e owe it to our children to have the financial support of both parents and to the taxpayers who fund the irresponsible behavior of deadbeat parents" (ibid., H3367); statement of Rep. Hutchinson noting resentment by the working poor of able-bodied welfare recipients (ibid., Mar. 22, 1995, H3506); statement of Rep. Funderburk referring to "three generations of Americans who do nothing but sit at home waiting for the next government check to arrive" (ibid., Mar. 24, 1995, H3793);

statement of Rep. Foley describing food stamp fraud and use of food stamps to buy junk food (ibid., Mar. 21, 1995, H3394–95).

50. *Contract with America,* 65.

51. Joel F. Handler and Yeheskel Hasenfeld, *The Moral Construction of Poverty* (Newbury Park, Calif.: Sage Publications, 1991); Michael B. Katz, *The Undeserving Poor: From the War on Poverty to the War on Welfare* (New York: Pantheon Books, 1989).

52. Andrew Hacker, "The Crackdown on African-Americans," *Nation,* July 10, 1995, 45; Williams, "Race, Rat Bites, and Unfit Mothers," 1168.

53. Fineman, *Neutered Mother,* 107–8; Dorothy Roberts, "Racism and Patriarchy and the Meaning of Motherhood," *American University Journal of Gender and the Law* 1 (1993): 1–38, 25.

54. Hacker, "Crackdown on African-Americans," 45. Statistics on the racial breakdown of parents receiving AFDC in 1992 are as follows: white, 38.9 percent; black, 37.2 percent; Hispanic (who can be of any race), 17.8 percent; Native American, 1.4 percent; and Asian, 2.8 percent (*Green Book,* 402).

55. Dowd, "Stigmatizing Single Parents," 45–46.

56. Roberts, "Meaning of Motherhood," 7–15. One illuminating historical study of the differential societal interpretation of single black versus single white women's pregnancies indicates that black women who became pregnant were viewed as more culpable and deserving of punishment. Rickie Solinger, *Wake up Little Susie: Single Pregnancy and Race before Roe v. Wade* (New York: Routledge, 1992).

57. Lucy A. Williams, "The Ideology of Division: Behavior Modification Welfare Reform Proposals," *Yale Law Journal* 102 (1992): 740–41.

58. Personal Responsibility and Work Opportunity Reconciliation Act, H.R. 4, § 101.

59. Murray, *Losing Ground,* 154–66; Robert Rector, "Memo to: President-Elect Clinton," *Heritage Foundation Reports* 12, Jan. 18, 1993, 1.

60. William Julius Wilson, *The Truly Disadvantaged* (Chicago: University of Chicago Press, 1987); Rebecca M. Blank, testimony, Hearings on Welfare Reform of the Subcommittee on Human Resources, House of Representatives Ways and Means Committee, Jan. 20, 1995.

61. Mark R. Rank, *Living on the Edge: The Realities of Welfare in America* (New York: Columbia University Press, 1994), 72–73; *Green Book,* 401.

62. Michael C. Laracy, "If It Seems Too Good to Be True, It Probably Is," Annie E. Casey Foundation, June 21, 1995, 10. However, a subsequent report found that since the adoption of the Family Cap in New Jersey, there was an increase in abortions among women receiving public assistance and a slight decline in the birth rate. Several years later the General Accounting Office issued a report finding that none of the available studies on the family cap "can be used to cite conclusive evidence about the effect of the family cap on out-of-wedlock births." General Accounting Office, *Welfare Reform: More Research Needed on TANF Family Caps and Other Policies for Reducing Out-of-Wedlock Births,* GAO-01-924, Sept. 2001, 20.

63. In the Senate, Sen. Paul Wellstone raised the issue of the lack of empirical support for the claim that benefits induce births and referred to the preliminary results from the Rutgers study (Laracy, "If It Seems Too Good to Be True," *id.*). *See also* the statement of Sen. Wellstone, *Congressional Record* (daily ed.) Aug. 7, 1995, S11744, 11750. Senator Moynihan also referred to the Rutgers study during the Senate debate and repeatedly expressed skepticism about such causal claims. *See* his statement in *Congressional Record* (daily ed.) Aug. 7, 1995, S11750; Daniel P. Moynihan, "Congress Builds a Coffin," *New York Review of Books,* Jan. 11, 1996, 34–35.

64. Bennett, written testimony.

65. General Accounting Office, "Families on Welfare. Sharp Rise in Never-Married Women Reflects Societal Trend," GAO/HEHS-94-92, May 1994.

66. Blank, testimony, 2–4.

67. Mickey Kaus, "Life Rift," *New Republic,* Feb. 13, 1995, 6.

68. Dorothy Roberts, "Exploding the Myths behind New Jersey Welfare Reform," *New Jersey Law Journal,* Jan. 25, 1993, 21.

69. Charlotte Rutherford, "Reproductive Freedoms and African American Women," *Yale Journal of Law and Feminism* 4 (1992): 255–90.

70. For a discussion of the "responsible fatherhood" movement, see the section of this essay titled "Coda."

71. Irving Kristol, "Life without Father," *Wall Street Journal,* Nov. 3, 1994, A18; George Gilder, *Wealth and Poverty* (New York: Basic Books, 1981), 114–23.

72. Gilder, *Wealth and Poverty,* 122, 136; Blankenhorn, *Fatherless America,* 3, 4, 25, 66.

73. Gilder, *Wealth and Poverty,* 71–72, 115.

74. Compare this with the famous statement by National Welfare Rights Organization founder Johnnie Tillmon: "AFDC is like a supersexist marriage. You trade in *a* man for *the* man." Johnnie Tillmon, "Welfare," *Ms.,* July/August 1995, 50.

75. Kristol, "Life without Father," A18.

76. William Raspberry, "Women Taming Men," *Washington Post,* Nov. 24, 1993, A17.

77. Moynihan, "Defining Deviancy Down," *supra* note 7, at 26; Murray, "Coming White Underclass," *supra* note 7, at A14.

78. Mary Anne Case, "Of Richard Epstein and Other Radical Feminists," *Harvard Journal of Law and Public Policy* 18 (1995): 390–96, which suggests that an optimistic reading of sociobiological evidence would lend support to making the mother–child unit the basic family model, as proposed in Fineman, *Neutered Mother,* 230–33; Alan Ryan, "Only Connect," *New Republic,* Oct. 4, 1994, 36–37, which suggests that "if men are by nature irresponsible and women are by nature caring, then surely one-parent families ought to be preferred over traditional ones."

79. Mimi Abramovitz, *Regulating the Lives of Women: Social Welfare Policy from Colonial Times to the Present* (Boston: South End Press, 1988), 315–18.

80. Martha F. Davis and Susan J. Kraham, "Protecting Women's Welfare in the Face of Violence," *Fordham Urban Law Journal* 22 (1995): 1141–57; Katha Pollitt, "Welfare Reform," *Nation,* July 11, 1994, 45.

81. Wilson, *Truly Disadvantaged;* Maxine Baca Zinn, "Family, Race, and Poverty in the Eighties," *Signs* 14 (1989): 856–74.

82. Blankenhorn, *Fatherless America,* 32–42.

83. Gwendolyn Mink, "Welfare Reform in Historical Perspective," *Connecticut Law Review* 26 (1994): 898–99.

84. Herbert Gans, *The War against the Poor* (New York: Basic Books, 1995), 96–97.

85. For example, reports on economic conditions in the mid-1990s indicated that declining real wages at the low end of the labor market practically ensured that a minimum-wage job would increasingly do no more than shift welfare recipients to the ranks of the "working poor." Peter T. Kilborn, "Take This Job. Up From Welfare: It's Harder and Harder," *New York Times,* Apr. 16, 1995, sec. 4, p. 1. Moreover, there is considerable competition for even those low-wage jobs, which allows employers to weigh job qualifications in ways that may disadvantage significant numbers of welfare recipients. Katherine Newman and Chauncey Lennon, "The Job Ghetto," *American Prospect,* Summer 1995, 66. Factors creating economic insecurity even for the most educated and skilled American workers and their families include the effects of corporate downsizing and record levels of wealth and income inequality in society. Kilborn, "Take This Job"; Louis Uchitelle and N. R. Kleinfeld, "On the Battlefields of Business, Millions of Casualties," *New York Times,* Mar. 3, 1996, 1; Edward N. Wolff, "How the Pie Is Sliced: America's Growing Concentration of Wealth," *American Prospect,* Summer 1995, 58.

86. Jencks and Edin, "Do Poor Women Have a Right to Bear Children?" 43. By contrast, some conservatives contend that "if poor mothers married the fathers of their children, almost three-quarters would immediately be lifted out of poverty." Robert E. Rector and Kirk A. Johnson, "Understanding Poverty in America," *Backgrounder* (Heritage Foundation), no. 1713, Jan. 5, 2004, 1–17.

87. Austin, "Sapphire Bound!" 569; Michael B. Katz, "Reframing the "Underclass" Debate," in *The Underclass Debate,* ed. Michael B. Katz (Princeton: Princeton University Press, 1993), 457–66; Dowd, "Stigmatizing Single Parents," 34–35, 51–81.

88. Fineman, *Neutered Mother,* 101–5; Dowd, "Stigmatizing Single Parents," 26–35.

89. Fineman, *Neutered Mother,* 161–76.

90. Ibid., 161–69, 226–27.

91. Ibid., 226–36; Martha Albertson Fineman, *The Autonomy Myth: A Theory of Dependency* (New Press, 2004), 123–41.

92. Rather than abolishing marriage, I argue that the government should foster greater sex equality within marriage and also foster greater equality among families by recognizing same-sex marriage and adopting a kinship registration system available for a range of family and close personal relationships. I elaborate this in my forthcoming book, *The Place of Families.*

93. Linda Gordon, *Pitied but Not Entitled* (New York: Free Press, 1994), 31–32.

94. Sylvia A. Law, "Rethinking Sex and the Constitution," *University of Pennsylvania Law Review* 132 (1984): 996–97; Dowd, "Stigmatizing Single Parents," 60–62; Patricia Hill Collins, *Black Feminist Thought* (New York: Routledge, 1991), 116.

95. The Personal Responsibility and Work Opportunity Act of 1995 had extensive provisions addressing establishment and enforcement of child support obligations, as does the final version, PRWORA. Some feminists raise concerns that attention to "deadbeat dads" is contrary to women's interests when it takes the form of mandatory paternity establishment and child support enforcement. It also exaggerates the extent to which some men actually could contribute enough resources to alleviate poverty and reinforces the assumption that provision for children is exclusively a private, rather than also a collective, responsibility. Fineman, *Neutered Mother,* 208–17.

96. Jill Duerr Berrick, *Faces of Poverty: Portraits of Women and Children on Welfare* (New York: Oxford University Press, 1995); Valerie Polakow, *Lives on the Edge* (Chicago: University of Chicago Press, 1993); Barbara Omolade, *The Rising Song of African American Women* (New York: Routledge, 1994).

97. Davis and Kraham, "Protecting Women's Welfare in the Face of Violence," 1143–50.

98. Catharine A. MacKinnon, *Feminism Unmodified* (Cambridge: Harvard University Press, 1987), 32–45.

99. Catherine A. MacKinnon, "Reflections on Sex Equality under Law," *Yale Law Journal* 100 (1991): 1281–1328, 1312.

100. Kathryn Abrams, "Ideology and Women's Choices," *Georgia Law Review* 24 (1990): 761–801.

101. Ruth Colker, *Abortion and Dialogue: Pro-Choice, Pro-Life, and American Law* (Bloomington: Indiana University Press, 1992), 43–57.

102. For example, in her examination of the life of one woman on welfare, Darlene Berrick details how the sexual abuse the woman suffered as a child at the hands of her father made her vulnerable to sexual involvement with irresponsible men (*Faces of Poverty,* 87–97). Another woman, Sandy, recounted the sexual molestation of her daughter by the father of the child (ibid., 56–57). Polakow's study offers similar stories (*Lives on the Edge,* 86–91).

103. Jennifer Steinhauer, "Study Cites Adult Males for Most Teen-Age Births," *New York Times,* Aug. 2, 1995, A10.

104. Frances Hudson and Bernard Ineichen, *Taking It Lying Down: Sexuality and Teenage Motherhood* (London: Macmillan, 1991); Bob Herbert. "Battered Girls in School," *New York Times,* Nov. 24, 1993, A25; Barbara Dafoe Whitehead, "The Failure of Sex Education," *Atlantic Monthly,* October 1994, 73–74.

105. Hudson and Ineichen, *Taking It Lying Down,* 19–77; Tracy E. Higgins and Deborah L. Tolman, "Feminism, Rape Law, and the Missing Discourse of Desire," in *Feminism, Media, and the Law,* ed. Martha Fineman and Martha McCluskey (New York: Oxford University Press, 1996).

106. Rhode and Lawson, introduction to *Politics of Pregnancy,* 8.

107. Berrick, *Faces of Poverty,* 68.

108. Rosalind Pollack Petchesky, *Abortion and Woman's Choice* (Boston: Northeastern University Press, 1990), 168–204; Kristin Luker, *Taking Chances: Abortion and the Decision Not to Contracept* (Berkeley: University of California Press, 1975), 78–111.

109. Polakow, *Lives on the Edge,* 79; Sharon Thompson, *Going All the Way: Teenage Girls' Tales of Sex, Romance, and Pregnancy* (New York: Hill and Wang, 1995), 113–14.

110. Fineman, *Neutered Mother,* 125.

111. Roberts, "Meaning of Motherhood," 28–29.

112. Fineman, *Neutered Mother,* 124–25.

113. Omolade, *Rising Song of African American Women,* 88–89.

114. In the aftermath of Quayle's Murphy Brown speech, the media featured many stories of women, often in their thirties and forties, often white, in professional jobs, who had not married and/or not found the "right" man but did not want to give up the experience of having a child and being a mother. Marsha King, "Single Motherhood—There's a Boom in Those Starting Families on Their Own," *New York Times,* July 30, 1993, F1. For a recent, thorough study of such unmarried older mothers, which appeared after the full-length version of this essay was published, see Melissa Ludtke, *On Our Own: Unmarried Motherhood in America* (New York: Random House, 1997). Although they face continued discrimination, lesbians have had some success in using adoption to secure joint parental rights for one partner's biological child. Adoption of Tammy, 619 N.E. 2d 315 (Mass. 1993); *In re* Jacob, 86 N.Y. 2d 651 (1995).

115. Jane Mattes, "Many Single Moms Make Doubly Good Parents," *Daily News,* Sept. 23, 1994, 29; Omolade, *Rising Song of African American Women,* 69–73.

116. Abrams, "Ideology and Women's Choices."

117. Seyla Benhabib, *Situating the Self* (New York: Routledge, 1992); Sarah Lucia Hoagland, *Lesbian Ethics* (Palo Alto: Institute of Lesbian Studies, 1988); Claudia Card, ed., *Feminist Ethics* (Lawrence: University Press of Kansas, 1991).

118. Annette Lawson, "Multiple Fractures: The Cultural Construction of Teenage Sexuality and Pregnancy," in Lawson and Rhode, *Politics of Pregnancy,* 101–25.

119. Berrick, *Faces of Poverty.*

120. For example, in her study, Berrick concludes that at one end of the spectrum of AFDC recipients are large numbers of women with "strong job skills" who "simply need welfare to tide them over until their economic fortunes change"; at the other end are women who, "owing to a combination of personal characteristics and environmental conditions," have "many and great needs" requiring individualized services" (ibid., 147).

121. Pearce, "Children Having Children," 46–47. Michelle Fine argues that approaches to teen sexuality focusing only on a discourse of female victimhood—for example, sex education programs that treat sex as a source of danger and fear, and keep out any discourse of female desire—may serve to perpetuate rather than challenge such problems. Michelle Fine, "Sexuality, Schooling, and Adolescent Females: The Missing Discourse of Desire," *Harvard Education Review* 58 (1988): 29, 31.

122. Kristin Luker, *Dubious Conceptions: The Politics of Teenage Pregnancy* (Cambridge: Harvard University Press, 1996); Pearce, "Children Having Children," 46–58.

123. Thompson, *Going All the Way,* 109–42; Elijah Anderson, *Streetwise: Race, Class, and Change in an Urban Community* (Chicago: University of Chicago Press, 1990), 113–15.

124. Studies suggest that poor teens (disproportionately teens of color) are far more likely than other teens to have uncontracepted sex, to become pregnant, and to continue rather than to terminate those pregnancies. Alan Guttmacher Institute, *Sex and America's Teenagers* (1994), 64–72.

125. Austin, "Sapphire Bound!" 563–64; Deborah A. Rhode, "Adolescent Pregnancy and Public Policy," in Lawson and Rhode, *Politics of Pregnancy,* 301–35. In the last decade, the National Campaign to Prevent Teen Pregnancy has undertaken research to understand some of these constraints and circumstances.

126. Sara Ruddick, *Maternal Thinking: Toward a Politics of Peace* (New York: Ballantine Books, 1993), 126, 129; Berrick, *Faces of Poverty,* 65–86.

127. Ruddick, *Maternal Thinking,* 51–52.

128. Fineman, *Neutered Mother,* 234.

129. Collins, *Black Feminist Thought*, 118–19, 123–29; Patricia Hill Collins, "Shifting the Center: Race, Class, and Feminist Theorizing about Motherhood," in *Mothering: Ideology, Experience, and Agency*, ed. Evelyn Nakano Glen, Grace Chang, and Linda Rennie Forcey (New York: Routledge, 1994), 45, 49–52.

130. Collins, *Black Feminist Thought*, 133–37.

131. Martha Minow, "The Welfare of Single Mothers and Their Children," *Connecticut Law Review* 26 (1994): 817–42; Lucie White, "On the 'Consensus' to End Welfare: Where Are the Women's Voices?" *Connecticut Law Review* 26 (1994): 843–56.

132. Polakow, *Lives on the Edge*. For another account of such obstacles, see Theresa Funiciello, *Tyranny of Kindness: Dismantling the Welfare System to End Poverty in America* (New York: Atlantic Monthly Press, 1993), 24–53.

133. Aida Torres and Jacqueline D. Forrest, "Why Do Women Have Abortions?" *Family Planning Perspectives* 20 (1988): 169.

134. Petchesky, *Abortion and Woman's Choice*, 352–53, 369–70.

135. In the full-length version of this essay, appearing in *Hastings Law Journal*, I discuss the tensions in the rhetoric of irresponsible reproduction created by the intersection of the abortion issue with efforts to deter "illegitimacy" through family caps.

136. I have been critical of some of these attempts, in part because of their devaluation of autonomy and in part because of the practical problems of persuading a larger audience that women's decisions are morally responsible. Linda C. McClain, " 'Atomistic Man' Revisited: Liberalism, Connection, and Feminist Jurisprudence," *Southern California Law Review* 65 (1992): 1171–1264, 1244–56.

137. Robin West, "Foreword: Taking Freedom Seriously," *Harvard Law Review* 104 (1990): 79–85; Carol Gilligan, *In a Different Voice* (Cambridge: Harvard University Press, 1982), 70–105.

138. *See* Amicus Brief for National Abortion Rights Action League (NARAL), *Thornburgh v. American College of Obstetricians & Gynecologists*, 476 U.S. 747 (1986) (nos. 84-495 and 84-9); *Amicus* Brief of NOW Legal Defense and Education Fund and NARAL, *Webster v. Reproductive Health Services*, 492 U.S. 490 (1989) (no. 88-605).

139. Julia E. Hanigsberg, "Homologizing Pregnancy and Motherhood: A Consideration of Abortion," *Michigan Law Review* 94 (1995): 371–418; MacKinnon, "Sex Equality under Law," 1318.

140. West, "Taking Freedom Seriously," 85; Joan Williams, "Gender Wars: Selfless Women in the Republic of Choice," *New York University Law Review* 66 (1991): 1589–94.

141. For example, Rickie Solinger's analysis of the sharply divergent treatment of white and black single pregnancy from the 1920s into the 1960s reveals that women in the helping professions played a prominent role in diagnosing and treating the problem of single pregnancy. Preconceived diagnoses precluded assessing agency, rationality, responsibility, and the meaning of motherhood from the perspectives of the women themselves. Thus, although pregnant black single females were expected to keep their children and suffer the social consequences, pregnant white single females were not regarded as mothers but were urged to relinquish their children for adoption (Solinger, *Wake up Little Susie*, 41–102).

142. Martha Minow, *Making All the Difference: Inclusion, Exclusion, and American Law* (Ithaca: Cornell University Press, 1990), 239–60.

143. White, "On the 'Consensus' to End Welfare," 851–56.

144. "Woman to Woman: On Welfare Reform," CUNY television broadcast, 1994; Polakow, *Lives on the Edge*, 592.

145. For example, an article in *Ms.* magazine by a former welfare mother, journalist Rita Henley Jensen ("Welfare," *Ms.*, July/Aug. 1995), triggered a letter to the editor inquiring why Jensen "failed to take precautions and got pregnant at 18 when she had no support," why she was drawn to an "abusive" mate, and why she had a second child ("Welfare Debate," *Ms.*, Nov./Dec. 1995, 5). Another writer observed that we "avoid discussion of the most difficult questions: Why do

people have children whom they are not prepared to support? . . . How do we assist people in their time of need while holding them to high standards of effort and responsibility?" (ibid.).

146. Allan Luks, "Advice From Welfare Mothers," *New York Times*, Aug. 24, 1995, A23; Isabel Wilkerson, "An Intimate Look at Welfare: Women Who've Been There," *New York Times*, Feb. 17, 1995, A1.

147. Berrick, *Faces of Poverty*, 30–32; Melinda Henneberger, "Washington's Bad Vibes: Welfare Bashing Finds Its Mark," *New York Times*, Mar. 5, 1995, sec. 4, p. 5.

148. Responsible Fatherhood Act of 2000, H.R. 4671 (proposed legislation).

149. Blankenhorn, *Fatherless America*, 1. Some of the organizations associated with this movement are the National Fatherhood Initiative, the National Institute for Responsible Fatherhood and Family Revitalization, National Center for Fathering, and Promise Keepers; Susan Chira, "War over Role of American Fathers," *New York Times*, June 14, 1994, A22; Gustav Niebuhr, "Men Crowd Stadiums to Fulfill Their Souls," *New York Times*, Aug. 6, 1995, 1; Tamar Lewin, "Creating Fathers Out of Men with Children," *New York Times*, June 18, 1995, 1.

150. President Clinton, Memorandum for the Heads of Executive Departments and Agencies on Supporting the Role of Fathers in Families, June 16, 1995, http://aspe.os.dhhs.gov/fathers/pclinton.txt; "Fathering: The Man and the Family. The Department of Health and Human Services' Response to President Clinton's June 16, 1995, Memorandum to Strengthen the Role of Fathers in Families," http://aspe.os.dhhs.gov/fathers/hhsresp.htm.

151. William J. Clinton, Statement on Welfare Reform, Aug. 28, 2000, Weekly Compilation Presidential Documents 1908, 2000 WL [Westlaw] 13131444; "Vice President Calls for 'Father-Friendly' Workplaces," *U.S. Newswire*, May 3, 1996.

152. National Center for Children in Poverty, "Map and Track: State Initiatives to Encourage Responsible Fatherhood. 1999 Edition," http://cpmcnet.columbia.edu/dept/nccp/MT99text.html.

153. Since 1999, various "responsible fatherhood" bills have been introduced in Congress but not passed, for example, the Fathers Count Act of 1999, H.R. 3073 and S. 1364, and the Responsible Fatherhood Act of 2000, H.R. 4671. As this volume goes to press, the welfare reauthorization bill passed in the House of Representatives, the Personal Responsibility, Work, and Family Promotion Act of 2003, H.R. 4, resembles Bush's plan in funding marriage promotion. It also creates a responsible fatherhood program. The Senate has not been able to agree on a bill, but the various proposed bills (e.g., the Strengthening Families Act of 2003, S. 657, and the Compassion and Personal Responsibility Act, S. 5) also include marriage promotion and responsible fatherhood programs.

154. Information on the federal government's responsible fatherhood and marriage initiatives appears on the Department of Health and Human Services website, http://www.acf/hhs.gov/healthymarriage. Bush's welfare plan, Working Toward Independence, is available at http://www.whitehouse.gov/news/release/2002/02/20020212-7.html.

155. Personal Responsibility, Work, and Family Promotion Act of 2003, H.R. 4, § 446.

156. Jacqueline K. Payne, Policy Attorney NOW Legal Defense and Education Fund, prepared testimony, Senate Finance Committee Social Security and Family Policy Subcommittee, July 25, 2000, http://web.lexis-nexis.com/congcomp/printdoc.

157. Ibid.

158. Blankenhorn, *Fatherless America*, 117, 124–47, 212–21.

159. "Vice President Calls for 'Father-Friendly' Workplaces," *U.S. Newswire*, May 3, 1996.

160. "Governor Bush Addresses National Summit on Fatherhood," presidential campaign press materials, June 2, 2000; "Al Gore Proposes Next Step in Welfare Reform: Help for Responsible Parents, Crackdown on Deadbeats," http://www.algore2000.com/briefingroom/releases/pr_102099_welfare_reform.html.

161. Susan Moller Okin, *Justice, Gender, and the Family* (New York: Basic Books, 1989), 170–86.

162. Blankenhorn, *Fatherless America*, 117–23.

163. Ellen Goodman, "Female Submissiveness a Subtext to 'New' Men's Movement," *Liberal Opinion Week*, Oct. 30, 1995, 1; Donna Minkowitz, "In the Name of the Father," *Ms.*, Nov./Dec. 1995, 64–69.

164. Discussion of Fathers Count Act of 1999 by Rep. Wynn, *Congressional Record*, Nov. 10, 1999, H118701 (http://thomas.loc.gov/cgi-bin/query/C?r106:./temp/~r106G3MSFk.

165. In other work, I argue for the importance of care as a public value and for governmental support of care work. Linda C. McClain, "Citizenship Begins at Home: The New Social Contract and Working Families," in *Progressive Politics in the Global Age*, ed. Henry Tam (London: Polity Press, 2001); Linda C. McClain, "Care as a Public Value," *Chicago-Kent Law Review* 76: 1673–1731 (2001).

166. William Marsiglio, Paul Amato, Randal D. Day, and Michael E. Lamb, "Scholarship on Fatherhood in the 1990s and Beyond," *Journal of Marriage and the Family* 62 (Nov. 1, 2000): 2000 WL 23509773.

167. Ibid.

168. Ibid.

CHAPTER 12

Feminist Economics

Implications for Education

Myra H. Strober

Mainstream economic concepts and modes of analysis have come to play a major role in structuring how we think not only about markets and material goods, but also about political and social institutions.[1] Indeed, mainstream economists (also known as neoclassical economists) write with pride about their imperialist invasion of intellectual territory in provinces as diverse as religion, the allocation of time, marriage, fertility, law, international relations, politics, linguistics, discrimination, the value of life, health, voting behavior, and education.[2] Key neoclassical economic constructs, such as self-interest, scarcity, maximization, choice, efficiency, value, and competition, originally developed to understand market transactions, have come to influence, and in some cases dominate, education policies. For example, because of the inroads that mainstream economic concepts and modes of analysis have made in our society, many believe that the primary function of the education system is to train workers for the economy.

It is probably inevitable that the economic system will affect major noneconomic institutions of society, such as education.[3] But the increased intellectual influence of mainstream economics, combined with heightened interest in money and economic activity in our society, have spawned proposals to further and more purposefully increase the use of neoclassical economic concepts and reasoning in the educational arena. Extending the critique of feminist economics, this essay elaborates some of the difficulties with core economic concepts and modes of analysis and argues that incursions of mainstream economics into education often interfere with the ability of educational institutions to fulfill their broad missions.

Certainly the mainstream economic model may be appropriate for the business side of education, and certainly part of the purpose of education is to prepare students for employment.[4] But the neoclassical economic model's narrow framing of human character, human purpose, and means to achieve well-being is ill suited to convey the complex and transformational goals of the education sector. This is not to say that neoclassical economic analysis may not provide some insights for educators. But these insights are often incomplete, and sometimes they are simply wrong.[5]

Some economists argue that the accuracy of neoclassical economics' assumptions about human behavior is irrelevant, that what matters is simply the ability of the mainstream model to predict behavior.[6] Without venturing into the question of how well neoclassical economic models in fact are able to predict, I make the point here that the behavioral assumptions of the model are inextricably tied to its constructs and policy prescriptions. As mainstream economics has colonized other disciplines and public discourses, those assumptions have permeated public consciousness. Educators cannot expect to use the economic model without its attendant behavioral assumptions having an impact on educational behavior.

Educators should not underestimate the ability of the neoclassical economic model to affect the perceptions and behavior of those exposed to its teachings. For example, in experimental research using games, economists have shown that the more neoclassical economics courses students take, the less likely they are to be public-spirited, as measured by the proportion of the tokens they contribute to support a particular public good.[7] Analysis suggests that this relationship is not simply correlative but, rather, causal.[8] Interestingly, among both economics and noneconomics majors, women are more likely to be public-spirited than men.[9]

Like mainstream economists, I believe that all choices have trade-offs. We need to ask what we give up when we choose to see students and the educational process through the mainstream economics lens. What are the gains and losses for the education sector of developing policies and practices based on neoclassical economics' views of human motivation and behavior?

In this essay, using some of the insights of feminist economics, I hope to raise our collective consciousness about the frequent mismatch between the worldview of mainstream economics and the purposes of education. In so doing, I aim to stimulate an on-going dialogue about the appropriateness of allowing the mainstream economic model to be exported to the education sector.

Overview

The critique of neoclassical economics by feminist economics began for the purpose of improving women's economic condition,[10] but the rethinking that has resulted has led to a questioning of the discipline's core concepts, central assumptions, methods of analyses, policy recommendations, and pedagogy.[11] The reconceptualization is meant to benefit not only women but also men, children, and indeed our society as a whole.[12]

The critique of mainstream economics from feminist writings is extremely varied and wide-ranging, and its practitioners come from multiple countries and numerous schools within economics: mainstream, institutional and

Marxist, to name a few. They also come from various schools of feminism: liberal, radical, Marxist, and separatist. Moreover, many feminist economists are as interested in race-gender, or race-gender-class, as they are in gender alone, and there are multiple cultural and ethnic visions of what feminist economics means. The feminist analyses brought to bear in this essay should not, therefore, be taken to represent all of feminist economists' thinking about these matters.

To avoid misunderstanding, we must know what feminist economics is not. It is *not* essentialist;[13] it does not hold that there are fundamental (essential) differences between women and men, and therefore it does not think that women need a different economics than men.[14] Feminist economics is also *not* about fundamental differences between women and men economists, and therefore it does not hold the view that women economists do economics in a way that is different from what men economists do, or even that women economists have a special pipeline to understanding women's economic oppression. Some of the insights that women have, however, may come from experiences that most men do not have.[15]

Mainstream economists argue that first and foremost, economics is the study of people's choices. But this was not always so. Adam Smith saw economics not only as a problem of exchange but also a problem of provisioning, "the creation and distribution of the 'necessaries and conveniences of life.' " One of the fundamental insights of feminist economics is that economics should be first and foremost the study of provisioning.[16]

What does it mean to be concerned with provisioning? It means being concerned with everyone having the basic goods and services consistent with a society's social norms. It means being concerned not only with one's own goods and services but also with those of others. It means speaking out when some people go hungry or malnourished even though there is enough food produced to ensure all the world's population an adequate diet. It means being willing to regulate and monitor trade and commerce so that producers provide adequate information to consumers and that the basic quality of goods and services is ensured. It means opening educational and economic opportunities to all. It would be a giant step for mainstream economics to consciously change its definition from a social science concerned with analyzing choices to one concerned with studying the provision of material well-being.

What would it mean for education to be fundamentally about provisioning? It would mean that education would provision every single student, regardless of race, gender, or socioeconomic status, with knowledge for living life. It would give them information and understanding to make better-informed decisions about such diverse matters as love, friendship, family relationships, parenting, community involvement, jobs and careers, leisure, political involvement, health, and financial planning. It would help them to develop a moral compass and a basis for discovering life's meanings.

Clearly, educators' definitions of well-being are far more complex than the definition used by mainstream economists. Mainstream economists equate well-being with the accumulation of goods and services. For educators, achieving well-being means far more than this; they would actively disagree with the bumper-sticker view that the man who dies with the most toys "wins." The goals of educators include not only teaching students cognitive and manual skills to aid them in the workplace, but also, more broadly, helping them to initiate an examination of the meaning of their lives, and helping them to fulfill both their sense of responsibility and their human potential. The mission of educational institutions includes teaching students to develop deep relationships that include mutual caring and to become integral members of their community and polity.[17] Educators want to initiate students into a life-long quest for knowledge and appreciation of the life of the mind. They see educational institutions as places to seek wisdom and self-understanding as well as knowledge. They wish to develop students' emotional intelligence, helping them to understand that a rich life includes not only experiencing the "good" emotions of happiness and love but also learning to deal with the more difficult feelings of anger, sadness, fear, envy, and apathy.[18]

Although economic theory treats altruism as anomalous (except insofar as the altruist egotistically benefits from the altruistic act), many educators find that individuals, including young children, behave altruistically because they have a genuine concern for other people's welfare.[19] In higher education, in particular, numerous institutions are seeking to educate for civic responsibility and to help students develop strong ethical values.[20] These educators wish to enhance altruism in their students; they certainly don't wish to treat it as anomalous.

In summary, in many instances the education and mainstream economic models are at odds. Although both seek to increase well-being, in practice, neoclassical economics defines well-being much more narrowly than does education, and the neoclassical economic definition often crowds out the more expansive and more difficult-to-measure definitions of educators. The next several sections examine in some detail the feminist critique of four constructs of the mainstream economic model and the application of this critique to the field of education. Understanding the ways in which the underpinnings of the economic model clash with the underlying purposes of educators should lead to a reassessment of the wisdom of importing economic thinking into education.

Well-Being and Value

Adam Smith recognized two types of value, use value and exchange value. Exchange value is the value that a good or service commands in the marketplace and is measured by its price.[21] Use value, on the other hand, is the value of a good or service to an individual regardless of its exchange value. For example, a particular photo may have high use value to an individual, even though its price in the market might be zero.

Mainstream economists today justify ignoring use value and concentrating solely on exchange value on the grounds that economics is interested only in *economic* value and *economic* well-being and that exchange value comes closest to measuring these economic concepts. Mainstream economists then go on to use an individual (or family's) income as a measure of individual (or family) well-being. In the aggregate, well-being is measured by per capita income, the so-called standard of living, which is gross domestic product (GDP) or national income (NI), divided by population. Of course, even mainstream economists recognize that there is economic value in nonmarket goods and services—household production and volunteer work being the most obvious examples. Still, despite this recognition, they equate value with exchange value.[22]

In addition to ignoring the value of nonmarket work, by focusing exclusively on exchange value, neoclassical economists also tend to ignore quality of life issues. Marilyn Waring presents the paradox that, according to neoclassical economists' definitions, a pristine forest, open to everyone and owned by no one, has no value. As soon as someone buys it, it does have value, as measured by the purchase price. And if the new owner begins cutting down the trees to sell as lumber, its economic value is likely to increase, for now it is producing income as well as having capital value.[23] If the deforestation results in landslides or floods with measurable damage, mainstream economists might count its negative external costs. But the cost of the forest becoming an eroded eyesore, with consequent loss of its visual and recreational pleasure, would be ignored, as would possible loss of animal and bird habitats.

Over time, by repeatedly equating value with exchange value, mainstream economists have given markets the power to become the arbiters of economic value. If one item commands a price in the market that is twice as high as another, the first item is said to have an economic value that is two times greater than the second. Eventually, the qualifier "economic" is omitted when speaking of value, and if a price of one item is twice the price of a second, the first is simply said to have twice the value of the second.[24]

Since data first began to be compiled to calculate GDP, some economists have been concerned about the equation of that figure with economic well-being, let alone well-being in general.[25] Feminist economists, particularly, have been concerned with developing new ways of more accurately measuring the quality of life, particularly across countries.[26] Nonetheless, the vast majority of mainstream economists continue to equate income or GDP with economic well-being. And as neoclassical economics becomes hegemonic, national income or GDP becomes not simply a measure of economic well-being but of well-being in general.

Well-Being and Value in Education

All of this is mirrored in the education sector with respect to the value of education. Mainstream economists divide the value derived from education into three categories: investment benefits to the individual, consumption benefits to the individual, and benefits to society above and beyond those that go to individuals, so-called external benefits. Investment benefits have exchange value; consumption benefits have only use value. Only investment benefits (and external benefits) are of interest to neoclassical economists, who tend to ignore the consumption benefits of education.

External benefits of education, perhaps exemplified by a person's ability to evaluate political candidates' positions and promises, read a ballot and vote, and generally appreciate the importance of political democracy, are seen as generating value for society as a whole. Education that results in some people having new insights or inventing new devices, products, or procedures, for example, in the medical field, would also be viewed as producing external benefits. In addition, to the extent that on average more highly educated individuals are also more highly paid, some economists view the higher tax payments on these higher salaries as another type of external benefit of education.

Except for empirical work in developing economies, however, human capital theory sees the primary benefits of education as investment benefits to individuals, as measured by their increased lifetime earnings. Skills taught in school are seen as enabling people to increase their job productivity, and in a market system, that increased productivity translates into increased earnings. From this perspective, when students go to school, the main thing they are doing is making an investment in their own future earnings. There may also be consumption benefits to individuals—for example, the ability to appreciate music, art, and literature, or the ability to understand new scientific developments, or the opportunity to make friends—but mainstream economists do not see these as central.

The hegemony of human capital theory may be seen in the budget allocations of the education sector. The subject areas that receive the greatest resources are those associated with earning a living. Conversely, those subjects that are not associated with vocational development are often starved for resources, particularly when it is necessary for educational institutions to tighten their belts. For example, because few people earn income by pursuing music and art, these subjects are thought to yield merely consumption benefits and are far more likely to be targeted for budget cuts in K–12 education than math or science, which is viewed as central to preparation for work. In higher education, the humanities suffer at the expense of the sciences. In the same vein, human capital theory helps shape such decisions as who is admitted to graduate programs; people who are "too old" to get a return on their investment are not admitted.

There are few places in the curriculum for teaching students the skills they need to be good friends, mates, or parents. Young children may get report cards that grade their ability to "work and play well with others," but for older children, adolescents, and young adults, the development of such abilities is viewed as outside the central mission of the education system.

In other words, the purpose of education has become to create workers. Few and far between are courses that help students draw lessons from great literature about unraveling moral dilemmas or finding meaning in life.[27] Art and music are marginalized and seen as expendable. Programs that teach emotional intelligence are truly rare.[28]

The struggle to view education as important beyond its human capital investment implications is tied to the broader struggle to stop equating well-being with income or GDP. The more that feminist economics can show that value is not the same as economic value, the more the so-called consumption benefits of education may be seen as vitally important.

Scarcity, Self-Interest, and Competition

At the heart of the neoclassical economic model is economic man, *homo economicus*. Portrayed as a wholly self-interested person with unlimited wants, living in a world in which resources (and therefore the goods and services these resources produce) are limited, *homo economicus* faces ever-present scarcity and must compete with others to fulfill his or her wants.[29]

Scarcity results from an imbalance between what one has and what one wants. Because neoclassical economic theory postulates that all human beings have unlimited material wants but finite resources, each must, by definition, face scarcity. Affluence cannot end scarcity; mainstream economics views even affluent people as wanting ever more material goods and services.[30]

A psychological feeling of scarcity that persists long after basic material needs have been met is not a natural condition of the world. It is created by human beings. This is why spiritual leaders in an affluent society argue that the sole source of scarcity is to be found in the human soul.[31] It is odd that although mainstream economics is ostensibly about well-being, it postulates a world in which human beings can never be content, can never truly attain well-being; they will always want more. Indeed, sometimes these insatiable needs are so intense that they lead to war.

In the more imperialistic versions of neoclassical economic theory, which deal not only with the material realm but with all human wants, the assumption is that even if material needs are met, human beings have other unlimited wants, for example, for more time. No matter whether we limit scarcity to the material world or to all of life, in neoclassical economic analysis, it can never be eliminated.

In fact, however, when we look at the nonmaterial world, we find many aspects of life that don't obey the "laws" of scarcity. Love, may be a scarce resource in the sense that some people may always crave more of it, but it is not scarce in the sense that once you give it to others you have less of it for yourself. Indeed, as the song goes, "Love is something, if you give it away, you end up having more." Empathy is yet another example of a resource that multiplies itself as it is practiced. So is prayer.

Scarcity, competition, and selfishness each describe behavior at one extreme of the spectrum. Scarcity is on a continuum that includes, in order of decreasing desire, scarcity–sufficiency–prosperity–abundance. The selfishness continuum might be described as selfishness–sympathy–empathy–altruism. The continuum on which competition sits might be competition–support–cooperation–collaboration–collusion. Mainstream economic analysis concentrates on only one end of the spectrum in the cases of scarcity and selfishness and on only two ends (competition and collusion) in the third case. It relegates the other parts of the continuum to a place outside of neoclassical economic analysis. This focus on scarcity, selfishness, and competition justifies the status quo and takes attention away from the possibility of and need for redistribution. There is little discussion among mainstream economists that, in an affluent society, scarcity is not natural but rather created, particularly through advertising.

Mainstream economic theory does not lead to the idea that those whose basic needs have already been met could increase their well-being by cultivating the art of enjoying what they already have, or that endless seeking after more goods and services can *decrease* well-being. Similarly, the neoclassical economic model's failure to recognize empathy and altruism as human characteristics means that it fails to suggest the possibility of redistribution and the extent to which it could improve well-being overall.

In many places, in both first-world and third-world countries, people do not have enough to eat. Yet there is at the present time enough food produced on earth to give the entire global population 3,500 calories per day. The problem of providing adequate food for every human being is no longer the mismatch between population and food production that haunted Malthus. There is no longer a true scarcity of food. Rather, the problems are maldistribution of resources and the absence of political will and know-how (in both the affluent and poor countries). Insisting that there is always scarcity and that people are always selfish takes our collective eye off the possibility that focusing on redistribution might be a tremendous source of increased well-being.

Economic theory has not always construed human character as so narrowly self-interested.[32] Adam Smith, generally taken to be the father of economics, wrote not only *The Wealth of Nations,* for which he is best known, but also *The Theory of Moral Sentiments,* in which he certainly recognized altruism.[33] The first sentence of *The Theory of Moral Sentiments* reads: "However selfish

soever man may be supposed, there are evidently some principles in his nature, which interest him in the fortune of others, and render their happiness
necessary to him, though he derives nothing from it, except the pleasure of
seeing it."[34]

Nor did Alfred Marshall, arguably the most prestigious nineteenth-century
economist, begin from the premise that people were inherently selfish; rather,
he thought people were shaped by their work. And he thought that religion as
well as the material world shaped people's nature: "For man's character has
been moulded by his every-day work, and the material resources which he
thereby procures, more than by any other influence unless it be that of his religious ideals."[35] Perhaps today, more than a hundred years later, we would
say that a combination of biological, cultural, psychological, spiritual, and
economic factors shapes human nature; surely most of us would agree that we
are not shaped simply by economic factors, and certainly not simply by self-
interest.

Mainstream economics has little to say about an individual's aspirations for
another's well-being. It talks frequently about envy, the so-called Jones effect,
whereby the increased well-being of others induces people to seek additional
goods and services for themselves. But there is no flip side to the Jones effect,
no empathy. Are people never genuinely pleased to see others improve their situation? If my neighbor buys a new car that I know she has wanted for a long
time, is my only possible reaction to wish I had one too? Can I not simply take
pleasure in her pleasure?

Neoclassical economics teaches that people feel better off if they use additional income to buy themselves an additional pair of shoes or take an additional vacation, but it does not examine the extent to which people might feel
better off if, for example, that additional income were used to provide a single mother with needed medical care. It does not inquire, to use neoclassical
language, how a reduction in the overall inequality of economic well-being
might affect my utility function.[36] Yet a reduction in income inequality might
profoundly affect my well-being. How many of us, particularly women, would
gladly give up some market goods and services to improve the economic well-
being of others, if that would result in greater physical security when we walk
down the street at night?

Finally, mainstream economics' fixation on the importance of competition
in creating economic well-being and its fear of cooperation lest it become collusion, to the detriment of the consumer, leads to a failure to consider cooperation as a mode of motivating and organizing economic activity. Yet as
experiments with game theory have shown, there is a great deal of cooperative
behavior in economic situations. Moreover, markets cannot flourish without
some degree of trust and cooperation among buyers and sellers.[37] The tasks
facing economics are to stop treating cooperation and competition as dichotomous and start asking intelligent questions about how much of each works

best under which conditions. And these same questions must be answered in the education sector.

Scarcity, Selfishness, and Competition in Education

By creating a scarcity of good grades and other rewards, educators have grafted the notions of scarcity and competition onto the educational system. There is no inherent scarcity of good grades or other rewards, such as prizes. The norm that not everyone can have an A, that some students must get grades lower than A, has been socially constructed. By creating a scarcity of good grades and therefore competition for those grades, educators consciously or unconsciously have emulated the reward system of the competitive model. School teaches students to march to the beat of extrinsic motivation, where the reward is not simply learning the material but rather competing with others to get a good grade.

The norm that good grades must be scarce is strong. For example, in recent years more students have been receiving A's in college courses than was true previously, which has resulted in the well-publicized consternation about grade inflation. Rarely mentioned is the possibility that the greater number of A's stems from better teaching or more effective learning partnerships between students and faculty, or from students having learned the required material more thoroughly or more quickly than in earlier times.

The closer the educational venue is to the competitive market, the stronger seems to be the enforcement of the scarcity norm. For example, in many business schools and law schools, faculty members are required to grade according to a pre-set curve. Indeed, in at least one highly prestigious business school, in required first-year courses, faculty must give a failing grade to a predetermined percentage of students.

In the same way that the education system creates a scarcity of good grades and encourages students to compete for them, it creates various types of other scarce rewards. For example, only a small percentage of students with high grades can be on the dean's list. Only one student can be singled out to give the valedictory address to fellow students at high school commencement. Each year, only one economist can win the award for the "best" (?) economist under the age of forty.[38] Only one scientist or writer can win a Nobel Prize in any one year in a particular field.

What is the purpose of creating scarcity in academic rewards? One possible purpose is to foster competition and teach students to vie with one another for extrinsic rewards so as to prepare them for the work world, where they will face both keen competition and an extrinsic reward system in which money and/or position are far more sought after than, for example, intrinsic job satisfaction. A second possibility is that scarce rewards provide learning incentives. Perhaps competition enhances learning, so that striving for good grades helps students to learn material either more quickly or more thoroughly, or both, or helps them to be better able to use what they learn more creatively (for example, to build new knowledge). A third possibility is that manufactured scarcity in the classroom has no beneficial effects on learning but merely performs a sorting service for the next level of education or the labor market.

What grade competition does not promote is learning to cooperate. To the extent that good grades are rationed, educators have created a zero-sum game. Students who help other students to learn may reduce their own grades. This may not have much effect on students who are far apart on the grade hierarchy; if I am an A student, I may have no hesitation in helping a D student, but I may decline to work closely with another A student, or even a B student. This failure to cooperate may limit what would otherwise be beneficial peer learning.[39]

Educational psychologists John Krumboltz and Christine Yeh argue that the competitive grading system has ill effects for teachers as well as for students. Instead of permitting a learning process in which students and teachers form a partnership, which the authors contend would enhance teachers' job satisfaction, the competitive grading system forces teachers into the far less satisfying role of a critic who must seek and find fault with students' work. Moreover, Krumboltz and Yeh think the current system places too little onus on teachers when students do not learn. As they put it, "[i]f every student achieved all the objectives of a given course, every student would earn an A— an unacceptable state of affairs in the current view. Thus teachers are reinforced for using methods that ensure that some students will not succeed."[40]

Related to competitive grading is classroom competition, which is so engrained in our education system that most people don't even notice it. Every time a teacher or professor asks the class a question, the multiple hands that go up are competing, each student hoping that the one who is called on will answer incorrectly so that he or she will get the chance to be "right." Sometimes, young children are so intent on the competition that when they are called on they can't even remember the question that was asked. Does all of this competition promote excellence? Would students work less hard if they were not competing with one another? Does competition promote better learning? An extensive review of the literature leads Alfie Kohn to the following clear conclusion: "Superior performance not only does not *require* competition; it usually seems to require its absence."[41]

Moreover, the competitive model sends the wrong message to students about learning. Learning to think, to reason, to question, to search for and evaluate evidence are not competitive activities. Why should a student have to engage in competition to learn? Do we maximize well-being for students or for our society as a whole when we tie the inclination to raise questions and puzzles, the ability to communicate with others, and the will to create new knowledge to competitive norms? These are questions we should ponder seriously as we consider the relevance of the economic model for education.

An alternative to classroom competition is cooperative learning. Instead of pitting students against one another to provide the correct answer for the class, the instructor puts students into teams that work together cooperatively. Students succeed when both they and their teammates can demonstrate that they understand the material. Sometimes, in the so-called jigsaw exercise, the instructor shapes the learning by providing each student with a crucial piece required to solve a group puzzle, so that only those groups that cooperate complete the task.[42]

Research shows the effects of cooperative learning to be positive. Robert Slavin concludes that as long as cooperative learning incorporates individual accountability as well as group goals, most studies find "moderate, but important" positive effects of cooperative learning methods on student achievement (as compared with the achievement for students in control groups).[43] He also finds that there are "impressive" positive effects on noncognitive outcomes such as self-esteem, pro-academic peer norms, cooperation, altruism, the ability to take another's perspective, and race relations.[44]

What might a grading system without scarcity and competition look like? Imagine a math class (say algebra). At the beginning of the class, the teacher and students (and perhaps in K–12 the students' parents) would agree on the learning goals for the class. Students would commit to working to learn a specified curriculum. After the first week, students would take a test on the material they had studied that week. Some students would demonstrate that they understood the material sufficiently to go on to new material. The ones that did not would be told that they need to repeat the test until they exhibit the mastery required. And so on for the entire course. Almost everyone ultimately would get a passing grade, but some students would get it more quickly than others. Cooperation would be encouraged, and each student would know that his or her success would not be negatively affected by anyone else's success. Teachers might wind up grading more tests than they do now, but that would be a small price to pay for enhancing the learning of more students. Some might think it unfair that some students get to take the test more than once but get the same grade as a student who passed it on the first round. But fairness is a matter of norms. If it were made clear that what is important is learning, not grades, the fairness argument would quickly evaporate.

In contemplating a system with no scarcity of good grades, it is useful to weigh costs and benefits (one aspect of the mainstream economic model that *is* worth maintaining). Socialization to the ethos of competition would be reduced, but socialization to cooperation would be enhanced. This would be especially so if grades were more frequently given to groups rather than only to individuals. Reduced competition would probably also result in more learning by more people (through peer effects as well as through more powerful motivation). In addition, for many students there would be more positive feelings about learning, which might translate into more desire for learning through-out life.

There might also be some important positive effects on risk taking and cre-ativity. A scarcity mentality can lead to fear, a sense of possible loss, a sense of needing to carefully conserve what one has and not take risks. A student may not take physics or calculus (or economics!) because he or she fears getting a grade lower than an A. Or a student may write an essay or do a project in the traditional way rather than risk a more creative approach that the teacher or professor may not like. Our schools are notoriously poor in fostering creativ-ity. The fact that some of our most creative thinkers and inventors (Bill Gates, Buckminster Fuller, Steve Jobs) have dropped out of some of the most presti-gious colleges should, in itself, give us reason to rethink the possible negative effects of schooling practices on creativity.

Ending the scarcity of good grades would not result in the education system abdicating its responsibility to prepare students for the work world, but it might play havoc with educational institutions' traditional role as a sorting system. This would be particularly so if the nascent movement to abolish the SAT as a screening device were successful. But abolishing competition for grades would allow the learning environments themselves to stress learning, not competition for the next stage.[45]

Teaching that learning is a cooperative rather than a competitive activity could be a major contribution from the education sector to our society, includ-ing the workplace. As we move to a knowledge economy, more and more workplaces are engaged in moving new ideas rapidly forward, and most of them operate with the same competitive norms as academic institutions.

Recently, a colleague and I were brought in to consult at a research labora-tory of a major corporation that was having difficulty retaining women scien-tists. In preliminary meetings, we learned from the few women there that they found the competitive atmosphere at the lab exceedingly unpleasant and stifling of creativity. For example, when someone came to give a seminar, the name of the game was to tear the presentation apart. Those who were the most ruthless in doing so were seen as the smartest, the most valuable to the organ-ization. The women questioned the value of this model of knowledge produc-tion. Later, when we brought the women and men scientists together for a workshop, we asked them to tell us what they found useful about the compet-itive ethos. Several men argued that it ensured excellence, that a presenter who knew that his or her paper would be ripped apart would be much less likely to present "sloppy science."

At a coffee break, much to my surprise, the man who headed the lab took me aside. He said that he had never thought about this issue and that our rais-ing it made him recall that for all the years he'd been at the lab, he had expe-rienced painful stomach aches both before and after he presented his work. He had come to hate making presentations to his colleagues. He was sure that his presentations would be better if the seminars were cooperative endeavors to improve his work rather than shoot it down. He was willing to try a cooperative model. We spent the rest of the workshop fleshing out what that would look like in this particular lab. I no longer underestimate the power of raising questions about sacred cows.

Efficiency and Well-Being

According to neoclassical economic theory, the more efficient are production and distribution, the greater the output of goods and services. And because producing more goods and services is equated with greater welfare, efficiency is seen as leading to enhancement of well-being. In fact, however, this argument needs careful scrutiny, for it assumes not only that more goods and services lead to greater economic well-being, but also that an increase in economic well-being implies an increase in total well-being. This may not be the case.

When surveyed, people in industrial societies often say they believe that an increase of 10 to 20 percent in their income would make them happier. But when social scientists look at the relationship between income and happiness, they find little evidence to support such a belief. In industrial societies, those in poverty are less happy than are others, but for those in the top four quintiles of income distribution, there is little correlation between income and happiness. Similarly, individuals in richer industrialized countries do not necessarily have a higher average level of happiness than do individuals in industrialized countries living at a somewhat lower level of per capita income. For those not in poverty, happiness is more strongly related to having good health, self-esteem, a loving relationship, friendship, and challenging work with adequate leisure than it is to level of income.[46] The 1992 National Survey of the Changing Workforce asked workers, "Would you be willing to give up a day's pay each week for an extra day of free time?" Almost 30 percent (28.8 percent) answered yes to this question.[47]

Neoclassical economics argues that it is legitimate for a social science to concentrate on material well-being and leave other sorts of well-being to other disciplines. But when these mainstream economic analyses are done and the policy prescriptions announced, the caveat that the analysis applies to only the material sector, not to "life," is forgotten. Or it is honored in the breach, with some rhetoric about the primary importance of material well-being for happiness. Because the social sciences have split off the study of economic well-being from other types of well-being, and because there is little or no interaction among social sciences, there is no serious dialogue about the trade-offs among various types of well-being.[48]

Even if reducing efficiency resulted in a decrease in total output of goods and services, it might not result in a lowering of total well-being. Indeed, the opposite might be true. Although neoclassical economists see efficiency as simply a means to increase output, in fact efficiency represents a particular style of operation and way of being. In order to decide whether it is worth being maximally efficient, so that maximum output (or income) can be attained, it is necessary to look at the trade-off between the benefits and costs of efficiency.

What are some of the costs of efficiency? One of them is pleasure. It is ironic that neoclassical economics, which is so strongly rooted in utilitarianism, has such a constricted analysis of pleasure. In mainstream economic analysis, pleasure is examined only insofar as consumers are assumed to obtain well-being from goods and services. The fact that producing in the most efficient way may lead to a boring and alienating production process is disregarded, as is the possibility that many people might be quite willing to sacrifice some "product" (goods and services) to have a more enjoyable work process.

Focusing on efficiency as simply a means to achieving more output puts all of the emphasis on the product and none on the process. But as John Lennon suggested, life is what happens to you while you're busy making other plans. Well-being may well be increased by trading off some efficiency to have some time to "smell the roses," to have positive relationships with co-workers, and to have adequate family leave time.

In analyzing these matters and computing these trade-offs, we must ask exactly who it is that benefits from efficiency. In the market sector, it is clear that the owners of businesses do. To the extent that efficiency raises productivity and the fruits of the increased productivity are shared with workers, workers benefit as well. But who benefits when parents are unable to take parental leave because employers fear a loss of efficiency? Certainly not the parents; certainly not their children; and certainly not society as a whole, which has an interest in children being well cared for. The market system does not take into account the well-being of parents, children, or society as a whole. It requires intervention from the government sector to safeguard those interests and insist on a trade-off between efficiency and well-being. Yet neoclassical economics is in favor of as little government intervention as possible.

Because women's work is so often in the nonmarket sector of the economy, its contributions to well-being and the quality of life are often overlooked, and it has generally not emphasized efficiency. As a result, it has been downgraded in importance. As feminist economics recognizes the importance of nonmarket production and questions the association between efficiency and well-being, it makes room for an enhanced valuation of nonmarket work and the work of nurturing and care-giving activities.

Efficiency and Education

Because school is seen so strongly as preparation for the workplace, notions of efficiency that dominate in work organizations have come to dominate in schools. Education is viewed in terms of a production function in which the "output" is produced by a series of "inputs," which are teachers, educational materials, buildings, administrators, and students themselves. Emphasis is placed on efficiently using inputs to maximize output.

One problem is that "output" is such a fuzzy concept in education. The output of the education system is, presumably, knowledge (just as the output of the medical system is, presumably, good health). However, it is exceedingly difficult to measure "knowledge." For what we really want to measure is not just cognitive knowledge that is learned and retained for a test, but the extent to which cognitive and affective knowledge are retained over a period of time and the ways in which the learner puts them to use.

Focusing on efficiency causes us to lose sight of these complexities. Ensuring efficiency requires that we measure output, and if that is too difficult, we settle all too quickly for those aspects that are relatively easy to measure. The output of the education system comes to be short-term cognitive recall that can be measured by performance on standardized (multiple choice) tests.

In recent years, in both K–12 and higher education, the "accountability" movement's interest in efficiency has taken the form of pushing for more and more standardized testing. Affective knowledge (including self-esteem and caring about others), emotional intelligence (including anger management), love of learning, ability to express oneself in front of a group, and ability to work cooperatively have all been sacrificed as outcome variables because they are too difficult to measure. Similarly, little or no concern is evidenced toward the negative effects of frequent testing on curriculum when teachers teach "to the test," putting nothing into lesson plans except what will later require recall for standardized tests. There is even less concern about discouragement felt by those children who experience repeated failure when, for one reason or another, they are not ready or able to learn the tested material.

In the 2000 presidential candidate debates, Gore and Bush sought to outdo each other in calling for more testing as the way to improve the efficiency of the K–12 education system. The focus was not on improving the system, for example, by putting more resources into education, but on more testing. The assumption seemed to be that if students had more tests to take, teachers and administrators would somehow have the right incentives to improve the efficiency of the system on their own.

As a result of an emphasis on efficiency and learning what can be easily measured, there is very little in the secondary school curriculum, for example, that is geared toward simply having fun with learning or toward appreciating learning for its own sake. Except for the hidden curriculum (playground activities, the formation of friendships, etc.), many find school a boring and dour place. And for the rest of their lives, they may view the subjects taught in school as "other"—for "eggheads," not for them—and have an ongoing distrust for people who excel at "book learning."

Worrying about affective learning in school is bound to decrease the efficiency of knowledge production that can be gauged by a standardized test. In a world in which output is measured by performance on standardized tests, learning is most efficient when teachers concentrate on cognitive learning and disregard the emotional content of their material. The message of standardized testing is that it doesn't matter how students *feel* about what they learn, or indeed how they feel about learning in general. What is important is that they be able to answer cognitive questions correctly on tests. But the separation of cognition and emotion in the quest for efficiency in learning contributes to a diminishment of excitement in the classroom and contributes to students' alienation from learning. The quest for efficiency thus defeats one of the major purposes of education, the creation of a lifelong love of learning.

It is impossible to divorce emotion from reason. Those who seek to be unemotional when they convey information about such situations as poverty and unemployment, for example, simply convey to their readers and listeners a deadening apathy, clearly an emotional state.[49] If feminist economists (along with feminists in other disciplines) succeed in breaking down the emotion–reason dichotomy, students will be taught not only to think about their lessons but also to feel about them. Instead of schooling being disconnected from their "outside" life and experiences, it will come to be integral to the experience of education.

In higher education, state legislators seeking to emulate the recent push for tests in K–12 are beginning to require that college students take standardized tests so that the value-added of college courses can be quantified and efficiency of resource utilization can be compared across institutions. At the same time, some institutions (private as well as public) are beginning to question the "efficiency" of learning in doctoral programs and are calling for more frequent review of faculty, including annual measurement of publication rates. No doubt some increases in efficiency in higher education may be warranted in some places. But focusing on easy-to-measure variables (number of years to a Ph.D. or number of articles published) will not get at the underlying problems. What is needed in most instances is for faculty at research universities to redirect their attention, to publish *less,* and to spend more time supervising doctoral students, preparing their courses, and working with students. Moreover, even with the best faculty mentorship, given the increased complexity of knowledge and the necessity for many doctoral students to work for pay while they attend school, it may be impossible for doctoral students to learn what they need to know in only four years.

A great deal would be lost if efficiency of knowledge production became the watchword in higher education. Creativity does not march to the drum of efficiency. Neither does the attainment of wisdom. On the contrary, wisdom requires extended contemplation. Moreover, faculty whose pay increases are tied to research output that is measured annually will be much less likely to undertake complex, risky, or long-term projects, in many cases to our collective detriment. We should be careful what we wish for.

Choice and Markets

Choice is central to neoclassical economic theory, for faced with perpetual scarcity and unlimited wants, it is through the making of choices that *homo economicus* maximizes well-being. Being quintessentially rational, *homo economicus* spends life evaluating options, weighing costs against benefits, and making choices that maximize utility.

Markets are also a paramount construct, because maximization of economic well-being requires that *homo economicus* and the businesses he or she creates specialize in production and then go to markets to exchange goods and services with others. Those markets, taking account of both supply and demand, ensure prices and quantities that create equilibrium conditions (at least until some factor that affects supply or demand changes). And if they are properly competitive, markets not only yield the lowest possible price for consumers but ensure that successful producers earn just enough to stay in business. Those who are unsuccessful must exit that market and try their hand at something else.

In determining prices of all goods and services and also all factors of production, including labor, markets determine their value and hence the distribution of income and wealth. Unless the sellers have monopoly power or collude, markets must be allowed to operate without interference.

This story of how choice and markets operate is appealing on several dimensions. It has elements of both the supernatural and hard science and simultaneously salves the conscience by varnishing the status quo with a veneer of justice.

The supernatural quality of markets is best seen in Adam Smith's concept of the invisible hand. A kind of secular deity magically transforming individuals' inherent self-interest into societal beneficence, markets determine not only everyone's fair share of goods and services, but also the value of those goods and services and the value of everyone's labor and capital.

But that's not all. The neoclassical economic model, which intentionally imitates physics, with its various "laws" of behavior and its emphasis on the concept of equilibrium, appeals to the modern desire for scientific specificity. There is something reassuring about human behavior that obeys well-understood laws and is so orderly that it can be conceptualized as coming to "rest" when various forces have all been accounted for.

Numerous choices lie behind the operation of markets. Producers make choices about what to produce, how much to produce, and what inputs to use in what combination. Consistent with their incomes, consumers choose the quantity and quality of the products they will purchase. And because people are assumed to make rational choices designed to improve their well-being, the outcomes of market transactions are viewed as optimal. If the system is left to operate without interference, people get what they "deserve." If some people have more felicitous outcomes than others do, it is likely the result of their superior abilities and choices.

The cards are stacked against redistribution in the economic story, because it insists that it is impossible to make interpersonal utility comparisons.[50] That is, if you propose taking a dollar from a rich woman and giving it to a poor woman, it is impossible to tell whether the increase in the poor woman's utility exceeds the decrease in the utility of the rich woman. Therefore, the argument continues, one cannot tell whether a redistribution of income or wealth is beneficial overall.

The outcomes of the model seem to produce a comforting sense of rightness, even justice. Except for income, there is little discussion of the constraints on choice. For example, the model teaches that discrimination by gender, race, and/or ethnicity, if it exists at all, will be "cured" by competition because businesses that indulge their desire to discriminate lose out to businesses that have lower costs because they don't discriminate. The notion that perhaps all businesses will indulge their desire to discriminate is not considered. Surely, the reasoning goes, some enterprising entrepreneur will note the profit opportunity, stop discriminating, and drive the others out.

Because of its unsophisticated assumptions about human behavior, the neoclassical economic model is seductively simple, and in an increasingly complex world, simplicity is often attractive. Those who extend this model to nonmarket behavior assume that human beings and markets behave the same way in the market and nonmarket sectors. Human behavior may seem complicated, these economists argue, but in essence it can be boiled down to utility maximization, trade-offs, and choices, so that it becomes really quite easy to understand the incentives that would motivate people to behave in desired ways. For example, if people engage in criminal behavior because it makes them better off, an increase in the price (penalty) for such behavior will surely reduce the crime rate. And, by extension, if the crime rate has not been reduced, then the price (penalty) is surely not high enough and needs to be raised.

Choice and Markets in Education

The notion that learning could be improved by introducing a competitive market model into K–12 public education was first put forward by conservative economist Milton Friedman in the 1950s and early 1960s.[51] Public education, he argued, was a monopoly that provided too little choice for parents. If public schools had to compete with one another, and particularly if they had to compete with private schools for public dollars, they would produce "output" that was more to parents' liking.

Of course, parents with high incomes have always had choices with respect to their children's education. They can choose to send their children to an excellent (and expensive) private school, or they can choose to move to a school district with high-priced homes that provide sufficient property tax revenues to support high-quality schools. The current "choice" movement in education argues that parents with low incomes should also have choices about where their children go to school and that having choices will improve their children's educational outcomes.

The schools available for inclusion in a choice system could, of course, all be public, but most frequently proponents argue strenuously for private schools to be included. One vehicle that permits low-income parents to choose private schools, which they otherwise couldn't afford, is a voucher, a document from the state or locality that parents present to the private school, which in turn redeems it for some dollar amount. A second vehicle is a charter school, a nonpublic school (either nonprofit or for-profit) funded by the state.

The argument for including private schools in parents' choice set is often that private schools have better average test scores than public schools. However, this claim needs careful evaluation.[52] Because of the positive correlation between student test scores and family socioeconomic level, it is necessary to account for differences in family socioeconomic level when looking at differences in test scores between public and private schools. Also, families who send their children to private school may, all else being equal, be more interested in education than other parents, so that their children's higher test scores may reflect parental interest and assistance in addition to any value-added from the private school itself. Finally, selection bias must be accounted for in comparing test scores of private and public school students. Because private schools are selective, children with learning or behavior problems are often excluded. Thus, the average test scores for private and public schools are not based on the same kind of population.

In extending the market metaphor to education, those advocating school choice argue that if parents have choice, they will take their children out of poor schools (where average test scores are low) and enroll them in better schools (where average test scores are high). As a result, better schools will expand and poor schools will contract or go out of "business" altogether, and everyone will be better off.

However, if we abandon abstract theory and look at the real people behind the supply and demand curves and the particular service that is being provided, it is unclear how either increasing the size of "good" schools or decreasing the size of "bad" schools (or closing them altogether) would improve student test scores. What we know about so-called effective schools, those that have fewer behavior problems, higher test scores, and lower drop-out rates, particularly in low-income neighborhoods, is that they have excellent principals who are able to motivate teachers, parents, and students with a personal, "hands on" management style. If such schools were to admit more pupils, perhaps by running double sessions, adding portable classrooms, or taking over an additional school, it is likely that the very resource that is so fundamental to their success would be changed. The effective principal would be unable to have a personal hands-on style in a large school. Indeed, research indicates that large schools are not effective, in part because they are too difficult to manage well and in part because students feel lost and "unmonitored" in them. Parents might well apply to have their children admitted to a successful school, but if the school admitted the many that applied, new students would be disappointed and old students would find that their situation had worsened.

If improving schools overall by making successful ones larger is not a sensible strategy, neither is improving schools by reducing the size of, or closing, unsuccessful ones. If a school is reduced in size because some parents choose to withdraw their children, it might well decline in quality. It is likely that the children with the highest test scores, whose parents might be more knowledgeable about and interested in their children's education, would be the most likely to leave. If the high-test-score children leave, and if peer learning is important, those children who remain in the poor school will have even fewer resources than before. Similarly, as morale declines, the best teachers in such a school might well leave, if they have job opportunities elsewhere that the poorer teachers don't have. Perhaps, ultimately, the school would be so "bad" that it would be closed. Then what?

Despite all of the rhetoric in the United States about the market model, we don't allow institutions that provide critical services to disappear. For example, in recent years we have almost always bailed out railroads and public utilities that are failing. If we closed a school, we would have to immediately reopen it, presumably with better management and better teachers. But the problem is that we don't have better principals and better teachers. If we did, they would already have been at the school. The problem is not that parents and children don't have choice, it's that they don't have good schools.

Proponents of choice believe that there are good managers and good teachers out there, but that they don't want to (or can't) work effectively in a system that is bureaucratized and heavily unionized. They want education to be improved by reopening schools that have been closed and running them as new entities.

Given that existing good schools, both public and private, are unlikely to expand to accommodate all the children whose parents want them to attend good schools, parents who wished to move their children would have to find new schools with an unproven track record. These schools might not be in their neighborhood. Their children might have long commutes to get there. They might not be able to get there unless their parents had a car. They might have to be separated from old friends and be fearful of making new ones. With all these negatives and an unknown outcome from a new school, how many parents would choose to move their children? Moving one's children to a new school is not exactly akin to changing one's shoe repair shop when the old one goes out of business. And why *should* parents have to move their kids? Why shouldn't their own school district provision children with good education?

Although some are pushing for a market model that requires individual parents to take action to improve their children's schooling, there is no discussion of either the most needy or the common good. Under a market model of schooling, who takes care of the requirements of the most needy children, those whose parents are incapable for one reason or another of helping them attend a better school?[53] Is it likely that school choice will increase the disparity in educational quality? Why are we willing to sacrifice our fundamental belief in the necessary separation of church and state to provide public subsidies for private schools? Why are we willing to abandon the strength that public schools have provided by socializing all children to be citizens of a single national entity?

There are serious problems in education. Some of them have to do with the fact that many children are not learning the cognitive material they need to succeed in the labor market. Others have to do with the fact that children are not learning what they need to succeed in life. To solve these problems we need provisioning, not choice, more resources, not a market model.

None of the discussions about choice and markets mentions more resources. Indeed, some of the attraction of private schools and for-profit entities is that they pay teachers even less than do the public schools. Particularly religious schools ask their teachers to take low salaries and in effect subsidize their students. In the case of for-profit schools, lower pay for teachers is what enables the school to make a profit without charging more to educate a student than the average cost of education in a public school.

One of the problems that schools face today is that they cannot attract and retain excellent teachers. Eighty percent of K–8 teachers and half of high school teachers are women. Before the 1970s, when medicine, law, academia, and business were closed to women, teaching was the most attractive occupation for bright women. For decades, schools had a bargain; they could employ women at low wages and be assured that they would not be bid away by more lucrative possibilities. Those days are over. To compete for excellent teachers who are competent in their subject matter and also know how to teach, school districts must raise salaries. Of course, increasing teacher salaries would not solve all of the problems of attracting and retaining excellent teachers. Poor working conditions, including quality of management, opportunity to grow as

a teacher, and student behavior, including violence, would still remain as negative factors. But higher salaries would certainly help, as would greater flexibility on the part of the educational establishment, including making it
possible to teach part time and to learn pedagogical information and techniques on the job.

Other resources also need to be increased, particularly to permit the renovation of buildings, but providing more resources to the education sector
won't be enough. The resources must be well managed not only at the school
level but also at the district and state levels. Figuring out how to manage
school systems in our largest cities is one of the most daunting challenges our
nation faces.

For the most part, voters have steadfastly rejected ballot measures to initiate voucher systems, and now courts have begun to question the con-
stitutionality of providing public subsidies for religious education.[54] Those
developments, together with the fact that thus far the evidence does not show
that school choice systems improve student achievement,[55] tell us that school
choice is not a panacea for our educational problems. It may well be time to
lay the mainstream economic model aside and focus our collective eye on the
real challenges, the need to provision education by increasing its resources and
developing effective educational management systems.

Conclusion

Neoclassical economics panders to the most self-serving, least lofty, goals of
humanity. Indeed, for most of Western history, greed was seen as a vice, not to
be indulged, but to be controlled and redirected. Making the fulfillment of unlimited individual wants the centerpiece of theory is not only quintessentially
narcissistic, as Susan Feiner has suggested;[56] it is also potentially dangerous,
as when failure to curb insatiable wants leads nations to war and to destruction of the environment. Moreover, it shortchanges human development.
Abraham Maslow's theory suggests that once people have fulfilled their more
basic human needs, they turn their attention to self-actualization. But if they
are told by neoclassical economics writ large in the society that it is normal
and admirable to develop and indulge an ever-present desire for more material
goods and services, they may never take the opportunity to seek greater fulfillment of their human potential.

Of course, there are often benefits to "thinking like an economist" (a phrase
mainstream economists like a lot), and some of the lessons that economics
teaches are surely worth remembering: opportunity costs (and hence trade-
offs) always exist; money should be spent where it is most beneficial; people
respond to incentives; second- or third-round unintended effects need to be anticipated; and market mechanisms are a means of holding people accountable.

But just as economics teaches that individual and business decision-making involves balancing costs and benefits, so too extending the economic model and particular economic constructs to nonmarket behavior also requires weighing costs against benefits. There is a curious blind spot in mainstream economic analysis that permits a discipline so imbued in benefit–cost analysis to ignore the considerable negative effects of the extension of neoclassical economic analysis to nonmarket sectors.

In the same way that education should not be a prisoner of any particular segment of society (government, business, labor, religious interests), so too it should not be dominated by a particular disciplinary ideology. Education has a choice about which characteristics of human beings it wishes to endorse and elaborate and which it seeks to change. Education may need the insights of mainstream economics, but those insights need frequent challenge from other social sciences, from the humanities, including moral philosophy, and from feminist scholarship.

Debating the downsides of neoclassical economics' imperialistic invasion of education requires complex analyses. A beginning has been made here. It is hoped that others will continue.

Bibliography

Aerni, April L., and Kim Marie McGoldrick, eds. *Valuing Us All: Feminist Pedagogy and Economics*. Ann Arbor: University of Michigan Press, 1999.

Anderson, Elizabeth. *Value in Ethics and Economics*. Cambridge: Harvard University Press, 1993.

Bellah, Robert N. "The True Scholar." *Academe* (Jan.–Feb. 2000): 18–23.

Bergmann, Barbara. *The Economic Emergence of Women*. New York: Basic Books, 1986.

——. " 'Measurement' or Finding Things Out in Economics." *Journal of Economic Education* (Spring 1987): 191–201.

Blau, Francine D. "On the Role of Values in Feminist Scholarship." *Signs: Journal of Women in Culture and Society* 6, 3 (1981): 538–40.

Blau, Francine D., and Marianne A. Ferber. *The Economics of Women, Men, and Work*. Englewood Cliffs, NJ: Prentice Hall, 1992.

Bowles, Samuel, and Herbert Gintis. "Walrasian Economics in Retrospect." *Quarterly Journal of Economics* (Nov. 2000): 1411–39.

Breathnach, Sarah B. *Simple Abundance*. New York: Warner Books, 1995.

Carnoy, Martin, "School Choice? Or Is It Privatization?" *Educational Researcher* (Oct. 2000): 15–20.

Carter, John R., and Michael D. Irons. "Are Economists Different, and If So, Why?" *Journal of Economic Perspectives* 5, 2 (1991): 189–208.

Chandler, Louis. "Traditional Schools, Progressive Schools: Do Parents Have a Choice? A Case Study of Ohio." Washington, D.C.: Thomas B. Fordham Foundation, 1999.

Chodorow, Nancy. *The Reproduction of Mothering*. Berkeley: University of California Press, 1978.

Cobb, Clifford, Ted Halstead, and Jonathan Rowe. "If the GDP Is Up, Why Is America Down?" *Atlantic Monthly*, Oct. 1995, 59–79.

Colby, Anne. "Moral and Civic Education for College Students." Manuscript. Carnegie Foundation for the Advancement of Teaching, Menlo Park, CA, July 2000.

Colby, Anne, and William Damon. *Some Do Care: Contemporary Lives of Moral Commitment.* New York: Free Press, 1992.

Daly, Herman, and John Cobb. *For the Common Good.* Boston: Beacon Press, 1989.

Feiner, Susan. "Reading Neoclassical Economics: Toward an Erotic Economy of Sharing." In *Out of the Margin: Feminist Perspectives on Economics,* ed. Edith Kuiper and Jolande Sap. London: Routledge, 1995.

Feminist Economics. July 1999 issue. Explorations on Quality of Life Indicators.

Ferber, Marianne A. "Guidelines for Pre-College Economics Education: A Critique." *Feminist Economics* (Nov. 1999): 135–42.

Ferber, Marianne A., and Julie A. Nelson, eds. *Beyond Economic Man: Feminist Theory and Economics.* Chicago: University of Chicago Press, 1993.

Ferguson, Ann. *Blood at the Root: Motherhood, Sexuality, and Male Dominance.* London: Pandora Press, 1989.

Fisher, Roger, and Scott Brown. *Building Relationships as We Negotiate.* London: Penguin Books, 1988.

Fisher, Roger, and William Ury. *Getting to Yes: Negotiating Agreement without Giving In.* London: Penguin Books, 1981.

Frank, Robert H., Thomas Gilovich, and Dennis T. Regan. "Does Studying Economics Inhibit Cooperation?" *Journal of Economic Perspectives* 7, 2 (1993): 159–71.

Friedman, Milton. *Capitalism and Freedom.* Chicago: University of Chicago Press, 1962.

——. "The Role of Government in Education." In *Economics and the Public Interest,* ed. Robert A. Solo. New Brunswick, NJ: Rutgers University Press, 1955.

Goldhaber, Dan. "School Choice: An Examination of the Empirical Evidence on Achievement, Parental Decision Making and Equity." *Educational Researcher* (Dec. 1999): 16–25.

Goleman, Daniel. *Emotional Intelligence.* New York: Bantam Books, 1995.

Granovetter, Mark. "The Old and the New Economic Sociology: A History and an Agenda." In *Work and Personality: An Inquiry into the Impact of Social Stratification,* ed. Melvin Kohn and Carmi Schooler. Norwood, NJ: Ablex Publishing Corporation, 1983.

Jacobs, Jerry, and Kathleen Gerson. "Who Are the Overworked Americans?" *Review of Social Economy* 56, 4 (Winter 1998).

Kuiper, Edith, and Jolande Sap, eds. *Out of the Margin: Feminist Perspectives on Economics.* London: Routledge, 1995.

Lazear, Edward P. "Economic Imperialism." *Quarterly Journal of Economics* (Feb. 2000): 99–146.

Marshall, Alfred. *Principles of Economics.* Philadelphia: Porcupine Press, 1990. Originally published in 1890.

Marwell, Gerald, and Ruth Ames. "Experiments on the Provision of Public Goods I: Resources, Interest, Group Size, and the Free Rider Problem." *American Journal of Sociology* 84, 6 (1979): 1335–60.

McEwan, Patrick J., and Martin Carnoy. "Competition, Decentralization, and Public School Quality: Longitudinal Evidence from Chile's Voucher System." Manuscript. Stanford University, 1999.

Meyers, David. *The Pursuit of Happiness.* New York: William Morrow, 1992.

Nelson, Julie. "The Study of Choice or the Study of Provisioning? Gender and the Definition of Economics." In *Beyond Economic Man,* ed. M. Ferber and J. Nelson. Chicago: University of Chicago Press, 1992.

Nordhaus, William, and James Tobin. "Is Growth Obsolete?" In *Economic Research: Retrospect and Prospect,* vol. 5: *Economic Growth.* National Bureau of Economic Research. General Series 96. New York: Columbia University Press, 1972.

Pujol, Michele A. *Feminism and Anti-Feminism in Early Economic Thought.* Aldershot, UK: Elgar, 1992.

Seguino, Stephanie, Thomas Stevens, and Mark A. Lutz. "Gender and Cooperative Behavior: Economic *Man* Rides Alone." *Feminist Economics* (Spring 1996): 1–21.

Simon, Kathy. "The Place of Meaning: A Study of the Moral, Existential, and Intellectual in American High Schools." Ph.D. dissertation. Stanford University, 1997.

Smith, Adam. *An Inquiry into the Nature and Causes of the Wealth of Nations.* Chicago: University of Chicago Press, 1976. Originally published in 1776.

———. *The Theory of Moral Sentiments.* Indianapolis, IN: Liberty Classics, 1969. Originally published in 1759.

Sobel, Elliott, and David Sloan Wilson. *Unto Others: The Evolution and Psychology of Unselfish Behavior.* Cambridge: Harvard University Press, 1998.

Strober, Myra H. "The Application of Mainstream Economics Constructs to Education: A Feminist Analysis." In *Feminist Economics Today: Beyond Economic Man,* ed. Marianne A. Ferber and Julie Nelson. Chicago: University of Chicago Press, 2003.

———. "Rethinking Economics through a Feminist Lens." *American Economic Review* (May 1994).

———. "The Scope of Microeconomics: Implications for Economic Education." *Journal of Economic Education* (Spring 1987): 135–49.

Waring, Marilyn. *If Women Counted: A New Feminist Economics.* San Francisco: Harper and Row, 1988.

West, E. G. *Introduction to* The Theory of Moral Sentiments, *by Adam Smith.* Indianapolis: Liberty Classics, 1969.

Notes

1. For helpful conversations and email discussions, I thank Cecile Andrews, Eamonn Callan, Jay Jackman, Biddy Martin, Julie Nelson, Elizabeth Strober, David Tyack, and Rick Wilk. For comments on an earlier version, I thank Judith Brandenburg, Elizabeth Cohen, Anne Colby, Larry Cuban, Edie Gelles, Deb Figart, Cassie Guarino, John Krumboltz, Lisa Petrides, Marilyn Power, and members of the Feminist Studies Seminar at Stanford University (particularly, Carol Delaney, Estelle Freedman, Barbara Gelpi, Patricia Karlin-Newman, Paula Lee, Joanne Martin, and Cecilia Ridgeway). For a related discussion, see Strober, "Application of Mainstream Economics Constructs."

2. Edward P. Lazear, "Economic Imperialism," *Quarterly Journal of Economics* (Feb. 2000): 99–146.

3. Marxists would explain this by pointing out that the economic "base" invariably determines the ideology and behavior of the "superstructure." But even without a Marxist framework, one can note the influence of the economic system on noneconomic institutions, such as the education system. For a discussion of ways in which capitalism affects the education system in the United States, see Samuel Bowles and Herbert Gintis, *Schooling in Capitalist America* (New York: Basic Books, 1976).

4. The rationale for public schooling in the United States has always included a vocational mission, and it was always assumed that education would promote individual success. But these were never viewed as the sole purpose of education, or even its primary purpose. Building a better society and furthering democracy were always at the forefront of intent. See William J. Reese, "Public Schools and the Elusive Search for the Common Good," in *Reconstructing the Common Good in Education: Coping with Intractable American Dilemmas,* ed. Larry Cuban and Dorothy Shipps (Stanford: Stanford University Press, 2000), 13–31. The missions of higher educational institutions in the United States are more difficult to summarize because they are so widely varied. Still, it would be close to the mark to say that preservation, dissemination, and furtherance of knowledge have been their collective aim. And there has been wide agreement that not only students themselves but also the society as a whole would benefit from fuller use of knowledge and more educated leaders. See, e.g., the collection of documents in Richard Hofstadter and Wilson

Smith, *American Higher Education: A Documentary History*, vol. 1 (Chicago: University of Chicago Press, 1961).

5. See, e.g., Gordon Winston, "Subsidies, Hierarchy, and Peers: The Awkward Economics of Higher Education," *Journal of Economic Perspectives* (Winter 1999): 13–36, for a discussion of why the economic theory of the firm does not apply in higher education.

6. Indeed, feminist economist Diana Strassmann has pointed out that neoclassical economists often see it as "bad manners" to critique the model's assumptions. Diana Strassmann, "The Stories of Economics and the Power of the Storyteller," *History of Political Economy* 25 (1993).

7. Gerald Marwell and Ruth Ames, "Experiments on the Provision of Public Goods I: Resources, Interest, Group Size, and the Free Rider Problem," *American Journal of Sociology* 84, 6 (1979): 1335–60; John R. Carter and Michael D. Irons, "Are Economists Different, and If So, Why?" *Journal of Economic Perspectives* 5, 2 (1991): 189–208; Robert H. Frank, Thomas Gilovich, and Dennis T. Regan, "Does Studying Economics Inhibit Cooperation?" *Journal of Economic Perspectives* 7, 2 (1993): 159–71; Stephanie Seguino, Thomas Stevens, and Mark A. Lutz, "Gender and Cooperative Behavior: Economic *Man* Rides Alone," *Feminist Economics* (Spring 1996): 1–21.

8. Seguino, Stevens, and Lutz, "Gender and Cooperative Behavior."

9. Seguino, Stevens, and Lutz (ibid.) offer several theoretical explanations for women's higher degree of cooperative behavior. Nancy Chodorow, *The Reproduction of Mothering* (Berkeley: University of California Press, 1978), argues that women's greater tendency toward cooperation stems from the fact that women are the primary caretakers of children. The developmental task of girls then is to emulate and identify with their mothers (permitting them to develop empathy and connectedness), whereas boys' developmental task is to separate from their mothers; boys therefore need to develop boundaries in interpersonal interactions, which lead to less cooperation. Mark Granovetter, "The Old and the New Economic Sociology: A History and an Agenda," in *Beyond the Marketplace: Rethinking Economy and Society*, ed. R. Friedland and A. F. Robertson (New York: Aldine de Gruyter, 1990), suggests that girls and boys develop different degrees of caring, nurturing, and self-centered behavior by emulating their same-sex parent. Melvin Kohn and Carmi Schooler, *Work and Personality: An Inquiry into the Impact of Social Stratification* (Norwood, NJ: Ablex Publishing, 1983); and Ann Ferguson, *Blood at the Root: Motherhood, Sexuality, and Male Dominance* (London: Pandora Press, 1989), point to the kinds of caring jobs that women perform in the labor market as enhancing the development of their caring skills (which may lead to more cooperative behavior).

10. Myra H. Strober, "Rethinking Economics through a Feminist Lens," *American Economic Review* (May 1994).

11. With regard to pedagogy, feminist economists have been concerned about the definition of economic literacy in the design of economics curriculum in secondary school. See Myra H. Strober, "The Scope of Microeconomics: Implications for Economic Education," *Journal of Economic Education* (Spring 1987): 135–49; and Marianne A. Ferber, "Guidelines for Pre-College Economics Education: A Critique," *Feminist Economics* (Nov. 1999): 135–42. They have also been concerned with making economics hospitable to a wider audience at the college level and reducing the gap between those who know how the economic system works and those who don't; see April L. Aerni and Kim Marie McGoldrick, eds., *Valuing Us All: Feminist Pedagogy and Economics* (Ann Arbor: University of Michigan Press, 1999).

12. Indeed, the mission statement of the journal *Feminist Economics* states: "The goal of *Feminist Economics* is not just to develop more illuminating theories, but to improve the conditions of living for all children, women, and men."

13. One of the advantages for feminist economics in developing later than other feminist thought is that it has avoided the pitfalls of essentialism.

14. For this reason, I do not like the terms *masculine economics* and *feminine economics*. They simply perpetuate old stereotypes (e.g., men are mathematical and women are not) and serve to confuse the issues. It is clearer to call mainstream economic theory sexist than to call it masculine.

15. For example, many women economists have a direct understanding of sexism gained through direct personal experiences in academe. And as bearers and rearers of children, some women economists may well be more likely to question the economic assumptions of a separative self and selfish utility maximization. Men economists who spend a great deal of time and effort rearing children may also find themselves questioning these assumptions for the same reason. The insights come not from gender but from experiences.

16. Julie A. Nelson, "The Study of Choice or the Study of Provisioning? Gender and the Definition of Economics," in *Beyond Economic Man,* ed. Marianne A. Ferber and Julie A. Nelson (Chicago: University of Chicago Press, 1993). Nelson took the term *provisioning* from Kenneth Boulding, "What Went Wrong with Economics?" *American Economist* 30 (1986): 5–12, who cited Adam Smith.

17. See Nel Noddings, *Caring: A Feminine Approach to Ethics and Moral Education* (Berkeley: University of California Press, 1984); Elizabeth Anderson, *Value in Ethics and Economics* (Cambridge: Harvard University Press, 1993); Robert N. Bellah, "The True Scholar," *Academe* (Jan.–Feb. 2000): 18–23.

18. Daniel Goleman, *Emotional Intelligence* (New York: Bantam Books, 1995).

19. See Elliott Sobel and David Sloan Wilson, *Unto Others: The Evolution and Psychology of Unselfish Behavior* (Cambridge: Harvard University Press, 1998); Anne Colby and William Damon, *Some Do Care: Contemporary Lives of Moral Commitment* (New York: Free Press, 1992). It is interesting that in Colby and Damon's study, people who had spent decades leading lives of exceptional moral commitment did not make a distinction between their moral goals and their personal and work-oriented goals. Their moral goals were primary, and in their personal and professional lives they behaved in accordance with their moral principles, a far cry from the portrayal of *homo economicus* in the neoclassical economic model.

20. For a review, see Anne Colby, "Moral and Civic Education for College Students," manuscript, Carnegie Foundation for the Advancement of Teaching, Menlo Park, CA, July 2000.

21. There has, however, been a long and on-going debate in economics regarding the appropriateness of price as a measure of value (the so-called transformation problem.)

22. Because the lion's share of nonmarket work is still done by women, whether they are employed for wages or not, women's contribution to economic well-being is vastly undervalued by the economic calculus.

23. Marilyn Waring, *If Women Counted: A New Feminist Economics* (San Francisco: Harper and Row, 1988).

24. The ill effects for women of the notion that the market price reflects economic value or, worse still, just plain value can be seen in the debate about comparable worth, equal pay for work of comparable value. Those opposed to comparable worth argue that in a market economy, the value of jobs is whatever the market assigns to them, the market is the final arbiter of value, and "monkeying with the market" is a sure road to diminished economic well-being.

25. Efforts to broaden the notion of well-being through indices supplementary to those of GNP are the index of Net Economic Welfare (see William Nordhaus and James Tobin, "Is Growth Obsolete?" in *Economic Research: Retrospect and Prospect,* vol. 5: *Economic Growth,* General Series 96 [New York: Columbia University Press for the National Bureau of Economic Research, 1972]); the Indicator of Sustainable Economic Welfare (see Herman Daly and John Cobb, *For the Common Good* [Boston: Beacon Press, 1989]); and the Genuine Progress Indicator (see Clifford Cobb, Ted Halstead, and Jonathan Rowe, "If the GDP Is Up, Why Is America Down?" *Atlantic Monthly,* Oct. 1995, 59–79). Feminist economists have devoted considerable effort to broadening the notion of economic well-being and thereby the determination of what has value. Nelson's desire to change the study of economics from one of choice to one of provisioning is an example of an effort to incorporate into economics some sense that an individual's well-being depends not only on his or her personal income but also on other people's well-being and on the common good.

26. See the special issue of *Feminist Economics* (July 1999) devoted to this subject.

27. Kathy G. Simon, "The Place of Meaning: A Study of the Moral, Existential, and Intellectual in American High Schools," Ph.D. dissertation, Stanford University, 1997.

28. Goleman, *Emotional Intelligence.*

29. Because mainstream economists make no distinction between the choices available to women and men and consider both to be rational, *homo economicus* can be either male or female, although the telltale pronoun *he* is usually used in neoclassical economic analysis. For a contrary, feminist, view, see Gillian J. Hewitson, *Feminist Economics: Interrogating the Masculinity of Rational Economic Man* (Cheltenham, UK: Edward Elgar, 1999).

30. For a fascinating discussion of how economics came to view human needs as insatiable, see Regenia Gagnier, *The Insatiability of Human Wants: Economics and Aesthetics in Market Society* (Chicago: University of Chicago Press, 2000).

31. Sarah B. Breathnach, *Simple Abundance* (New York: Warner Books, 1995).

32. Furthermore, not all stripes of neoclassical economic theory make the assumption of extreme self-interest that current mainstream economics does. For a discussion of how modern mainstream economics came to privilege the Walrasian notion of extreme self-interest rather than Marshall's more moderate view of human motivation, see Samuel Bowles and Herbert Gintis, "Walrasian Economics in Retrospect," *Quarterly Journal of Economics* (Nov. 2000): 1411–39.

33. Adam Smith, *The Theory of Moral Sentiments* (Indianapolis: Liberty Classics, 1969). Originally published in 1759, this book apparently found favor in France, particularly among women readers. In 1764, a friend of David Hume's, the Comtesse de Bouffler-Rouvel, is to have said that the book "had come into great vogue in France, and that Smith's doctrine of sympathy (therein) bade fair to supplant David Hume's immaterialism as the fashionable opinion, especially with the ladies." See E. G. West, introduction to *The Theory of Moral Sentiments,* by Adam Smith (Indianapolis: Liberty Classics, 1969), 20.

34. Adam Smith, *An Inquiry into the Nature and Causes of the Wealth of Nations* (Chicago: University of Chicago Press, 1976), 47. This volume was originally published in 1776.

35. Alfred Marshall, *Principles of Economics* (Philadelphia: Porcupine Press, 1990), 1. This volume was originally published in 1890.

36. I once sat on a committee to make up a national economics examination and pushed for several questions on the distribution of income and wealth. The other economists on the committee told me that those were not economics questions.

37. See, e.g., Roger Fisher and Scott Brown, *Building Relationships as We Negotiate* (London: Penguin Books, 1988).

38. There has been an interesting debate among feminist economists about the wisdom of creating an annual prize for the "best" article by a junior scholar in the journal *Feminist Economics.* The initial proposal was that the editors of the journal would choose the prizewinner. Some of the editors were in favor of such a prize, arguing that it would help the author receive tenure and promotion. Other editors were opposed, concerned about the implications for tenure and promotion for all the many junior authors who would not win the prize and also about the implication that doing feminist economics is a competitive activity. No one suggested that the prize would offer an incentive to write better articles. Interestingly, when the matter was brought to a meeting of the membership of the International Association for Feminist Economics, the owner of the journal, the membership overwhelmingly rejected the idea of a prize.

39. The economics department at the University of Pennsylvania recently announced that it was ending its required grading curve in its introductory economics course because it had created a hostile environment in which students have "engaged in cutthroat competition, refusing to share notes or help confused classmates." *Chronicle of Higher Education,* Feb. 9, 2001, A8.

40. John D. Krumboltz and Christine J. Yeh, "Competitive Grading Sabotages Good Teaching," *Phi Delta Kappan,* Dec. 1996, 325.

41. Alfie Kohn, *No Contest* (Boston: Houghton Mifflin, 1986), 46–47.

42. Another example of cooperative learning is the Talmudic tradition, in which study takes place in a community and the meaning of the text is derived by arguing about it. There is no one

right answer, and no grades are given. Scholars know how well they have learned by how well they can teach the material to others the next time around.

43. Robert E. Slavin, *Cooperative Learning: Theory, Research, and Practice* (Englewood Cliffs, NJ: Prentice Hall, 1990), 32.

44. Ibid., 53.

45. Progressive educators, beginning with John Dewey and his colleagues in the 1890s at the University of Chicago and continuing throughout the twentieth century with educators such as William Kirkpatrick at Teachers College at Columbia University in the 1930s, and Theodore Sizer's Coalition of Essential Schools and Deborah Meier's public school in New York City in the 1990s, have argued the importance of cooperative learning, educating the whole child including artistic and emotional education, and not allowing education to be seen simply as preparation for work. See http://www.uvm.edu/-dewey/articles/proged.html. A recent article by Louis Chandler reports on a survey of principals in 336 elementary schools (124 public schools, 133 Catholic schools, 22 independent noncharter schools, and 57 independent charter schools) in Ohio to determine the degree to which their schools practiced ten principles of progressive education, including cooperative learning, curriculum that focuses on educating the whole child, teacher reports of student progress substituting for grades, and assessments that rely on portfolios of individual and collaborative projects and take into account the readiness of individual children for particular kinds of learning. Creating a scale that ranged from 10 (highly traditional) to 50 (highly progressive), Chandler found that most schools fell in the middle range and that there was considerable variation within each of the four types of schools with respect to how traditional or progressive they were. Nonetheless, there were statistically significant differences among the four types of schools, with independent noncharter schools having a mean score of 23.0, independent charter schools a mean score of 24.5, public schools a mean score of 26.9, and Catholic schools a mean score of 28.7. See Louis Chandler, "Traditional Schools, Progressive Schools: Do Parents Have a Choice? A Case Study of Ohio" (Washington, D.C.: Thomas B. Fordham Foundation, 1999).

46. David G. Myers, *The Pursuit of Happiness* (New York: William Morrow, 1992).

47. Jerry A. Jacobs and Kathleen Gerson, "Who Are the Overworked Americans?" *Review of Social Economy* (Winter 1998): 453.

48. It is interesting that education is one of the few interdisciplinary fields in the social sciences and that schools of education are some of the few places in the academic world where economists and social scientists from other disciplines are brought together.

49. Strober, "Scope of Microeconomics."

50. See Paula England, "The Separative Self: Androcentric Bias in Neoclassical Assumptions," in Ferber and Nelson, *Beyond Economic Man*; see also, England, ch. 3, this vol.

51. Milton Friedman, "The Role of Government in Education," in *Economics and the Public Interest,* ed. Robert A. Solo (New Brunswick, NJ: Rutgers University Press, 1955); Milton Friedman, *Capitalism and Freedom* (Chicago: University of Chicago Press, 1962).

52. See Dan Goldhaber, "School Choice: An Examination of the Empirical Evidence on Achievement, Parental Decision Making and Equity," *Educational Researcher* (Dec. 1999): 16–25; and Martin Carnoy, "School Choice? Or Is It Privatization?" *Educational Researcher* (Oct. 2000): 15–20.

53. A mayor of a city that was considering vouchers once told me that if parents couldn't be interested enough in their children's education to help them choose the right school, then, as a government official, he would just have to let those children "go by the wayside." He couldn't substitute for what their parents were failing to provide.

54. See *Zelman v. Simmons-Harris,* 536 U.S. 639 (2002) (Cleveland program permitting parents to use publicly funded vouchers to pay tuition at private schools, including religious schools, does not violate the Establishment Clause of the U.S. Constitution where the voucher program is "neutral in all respects toward religion," any tax funds flowing to religious schools as a result of the program does so as a result of individual choice, and the program provided genuine secular schooling options); *Locke v. Davey,* 540 U.S. 712 (2004) (a state can permissibly prohibit state

scholarship funds from being used by a student for religious instruction without violating the Free Exercise clause of the U.S. Constitution).

55. The evidence on the effects of voucher and charter school experiments in raising student test scores is just emerging, but because many charter schools are not required to give their students the usual achievement tests, the evidence may be a long time in coming. What evidence there is does not show significant increases in test scores when socioeconomic level and selection bias are accounted for. Evidence from Chile, which has had a choice system for twenty years, is mixed. Patrick J. McEwan and Martin Carnoy ("Competition, Decentralization, and Public School Quality: Longitudinal Evidence from Chile's Voucher System," manuscript, Stanford University, 1999) found significant positive effects in one lower-middle-class area in Santiago but no significant effects in the rest of Santiago and significant *negative* effects in the rest of the country.

56. Susan Feiner, "Reading Neoclassical Economics: Toward an Erotic Economy of Sharing," in *Out of the Margin: Feminist Perspectives on Economics*, ed. Edith Kuiper and Jolande Sap (London: Routledge, 1995), 151–66.

PART IV

FEMINISM, ECONOMICS, AND LABOR

L abor and productivity have always been focal points for both feminist and economic theory. Women's participation in the labor force has been measured both by looking at their access to jobs and pay on a par with men and by assessing the impact of their historical responsibility for caretaking within the family on their participation in the labor force. Women's relatively disadvantaged position in the labor force is strongly related to their general lack of power within American society.

The essays in this part consider both "market" and "nonmarket" labor. Katherine Stone's essay, "The New Face of Employment Discrimination," and Risa Lieberwitz's essay, "Contingent Labor: Ideology in Practice," examine fundamental recent changes in the labor force that result in part from globalization and privatization. These changes have led to an increasingly volatile work environment. Stone's essay focuses on this process of change from the perspective of the employee, noting the manner in which employees in the new economy have less and less job security.

Interestingly, in this state of heightened insecurity, some employees are still increasingly able to make greater demands on their employer to assist in the development of their human capital. Having no expectation of job security,

they are released to use their developed human capital as free agents nav-
igating an open and accessible employment market. On the one hand, the empowerment of skilled employees as individual agents not tied by bonds of
loyalty to specific employers has the potential to foster a more egalitarian meritocracy within the workforce. Stone points out, however, the many ways in
which the new rules can adversely affect those who historically have been marginalized in the workplace, such as women. Stone points out the implications
of this new arrangement for patterns of employment discrimination and discusses the need for new methods for redressing discrimination.

While Stone focuses on the impact of new employment arrangements on
specific employees, Lieberwitz focuses more on employer/employee labor relations. Lieberwitz examines the manner in which the increasing lack of job protection characteristic of the new employment model has been justified as being
more of a "natural" unregulated economy and thus inherently more efficient.
Lieberwitz counters that employers hide behind notions that this current
model is more natural in order to obscure the increasingly skewed power relations underlying the new employment model. It is not the market that is
maximizing profits but rather employers making choices in order to both increase their own profits and further cement their power vis-à-vis the employee.
Lieberwitz argues that because the superiority (and inevitability) of capitalism
is completely unquestioned within our political democracy, the power dynamic
behind the new employment market is easily obscured.

Within traditional economics, labor has generally been defined to include
only the for-pay labor performed outside the family. Feminists have asserted
that a focus on only market forms of labor fails to acknowledge the significance of women's caretaking contributions to society and that such a failure
devalues such contributions and plays a role in women's access to power in society relative to men.

Some feminists have further outlined the contours of this dynamic through
the use of economic methodology. By focusing on women's caretaking work as
something productive and of significant value to society, these feminists have
argued that women should be entitled to reap the economic benefits of their
contributions of labor. Others, by contrast, reject the impulse to commodify
caretaking work, which they argue is the result of viewing this work solely in
economic terms. These feminists assert that "certain human attributes or certain resources should lie wholly or partially beyond exchange." Katharine Silbaugh's essay, "Commodification and Women's Household Labor," represents
an important contribution to this debate.

Noting that the actual caretaking tasks performed within the home by paid
domestic workers and unpaid caretakers (generally mothers and grandmoth-
ers) is identical, Silbaugh points out the fundamental absurdity of not viewing
the unpaid caretaking work in economic terms. Silbaugh also notes the lost
benefits to women, including Social Security, when such work is not viewed as

productive labor. Silbaugh, however, does take seriously the commodification critique. But rather than concluding that the commodification critique requires a refusal to view unpaid caretaking work in economic terms, Silbaugh argues that unpaid work can be viewed through both noneconomic and economic lenses, rejecting the universality intrinsic to traditional economics.

Laura Kessler, in her essay "Is There Agency in Dependency? Expanding the Feminist Justifications for Restructuring Wage Work," appears somewhat more skeptical of the use of neoclassical methodology. Kessler focuses not on the proper treatment of unpaid forms of labor but rather on how such labor prevents women from participating in the paid labor market on equal terms with men. Kessler notes that certain key economic concepts and extensions, particularly rational choice theory, are incompatible with certain biological issues, such as pregnancy and child rearing. One cannot equate the decision to have a child or to provide care to such a child as a "choice" women make, thus justifying the social policy conclusion that they should be solely responsible for any adverse consequences.

Kessler also looks at specific legislative and court-facilitated attempts to remedy inequality resulting from reproduction, discussing Title VII sex discrimination cases, the Pregnancy Discrimination Act, and the Family Medical Leave Act. She argues that notwithstanding such laws, both neoclassical economics and liberal theory, which have a singular focus on the autonomy and equality of the liberal individual, render women's caretaking work invisible within our current legal framework. Kessler argues that the law should move away from economics and liberal theory and suggests a movement toward a notion of participation in caretaking work as a possible manifestation of women's political agency.

CHAPTER 13

The New Face of Employment Discrimination

Katherine V. W. Stone

Over the past ten years, the employment relationship has undergone a profound transformation.[1] No longer is employment centered on a single, primary employer. Instead, employees expect to change jobs frequently. No longer do employees derive their identity from a formal employment relationship with a single firm; rather their employment identity comes from attachment to an occupation, a skills cluster, or an industry. Firms now expect a regular amount of churning in their workforces. They encourage employees to look on their jobs as short-term arrangements and to manage their own careers. Employees no longer expect long-term career-long job security.

Management theorists and industrial relations specialists speak of the new employment relationship as a "new psychological contract" or a "new deal at work." In the new deal, the long-standing assumption of long-term attachment between an employee and a single firm has been broken. In its idealized form, the new deal is a move to a free agency model of employment, in which each individual operates as a rational economic actor in a labor market unmediated by institutions, customs, and norms. In this setting, both the individual and the firm maximize utility and advantage, without regard for long-term ties or mutual loyalty.

We can see evidence of this change in many places. For example, employees are no longer "workers" or even "employees"—they are professionals in a particular skill or line of work. Cafeteria workers are now termed "members of the culinary service team." Salespeople are now "sales associates," clerical workers are "administrative assistants," and cashiers are "cash register professionals." These new-breed professionals have their own web pages, magazines, and trade conferences in which they network with others like themselves and keep abreast of opportunities and developments.

We also see evidence of change in the methods and strategies of job seekers. Resumes are no longer crisp chronological lists of schools attended and positions held. Today, resumes are narratives about skills mastered and tasks performed. Resume preparation services advise applicants to organize their resumes on a functional rather chronological basis, emphasizing abilities and potentials rather than work history. Such a resume does not highlight either past employers or the sequence of jobs. Indeed, one has to read a resume carefully to find such information.

Evidence of change is also apparent in employer recruitment tactics. Employers are using new approaches to attract applicants and are offering incentives tailored to the new sensibilities. McDonald's advertises on the radio, offering training in skills such as management and finance, areas that go far beyond the immediate tasks of operating a register or making fast food. Burger King offers to help with college tuition.

At the other end of the spectrum, business consultants talk about the "talent wars" of recruitment. They advise firms to restructure human resource policies in order to attract the top talent by offering learning opportunities, lifestyle perks, and performance incentive compensation. For example, in the recent book *Winning the Talent Wars,* Bruce Tulgan advises firms that to retain valued employees, they need to permit people to customize their jobs to suit their own ambitions and lifestyles.[2] A firm should let its employees select their work tasks, work location, schedule, and learning opportunities. Tulgan refers to employees as free agents operating in a free talent market, and he urges firms to offer whatever it takes to attract and keep the best of them—whatever it takes *except* job security.[3]

Rosabeth Moss Kanter also advises firms that to attract committed workforce, they need to make employees feel welcome and valued. She suggests giving employees gifts to welcome them into the workplace community, giving them buddies and mentors to cement their bond, staging periodic formal and informal recognition ceremonies to foster positive feelings, providing family-friendly schedules to accommodate private lives, and in other ways creating a culture of respect and trust.[4] Conspicuously absent from her proposals are promises of job security. Kanter says firms need to build commitment, not blind loyalty.[5]

Many have written about the new deal at work in recent years, but few have considered the policy implications. From a policy perspective, it is important to define precisely what the new deal is and how it differs from the old deal. Once we understand the terms of the new employment relationship—the explicit and implicit promises, terms, obligations, and expectations that both parties bring to bear—we can evaluate the new workplace from the perspective of fairness to individuals, equity between individuals, and justice society-wide. Such an understanding will also enable us to reconsider existing labor and employment laws and to determine which aspects of the regulatory framework need to be retained, which ones abandoned.

This essay examines the impact of the new workplace practices on the problem of employment discrimination. It discusses how the nature of employment discrimination is changing in the new workplace, and it argues that new approaches to eliminate the new forms of discrimination must be devised. In order to see the ways in which discrimination now operates, I begin with a description of the new workplace.

The Contours of Change

In the past, most large corporations organized their workforces into what has been termed an "internal labor market." In internal labor markets, jobs were arranged into hierarchical ladders, and each job provided the training for the job on the next rung up. Employers who used internal labor markets hired only at the entry level, then used internal promotion to fill all of the higher rungs. Employers wanted employees to stay a long time, so they gave them implicit promise of long-term employment and of orderly and predictable patterns of promotion. Consistent with internal labor market job structures, employers structured pay and benefit systems so that wages and benefits rose as length of service increased.[6]

In recent years, employers have dismantled their internal labor market job structures and abandoned the implicit promises that went along with them. In their place, they are creating new types of employment relationships that do not depend on, or encourage, longevity. Employers make these changes in order to gain the flexibility to cross-utilize employees and make quick adjustments in production methods as they confront increasingly competitive product markets. Work has thus become contingent not only in the sense that it is formally defined as short term or episodic, but in the sense that the attachment between the firm and the worker has been broken. Employment no longer depends on having an ongoing relationship with an employer. Rather, we are witnessing the "recasualization" of the regular, full-time employment relationship.

The changes in the employment relationship are evident in the employment data on job tenure and turnover. Labor economists report a significant decline in job tenure in the 1990s.[7] Thus, for example, the Bureau of Labor Statistics of the Department of Labor found that between 1983 and 1998, a significant decline occurred in the proportion of men who had been with their current employer for ten years or more.[8] For men ages 40 to 44, the proportion declined from 51 percent in 1983 to 39 percent in 1998. Similar large declines occurred for men in every age group over 45. Men between age 55 and 64 have also seen their median years on their current job decline, from 15.3 years in 1983 to 11.2 years in 1998. For men ages 45 to 54, the decline was from 12.8 years to 9.4 years.[9] These are dramatic changes. For women, there was not such a marked decline, and in some cases even a modest rise, but because women have not traditionally been part of the long-term employment system, the overall percentages of women working for ten years or more is significantly lower than men in any event.

In addition to the aggregate economic data, we know a lot about the contemporary labor market from the accounts of journalists, scholars, and corporate executives. These informants report that there is a fundamental change in the implicit, psychological contract under which most Americans are now employed. For example, the sociologist Richard Sennett interviewed a number of younger employees about their experiences in the labor market, and he reports that "[t]he most tangible sign of that change might be the motto 'No long term.' In work, the traditional career progressing step by step through the corridors of one or two institutions is withering: so is the deployment of a single set of skills through the course of a working life."[10] Sennett also interviewed an executive at ATT who told him, "[i]n ATT we have to promote the whole concept of the work force being contingent, though most of the contingent workers are inside our walls. 'Jobs' are being replaced by 'projects' and 'fields of work.' "[11]

The same sentiment was expressed eloquently by Jack Welch, the miracle-maker CEO of General Electric Company, who was asked by the *Harvard Business Review* in 1989, "What is GE's psychological contract with its people?" Welch replied:

> Like many other large companies in the United States, Europe, and Japan, GE has had an implicit psychological contract based on perceived lifetime employment. People were rarely dismissed except for cause or severe business downturns. . . . This produced a paternal, feudal, fuzzy kind of loyalty. You put in your time, worked hard, and the company took care of you for life. That kind of loyalty tends to focus people inward. But given today's environment, people's emotional energy must be focused outward on a competitive world where no business is a safe haven for employment unless it is winning in the marketplace. The psychological contract has to change.[12]

Peter Drucker, the popular management theorist, stated bluntly: "There is no such thing as 'lifetime employment' anymore—such as was the rule in big U.S. or European companies only a few years ago."[13] Thomas Davenport, a principle in the leading management consulting firm Towers Perrin, writes, "Has the psychic contract evolved since 1983? You bet it has."[14]

Why are corporations restructuring their employment practices? Work practices are being adjusted to production requirements. As firms are forced into a more competitive environment through increased trade and global competition, they have to pay more attention to short-term cost reduction. In addition, the takeover battles in the market for corporate control force firm managers to be responsive to short-term change in revenues and demand. Part of this responsiveness involves just-in-time production, just-in-time product design, and just-in-time workers.

The View from Organizational Theory

The essential features of the new employment relationship are best understood in the terminology of organizational behavioral theory. These theorists both study contemporary human resource practices and advise human resource professionals about how to create a workplace that can function smoothly and efficiently in today's competitive environment. The core building blocks of their approaches are three concepts—the psychological contract, the boundaryless career, and organizational citizenship behavior. It is important to understand these concepts in order to address questions of discrimination in the new workplace.

The New Psychological Contract

To understand these changes in the employment relationship, scholars of organizational behavior have developed the concept of a psychological contract between an employee and the firm. The term *psychological contract* refers to an individual's *beliefs* about the terms of his or her employment contract, the employee's perceptions of the terms of a reciprocal exchange.[15] A psychological contract is distinguished from mere expectations, which reflect the employee's hopes and aspirations, but not the belief in mutual obligation. When expectations are not met, an employee is disappointed; when a psychological contract is breached, the employee feels wronged.[16] Researchers find that "[f]ailure to honor a contract creates a sense of wrongdoing, deception and betrayal with pervasive implications for the employment relationship."[17]

Academic interest in the notion of psychological contracts developed during the period in which middle management in large American corporations was the victim of large-scale downsizing and corporate restructuring. In studying those left standing after massive layoffs in their firms—a group referred to by the evocative term *layoff survivors*—as well as those who lost their jobs but were later reemployed at new firms—termed *expatriate managers*—organizational sociologists theorized that these employees' intense sense of unfairness and anger was a result of the fact that the changes in their employment were inconsistent with their tacit assumptions about the terms of their employment contracts.[18]

For present purposes, the important fact of the psychological contract is that it is undergoing a profound transformation. According to one scholar:

[Under] the old psychological contract, the employer was seen as a caretaker for the employee . . . employees who were good performers were virtually guaranteed a job by their employer until retirement . . . the employer gave career development and promotions and the employee gave loyalty and commitment to the job and the organization. In the new

psychological contract, both employees and employers have lower expectations for long-term employment, employees are responsible for
their own career development, and commitment to the work has replaced commitment to the job and organization.[19]

Researchers have attempted to characterize the new set of expectations that
managers impart to their employees—expectations not of long-term job security and continuous promotion along a job ladder but of something else. The
terms of the new psychological contract can be found in the management literature about competency-based organizations, total quality management, and
other high-involvement work practices that define the new workplace as it is
imagined, and currently being constructed, by management and management
consultants. The new expectations shape workplace behavior and workplace
norms.

The Notion of the Boundaryless Career

Another concept that is central to understanding the new employment relationship is the concept of the boundaryless career. A boundaryless career is a
career that does not depend on traditional notions of advancement within a
single hierarchical organization. It includes an employee who moves frequently across the borders of different employers, such as Silicon Valley technicians, or one whose career draws its validation and marketability from
sources outside the present employer, like professional and extra-organiza-
tional networks. It also refers to changes within organizations, in which individuals are expected to move laterally, without constraint from traditional
hierarchical career lattices.[20] It has been defined as "a career which unfolds
unconstrained by clear boundaries around job activities, by fixed sequences of
such activities, or by attachment to one organization."[21]

The advent of boundaryless careers is said to correspond to the growth in
joint ventures, outsourcing, and other forms of network production that permit and sometimes even encourage mobility between related enterprises. It is
also related to change within firms where departmental boundaries and job
definitions are becoming replaced with broadly defined bands.[22] Whereas previously, careers were understood to unfold in structured ways, either with internal labor markets or along fixed lattices on organizational flow charts, recent
research on careers has found fluidity. One scholar writes that "[i]nside firms in
the United States, decentralization and increasing emphasis on cross-functional
coordination and teams have blurred previously rigid departmental boundaries.
Many American employers have moved to more general job descriptions, emphasizing key values, rather than precise, predetermined duties."[23]

The concept of a boundaryless career is a major departure from the internal labor markets of the past one hundred years. Instead of job ladders along

which employees advance within stable, long-term employment settings, there are possibilities for lateral mobility between and within firms, with no set path, no established expectations, and no tacit promises of job security.

The Concept of Organizational Citizenship Behavior

The concept of organizational citizenship behavior is another prominent concept in contemporary organizational theory. Organizational citizenship behavior (OCB) means behavior that goes beyond the requirements of specific role definitions.[24] Researchers have found that OCB is a significant feature in organizational effectiveness.[25] Indeed, it has been suggested that OCB is the defining feature of those companies rated as "excellent" for their management practices.[26] Organizations need predictable role performance; they also need spontaneous and innovative activity that goes beyond role requirements. Firms want employees to take an entrepreneurial approach to their jobs, to pitch in, to give something extra. They want to induce employees to exercise creativity on behalf of the firm. They want to give employees discretion, but they also want to ensure that the discretion is exercised on the firm's behalf. Much of current human resource policy is designed to encourage OCB, but to do so without making promises of job security. That is, the goal of today's management is, in the words of one consultant, to engender "commitment without loyalty."[27]

The Nature of the New Employment Relationship

The concepts of the new psychological contract, the boundaryless career, and organizational citizenship behavior are used by management and organizational theory to address a fundamental paradox in today's workplace: firms need to motivate employees to provide the commitment to quality, productivity, and efficiency while at they same time they are dismantling the job security and job ladders that have given employees a stake in the well-being of their firms for the past hundred years. In the past, internal labor markets were adopted by firms to solve problems of employee motivation, encourage skill acquisition, and discourage employee oppositional behavior. In the new era, what in the new employment systems will accomplish these goals? What type of psychological contract can replace the old implicit contract for job security in engendering the OCB necessary for success in today's firms?

Rosabeth Moss Kanter acknowledges that the new high-commitment management models are colliding with "the job insecurity reality" found in American corporations.[28] She resolves the paradox by advocating that firms offer "employability security" instead of employment security. She says firms should provide lifetime training and retraining opportunities.[29] She claims that this will enable them to attract high-caliber talent and will give those employees who are downsized other opportunities.[30]

Peter Drucker also tries to confront the paradox of employee motivation in the "no long-term" world.[31] He recommends that employees market themselves for their knowledge and their human capital. They should plan to work in networks—for corporations, but not as employees of the corporations. He says high management needs to stop emphasizing loyalty and instead learn how to instill trust.[32]

Janice Klein, a former G.E. executive turned M.I.T. Sloan School professor, also attempts to provide an answer. She advocates a flattening of hierarchies and elimination of executive dining rooms, managerial parking spaces, and other status-linked perks. She says firms must make a visible commitment to equity of sacrifice in times of workforce reductions. The task, she states, is for managers to "find other means to convince employees that they are in the same boat together."[33]

From these and other management theorists, it is possible to enumerate the elements of the new employment relationship. One important element is the promise of training to enable employees to develop their human capital. Employers promise employability, that they will enable employees to develop their human capital. Another feature of the new employment relationship involves the promise of networks. Not only can employees raise their human capital; they can raise their social capital by meeting and interacting with others from other departments within the firm, with customers and suppliers of the firm, and even with competitors.

The new employment relationship also involves compensation systems that peg salaries and wages to market rates rather than internal institutional factors. The emphasis is on differential pay to reflect differential talents and contributions.[34] Thus, for example, the management consulting firm Towers Perrin urges its clients to "reward results, not tenure, even at the hourly level."[35] It advocates a "significantly disproportionate share of all pay programs for high-performing employees" and "differen[t] deals based on employee contribution."[36] It acknowledges that these recommendations will create dissatisfaction among lower-performing employees and says, "Top Companies also plan for and achieve higher turnover rates. This strategy is based on the hypothesis that significant pay differentiation provides more motivation for the average and poor contributors to leave as they can get a better deal at other companies which tend to offer higher levels of pay."[37]

Other features of the new employment relationship are a flattening of hierarchy, the provision of opportunities for lateral as well as vertical movement within and between organizations, and the promotion of contact between employees at all levels and firm constituents, including suppliers and customers. It also involves the company-specific use of dispute resolution devices to redress perceived instances of unfairness.

We can thus make a chart comparing the new to the old psychological contract:

Old Employment Relationship	New Employment Relationship
job security	employability security
firm-specific training	general training
de-skilling	upskilling
promotion opportunities	networking opportunities
command supervision	micro-level job control
longevity-linked pay and benefits	market-based pay
collective bargaining and grievance procedures	dispute resolution procedures for individual microdisputes

The New Workplace and the Old Labor Laws

The new employment system has many implications for labor and employment regulation. Many aspects of the present system of labor and employment law assume the existence of strong firm–worker attachment, long-term jobs, and promotion ladders to define progress throughout a career. Throughout most of the twentieth century, the law and the institutions governing work in America have been based on the assumption that workers are employed by corporations that have stable work forces and value long-term attachment between the corporation and the worker.

For example, the collective bargaining laws were designed to promote the self-organization of workers so they could constitute a countervailing power that could bargain with employers about the operation of internal labor markets. Unions negotiated agreements that contained seniority and just-cause-for-discharge clauses that enabled them to enforce the firms' promises of lifetime employment security. Unions also negotiated other terms that were consistent with a lifetime employment commitment, such as longevity-based wages, vacation and sick leave policies, and other benefits. Long vesting periods for pensions also assumed and reinforced the norm of long-term employment.

At the same time, the New Deal social security and unemployment programs tied crucial social insurance protections to employment, thereby reinforcing the bond between employee and firm. There thus evolved an employment system comprised of rising longevity-based wages, health insurance, and retirement security. For American workers, the promises of such a system embodied the epitome of a good life. These promises were not always given freely or gratuitously—workers often fought hard for them. Nonetheless, once in place, the lifetime employment system with the multiple forms of job and livelihood security it offered was beneficial to both management and labor.

While the old employment system provided job security and relative prosperity to many, it also created an invidious form of labor market dualism—a sharp division between insiders and outsiders that strongly fell along racial and gender lines. The primary sector—the unionized work force within large firms—was the privileged core. As a core, it generated a periphery comprised of women, minorities, migrant workers, and rural Americans, groups that were largely left outside. The labor laws and large-firm employment practices reinforced a sharp divide between those inside and those outside the corporate family. The insiders benefited from the collective bargaining laws; the outsiders were protected by the other two types of labor laws—minimal individual employment standards, such as the Fair Labor Standards Act and OSHA, and employment discrimination laws.

The change in the nature of the workplace requires us to reassess and reinvent many aspects of labor and employment law. For example, in the law of individual employment contracts, it is becoming necessary to shift focus from the at-will contract and its exceptions to issues of restrictive covenants and ownership of human capital.

In addition, the new workplace has changed the nature of employment discrimination. Whereas in the past discrimination often took the form of keeping women and minorities out of internal labor markets or constraining them to the lower rungs of the job ladders, discrimination today takes the form of more subtle forms of exclusion. Therefore, in order to make further strides toward equality, we must develop new theories of liability and new remedial approaches.

Third, the old regulatory system erected a system of employment-based social insurance, which provided health insurance, old-age assistance, workers' compensation, and unemployment insurance to those employed within the primary sector. The new system threatens to undermine these features of the private welfare state. With boundaryless careers instead of job security, many of the workers who had employer-provided insurance lose their health insurance and long-term disability insurance, as well as unvested pension benefits, each time they move across the boundary from one employing establishment to another. Furthermore, the decline of unions means that union-negotiated benefit packages are becoming scarce. Yet the disintegration of the private social welfare system has potentially large social costs. If a large number of workers who formerly had employer-provided health insurance and pension benefits no longer do, then there are potentially serious social costs.

Fourth, the new employment relationship and its attendant job structures was initially constructed in nonunion environments, and it continues to operate almost exclusively in nonunion environments to this day. Unions are a valuable form of voluntary association because they provide democratic participation and voice to a large sector of the population, both in the workplace and in the political process. Yet many of the features of unionism under the

National Labor Relations Act, such as narrowly and precisely defined bargaining units, are not suited to boundaryless careers.[38] If we want to preserve institutions for employee representation, a new model of unionism and a new legal structure to support it need to be imagined.

Finally, the new workplace is arising at the same time that income distribution is becoming ever more unequal. The impact of the new psychological contract and the other new work practices on income distribution needs to be analyzed and addressed.

In a longer work, I address the impact of the changing workplace on all these issues.[39] In this essay, I discuss the implications of the boundaryless workplace for efforts to eliminate employment discrimination.

The Changing Face of Employment Discrimination

Much of the civil rights legislation and enforcement efforts of the past three decades have been directed toward eliminating employment discrimination as it was manifest in the old workplace under the old employment relationship. The boundaryless workplace does not eliminate the problem of employment discrimination, but it does change the nature of discrimination and renders many of the older civil rights strategies ineffective.

Historically, employment discrimination has taken the form not merely of pay differentials between men and women, and blacks and whites, but also, and more significantly, of job segregation along gender and racial lines.[40] Jobs occupied primarily by women or minorities have lower pay, fewer benefits, and lesser status than jobs occupied by white males.[41] The civil rights legislation of the 1960s was aimed at eliminating both disparate pay and job segregation. The Equal Pay Act of 1962 addressed the problem of disparities in compensation between women and men doing the same job, and Title VII of the Civil Rights Act of 1964 addressed the issue of equal employment opportunities for women and minorities. Title VII provided a means for women and minorities to challenge discrimination in hiring, testing, promotion, training, remuneration, benefits, and other aspects of the employment relationship. As a result, it became the primary weapon in the struggle to achieve equality in the workplace.

Civil rights enforcement efforts were initially directed at corporate hiring and compensation practices, and aimed to obtain equal pay and access to jobs for women and minorities. But it quickly became apparent that women and minorities needed not simply jobs, but good jobs. They needed access to jobs in the primary sector that offered promotional opportunities, training, job security, and benefits—that is, jobs that were part of internal labor markets.[42] Hence, Title VII plaintiffs sought not only hiring mandates but also affirmative action to help women and minorities enter the primary labor market and move up the advancement ladders.

In an era of promotional ladders within firms, it was logical and appropriate for Title VII plaintiffs to seek remedies that gave women and minorities access to the upper rungs of the promotion ladders. Hence, many lawsuits challenged employers' use of discriminatory tests and other selection devices as well as subjective supervisory assessment measures in promotion decisions.[43] These antidiscrimination strategies assumed that there were identifiable job ladders to define advancement opportunities within firms, and sought to move women and minorities up within them.[44]

Title VII remedies for employment discrimination were thus tailored to redressing discrimination within firms that used internal labor markets. The link between Title VII and internal labor markets becomes apparent when we examine the role of internal labor markets in creating and perpetuating employment discrimination. This examination demonstrates that existing Title VII remedies, although effective in the old workplace, are not well suited to the new one.

Employment Discrimination and Internal Labor Markets

Long ago, Gary Becker explained employment discrimination as a product of employers' "taste for discrimination."[45] He hypothesized that some employers had an irrational taste for an all-white or an all-male work force, and that this taste factored into their utility function when making profit-maximizing employment decisions. Those employers, he posited, were willing to pay higher wages for their "taste" preference.[46] In this view, discrimination is both irrational and inefficient.

A number of economists have since pointed out that if discrimination were merely a product of irrational employer behavior, namely, the result of employers exercising a nonmarket preference, then over time, competition would eliminate it.[47] Employers of white men would find that they could operate just as well with minorities or women, who would cost them less. They would therefore lay off white men and hire minorities and women. Eventually wages of white males would fall and those of minorities and women would rise until parity was achieved. However, this has not occurred.[48] Therefore, various modifications of Becker's theory have been offered to explain the intractable nature of discrimination in the labor market.[49]

One concept that has been used to explain the persistence of employment discrimination is the concept of statistical discrimination. Statistical discrimination occurs when two groups vary on average in terms of some relevant characteristic, and an employer treats all members of each group as if they all possess that average characteristic.[50] For example, if employers assume all women will have short job tenure and treat all women on the basis of that belief, then employers will avoid hiring women for jobs for which they value longevity.[51] In particular, they will not hire women for jobs that require on-the-job training or that are organized into job ladders.[52]

Internal labor markets came to dominate American industry in the early twentieth century. Under the internal labor market employment system, employers valued longevity; they wanted to hire employees who would stay on the job a long time. Yet, for most of this century, women as a group have had a pattern of short job tenure relative to men.[53] According to economic historian Claudia Goldin, "firms often used sex as a signal of shorter expected job tenure."[54] Thus, by operation of statistical discrimination, employers avoided hiring women for jobs in internal labor markets.[55] In this way, the system of job ladders, internal promotion, and limited ports of entry has operated to keep women out of the best jobs.

The interaction between statistical discrimination and internal labor markets is explained by sociologists Patricia Roos and Barbara Reskin as follows:

> With respect to women, [statistical discrimination] is most often manifest in employers' reluctance to hire *any* woman for jobs that require appreciable on-the-job training, because they believe many young women leave the labor force to have children. As a result, newly hired females are often assigned to low-skilled dead-end jobs. Because transferring across internal labor markets is very difficult, if not impossible, . . . statistical discrimination has long-lasting implications for women's occupational outcomes.[56]

Internal labor markets not only limited women's entry-level job prospects; they limited women's later employment prospects as well. This is because internal labor markets required that employers hire only at the bottom rung of the job ladder and then promote from within existing employment ranks.[57] Therefore, when women were excluded from entry-level jobs within internal labor markets, they were excluded from the best jobs forever.[58]

Thus a great deal of contemporary employment discrimination has its roots in the internal labor market job structures of the past. Employers that used promotion ladders did not hire women because they wanted workers who would learn skills as they went along. Those that used Fordist-style assembly lines, in which job ladders were flat, did not hire women because their early twentieth-century human resource practices were designed to discourage turnover and encourage longevity.[59]

One can see evidence of women's exclusion from internal labor market jobs in the pattern of women's employment.[60] In the past, women workers have tended to cluster into two types of jobs. First, women were heavily concentrated in jobs for which they could obtain the necessary training *outside* the workplace. Thus, women were overwhelmingly found in occupations such as child care, nursing, cooking, and sewing—all of which involved skills learned in the traditional gendered home. Similarly, women were hired for jobs for which they received training through the public school system, such as teaching or bookkeeping.

Second, women have historically been hired into jobs for which employers do not value longevity. Indeed, in some jobs, employers had policies that prevented women from remaining on the job for long. For example, airlines hired women as flight attendants from the early days of commercial air flight, but until the early 1970s the carriers required women to quit as soon as they reached age thirty or were married.[61]

Throughout most of the twentieth century, then, women were not hired into large corporate internal labor market jobs. Rather, the dominant labor relations practices, based on the theories of scientific management, kept women out of the good jobs in manufacturing. The use of internal labor markets and the operation of statistical discrimination led employers to hire men for the primary labor market jobs. When women finally were permitted in, union-negotiated promotion rights and job ladders dictated that they come in at the bottom.[62]

Some economists have argued that the operation of statistical discrimination might explain short-term employment discrimination, but it cannot explain long-term employment discrimination because hiring on the basis of average group characteristics is inefficient for employers if there are better methods of assessment available. Thus, some economists have claimed, employers have an incentive to improve their assessment methods rather than rely on statistically average characteristics.[63] However, even if better assessment methods were available, statistical discrimination can explain the *initial* exclusion of women and minorities from internal labor markets on the basis of hiring decisions made before improved assessment techniques became available, or exclusionary hiring decisions made as a rough first cut in a time of rapid expansion. Once that first cut occurs, a vicious cycle develops. Women learn they are not eligible for primary labor market jobs and do not invest in the necessary training to get them. Because women underinvest in education and training, employers come to believe, sometimes correctly, that women lack the necessary human capital for the primary labor market jobs.[64] At that point, even improved, individualized assessment techniques do not lead to equal labor market opportunities.[65]

Labor economist Francine Blau suggests an additional dynamic. She concedes that it might be true that women, knowing that certain better jobs are not available to them, do not invest in the training necessary to perform them. However, she contends it is also possible that

> employers' view of female job instability leads them to give women less training and to assign [women] to jobs where the cost of turnover is minimized. [As a result,] women may respond by exhibiting the unstable

behavior employers expect. This in turn confirms employer perceptions.
. . . Viewing the matter somewhat differently, the employers' *ex post*
"correct" assessment of sex differences in average productivity may be
seen to result from their own discriminatory actions.[66]

Under either scenario, employers' initial perceptions that women's labor
market characteristics are unsuitable to internal labor market job structures
set in motion a feedback loop that leads employers to refuse to hire women for
primary labor market jobs.

There is another respect in which the old psychological contract and internal labor market job structures have played a role in sustaining job segregation. Sociologist Jerry Jacobs has posited that the implicit contract between
employers and employees under the internal labor market system involved not
only a promise of job security, but also a promise that existing working conditions and status and pay differentials would be maintained.[67] Jacobs maintains that male workers derived both tangible and symbolic benefits from
sex-segregated workplaces, including status rewards, camaraderie, and the job
and income security that resulted from not having to compete with lower-paid
women workers.[68] These implicit contracts were used to instill morale, motivation, and trust. They operated within internal labor markets to induce employees to invest in firm-specific human capital and to expend effort on behalf
of the firm.[69] Thus, if an employer were to integrate a formerly all-male workplace, he ran the risk that the existing work force would see it as a violation
of these implicit contracts, with a resulting cost in terms of morale, productivity, and labor peace.[70]

A similar dynamic of discrimination that has curtailed women's employment opportunities operates with respect to minorities. Minority employment
opportunities have been curtailed by the same pernicious combination of internal labor markets, implicit contracts, and statistical discrimination that engendered the exclusion of women. In addition, minorities were excluded from
internal labor markets by the overtly racist policies of American employers and
unions. Until the 1960s, many unions either excluded minorities altogether or
kept them in low-wage, low-skill job categories.[71] In the building trades, for
example, unions kept minorities and women out of apprenticeship programs
and out of union hiring halls. Thus minorities, like women, were excluded
from the core good jobs and relegated to the secondary labor market periphery in which the pay was low, the jobs were dirty, and job security did not exist.

In the 1970s and 1980s, employment patterns began to change. First,
women became more attached to the labor market,[72] so employers had less
reason to practice statistical discrimination.[73] Also, equal employment opportunity laws forced many firms to hire women and blacks for previously all-
white-male jobs.[74] Overt discrimination in hiring became unlawful unless it
was pursuant to a "bona fide occupational qualification," which was narrowly

defined.[75] Early on, the Equal Employment Opportunity Commission (EEOC) took the position that Title VII prohibited statistical discrimination by declaring that it was unlawful for employers to make hiring decisions based on real or perceived group characteristics.[76] For all of these reasons, the sex segregation of jobs as well as the pay gap between men and women declined.[77] Minorities also made strides under the civil rights laws, at least in the early years.[78] In particular, the pay gap between black and white women narrowed substantially, so that by 1981 black women were earning 90 percent of what white women earned—a dramatic increase from the mere 69 percent of 1964. In the same period, the gap between the earnings of black men and white men narrowed from 66 percent in 1964 to 71 percent in 1981.[79] Occupational segregation, which has not been as extreme for minorities as it has been for women, also declined.[80]

Even after the most blatant pay differentials and explicit barriers to hiring women and minorities were broken, those groups continued to be disadvantaged within major corporations. Because jobs were arranged in hierarchical progression, latecomers came in at the bottom and had the farthest to rise. Thus they did not have access to the higher rungs of the internal labor markets.[81] Also, because they were at the bottom, the latecomers were the first to be laid off in times of cutbacks. Efforts by women and minorities to jump over established arrangements for hierarchical progression generated intense and bitter disputes about affirmative action. White male workers resisted because they felt that their psychological contract gave them an entitlement to a certain sequence of advancement and that affirmative action was thus a violation of their rights.

The Dynamics of Discrimination in the Boundaryless Workplace

Because many aspects of employment discrimination originated in or were perpetuated by the old employment system, there is reason to hope that it might subside in the future. The new workplace, with its depreciation of long-term employment and its rejection of job ladders, offers the possibility of creating new opportunities for women and minorities. To the extent that the old labor system locked them out, the demise of that system could be a major improvement. The new psychological contract could spell the end of labor market dualism and the beginning of more egalitarian job structures. However, there are new impediments to the achievement of equal opportunity for women and minorities in the new workplace that need to be addressed.

THE PROBLEM OF TRAINING

Success under the new psychological contract requires employees to manage their own careers and constantly develop new skills. Workers can only succeed in this system if they have an opportunity to develop skills. Yet there is evidence that women are not receiving equal access to employer-sponsored training programs.[82] When training is offered after hours, women's nonparticipation can be explained by the time squeeze that many women experience as a result of family obligations. But when training is offered during the work day, women are still not gaining as much training as men. It is important to identify gender differences in participation in training programs, as well as aspects of employer training programs that discourage female participation.[83] It is also important to determine whether there are differences between the propensity of minority and white employees to take advantage of employer-sponsored training.

To attain equality in the new workplace, women and minorities need access to improved job-related training. Civil rights litigation needs to focus on ensuring equal access to training and skills. Minorities and women should advocate a leveling of skills training and broad access to educational opportunities. They should support expanded public adult education programs, apprenticeship systems for teenagers and young adults, local and regional job training centers, and technical courses in the summers and evenings at community colleges. If publicly funded training is not made available, there is a danger that employers will favor employees who pay for training themselves.[84] Because white males are more highly paid than the others, they would be in a better position to self-finance their training. This would reinforce and create a new kind of labor market dualism—a dualism of knowledge.

THE PROBLEM OF INVISIBLE AUTHORITY

In the past, much employment discrimination was rooted in the hierarchical job structures of internal labor markets. Today's workplace does not have defined job ladders, and the criteria for advancement are not clearly specified, so it is difficult for someone to claim that she has been bypassed for advancement because of her gender or race. In the boundaryless workplace, everyone makes lateral movements, but some move in circles while others spiral to the top. The diffuse authority structure of the new psychological contract makes discrimination hard to identify.

In addition, the new nonhierarchical workplace makes lines of authority and power invisible. Although ostensibly all employees have opportunities to make lateral movements, increase their responsibilities, and enhance their skills, there is still a hidden core of top managers who allocate responsibilities and rewards. Under the new psychological contract, these decision makers have no clear designation or location on the organizational chart, rendering their decisions to a great extent unaccountable. Thus it is difficult to know to whom to make appeals, with whom to lodge complaints, or how to bring about change.

Sociologists of organizations note that when there is no visible power structure, the invisible structures rule. In the new workplace, these invisible and secret power structures may well turn out to be more remote and impenetrable for women and minorities than the old power structures. Responsibility for discriminatory decisions has become difficult to assign and even more difficult to remedy. Title VII remedies, such as decrees requiring employers to promote women and minorities up job ladders, are not useful to redress these forms of discrimination in a boundaryless workplace.

THE PROBLEM OF CLIQUES

A related problem for women and minorities in the new workplace stems from the trend toward delegating major employment decisions to peers. Several sociologists of work have focused on the role of networks in perpetuating sex and racial segregation in employment. Mark Granvitter, Jerry Jacobs, and others have observed that workplaces are social organizations in which people interact with each other to learn the tricks of the trade, share necessary information, assist in tasks, and coordinate performance.[85] The need for cooperation and teamwork in the workplace makes it difficult for employers to incorporate women and minorities when there is resistance from incumbent white males.[86] Yet when women and minorities are denied access to informal forms of training and networking, their ability to succeed is severely compromised.[87] The phenomenon of women being shunned, ignored, and frozen "out of the loop" when they enter predominately male workplaces has been well documented.[88] Many first-person accounts attest to the power of workplace cliques to exclude, disempower, demoralize, or otherwise disable those who are targeted for exclusion.[89] Clique members use the tools of ostracism, belittlement, verbal harassment, innuendo, nefarious gossip, and shunning—tools that are difficult to identify or remedy. Often the targets are newcomers, atypical employees, and those who are not part of the old crowd, namely, women and minorities. Reports of such conduct are becoming increasingly prevalent.[90]

The new workplace exacerbates the age-old problem of cliques because it involves empowering peer-based decision making. Current management theorists advocate using peers to decide many important issues such as hiring, evaluation, job allocation, and pay.[91] Some firms are using peer review panels to decide employees' appeals of disciplinary actions.[92] Although peer-based decision making may work well in some situations, it can also promote cliquishness and lead to patronage systems, bigotry, and corruption. In such a workplace, women and minorities could again find themselves excluded.

THE PROBLEM OF LAWLESSNESS

One of the achievements of unionism has been to facilitate the introduction of rules into industrial life. The great organizing drives of the Congress for Industrial Organization were often precipitated by acts of petty tyranny and arbitrary mean-spiritedness by lower-level supervisors.[93] The industrial unions created an industrial jurisprudence, a common law of the shop, enforceable by outside arbitrators.[94] Although this law of the shop remained invisible to outsiders, it enabled third-party neutrals—arbitrators—to erect a rule-based system for the day-to-day conduct of affairs in unionized workplaces.[95]

Later, equal employment laws also provided a mechanism for orderly, rule-based, and accountable decisions about such matters as hiring, promotions, and pay rates. These rule-based systems injected an external order into the otherwise private and often anarchic domain of the workplace. In particular, the equal employment laws provided rules by which women and minorities could break into workplaces that had been white, male, privileged clubs.[96]

Currently, the systems of external rules that penetrated the workplace in the past are breaking down. Unionism has declined precipitously, and with it, collectively bargained arbitration systems. In addition, Title VII is losing its effectiveness in light of the Supreme Court's 1991 decision in *Gilmer v. Interstate/Johnson Lane Corp.*,[97] holding that an employer can compel an employee to use a private arbitration system to decide an age discrimination complaint.[98] Since *Gilmer,* the lower courts have generally upheld employers' efforts to require their employees to use employer-crafted arbitration systems to resolve all types of discrimination complaints instead of bringing such complaints to the EEOC or a court.[99] As the systems of external rules to govern the workplace fade, there is a danger that the workplace will become a bastion of patronage and favoritism.

Proposals for Redressing Discrimination in the New Workplace

Women and minorities need legal strategies to combat the dangers facing them in the new workplace. A few legal scholars have recently addressed some of these dangers and proposed solutions. Vicki Schultz has focused on the problem of workplace cliques sabotaging the work efforts of women who enter traditionally male workplaces.[100] She advocates that actionable sexual harassment be reconceived not as a sexual affront per se but as "conduct designed to undermine a woman's competence."[101] She proposes a legal standard by which actions by an employer or its agent that deliberately undermine the competency of a person because of his or her gender would be actionable under Title VII. In cases in which it is difficult to prove whether the challenged conduct is motivated by gender, she proposes a presumption that it is improperly motivated in contexts in which women work in traditionally male jobs.[102] Schultz finds support for her view in Justice Ruth Bader Ginsburg's concurring opinion in *Harris v. Forklift Systems, Inc.,*[103] in which Justice Ginsburg stated that to establish a hostile work environment, a plaintiff must "prove that a reasonable person subjected to the discriminatory conduct would find . . . that the harassment so altered working conditions as to '[make] it more difficult to do the job.' "[104]

David Yamada has focused on the problem of abusive supervisors who undermine a worker's morale and confidence.[105] Yamada's discussion is not limited to gender- or race-based harassment claims but rather applies to all types of bullying by supervisors. He proposes a new cause of action, called the Intentional Infliction of a Hostile Work Environment, which would make an employer liable for "intentionally subject[ing] the plaintiff to a hostile work environment." If a work environment were found to be "hostile by both the plaintiff and by a reasonable person in the plaintiff's situation," the employer would be liable unless he could show (1) that he exercised reasonable care to prevent and correct the challenged conduct and (2) that the plaintiff failed to use any preventive or corrective opportunities provided by the employer.[106] Although Yamada's proposal is not limited to gender or racial discrimination claims, it is an attempt to address the kinds of pernicious conduct that are particularly problematic for women and minorities in the new workplace.

The proposals by Schultz and Yamada are bold and creative efforts to reach beyond existing discrimination law and address heretofore unacknowledged forms of workplace injustice. Both Schultz and Yamada have called attention to the problem of subtle, yet powerful, forms of disempowerment that in today's workplace can make the difference between an individual's success or failure. The virtue of the proposals is that they attempt to identify, name, define, and constrain some of the forms of harmful conduct that appear to be increasing in the workplace. However, neither proposal addresses all the problems women and minorities face in the boundaryless workplace. They both propose theories of liability to constrain actions by *supervisors* who intimidate, harass, sabotage, or otherwise bully a subordinate. But as the earlier discussion highlights, the most serious forms of discrimination in the new workplace are often not the result of *supervisor* conduct but of *coworker* conduct.

In addition, both of the proposals, although thought provoking, are difficult to apply. The standards they propose for liability—Schultz's competence-undermining test and Yamada's hostile work environment test—are vague. To base liability on such standards could pose difficult issues of proof, create uncertainty, foment litigation over trivial insults, and run the danger of judicial micromanagement of employee relations. For these reasons, their proposals are best understood as providing broad new conceptions of workplace justice rather than detailed blueprints for legal reform.

The new types of employment discrimination that appear in the new workplace are not easily treated with the existing Title VII framework. Currently, Title VII is directed to harm caused by employers or their agents, and it assumes a hierarchical authority structure. Title VII only reaches coworker harassment when the employer knew, or should have known, of the harassing conduct and failed to take adequate remedial measures.[107] This is because the law prohibits those who have authority in the employment relationship from exercising their power in a discriminatory fashion.[108] It is not a generalized code of workplace civility.[109]

Although there is authority and power in the new workplace, it is often exercised through cliques and peer groups, defying traditional tools for assigning accountability. Therefore to redress the new forms of employment discrimination, it is necessary to combine new concepts of substantive liability, such as Schultz's redefinition of sexual harassment or Yamada's proposed tort of intentional creation of a hostile work environment, with new procedures and remedies.

Any new procedures to redress employment discrimination cannot delegate responsibility for identifying and remedying discriminatory conduct to the work group, because the work group is often the source of the problem. Similarly, it cannot delegate those tasks to high management officials, because they have an interest in smooth operations, which often means condoning the discriminatory conduct. It is also difficult to imagine a court imposing civil liability on a worker for ganging up on a coworker unless the conduct constitutes a crime or tort, like assault or rape. For a court to judge the subtle aspects of exclusion and marginalization that debilitate women and minorities in the workplace would involve it in micromanaging workplace etiquette. It is not likely that a court would be willing to do this, nor that it could do it well. Therefore it is necessary to devise a system of workplace-specific alternative dispute resolution that uses a neutral outsider to scrutinize workplace conduct and apply equal opportunity norms.

One approach that could address the new forms of discrimination in the new workplace is to encourage firms to develop meaningful dispute resolution systems that address worker–coworker as well as worker–supervisor complaints. These systems would have to use external decision makers to hear allegations of coworker- as well as supervisor-instituted bullying, exclusion, and harassment. By bringing outside neutrals to adjudicate workplace disputes, such a system would offer the possibility of injecting an external standard of fairness that can transcend the rule of the clique. Some corporations are already designing dispute resolution systems to resolve both grievances between the employee and the firm and disputes between employees. If properly structured, internal dispute resolution systems could help counteract the development of workplace fiefdoms and cliques, redress abuses of hidden authority, and bring external norms to the workplace.

The Supreme Court has recently given an impetus to the development of such systems in its decisions in *Farragher v. City of Boca Raton*[110] and *Burlington Industries v. Ellreth*.[111] In those cases, the Court held that employers can avoid liability for sexual harassment if they have internal procedures in place to deal with harassment claims and if employees unreasonably fail to use them. These decisions encourage employers to develop meaningful procedures to address harassment complaints against supervisors. If the Court extended the reasoning to coworker claims, then employers would have a powerful incentive to use a neutral dispute resolution mechanism for these new types of discrimination claims.

Although the use of internal dispute resolution procedures for employment discrimination complaints is growing, at present these systems are often biased toward employers and serve to evade, rather than enforce, external norms.[112] Also, under current interpretations of the Federal Arbitration Act (FAA), arbitral awards receive virtually no judicial review.[113] Under the FAA, an arbitral award may not be vacated for an error of law or erroneous fact-finding, but only if the arbitral award displayed a "manifest disregard of the law."[114]

If internal dispute resolution systems were properly structured, however, they could address the subtle but powerful forms of discrimination in today's boundaryless workplaces. To do so, the legal framework governing employment arbitration would have to be revised to permit de novo judicial review of issues of law and to require outside, neutral arbitrators. Courts would also have to require some minimal standards of due process in the arbitrations themselves.[115] In addition, employment arbitration systems would have to include disputes between coworkers as well as disputes between employees and employers. To succeed in providing redress for subtle forms of employment discrimination, the outside arbitrator would have to not merely apply internal norms but also serve as a check on the possibility of tyranny and capture by insider cliques. The proposal to permit de novo judicial review for arbitral rulings on issues of law would ensure that Title VII and other employment laws were applied to the workplace.

This proposal does not provide a new test for liability but rather a new mechanism for resolving discrimination disputes. It is a mechanism that would enable each workplace to identify and prevent competency sabotage, bullying, shunning, harassing, and other forms of gender-based or race-based conduct that threaten to once again undermine the employment prospects of women and minorities. And by doing so, it is hoped that it would provide an approach to employment discrimination that would enable women and minorities to achieve true equality of opportunity to pursue an unbounded career.

Notes

1. Portions of this chapter appeared in Katherine V. W. Stone, *From Widgets to Digits: Employment Regulation for the Changing Workplace* (Cambridge U. Press 2004) (reprinted with the permission of Cambridge University Press).

2. Bruce Tulgan, *Winning the Talent Wars* 155–57 (2001).

3. *Id.* at 176–66.

4. Rosabeth Moss Kanter, *e-Volve* 211–14 (2001).

5. *Id.* at 225–26.

6. *See* Peter Doeringer & Michael Piore, *Internal Labor Markets and Manpower Analysis* (1971). For a discussion of the history of internal labor markets in American industry, *see* Katherine Stone, *The Origin of Job Structures in the Steel Industry*, in *Labor Market Segmentation* 27 (Richard C. Edwards et al. eds., 1975) [hereinafter Stone, *Job Structures*]. For a thoughtful review of the recent economic literature on internal labor market institutions, *see* Claudia Dale Goldin, *Understanding the Gender Gap: An Economic History of American Women* 247 (1990).

7. *See* David A. Jaeger & Ann Huff Stevens, *Is Job Stability in the United States Falling? Reconciling Trends in the Current Population Survey and the Panel Study of Income Dynamics*, J. Lab. Econ. S1, S24–25 (Oct. 1999).

8. BLS News Releases, *Employee Tenure in 2000*, http//146.142.4.23/pub/news.release/tenure.txt (Aug. 9, 2000).

9. *Id.*

10. Richard Sennett, *The Corrosion of Character* 22 (1998).

11. *Id.*

12. Noel Tichy & Ram Charan, *Speed, Simplicity, Self-Confidence: An Interview with Jack Welch*, Harv. Bus. Rev. 112, 120 (Sept.–Oct. 1989) (emphasis omitted).

13. *See* Peter Drucker, *Managing in a Time of Great Change* 71 (1995) (describing change in composition of temporary workers).

14. Thomas O. Davenport, *Human Capital: What It Is and Why People Invest in It* 26 (1999).

15. Sandra L. Robinson & Denise M. Rousseau, *Violating the Psychological Contract: Not the Exception but the Norm*, 15 J. Organizational Behav. 245, 246 (1994).

16. *See id.* at 247.

17. *Id.*

18. *See generally* Neil Anderson & René Schalk, *The Psychological Contract in Retrospect and Prospect*, 19 J. Organizational Behav. 637, 643–44 (1998) (summarizing studies on the impact on employees of employer breach of psychological contracts).

19. Marcie A. Cavanaugh & Raymond A. Noe, *Antecedents and Consequences of Relational Components of the New Psychological Contract*, 20 J. Organizational Behav. 323, 324 (1999).

20. *See* Michael B. Arthur, *The Boundaryless Career: A New Perspective for Organizational Inquiry*, 15 J. Organizational Behav. 295, 296 (1994).

21. Anne S. Miner & David F. Robinson, *Organizational and Population Level Learning as Engines for Career Transitions*, 15 J. Organizational Behav. 345, 347 (1994).

22. *See id.* at 345; *see also* Davenport, *supra* note 14, at 152–56 (urging firms to create "communities of practice").

23. Miner & Robinson, *supra* note 21, at 347.

24. *See* Dennis W. Organ, *Organizational Citizenship Behavior: The Good Soldier Syndrome* 4–5 (1988).

25. *See id.* at 6–7. Organizational effectiveness is comprised of features such as efficiency, ability to attract valuable resources, good will, external image, reputation, innovativeness, and adaptability. *See id.*

26. *Id.* at 24.

27. Peter Cappelli, *The New Deal at Work: Managing the Market-Driven Work Force* 217 (1999). *See also* Kanter, *supra note* 4, at 225–26.

28. Rosabeth Moss Kanter, *On the Frontiers of Management* 190 (1997).

29. *Id.* at 192.

30. *Id.*

31. *See* Drucker, *supra* note 13, at 71–72.

32. *See id.*

33. *See* Janice Klein, *The Paradox of Quality Management: Commitment, Ownership, and Control*, in *The Post-Bureaucratic Organization* 178–79 (Charles Heckscher & Anne Donnellon eds., 1994).

34. *See, e.g.,* Kanter, *supra* note 28, at 175 (reporting that the tide is moving "toward more varied individual compensation based on people's own efforts").

35. *Pay Attention! How to Reward Your Top Employees; Sleep Well Last Night?* Persp. on Total Rewards (Jan. 2000), http://www.towers.com/publications/publications_frame. asp?target' pubs_date.htm.

36. *Id.*

37. *Id.*

38. 29 U.S.C. § 150 et seq. The National Labor Relations Act establishes the National Labor Relations Board, a federal agency that certifies labor unions, defines bargaining units, and requires employers to bargain with the certified union concerning wages, hours, and other terms and conditions of employment for all employees in the bargaining unit.

39. *See* Katherine V. W. Stone, *The New Psychological Contract: Implications of the Changing Workplace for Labor and Employment Regulation,* 48 UCLA L. Rev. 519 (2001).

40. *See* Vicki Schultz, *Life's Work,* 100 Colum. L. Rev. 1881, 1894–95, and n. 40 (2000) (summarizing data on sex segregation and pay differentials).

41. *See* Committee on Women's Employment and Related Social Issues, *Women's Work, Men's Work: Sex Segregation on the Job* 49–50 (Barbara F. Reskin & Heidi I. Hartmann eds., 1986); Jerry A. Jacobs, *Revolving Doors: Sex Segregation and Women's Careers* 28–30 (1989) (finding significant gender segregation of workplaces throughout the 1980s). *See generally* Vicki Schultz, *Reconceptualizing Sexual Harassment,* 107 Yale L.J. 1683, 1756–57 (1998).

42. *See* Doeringer & Piore, *supra* note 6, at 133–37.

43. *See, e.g., Price Waterhouse v. Hopkins,* 490 U.S. 228 (1989) (upholding a challenge to the denial of partnership to a woman on the basis of sex stereotyping); *Griggs v. Duke Power Co.,* 401 U.S. 424 (1971) (upholding a challenge to racially discriminatory testing and selection devices).

44. They were, however, strategies that triggered conflict between more senior white male employees and the newcomers who were seeking to jump rungs on the ladder. These disputes crystallized into conflicts over affirmative action.

45. Gary S. Becker, *The Economics of Discrimination* 14–15 (1957).

46. *Id.*

47. *See* Kenneth J. Arrow, *What Has Economics to Say about Racial Discrimination?* 12 J. Econ. Persp. 91, 94 (1998).

48. *See id.* at 92–93; William A. Darity Jr. & Patrick L. Mason, *Evidence of Discrimination in Employment: Codes of Color, Codes of Gender,* 12 J. Econ. Persp. 63, 63–76 (1998).

49. *See* Arrow, *supra* note 47, at 94–98; Darity & Mason, *supra* note 48, at 84–87.

50. For a concise account of statistical discrimination, *see* Arrow, *supra* note 47, at 96–97.

51. *See* Francine D. Blau, *Occupational Segregation and Labor Market Discrimination,* in *Sex Segregation in the Workplace* 117, 122–23 (Barbara F. Reskin ed., 1984); Karen Oppenheim Mason, *Commentary: Strober's Theory of Occupational Sex Segregation,* in *Sex Segregation in the Workplace, id.* at 157, 165.

52. *See* Blau, *supra* note 51. Historically, women tended to be placed in jobs that required few skills, and they were provided with little or no on-the-job training. *See* Claudia D. Goldin, *Understanding the Gender Gap: An Economic History of American Women* 100–103 (1990).

53. Claudia Goldin found, on the basis of available data, that around 1900, males had almost three times the duration in their current occupation, and one and one-half times the years with their current employer than did women. Goldin, *supra* note 52, at 101.

54. *Id.* at 116.

55. *See* Jeremy I. Bulow & Lawrence H. Summers, *A Theory of Dual Labor Markets with Application to Industrial Policy, Discrimination, and Keynesian Unemployment,* 4 J. Lab. Econ. 376, 401 (July 1986); *see also* Lester C. Thurow, *Generating Inequality: Mechanisms of Distribution in the U.S. Economy* 178 (1975).

56. Patricia A. Roos & Barbara F. Reskin, *Institutional Factors Contributing to Sex Segregation in the Workplace,* in *Sex Segregation in the Workplace, supra* note 51, at 235, 241 (citations omitted).

57. *See* Stone, *Job Structures, supra* note 6, at 45–49.

58. *See* Doeringer & Piore, *supra* note 6, at 2.

59. *See* Sanford M. Jacoby, *Modern Manors: Welfare Capitalism Since the New Deal* (1997).

60. *See* Blau, *supra* note 51, at 134 (on the clustering of women's jobs throughout the twentieth century).

61. *See* Georgia Panter Nielsen, *From Sky Girl to Flight Attendant: Women and the Making of a Union* 83–89 (1982) (writing on the pervasiveness of the no-marriage rule and the protracted struggle by the flight attendants' union to eliminate it). Other women's occupations also had no-marriage policies, including teaching, nursing, and secretarial work. *See* Jacobs, *supra* note 41; *see also Zipes v. Trans World Airlines, Inc.,* 455 U.S. 385, 388 (discussing the airline's no-children rule); *United Airlines, Inc. v. McDonald,* 432 U.S. 385, 387 (1977) (discussing the airline's no-marriage rule).

62. *See, e.g.,* Ruth Milkman, *Farewell to the Factory: Auto Workers in the Late Twentieth Century* 37 (1997) (noting that women at General Motors auto plants do not get the highly desirable jobs because their average seniority is considerably less than that of men).

63. *See, e.g.,* Darity & Mason, *supra* note 48, at 83.

64. *See id.* at 84.

65. William Darity and Patrick Mason term this a self-fulfilling prophecy that operates as follows: Suppose employers believe, for whatever reason, that Group A is more productive, on average, than Group B. They therefore hire Group A workers for the more challenging and lucrative jobs. Seeing this pattern, members of Group B become less motivated to acquire additional human capital through schooling or training. *See id.* These effects would be passed along within Group B from generation to generation. *See id.* at 84–85. Thus, the group-typed beliefs held by employers can have a strong and enduring effect on the human capital of the disadvantaged group. *See id.* at 176–77.

66. Blau, *supra* note 51, at 117, 123.

67. *See* Jacobs, *supra* note 41, at 179.

68. *See id.* at 153–55. For a description of male workers' reaction to the presence of women auto workers, *see* Milkman, *supra* note 62, at 37.

69. *See* Jacobs, *supra* note 41, at 179–80.

70. *See id.* at 181.

71. *See Steele v. Louisville & Nashville R.R. Co.,* 323 U.S. 192, 195 (1944) (holding that a whites-only railroad union that negotiated a collective agreement designed to exclude blacks from desirable jobs violated the duty of fair representation). *See generally* William B. Gould, *Black Workers in White Unions: Job Discrimination in the United States* (1977); *The Negro and the American Labor Movement* (Julius Jacobson ed., 1968); Joseph F. Wilson, *Tearing Down the Color Bar: A Documentary History and Analysis of the Brotherhood of Sleeping Car Porters* (1989).

72. *See* Blau, *supra* note 51, at 125 (summarizing studies).

73. *See* Blau et al., *The Economics of Women, Men, and Work* 207–8 (3d ed. 1998).

74. *See* Committee on Women's Employment, *supra* note 41, at 128–29 (reporting on the effectiveness of enforcement of equal employment laws in reducing employment discrimination on the basis of gender); Darity & Mason, *supra* note 48, at 63–90 (summarizing studies that demonstrate that the change in the black–white earnings differential is the result of the enactment of the Civil Rights Act of 1964).

75. 42 U.S.C. §§ 2000e to 2000e-17. The bona fide occupational qualification (BFOQ) exception permits employers to make hiring decisions based on otherwise prohibited reasons, if such decisions are necessary to the "essence of the business." *Int'l Union, UAW v. Johnson Controls, Inc.,* 499 U.S. 187, 203 (1991).

76. *See* EEOC Guidelines, 29 C.F.R. § 1604.2(a)(1) (1968).

77. *See* Blau et al., *supra* note 73, at 127–29 (noting decline in job segregation and pay gap).

78. Minorities experienced a significant narrowing of the pay gap between 1965 and 1975, but it flattened after that. *See* John Donahue & James Heckman, *Continuous vs. Episodic Change:*

The Impact of Civil Rights Policy on the Economic Status of Blacks, 29 J. Econ. Literature 1603, 1604 (1991).

79. *See* Blau, *supra* note 51, at 126.

80. *See id.* at 135–36.

81. *See* Blau et al., *supra* note 73, at 126 (noting that even when women gain access to an occupation, they are often at the bottom of a hierarchy).

82. *See* David Knoke & Yoshito Ishio, *The Gender Gap in Company Job Training,* 25 Work & Occupations 141, 161 (1998).

83. *See* Rosemary Batt et al., *Net Working: Work Patterns and Workforce Policies for the New Media Industry* (2001) (studying women in computer-related fields and finding that women are less interested in acquiring technical skills and more interested in acquiring managerial skills).

84. For a description of a wide array of publicly funded and for-profit training programs, *see generally* Cappelli, *supra* note 27, at 202–10 (1999).

85. *See* Mark S. Granovetter, *Getting a Job: A Study of Contracts and Careers* 45–48 (1974); Jacobs, *supra* note 41, at 182.

86. *See* Jacobs, *supra* note 41, at 181–82.

87. Susan Sturm, *Race, Gender, and the Law of the Twenty-First Century Workplace,* 1 U. Pa. J. Lab. & Emp. L. 639, 642 (1998).

88. Jacobs, *supra,* note 41, at 181–82; *see, e.g.,* Rosabeth Moss Kanter, *Men and Women of the Corporation* 207 (1977). *See generally* Roos & Reskin, *supra* note 56, at 235, 236–56 (citing studies); Schultz, *supra* note 41, at 1704 (citing examples of ways in which gender dynamics can sabotage women's ability to function on the job).

89. *See* Schultz, *supra* note 41, at 1704; *see also* Vicki Schultz, *Telling Stories about Women and Work,* 103 Harv. L. Rev. 1750, 1832–39 (1990) (citing first-person accounts).

90. *See* Schultz, *supra* note 41, at 1694–95; David C. Yamada, *The Phenomenon of "Workplace Bullying" and the Need for Status-Blind Hostile Work Environment Protection,* 88 Geo. L.J. 475, 477–78 (2000).

91. *See* Edward E. Lawler III, *High Involvement Management* 191–233 (1986).

92. *See, e.g.,* Masanori Hashimoto, *Employment-Based Training in Japanese Firms in Japan and the United States: Experiences of Automobile Manufacturers,* in *Training and the Private Sector* 109, 140 (Lisa M. Lynch ed., 1994) (describing peer review at a Honda plant in Ohio); *id.* at 142 (describing peer review at a Toyota Motor plant in Kentucky).

93. *See, e.g.,* Clinton Golden & Harold Ruttenberg, *The Dynamics of Industrial Democracy* (1942).

94. *See* James B. Atleson, *Labor and the Wartime State* 55–57 (1998).

95. *See* Archibald Cox, *Some Aspects of the Labor Management Relations Act, 1947,* 61 Harv. L. Rev. 274, 276–77 (1948); Harry Shulman, *Reason, Contract, and Law in Labor Relations,* 68 Harv. L. Rev. 999, 1001 (1955); *see also* Katherine V. W. Stone, *The Post-War Paradigm,* in *American Labor Law* 90 Yale L.J. 1509, 1523–25, 1531–35, 1559–65 (1981). I have argued in previous work that the grievance and arbitration system did not go far enough in bringing external norms into the workplace. *See id.* at 1517; Katherine V. W. Stone, *The Legacy of Industrial Pluralism,* 59 U. Chi. L. Rev. 575, 577 (1992). However, that is not to deny that the system brought some modicum of external scrutiny and judgment to bear on what was otherwise an insulated and autocratic domain.

96. *See* Cynthia L. Estlund, *Working Together: The Workplace, Civil Society and the Law,* 89 Geo. L.J. 31–32 (2000) (arguing that Title VII has supplied a normative vision of equal opportunity that has helped transform discriminatory workplace practices).

97. *Gilmer v. Interstate/Johnson Lane Corp,* 500 U.S. 20 (1991).

98. *Id.* at 24–35.

99. *See* Katherine V. W. Stone, *Mandatory Arbitration of Individual Employment Rights: The Yellow Dog Contract of the 1990s,* 73 Denv. U. L. Rev. 1017, 1033 (1996) [hereinafter Stone, *Mandatory Arbitration*].

100. *See* Schultz, *supra* note 41, at 1756–69.

101. *Id.* at 1769.

102. *See id.* at 1801.

103. 510 U.S. 17 (1993).

104. *Harris v. Forklift Sys. Inc.,* 510 U.S. 25 (1993) (Ginsburg, J., concurring).

105. David C. Yamada, *supra* note 90, at 475, 480–83.

106. *See id.* at 524–27.

107. *See Gunnell v. Utah Valley State Coll.,* 152 F.3d 1253, 1265 (10th Cir. 1998); *Blankenship v. Parke Care Ctrs.,* 123 F.3d 868, 873 (6th Cir. 1997); *Yamaguchi v. United States Dep't of Air Force,* 109 F.3d 1475, 1483 (9th Cir. 1997).

108. *See Burlington Indus. v. Ellreth,* 524 U.S. 742, 761–62 (1998).

109. *See Harris* 510 U.S. at 16, 21 (stating that Title VII does not make actionable conduct that is merely offensive).

110. 524 U.S. 775 (1998).

111. 524 U.S. 742 (1998).

112. For criticisms of employer-designed arbitration systems that are imposed on nonunion employees, *see generally* Stone, *Mandatory Arbitration, supra* note 99; Joseph R. Grodin, *Arbitration of Employment Discrimination Claims: Doctrine and Policy in the Wake of* Gilmer, 14 Hofstra Lab. & Emp. L.J. 1 (1996); and David S. Schwartz, *Enforcing Small Print to Protect Big Business: Employee and Consumer Rights Claims in an Age of Compelled Arbitration,* Wis. L. Rev. 33 (1997).

113. *See* Katherine V. W. Stone, *Rustic Justice: Community and Coercion under the Federal Arbitration Act,* 77 N.C. L. Rev. 931, 954–55 (1999) [hereinafter Stone, *Rustic Justice*] (citing cases that establish the narrow standard of review under the Federal Arbitration Act).

114. *Wilko v. Swan,* 92 U.S. 427, 436 (1953), overruled on other grounds by *Rodriguez de Quijas v. Shearson/Am. Express Inc.,* 490 U.S. 477 (1989).

115. *See* Stone, *Rustic Justice, supra* note 113, at 1024–28 (suggesting a mechanism to provide increased scrutiny and to inject external norms into private arbitration tribunals).

CHAPTER 14

Contingent Labor

Ideology in Practice

Risa L. Lieberwitz

Much has been said over the past decade about the "new economy," based on the impact of globalization and technological advances.[1] In the field of labor relations, the pressures of global competition have been identified as rationales for increased "flexibility" for employers to relocate, to set working conditions, and to be free from government workplace regulation. The new technology has been viewed as the basis for a new kind of skilled workforce desiring independence from long-term employment relationships. The most extreme rhetoric of this kind originated in the United States, corresponding to the United States' historically strong support of unilateral employer control over the workplace. The increased rhetoric concerning the requirements of globalization also coincided with the demise of the Soviet Union and other socialist economies. With the United States' current position as the dominant country in this global market, the U.S. call for "flexibility" for employers poses important concerns for American workers and for labor in other countries, which feels the pressure to conform to American practices. American domination may also provide fodder for politicians and capitalists in other countries seeking a rationale for limiting the benefits of the welfare state.

This essay addresses the questions of whether there is really a "new" economy and whether the related calls for flexibility present new issues for labor. In addressing the question of what is new, the essay examines capitalist goals and tactics, distinguishing between them to separate new issues from familiar ones. The discussion of goals and tactics focuses most closely on the growth of "contingent labor" in the United States during the 1990s, as an example of changing tactics to achieve stable capitalist goals. Finally, the essay addresses the means for combating such tactics in order to promote alternative goals.

What's New about the "New Economy"?

Capitalist Goals and Tactics

The "newest" characteristic of the economy is the virtual absence of alternative economic structures. In this context, discussions of political and economic reform eliminate the foundational questions about choices of economic arrangements, to assume a current and ongoing reality of capitalism as the sole economic model. Further, this narrowed worldview strengthens the hold of capitalist ideology, avoiding challenges to basic inequities of capitalist economic structures by destroying alternative visions of economic arrangements. The almost total domination of capitalist ideology also stifles the critique of the contradictions between capitalism and political democracy by treating the pairing of the two as inevitable and representative of the limits of democratic structures. Within this context, economic and political reforms are limited to redistributing wealth by improving working conditions and raising workers' standard of living. Although these are important reforms, they do not address the fundamental issues of creating a democratic economic workplace, which would challenge the distribution of power between labor and management.

Thus, the "new economy" does not present new economic goals. Capitalist goals remain stable and, if anything, more entrenched in the current global economy, which emphasizes private markets and private national and multinational economic institutions. The two main goals of capitalism are based on distribution of power and wealth. In the employment setting, the capitalist goal of retaining the lion's share of the profits is clear and has been a focus of the labor movement's attempts to redistribute wealth through wages and benefits to labor. In the United States, such inequality has reached extreme proportions, with this country experiencing "the most unequal income distribution and one of the highest poverty rates among all the advanced economies in the world."[2] Equal attention, though, should be given to the capitalist goal of retention of power and control over the workforce. Although the political and economic goals may be related, their order of priority is often confused. That is, employer tactics, such as increased hiring of temporary workers, are often identified as means to control workers toward the goal of increasing and retaining profits. Regardless of the impact on profits, however, employers would still use such tactics to maintain unilateral control over the workplace. The importance of this order of priorities is captured by Justice Holmes's statement, "[t]he only prize much cared for by the powerful is power. The prize of the general is not a bigger tent, but command."[3] In the workplace context, one example of the primary importance of control and power is the long and ongoing history of vehement anti-union ideology among employers in the United States. Regardless of the economic profitability of a business, employers in the United States engage in active anti-union campaigns to maintain unilateral control over the workplace, including unilateral control over wages, working conditions, and business decisions.

Although capitalist goals of maintaining power and wealth remain intact, the "new economy" presents new tactics to serve stable goals. Within the current economic and political context, employer tactics can build on the exclusive position held by capitalist models. From a perspective that describes capitalism as the sole sustainable economic system, the role of the private market dominates all explanations of employer choices; that is, the market is presented as a neutral and inevitable external force that drives business decisions toward the goal of profit maximization. Assumptions that the market is an objective force driving employer decisions toward the overriding goal of profit maximization pervade neoclassical economics literature[4] and mainstream media reporting.[5] The view of the market as neutrally driving business decisions toward the primary objective goal of profit maximization, though, is a unidimensional description of employer tactics. Although economists describe employer choices as involving a cost–benefit analysis, they do not include employer control and power over the workforce either as an employer goal or as an important benefit to employers. Thus, an employer's actions, including anti-union campaigns, are envisioned strictly in terms of a profit-maximization goal.

The characterization of an overriding goal of market-driven profit maximization hides the primary nature of the goal of power maximization in driving decisions. It may be true that employer tactics are constrained by market conditions that promote or inhibit their ability to demand certain employment arrangements. Taking both goals of maximizing control and profits into account, however, provides a fuller explanation of employer tactical choices in relation to market conditions. Thus, under some economic conditions, such as a period of high unemployment, an employer may have certain tactics available to maximize both control and profits. In such an economic cycle, an employer may maintain a low-paid non-union workforce through threatening to discharge employees who attempt to unionize, implementing large-scale layoffs, or hiring mostly part-time employees. In a period of low unemployment, other tactics may be more functional toward achieving employers' goals, including demands that employees work mandatory overtime hours, which enables the employer to avoid the costs of hiring new employees and maintains control over the current workforce. In each case, the employer's economic tactics serve the goal of profit making as well as the deeper goal of maintaining power and control. The goal of power maximization may also provide an analysis in which profit maximization explanations fail. For example, neoclassical economists describe race or sex employment discrimination as inconsistent with the goal of profit maximization, and therefore, as inefficient behavior that should be eliminated by market forces. Economists consequently recognize the need to look to other reasons, such as employer, coworker, and customer discrimination, to explain the persistence of race and sex discrimination in employment.[6] An analysis that also focuses on employer power provides a more full account, as employers increase their control over the workforce by creating hostile divisions within the workforce along racial and gender lines, regardless of the effects of such practices on business profitability.[7]

As discussed further in the next section, recent employer tactics in the United States include increased contingent employment arrangements. Although the growth in the contingent workforce may be related to increasing employer profits, it functions, most powerfully, to expand employer control by creating a fragmented and non-unionized disposable workforce.

Flexibility on the Employer's Terms

The call for flexibility has become the most recent cliché of employer assertions of the freedom to adjust workplace practices to remain competitive in the global marketplace.[8] Part of the employer demand for increased flexibility has been a growth in "flexible" employment arrangements in the form of contingent employment. The term *contingent employee* has been used to identify a variety of employment arrangements, including part-time employees, temporary employees hired through a temporary employment agency, and employees hired as independent contractors.[9] Given the lack of an agreed-upon definition of the scope of employees within the category of contingent employees, it is difficult to arrive at a clearly defined rate of contingent employment. There is consensus, though, that the rate of contingent employment increased dramatically during the 1990s, although there was some slowing of the growth of contingent employment in the latter part of the past decade.[10]

In translation, the flexibility called for by employers, including the increase in contingent employment, is a call for expansion of employer control over the workforce. In the United States, this power is still found in the continued strength in legal and political rhetoric of the doctrine of employment-at-will, under which the employer has the unlimited power to hire and fire employees. This doctrine is often expressed as a litany of the power to hire and fire for "a good reason, a bad reason, or no reason at all." At the core of employment-at-will doctrine is a view of workers as contingent, that is, employed or discharged at the will of the employer. Thus, the corollary of employee contingency is employer power and control. In the United States, the employment-at-will doctrine underlies the general lack of statutory regulation of the employment relationship. Outside the discrete statutory limitations on employment-at-will provided by legislation prohibiting employment discrimination on the basis of race, sex, national origin, religion, age, and disability, employees are provided no statutory protection from unjust treatment by their employer. Private-sector employees and most public-sector employees have a statutory right to form and join unions, although such statutes, especially in the private sector, provide for weak remedies and are seriously under-enforced. Only through unionization can employees in the United States win the contractual rights in collective bargaining agreements to "just cause" for discipline or discharge, as well as basic benefits such as health insurance, paid sick leave, and paid vacations.[11]

Against this background, the term *contingent employee* seems redundant. Perhaps the term used to describe temporary employees or "independent contractors" should be "even more contingent employees." Such a term would express the reality of the general vulnerability of most employees in the United States, who are subject to employment-at-will doctrine and could not be called "permanent" employees with any entitlement to basic benefits or protection from layoff or discharge. Given this reality, *contingent employee* is a term with several functions. First, the explicit use of the term *contingent* expresses an even greater degree of expendability of those employees classified as contingent employees; the term *contingent* also expresses a contrast between the "regular" workforce and the contingent employees, demonstrated through lower wage rates and lack of any benefits for contingent workers.[12] By hiring temporary employees through temporary employment agencies or as "independent contractors," the employer also seeks to avoid a traditional employer–employee relationship for the purpose of escaping statutory obligations such as payment of unemployment compensation or respecting employee rights to unionize and bargain collectively.[13]

The growth of the contingent workforce has affected a broad spectrum of employees, ranging from low-wage workers to higher-paid professional and technical employees.[14] Two types of employment arrangements that affect workers across this spectrum are temporary employment and independent contracts. Both of these categories of contingent employment are similar in that they are both employers' tactics for further destabilizing the employment relationship. An important difference between them is the concentration along gender and racial lines, with a heavy representation of women and minorities in the temporary employee category and white men represented more heavily in the independent contractor category.[15]

The growth in the temporary workforce has taken place most significantly through contracts between a "user" employer and a third-party temporary employment agency (TEA) as the "supplier" of temporary employees.[16] Critiques of temporary employment have identified the specific economic injustices of the inferior economic treatment of such temporary employees as compared with the "regular" workforce. But more fundamentally, some critiques have also focused on the ideological content underlying the growth of this form of contingent employment and the acceptance of its legitimacy. In particular, the use of labor-only contracts through TEAs or other "leased" arrangements represents a rejection of the ideological position that "labor is not a commodity."[17] Rather, these arrangements view the employees only in relation to the commodity of labor purchased by the "user" employer.

The ideological critique of temporary employment through TEAs starts to capture the way that this hiring practice serves capitalist goals. Certainly, employers may have an economic motive in hiring temporary workers. In creating such "second-class" workers, a "user" employer has a rationale for failing to provide wages and benefits to the temporary employees that are equal to those paid to the regular employees.[18] The user employer also shifts the costs of employer statutory obligations, such as paying workers' compensation premiums, to the TEA as the direct employer.[19] The actual cost savings of temporary contract labor, however, may be simply secondary in comparison with the way it serves the goal of increasing the employer's power and control at the workplace. Although the existence of any wage labor system commodifies labor through hiring in a labor market, the growth in the temporary labor workforce exacerbates the commodification of labor by further alienating a person's labor from himself. The terminology of the "supplier" and "user" employers describes a commercial relationship in which labor is delivered from the supplier to the user employer as a commodity. The fact of the labor being packaged in the form of human beings is incidental to the transaction.

In further commodifying labor through the expansion of the contingent workforce, the employer dehumanizes the employment relationship, increasing employer power over a second-class workforce that is even more vulnerable than that of the regular employees. This tactic divides the workforce along these status grounds and along racial and gender lines, given the overrepresentation of women and people of color in the low-wage temporary workforce.[20] The presence of temporary employees from TEAs also serves as a reminder to the regular employees of their own vulnerability to replacement by temporary employees, who may work for years in a "temporary" job alongside regular employees doing similar work. Thus, in addition to temporary employees' fear of unionizing, regular employees may feel more insecure and more fearful of unionizing. Further, unionization of the temporary employees alone or combined with regular employees will be difficult, given the multiple employment relationships and the inherent instability of the user employer's contract with the TEA.[21]

Similarly, employers may hire employees as independent contractors to save costs of paying benefits and of fulfilling statutory obligations such as paying workers' compensation premiums, payroll taxes, or Fair Labor Standards Act overtime premiums.[22] The increase in employer power from such a tactic, though, again is greater than the financial cost savings. Union avoidance is guaranteed, given the exclusion of independent contractors from the protection of the NLRA. By defining employees as independent contractors, the employer creates an image of atomized units performing work for the employer, but with no employment relationship with the employer. This arrangement replicates the sale of a commodity by the independent contractor to the employer through an arm's-length transaction that involves no ongoing employee status.

Although independent contractor status has gained the most recent attention in the high-technology industries, employers have attempted to classify low-wage workers as independent contractors as well. One well-publicized example comes from the poultry-processing industry, with Perdue Farms' denial of overtime pay to "chicken catchers," arguing that the workers were exempt from the Fair Labor Standards Act as independent contractors. In February 2000, a federal district court held that the chicken catchers and their crew leaders came within the common law definition of employees, given Perdue's control over their work.[23] In May 2001, Perdue Farms entered into a $2.4 million settlement of the suit, which covered a hundred chicken catchers at three Perdue poultry-processing plants.[24] Other current trends in labeling low-wage employees as independent contractors include the increase in home work, performed primarily by women paid on an hourly or piece-rate basis.[25]

In the high-technology industry, employers present independent contractor status as beneficial, providing optimal flexibility to both parties. The rhetoric builds on the image of the "information technology" society, in which highly skilled technical and professional employees will benefit from their status as independent agents, selling their skills to the highest bidder and moving easily among independent contractor jobs for multiple clients. Reality is quite different for the employees working in high-technology jobs that do not provide these high levels of remuneration. The reality shows that employers have manipulated employee status to label them as independent contractors, although they may be performing the same work as the regular employees over long periods of time. The results are serious exploitation of such "independent contractors," who do not receive the benefits provided to the regular employees, are excluded from NLRA protection if the label of independent contractor sticks, and who in no way fit the image of the flexible high-tech professional.

A recent case at Microsoft illustrates employer manipulation of both temporary employee and independent contractor status by creating "perma-temps." Microsoft had hired technical employees in its Washington State office to work as independent contractors, although they were performing the same work as Microsoft's regular employees. After the Internal Revenue Service found that these "independent contractors" were "common law" employees, based on Microsoft's control over their work, Microsoft rehired some of the independent contractors as regular employees and some as temporary employees through a TEA. A federal circuit court held that these temporary employees also met a "common law" definition of employee in relation to Microsoft and were, therefore, entitled to a stock purchase plan offered to the regular Microsoft employees. The court recognized that the realities of the employment relationship should govern the status of the employee, rather than a label created by an employer seeking to avoid providing equal benefits to all employees.[26]

Adjunct university faculty are another example of employers' manipulation of professional employee status. The percentage of non-tenure-track part-time faculty in the United States has expanded rapidly, with estimates indicating a growth of 133 percent from 1971 to 1986,[27] and an increase of part-time faculty from 22 percent of the professorate in 1970 to 46 percent in 2001.[28] As so-called independent contractors or as part-time faculty, adjunct faculty have a precarious professional existence; they are paid at extremely low rates for their "piece work" of teaching classes for one or more universities, with no traditional employment relationship with a university, usually without benefits, and no assurance of future employment.[29] Again, the university employer cuts costs but, more importantly, increases power over a vulnerable faculty workforce without the job security needed to assert rights of academic freedom.[30]

What explains the growth of the contingent workforce over the past decade? Employers assert that hiring temporary contract labor and independent contractors increases their ability to save the costs of benefits and higher wages and to respond quickly and "flexibly" to changes in the competitive global market. However, the narrow focus on market competition for profits masks the equally important, or even primary, function of contingent labor as a means to serve the capitalist goal of control over the business and workforce. But these capitalist goals of control and profits existed before the recent growth in the contingent workforce, raising the question of why employers have chosen to increase the contingent workforce as a means to further their goals at this time. Again, the global dominance of private-market ideology and rhetoric provides an explanation. The current view of the inevitability of private markets provides a justification for applying market forces to determine the nature of the employment relationship. According to such rhetoric, the market determines whether labor will take the form of a traditional employment relationship or whether it will be bought and sold in the form of contingent labor.[31] Thus, the further commodification of labor is simply an inevitable application of the laws of the market, particularly under the pressures of increased global competition. This perspective, though, denies the reality that employers make choices not simply to maximize profits in response to market forces but to maximize control over the workforce in all market conditions. Employers justify contingent employment during economic downturns as well as during economic rebounds. During economic downturns, employers assert the need to preserve maximum flexibility to hire on a temporary basis. During economic upswings, hiring on a temporary basis is still useful "to test-drive employees before making a commitment."[32] The broadened scope of the contingent workforce provides further evidence of the importance of employers' choices that function to maximize control. Temporary, part-time, and independent contractor status of employees has expanded across the economic spectrum, from low-skilled jobs to professional occupations such as engineering and university teaching, with similar results of increased job insecurity and decreased wages and benefits.

Reliance on the market as an objective external force also avoids an evaluation of the morality of employer choices. In hiring contingent labor, employers further dehumanize employees by creating an employment relationship that establishes a vulnerable second-tier status for temporary employees and many independent contractors, including lower wages, a lack of benefits, increased job insecurity, and further divisions along gender and racial lines. This precarious status creates almost insurmountable obstacles for contingent employees to address their needs through collective action, either because they are statutorily excluded from protection or because their vulnerability increases their fear of employer retaliation. Under a private-market analysis, though, employers and economists can present such treatment of contingent employees as a rational choice in the furtherance of flexibility and cost savings within a market economy, rather than as a choice open to moral scrutiny.

What Is to Be Done?

Combating the problem of the expanded contingent workforce must be done through the use of multiple tactics. Just as employer tactics should be understood as serving the employer goal of maintaining power, so the tactics of the labor movement and other progressive organizations should be chosen to achieve broad goals. In opposition to employer goals, a progressive movement for worker rights should not shy away from an ideological position that asserts collective demands for a redistribution of power and wealth. Demands only to share the wealth will leave capitalism intact. Demands for a just and equitable distribution of power and wealth can present alternatives to capitalism that promote democratic values across political and economic institutions.

Expanded Union Organizing

With this broader ideology as a guide, specific tactics for combating the problem of the increase in contingent work should include focused efforts on union organizing across all job categories and professions. Broad-based unionization will enable workers to resist employer actions to divide them along race and gender lines and will build a common identity for workers at all wage levels in all kinds of jobs. Through collective bargaining and collective political strength, unionized workers can resist employer tactics to increase contingent work. Unions can also press for real flexibility for workers in their choices of working arrangements. Important efforts in these directions can be seen in the following examples: The Service Employees International Union's (SEIU) Justice for Janitors campaign organizes janitors working for cleaning companies that contract with commercial building owners. The SEIU has targeted the creation of more full-time jobs, with corresponding benefits, as one of its current goals in collective bargaining.[33] The SEIU also recently won a union-organizing campaign among 75,000 home health care workers in Los Angeles

County.[34] Recently enacted California state legislation requires that counties designate an employer of record, such as a public authority or a contracting provider agency, for home health care workers employed in the state's program, rather than identifying the individual clients as the employer.[35] Following their win in federal district court, the chicken catchers who brought the overtime pay lawsuit against Perdue Farms unionized in all three poultry-processing plants involved in the litigation.[36] The Microsoft technical employees in Washington State formed a union, the Washington Alliance of Technical Workers (WashTech), affiliated with the Communications Workers of America (CWA).[37] CWA is also engaged in unionizing efforts among contingent employees at other companies, including IBM.[38] Adjunct university faculty have also engaged in efforts toward unionization.[39]

The Role of Legislatures and Courts

Legislative and judicial actions are needed to protect workers against exploitation in working arrangements. Through such actions, legislative and judicial institutions can restrict employers' tactical choices such as "leasing" employees through temporary employment agencies or hiring employees as independent contractors.[40] Various countries are at different starting points in creating restrictions on contingent employment; the spectrum includes prohibitions on temporary employment beyond a defined time period;[41] requirements that equal wages and benefits be paid to regular employees and contingent employees performing similar work;[42] regulation of both the supplier and user employers to ensure health and safety protections and payment of social security contributions;[43] and limitations on contract labor that undermines the status and conditions of unionized employees.[44] While providing protections, such legislation accepts the legitimacy of the triangular employment relationship.[45]

The United States lacks effective regulation of contract labor arrangements. Thus far, such questions have been addressed primarily through administrative and judicial interpretations of existing legislation, such as whether employees are actually independent contractors or whether they fit a common law definition of employee. A recent NLRB decision in the year 2000 expanded the potential of temporary employees to unionize, only to be overruled in 2004. The first NLRB decision, *M. B. Sturgis, Inc.,*[46] re-examined the definition of the employment relationship in light of the growing use of subcontracting work, including contracts between employers and TEAs. Before *Sturgis,* the union faced obstacles when organizing in workplaces that employed temporary employees, as temporary employees would be included in the same bargaining unit as the "regular" employees only with the consent of the TEA and the user employer. According to *Sturgis,* in instances in which the supplier TEA and user employer are joint employers of the temporary employees, the union may seek to represent a mixed bargaining unit of temporary employees and employees employed solely by the user employer. This arrangement recognizes the economic realities of the user employer's control over the temporary employees and the common interests of the temporary and regular employees. In *H.S. Care L.L.C., d/b/a Oakwood Care Ctr.,*[47] however, the NLRB overruled *Sturgis*, returning unions to the difficult circumstances of either obtaining the consent of the user employer and TEA to a mixed bargaining unit or organizing the temporary employees in a separate unit, with the TEA as the employer.

Conclusion

It should come as no surprise that employers continue to develop new tactics to achieve capitalist goals of maintaining and increasing power and wealth. Management's desire for "flexibility" is equivalent to its traditional goal of unilateral control over the workplace. The tactic of expanding the contingent workforce promotes this goal by creating an expendable and fragmented workforce. By hiring through temporary employment agencies and by transforming employees into independent contractors, employers avoid the social and economic obligations attached to the employment relationship, while maintaining maximum power over a vulnerable workforce.

Opposition to such employer tactics should be launched from a broad perspective. Within this broad context, the issue of contingent labor can be seen not simply as a fight to force employers to share more wealth, but as part of a deeper struggle for democratic economic institutions. Specific political and legislative reforms that limit employers' ability to use contingent labor have the potential to achieve more than a fairer distribution of income. Such reforms can be part of a broader approach to enhancing workers' ability to gain collective power through unionization, creating the foundation for redistributing both wealth and power from management to labor.

Notes

1. This essay was first presented at the conference Gross Domestic Product vs. Quality of Life: Balancing Work and Family, sponsored by the Institute for Women and Work of the Cornell University School of Industrial and Labor Relations, held at the Rockefeller Center in Bellagio, Italy, Jan. 29—Feb. 2, 2001.

2. Jared Bernstein, Lawrence Mishel, & John Schmitt, *State of Working America 2000–01* 18 (Economic Policy Institute 2000), http://epinet.org/books/swa2000/swa2000intro.html.

3. Fred R. Shapiro, *The Oxford Dictionary of American Legal Quotations* 184 (1993).

4. *See, e.g.,* Joseph E. Stiglitz, *Economics* 28–29, 723–26 (1993); Ronald G. Ehrenberg & Robert S. Smith, *Modern Labor Economics: Theory and Public Policy* 4, 6 (6th ed. 1996); Richard G. Lipsey & Peter O. Steiner, *Economics* 191–92 (4th ed. 1975).

5. *See, e.g.,* Lewis M. Segal & Daniel G. Sullivan, *The Temporary Labor Force,* 19 Econ. Persp. 2 (March 1995); *Career Evolution,* Economist (Jan. 29, 2000); Louis Uchitelle, *U.S. Jobless Rate Hit 4.5% in April: 223,000 Jobs Lost,* N.Y. Times 1 (May 5, 2001); *see* critique in Alice De Wolff, *The Face of Globalization: Women Working Poor in Canada,* 20 Canadian Woman Stud. 54 (Fall 2000).

6. *See* Ehrenberg & Smith, *supra* note 4, at 433–50.

7. *See* Michael Reich, David M. Gordon, & Richard C. Edwards, *A Theory of Labor Market Segmentation,* in *Problems in Political Economy: An Urban Perspective* 108–13 (2d ed., David M. Gordon ed., 1977); Robert Cherry, *Economic Theories of Racism,* in *Problems in Political Economy, id.* at 170–82; Michael Reich, *The Economics of Racism,* in *Problems in Political Economy, id.* at 183–88.

8. *See* Reinhold Fahlbeck, *Flexibility: Potentials and Challenges for Labor Law,* 19 Comp. Lab. L. & Pol'y J. 515, 526 (1998).

9. *See id.* at 526; Leah F. Vosko, *Leased Workers and the Law: Legitimizing the Triangular Employment Relationship: Emerging International Labor Standards from a Comparative Perspective,* 19 Comp. Lab. L. & Pol'y J. 43, 46 (1997); Bernstein, Mishel, & Schmitt, *supra* note 2, at 3.

10. *See* Bernstein, Mishel, & Schmitt, *supra* note 2, at 3 (in the United States, "the share of workers employed by temporary agencies grew 60% from 1991 to 1995 but by just 26% from 1995 to 1999. . . . In terms of all types of nonstandard work—including regular part-time, temporary help agency, on-call, independent contracting, and contract firm work—the share of workers in these arrangements fell from 26.4% to 24.8% of total employment during 1995–99"); Melissa A. Childs, *The Changing Face of Unions: What Women Want from Employers,* 12 DePaul Bus. L.J. 381, 411–12 (2000); Renate M. de Haas, *Business Law: Employee Benefits: Vizcaino v. Microsoft,* 13 Berkeley Tech. L.J. 483 (1998) (citing estimates of temporary workers as 20–30 percent of the United States workforce and placing the growth rate of contingent employment in the United States at "at least 40% greater than that of the workforce as a whole during 1998"); Fahlbeck, *supra* note 8, at 526 (describing "atypical" workers, who "represent an important and increasing proportion of the workforce, anywhere from 15–20 to some 35–40% of the entire working population").

11. The rate of union membership in the United States remains low, at an estimated 13.9 percent in 1999. Bureau of Labor Statistics News Release (Jan. 19, 2000), http://stats.bls.gov.newsrels.htm. *See also* Fahlbeck, *supra* note 8, at 517–18 (describing the United States at one end of a "flexibility spectrum," providing the greatest power for employers, given that "[f]lexibility is at the very heart of the system" in the United States).

12. *See* Childs, *supra* note 10, at 413–14; Frances Raday, *The Insider-Outsider Politics of Labor-Only Contracting,* 20 Comp. Lab. L. & Pol'y J. 413, 416 (1999).

13. *See* cases cited in Childs, *supra* note 10, at 406–15 and n. 124; de Haas, *supra* note 10, at 490–93.

14. Childs, *supra* note 10, at n. 141; Fahlbeck, *supra* note 8, at 523, 537.

15. *Contingent and Alternative Employment Arrangements,* Bureau of Labor Statistics News Release (Dec. 21, 1999), <http://stats.bls.gov.newsrels/conemp.nws.htm>; Childs, *supra* note 10, at 411–14.

16. *See* Fahlbeck, *supra* note 8, at 524, stating that "the single biggest—or one of the biggest—employer in many countries in terms of the number of employees is the leading temporary work agency, Manpower. Significant is also that the number of temporary work firms has mushroomed in recent years."

17. *See id.* at 522 (basing this argument on language from the United States federal Clayton Act, an antitrust statute, 15 U.S.C. §§ 12–27); Vosko, *supra* note 9, at 48–49 (citing this language as "a particularly salient theme in the evolution of the ILO," leading to its original position against private employment agencies); Raday, *supra* note 12, at 413 (critiquing the ILO for reversing its original policy against employment agencies by adopting Convention 181 in 1997, which

"legitimized private intermediaries, not only as job placement agencies, but also as direct providers of labor services").

18. *See* Childs, *supra* note 10, at n. 130 (describing the addition of the contingent workforce as creating "a two-tiered workforce").

19. The Building and Construction Trades Department of the AFL-CIO recently released a report alleging that Labor Ready, a major temporary employment agency, has been systemically misclassifying employees' work to lower workers' compensation premiums. *See* news release, *New Report Shows Labor Ready Inc. Workers Com Misclassification Widespread, Long-Term* (May 18, 2002), available at http://www.bctd.org/news/newsreleases/2002/5.28.02.html.

20. *See* Raday, *supra* note 12, at 418 (discussing the "double discrimination" against women and minorities in the area of "labor-only contracting").

21. *See id.* at 416, 418–20 (discussing the employer's use of leased workers to undermine the position of unionized employees, and discussing the difficulties of organizing leased workers).

22. *See* Childs, *supra* note 10, at n. 124.

23. *See* Elizabeth Walpole-Hofmeister, *Court Finds Chicken Catchers Are Employees Covered by FLSA for Overtime,* 41 Daily Labor Report A-5 (Mar. 1, 2000); *see also* cases from other industries, discussed in de Haas, *supra* note 10, at 490–93.

24. Elizabeth Walpole-Hofmeister, *FLSA: Perdue Farms Settles Overtime Suit, Will Pay Chicken Catchers $1.7 Million,* 92 Daily Labor Report A-1 (May 11, 2001).

25. Childs, *supra* note 10, at 414–15.

26. *See* Vizcaino v. Microsoft, 97 F.3d 1187 (9th Cir. 1996); modified en banc, *Vizcaino v. Microsoft Corp.,* 120 F.3d 1006 (9th Cir. 1997); cert. denied, 118 S.Ct. 899 (1998); enf'd by mandamus, *Vizcaino v. U.S. Dist. Ct.,* 173 F.3d 713 (9th Cir. 1999). For discussions of the Microsoft case, *see* Danielle D. van Jaarsveld, *Nascent Organizing Initiatives among High-Skilled Contingent Workers: The Microsoft-Washtech/CWA Case* (master's degree thesis 2000) (thesis on file with the author); Danielle D. van Jaarsveld & Lee H. Adler, *A Discussion of Organizing and Legal Strategies in a High Technology Environment: The Microsoft-WashTech/CWA Case* (Nov. 18–19, 1999) (paper delivered at the Subcontracted Work Initiative Strategy Forum, sponsored by the National Employment Law Project and the Farmworkers Justice Fund, Washington, D.C.)(paper on file with the author); de Haas, *supra* note 10, at 484–88. Microsoft agreed to a $96.9 million settlement of this litigation, which was given final approval by a federal district court. *See* Jo-el J. Meyer, *Ninth Circuit Affirms Award of $27 Million in Attorney's Fees in Microsoft Benefits Suit,* 96 Daily Labor Report A-3 (May 17, 2002).

27. John C. Duncan Jr., *The Indentured Servants of Academia: The Adjunct Faculty Dilemma and Their Limited Legal Remedies,* 74 Ind. L.J. 513, 521 (1999). During that same period, full-time faculty increased by 22 percent. *Id.* at 521. *See also* Ann Marie Cox, *Report Details Colleges' Heavy Reliance on Part-Time Instructors,* Chron. Higher Educ. (Nov. 22, 2000).

28. Jane Buck, *The President of the AAUP Looks Back and Around on February 24: In Many Ways, the Changes in Academic Life Recently Haven't Been for the Better,* 28 New York Academe 1, 10 (Spring 2001).

29. Duncan, *supra* note 27, at 524–28.

30. Risa L. Lieberwitz, *The Corporatization of the University: Distance Learning at the Cost of Academic Freedom?* 12 Boston U. Pub. Int. L.J. 73, 96–99 (2002).

31. *See, e.g.,* Segal & Sullivan, *supra,* note 5; David Leonhardt, *Temporary Jobs Have Become the Victims of a Slow Market,* N.Y. Times sec. C, at 1 (May 19, 2001).

32. Max Jarman, *Temp Job Layoffs Set 19-Year Record,* Ithaca Journal 6A (May 25, 2001).

33. *See* Elizabeth Walpole-Hofsmeister, *100,000 Janitors Covered in SEIU Pacts Bargained during 2000 in Two Dozen Cities,* 229 Daily Labor Report C-1 (Nov. 28, 2000). In April 2000, the SEIU led a successful three-week strike of 8,500 janitors against commercial building owners and operators. *Id. See also* Karl E. Klare, *New Approaches to Poverty Law, Teaching, and Practice: Toward New Strategies for Low-Wage Workers,* 4 B.U. Pub. Int. L.J. 245, 269–72 (1995).

34. *Los Angeles Home Care Workers Vote to Organize by Huge Majority,* 39 Daily Labor Report A-4 (Mar. 1, 1999).

35. *Id.*

36. Walpole-Hofmeister, *supra* note 24.

37. *See* van Jaarsveld & Adler, *supra* note 26, at 7–16.

38. *Id.* at 6–7.

39. *See, e.g.,* Mark Cutler, *Eight Circuit Reverses Order Reinstating Instructor Who Organized Adjunct Faculty,* 209 DLR A-7 (Oct. 27, 2000); Michael Bologna, *Part-Time Roosevelt University Professors Vote For Representation By IEA/NEA Affiliate,* 50 DLR A-9 (Mar. 14, 2000); Mark Bologna, *Part-Time Faculty at Columbia College in Chicago Approves First-Ever Contract,* 54 DLR A-4 (Mar. 22, 1999).

40. *See* Raday, *supra* note 12, at 416.

41. *Id.* at 423, citing legislation in the Philippines, India, Malaysia, Belgium, Spain, Luxembourg, France, Germany, and Italy regarding the use of temporary labor-only contracting.

42. *Id.* at 424–25, citing legislation in Belgium, France, Austria, Denmark, Portugal, Mexico, Italy, and the Netherlands.

43. *See* Vosko, *supra* note 9, at 67–69, citing legislation in Japan, Norway, Sweden, France, Spain, and by directive in the European Parliament.

44. *See* Raday, *supra* note 12, at 425–26, citing legislation and interpretation of legislation in the United States, Canada, France, Italy, Japan, Finland, and Sweden.

45. *See* Vosko, *supra* note 9, at 70–73; and Raday, *supra* note 12, at 420–22, both criticizing the ILO's change in policy, shifting from a policy against labor-only contracts to the 1997 adoption of Convention 181, the Private Employment Agencies Convention, accepting the role of employment agencies. Convention 181 provides some protections of employees, but does not have a provision for equal treatment of the agency employees and the user's regular employees doing similar work. The ILO Draft Convention on Contract Labor does include such an equality provision, but the Draft Convention excludes private employment agency employees.

46. 331 NLRB 173 (2000).

47. 343 NLRB 76 (2004).

CHAPTER 15

Commodification and Women's Household Labor

Katharine B. Silbaugh

A woman washes a kitchen floor.[1] She puts the mop away and drives to the corner market. She consults a shopping list and purchases groceries, carefully choosing the least expensive options. A four-year-old child is tugging at her leg while she does this, and she tries to entertain him, talking to him about the mopped floor, the grocery items. When she returns from the store, she prepares lunch from what she has brought home with her. She and the child both eat lunch. After lunch, she and the child collect laundry, and she runs a load. She takes the garbage out to the curb. Then she reads him a story. They play a game where she comes up with a word, and he tries to name its opposite. Sometimes there is no opposite, and that is particularly funny to both of them. She has done housework.

There is no way to tell from this description whether these activities are market or nonmarket, whether her work is a commodity or not. Would it help to categorize her work if you knew the location? Is this her home? Suppose she is a paid domestic worker, and this housework is a commodity. She leaves her employer's home. She goes home and does exactly the same thing there, but this time she is preparing dinner. The second child is her own. Whether these activities are viewed as a commodity is contextual, not activity based.

Should we think and talk about unpaid domestic labor—housework—using market, or economic, language? What follows is a defense of economic discourse on the subject of law and housework. It is written in response to the common criticism aimed at scholars who have examined domestic labor through an economic lens. It is a response to what is commonly called a commodification critique, and particularly as that critique is formulated within feminist discourse.

Characterizations of domestic labor by legal actors almost never include an emphasis on its economic productivity, but instead focus on housework as an expression of the affectionate emotions associated with the family setting in which the housework occurs.[2] By setting up a dichotomy between the language of economic productivity and the language of emotions, legal actors have used the language of emotions to deny material security to those who perform domestic labor. A more clearly articulated understanding of the economically productive aspects of home labor, the kind used by economists and sociologists, would benefit those who perform the labor, who are still primarily women.

I question current categorical thinking about women's home activity. I argue that economic understandings are very useful, and that they do not and need not supply a complete understanding of human activities. I will make the case that economic understandings are representations of a given activity, as are sentimental or emotional understandings, and that they can and should coexist. Margaret Jane Radin, the foremost legal scholar who has addressed commodification concerns, has also argued that multiple understandings can coexist.[3] Her goal, however, is to bring nonmarket understandings to market activities, in search of a less commodified society.

This essay questions that goal. My central argument is that the entirely emotional understanding of home labor is itself an impoverished one. If one conceded that the use of economic rhetoric could habituate people to thinking about a topic differently, as critics of economic language assert, that would not necessarily make the case against the use of such rhetoric in all contexts. I make the uncommon case here for the value of bringing market understandings to nonmarket activities, where they can coexist with noneconomic conceptions. The broader implication of the thesis is that we should not assume that analyses that can remake relations are always doing a disservice where those relations are already fraught with problematic analyses. In certain contexts it may be a very conservative claim that economic analysis is bad because it has the power to change the way we view something.

My claim is that gender equality requires us to take the economics of home labor seriously. This argument turns on a comparison between wage labor and home labor, which are similar both in content and in many of the motivations that drive workers. I argue that the difference in the treatment of these workers may be difference based on gender. I discuss the tendency to raise commodification concerns when women's interests are at stake, and I question whether resistance to market reasoning in these contexts is a form of resistance to women's economic power. I then examine some legal doctrines touching on home labor that could benefit from economic analysis. If importing economic reasoning into these areas transforms our understanding of them, I posit that women would benefit from that transformation. I conclude that as long as so many of women's activities remain nonmarket and as long as women's economic welfare is a concern of feminists, economic analysis of nonmarket activities is affirmatively desirable. My objective is to show what can be gained by allowing economics to inform, without dominating, the discourse on policy and doctrine surrounding home labor. Concern over women's lives becoming entirely commodified seems by comparison an abstract worry.

The Basic Problem with Commodification

The standard argument against commodification, often referred to as the commodification critique, is that certain human attributes or certain resources should lie wholly or partially beyond exchange, because to allow exchange would be inconsistent with a vision of personhood or human flourishing. Prohibiting exchange may not be enough; it may be necessary to discourage economic analysis and discourse about these attributes. "[M]any kinds of particulars—one's politics, work, religion, family, love, sexuality, friendships, altruism, experiences, wisdom, moral commitments, character, and personal attributes [are] . . . integral to the self. To understand any of these as monetizable . . . is to do violence to our deepest understanding of what it is to be human."[4]

Elizabeth Anderson defines a commodity as something to which "the norms of the market are appropriate for regulating its production, exchange and enjoyment." The application of market norms is inappropriate where they "fail to value [the thing] in an appropriate way." If it is appropriate to apply "use" as the proper mode of valuation, then market norms are acceptable and we may treat something as a commodity. To value something differently than as a commodity is, according to Anderson, to recognize a "special intrinsic worth" to that item. This essentialist notion that things have an intrinsic worth turns out to be important to anticommodification arguments. Anderson argues, "when women's labor is treated as a commodity, the women who perform it are degraded." Degradation means that "something is treated in accordance with a lower mode of valuation than is proper to it." Finally, Anderson believes that commodifying women's labor leads to exploitation of women, because women's noncommercial motivations are taken advantage of without offering anything in exchange but commercial responses.[5]

Anderson's work draws on a notion of incommensurability of value that is seen in the work of Martha Nussbaum.[6] As applied to the domestic labor context, the problem of incommensurability would arise with the need to give the labor a market value when it is not commensurable to market goods or services. The two may not be commensurable if, for example, one is measured on a valuation scale that can translate into dollars, whereas another is measured on one that cannot, such as love, admiration, wonder, or respect. Although these scholars have not applied their critiques directly to housework, it can be argued that there is no perfectly accurate market replacement for unpaid work, such as, for example, child care, that a family member performs.

The commodification critique applies to an analysis of the economy of the home and the family labor that occurs there, as well as to the actual purchase and sale of that labor. To Anderson, market norms have an "expressive significance" as well as a practical one, and can thus infect nonmarket conceptions of women's labor. The argument posits that talk matters: you can pervert the personalness of something by talking about it as if it were fungible. Identifying an "economy," meaning a set of implicit valuations and exchanges, is possible even where "real markets" are either prohibited or practically impossible to imagine: organs for transplantation, sexual contacts, candidates for marriage partnerships, religious convictions, love, or a person's politics. Although in many cases this is just talk, to a commodification skeptic, that talk itself damages the integrity of the attribute in question: sexuality, love, marriage, health.

James Boyd White has made this case most powerfully, arguing that expression is never transparent but instead constitutes and transforms the reality it describes. Says White: "the languages we speak, and the cultural practices they at once reflect and make possible, form our minds by habituating them to certain modes of attention, certain ways of seeing and conceiving of oneself and of the world." White concludes that economic language should be "vigorously resist[ed]" because "[t]he conventions of this discourse necessarily habituate its user[s] to thinking in terms of self-interest as a central principle." In passing, he applies this critique to an economic understanding of home labor, noting that

> [t]he segmentation of the exchange model tends to misvalue the work we do for ourselves, which is most of the traditional work of women. . . . This is especially true of people who raise their own children. Such work cannot be segmented into functions and then made the material of the market process, actual or hypothetical, for what the child requires is the sustained presence of, and interaction with, a loving and respectful person, something no alternative can supply. Similarly, housework has a different meaning when one is maintaining one's own home rather than acting as a servant for others.[7]

To those who see a difference between real and rhetorical markets, the difference tends to be treated as one of degree. Under this view, it might not hurt personhood as much to talk about markets in certain attributes as it does to create such markets, but talk certainly doesn't help. By condemning talk as well as trades, skeptics take away the opportunity to make the affirmative case for the benefits of an economic perspective. For legal analysts, this conflation of actual buying and selling and market analysis proves problematic, as we will see later.

A Taxonomy of Anticommodification Discourse

Margaret Radin set out a number of useful categories of thought about commodification.[8] She uses the term *radical noncommodification* to refer to a utopian vision in which people and things are embodied with unique personalities and cannot be exchanged under any circumstances. The ideal of universal noncommodification is associated with Marx and arguably lurks in the background of Radin's early work, which idealizes a future world without commodification but acknowledges the distance between this world and that one. Radical commodification describes an ideal where anything of value will be ownable and freely exchangeable. To radical commodifiers, every objection to markets other than on administrability grounds is misguided, mushy sentimentality that hurts the people it is intended to help. Real welfare, both individual and societal, will always be promoted by permitting exchange. Nothing is off the table: babies, organs, surrogacy, sex, justice, and so on.[9]

Finally, "partial commodification" describes Radin's understanding of our current world. She uses employment law and housing market regulation as examples because both are traded in the market, but that trade is subject to extensive regulation. Radin points to ways in which the idea of partial commodification can be used. First, we might have spheres of commodification, where some areas of experience are inappropriate for commodification altogether, but those things that can be commodified are commodified completely. Radin calls this "liberal compartmentalization," identifies Michael Walzer as its most distinguished proponent, and disapproves of it as both impossible and undesirable. Liberal compartmentalization is most clearly illustrated by the desire to establish the home and the political sphere as spaces that are entirely nonmarket, with much of what is outside the home and the government as presumptively a market domain. This kind of partial commodification is one way to remedy the uneasiness most people have with radical commodification. Radin dislikes it because it permits unfettered commodification in those areas that do not receive complete market immunity. I dislike it because it permits unfettered noncommodification of large segments of women's labor, as I argue later.

The other kind of partial commodification is called "incomplete commodification" by Radin, and she believes that it provides a better descriptive and normative view. Incomplete commodification applies if the same attribute or thing is thought of in both market and nonmarket terms. There are no spheres in which the market is completely banished or completely dominant. Competing market and nonmarket conceptions of the same thing can be held in two ways. In the first, different segments of society contest either the commodified or the noncommodified understanding held by others but neither segment can claim a consensus. In the second, a person or persons understand the commodity aspects of a thing or attribute and its noncommodity aspects; here the two understandings are simultaneously at work within the same person. Radin says that both of these types of coexistences have led to pubic policy choices that embody or accommodate the plural meaning at play. Radin argues that these multiple meanings can achieve stability, and when they do we are better off than if we require that one conception extinguish others. She is particularly concerned with making sure that market understandings do not extinguish nonmarket ones.

Radin identifies what she calls the "domino theory" in the discourse on commodification. This is the idea, held by many, that if any commodified version of an attribute or thing exists, noncommodified versions will cease to exist. Where incomplete commodification exists, the market understanding will eventually prevail over the nonmarket understanding, and the nonmarket understanding will be extinguished. Although the inevitability of extinguishing nonmarket understandings is never well explained, the argument is used to support prohibitions on all commodification of an activity. For example, if it is important to the culture that a noncommodified version of sexuality exists, and if any commercialized sexuality will extinguish or infect the noncommodified version by making all people understand their sexuality as having a price, all commercialized sex must be prohibited to honor the greater societal value placed on the continued existence of noncommodified sex. The domino theory posits that both cannot exist without changing each other.

Another example of the domino theory argument is one against surrogate mothering or markets in adoption. These arguments proceed as follows: it would be awful for children to understand themselves as having a price. If any children are traded through the process of surrogacy or markets in adoption, all children will come to understand that they too are marketable. This understanding would extinguish the nonmarket norm in familial relations. Because the latter norm is extremely valuable to us, we should not allow any commodification of either reproductive capacity or adoption, lest the noncommodified conception cease to exist even in that majority of cases in which markets played no role in the formation of a family.

Radin identifies what she calls the problem of the double bind: one might idealize noncommodification in a utopian world, but in this world decommodifying only certain things may do more harm than good. For example, total decommodification of sexuality may be an ultimate goal, but as long as it is partially commodified, prohibiting prostitution may do more harm than good by hurting a particularly vulnerable class of people: those engaged in the commercial sex industry. She calls this a problem of transitional balancing, where the transition is from our world to an ideal world. The balancing trick is to consider the damaging effects of noncommodification in the present world and thus tend toward permitting commodification, while also considering the domino effect whereby commodifying might change the nature of the thing for the worse, so that we find ourselves moving farther from the ideal. How to decide between these two pulls of the double bind? Says Radin, there is no formula. We must engage in a context-specific, factual inquiry to tell us whether commodification or decommodification will do more good than harm, all things considered, for each given contested attribute or thing. Her formula gives us no real criteria for making the decision, but it does invite us to go straight to the facts and not to force the conversation onto a broader theoretical plane.

The idealized future world, in Radin's view, seems implicitly to be one without commodification, but she has become increasingly open to the limited use of markets and market language in contested cases. She argues that there are many ways in which partial commodification can thrive and remain stable.

Ultimately, though, Radin makes a one-way claim: for the value of importing nonmarket understandings into market activities. She believes that improvement of personhood will come from a better grasp of those nonmarket attributes. I thoroughly agree with Radin's conclusion that multiple conceptions are possible and beneficial, but I seek to turn her conclusion around. I argue for a better recognition of and understanding of the economic aspects of nonmarket activities. Under this view, plural meanings are not a matter of transition; either market or nonmarket understandings are functional representations, not ideal models.

Feminism and Economic Skepticism

Feminists rank high among those who are skeptical of economists. This skepticism proceeds on two fronts in the domestic labor context. The two parts are a negative reaction to economics as a way to describe home activities, and an affirmatively positive response to love and affections as a descriptively accurate way of understanding and explaining productivity in the home.

Offense at Economics

Some feminists have a visceral dislike for economic analysis. Although there are many reasons for this, I believe two are most strongly at play. The first is situational: many feminists don't trust the current practitioners of economic analysis. The second is more substantive: many feminists do not accept the implicit notion of fungibility at play in economic analysis.

The problem of distrust may come from two characteristics of economic discourse. The first is an apparent essentialism among many economists. Some economic literature reads like more than a useful tool with which to explain certain phenomenon. It instead reads like the raison d'être of that phenomenon, its beginning and end. Everyone has her favorite example of a social phenomenon being mercilessly pushed into an economic model, producing logically clean but absurd explanations: adoption, marriage, heroic rescues, voting, altruism, religion, childbirth, sexuality. This kind of relentless essentialism among economists leaves reasonable people with what appears to be a decision to either embrace the whole absurd end of the spectrum or jump ship entirely. It is fully possible and desirable to use economics to assist in understanding social phenomena, even the ones mentioned above, without turning away from other possible explanations or understandings. But this does not describe much of the economic analysis practiced in the legal academic community. The idea of extending this sort of essentialism into the social relations surrounding family labor seems to carry the risk of damaging the complex context of dependencies and moral and emotional commitments made there.

The second reason many feminists distrust practitioners of economic analysis is that they often employ assumptions with suspect origins. Moreover, although these are almost always identified at the outset as assumptions, by the end of the equation they sometimes seem to have assumed the status of fact. In legal discourse, when an assumption is used in an economic model, we usually see the burden of proof implicitly shifted to critics of the model to disprove the factual assumption, despite the frequent lack of evidence in favor of the assumption from the outset. There is the well-known joke about the economists on a desert island with a case of food in tin cans. They begin their plan for opening the cans by saying, "First, let's assume a can opener." It's funny when it's a can opener. It is not so funny, or at least it shouldn't be, when the empirically unsupported assumption is that women want children more than men do, that women have higher inherent value when they are young and men are worth more when they are older, that husbands and wives in most cases have the perfect trust and agency necessary to treat them as a single economic unit (individuals are selfish and self-interested but family heads are altruistic), or that rapists would pay for sex somehow if they had the necessary wealth of money, power, or looks.[10] Having those assumptions implicitly raised to the level of facts over the course of an economic argument is particularly problematic.

I think of the implicit elevation of assumption to fact as "assumption slippage." This slippage is a dynamic process: readers of economic texts, particularly in the legal community, are participants in its occurrence as much if not sometimes more so than economic authors. Much of the most prominent economic analysis of family and gender relations, particularly that associated with Gary Becker, relies on very questionable assumptions that appear to come right out of the pages of *The Total Woman*,[11] and from there they help to build economic rationalizations for very conventional mid-twentieth-century middle-class suburban gender relations. In the words of Barbara Bergmann, "to say that New Home Economists [Becker et al.] are not feminists in their orientation would be as much of an understatement as to say that Bengal tigers are not vegetarians."[12] Isabel V. Sawhill has offered a critique of the lack of empirical basis for some of the basic assumptions of the New Home Economists who are prominent in the field.[13] As economists know from their training but their legal readers quickly forget, an economic model is only as good as its assumptions. Hence, the implicit standard in economic scholarship is that unproved assumptions must be plausible before a model based on them is acceptable, even with caveats. In the context of home labor, those assumptions are very important. Assuming altruistic heads of households reduces the need to worry about disparate human capital investments made within the family. The assumption that women desire children more than men do provides an explanation for what otherwise might be tricky distributional results that occur within families. If these are to be the assumptions on which an economic analysis of home labor is to proceed, many people do not want any part of it.

I cannot join the routine conclusion that the problems with Gary Becker's work are so far-reaching as to make his work as a whole of limited use. We are indebted to Becker for raising extraordinarily important economic questions about the functioning of the family. Becker has brought us many ideas that are extremely helpful in thinking about family relations, including the very notion that in economic terms the home is a place of production and not just a place of consumption. If he has proceeded from unsupportable or incomplete assumptions, those can be corrected and the analysis and its outcomes adjusted accordingly. Indeed, examining and critiquing these assumptions have been a large implicit part of the feminist response to Law and Economics already, and should continue to be so. However, critiquing assumptions does not inflict a fatal blow to methodology. It would be a mistake to hold these questionable assumptions out as an indictment of an entire mode of analysis. This is a standard to which most scholars would not wish to be held, and feminists are no exception.

An important lesson about the scope of the usefulness of economic analysis can be learned from assumption slippage and the response to it: empiricism counts. Empirical research and data need to drive any real search for policy solutions to basic problems, or even to clear understandings of the problems themselves. Law professors are not in a great position to do empirical research and must rely on fields outside of law or economics, such as sociology, to inform economic understandings. This dependence is not without its own difficulties for lawyers untrained in the understanding and sorting of sociological research. The most that economic understandings can do is to highlight some empirical questions that need to be answered. Even answers to empirical questions do not close debates over facts. If we are confident that a resource is scarce as a matter of empirical fact, we can either treat that information as a given or instead ask why the resource is scarce. That which has an empirical basis is not thereby natural or inevitable, and so even provable assumptions should be open to well-framed criticisms. But once again, economics can assist in the framing task itself.

I do not wish to be understood as overstating the ease of remembering that we are dealing with hypothetical models when we use economic analysis. I think the risk of forgetting is more serious when we cannot verify the empirical assumption. We move quickly on from it, sensing that the unavailability of data threatens to make an otherwise elegant model useless. At times it seems that, perversely, the less supportable an assumption, the less contestable it is, and the more it acquires the status of fact. It may be that James Boyd White's concern about the culture of economic discourse is played out most seriously when data are least available.

The next level of concern over economic analysis does not center solely on the supposed "priors" of its practitioners. It is a more substantive criticism: a rejection of the suggestion that many attributes of family life and work are fungible and thus that the study of value can proceed by observing choices people make. Fungibility is the idea that goods, services, or attributes can be placed on a single metric of value and then traded off against one another on that metric. Fungible things can be replaced by something else that falls in the same place on the metric, such as similar services by a different person, or simply money measured in the right amount, without regret. On this account, economics is entirely concerned with theoretically measurable maximized choice among alternatives, rather than being concerned with the personal experience of choice, methods of provisioning in general (whether by voluntary exchange, gift giving, or coercion),[14] or the process of developing what economists call preferences. Radin concedes that whether we think the fact of choice between alternatives proves fungibility, as many economists believe, or instead proves nothing about fungibility, is largely a matter of intuition. Joseph Raz argues that the meaning we give to a choice is its conventional understanding, and if that does not include a trade along a single metric, then no such fungibility can be inferred.[15] Raz taps into many people's response to the talk of fungibility when thinking about marriage, romantic partners, and family work choices that are implicit in an economic analysis of home labor.

There is similar negative response to the notion of bargaining within marriage or within family relations, which is an important element of an economic understanding of home labor. Though a bargaining model is often thought of as an improvement on Becker's notion of an altruistic head of household, which can justify a failure to examine interspousal conflict, the bargaining model itself draws a negative response from many.[16] Although many would acknowledge much day-to-day bargaining within the family, it is also thought that a bargaining analysis fails to capture the altruistic behavior layered alongside self-interested behavior in family relations. It is difficult to predict much about behavior if one can rely on neither complete self-interest nor complete altruism, and a bargaining analysis of family labor puts forward assumptions about family behavior to which many respond negatively.[17]

The Aptness of the Emotional Understanding

The former critique, that family labor is not fungible and not always strategic, is also frequently stated in the affirmative: family labor is uniquely emotional.

What is wrong with the affections characterization? Family care is all about affections. Should courts ignore the emotional motivations behind caring for a child or preparing a meal for a partner or spouse? Although I argue that this idea can coexist with an economic understanding of home labor, many think that an economic understanding demotes or denigrates the emotional significance of home labor; this is the essence of the domino theory. These criticisms of the commodification of home labor through the use of economic rhetoric and analysis represent a subset of criticisms of all commodification and economic rhetoric. The family context, however, raises the concerns in a particularly bright light.

I believe that feminist skepticism of economics is understandable but should be avoided. Keeping economic understandings away from women's activities represents a particularly gendered understanding of those activities that is itself costly.

A Defense of Market Concepts

The feminist legal discourse should be open to economic understandings of home labor. The argument proceeds on several fronts. First, a claim for economic understandings is not a claim against other understandings. Here I build on Radin's ideas that phenomena have plural meanings. Next, within legal discourse, the transformative effect of language may not operate with the all-consuming power that some might expect from language in other areas of study. Furthermore, to the extent that economic analysis has the transformative power that skeptics of economics attribute to it, I question the general assumption that these transformed norms are inherently negative if they highlight market understandings. I argue that home labor and wage labor are in many ways similar. That similarity includes both the content of the work and the mixed motivations behind the work. Both waged and unwaged labor contain market and nonmarket aspects. I posit that differences between their treatment ought to be understood as differences related to gender, given the history and current practices surrounding home labor. I ask for skepticism toward that different treatment, given its tendency to leave women without cash in the name of noncommodification. I explore the tendency of the noncommodification argument to be economically disempowering to women in other areas in support of the claim that is has this effect on home labor. I then return to the claim that transformation of current understandings is not always a ground for criticizing language, and that in the home labor context it may be a ground for embracing economic language. I end with a set of policy debates I believe can be enhanced by viewing home labor as economic activity.

Plural Meaning

The most important response to the commodification critique, and one that Radin embraces, is the notion of plural meanings, or multiple understandings of a single activity that can coexist. According to Radin, "[t]he way to a less commodified society is to see and foster the non-market aspect of much of what we buy and sell, to honor our internally plural understandings, rather than to erect a wall to keep a certain few things completely off the market and abandon everything else to market rationality."[18]

Although Radin's insight into the possibility of plural meaning is useful, it is impossible not to notice her hierarchy among models. She seeks a less commodified society, not plural conceptions of human activity. Radin gives little encouragement for us to bring out the market aspects of nonmarket activity such as home labor. Her claim falls short of a richness of understanding that includes economics as a creative force in personality. I make the claim for that possibility by bringing forward some of the negative aspects of nonmarket understandings, while maintaining the notion that neither an economic nor an emotional understanding of nonmarket activities is intrinsic to the activities themselves. This latter point saves room for Radin's desire to promote plural meaning, but it rests less on an implicit trajectory toward an ideal of a singular, and for her nonmarket, conception.

Suppose human activity is multifaceted and resists any singular, encompassing description. Home labor, as with so many human activities or attributes, cannot be understood entirely with economic reasoning. Economic reasoning, however, can be one of several ways to interpret human activity that will show us a facet of that activity and enrich our understanding of it. We probably experience many things as such; the question is whether we are able to highlight that experience. Although this point might be raised by a critic of economics because of the tendency among some economists to be essentialist in their thinking, it also should rescue economic analysis for those who would banish it entirely from legal discourse. If the problem is a lack of nuance among economists, feminists should not employ a similar lack of nuance by rejecting economic reasoning or, as in Radin's case, looking for its gradual demise.

Radin asks if we can both know the price of something and simultaneously know that it is priceless. I believe the answer is yes. An important illustration of this point can be found in Viviana Rotman Zelizar's historical examination of the life insurance industry.[19] In the first half of the nineteenth century there was tremendous public resistance to the sale of life insurance in the United States because the public took offense at the suggestion that a life could be valued in monetary terms. The insurance industry responded to the resistance with a pitch that was aimed at the idea that the life was not worth the money. Widows needed to be cared for after the death of a spouse, and insurance would help with that, although it would in no way replace the life lost. Under this conception, the life insurance market took off. Today's life insurance market does not offend most people on commodification grounds, despite its known actuarial focus. Life insurance is considered a kind and responsible purchase for family members, who do not thereby come to view the insured loved one as bearing a price. Students of insurance would argue that it is not about pricing life at all but about subjectively chosen levels of risk. Thus, a "price" does not unseat the understanding of pricelessness. The fact of a price does not create a market: we would not accept the argument that because we price lives for insurance purposes, we may also buy and sell people. Such an idea would only serve to show us that the "price" does not capture the value. It instead serves a limited purpose that is unrelated to real value.

Radin makes the interesting point that by promoting the exile of economic understandings entirely, we implicitly grant too much power to that mode of analysis. If we believe that the very existence of an economic discourse destroys other understandings of a phenomenon, we grant that economic discourse has become a baseline that will always extinguish other understandings if it is permitted to thrive. Elizabeth S. Anderson's analysis displays this belief. That economics need not extinguish other perspectives is an important idea when thinking about the potentially important emotional perspective on family labor.

Economics is a tool for identifying the allocational issues at play in a given social setting. An important implication of Radin's notion of plural meaning is that where a plural or multifaceted understanding is employed, policy and legal choices can be made that embody those plural understandings. This should be important when thinking about the policy issues surrounding home labor. I argue that the addition of some understanding of the economic significance of home labor, without moving it into an unregulated market, would positively inform legal discourse on the home.

Anderson is concerned that commodification of women's labor leads to the exploitation of women because it gives only a commercial response to women's noncommercial motivations. Anderson's analysis does not account for the possibility of women's mixed motivations. Anderson's analysis also does not allow for the possibility that responses that are noncommercial may exist even where commercial responses exist.

Consider the benefits gained in the fields of sociology and economics from a shift in understandings of home activity. Before either field had made the transition from seeing the home only as the site of consumption and affections to seeing home activity as work, neither field had the occasion to ask the questions that arise from that observation: What is this work like? Is it safe, efficient, stressful? What are its standards and practices? How does it compare to market work in terms of needed human capital development, productivity, and job satisfaction? We ought to care very much about the answers to these questions. The questions were not available to the eye of the economist or so-ciologist until the notion of work was imported into the home. Legal analysis is very much in need of the same opening up to questions.

The Limited Influence of Talk in Legal Discourse: Plural Meaning as the Norm

Does talking about home labor as productive mean commodifying it? It be-comes important to think about what is meant by commodification. To as-sume that there is no important difference between analyzing the economics of something and creating an unregulated market for that same thing is terribly damaging to intellectual discourse. "Wages for housework" is not the only possible outcome of this exercise. Even if there is only a difference of degree between talk and real markets, as the commodification literature suggests, that difference should matter for the purposes of legal analysis.

Rhetoric and real markets differ particularly in the legal context. We rou-tinely ask questions about value in legal practice as if a market exists where one does not. Consider the wrongful death suit or any tort suit that includes a claim for pain and suffering damages. The value of these claims is obviously not established by a real market. Moreover, it is not difficult for most people to accept that there should not ever be a real market in these things. Nonethe-less, in a tort action, we allow money to change hands as if a market value were placed on these things. This is a clear practical example of the existence of what Radin calls plural meanings.

Monetization of things for which there is no market and no push for a mar-ket for the purpose of providing a remedy within the law is an illustration of the resilience of nonmarket conceptions. Although legal academics may fret about the message we are sending by placing a value on the loss of an arm, the nonlegal world does not appear to have been influenced into believing that arms are worth x amount of money, despite the many years that a monetary remedy has been provided for the loss of an arm. Loss of consortium damages are an even better example of this phenomenon. This routine fact of legal dis-course should deflate somewhat the worry over the domino effect if we decide to analyze, by the use of economic understandings, those legal policies affect-ing home labor. Law's pragmatic focus on remedies has not had an enormous spillover effect into social understandings in nonlegal discourse.

Consider the benefits of economic discourse in law that concerns those things we generally view as noncommodifiable. Accident victims who receive pain and suffering damages are not likely to want those remedies taken away on the grounds that the hedonic experience of pain is nonfungible or priceless. Pretending that there is a market value to pain, although there is not a true market in pain, is a necessary part of improving the welfare of accident victims. This is a partial answer to the question of whether we can know both the price of something and that it is priceless. As lawyers we already do. Incommensurability does not disappear; it simply does not paralyze.

The case of legal remedies is one illustration of a central argument of this essay. It is not enough to say that economic rhetoric has an impact on the imagination and to give examples of where that impact is negative. Conceding that rhetoric has an impact is not to concede that in all contexts that impact is negative. It is a conservative leap, grounded in preserving current understandings, to assume that it must be so. We see the creative potential of economics as applied to well-known conventional legal remedies in the tort context. The point is made more salient by looking at the context of home labor in particular.

The Need for Economic Understandings of Home Labor in Particular

Consider critics who argue that love and affection are a descriptively accurate way of understanding and explaining productivity in the home. If plural meaning is possible, the emotional account of home labor does not disappear in the face of the economic account. It seems obvious that most labor, including most wage labor, can be multifaceted. It is usually performed in furtherance of some family commitment and is often substantively rewarding at a personal level as well.

Having relieved ourselves of the burden of holding a singular conception of home labor, we can move on to aspects of home labor that justify the need for economics as one of the plural understandings associated with that labor.

Comparison between Commodification Concerns over Wage Labor versus Home Labor

SIMILARITIES BETWEEN WAGED AND UNWAGED LABOR

What do waged and unwaged labor have in common? Both improve the welfare of an individual or a family, and neither is leisure. Goods that are made in the home and services that are provided by those who work in the home produce value that improves the standard of living for all in the home in the same way that a wage buys goods and services that improve the standard of living in a home. A meal is prepared and clothes are cleaned because both contribute to individual or collective welfare. Either can be performed at home or purchased as a service with wages earned in the market. Purchase or self-performance will lead to a similar result: an improvement in welfare.

A person is engaged in leisure activity or simply consuming if the only benefit of her activity goes to her but she would receive no benefit if a third party engaged in that activity for her. Thus, preparing a meal is not leisure because it produces a meal that a worker might still enjoy if it were prepared for her. This is different from true leisure, such as watching a movie, which can only be enjoyed if a person does it for herself. Some people may enjoy meal preparation. Much labor, paid and unpaid, has a leisure component in addition to a labor component, but there is nothing unique about unpaid labor in this respect.

Substantial sociological literature documents the way women's work is divided between paid and unpaid labor.[20] Women spend substantially more than half of their working hours doing unpaid labor. Women enjoy fewer leisure hours than do men. Allocating time to unpaid labor is a choice that women make in considering how to improve the circumstances of their families as well as their own circumstances. The social organization whereby more of women's work is performed in the home than men's may result from historic or current gender discrimination in law and culture, from women's socially or biologically determined greater commitment to children, or from other unexplored causes.

Nonetheless, the fact that women perform more home labor should not reduce the value of that work. Second-wave feminism from the 1960s to the present and the antidiscrimination laws of the same time period have brought substantial changes in women's paid labor force participation, with a particular increase among middle-class women, who previously had spent less time in the paid labor market than lower income women. Yet this radical change in paid labor force participation has not brought a similar change in the distribution of home labor. The time men spend at home labor, reported as a fraction of the time women spend, has changed only slightly, and that change is accounted for by a slight drop in the amount of women's home labor, not an increase in men's absolute hours.[21] Home labor as an area of significant concern to women's working lives does not appear to be temporary. Therefore, it is critical to push for that work to be treated equally with paid work, and not just to seek the equality of treatment of both men and women in the paid labor force.

THE CASE FOR EQUAL TREATMENT OF MEN'S AND WOMEN'S WORK

The significance of home labor in women's working lives endures, just as the significance of wage labor in men's lives endures. The increasing significance of wage labor in women's lives does not change this reality. Thus if we wish to be vigilant in pursuit of gender equality, we should be vigilant in asking that unwaged labor be subject to the same benefits and burdens as waged labor. If we are willing to live with partially commodified wage labor or if we see a benefit to it, we must have partially commodified home labor. This call for equal treatment between waged and unwaged labor with respect to commodification concerns is supported by several observations. The first observation is that wage labor is not entirely commodified. The second is that home labor is already partially commodified. The third is that affections motivate workers in the wage labor market as they do in the home, because wage laborers work both on behalf of and for the benefit of those with whom they have intimate relations.

Wage labor is not entirely commodified. Although we might expect some Law and Economics scholars to use wage labor as an example of reasonably complete commodification, Radin would contest that description. According to Radin, we as a culture are conflicted between those aspects of wage labor that we recognize as both fungible and removed from personhood and those that we consider integral to personhood. As a result, we do not have an actual free market in wage labor, but instead regulate heavily in areas ranging from occupational safety to collective bargaining to racial discrimination. Those regulations reflect a societal understanding of employment as having plural meaning, with both marketable and nonmarketable attributes coexisting. No doubt there is no societal consensus on where the line of regulation should be drawn, but it is easy to see that plural meanings have been and continue to be accommodated in the paid labor field.

Radin discusses wage labor in this respect, drawing on Hannah Arendt's terminology of "work" versus "labor" but using the terms differently. To Radin, work is partially commodified but has a noncommodified aspect, whereas labor is entirely commodified—"Laborers are sellers: fully motivated by money, exhausting the value of their activity in the measure of its exchange value."[22] Fortunately, Radin thinks most people are workers. For workers, "there is an irreducibly non-market or non-monetized aspect of human interaction going on between seller and recipient, even though a sale is taking place at the same time."[23] Unlike laborers, money does not fully motivate workers, and the value of their activity cannot be fully understood by its price.

Although Radin does not discuss a scale by which one is a worker at one end and a laborer at the other, she does discuss artists first and shoe salespeople later. The difference between these, however, might matter to the culture at large when deciding whether to worry about commodification. By this taxonomy, family labor is toward the artists' end of the spectrum; its nonmarket or personal attributes dominate in the popular understanding. We might, however, want to object to the categorical assumptions made along this spectrum. Probably some artists, and some family members, are almost entirely mercenary, and probably some salespeople are "artists." Our policy understandings will be shallow if we fail to see nonmarket aspects at work not only when they are obvious, as in the case of the artist or the family laborer, but also when they are not obvious, as in the case of the shoe salesperson. Radin wants to encourage us to foster the nonmarket aspects of all activities.

Although I agree with Radin on this goal, I think the inverse goal is also important: to see the economic aspect of activities that do not appear to be economically motivated. If plurality of understanding is the goal, not just noncommodification, the goal is justified. For this reason, I encourage some attention to the economics of home labor when making policy decisions, without forfeiting what is uniquely personal about it.

What works for paid labor ought to work for domestic labor. The claim I wish to make is that domestic labor embodies attributes of personhood that we may think imprudent to commodify in a real market; but, at the same time, we can understand domestic labor as susceptible to economic reasoning. The comparison to wage labor is apt not only in bringing unwaged labor closer to the wage labor standard but also in understanding that the wage labor standard contains seeds of the rejection of commodification that many feel should attach to home labor.

Just as important to the call for equality between wage and home labor is the observation that domestic labor is already commodified. There is already a market (or could reasonably be a market) for almost every task that falls within my description of home labor. Clear concrete problems for paid domestic workers arise from a cultural desire to deny that this is so, as I discuss later in the chapter. There is also an interesting desire to distinguish paid domestic work from unpaid domestic work, to distinguish what Dorothy Roberts calls the menial from the spiritual.[24] Consider commodification critic James Boyd White's analysis of the child care people provide to their own children: "Such work cannot be segmented into functions and then made the material of the market process, actual or hypothetical, for what the child requires is the sustained presence of, and interaction with, a loving and respectful person, something no alternative can supply."[25] This distinction does not square with many people's experiences. Race, class, and immigration status come to the forefront when we consider why the line between spiritual and menial labor is drawn around paid domestic work; Roberts makes the case that this line is racialized. In addition, the important gender roles of the middle-class household, where there is no paid domestic labor, may be supported by a denial of the reality of an existing market in home labor. Denying the reality of an existing market assists in maintaining the image of the unpaid household laborer as a nonworker and creates an illusion of her work as primarily an expression of affections demonstrated through her activities.

A final potential substantive difference between waged and unwaged labor, which could be the implicit ground on which to treat them differently, may be the relationships surrounding home labor: the emotional relationship between the worker and the beneficiaries. However, we cannot universalize wage labor as functioning without those relationships. Work in a family business can be waged as can work in a small business, work in a sole proprietor business, or work in the home as a paid domestic laborer. Even work in a large business includes important localized relationships among workers. Moreover, most people in the wage labor market probably consider family members to be beneficiaries of their work through wages returned to the family. Indeed, Arlie Hochschild, who popularized the concern about women's double work day in her 1989 book *The Second Shift,* has turned her focus to the study of the relational significance of wage labor.[26] She concludes that individuals today seek and find many of the emotional benefits of family life in the workplace now that the home carries the burden that was once associated with the rushed workday.

The claim for equality in how we treat work, both men's and women's, proceeds on several fronts. It cannot be especially harmful to commodify women's work; instead, such commodification carries the same risks, not qualitatively worse ones, as other types of work. In saying this, we must be mindful of several things. First, wage labor is not fully commodified, and domestic labor is already partially commodified. Second, it may be argued that the relationships between workers and beneficiaries is substantively different for paid and unpaid workers. But we may decide that that is a line too starkly drawn. Not only do most workers in the paid labor market consider family members to be the beneficiaries of their work, but much paid work also involves family-like relationships, sometimes literally, as in a family business, and sometimes metaphorically.

Finally, we should question why the substantive line between commodifiable and noncommodifiable labor is also a substantive gender line. This point is discussed in the following section, in which I note that many of the areas where commodification concerns arise touch on women's labor. Given that fact, we need to question what notions of femininity govern in those situations.

Women as Noncommodifiable: Questioning the Origins of an Idea

Does concern about the comparison between wage labor and home labor commodification grow out of an implicit assumption that there is something intrinsically different about home labor? We might want to ask whether it is coincidental, or instead highly relevant, that the intrinsic difference at play in analysis also cuts along gender lines: women's work, hereby, would be essentially nonmarketable. Consider the problems with assuming that women are inclined to make gifts of attributes of their personalities. Women serve, men sell. It is a familiar notion about which many feminists have been skeptical.

THE GENDER LINE: CASHLESS WOMEN

At a practical level, women should at least be wary of anti-commodification arguments, because these arguments arise when women receive money for something, not when women are paying money for something. The argument is used most frequently in legal discourse when talking about women receiving money for surrogate parenting and sexual contact, and herein for household labor. Although Radin extends the argument into gender-neutral territories such as housing, most of the commodification red flags are raised by her and by others when discussing women's commodification.

One might respond that the emphasis of the anticommodification argument is that some aspect of women's personhood is going to be sold, not that women are about to receive money. It is the sale that is objectionable, not that women may end up with cash. Consider, though, that it is not uncommon to find people who approve of altruistic transfer in these same areas, for example, human egg donation and surrogacy. In fact, the current fee caps in both of these fields reflect that ideal in practice: donors are not supposed to be too motivated by money, so fees are held down to ensure that there is a partially altruistic motivation for donating. In these cases, it seems arguable that the difference a woman experiences may simply be whether money comes to her, and how much, as compared to other wage labor that she might similarly perform from partially altruistic motivation. This difference occurs in the name of noncommodification. It is worth asking whether Anderson's concern about exploitation as a result of the commodification of women's reproductive capacity might just as easily turn into exploitation from noncommodification, and not just in a "non-ideal" world. Here the mixed motivations of women are exploited by highlighting the altruistic aspects of those motives in a discriminatory fashion. Only *women's* mixed motives relating to feminine activities are highlighted and offered as justification for leaving women without cash. Mixed motivations in the labor force at large do not require regulatory practices aimed at keeping wages down.

Social practices also exist in which the characterization of the problem as "withholding money from women" seems even more apt at the practical level than "preventing the sale of women," given the particular form that current decommodification takes. Prostitutes and pimps have a relationship that results where prohibition on sale ensures that although a female attribute is being sold, a woman is not getting most of the money. The "transitional balancing" questions raised by commodification and prostitution have been widely debated elsewhere. I raise it to illustrate that protecting women from sale does not necessarily go hand in hand with preventing women from receiving cash. Women can be sold and remain relatively cashless. Few would argue that the current form of the criminalization of prostitution is intended or designed for the protection of prostitutes, and so the lack of connection between noncommodification (and its female cashlessness) and sale is hardly remarkable. But in the reproductive areas of surrogacy and egg donation, noncommodification ideals drive the policy of leaving women relatively cashless despite their (partial?) sale.

We do not usually see the anticommodification argument raised as forcefully when things typically associated with male personhood are being sold.

Although it may be that women's personhood is more at risk for being inappropriately objectified and commercialized, we should at least consider an alternative understanding of why commodification concerns focus on women's issues. It may have as much to do with notions of femininity and a desire to elevate a romantic essentialism about femininity as it does with a desire to protect women's integrity. Consider Anderson's argument that women's reproductive labor is inappropriately alienated by surrogacy because a surrogate mother must "divert [her labor] from the end which the social practices of pregnancy rightly promote—an emotional bond with her child."[27] It is not clear why the end Anderson prefers for women's labor must be extinguished by money, but it is clear her argument leaves women without money for their labor. If a reinscription of the public–private sphere ideology on which market rhetoric thrives occurs around women's home labor, it may depend on a particular notion of femininity that has as one of its characteristics cashless women. Perhaps Anderson recognizes this but sees it as a necessary trade-off for the preservation of familial bonds. She does not explain, though, why it is a trade-off, and why markets and monetary exchange cannot coexist with expressions of affection in a realistic reflection of women's mixed motivations. We have the example of wage labor as an area in which monetary exchange and mixed motivations coexist.

This is not to say that the anticommodification argument is insincere. But at least Radin readily admits that gut instinct plays a significant, perhaps deciding role in drawing a line between things essential to personhood that should not be commodified and things that are less essential to personhood and therefore can be commodified.[28] These "gut instincts" must be informed by cultural gender understandings.

It certainly seems plausible that what makes us uncomfortable about selling female reproductive capacity, for example, is its subversion of the motherhood role, not just its potential to lead to exploitation. In contrast, consider the rather dull academic reaction to the sale of sperm. Attaching anticommodification concerns only to women is a reincarnation of the old public–private split whereby things feminine are nonmarket. Domestic labor has such a strong parallel with wage labor in terms of its content and the role it plays in a worker's life that the anticommodification concern raised against only home labor seems a clear case of reinscribing gender roles.

Certainly there is room for the argument that commodification of things such as housing and wage labor harms male personhood. The fact that we are more concerned about commodification of women's personhood does not mean that we have erred with respect to women; we might have erred with respect to men. Radin's work suggests this. But we must at least consider the gender line in the anticommodification discourse and its possible origins in gut instincts, including our own, which we might not want to trust. And in deciding whether we are right to permit partial commodification of "men's" personal attributes, such as wage labor, we need to ask which gut instinct is stronger: the one that permits wage labor, or the one that doesn't permit market analysis of home labor. The partial commodification of wage labor is acceptable to most people in a world of scarce resources that is as thoroughly organized around markets as our own. Much that is personal is created and produced on the market, and home labor is not special in that respect.

This argument reinforces my claim for the equality of treatment between home and wage labor, and further suggests that different treatment on commodification grounds tracks different treatment in other areas, such as reproductive capacities, while falling straight along gender lines.

HELP FROM THE HISTORY OF NOTIONS OF DOMESTIC LABOR

We should care why surrogacy contracts are deemed illegal: is it because the human dignity of child and mother are threatened, or because, by selling her reproductive capacity, the mother undermines traditional family roles? We must be skeptical of our ability to produce a coherent answer to that question. Similarly, we need to know why we instinctively resist the commodification of home labor. There may be a difference between noncommodified values at a deep level and sentimentalization.

To sort out that difference, we have to scrutinize what women are actually doing in the home and not romanticize it. It is dangerous to pretend that the reason domestic labor is not understood as work is that there is something essentially too close to personal human identity involved in performing it. The crucial question is whether work in the home is not understood as work because women do it; that is, is work in the home doctrinally cast as an expression of affection at least in part because that explanation justifies women's inferior economic status?

One way to explore the question is through a search of doctrinal origins. Reva Siegel's work is particularly useful for this project.[29] She claims that sentimentalization of women's home labor occurred as a mechanism for maintaining gender stratification in the face of a moment of possible transformation in status relations. If the sentimental notion of home labor in law is arguably born out of instrumentalism working against women, then we want to be careful when saying that those sentimental notions are integrally connected to women's human dignity. Siegel has tracked the legal response to the Married Women's Property acts and the earnings statutes of the nineteenth century. Before their enactments, legal understanding of women's home labor had been clearly and openly economic, with men owning their wives' labor and that labor viewed primarily as having monetary value. Both statutory reforms had the potential to completely change the status relationships between husbands and wives, and the texts of the statutes suggested they could do so by giving wives economic rights in all their labor, including their labor at home. Siegel carefully examines the early judicial interpretations of those statutes and concludes that judges limited them by minimizing the economic significance of home labor so as not to disrupt labor relations within the home. Although the economic value of home labor had been openly acknowledged in the past, judges introduced a sentimentality to home labor that had not previously informed legal discourse, even though it was available in the discourse outside of law at the time. The history of how this work became sentimentalized tells us that it was not women who infused the work with its aura of domestic love.

This is not to say that the suspicious origins of the idea that home labor is not wealth generating should determine how we look at home labor today. Origins are not decisive. I have, for example, argued that the questionable gender presumptions of Gary Becker and the original proponents of economic understandings of the family should not prevent feminists from employing economic understandings. But if the different understandings of unwaged home labor and wage labor are not intrinsic, if they are historically placed within women's struggle for economic rights, then we should be asking whether it is particularly helpful or instead harmful to be viewing home labor as different from wage labor.

The foregoing serves as a partial response to Anderson's concern that commodification invites exploitation. It seems just as plausible to argue that pricelessness invites exploitation. Refusing to consider the economics of home labor perpetuates the idea that women are inclined to serve and to gift their work. It would be a strange scenario whereby affections that accompany labor penalize rather than enhance the value of that labor, admitting that value has a material component for women as well as for men.

Even if rhetoric influences relations, the foregoing should leave us wondering why those who are interested in the impact of rhetoric dislike economics so strongly. The belief that rhetoric may reorganize understanding does not demonstrate that there is no role for economics if reorganization is in order. To the contrary, if there is power in the observation that analysis can remake relations, economic analysis may be an important creative force in this particular context in which current relations are not ideal. This single context, in which gender relations might benefit from the reimagining that economics might provide, throws a wrench into the general claim that economics should be "vigorously resist[ed]" because language may be constitutive.[30] That claim must instead recognize context.

Applications of the Argument

The anticommodification literature routinely treats commodification, or partial commodification, as a necessary evil where it applies. Radin has identified this as the double bind: wanting a perfect world of noncommodification but accepting that commodification may be necessary in an imperfect world. I think the case for economic or market reasoning can be made more affirmatively than that.

Consider White's argument that the way we speak has a constitutive effect on what we speak about. To White, this is a strong argument against economic rhetoric. But it is not evident why this conclusion must follow from his analysis. Even if economic rhetoric remakes relations, that may be a positive development in some areas, with domestic labor being a prime example. White's analysis purports to critique economic rhetoric as an abstract idea to be "vigorously resist[ed]."[31] There is something conservative about this conclusion: it depends on the idea that there is something very valuable to preserve in current discourse. That discourse does not float in the air but has a particular context, and we need to look at that context to know whether remaking understandings would be a positive or negative development.

I think it is important to consider the costs of sentimentality. What harms are created by an ideal of noncommodification? One answer might be found in the gender equality argument made earlier. A second might lie in concrete doctrine: economics is not a necessary evil but an additional tool of analysis that permits us to see one more facet of a phenomenon. That new angle opens up additional creative opportunities for problem solving. My task in this essay is not only to make a space for economic understandings in the abstract. I am interested in the benefits of an economic perspective on domestic labor. In that light, consideration should be given to what economics can add to the following concrete doctrinal problems associated with home labor.

Welfare

Nowhere is the need for an economic perspective on women's domestic labor more pressing than in the welfare discourse. Mothers who receive Temporary Assistance for Needy Families (TANF) are almost by definition caregivers to those children. Children in poverty who are eligible for aid need not only marketable goods, such as food, shelter, and clothing; they also need supervision, education, household management including food preparation and laundry, and caregiving to ensure a measure of personal welfare. Typically, they receive the latter from a parent, usually a mother or another woman who plays a mothering role.

It is not a difficult task for an economist to attach economic value to this contribution by a TANF parent. The New Home Economists have brought an analysis to divorce law that gives an account of women's caregiving and home management as contributing to family wealth and welfare in a manner that is economically equivalent to wage labor. Although these economists have focused their energies on divorce law that applies primarily to the middle and upper classes, the work performed by caregivers is in many ways similar across class lines. To the late twentieth-century economist, there is moral equivalence between paid and unpaid work in terms of productivity. The economist also brings an understanding of what will be lost in terms of nonmonetary income and material welfare if an unpaid worker must reallocate her time to paid labor.

In contrast, the all-too-familiar complaint that the welfare system itself is responsible for poverty is built on an understanding that home labor is not, in fact, work. In the words of former presidential candidate Robert Dole, "real welfare reform must include a real work requirement, which in no uncertain terms requires able-bodied welfare recipients to find a job, not stay at home, and not stay in a training program forever, but to go to work in a job, hopefully in a real job in the private sector. When it comes to escaping poverty, we know that the old American work ethic was true, because work works."[32]

Dole's comments reflect the common refrain in the public discourse on welfare: welfare recipients by definition do not work; a work ethic must be cultivated among welfare recipients, and real work is at a job in the private sector, not "stay[ing] at home." If we bring an economic understanding to home labor, Dole's comments seem fraught with troubling analysis. Moreover, potential solutions to the welfare "problem" would be much better crafted were the productivity of child rearing a factor in the analysis.

For those who think that the role of caretaking in the home is significant, this common spin on welfare is problematic. But one might respond with a case for public support of child rearing that does not use economic rhetoric. We might instead argue that mothering is a competing value with work, equally deserving of society's active support. We would not be arguing that child rearing is itself work but only that Dole is wrong in placing work above all else. What is gained by arguing that home labor is economically and morally equivalent to wage labor?

The answer is partially strategic. If the moral claim for societal support of wage labor proceeds on the theory that wage labor can be judged by a certain set of criteria, if unpaid domestic labor measures up to wage labor on these same terms, then society should support home labor. If this were a purely instrumental point, it might seem an inappropriate argument at the academic level, being appropriate instead only for a strategy room. But more might be said for this approach, if Dole's basic instinct that work is valuable has any merit.

Sociologist William Julius Wilson has argued that work is the organizing structure of the human biography.[33] In this regard, he sounds like many neoconservative academics and commentators who fault a "culture of poverty," meaning a culture in which work is not valued, for the economic plight of the very poor in American urban areas. But unlike these neoconservatives, Wilson argues that joblessness is a result of economic structure, which creates social isolation among those who cannot find work.[34] Wilson is friendlier than most liberals to the notion that there may be a distorted work ethic among the "truly disadvantaged," but he views that ethic as the result of joblessness, not the cause of joblessness. Unfortunately, Wilson does not go the extra step in asking whether uncompensated labor in the home demonstrates a healthy work ethic. Instead, he favors policies that promote paid employment on an equal basis for all Americans. Wilson taps into an understanding of the importance of work on which there is a broad societal consensus. Wilson may be right that work is deeply understood as an organizing structure of human biography, and he may be very much in need of a better understanding of unpaid home labor in order to bring it within his definition of work.[35]

Consider the argument put forward by Mark Kelman.[36] Kelman defends the decision not to tax imputed income because such a decision preserves individual liberty to conduct private activities outside the market. His line is market and nonmarket, rather than productive versus unproductive. Kelman makes no distinction here between a person's underutilization of skills by, for example, training as a physician but spending her days on the beach versus working without pay in the home. This is an insult to the unpaid home laborer and highlights the difficulty with de-emphasizing the economic nature of home labor. Should the value of home labor rise and fall with the value on sunbathing? Even most people who are truly sympathetic to welfare recipients would agree with Wilson in putting work above leisure as a personal good. Consequently, it is particularly important to appreciate the economic aspects of the activities of a TANF mother who is taking care of her children.

In this context, dignity is an important component of economic rhetoric. Economic rhetoric recovers women's work from the misunderstanding that it is unproductive and that the ethic it reflects is similar to that of the sunbather. Economic rhetoric also has an important pragmatic, policy component. The need for substitute care should not be an afterthought but a core economic difficulty with workfare programs, and it must be better understood in the mainstream debate on welfare.

Paid Domestic Workers

Paid domestic labor is still almost exclusively performed by women, but as a profession it is not representative of women across racial and socioeconomic lines. Instead, paid domestic laborers are historically and presently overwhelmingly women of color, immigrants, or both. According to the Bureau of Labor Statistics, 691,000 people are "private household workers" in the United States, meaning that they perform either child care or cleaning in a private home for pay.[37] There are another 555,400 recorded as doing home health care for pay, and 501,900 as providing child day care outside of the home for pay.[38] These three categories alone represent 1,748,300 workers of record, almost all of whom are women. For example, of the 691,000 private household workers, 96.3 percent are women.[39] The majority of those who perform housecleaning are classified by the Census Bureau as Black or Hispanic (51 percent). A substantially disproportionate number of private household workers overall are Black or Hispanic (nearly 44 percent). These statistics do not include launderers, drivers, secretaries, gardeners, dog walkers, grocery delivery workers, or the numerous other job classifications that encompass the work of the unpaid household worker.[40]

Thus, discussions of whether home labor should be commodified proceed from the outset on a premise that insults the population of women who already perform domestic labor for pay. Quite simply, the market already exists. Paid domestic workers bear an extremely unfair burden generated by the precise mode of analysis I criticize: the desire to construe home labor as something other than work. The problem of the pricelessness of unpaid home labor bears down on the paid domestic laborer, both in broad social understandings and concretely through impairment of the ability to achieve an even remotely level playing field on which to sell her labor. The former point can be illustrated through an examination of a few of the labor laws that apply to paid domestic workers. The latter point can be illustrated through a look at the tax treatment of unpaid labor.

Domestic workers are explicitly exempted from coverage by the National Labor Relations Act (NLRA), the Occupational Safety and Health Act (OSHA), and to some extent almost all workers' compensation statutes. The exemptions are not on grounds related to the size of the employer or the number of employees. There is no available legislative history explaining the NLRA's exemption, although racial discrimination played a significant role. Early state labor law suggests that the exemption is related to the idea that the home is about emotions, not industry. In a 1939 decision, a judge refused to give a domestic worker the right to picket his worksite under state labor law because the home is the "abiding place of affections, esp[ecially] domestic affections."[41] This notion of affections, so prevalent in describing the home labor of the unpaid houseworker, stripped the paid domestic worker of basic employment rights under labor laws. The OSHA exemption applies only to "ordinary domestic household tasks" such as cooking, child care, and cleaning.[42] OSHA's exemption is said to be "on public policy grounds," which go entirely unstated. If this means that the grounds are obvious, we can only wonder why it should be obvious that paid domestic workers are different from all other paid workers to whom society feels it should guarantee a safe work environment. The attempt to remove paid domestic workers from the formal economy is one serious consequence of the general desire to view household labor of either sort as being without economic consequence.

Economic understanding can help us even more concretely to understand some of the reasons, in addition to those of race and class stratification, why paid domestic labor is so poorly compensated. There is a reasonable argument that unpaid domestic labor receives a tax subsidy, whereas paid domestic labor does not. As a result, the price that can be charged for paid domestic labor must be lower than it otherwise could be in order to compete with the tax subsidy given to unpaid domestic labor. Once explained, this point underscores the benefits of economic analysis applied to domestic labor, in this case revealing a market distortion that works against paid domestic workers.

Housework performed in the home by a family member is not taxable income for the purposes of the federal income tax, despite the general rule that nonmonetary income and income from informal economies is taxable.[43] The exception is for income that does not come from a market bargain, whether it is monetary or not. This is thought to exclude household labor, which is prejudged as unbargained-for labor. Economists and many tax scholars have recognized the difficult distortions that the failure to tax imputed income introduces into the family economy both in terms of decision making about paid labor force participation versus home labor and in terms of distributional issues surrounding government benefits.[44] The failure to tax imputed income from unpaid household labor works as a tax subsidy that favors unwaged over wage labor, and a tax subsidy that favors unpaid home labor in particular. As a result, a person deciding whether to allocate time to paid or unpaid labor may take into account the extent to which wages from paid labor will be reduced by taxes, whereas value produced by home labor will be enjoyed in full. It seems plausible that there are cases where this calculation does occur, as women figure out the high cost of returning to the paid labor force after the birth of a child and consider the cost of purchasing child care out of after-tax wages when they could provide that child care themselves without taxation. Recent scholarship on this topic relies on an understanding of the economic productivity of home labor and is an example of the insights that can come from an economic understanding.

So far analysis within the tax context has only examined the impact of tax subsidies on the unpaid house worker. However, the failure to tax unpaid housework also impacts the paid domestic worker. Because the majority of home labor is unpaid, the paid domestic worker competes for a wage against a tax-subsidized unpaid worker. This may be one of the factors that drives down the wages of paid domestic workers. This hypothesis should be explored by economists and, if it appears valid, should be an important public policy issue for law reform. This issue could not be understood without an understanding of the economic productivity of home labor and the wealth created by it.

The paid domestic worker is the victim by association with the unpaid domestic worker, both by suggestion and directly. First, the paid worker is denied the benefits of labor law, in some cases explicitly on the grounds that the home is the site of affections, or that housework, as distinct from other work in the home, raises unique but unspecified public policy concerns. Like the unpaid worker, the paid domestic worker's job is something different from all other work, whether performed in a house, as a sole employee, or part time. The waged and unwaged domestic workers are conflated. When one fails to see the unpaid domestic laborer in economic terms, it becomes more difficult to see the paid domestic laborer in economic terms. This might help to explain the absence of labor law protections to paid domestic workers. The families who employ domestic workers join in this perspective; the household that is safe enough for their domestic life must be beyond government safety regulations for their employees. Second, in addition to that suggestive function, the failure to understand unpaid labor in economic terms has a more direct impact. By not taxing unpaid home labor, the competitive price of paid home labor is reduced. This reduction may assist in perpetuating poverty among paid domestic workers. Conversely, at those times when a price might be placed on unpaid home labor in law, as in the wrongful death suit or the divorce context, that price has been deflated by distortions in the market for paid domestic labor.

Social Security

The system of compensating unpaid home laborers through spousal and survivor's benefits reveals a legal and cultural reliance on the family economy to provide old-age security to home laborers. Home laborers receive Social Security only if they are married or were once married for at least ten years to the same person, and they cannot combine that benefit with credits in the Social Security system accrued on their own accounts in the paid labor market if they have spent some time working in each place. This makes home laborers vulnerable to the vicissitudes of family structure, thereby both limiting their choices as to family structure and placing the burden of an unchosen unconventional family structure on the shoulders of home laborers. For the paid worker, these family structure issues are irrelevant to entitlement under the system.

A Social Security system that provides for unpaid domestic workers on their own account would be far superior to the system we currently have. One option would be a guaranteed income support to all citizens. This system, however, would be a huge departure from our current work-based system because it would need to include both the sunbather and the child rearer on equal footing. Less of a departure is possible. An economic understanding of the productivity of home labor could permit home laborers to stand on their own in the Social Security system just as wage laborers do. Contributions could be made to the Social Security system for being materially productive. These contributions could be made on either a voluntary or a mandatory basis, just as the participation of wage laborers is mandatory. But contributions from unpaid laborers cannot be assessed without some method of calculation. Economic valuation on which to base contributions in the absence of a real market is complicated but possible, but not if we foreclose economic understandings of home labor on commodification grounds.

Contracts

The area of contract law that most directly implicates home labor is the law of premarital or marital agreements. This peculiar set of rules reveals a rejection of an economic understanding of home labor in favor of a highly sentimental one. Although this has not always been the case, when spouses today sign an agreement about the disposition of either property or income in the event of death or divorce, courts generally will enforce it. However, when spouses sign an agreement whereby one will pay the other for home labor, courts will not enforce it. Courts reason that despite the parties' agreement to monetize the home labor, it is of a personal nature that removes it from the sphere of ordinary premarital agreements.

The result of courts' treatment of home labor is a striking inequality in the treatment of waged versus unwaged labor, or traditionally male versus traditionally female labor. The fact that wage labor is "financial" hardly makes it irrelevant to familial care and emotions. Most people work for wages in order to spend those wages caring for family. In this respect, we are permitting agreements now that are deeply personal simply because we perceive them as economic in nature.

Once again, the question arises: Are enforceable housework agreements a utopian vision? The preceding analysis, in that it is about the substance of legal marriage, cannot answer that question. However, my analysis insists that the answer be the same for unwaged labor as it is for waged labor. To create equality between waged and unwaged labor, one must have an economic understanding of home labor. Economics advances our understanding of the multifaceted nature of activities within the home.

Those things that can be monetized can be owned in premarital agreements and protected from a spouse in premarital agreements. Those things not monetized cannot be bargained for legally, carry no personal entitlement, and receive no protection. Whatever commodification risks attend to enforcing housework agreements attend equally to enforcing agreements that keep wages and property inaccessible to a spouse.

Divorce

Divorce law presents more opportunities to use economic understandings of home labor, and in this area legal academics have done so with increasing frequency. However, more opportunities remain. For example, the division of property at divorce shows what an economic understanding can bring to a discussion of family law policy that is currently missing. Although most families

have no substantial assets to divide at divorce and instead live off of earned income, the following property example illustrates the tendency of judges to ignore the economic understanding of home labor. Before the divorce reform of
the last thirty years, divorce meant that property, when there was any to distribute, remained with its owner of record, usually the male wage earner. After
the divorce-law reforms in many states, courts began to consider the source of
wealth as relevant to distribution upon divorce, in addition to record of ownership. This change is beneficial to women because these reformed statutes require courts to consider not only the contributions of a wage earner to the
accumulation of wealth but also the contributions of a homemaker. This development shows a subtle understanding of the role of home labor in wealth
creation. When the family owns property, not only the wage earner but the
home laborer as well has worked to accumulate that property, whether directly by increasing the value of the asset through unpaid labor (as through
home improvements) or indirectly by providing day-to-day family subsistence
that freed up cash for the purchase of assets. The statutes have increasingly
been interpreted to mean that full-time homemakers, under this specific provision, can receive a substantial portion of family wealth even if it was purchased with cash held in the name of a full-time wage-earning spouse. In some
states, this has become a presumption of a 50–50 split of assets.

One might guess from this emerging jurisprudence that courts are compre-
hending the economic significance of home labor, but there are hints that this
is not the case. It appears that courts are instead reinterpreting marital obligations as requiring wealth sharing without regard to contribution. If this is the
case, I do not argue that this reinterpretation is normatively undesirable. There
could be an argument that deemphasizing each person's contribution altogether may reflect some aspects of a better substantive marriage law. But under
current law, in which contribution to wealth does matter, I argue that present
interpretations mean that courts have failed to grasp fully the economic contribution of home labor. This is evidenced by courts' curious treatment of
women who both work in the wage labor market and also perform a substantial amount of the home labor, thus contributing to family wealth with wages
and with home labor. This mixture of contributions, as discussed earlier in the
essay, describes most women today. But when wage-earning women try to invoke additional considerations for contribution to wealth generated by home
labor, courts have responded that despite the language of the statute, those
provisions only cover the full-time homemaker.[45]

This judicial response indicates that courts are not recognizing the wealth
created by home labor but instead wish to show compassion for the very real
financial straights in which a full-time homemaker can find herself after divorce. If judges understood home labor as creating actual material wealth, the
home labor as well as the wage labor of a wage-earning homemaking spouse
would have to be counted as contributing to wealth creation. Women are

working longer combined hours than are men. Although this does not necessarily mean that they are contributing more economic value, that conclusion
is possible. The proposition is at least worth exploring. By refusing to credit
the home labor contributions of the wage-earning homemaking spouse, judges
are ignoring the economic value of the home labor of the majority of women.
The full-time homemaker is the exception today, not the rule, and divorce law
has no provision whatsoever for capturing the economic value generated by
home labor in the majority of cases. This results, at least in part, from a failure to bring a proper economic understanding of that labor into legal analysis, relying instead on an understanding of marriage roles as described by the
terms *breadwinner* and *homemaker*. Despite their apparent economic base,
these role designations have a social significance from which economics is almost entirely removed.

It is important to remember that we might decide that the amount of contribution should not be the decisive factor in determining property allocation
at the time of divorce. However, we may benefit from a clearer examination of
the proper outcomes of such policy options when informed by an economic
understanding. This exercise might help us to clarify our goals in divorce law
by presenting the possible understandings of legal obligations associated with
marriage, and force us to further examine the strengths and weaknesses of
marriage as the relevant institution for financially supporting the dependencies
arising from childhood, illness, and aging.

Caveats on the Use of Economics

Some practical risks attend the use of economic understandings of home labor.
First, there is a concrete risk that the deflated wages of the paid domestic
worker will be used to estimate the value of unpaid work, as they are in
wrongful death and divorce contexts. Analysts have to be cautious in deciding
which measure of the value of home labor to use. One might prefer opportunity cost as a measure—or a measure that aggregates the price of experts, such
as nurses, teachers, launderers, and cooks—in order to figure out the value of
home labor, rather that the price of generalist housecleaners in the domestic
labor market.[46] More importantly, reformers should be deeply concerned
about the low wages of paid domestic workers and place efforts at raising
those wages at the forefront of the debate over activity within the home. Finally, the use of economic understandings may, as some fear, diminish other
understandings in practice.

The answer to these concerns is to note carefully and be constantly mindful of distortions both in present valuation of home labor and in the alternative noneconomic understandings of the work. None of these reservations
justifies foregoing the very useful insights economics brings to the public policy questions surrounding women's home labor. We must remember the

distinction between identifying questions through economic understandings and producing answers. Producing answers requires that all conceptions of an activity be considered together. It also requires an extremely detailed examination of the empirical data, with attention to the limitations of empirical knowledge that come both from data collection methodology and from the fact that facts do not explain their own causes and cannot be taken as static starting points, even when they are verifiable.

Conclusion

The commodification critique is often a conversation stopper. Because markets do not capture the entire experience in question, they are thought to threaten the existence of what they cannot describe. In the context of a phenomenon that is highly commodified, this argument might lead to fruitful discussions of the appropriate methods of preserving nonmarket understandings. In the context of phenomena that are almost entirely nonmarket, however, the objection to commodification seems much weaker because it fails to consider the potential benefits that economic understandings can bring to the social relations surrounding that nonmarket phenomenon. Because many of women's activities have historically occurred outside of the market, a normative position against market reasoning about home activities is nearly equivalent to a normative position against market reasoning about women's activities. As long as women's economic power remains a central concern of feminist discourse, this aversion to market analysis is detrimental to feminist reform. Understanding the economic aspects of women's nonmarket activity is an important part of the transformative vision of a progressive feminism. Only after asking questions about the relationship between nonmarket reasoning and women's economic weakness can we decide what kinds of policy changes will benefit women both as a class and as divided by differences that are relevant to economic status. By comparison, concern about a world in which women's lives are stripped of all but their monetary value seems a fairly abstract one.

Notes

1. This essay was originally published at 9 Yale J. L. & Fem. 81, © 1997 Katharine B. Silbaugh. Reprinted with permission.

2. Katharine Silbaugh, *Turning Labor into Love: Housework and the Law,* 91 NW. U. L. Rev. 1 (1996).

3. *See* Margaret Jane Radin, *Contested Commodities* 104 (1996).

4. *Id.* at 105–6. The commodification literature is far too expansive to review in detail here.

5. Elizabeth Anderson, *Value in Ethics and Economics* 72–81 (1993).

6. *See* Martha Nussbaum, *Love's Knowledge* 106–24 (1990).

7. James Boyd White, *Heracle's Bow* 166, 164–174, 190 (1985).

8. Radin, *supra* note 3.

9. *See* Elisabeth M. Landes & Richard A. Posner, *The Economics of the Baby Shortage*, 7 J. Legal Stud. 323 (1978); *see* Lloyd R. Cohen, *Increasing the Supply of Transplant Organs: The Virtues of a Futures Market*, 58 Geo. Wash. L. Rev. 1 (1989).; *see* Comments, *Baby-Sitting Consideration: Surrogate Mother's Right to "Rent Her Womb" for a Fee*, 18 Gonz. L. Rev. 539 (1983); *see generally* Richard A. Posner, *Sex and Reason* (1992); *see* Gary S. Becker & George J. Stigler, *Law Enforcement, Malfeasance, and Compensation of Enforcers*, 3 J. Legal Stud. 1 (1974).

10. *See* Richard A. Posner, *Economic Analysis of Law* 201 (4th ed. 1992).

11. Mirabel Morgan, *The Total Woman* (1973).

12. Barbara Bergmann, *The Task of a Feminist Economics: A More Equitable Future*, in *The Impact of Feminist Research in the Academy* 132–33 (Christie Farnham ed., 1987).

13. Isabel V. Sawhill, *Economic Perspectives on the Family*, 106 Daedalus 115, 120–24 (1997). Others have followed. *See generally Beyond Economic Man* (Marianne A. Ferber & Julie A. Nelson eds., 1993).

14. *See* Julie A. Nelson, *The Study of Choice or the Study of Provisioning? Gender and the Definition of Economics*, in *Beyond Economic Man*, *supra* note 13, at 23.

15. *See* Joseph Raz, *Value Incommensurability: Some Preliminaries*, 86 Proc. Aristotelian Soc. 117, 128, 132–34 (1985–86).

16. *See* Marilyn Manser & Murray Brown, *Marriage and Household Decision-Making: A Bargaining Analysis*, 21 Int'l Econ. Rev. 31 (1980).

17. A bargaining analysis assumes complete self-interest as between spouses, an assumption that is probably no more plausible than one of complete altruism. *See* Paula England, *The Separative Self: Androcentric Bias in Neoclassical Assumption*, in *Beyond Economic Man*, *supra* note 13, at 37, 48. In *Rational Fools: A Critique of the Behavioral Foundation of Economic Theory*, 6 Phil. & Pub. Aff. 317 (1977), Amartya K. Sen first made this point about the limitations of economic thinking after one drops the implausible assumption of purely self-interested human behavior.

18. Radin, *supra* note 3, at 107.

19. *See* Viviana Rotman Zelizar, *Morals and Markets: The Development of Life Insurance in the United States* (1979).

20. *See* Silbaugh, *supra* note 2, at 10–13 (describing sociological literature on division of women's labor).

21. *See* Victor R. Fuchs, *Women's Quest for Economic Equality* 78 (1988); Silbaugh, *supra* note 2, at 8–9.

22. Radin, *supra* note 3, at 105.

23. *Id.* at 107.

24. *See* Dorothy E. Roberts, *Spiritual and Menial Housework*, 9 Yale J.L. & Feminism 51 (1997).

25. White, *supra* note 7, at 190.

26. *See* Arlie Russell Hochschild, *The Second Shift: Working Parents and the Revolution at Home* (1989); Arlie Russell Hochschild, *Work: The Great Escape*, N.Y. Times Magazine 50 (Apr. 20, 1997).

27. Anderson, *supra* note 5, at 82.

28. *See* Radin, *supra* note 3, at 11–12.

29. *See* Reva B. Siegel, *Home as Work: The First Woman's Rights Claims concerning Wives' Household Labor, 1850–1880*, 103 Yale L.J. (1994); Reva B. Siegel, *The Modernization of Marital Status Law: Adjudicating Wives' Rights to Earnings, 1860–1930*, 82 Geo. L.J. 2168, 2181–96 (1994). *See also* Amy Dru Stanley, *Conjugal Bonds and Wage Labor: Rights of Contract in the Age of Emancipation*, 75 J. Am. Hist. 472 (1988).

30. White, *supra* note 7, at 166.

31. *Id.* at 161, 164.

32. *Excerpts from Dole and Clinton Speeches on Redoing Welfare,* N.Y. Times A10 (Aug. 1, 1995).

33. *See* William Julius Wilson, *When Work Disappears* 73–75 (1996).

34. *See* William Julius Wilson, *The Truly Disadvantaged* 55–62, 109–24, 137–39 (1987).

35. *See id.;* Wilson, *supra* note 33, at 73–75.

36. Mark G. Kelman, *Personal Deductions Revisited: Why They Fit Poorly in an "Ideal" Income Tax and Why They Fit Worse in a Far from Ideal World,* 31 Stan. L. Rev. 831, 880 (1979).

37. Bureau of Labor Statistics, U.S. Department of Labor, *Employment and Earnings* A-25 (Feb. 1996).

38. Bureau of Labor Statistics, U.S. Department of Labor, *Employment, Hours and Earnings, U.S. 1990–1995* (Sept. 1995).

39. Bureau of Labor Statistics, U.S. Department of Labor, *Employment and Earnings* table 649 (Jan. 1994) (monthly).

40. I could only obtain racial classifications for the private household worker data, not for the home health care or public day care data, thus the incomplete reporting of race data here.

41. *State v. Cooper,* 285 N.W. 903, 905 (Minn. 1939) (quoting *Webster's New International Dictionary* (2d ed.)).

42. 29 C.F.R. § 1975.6 (1995).

43. *See* Nancy Staudt, *Taxing Housework,* 84 Geo. L.J. 1571, 1575–76 (1996).

44. For the decision-making component, *see* Edward J. McCaffrey, *Taxation and the Family: A Fresh Look at Behavioral Gender Biases in the Code,* 40 UCLA L. Rev. 983 (1993); and Richard A. Posner, *Conservative Feminism,* 1989 U. Chi. Legal F. 191. For the issue of the distribution of government benefits, *see* Staudt, *supra* note 43.

45. E.g., *In re Marriage of Banach,* 489 N.E. 2d 363, 369 (Ill. App. Ct. 1986); *In re Marriage of Stice,* 779 P. 2d 1020, 1027–28 (Ore. 1989).

46. *See generally* Euston Quah, *Economics and Home Production: Theory and Measurement* (1993) (exploring various studies that have measured the value of home labor and various techniques that can be used, along with strengths and weaknesses).

CHAPTER 16

Is There Agency in Dependency?

Expanding the Feminist Justifications for Restructuring Wage Work

Laura T. Kessler

Women, more so than men, perform the unpaid family caregiving work within our society.[1] This statement is supported by both a voluminous body of social science research and a cursory survey of the world around us. Women are primarily responsible for the care of children and housekeeping, whether or not they work outside the home for wages.[2] It is women, more so than men, who care for sick or disabled family members,[3] including elderly parents.[4] Although recent studies indicate that the amount of time spent by women on caregiving and housework has declined since the 1970s, women continue to spend considerably more time than men doing such work.[5] From the 1970s to the 1990s, the amount of time spent by women on such work declined from four times that spent by men to two or three times that spent by men.[6] Much of this small improvement is attributable to an overall decline in the hours of housework performed by women, rather than to an increase in such work performed by men.[7] When childcare and routine, stereotypically female tasks are considered, progress with regard to the gendered division of household labor is less remarkable still.[8]

The American workplace and employment discrimination laws have yet to address seriously this profound existential difference between men and women with regard to caregiving. Title VII has prohibited employment discrimination on the basis of pregnancy since 1978,[9] when Congress passed the Pregnancy Discrimination Act,[10] but it does not require employers to recognize women's caregiving responsibilities beyond the immediate, physical events of pregnancy and childbirth. The passage of the Family and Medical Leave Act of 1993 (FMLA),[11] which requires covered employers to provide employees up to twelve weeks of unpaid leave per year for the birth or adoption of a child or for the care of seriously ill family members, seemed to alter this state of affairs. However, a close examination of the FMLA reveals that it does little more than provide job security to some women in the case of childbirth. Neither of these statutes, which constitute the bulk of the United States' maternity and parental leave policies, provides for the most common employment leave needs of caregivers, who by all measures are disproportionately women. This lack of protection has resulted in a persisting labor force attachment gap between men and women that has had serious economic and social consequences for both women and children.

Why has employment discrimination law failed to address the conflicts between work and family that continue to disproportionately burden women? In particular, what explains the law's inability to recognize women's cultural caregiving? By cultural caregiving, I mean women's nonbiological care work that is understood by the law and society more broadly to be a function of gender socialization, an ethic of care, or love. The answer lies, in part, in the pervasive influence of certain core concepts underlying liberal and economic theory on cultural and legal discourse, and in the way legal decision makers rely on these concepts. Specifically, the theoretical constructs of autonomy, equality, and rational choice which constitute the foundations of our legal system possess a limited ability to recognize women's experiences that are not grounded in immutable biological difference.

The assumption underlying both liberal and neoclassical economic theory that humans are autonomous, unencumbered actors has formed the foundation for the current structure of the workplace and our employment discrimination laws, which are modeled on an "ideal worker" who has no caregiving responsibilities.[12] Equality theory similarly possesses a limited ability to recognize cultural differences between men and women such as women's caregiving, because cultural differences that are not universally true for all women escape categorization as sex-based classifications under the law. Finally, the oversimplified strain of neoclassical economic theory that has come to pervade our country's political and legal discourse has served to construct women's caregiving as a freely chosen endeavor that is undeserving of protection from discrimination within the workplace.

Legal feminists have responded to the assumptions of autonomy, equality, and choice with a rich set of critiques. Among them has been a call for the collective societal responsibility for dependency on the basis of social contract theory[13] and the assertion that care is a public good[14] or value.[15] The merits of such conceptualizations of care work have been hashed out extensively within the discourse, with the primary emergent concern focusing on the dangers of seeking public remedies for the problem of devalued care work.[16] I share this concern.[17] But the feminist critique of autonomy, equality, and choice I wish to focus on in this chapter is the suggestion by some scholars that women's caregiving is a condition of impaired agency arising from biological or social forces.[18] I call these responses the "stories of biology and gender socialization." According to these stories, women are propelled into caregiving work by their unique biological role in reproduction and by a pervasive societal system of gender. Further, women merit relief from these biological and social conditions through a more equal distribution of care work among women, men, employers, and the state.

The stories of biology and gender socialization successfully contest certain aspects of the prevailing theoretical construct, particularly the assumption of human autonomy. However, these stories cannot fully contest the existing paradigm. Although the dominant account of constrained agency at the center of much feminist theorizing has served as a valuable organizing principle for obtaining legal recognition of pregnancy and childbirth, it has proved less capable of addressing the rhetoric of choice that legitimates discrimination on the basis of women's cultural, that is, nonbiological, caregiving work.

If feminist legal theorists more fully explore the positive value and meaning of caregiving work to women, in addition to highlighting the undeniable experience of caregiving as a condition of oppression, then they could make more headway against rational choice justifications for discrimination against caregivers. My aim is to recover women's agency, however restricted and distorted by gender-based domination, from recent legal feminist accounts of women's care work. Such a thicker, more positive account of caregiving work may better serve to contest the rhetoric of choice that constructs women's caregiving as an invisible activity unworthy of legal recognition or public support and may serve to bring more women together across their differences. This chapter is part of a larger project in which I seek to develop a theory justifying support for care work on women's capacity for political agency within the context of their nurturing functions.

Women's Cultural Caregiving Work
and the Labor Force Attachment Gap

In an effort to garner societal recognition of women's caregiving, feminist theorists have worked to provide a rich, complex, problematized account of women's nurturing experiences. Liberal feminism began this project more than two decades ago by depicting the confinement of women to the private sphere of nurturing and homemaking as stultifying and oppressive.[19] As the liberal feminist critique has highlighted, caregiving is intensely physical. Because much caregiving work focuses on attending to bodily functions, such work often involves unpleasant, messy, and strenuous physical tasks.[20] It is women, primarily, who come into contact with feces, urine, vomit, blood, saliva, and mucus.[21] It is women, primarily, who literally carry, lift, and support others' bodies, whether young children or persons who are sick or elderly. Caregiving is also mentally taxing. Caregiving requires the ability to focus simultaneously on multiple tasks and to be attentive to the emotional needs of others. Such work can be self-annihilating, mind deadening, and repetitive. Caregiving can be dream deferring and socially isolating. This critique of the oppressive nature of women's caregiving responsibilities—caring for children, the sick, and the aged; cooking and cleaning; and the sexual and emotional nurturance of men—continues today.[22]

A more recent feminist project, both within law and other disciplines, explores the positive side of women's caregiving, if not by depicting caregiving work as necessarily or exclusively pleasurable then at least by asserting the fundamental morality of such work. Carol Gilligan's research showing that women and girls possess a unique ethic of care and responsibility is a classic example.[23] In law, Martha Fineman has articulated the moral basis for a theory of collective societal responsibility for dependency.[24] Critical Race Feminism has highlighted the social, political, and spiritual importance of family caregiving work for women of color, who historically have been deemed unfit to nurture their own children and who have never had the luxury of receiving state "protection" from the labor market.[25] Still other feminist scholars have depicted women's caregiving experiences as simultaneously pleasurable and painful, leading women both to fear separation from those they nurture and to seek independence from them,[26] and as both a source of power and oppressive role conformity for women.[27]

Concomitant with the wealth of feminist scholarship exploring the significance of caregiving to women has been a parallel exploration of the meaning in women's lives of wage work. Feminist scholars have depicted wage work as a source of intellectual fulfillment, empowerment, individuation, and social connection for women.[28] Yet feminist legal scholars also have criticized this positive depiction of wage work for ignoring the real harm, degradation, and oppression of the workplace experienced by less privileged women,[29] and most acutely experienced by women of color living in poverty.[30]

As this rich body of scholarship demonstrates, a woman's experiences of wage work and caregiving are dependent on her place within the larger social context and are as complex as the institutions of work and family themselves. Any consideration of the problems confronted by women caught in the intersection of family and market work must be attentive to differences among women both in its theoretical understanding and proposed solutions. Yet there is also a compelling need to identify commonalities among women and to resist the current trend, within the academy and without, to dismiss the continuing relevance of "women" as an analytic category.[31]

One such commonality is the fact that today, most women must work in order to support their families. Given the decrease in real wages over the last several decades, the breakdown of the family wage system,[32] and the emergence of the single-parent family as a prominent family form, the recent explosion of women's labor force participation can be explained as a matter of sheer economic necessity. An unprecedented divorce rate of 50 percent and an increase in out-of-wedlock births have left millions of women to struggle as the heads of households to support themselves and their children. Of families with children less than eighteen years old, about one-third are single-parent households.[33] Single women heads of household must work full time in the paid labor force to keep their families above the poverty line; many are unsuccessful.[34] Today, even married women's paid work is necessary to provide the basics for their families,[35] given the stagnation or, in the case of the least skilled, the substantial decline in the real wages of men.[36] Finally, studies show a correlation between married women's labor force participation and the rise of no-fault divorce.[37] With decreased opportunities under modern no-fault rules for women to receive alimony upon divorce,[38] married women's work serves as a form of insurance against impoverishment in the eventuality of divorce.[39] By 1998, more than three-quarters of mothers were participating in the labor force, including two-thirds of those with children under age six.[40]

These dramatic social and economic changes, however, do not tell the whole story. Labor force participation rates merely indicate whether women are working.[41] They do not reveal the extent of women's labor force participation, that is, whether it is full time or part time, permanent or temporary, or how much time women spend engaged in market work over any extended period.[42] Herein lies a second important commonality among women: women's disproportionate share of family caregiving and housework has resulted in a persistent labor force attachment gap between men and women. Although women's labor force participation has increased dramatically over the past three decades, only 50 percent of women actually negotiate full-time, year-round jobs together with family responsibilities.[43] The extent of involvement in paid work is even less for women with children under six years old; only 35 percent of such women participate in the labor force on a full-time, year-round basis.[44] Nearly three-fourths of part-time workers are women.[45] Women are more likely than men either to accept voluntarily or to be funneled into lower paying "mommy-track" professional jobs[46] and noncommissioned retail work.[47] "Contingent" workers—basically, workers with jobs that are not expected to last—are more likely than noncontingent workers to be women.[48] More than one-third of married mothers and nearly one-half of single mothers with children under age six do no market work.[49] In 1996, three out of four persons not in the labor force were women,[50] the majority, 70 percent, because of home or family responsibilities.[51]

The persistent attachment gap resulting from women's disproportionate caregiving responsibilities at home has had tangible negative economic and social consequences for women. The part-time, temporary, or otherwise contingent jobs to which women are often limited generally provide lower hourly wages than full-time positions,[52] tend to be less stable,[53] and are less likely to offer health insurance,[54] childcare benefits,[55] pension benefits,[56] or opportunities for advancement.[57] Even for women who work full time, career interruptions for nurturing responsibilities often translate into lower seniority, wages, and salaries in relation to male coworkers.[58] Such interruptions occur not just during a woman's childbearing years but later in life as well. Older women

who reduce their work hours or exit the workforce at the height of their earning capacity to care for elderly parents experience not only short-term losses
of wages but also potentially long-term reductions in pension income.[59]

Furthermore, women's disproportionate responsibility for caregiving at
home has consequences well beyond their reduced economic well-being. The
"feminization of poverty"[60] weakens women's bargaining power within marriage,[61] leaves women vulnerable to sexual abuse and domestic violence,[62] and
can decrease the likelihood of women gaining or keeping the custody of their
children upon divorce. Moreover, because women are the primary caretakers
of children in our society, the marginalization of women's wage work has resulted in the widespread poverty of children in America.[63] Finally, the failure
of our law to recognize women's work–family conflicts has, in large part,
shifted the burden of caregiving from one class of women to another—that is,
from economically privileged women able to conform to the rigid expectations
of the American workplace to low-paid domestic and childcare workers who
disproportionately are poor women and women of color.[64] As demonstrated
in the following section, the law's response to the labor force attachment gap
and the resulting marginalized economic status of women and children has
been minimal.

The Limited Response of Employment
Discrimination Law to the Attachment Gap:
Title VII, the Pregnancy Discrimination Act,
and the Family and Medical Leave Act

Current protections for women's disproportionate caregiving within the family, insofar as these responsibilities conflict with their ability to work for
wages, are limited to two different statutory enactments, Title VII and the
Family and Medical Leave Act, neither of which provides adequate support for
the most common leave needs of caregivers, who typically are women.

The model of formal equality and the categorical framework on which Title
VII is based have made it difficult for women to obtain workplace reforms that
recognize their cultural caregiving. Title VII, as amended by the Pregnancy
Discrimination Act (PDA), provides only limited protections for the physical
and immediate events of pregnancy and childbirth. It does little to address the
issue of women's most common caregiving responsibilities.

Courts have uniformly held that needs or conditions of a child that require
a mother's presence are not within the scope of the PDA. Thus, for example,
courts have held that women whose employers terminate, demote, or otherwise discipline them because of their need for workplace flexibility or time off
to breast feed, provide medical care to, adopt, or simply "rear" their children
are not protected by the PDA.

Title VII's disparate treatment theory has served women only to the extent that they can demonstrate that their family obligations will not interfere with their wage work. Thus, plaintiffs have been moderately successful in cases concerning hiring or promotion, where, absent any employment record, or at least any employment record for the job in question in the case of promotion, the perceived threat of a woman's family caregiving responsibilities can be dismissed as a stereotype. In contrast, plaintiffs have been far less successful in cases concerning demotion or termination, where either the plaintiff's direct requests or her employment record reveals that she requires an alternative work structure because of her family obligations.

Title VII's disparate impact theory, which does not require proof of discriminatory motive, is seemingly well suited to address the discrimination women experience at work on the basis of their cultural caregiving. For caregiving discrimination is typically the product not of hostile intent but of the distinctly American structure of work, which assumes that workers do not have competing family obligations. But even the disparate impact theory of discrimination is limited in its ability to address women's work–family conflicts. Most significantly, this theory possesses only a limited ability to address employer inaction, that is, the failure to provide adequate leave, a major source of harm to women who have significant caregiving obligations. Further, plaintiffs attempting to proceed under a disparate impact theory have been hindered by insurmountable problems of proof and the formidable business necessity defense.

Under the FMLA, women receive limited, unpaid job protection for instances when they or their family members are incapacitated due to pregnancy, childbirth, or serious illness. But women's typical caregiving responsibilities—caring for young but healthy children or elderly but not seriously ill parents, dealing with minor family illnesses, cooking and cleaning, transporting children or parents to routine medical appointments, and coping with unexpected family emergencies, that is, all the work that women disproportionately and invisibly perform within the family—does not even register as a blip on the radar screen of the U.S. legal system.

In a law review article, I review these statutes and judicial decisions applying and interpreting them in far greater detail.[65] In doing so, I demonstrate that our employment discrimination laws have failed to transform the male-centered norms that structure the American workplace beyond a minimal concession to women's experiences of pregnancy and childbirth.

To be sure, such statutes, particularly Title VII, facilitated the mass entrance of women into the workforce over the last three decades.[66] Employment discrimination laws were central to effecting this social transformation. Title VII has challenged discrimination in the hiring and promotion of women based on the stereotypical view that their status as caregivers makes them unsuitable for market work, both by reinforcing the perception of women as wage earners

and by providing some formal legal protections to women. The FMLA also
has afforded some women job security with regard to the significant life event
of childbirth. Still, an examination of judicial decisions applying and interpreting Title VII and the FMLA reveals that these laws are of limited use to women
who, once in the labor force, are demoted or terminated on the basis of their
cultural, that is, nonbiological, caregiving responsibilities to their families.

Root Causes: The Limits of Liberal and Economic Theory

A gap between a law's reach and the aspirations of those who seek
to use it to accomplish substantial societal reform is a common
enough phenomenon, but this is small consolation, and critics look
for explanations.

Katharine T. Bartlett, *Only Girls Wear Barrettes: Dress and
Appearance Standards, Community Norms, and Workplace Equality*
(Mich. L. Rev. 1994)

The current legal framework is unable to recognize women's cultural caregiving work as it impacts their labor force attachment. This section seeks to explain this failure. I propose that the liberal and neoclassical economic theories
that dominate our law have dictated the limited response to the conflict between women's private nurturing responsibilities and their wage work. There
is now a great wealth of literature critiquing the assumptions of liberal legal
and Law and Economic theory, both by feminist and other critical legal scholars. Among the tenets of liberal theory that have been examined exhaustively
are autonomy, neutrality, privacy, and equality. Elsewhere I have extensively
reviewed the existing critical legal studies and feminist legal theory literature
critiquing these ideals.

The law's failure to address the conflict between women's work and family
obligations is arguably a function of each of these assumptions. Recounting
each of these critiques in detail is beyond the scope of this essay. However, I
revisit here our law's foundational tenets of autonomy, equality, and rationality to make a specific argument about the law's inability to recognize women's
cultural caregiving. I suggest that the liberal and neoclassical economic theories that so greatly influence our law, including our discrimination laws, are
unable to account for women's experiences that are culturally based. By cultural, I mean those aspects of women's lives that are understood to be the
product of gender socialization, not biological forces. Caregiving, which
women disproportionately perform but which men are also capable of performing, is just such a cultural experience, at least according to modern social
scientific theory.

This prevailing view, of course, grew in large part out of modern feminism's challenge to the historical conception of women as biologically unsuited for wage labor or public participation.[67] The popular understanding that women's caregiving is attributable to gender socialization, not biological difference, can also be traced to the link between the civil and women's rights movements. Sex discrimination law grew out of the civil rights movement, which was grounded on the theory that all humans are inherently the same and thus deserving of the same liberties, rights, and privileges of citizenship.[68] At the core of the rejection of racial segregation were the powerful notions that blacks are fundamentally the same as whites and that it is irrational for surface differences such as skin color to carry any significant meaning. Indeed, the modern civil rights movement rested on a showing that race was socially constructed. The belief that discrimination was the result of irrational prejudice or historical disadvantages that grew out of irrational prejudice was a means of overcoming powerful dehumanizing ideas about blacks' natural or biological inferiority, which were the basis for treating them as chattel, the very root of slavery.[69] Sex discrimination law grew out of this scheme as a practical strategy among feminists working to include women within the existing model of formal equality underlying civil rights laws.[70] As with race, this political strategy was consistent with a developing consensus among anthropologists, sociologists, and psychologists that sex differences were illusory and not the proper basis for differential treatment.[71]

Although the "social construction" story underlying the women's rights movement of the 1960s and 1970s and our present sex discrimination laws made limited gains in breaking down the family wage and separate-spheres doctrines, I contend that this story is incapable of fundamentally challenging certain aspects of liberal and neoclassical economic theory that continue to perpetuate the labor force attachment gap between men and women. The concepts of autonomy, equality, and rationality, which form the foundation of our law, have the peculiar ability only to recognize women's immutable biological differences from men, leaving women's cultural caregiving beyond the law's reach. This explains, in part, the limited ability of Title VII, the Pregnancy Discrimination Act, the Family and Medical Leave Act, and judicial opinions interpreting these statutes, to recognize much beyond women's immediate, physical experiences of pregnancy and childbirth.

It is important to make clear that I am not intending to argue that women's biological difference should be the basis for workplace accommodation, although, unlike the formal equality position, I acknowledge that there are real differences between the sexes that are relevant to law. Rather, my ultimate point will be that even the "social construction" story of women's caregiving, at least as it has been marshaled by many feminist theorists, represents an acceptance of the premises underlying the biological inferiority model that has been so widely criticized. Both rely on a depiction of constrained agency, thereby failing to challenge the dominant framework that provides support only for "innocent" actors who have little control over their predicament. My assertion that the law as currently constructed respects only biological difference is thus a descriptive, not a normative, endeavor.

Autonomy

As other commentators have highlighted, the assumption within both liberal and economic theory that humans are individuals first, that "what separates us is epistemologically and morally prior to what connects us,"[72] has formed the basis for the model worker on which the workplace is structured.[73] That "ideal worker," as Joan Williams has identified him, is an individual unencumbered by childcare or other nurturing responsibilities.[74] This ideal worker is available for work at least forty hours a week and has no need for even intermittent time off to care for sick children, much less for more substantial leave to deal with the physical limitations of pregnancy and childbirth, to raise infants and young children, or to care for elderly relatives. The limited protections of Title VII and the FMLA, while representing an acknowledgment of the falsehood of the ideal worker, at the same time reinforce that ideal through their cramped definitions of the circumstances in which a worker is encumbered. Both statutes, at bottom, only recognize biological conditions—pregnancy, childbirth, and serious illness—and this recognition was achieved only after two decades of legislative advocacy and litigation.[75] Put simply, the powerful notions of the autonomous individual have worked to define biological incapacity as the outer limit of cognizable dependence within the current legal scheme.

Equality

The embeddedness of the concept of equality within our legal system—particularly the peculiar form of formal equality that has dominated judicial decision making over the past decade[76]—is a primary source of the law's failure to recognize the conflict between women's work and family responsibilities. The ideal of equality, that like things should be treated alike, is a fundamental concept underlying our liberal legal system. That similarly situated persons or groups of persons should be treated similarly is the goal of the equal protection clause of the Fourteenth Amendment.[77] This notion of equality is similarly at the heart of Title VII's prohibition of sex discrimination. The feminist critique of equality has not attacked the concept of equality itself—that like things should be treated alike—but rather has attacked the failure of legal decision makers to see difference where it exists.[78] As the feminist critique highlights, the process of classification is a precondition of equality analysis. For if justice requires that like things be treated alike, the object of the law must be categorized in order for the law to function justly.

Viewed through the categorical lens of equality analysis, women's nurturing poses a difficult problem for the law. Because the caregiving that women disproportionately perform is defined within the dominant discourse as a cultural not a biological phenomenon, it is difficult if not impossible for the law to recognize. Cultural differences are "more or less" differences, as Christine Littleton has described them,[79] that is, those experiences that are generally but not always true for women. Women's disproportionate responsibility for the care of dependents is such a "more or less" difference. Put simply, because not all women are necessarily caregivers, and because men can and do nurture others, even if such nurturing is the exception, the law is unable to equate nurturing with women and thus to recognize discrimination on the basis of nurturing responsibilities as sex discrimination. This phenomenon also has been called the problem of the "perfect proxy": because caregiving is not a perfect proxy for the female sex, discrimination on the basis of caregiving is not considered sex discrimination.[80] Title VII is plagued by this flaw.

Feminists are deeply divided over whether seeking the law's recognition of women's differences detracts from women's equality or is a necessary precondition to it. Some feminist legal scholars have cautioned against celebrating women's differences from men, whether biological *or* cultural, because difference has always meant women's difference and historically has provided the basis for treating women worse as well as better than men.[81] Other feminist legal scholars have opposed celebrating women's gender-specific experiences, because those experiences have been constructed and limited by patriarchy.[82] Still other feminist legal theorists argue for accommodation, but only with regard to biologically based differences such as pregnancy, menstruation, or rape.[83] Feminist theorists and legal advocates for women have been hesitant to urge recognition of strictly cultural differences for fear of essentializing women's experiences and reinforcing gender roles.

However, even if feminists could come to a consensus around a strategy that seeks recognition of women's cultural differences—and many have noted that, at least within the academic literature, such a consensus is beginning to develop[84]—the foundational tenet of equality underlying the dominant liberal legal framework will pose a major impediment to gaining legal recognition of women's nurturing work, which is a "more or less" difference. In other words, the law's inability to recognize women's caregiving is a fundamentally theoretical problem as well as practical one. This presents a far greater challenge for feminist legal theorists than the current understanding of the predicament would imply. For even if we could "[s]top fighting each other!" as Joan Williams has recently implored,[85] the categorization problem of equality theory on which our discrimination laws are founded presents an insurmountable epistemological obstacle to gaining recognition of women's cultural experiences.

As discussed earlier, Title VII, the PDA, and the FMLA plainly manifest this limitation of equality theory, and thus our law, to address the conflict between work and family experienced by women. Because women's caregiving is not an "all or nothing" immutable biological difference, our employment antidiscrimination laws possess a limited ability to recognize it.

Rational Choice Theory

The law's limited response to the conflict between women's disproportionate responsibility for caregiving and their wage work can also be attributed to the influence of the Law and Economics movement, which exploded into prominence in the 1980s.[86] Law and Economics is diverse in theory and perspective: there are the Chicago and New Haven schools, the Public Choice wing, first and second generations, and so on.[87] Yet common among these perspectives has been an embrace of rational choice theory, which has greatly influenced employment discrimination law.[88] Rational choice theory hypothesizes, first, that human beings universally are motivated by self-interest, that they are "utility maximizers." Second, it assumes that all human behavior is a result of rational decision making. In its most simplified form, rational choice theory posits that a person, in deciding to engage in any particular behavior, compares the costs and benefits of the action. If the benefit exceeds the cost, she will engage in the activity; she will refrain if the reverse is true. By definition then, according to rational choice theory, if a person engages in an action, it is in her self-interest. If it were not, she would not have acted.[89] "If consent can be observed, the benefit can be inferred, even if we do not understand the reasons for the transaction ourselves."[90]

Rational choice theory has outer limits, however. There are circumstances when even traditional economic theory and our law, which has been so greatly influenced by economic concepts, recognize that a person is not acting of her own free will. The traditional circumstances are narrowly defined as those in which an actor's agency is impaired by physical or psychological factors outside of her control. As expressed in contract and criminal law, for example, force, fraud, duress, incapacity, and "heat of passion" are commonly recognized defenses to liability.[91] Short of these limited conditions, our law presumes the actor is squarely situated within the rational choice model. As Richard Epstein has stated, "[t]he exchange need only be monitored [by the law] . . . to ensure that force and fraud and incompetence are not involved. When those minimum conditions are satisfied, then the consent of both parties guarantees that the transaction works to their common benefit."[92]

Viewed through the lens of rational choice theory, women's cultural caregiving is a mere choice, for which the state owes no support and employers owe no accommodation. Perhaps the most often-cited evidence of this reasoning can be seen in *Equal Employment Opportunity Commission (EEOC) v. Sears Roebuck & Co.*,[93] in which Sears successfully argued as a defense to a Title VII discrimination case that its female employees voluntarily "chose" low-paying, noncommissioned sales jobs so as to facilitate their family responsibilities.[94]

In contrast, rational choice theory has a limited ability to recognize women's biological differences, which are viewed as irrevocably bound up in nature and beyond women's control. Although women often "choose" to become pregnant, once this choice is made—even if we assume that all pregnancies are desired, which clearly they are not—short of abortion, women cannot "choose" to avoid birth. Understood in this way, the PDA and FMLA can be explained as examples of limited but traditional exceptions to the model of personhood that is at the heart of rational choice theory. Both statutes are focused on women's biological differences from men, despite the FMLA's gender-neutral language and provisions for "parental" leave.[95] Each represents a grudging recognition that women's experiences of pregnancy and childbirth—childbirth really—cannot be accommodated within a legal system and society so invested in the concept of the rational decision maker.[96] In such a world, women's other caregiving experiences, even those with a biological component such as breast feeding, to say nothing of the basic day-to-day care of children and other dependents, are defined as a choice undeserving of the law's recognition.

In summary, the foundational tenets of liberal and economic theory, particularly the concepts of autonomy, equality, and rational choice, have served to render women's caregiving responsibilities nearly invisible within the current legal framework. First, the assumption underlying both liberal and economic theory that humans are autonomous, unencumbered actors has formed the foundation for the current structure of the workplace, which is modeled on a worker who has no caregiving responsibilities. Second, equality theory possesses only a limited ability to recognize cultural differences such as women's caregiving, for the simple reason that such "more or less" differences between men and women escape categorization as sex-based classifications. Third, the influence of rational choice theory has served to construct women's caregiving not only as a freely chosen endeavor but one that by definition is assumed to benefit women.

Of course, the constructs of autonomy, equality, and rational choice are just that—constructs. Constructs are just ideas, after all. They must live in the world with real people, with real women. Although theoretical constructs have a tenacious ability to resist contradictory information, particularly when such constructs are controlled by those who benefit from them, even the most powerful theories must reckon with blatant, existential phenomena to the contrary. Women's unique biological experiences of pregnancy and childbirth—particularly childbirth—are such "in your face" phenomena that cannot be maintained within the prevailing theoretical constructs undergirding our employment discrimination law. In contrast, the myth of autonomy, the limits of equality analysis, and the culturally privileged account of the rational actor render women's gender-based caregiving experiences invisible and beyond the law's reach. Thus, although our legal system has yet to acknowledge women's cultural caregiving as it affects their workforce participation, it has produced limited job protections for women to the extent that the strictly biological conditions of pregnancy and childbirth limit their wage work.

In sum, Title VII, the Pregnancy Discrimination Act, and the Family and Medical Leave Act are able to perceive circumstances when women are not in fact autonomous, rational, or equal to men, but those circumstances are limited to the moment of "parturition,"[97] when a woman is literally connected to human life and totally overtaken by nature. Our country's employment laws protect women from workplace discrimination only to the extent that their agency is impaired due to physical factors outside of their control.

Feminism's Response

The constraining effect of liberal and economic theory on the law has received a great deal of attention from feminist legal theorists. As discussed earlier, feminist theorists have critiqued the elemental constructs underlying these predominant jurisprudential movements in an effort to show how they represent an androcentric conception of humanity and limit the law's ability to address the conflict between women's work and family obligations.[98] In this essay, I focus on two particular responses that seek to challenge the myths of autonomy, equality, and rationality by exposing the ways in which women's caregiving compromises their agency. The first such response is that women are not fully autonomous, equal, or rational because biological forces make women more inclined than men to nurture. I call this the "story of biology." Robin West's work provides an example of such a strategy,[99] although she is not alone.[100] According to West:

> [T]he biological relationship *of the mother to the newborn* is radically different from that of the father. . . . First, the mother, but not the father, is necessarily physically *there* when the baby is born. And second, the mother, but not the father, will lactate, and if she is to avoid painful engorgement of her breasts, will breast-feed. A newborn baby instinctually knows how to breast-feed and knows from which parent to do so. From the baby's birth, the mother is physically connected, and remains physically connected, to the baby in ways which are not true of the father, simply by virtue of physical proximity and her ability to lactate. Mothers are more inclined to nurture their children, perhaps, *in part* simply because

they are necessarily physically proximate and universally capable of doing so from the beginning of life.[101]

The story of biology has received little attention as a transformative device among feminist legal theorists, largely because of the history of discrimination against women on the basis of their perceived biological weakness.[102]

In contrast, a related but more common response to the rhetoric of autonomy, (formal) equality, and choice is that women are not fully autonomous, equal, or rational because gender socialization greatly influences their decisions to take on caregiving responsibilities. I call this the "gender socialization story." In an article critiquing the androcentric structure of the workplace, Nancy Dowd tells the story of gender socialization in this way:

If you are a woman, family is definitional, as much so as biology. It is the contingency, the possibility of family, as well as the scope of actual family responsibilities, that so strongly affects women's sense of time and self, and others' view of women's lives and potential. While connected to women's biological role of bearing children, the critical role of family is primarily based on women's social role as primary or sole parents. Nevertheless, women are viewed, and feel, that they take on family responsibilities automatically, "naturally": *this is not a matter of choice.* It is foremost a caretaking role. Women care for their partner, their children, their parents, and/or their partner's parents.[103]

A second example of the gender socialization story can be found in the work of Joan Williams. In her recent book presenting an eclectic array of strategies, legal and nonlegal, for restructuring family and market work to account for the needs of working parents, she states, "it is not surprising that women facing the constraints handed down by domesticity speak of having made a 'choice.' But the fact that women have internalized these constraints does not mean that they are consistent with our commitment to gender equality."[104] Later in the book, she elaborates:

[S]ocial forces . . . get encoded as women's choice to devote themselves to caregiving rather than to market work. These [include] objective factors such as the lack of affordable, high quality child care, employers' entitlement to marginalize anyone who does not live up to the ideal-worker norm, and fathers' felt entitlement to perform as ideal workers. These objective factors create strong force fields pulling mothers toward marginalization. . . . [M]en and women live in different force fields, and so experience very different social cues. As a result, most well adjusted people become gendered. Consequently, women develop various skills and traits required for the modern caregiving role, such as the ability to do six things at once, family executive skills . . . , and the ability to sustain the complex social relationships associated with childhood (with friends, parents, teachers, and so on). Are these skills evidence of women's ethic of care, or are they evidence that most rise to the occasion once they are assigned the role of primary caregiver? . . . Many women end up as they do not because they, from the beginning, shared an ethic of care. Maybe they were just making the best of a bad deal.[105]

Finally, Vicki Schultz's work on the "lack of interest" defense in Title VII cases presents another example of the story of gender socialization within legal scholarship, positing that women's employment preferences are molded by a powerful system of workplace socialization. She explains:

Title VII promised working women change. But, consciously or unconsciously, courts have interpreted the statute with some of the same assumptions that have historically legitimated women's economic disadvantage. Most centrally, courts have assumed that women's aspirations and identities as workers are shaped exclusively in private realms that are independent of and prior to the workworld. By assuming that women form stable job aspirations before they begin working, courts have missed the ways in which employers contribute to creating women workers in their images of who "women" are supposed to be. Judges have placed beyond the law's reach the structural features of the workplace that gender jobs and people, and disempower women from aspiring to higher-paying nontraditional employment.[106]

Examples of the gender socialization story can be found in the work of many feminists, both within[107] and outside of law.[108]

Note that none of these theorists explicitly argues that disadvantages arising from caregiving work should be eliminated *because* women are helpless to escape their socialization into such work (or in the case of Schultz, socialization out of traditionally masculine jobs). We would not expect feminist theorists explicitly to make such arguments given the fundamental importance of women's agency for feminist theory. Yet the story of gender socialization is at least in part a reaction to the autonomous, equal, rational chooser assumed by liberal legal and law and economic theory. In this sense, the concept of gender socialization can be seen as doing double duty, for it contests both older biological conceptions of women as naturally unsuited for public participation and market work,[109] and resists new theoretical threats of neoliberalism which construct women's family caregiving as an unencumbered choice undeserving of public support or legal protection. Further, the notion of a gendered world successfully contests the highly individualistic, victim-specific conception of who is harmed by sex discrimination. If the harm to women from discrimination is expanded to include all affected by a societal system of gender, then a space is opened for all women to lay some legal claim to protection, even if there are differences among them and even if all women have not individually experienced overt sex discrimination.[110]

Still, I suggest that this latter and widely accepted socialization story has had a limited ability to fundamentally challenge women's work–family conflicts, given our legal system's difficulty in recognizing socially constructed or "cultural" differences between men and women. Although an understanding of the "force field"[111] that gender exerts on women may challenge the myth of autonomy, it also may hamper women's ability to achieve justice through equality analysis. For if women's caregiving is simply a socially manufactured predisposition but not an inevitability, then laws that discriminate on the basis of women's caregiving escape categorization as sex-based classifications under equality analysis. Moreover, given the crude model of the rational decision maker that now pervades our law, choices constrained by gender socialization are typically not considered sufficiently bounded or coerced to justify protection or recognition by legal decision makers. After all, women can simply reject their culturally assigned roles as caregivers. Put another way, women can solve their work–family conflicts simply by ceasing the uncompensated "flow" of household labor to men.[112] Indeed, given the failure of men and society more broadly to support caregiving and housework, many women have adopted some formulation of this "strike" solution by delaying pregnancy,[113] delegating their caregiving work to relatively disadvantaged domestic workers,[114] or forgoing motherhood altogether. These solutions are fundamentally unjust to many women, particularly to the women least able to alleviate the burden of unpaid caregiving work or to negotiate the terms of their employment in the marketplace, and of course, to children.[115]

In sum, the gender socialization story is a powerful rhetorical tool to deconstruct dominant liberal legal paradigms that regulate and construct women's work–family conflicts, particularly the myth of autonomy. But this story cannot address the limiting effects of rational choice theory on our law. According to neoclassical economic theory, at least as it has been conceptualized in popular discourse and deployed by legal decision makers, little short of physical force, whether the force of a gun or the force of Mother Nature, warrants the law's recognition of dependence. Nor can the gender socialization story fully challenge the categorization problems inherent in liberalism's commitment to formal equality, for all women are not similarly constrained by gender norms.

In making this argument, it is not my intention to deny the complex combination of sociological, biological, economic, and political forces that constrain women's agency when it comes to caregiving. Moreover, it is not a simple matter to overcome socially assigned gender roles, as the current theoretical framework sometimes seems to assume. In fact, as Martha Fineman has pointed out, it may be harder to do so than to overcome biology.[116] Some women have gained control over their unique biological role in reproduction through technological innovation; they have made less progress challenging gender socialization.

Nor can we discount the distortion of women's agency within dominant societal and judicial discourses. Kathryn Abrams has noted that "women are presented either as fully autonomous choosers (sometimes even manipulative hyperagents) or as wholly compromised victims."[117] In contrast, the law has adopted a more balanced view of male subjects, recognizing that men sometimes must operate under "context-based restraint" not reflective of some "characterological" defect.[118]

Uncovering the divergent ways in which the law treats men and women who are constrained by systemic inequality is an important feminist project. First, such a project, like Fineman's and Williams's work, starts with the assumption of the universal nature of dependency and thus can challenge liberalism's limiting assumption of autonomy. Second, by focusing on how the law constructs women as legal subjects, Abrams's approach removes from the discussion the decades-old and ultimately irresolvable debate about women's essential nature. Such a disruption in the discourse could open a significant space for alternative theories of inequality, bring women with divergent interests and experiences together, and minimize the spillover costs for women that victories based on a universal theory of the legal subject often have on other areas of law. If successful, these achievements alone would be substantial.

Focusing on women's bounded agency alone, however, cannot fundamentally challenge the theoretical constructs that so effectively stunt the law's ability to respond to the experience of caregiving. Constraints on agency have been legally cognizable under only extremely narrow circumstances that typically involve physical force, threat of force, or serious psychological impairment.[119] While there certainly are exceptions that might prove fruitful for exploration, and while it is not my intention to deny the existence of gender as a powerful operating force on women and men alike, I suggest that our discrimination law and the theoretical framework that is its cornerstone possess a limited ability to recognize decisions constrained by conditions short of brute force. As such, with regard to women's conflicts between work and family, employment discrimination on the basis of biological difference is the primary target of the law. It is clear, then, that we must refine the theoretical constructs underlying our employment discrimination laws before such laws will recognize women's culturally based caregiving work.

One place to start might be to redefine the justifications for restructuring the workplace. At present, the primary justifications within our law for recognizing dependency are innocence and immutability. Where a woman is considered to have no responsibility for her predicament and little control over achieving self-sufficiency, within the prevailing construct the law might afford her a limited accommodation to the extent that she can demonstrate that men have received similar dispensations in similar circumstances. Thus, Title VII, the Pregnancy Discrimination Act, and the Family and Medical Leave Act provide women with limited protections from employment discrimination on the basis of their "incapacity" related to childbirth. However, because women's caregiving work is understood to be either a choice or a cultural activity, under the current theoretical framework there exists little justification for restructuring the workplace to account for family labor. Thus far, many reformers have approached this dilemma by depicting women's caregiving as a manifestation of constrained agency—either due to biological or sociological forces.

An alternative approach that might challenge the prevailing assumption that physical incapacity is the only legitimate form of dependency would involve an exploration of the fundamental importance of family caregiving work to women as individuals. Often, feminist theorists have been hesitant to discuss the positive meaning for women qua women of their cultural caregiving work, for fear of reinforcing harmful gender roles. This undertheorization limits our ability to respond to those who question the purported "special treatment" that parents, and women in particular, allegedly receive in the workplace.[120] Opponents of social welfare programs and workplace regulation, and women for whom having children may not be central to their life plans,[121] ask why they should subsidize the private choices of others to have children. The answer must provide a richer and more positive account of women's cultural caregiving work than can be conveyed by the stories of biology or gender socialization.

Given our country's record of exploitation and control of the mothering and wage work of working-class women, single women,[122] and women of color,[123] family caregiving work for some women might be understood as a form of powerful political resistance: a product of choice, not constraint or oppression. Similarly, the care work of lesbian women may be a form of contestation against dominant societal values that label their mothering and lovemaking as deviant.[124] Even relatively privileged, white heterosexual women may experience their family commitments as a means to resist, or at least balance, the pressured conditions of the modern workplace.[125] Feminists must begin to mine such complexity if we are to respond to the limited ability of economic and liberal legal theory to recognize women's cultural experience of caregiving.

In making the assertion that caregiving can be a manifestation of political agency, I do not mean to suggest that housework or the care of intimate relatives or partners is unidimensionally positive or empowering. Gender polices women of all classes, races, and sexual orientations into traditional caregiving roles; the family, like work, can be a site of oppression for women. Rather, my aim is to recover women's agency, however restricted and distorted by gender-based domination, from the dominant feminist accounts of women's care work within law in an effort to complicate the story of caregiving for women.

A theory that presents women's cultural caregiving in all its messiness as a condition of oppression and power, drudgery and deep satisfaction, constraint and choice, has the potential to be more transformative than one that rests on squeezing women's caregiving experiences into the limited exceptions to the autonomous, equal, and rational person assumed by our dominant theoretical paradigms. This is not to diminish the value of thinking about women's caregiving as a product of "domesticity."[126] The gender socialization story is important because it erodes autonomy as a legitimate principle for organizing market work and exposes the injustice of the gendered division of family labor. However, I worry that we lose many potential allies when we depict women's caregiving primarily as a condition of gender constraint, particularly women whose sexuality, reproduction, and mothering historically have been discouraged and regulated. Thicker conceptions of caregiving possess greater potential to bring women together across their differences.

Quite simply, reasons matter. Concrete outcomes achieved will always be a function of the justifications provided. In the face of the limits of formal equality analysis and the rhetoric of choice, justifying rights upon women's bounded agency is unlikely to produce anything greater than a legal regime protecting women from discrimination on the basis of their biological differences from men. For in the discourse over difference, women's cultural differences are erased because the theoretical frameworks that construct our law are blind to such differences. The implications of this problem with the current paradigm are serious: although unintended, justifications based on a concept of socially bounded agency will merely serve to reinforce the existing paradigm that relies on biological difference as a basis for limited accommodation (not to mention discrimination). Accordingly, an exploration of the meaning and value of caregiving work to *women* is imperative for the project of developing an alternative theoretical framework that will successfully move the existing order.

If women assert that they deserve rights because they are "equal" to men, they are likely to be afforded rights only when they are in fact equal. If women assert that they deserve rights because gender socialization or biological forces dictate their caregiving, they will receive rights only during the limited circumstances when society considers their agency to be bounded. But if women assert that they deserve rights because caregiving work is at least in part an assertion of the legitimacy of their identity and equality as citizens, then women—and men for that matter—will be afforded rights when they engage in caregiving.

Conclusion

U.S. employment antidiscrimination laws do not adequately address the conflict between women's labor force participation and their disproportionate responsibility for caregiving within the family. Title VII of the Civil Rights Act of 1964, the Pregnancy Discrimination Act, the Family and Medical Leave

Act, and judicial decisions interpreting these statutes provide job security to some relatively privileged women in the limited instances of pregnancy and childbirth. In contrast, women's experience of cultural caregiving is virtually unrecognized by laws prohibiting sex discrimination in the workplace. In particular, although women receive some limited protections if they can prove that they have not been hired or promoted based on "stereotypical" assumptions about their role as primary caregivers, once employed, women remain largely unprotected from demotion or termination on the basis of their culturally based, that is, nonbiological, family caregiving labor. This failure of our law has contributed to the perpetuation of a labor force attachment gap between men and women, persistent inequality in the economic status of women, and the widespread impoverishment of children in America.

This essay has suggested that the stunted response of U.S. employment discrimination law to women's work–family conflicts is influenced in part by certain core values and assumptions within our legal tradition, particularly the value of formal equality and the assumption that legal agents are rational decision makers. Such robust doctrines cannot be dislodged or even modestly disrupted through theoretical approaches that seek to fit women's experiences of caregiving into the existing paradigm. As such, the explicit or implicit suggestion by many feminist legal theorists that employers and the state should support women's family caregiving because the unfair distribution of such work is produced by the tug of biology or a ubiquitous system of gender likely will not significantly transform the existing framework. Such an approach, by focusing on women's bounded agency, merely serves to include women's cultural caregiving within the existing paradigm that defines biological incapacity as the outer limit of the law's protection.

An alternative approach that might achieve recognition of caregivers while at the same time challenging the existing framework would be to explore the positive meaning of caregiving to women *as women*. Such a reconceptualization of caregiving as a possible manifestation of women's political agency, however constrained, would provide a richer and more positive account of women's caregiving work than can be conveyed by the stories of biology or gender socialization. Only by complicating our understanding of women's caregiving work will we be able to fully disrupt the assumptions of equality, autonomy, and rationality, which serve to justify the continuing nonrecognition of women's caregiving in our law and society.

Notes

1. This research was supported by a grant from the the the S. J. Quinney College of Law Summer Research Program. My thanks to the faculty of the S. J. Quinney College of Law and to participants in the Feminism and Legal Theory Workshops on Discrimination and Inequality at

Columbia and Cornell who gave helpful feedback on portions of this project. Special thanks go to Terence Dougherty, Martha Ertman, Martha Fineman, Jack Greenberg, Susan Sturm, and Matthew Weinstein. This essay was submitted in partial fulfillment of the requirements for the degree of Juris Science Doctor in the School of Law, Columbia University. Portions of this chapter were originally published at 34 U. Mich. J.L. Ref. 371 (2001) (reprinted with permission).

2. Arlie Hochschild, *The Second Shift: Working Parents and the Revolution at Home* 3–4 (1989); Suzanne M. Bianchi et al., *Is Anyone Doing the Housework? Trends in the Gender Division of Household Labor,* 79 Soc. Forces 191, 196 (2000); Scott Coltrane, *Research on Household Labor: Modeling and Measuring the Social Embeddedness of Routine Family Work,* 62 J. Mar. & Fam. 1208 (2000).

3. Eliza K. Pavalko & Julie E. Artis, *Women's Caregiving and Paid Work: Causal Relationships in Midlife,* 52B J. Gerontology Series B: Psychol. Sci. & Soc. Sci. 170, 177–78 (July 1997).

4. *Id.; see also* Emily K. Abel, *Who Cares for the Elderly? Public Policy and the Experiences of Adult Daughters* 4, 128 (1991); Patricia Braus, *When The Helpers Need a Hand,* 20 Am. Demographics 66, 67 (1998); Nadine Taub, *From Parental Leaves to Nurturing Leaves,* 13 N.Y.U. Rev. L. & Soc. Change 381, 387 n. 26 (1984–85).

5. *See supra* note 2.

6. Francine D. Blau, *Trends in the Well-Being of American Women, 1970–1995,* 36 J. Econ. Literature 112, 150–55 (1998); Coltrane, *supra* note 2, at 1208.

7. John P. Robinson & Geoffrey Godbey, *Time for Life: The Surprising Ways Americans Use Their Time* 107–9 (1997); Bianchi, *supra* note 2, at 208 table 1.

8. Bianchi et al., *supra* note 2, at 209 table 1 (showing that although women performed about twice as much total housework per week as did men in 1995, they performed about four times the amount of "core housework," *i.e.,* cooking, meal cleanup, housecleaning, and laundry); Laura Sanchez & Elizabeth Thomson, *Becoming Mothers and Fathers: Parenthood, Gender, and the Division of Labor,* 11 Gender & Soc'y 747, 756 table 1 (1997) (showing that in 1994, women in families with children contributed almost two-thirds of the total family work hours).

9. In 1964, as part of the Civil Rights Act, Congress passed Title VII to prohibit employment discrimination on the basis of sex, among other classifications. Civil Rights Act of 1964, Pub. L. No. 88-352, §§ 701–16, 78 Stat. 253–66 (codified as amended at 42 U.S.C. § 2000e to 2000e-16 (2000)) [hereinafter Title VII].

10. Pub. L. No. 95-555, 92 Stat. 2076 (codified at § 42 U.S.C. § 2000e(k) (2000)). *See infra* the section titled "The Limited Response of Employment Discrimination Law to the Attachment Gap."

11. Pub. L. No. 103-3, 107 Stat. 6 (codified at 29 U.S.C. §§ 2601–54 (2000)). *See infra* the section titled "The Limited Response of Employment Discrimination Law to the Attachment Gap."

12. Joan Williams has described the theoretical employee unencumbered by caregiving responsibilities as the "ideal worker." Joan Williams, *Deconstructing Gender,* 87 Mich. L. Rev. 797, 822 (1989) [hereinafter Williams, *Deconstructing Gender*].

13. *See* Martha Albertson Fineman, *Contract and Care,* 75 Chi.-Kent L. Rev. 1403 (2001).

14. *See* Mary Becker, *Care and Feminists,* 17 Wis. Women's L.J. 57, 63 (2002); Martha Albertson Fineman, *Cracking the Foundational Myths: Independence, Autonomy and Self-Sufficiency,* ch. 9, this vol. [hereinafter Fineman, *Cracking Foundational Myths*].

15. *See* Linda C. McClain, *Care as a Public Value: Linking Responsibility, Resources, and Republicanism,* 76 Chi.-Kent L. Rev. 1673 (2001).

16. *See* Martha M. Ertman, *Commentary: Changing the Meaning of Motherhood,* 76 Chi.-Kent L. Rev. 1733 (2001).

17. *See* Laura T. Kessler, *Transgressive Caregiving* (unpublished manuscript, on file with author).

18. *See infra* the section titled "Feminism's Response."

19. *See* Betty Friedan, *The Feminine Mystique* 19 (1963).

20. Studies show that within the family, women do the more routine physical tasks of child care whereas men do more play, discipline, and education. *E.g.*, Scott Coltrane, *Family Man* 48–49, 91 (1996).

21. My vulgarity here represents a purposeful attempt to bring home what more delicate descriptions such as "changing diapers" and "wiping runny noses" so well hide.

22. *See* Arlie Russell Hochschild, *The Time Bind: When Work Becomes Home and Home Becomes Work passim* (1997); Robin West, *Caring for Justice* 126 (1997) [hereinafter West, *Caring for Justice*]; Katherine M. Franke, *Theorizing Yes: An Essay on Feminism, Law, and Desire*, 101 Colum. L. Rev. 181, 183–85 (2001).

23. Carol Gilligan, *In a Different Voice* 100 (1982).

24. *See generally* Fineman, *Cracking Foundational Myths, supra* note 14.

25. Dorothy E. Roberts, *Spiritual and Menial Housework*, 9 Yale J.L. & Feminism 51, *passim* (1997).

26. Robin West, *Jurisprudence and Gender*, 55 U. Chi. L. Rev. 1, 14–21 (1988) [hereinafter West, *Jurisprudence and Gender*].

27. *See* Naomi R. Cahn, *Gendered Identities: Women and Household Work*, 44 Vill. L. Rev. 525, 526 (1999).

28. *See, e.g.,* Alice Kessler-Harris, *In Pursuit of Equity: Women, Men, and the Quest for Economic Citizenship in Twentieth-Century America* (2001); Vicki Schultz, *Life's Work*, 100 Colum. L. Rev. 1881, 1886–92, 1959–61 (2000) [hereinafter Schultz, *Life's Work*].

29. *See, e.g.,* Joan Williams, *Unbending Gender: Why Family and Work Conflict and What to Do about It* 152 (2000) [hereinafter Williams, *Unbending Gender*] ("Working-class women's identity is 'multifaceted,' framed not only around work but around family and other roles as well. This is true in part because some three-fourths of working-class women hold low-status, low-paying, traditionally female jobs.").

30. Evelyn Nakano Glenn, *Cleaning Up/Kept Down: A Historical Perspective on Racial Inequality and "Women's Work,"* 43 Stan. L. Rev. 1333, 1336–53 (1991); Roberts, *supra* note 25, *passim*.

31. Martha Albertson Fineman, *Feminist Theory in Law: The Difference It Makes*, 2 Colum. J. Gender & L. 1, *passim* (1992) [hereinafter Fineman, *Feminist Theory in Law*]; Christine Littleton, *Does It Still Make Sense to Talk about "Women"?* 1 UCLA Women's L.J. 15, 15–16 (1991).

32. *See* Barbara Ehrenreich & Frances Fox Piven, *The Feminization of Poverty: When the "Family-Wage System" Breaks Down*, 31 Dissent 162, 162–64 (1984).

33. Jason Fields & Lynne M. Casper, *America's Families and Living Arrangements: March 2000*, Bureau of the Census, U.S. Department of Commerce, Current Population Rep. P20-537, at 7 (June 2000).

34. Joyce Iceland, Dynamics of Economic Well-Being: Poverty, 1996 to 1999, in Current Population Reports P70-91 5 figure 6, Bureau of the Census, U.S. Department of Commerce (July 2003) (showing that 41.7 percent of female-headed single-parent households fell below the poverty line for at least two months in 1999, compared with 12.8 percent of married-couple families).

35. Peter Cattan, *The Effect of Working Wives on the Incidence of Poverty*, Monthly Lab. Rev. 22, 27–28 (Mar. 1998).

36. Frank Levy, *Incomes and Income Inequality*, in *State of the Union: America in the 1990s* 1, 43–45 (Reynolds Farley ed., 1995).

37. Allen M. Parkman, *Why Are Married Women Working So Hard?* 18 Int'l Rev. L. & Econ. 41, 48–49 (1998).

38. Lenore J. Weitzman, *The Divorce Revolution* 163–80 (1985); Jana B. Singer, *Alimony and Efficiency: The Gendered Costs and Benefits of the Economic Justifications for Alimony*, 82 Geo. L.J. 2423, 2424–28 (1994); Joan Williams, *Is Coverture Dead? Beyond a New Theory of Alimony*, 82 Geo. L.J. 2227 (1994).

39. Parkman, *supra* note 37, at 43.

40. *See* U.S. Dep't. of Labor, *Report on the American Workforce* 140 table 6 (1999) [hereinafter *DOL Report on the American Workforce*].

41. Howard V. Hayghe & Suzanne M. Bianchi, *Married Mothers' Work Patterns: The Job–Family Compromise*, Monthly Lab. Rev. 24 (June 1994).

42. *Id.*

43. *See* Philip N. Cohen & Suzanne M. Bianchi, *Marriage, Children, and Women's Employment: What Do We Know?* Monthly Lab. Rev. 27 table 2, 30 (Dec. 1999).

44. *Id.* at table 2.

45. Bureau of Labor Statistics, U.S. Department of Labor, *Summary 96-9, Issues in Labor Statistics: A Different Look at Part-Time Employment* (Apr. 1996).

46. Nancy E. Dowd, *Work and Family: The Gender Paradox and the Limitations of Discrimination Analysis in Restructuring the Workplace*, 24 Harv. C.R.-C.L. L. Rev. 79, 89–90 (1989) [hereinafter Dowd, *Gender Paradox*].

47. This issue arose most clearly in *EEOC v. Sears*, 628 F. Supp. 1264, 1305–8 (N.D. Ill. 1986), in which Sears successfully argued as a defense to a Title VII discrimination case that its female employees voluntarily "chose" lower-paying, noncommissioned sales jobs.

48. Bureau of Labor Statistics, U.S. Department of Labor, Contingent and Alternative Employment Arrangements 3 (May 24, 2001) (press release) [hereinafter BLS, Contingent Employment].

49. Bureau Labor Statistics, U.S. Department of Labor, Employment Characteristics of Families in 2003, table 4 (April 20, 2004) (press release); *see also* Howard V. Hayghe, *Developments in Women's Labor Force Participation*, Monthly Lab. Rev. 41 (Sept. 1997).

50. Bureau of Labor Statistics, U.S. Department of Labor, *Summary 98-4, Issues in Labor Statistics: Who's Not Working* 1 (May 1998).

51. *Id.*

52. *See* Michael K. Lettau, *Compensation in Part-Time Jobs versus Full-Time Jobs: What if the Job Is the Same?* 7 (Office of Research and Evaluation, Bureau of Labor Statistics, U.S. Department of Labor, 1994) (working paper no. 260); Jerome E. King, *Part-Time Workers' Earnings: Some Comparisons* 31 (Bureau of Labor Statistics, Compensation and Working Conditions, 2000).

53. *See* Susan N. Houseman & Anne E. Polivka, *The Implications of Flexible Staffing Arrangements for Job Stability* 12–13 (Upjohn Institute Staff, 1999) (working paper no. 99-056).

54. *See* BLS, Contingent Employment, *supra* note 48, at 4; Donald R. Williams, *Women's Part-Time Employment: A Gross Flows Analysis*, Monthly Lab. Rev. 36, 43 n. 8 (Apr. 1995).

55. Bureau of Labor Statistics, U.S. Department of Labor, *Summary 98-9, Issues in Labor Statistics: Employer-Sponsored Childcare Benefits* (Aug. 1998).

56. BLS, Contingent Employment, *supra* note 48, at 4.

57. *See Nonstandard Work: The Nature and Challenges of Changing Employment Relations* (Françoise Carré et al. eds., 2000).

58. *See* Joyce P. Jacobsen & Laurence M. Levin, *Effects of Intermittent Labor Force Attachment on Women's Earnings*, Monthly Lab. Rev. 18 (Sept. 1995).

59. E. R. Kingston & R. O'Grady-LeShane, *The Effects of Caregiving on Women's Social Security Benefits*, 33 Gerontology 230–39 (1993).

60. Diana Pearce, *The Feminization of Poverty: Women, Work and Welfare*, 11 Urb. & Soc. Change Rev. 28 (1978).

61. *See, e.g.*, Theodore Bergstrom, *Economics in a Family Way*, 34 J. Econ. Literature 1903 (1996); Shelly Lundberg & Robert A. Pollak, *Bargaining and Distribution in Marriage*, J. Econ. Persp. 139 (Fall 1996).

62. *See* Clare Dalton & Elizabeth M. Schneider, *Battered Women and the Law* 177–200 (2001).

63. In 1997, 19.9 percent of children in the United States were poor. John Iceland et al., *Are Children Worse Off? Evaluating Child Well-Being Using a New (and Improved) Measure of*

Poverty as of 1997 (U.S. Census Bureau, Apr. 1999) (Poverty Measurement working papers). The poverty rate for children in female-headed families was 49.0 percent in 1997. *Id.*

64. Ninety-six percent of private household workers, including child-care workers, cleaners, and servants, are women; almost one-half are black or Hispanic. Bureau of Labor Statistics, U.S. Department of Labor, *Current Population Survey: Household Data Annual Averages* 180 table 11 (2000). In 1998, the median annual salary of such workers was approximately $11,600. Bureau of Labor Statistics, U.S. Department of Labor, *Occupational Outlook Handbook 2000–2001* 357 (2000). Nonprivate child-care providers, *i.e.*, those who work in day-care centers, fare a little better, but not much: they earn about $16,000 a year. *Id.* at 355.

65. Laura T. Kessler, *The Attachment Gap: Employment Discrimination Law, Women's Cultural Caregiving, and the Limits of Economic and Liberal Legal Theory*, 34 U. Mich. J.L. Ref. 371, 389–429 (2001).

66. Married women's labor force participation nearly doubled from 1969 to 1998. *DOL Report on the American Workforce*, *supra* note 40, at 96, 98 chart 3-22. The increase was even more pronounced for married women with children less than three years of age, increasing almost three-fold over the same period. *Id.* at 96, 98 chart 3-23.

67. *See, e.g., Goesaert v. Cleary*, 335 U.S. 464 (1948); *Muller v. Oregon*, 208 U.S. 412 (1908); *Bradwell v. Illinois*, 83 U.S. 130 (1872); *see also Dothard v. Rawlinson*, 433 U.S. 321 (1977); *Rostker v. Goldberg*, 453 U.S. 57 (1981).

68. John Rawls, *A Theory of Justice* 5 (1971) ("institutions are just when no arbitrary distinctions are made between persons in the assigning of basic rights and duties").

69. *See, e.g.*, Franz Samelson, *From "Race Psychology" to "Studies in Prejudice": Some Observations on the Thematic Reversal in Social Psychology*, 14 J. Hist. Behav. Sci. 265 (1978).

70. *See, e.g.*, Ruth Bader Ginsburg, *Gender and the Constitution*, 44 U. Cin. L. Rev. 1, 16–23 (1975); Pauli Murray, *The Autobiography of a Black Activist, Feminist, Lawyer, Priest, and Poet* 356–57 (1987).

71. *See* Cynthia Fuchs Epstein, *Women's Place: Options and Limits in Professional Careers* (1970); Margaret Mead, *Sex and Temperament in Three Primitive Societies* 205–6 (1935); John Stuart Mill, *The Subjection of Women*, in *Essays on Sex Equality* 123–242 (Alice S. Rossi ed., 1970).

72. West, *Jurisprudence and Gender*, *supra* note 26, at 2.

73. *See, e.g.*, Kathryn Abrams, *Gender Discrimination and the Transformation of Workplace Norms*, 42 Vand. L. Rev. 1183, 1221–22 (1989); Dowd, *Gender Paradox*, *supra* note 46, at 100–101; Nancy E. Dowd, *Work and Family: Restructuring the Workplace*, 32 Ariz. L. Rev. 431, 466 (1990) [hereinafter Dowd, *Restructuring Work*]; West, *Jurisprudence and Gender*, *supra* note 26, at 2; Williams, *Deconstructing Gender*, *supra* note 12, at 822.

74. Williams, *Deconstructing Gender*, *supra* note 12, at 822.

75. *See* the section titled "The Limited Response of Employment Discrimination Law to the Attachment Gap."

76. *See, e.g., Bush v. Gore*, 121 S. Ct. 525, 530 (2000).

77. The Fourteenth Amendment provides that "[n]o state shall . . . deny to any person within its jurisdiction the equal protection of the laws." U.S. Const. amend. XIV, § 1.

78. *See, e.g.*, Martha Minow, *Making All the Difference* 50–74, 219 (1990); West, *Caring for Justice*, *supra* note 22, at 100; Herma Hill Kay, *Models of Equality*, U. Ill. L. Rev. 39, 66 (1985); Linda Krieger & Patricia Cooney, *The Miller–Wohl Controversy: Equal Treatment, Positive Action and the Meaning of Women's Equality*, 13 Golden Gate U. L. Rev. 513, 517 (1983); Sylvia A. Law, *Rethinking Sex and the Constitution*, 132 U. Pa. L. Rev. 955, 1007–13 (1984); Christine A. Littleton, *Reconstructing Sexual Equality*, 75 Cal. L. Rev. 1279 (1987) [hereinafter Littleton, *Reconstructing Sexual Equality*]; West, *Jurisprudence and Gender*, *supra* note 26, at 14–18; *cf.* Catharine A. MacKinnon, *Sex Equality* (2001) (page proofs at 4–24, on file with author).

79. Littleton, *Reconstructing Sexual Equality*, *supra* note 78, at 1324–28.

80. Mary Anne Case, *"The Very Stereotype the Law Condemns": Constitutional Sex Discrimination Law as a Quest for Perfect Proxies,* 85 Cornell L. Rev. 1447, 1449–50 (2000).

81. *See id.* at 1477–78; Wendy W. Williams, *The Equality Crisis: Some Reflections on Culture, Courts, and Feminism,* 7 Women's Rts. L. Rep. 175, 196–200 (1982); Wendy W. Williams, *Notes from a First Generation,* 1989 U. Chi. Legal F. 99.

82. *See, e.g.,* Catharine MacKinnon, *Difference and Dominance: On Sex Discrimination,* in *Feminism Unmodified: Discourses on Life and Law* 32 (1987).

83. *E.g.,* Herma Hill Kay, *Models of Equality,* 1985 U. Ill. L. Rev. 39, 81–87; Krieger & Cooney, *supra* note 78, at 517; Law, *supra,* note 78, at 1007–13.

84. *E.g.,* Joan Williams, *Do Women Need Special Treatment? Do Feminists Need Equality?* 9 J. Contemp. Legal Issues 279, 279 (1998) [hereinafter Williams, *Special Treatment*].

85. *Id.* at 319.

86. *See* Gary Minda, *The Jurisprudential Movements of the 1980s,* 50 Ohio St. L.J. 599, 604–14 (1989).

87. *Id.*

88. *See* Richard Posner, *An Economic Analysis of Law* 19–22 (1992) (summarizing the history and growing influence of Law and Economics theory).

89. The foregoing is largely based on Thomas Ulen's summary of rational choice theory set out in *Firmly Grounded: Economics in the Future of the Law,* 1997 Wis. L. Rev. 433, 457.

90. Richard A. Epstein, *Forbidden Grounds: The Case against Employment Discrimination Laws* 26 (1992) [hereinafter Epstein, *Forbidden Grounds*].

91. *See* 17A Am. Jur. 2d Contracts §§ 214–221 (2004); 21 Am. Jur. 2d Criminal Law §§ 34–36, 160–67 (2004); 40 Am. Jur. 2d Homicide §§ 49, 241 (2004).

92. Epstein, *Forbidden Grounds, supra* note 90, at 25.

93. 628 F. Supp. 1264 (N.D. Ill. 1986), *aff'd,* 839 F.2d 302 (7th Cir. 1988).

94. For a discussion of the Sears case, *see* Vicki Schultz, *Telling Stories about Women and Work: Judicial Interpretations of Sex Segregation in the Workplace in Title VII Cases Raising the Lack of Interest Argument,* 103 Harv. L. Rev. 1749, 1840–41 (1990) [hereinafter Schultz, *Telling Stories*]; *see also* Joan Williams, *Gender Wars: Selfless Women in the Republic of Choice,* 66 N.Y.U. L. Rev. 1559, 1608 (1991).

95. *See* the discussion in the section titled "Limited Response of Employment Discrimination Law to the Attachment Gap."

96. Normal pregnancy has been deemed by both administrative and judicial decision makers as beyond the reach of the FMLA. *See* 29 C.F.R. § 825.114(a)(2)(ii) (2000); *Gudenkauf v. Stauffer Communications, Inc.,* 922 F. Supp. 465, 475 (D. Kan. 1996).

97. *McNill v. New York City Dep't of Corr.,* 950 F. Supp. 564, 569 (S.D.N.Y. 1996).

98. *See* the previous section, "Root Causes: The Limits of Liberal and Economic Theory."

99. West, *Caring for Justice, supra* note 22, at 117.

100. *E.g.,* Judith G. Greenberg, *The Pregnancy Discrimination Act: Legitimating Discrimination against Pregnant Women in the Workforce,* 50 Me. L. Rev. 225, 230 (1998).

101. West, *Caring for Justice, supra* note 22, at 117; *see also id.* at 14 ("we can hardly . . . simply rul[e] out of bounds by fiat the existence and relevance of the natural world, both around us and within us, in toto").

102. *See supra* note 67 and accompanying text.

103. Dowd, *Restructuring Work, supra* note 73, at 451 (emphasis added).

104. Williams, *Unbending Gender, supra* note 29, at 37.

105. Id. at 188–89.

106. Schultz, *Telling Stories, supra* note 94, at 1756.

107. *See, e.g.,* Littleton, *Reconstructing Sexual Equality, supra* note 78, at 1292n77 ("Asymmetries in areas such as responsibility for childrearing need not, of course, be attributed to nature, but rather to the complex combination of legal, social, and psychological incentives presented to women and men").

108. *See, e.g.,* Sandra Bartky, *Femininity and Domination: Studies in the Phenomenology of Oppression* (1990); Claudia Card, *Gender and Moral Luck,* in *Identity, Character, and Morality:*

Essays in Moral Psychology (O. Flanagan and A. Oskensberg Rorty eds., 1990); Kathryn Pauly Morgan, *Women and Moral Madness,* in *Science, Morality, and Feminist Theory* (M. Hanen and K. Nielsen eds., 1987).

109. *Cf. Muller v. Oregon,* 208 U.S. 412, 422 (1908) ("The two sexes differ in structure of body, in the functions to be performed by each . . . in the capacity for long-continued labor"), *with Stanton v. Stanton,* 421 U.S. 7, 14–15 (1975) ("No longer is the female destined solely for the home and the rearing of the family, and only the male for the marketplace and the world of ideas").

110. For example, Martha Fineman uses the concept of the "gendered life" to describe women's common "socially manufactured" experiences that can bring together "women across our differences in areas where social and cultural definitions of 'Woman' operate to potentially oppress us all." Fineman, *Feminist Theory in Law, supra* note 31, at 4.

111. Joan Williams describes the disciplining nature of gender as a "force field." Williams, *Unbending Gender, supra* note 29, at 37–39.

112. *See* Williams, *Special Treatment, supra* note 84, at 287.

113. Francine D. Blau et al., *The Economics of Women, Men, and Work* 281–86 (1998) (describing the "negative substitution effect" of women's labor market earnings on fertility decisions).

114. *See supra* notes 25, 30, 64, and accompanying text.

115. Again, I acknowledge that not all women wish to become mothers and that motherhood is to a great extent "compulsory" in our society. *See* Franke, *supra* note 22, at 183–84. But the radical feminist position that motherhood and reproduction are primarily sources of oppression for women cannot be sustained unless we embrace the untenable notion that false consciousness fairly represents women's experience, and unless we callously discount women for whom motherhood and the family may serve, at least in part, as a respite from extrafamilial sources of oppression such as the workplace and the state. *See infra* notes 123–25 and accompanying text.

116. Fineman, *Feminist Theory in Law, supra* note 31, at 2.

117. Kathryn Abrams, Changing the "Subject" of Inequality, presented at the Feminism and Legal Theory Workshop on Discrimination and Inequality, Cornell Law School (June 17–19, 1999) (unpublished manuscript, on file with author).

118. *Id.* In particular, Abrams looks to areas of law where the legal subject is viewed with greater objectivity, such as the Uniform Commercial Code provision on unconscionability, for paradigms that might challenge the distorted depiction of women as legal subjects.

119. *See supra* note 91 and accompanying text.

120. *E.g.,* Elinor Burkett, *The Baby Boon: How Family-Friendly America Cheats the Childless* (2000).

121. *E.g.,* Franke, *supra* note 22, at 183–89 (questioning the repronormative assumptions of cultural feminists and arguing that society is reproduced through "countless reiterative practices" such as market-based consumption, not just biological reproduction).

122. *See* Martha Albertson Fineman, *The Neutered Mother, the Sexual Family, and Other Twentieth-Century Tragedies* 232 (1995).

123. *See* Dorothy Roberts, *Killing the Black Body: Race, Reproduction, and the Meaning of Liberty* (1997); Roberts, *supra* note 25; Glenn, *supra* note 30.

124. *See* Victoria Clarke, *Sameness and Difference in Research on Lesbian Parenting,* 12 J. Community & Applied Soc. Psychol. 210, 214–15 (2002).

125. *See* Deborah L. Rhode, *Balanced Lives,* 102 Colum. L. Rev. 834, 839 (2002) (detailing lawyers' discontent with long work hours, inflexible schedules, and their lack of connection to social justice causes in their work).

126. According to Joan Williams, "domesticity is a gender system comprising most centrally both the particular organization of market work and family work that arose around 1780, and the gender norms that justify, sustain, and reproduce that organization." Williams, *Unbending Gender, supra* note 29, at 1.

PART V

ECONOMICS AND INTIMACY

Gendered Economic Roles and the
Regulation of Intimate Relationships

D iscussions of the legal regulation of intimate relationships are inescapably often also discussions that impact relationships across gender. Legislation concerning the family has always played a role in constituting gender relationships. By entering into the spousal relationship, women traditionally were transferred as property from their father to their husband. To a significant extent, the rights and obligations of particular family members have been determined by each one's gender.

Traditional economics did not view the family as meriting much attention. Like liberal political theory, with its focus on the individual political actor, *homo economicus* was a solitary economic actor unconstrained by familial ties. In fact, the familial realm was defined as a nonmarket realm not subject to analysis on the same terms as the market. Neoclassical economics and Law and Economics, however, leave no stones unturned and imperialistically apply their methodology to traditionally nonmarket activities and realms, including the family. Beginning with Chicago school economist Gary Becker and continued by numerous other economists and legal academics, the family has been subjected to analysis using neoclassical economic tools as both a descriptive project and a mechanism for determining legal rules that are most efficient for regulating family relationships. Such inquiry has focused on issues that include why people chose to marry and divorce, have children, or accept certain allocations of labor within and without the family. Fundamental to the inquiry are the assumptions that the individual actors within the family are rational actors who make decisions based on choosing the most efficient of their available options.

Feminist responses to the interest of neoclassical economics and Law and Economics in the family have included exploring the plethora of social, cultural, psychological, and emotional determining factors beyond rational choice that guide people's behaviors within families. Additionally, feminist writers have radically questioned the very family unit that is the focus of the Law and Economics narrative. This family unit is a traditional, natural-law family unit, and although interactions between its members are subjected to the Law and Economics analysis, the unit itself is not subject to its scrutiny. This calls into question Law and Economics' ability to determine, in an abstract, scientific sense, the most efficient legal rules for regulating intimate relationships. Certain feminist writers, responding to this glaring lapse in scientific rigor, have turned the economic analysis on its head, looking at the manner in which market models, such as contract and other business models, can inform both an analysis of the family and at times provide a vision for new ways of regulating intimate relationships.

The first essay in this section, June Carbone's "What Do Women Really Want? Economics, Justice, and the Market for Intimate Relationships," explores Gary Becker's model of the family. Carbone discusses Becker's project as the creation of a grand narrative of the family, culminating in what is its ultimate decline. A basic principle of neoclassical economics is that as an economy becomes increasingly specialized, it becomes increasingly productive and moves toward efficiency. To Becker, so too within the family, where traditional gender roles of the man as breadwinner and the wife as homemaker are forms of specialization. To Becker, the growth of the earning power of women has cut against this traditional model, leading to increased divorce rates, declining fertility, increasing rates of "illegitimacy," and so forth. Writers in the Law and Economics school argue that legal action, such as repealing no-fault divorce laws, could help remedy this tragedy.

Carbone also discusses a leading feminist description of the family, based on the work of Susan Moller Okin, which alternatively views relationships within the family as based on economic relations of power, not economic actors moving toward specialization. Carbone notes that both Becker's and Okin's models focus primarily on a traditional family unit and that factors other than one's economic position inform individuals,' and particularly women's, decisions to form or to forego intimate relationships.

Ann Laquer Estin's essay "Can Families Be Efficient? A Feminist Appraisal" and Margaret Brinig's "Some Concerns about Applying Economics to Family

Law" discuss the interplay between Law and Economics and the family from a feminist perspective. Estin's essay primarily focuses on Law and Economics' claim to embody positivist scientific inquiry. Estin notes the difficulty of making a claim to positivism when the subject matter involves gender roles and the frequency with which Law and Economics writers fall back on essentialist biological notions of gender. Estin also discusses the manner in which rational choice theory as applied to the family and the celebration of specialization as a means toward efficiency do not take into consideration issues of power and violence within the family.

Brinig's essay also deals with the application of economics to the family, but focusing specifically on commodification and externalities. Brinig explores the limits of commodification, arguing that seeing actors within the family as persons who merely bargain with each other, much as they would in a business context, leaves out considerable aspects of familial relationships, including love. Alternatively, Brinig notes that the concept of externalities, or third-party effects, a concept that derives from economics, can be a useful methodological tool when evaluating legal rules as applicable to families.

The final essay in this part, Martha Ertman's "The Business of Intimacy: Bridging the Private–Private Distinction," is an example of the application of private law models to view intimate relationships. Although the use of contract or business law as a lens through which one may view the intimate realm can seem to be a jarring juxtaposition, it is in fact quite apt. Both business and contract law allow considerable flexibility to parties in structuring relationships. It thus can be an interesting source of ideas for creating new models for the family relationship. Further, private law contract and business models and methodology have developed alongside and in response to market considerations. Ertman notes that both the intimate and business realms are traditionally viewed as private realms within society. However, not taking the marital relationship as a given, Ertman views business models as having the potential to govern a wider variety of forms of intimate pairings (or triplings) than does the marital model. Ertman makes the case for incorporating business models into the law governing intimate relationships because, unlike family law, business law is not governed by underlying natural-law principles that impose religious, traditional, and morality-based constraints on forms of intimate relationships. Ertman further makes the case for using business models because such models are particularly able to adapt to changed circumstances and thus can provide fluidity, given the changing and evolving nature of family relationships. Ertman examines in detail three business models—the corporation, the partnership, and the limited liability company—and considers the applicability of the laws that define and regulate such models to the regulation of the entering into and the exiting from intimate relationships.

CHAPTER 17

What Do Women Really Want?

Economics, Justice, and the Market for Intimate Relationships

June Carbone

Many would describe the tensions between neoclassical economists and legal feminists as all out war, with battle lines hardened and neither side conceding the legitimacy of the other camp's starting assumptions. I prefer the metaphor of the Cape of Good Hope, which oversees the clash of two oceans, with opposing currents (and vocabulary) and raging storms, but at the end of the day a measure of integration.

Economics and feminism, at least when they turn their attention to the interaction of men and women, describe the same events. Both chart the transformation in the family from an insistence on marriage, as a realm of opportunistic men and dependent women that provided the only acceptable locus for childrearing, to a greater embrace of both egalitarian and single-parent families. Economics, however, tells the tale in tones of tragedy, arguing that women's greater labor force participation lessens the payoff from family investment and discourages the "efficient" division of labor that maximized utility through an emphasis on men's income and women's devotion to children. Feminists recount the same tale with notes of triumph, contending that women's greater independence gives them the ability to renegotiate the terms of an intrinsically oppressive relationship—or to leave if their concerns remain undressed.

Neoclassical economists and feminists disagree most emphatically on the morals of their respective stories, but even here there is some hope for integration. Recast in the language of economics, the feminist celebration of female independence becomes a description of efficiency-enhancing specialization among women that complements, rather than supplements, family arrangements and promotes overall welfare. Economics then sounds an appropriate precautionary note, predicting that the net result will be less marriage, fewer children, and only a relative increase in equality. The most truly irreconcilable differences in these accounts are the ones in emphasis.

Gary Becker and the Rise of Imperial Economics

Economics, widely referred to as the "dismal science," has long involved the study of commerce, trade, resource allocation, and anything else that can be profitably explained in terms of greed. For equally long a period, its contributions to the realms of love or emotion have been suspect. Forty years ago, Gary Becker, a University of Chicago economist, set out to change all of that. Imperial economics' leading colonizer, Becker declared that "the economic approach provides a framework applicable to all human behavior," from homicide to filial affection.[1] The centerpiece of his colonizing efforts within the family was his 1981 *Treatise on the Family;* a decade later, he was rewarded with the Nobel Prize in Economics.

Applying economics to the supposedly altruistic world of the family is controversial in part because of the assumptions at the core of economic theory. As a discipline, economics acquires its power, its ability to express insights in mathematical form and to predict human behavior with a physics-like appearance of precision, from its use of simplifying assumptions. The most important of these assumptions is the notion that people act rationally to maximize utility, or in other words, that they will do what is necessary to get what they want. If, for example, a suburban homeowner enjoys Star Trek reruns more than mowing the lawn, an economist would not be surprised to learn that she spends more time watching TV than cutting grass, or that she is willing to pay more for lawn mowing than her neighbor who enjoys the exercise. In the hands of an economist, such assumptions might be used to analyze the pricing structure of an entire industry.[2]

To be sure, these simplifying assumptions can be controversial even when applied to financial transactions. Robin West argued in the *Harvard Law Review* that the portrait of human motivation in Franz Kafka's novels presents at least as persuasive an alternative.[3] Kafka, one of the most distinctive of European novelists, delighted in featuring central characters absorbed, for example, by metamorphosis into a cockroach. His characters, West emphasizes, are often devoid of rational, let alone profit-maximizing, behavior. It would not be hard to imagine a Kafkaesque character who hated mowing the lawn and did it, whether needed or not, several hours a day. Richard Posner, invited by the *Harvard Law Review* to respond, disputed West's interpretation of Kafka,[4] but the classic answer is Milton Friedman's. Friedman argued in the 1930s that economics does not depend on people being rational or selfish. All that matters is that they act as though they are. Friedman maintained that economics was in the business of prediction, not psychology. If, on aggregate, people who hate lawn mowing are willing to pay others to do it for them, it does not matter whether Franz Kafka can find (or imagine) someone who defies prediction.[5]

Gary Becker, who worked with Friedman at Chicago, pioneered the use of rational actor analysis to explain presumably altruistic behavior within the family. Initially these efforts were met with ridicule. He describes "giving a paper on economics and population at a conference in 1957 and people laughing at me."[6] Becker nonetheless persisted, and particularly with the enhanced stature that attends a Nobel laureate, he has assumed a role as one of the traditional family's leading theorists. His work, in a fashion characteristic of the economic approach, attempts to explain the family in terms of "grand theory," that is, to reduce a large number of complex and sometimes seemingly inconsistent events to a single conceptual framework, and then to use that framework to explain how the existing system came to be and the form future changes are likely to take. What Becker discovers, repackaged in economic terms, is the rise and fall of the traditional family.

Becker's 1981 *Treatise on the Family* exalts, as the central feature of family life, the sexual division of labor and the evolution of a marriage as a long-term contract designed to promote and protect this division. Becker's idea of specialization will be familiar to anyone who has ever taken an undergraduate course in economics. Imagine two islands X and Y that produce two goods—guns and butter—or more productively, coconuts and eggs. The two islands can increase their joint production of the goods, the economic account maintains, if X specializes in one, Y specializes in the other, and they trade. Even if Island X is better at producing both coconuts *and* eggs, it can increase its overall wealth by specializing in the form of production in which it has the greatest comparative advantage over Y and encouraging Y to invest in production of the other good.

Becker uses the same approach to describe the advantages of the family. In chapter 2 of his treatise, he posits two types of human activity, H_1, defined in terms of market activity, and H_2, household production. He observes that within families, "[t]he most pervasive division is between married women, who traditionally have devoted most of their time to childbearing and other domestic activities, and married men, who have hunted, soldiered, farmed, and engaged in other 'market' activities."[7] With scientific precision, he then advances a series of theorems, along with supporting equations. Theorems 2.1 and 2.4, for example, provide the following:

> Theorem 2.1. If all members of an efficient household have different comparative advantages, no more than one member would allocate time to both the market and the household sectors.

> Theorem 2.4. If commodity production functions have constant or increasing returns to scale, *all* members of efficient households would specialize completely in the market or household sectors and would invest only in market or household capital.[8]

Although Becker's defense of specialization is economic orthodoxy, his application to the family is both innovative and controversial. It is difficult, for example, to visualize what "commodity production functions with constant or increasing returns to scale" would mean in the context of the family: the increasing marginal productivity of child rearing (five children do not cost five times as much to raise as one)? cookie baking (30 batches of chocolate chip cookies can be more efficiently produced than 29)? Nonetheless, even the weaker assumptions of theorem 2.1 result in the conclusion that to reap the greatest benefits only one parent should concentrate on a career; the other would be better off with no more than a part-time job. In Becker's world the most efficient families will be those in which Dad brings home the bacon and Mom cooks it.

Becker maintains that the advantages that proceed from this division of labor do not depend on testosterone or any other inherent differences between men and women. Gay or lesbian couples, for example, could also reap advantages from having one partner concentrate on the home and the other on the market. Nonetheless, in one of the most controversial parts of the book, Becker uses biology to explain why the intrafamily division is a sexual one. He writes:

> Although the sharp sexual division of labor in all societies between the market and household sectors is partly due to the gains from specialized investments, it is also partly due to intrinsic differences between the sexes.
>
> . . . [B]iological differences in comparative advantage explain not only why households typically have both sexes, but also why women have usually spent their time bearing and rearing children and engaging in other household activities, whereas men have spent their time in market activities. This sexual division of labor has been found in virtually all human societies, and in most other biological species that fertilize eggs within the body of the female.[9]

Becker acknowledges the societal role in promoting gender stereotypes and explains how this, too, is efficient. He reasons that "deviant investments [medical education for women?] would presumably be more common if deviant biology [women unable to have children, women unwilling to be homemakers, or women more likely than their husbands to succeed in the medical profession?] were more common—or if it were revealed at younger ages."[10] Given the inability to predict these matters from childhood, it is easier, and the utility-maximizing individual will be predicted, to assume that girls should take home economics while boys study auto mechanics. Different comparative advantages (those trained to be doctors—or auto mechanics—will find, upon marriage, that they can earn more than spouses trained to be homemakers) then become a self-fulfilling prophecy.

If, as Becker claims, the sexual division of labor is universal and the central advantage of family organization, why do so many scholars believe it is imperiled? Becker emphasizes that arranging an efficient division of labor is far from automatic and that much of the development of the family as an institution is designed to encourage the desired specialization. He observes:

Specialization of tasks, such as the division of labor between men and women, implies a dependence on others for certain tasks. Women have traditionally relied on men for provision of food, shelter, and protection, and men have traditionally relied on women for the bearing and rearing of children and the maintenance of the home. Consequently, both men and women have been made better off by a "marriage," the term for a written, oral, or customary long-term contract between a man and a woman to produce children, food and other commodities in a common household.[11]

Although this paragraph treats the relationship between men and women as symmetrical, elsewhere Becker writes that "[s]ince married women have been specialized to childbearing and other domestic activities, they have demanded long-term 'contracts' from their husbands to protect them against abandonment and other adversities. Virtually all societies have developed long-term protection for married women."[12] Marriage, and the traditional family, served as a guarantee necessary to persuade women to undertake their domestic tasks.

Lloyd Cohen puts it more bluntly. In an article subtitled, "I Gave Him the Best Years of My Life . . . ," Cohen notes that the investments men and women make in their respective spheres are not parallel.[13] Investment in market capital is portable; a man with a good job can take it with him to another marriage. Investment in household activities, on the other hand is "marriage specific"; the children from a first marriage are a liability to a second. In the marriage market Becker and Cohen describe, those commanding the greatest value are young women and wealthy men.[14]

Cohen argues that this asymmetry in marital contributions creates the risk of what economists call "opportunistic behavior" and what others have referred to as "wife stuffing." *Doonesbury*, though, almost certainly does a better job than the economists in depicting the phenomenon. Several years ago, Gary Trudeau, *Doonesbury*'s creator, ran a series of comic strips in which Mark Slackmeyer's middle-aged father divorces his wife of many years. Mark's mother, wrinkled, graying, and middle-aged, is drawn as the personification of Cohen's title "I Gave Him the Best Years of My Life . . ." In the final set of the series, Mr. Slackmeyer, short, balding, and just as middle-aged as the wife he left behind, is shown walking down the aisle with a stunningly attractive young professional. Slackmeyer, portrayed in the strip as a successful executive, has successfully "traded in" his wife of many years for a new model.[15]

Picking up Becker's mantle of economic analysis and applying it to family law, Allen Parkman, the Regents Professor of Management at the University of New Mexico, maintains that this scenario illustrates the answer to the question in the title of his book *No-Fault Divorce: What Went Wrong?*[16] Realization of the gains from specialization and trade require enforcement of the bargain, Parkman argues. If one party lives up to her end of the deal, becoming more vulnerable because of it, and the other party is free to walk away at any time—and can benefit from doing so—then the gains that occur from specialization will not be realized. Parkman uses this analysis to argue that no-fault divorce is dangerously misguided. If Becker is right that the foundation of the family is specialization, and Cohen is right that the exchange that follows is asymmetrical, then treating marriage as no more than a voluntary relationship that either party can end at will discourages the enterprise. Women will reject the path of efficiency and refuse to stay home and take care of the children.

Becker, skeptical about the impact of legal rules,[17] identifies an alternative culprit to explain increasing divorce, falling fertility, and other signs of decreasing domestic productivity. "I believe," he writes, "that the major cause of these changes is the growth of the earning power of women as the American economy has developed. . . . The gain from marriage is reduced by a rise in the earnings and labor force participation of women and by a fall in fertility because a sexual division of labor becomes less advantageous. . . . And divorce becomes more attractive when the gain from marriage is reduced."[18] At the margin where economists conduct their calculations, women enjoy more attractive alternatives to marriage and homemaking than they once did, and thus the price it takes to persuade them to marry and stay married has risen.

Becker himself, in a manner typical of economists, limits his analysis to description, reserving judgment about whether these changes in the family are for better or ill. Indeed, his last chapter has the feel of a Greek tragedy in which what happens to the central characters (at least to the extent it is tied to women's workforce participation) is the product of ineluctable forces beyond hope of control. Those using economic analysis in other disciplines, however, recognize no such limitations. Within law, which as a discipline addresses what the law *ought* to be as much it describes what the law is, the type of analysis Becker pioneered has been used to prescribe a more traditional family code. The law should encourage family stability, Ira Ellman argues in a lead article in the *California Law Review,* by protecting the exchange upon which the traditional family is based.[19] Eliminating fault from the system eliminated the traditional obligation to stay married in ways that work systematically to the disadvantage of women who devote their energies to the home. Reintroducing mutual consent as a prerequisite for divorce, which Parkman champions, or redefining alimony in terms of lost career opportunities, which Ellman advocates, should eliminate some of the "distorting incentives" that discourage women from devoting themselves to a domestic role and undermine the benefits of family life.

This legal analysis, which at most explains why family law may have accelerated the pace of family change, ultimately fails, however, to provide a comprehensive picture of how specialization within the family will coexist with the larger changes occurring in the world outside and to account for the fact that, with the advent of no-fault divorce, women, not men like Mark Slackmeyer's dad, are the ones most likely to want out of marriage.[20]

Susan Moller Okin and the Critique of Efficiency

If Becker is a seminal figure in the extension of economic analysis to the family, then Susan Moller Okin is an ovial one in applying principles of justice to the domestic sphere. Okin, a professor of political science at Stanford, provides what Michael Walzer describes as "the first sustained feminist account of distributive justice."[21] Okin's thesis, developed philosopher by philosopher, is that however justice is measured, if the same principles were applied to the family, the family could not pass muster. What is so startling about this thesis is that until the 1989 publication of Okin's book *Justice, Gender, and the Family,* no one else seemed to notice it.

Okin's introduction explains:

> Political theory, which had been sparse for a period before the late 1960's . . . has become a flourishing field, with social justice as its central concern. Yet, remarkably, major contemporary theorists of justice have almost without exception ignored the [family]. . . . They have displayed little interest in or knowledge of the findings of feminism. They have largely bypassed the fact that the society to which their theories are supposed to pertain is heavily and deeply affected by gender, and faces difficult issues of justice stemming from its gendered past and present assumptions. Since theories of justice are centrally concerned with whether, how and why persons should be treated differently from one another, this neglect seems inexplicable.[22]

Okin then reviews the work of the leading contemporary political theorists—Sandel, Bloom, MacIntyre, Nozick, Rawls, Walzer—and demonstrates how their conceptions of justice cannot be reconciled with the operation of the family. Her consideration of John Rawls occupies the literal and intellectual center of the book.

Okin begins her Rawls discussion by noting that his *Theory of Justice* "has had the most powerful influence of any work of contemporary moral and political theory."[23] Indeed, Rawls has been credited with single-handedly bringing about the revival of the political theory Okin describes in her introduction. Rawls's work champions the idea of "justice as fairness," and in determining what is fair, Rawls uses what Okin terms "a construct, or heuristic device, that is both his single most important contribution to moral and political theory and the focus of most of the controversy his theory still attracts, nearly twenty years after its publication."[24] Rawls's construct involves imagining an "original position" in which parties deliberate through a "veil of ignorance" in which they do not know the personal characteristics—wealth, class, intelligence, race, gender—they will have in the world governed by the principles they devise. He then assumes, among other things, that his representatives are risk averse, that is, that they fear loss of the basic necessities of life more than they value the opportunity for extraordinary gain. From these assumptions, Rawls derives two principles to which those in the original position would presumably agree: the principle of equal basic liberty for all individuals, and the "difference principle," which provides that for differences in authority, wealth, and other benefits to be justified, they must work to the greatest benefit of the least advantaged and must be attached to positions accessible to all under conditions of fair equal opportunity.[25]

Rawls makes no attempt to apply this construct to the family. Indeed, he makes the parties in the original position *heads* of families, rendering, as Jane English observes, "the family opaque to claims of justice."[26] Nonetheless, Okin argues, not only is there no reason in theory why Rawlsian principles should not be applied to gender, but the idea of the original position seems particularly well suited to testing the fairness of the consequences that flow from sexual difference. Okin then systematically critiques the ways in which a gendered society cannot meet the criteria of *A Theory of Justice*. The most important of her claims concerns the gendered operation of the family.

The family Okin describes should be immediately recognizable to anyone who has studied Gary Becker. Its central features are a sexual division of labor, and concomitant dependency and restricted opportunities for women. Whereas Becker addressed rational choice and efficiency, however, Okin's concern is power, and she invokes the work of another economist, Albert O. Hirschman, to explain the traditional family's power dynamics. Hirschman's 1970 book *Exit, Voice, and Loyalty* was a classic exposition of the role of asymmetry in relationships and, like Becker and Parkman, Hirschman used analogies drawn from international trade to illustrate his ideas.[27] Imagine, Hirschman posited, two islands, A and B, which specialize in different goods (eggs and coconuts? H_1 and H_2?) and trade. Imagine further that B, which has fewer outlets for its products, is more dependent on the trading relationship than is A. Although both parties benefit from their continuing trade, A has the greater ability to leave unharmed, and, Hirschman concludes, this threat gives A greater ability to dictate the terms of the relationship.

Okin spends the last several chapters of the book demonstrating how such asymmetries systematically disadvantage women. She emphasizes studies of power within the family, showing that for all but lesbian couples, "the amount of money a person earns—in comparison with a partner's income—establishes relative power" and that the housewife with preschool children is at the least powerful point in her marriage, with her power likely to decrease further only with the birth of additional children. Okin notes with some irony that the *more* a woman contributes in the form of domestic services, that is, the more she specializes in the production of a product of value to her husband alone, the *less* her influence is likely to be within the relationship.[28]

Although Okin titles her analysis "Vulnerability by Marriage," she take pains to show, in a manner strikingly similar to Becker's, the interactions between women's domestic role in marriage, their premarital education and socialization, their limited opportunities within the workplace, and their vulnerability by separation and divorce. Okin echoes Becker's conclusion that although no-fault divorce has probably not had much impact on the divorce rate itself, it has affected the allocation of resources thereby contributing to the impoverishment of divorced women and their children.[29]

Okin's ultimate conclusion is that women's systematic vulnerability because of, and within, marriage cannot be reconciled with any of the accepted accounts of justice in our society, and that "any just and fair solution to the urgent problem of women's and children's vulnerability must encourage and facilitate the equal sharing by men and women of paid and unpaid work, of productive and reproductive labor. We must work toward a future in which all will be likely to choose this mode of life. A just future would be one without gender."[30]

Okin's call for more egalitarian families resonates with the conclusions of scholars in other disciplines. Rhona Mahony's book *Kidding Ourselves: Breadwinning, Babies, and Bargaining Power* amplifies Okin's discussion of power.[31] Mahony draws on game theory to design strategies intended to implement the egalitarian future Okin advocates. Mahony advises women to (1) "train up," that is, to acquire the education and skills necessary for well-paying jobs; (2) "marry down," that is, marry otherwise desirable men likely to earn less than they will; (3) increase their BATNAS (best alternative to negotiated agreement) by refusing to cut back disproportionately on their labor market activity or to assume the major share of child rearing; and (4) revalue homemaking to make it more attractive for men as well women. Mahony acknowledges, however, in a way that Okin does not, the tension between gains from specialization within marriage, on the one hand, and egalitarian roles, on the other. Her solution is to focus on the elimination of the *sexual* division of labor in the belief that "when men are doing half the child care, more couples will choose to reap the gains of specialization that a homemaker gives his or her family. Breadwinner–homemaker couples will outnumber the oddballs who try to share parenting fifty-fifty."[32] In the meantime, however, women should avoid making the choices that consign them to a domestic role.

Mahony is sensitive to the charge that family life should be about more than maneuvering for personal advantage; she responds that the existing division of household labor is already the product of negotiation, and her book simply points out how women can become better at it. In similar fashion, movement toward the more egalitarian roles Okin and Mahony advocate has occurred more through individual decisions than from invocation of abstract principles or self-conscious gender reform. Consider two popular accounts of the very different sets of choices made by two famous American women:

> In the fall of 1919, [Rose] . . . became pregnant for the fourth time in four years. Sick of Joe's philandering and his absences, she declared she'd had enough. Early in January 1920 Rose left her children and her husband and returned to her parents in Dorcester.
>
> The separation lasted three weeks. But if Rose hoped her errant, perpetually absent husband would come crawling for forgiveness, she was to be disappointed. Joe did not come at all. It was thus left to her father, John F. Fitzgerald, to tell Rose her Irish-Catholic duty. . . . Rose [who had married Joe over her parents' objections], he felt, had made her own bed and she must lie in it. "What is past is past. the old days are gone. . . . You've made your commitment, Rosie, and you must honor it now."
>
> To her credit, Rose Kennedy did. She returned to Beals Street, her three children, and her husband. A few weeks later, on February 20, 1920, she gave birth to her fourth child, a second daughter, whom they christened Kathleen. Rose never again broke down or even complained. For good or ill, she would become the archetypal, stoic Irish-Catholic mother.[33]
>
> By now [the time of the Whitewater investment], it must . . . have been obvious that Hillary couldn't count much on financial contributions from her husband, given his earning prospects and lack of interest in making money. . . .
>
> According to friends of the couple, it was also at this time that Hillary expressed doubts about the future of her marriage, and, as a result, whether she could count on Bill to support her and a child. Their marriage, now in its third year, was at a low point. If Gennifer Flowers's account can be believed, she and Bill were in the passionate early stages of their affair that summer. People close to the Clintons were aware of other women in Bill's life, too.
>
> Bill and Hillary's move to the governor's mansion in January 1979 did little to ease these anxieties. If anything, Bill's greater celebrity status opened up more opportunities. He confided in Susan McDougal that he loved being governor: "This is fun. Women are throwing themselves at me. All the while I was growing up, I was the fat boy in the Big Boy jeans."[34]

However much one might discount the popular versions of their lives, Rose Fitzgerald Kennedy and Hillary Rodham Clinton clearly made very different choices based on their perceptions of the alternatives available to them. Rose "specialized" in the family (while her absent husband made millions) in almost precisely the way Gary Becker describes, and she appears to have occupied a role almost completely without power in the relationship. Hillary became a law firm partner—and invested in Whitewater, James Stewart believes—because of the type of reasoning Rhona Mahony advocates. Although Stewart reports that with Chelsea's birth, Hillary's "thoughts of leaving Bill were banished," she appears to have fashioned a more egalitarian and certainly more influential role than did Rose. Indeed, when First Daughter Chelsea needed permission at school to take some aspirin, she is widely to reported to have told the school nurse, "Call my dad, my mom's too busy."[35] Gary Becker would have nonetheless predicted the other striking difference between the two couples: Rose had nine children while Hillary has one.

Feminism *and* Economics: The Forces of Social Change

Despite differences in discipline and perspective, Gary Becker and Susan Moller Okin describe the same family—the nuclear family at midcentury. And despite occasional pretensions to universality (Becker: "the sharp sexual division of labor in all societies between the market and household sectors")[36] and diversity (Okin: "there are no shared meanings . . . about the appropriate roles of men and women, and about which family forms and divisions of labor are most beneficial for partners, parents and children"),[37] they could both take as their starting point the sitcom couples of the fifties: the Nelsons (*Ozzie and Harriet*), the Reeds (the *Donna Reed Show*), even the Ricardos (*I Love Lucy*). These shows played out the sexual division of labor Becker and Okin describe, with successful breadwinners, full-time homemakers, tensions that build to successful resolution, and only occasional yearnings for something more.

Becker and Okin achieve their greatest resonance when they describe the changes that take us away from the idealized families of the fifties. Becker, although he uses dramatic language ("the family in the United States changed more rapidly [from 1950 to 1977] than during any equivalent period since the founding of the colonies"),[38] concentrates most of his analysis, in proper economic focus, at the margin, that is, on the incremental changes that affect family decision making. Becker believes that the major cause of increased divorce, declining fertility, delayed childbearing, and greater illegitimacy is "the growth in the earning power of women as the American economy developed."[39] In short, with increasing pay for women's services, women work more. As a result, Becker argues, specialization within the family lessens, the gains from marriage drop, and divorce rates jump. Welfare state programs that subsidize the cost of child rearing increase the effect.

What is curious about Becker's analysis is that he could have described exactly the same developments in terms of *increased* specialization, and had he done so, the analysis would have been more accurate. Economist David Friedman explains that the increased workforce participation Becker emphasizes produces greater, not less, specialization as women trade in the largely undifferentiated role of wife and mother for a more complex array of activities.[40] In the sitcom families of old, Lucy Ricardo's activities differed only slightly from Donna Reed's. In the real world, Lucy was a successful executive and Donna a recognized actress (and by the eighties her TV character might have been a medical professional) in addition to their activities as wives and mothers. Moreover, while women's productivity gains as they become doctors, lawyers, day-care providers, office workers, fast food servers, and medical technicians are dramatic, any decrease in specialization between men and women is not. Barbara Bergmann reported in the mid-eighties that "husbands of wives with full-time jobs averaged about two minutes more housework per day than did husbands in housewife-maintaining families, hardly enough additional time to prepare a soft-boiled egg."[41] Women's increased specialization accordingly dwarfs any reallocation of responsibilities within the family. How then can decreased specialization explain Becker's parade of horribles? Becker's analysis requires translation, and Okin supplies the vocabulary.

Simply stated, Okin's book explains just how bad a deal traditional marriage has been for women. Surveys consistently show that married men are happier than single men; single women are happier than married women.[42] Unhappily married women remain married, Okin maintains, because the younger the children, the more of them, and the less the mother earns, that is, the greater her "specialization" within the family, the less the woman's ability to leave or credibly threaten to do so. Without the possibility of "exit," "voice"—and the ability to share the burden of changing diapers or making school lunches—diminishes as well.[43]

Becker acknowledges the circular reinforcement of women's domestic role as employers discriminate against women on the basis of their stereotypical expectations that women will devote more energy to home than market, girls invest less in education and training in response to such expectations, and women then choose to spend more time at home because of the lack of alternatives. What he does not acknowledge is that the same forces reinforce patterns of power and satisfaction within marriage. Joe Kennedy could get away with flagrant adultery and a highly visible affair with Gloria Swanson at least in part because Rose had no where to go.

Restated in terms of Okin's analysis of power, Becker's reference to "reduced gains from marriage" becomes an explanation of the increasing attractiveness of the alternatives.[44] Consider again the powerless mother with young children in Okin's book. If she works full time and hires a babysitter, the family may gain more from the extra income than it would from her domestic efforts. If, however, her husband drinks too much, stays out too late, or emotionally abuses her or the children, divorce becomes a more realistic option than it would be for her homemaker counterpart. The overall well-being of this couple may be greater than if she remained a homemaker, but the resources in their marriage will be distributed differently and the relative advantages to remaining married may be accordingly less. Proud, ambitious, college-educated Rose Fitzgerald, were she a young woman today, would almost certainly leave Joe Kennedy even if the potential benefits from staying were no less.

It is tempting at this point to conclude that Becker is right, that women's new jobs cause family breakdown; it is just that Okin better states the reasons—that once women acquire a measure of independence, they become unwilling to put up with the louts they married. Indeed, Okin's insights are easily translated into economics terms. Becker himself might note that as the gains women make from trading with each other (and McDonald's) increase, their price for continued participation in marriage rises, and fewer men are willing or able to pay. Shoshana Grossbard-Shechtman, who studied under Becker in Chicago, proposes a general theory of marriage in almost exactly such terms,[45] and empirical research confirms that women, particularly younger women, are more likely to initiate divorce than men. Lenore Weitzman's *Divorce Revolution*, in the midst of pessimism about everything else liberalized divorce has wrought, reports that "even the longer-married housewives who suffer the greatest financial hardships after divorce (and who feel the most economically deprived, most angry, and most 'cheated' by the divorce settlement) say they are 'personally' better off than they were during the marriage."[46]

If this were happening in isolation, the result would not necessarily have to be more divorce. Instead, with time, the terms on which marriages were conducted would change, women would acquire a greater measure of influence, society would shift toward the more egalitarian future Okin advocates, and the divorce rate would increase only temporarily until couples adjusted to the new power structure and men became more willing to wash the dishes. Okin's book would become not only prescriptive but predictive, driven by the forces Becker identified. The real world, however, is more complicated.

To begin with, relative power within marriage is not the only thing that shapes attitudes. Polls show that men and women have different expectations about the roles they and their spouses will play during marriage and that the size of the gender gap varies over time, race, and class.[47] Income and employment differences between African American men and women, for example, are smaller than those between white men and women without necessarily resulting in more egalitarian attitudes or gender roles.[48] Although the reasons for the racial differences are complex, the result of women's greater independence can be less marriage rather than renegotiation of its terms.[49] Joe Kennedy, after all, might find it harder to continue his affairs on the side, but he would also find it easier to divorce Rose and marry Gloria Swanson.

In addition, any decline in specialization between men and women is *only* at the margin. Despite women's relatively greater independence, they still bear the overwhelming responsibility for child rearing, whether they do it themselves or hire other women to help them. Okin requires dismantling the sexual division of labor, but although she puts forward a number of proposals that would make the child-rearing role less perilous, she does not persuasively explain how the elimination of gender differences is to occur. Victor Fuchs sounds a cautionary note. He argues that it is not the fact that women take care of children that is the source of their disadvantage but the fact that women care more about children.[50] If Fuchs is right, women's increased employment may result in greater autonomy, but it is unlikely to produce equality. Instead, it produces a recalculation of the curves that depict supply and demand. Both men and women enjoy greater alternatives to marriage as men enjoy more varied possibilities for sex and companionship and women have more varied opportunities for self-support. Even if the average person continues to experience greater benefits from married rather than single life, the marginal person contemplating engagement or divorce will insist on more in order for marriage to continue to be worthwhile. The effective price will be greater, fewer people will be willing to pay, and as Gary Becker correctly predicted, the ranks of the unmarried will skyrocket. A full assessment of the moral dimensions of the change, however, belongs to other disciplines.[51]

Notes

1. Gary S. Becker, *A Treatise on the Family* (Cambridge: Harvard University Press, 1981).

2. David D. Friedman, *Price Theory: An Intermediate Text,* 2d ed. (Cincinnati: South-Western Publishing, 1990).

3. Robin West, "Authority, Autonomy, and Choice: The Role of Consent in the Moral and Political Visions of Franz Kafka and Richard Posner," *Harvard Law Review* 99 (1985): 384.

4. Richard A. Posner, "The Ethical Significance of Free Choice: A Reply to Professor West," *Harvard Law Review* 99 (1986): 1431–48.

5. Milton Friedman, *Essays in Positive Economics* (Chicago: University of Chicago Press, 1935).

6. Richard Thomson, "Profile: Economist of the Mind," *Independent*, Oct. 18, 1992, 11.

7. Becker, *Treatise on the Family,* 14.

8. Ibid., 17, 19.

9. Ibid., 23.

10. Ibid., 25. Becker emphasizes "that 'deviance' is used only in a statistical, not a pejorative, sense" (24).

11. Ibid., 27.

12. Ibid., 14.

13. Lloyd Cohen, "Divorce and Quasi Rents: or, I Gave Him the Best Years of My Life," *Journal of Legal Studies* 16 (1987): 267.

14. Cohen emphasizes that another way of thinking about the asymmetry is that men reap the greatest advantages during the peak child-rearing years, which tend to come early in the relationship; women enjoy the greatest benefits as the children grow older and their husband's earning capacity reaches its peak (ibid., 287).

15. At the wedding, however, when Slackmeyer toasts his new bride, he explains that "my lawyers took most of what I saved through the years and my ex-wife got the rest. The only thing that I can offer my new bride is my unconditional devotion. God willing, that will be enough." One of the guests is pictured in the next caption looking shocked and speculating, "Do you suppose she knew?" Mark responds, "I don't get it. Why are we here?" *Doonesbury* comic strip, May 17, 1990.

16. Allen M. Parkman, *No-Fault Divorce: What Went Wrong?* (Boulder, CO:: Westview Press, 1992).

17. Becker invokes the Coase theorem to express skepticism about the impact of any legal change. An economic imperialist like Becker, Ronald Coase is a seminal figure in the introduction of economic analysis to law. See Ronald H. Coase, "The Problem of Social Cost," *Journal of Law and Economics* 3 (1960): 1. In the early sixties, Coase wrote that absent transaction costs, legal changes might redistribute wealth but were unlikely to affect outcomes. Coase gave the example of a railroad that ran through wheat fields, giving off sparks that occasionally caused fires. Without transaction costs, Coase argued, either the farmers would pay the railroad to take effective precautions or the railroad would pay the farmers for the damage to their crops. Either way, the parties would bargain until they reached the optimal outcome, that is, one that maximized the joint welfare from the farms and the railroad. Becker argues that married couples should similarly be expected to negotiate. In a fault-based system that effectively requires the consent of the other spouse for a divorce, the party who most wants the divorce would have to pay a higher price than in a no-fault system, *but,* Becker concludes, there would be no reason to believe that the overall divorce rate would change.

Coase also argued, however, that with transaction costs, the railroad could effectively be made to pay the farmers for their losses, but the farmers were unlikely to be able to organize in a way that would permit them to pay the railroad enough to stop its harmful activity. Coase's larger point was that it would often be the effect of transaction costs, rather than efficiency considerations, that should determine the choice of which laws to enact. Becker discounts the transaction costs that might prevent married couples from bargaining efficiently, but even a cursory examination of the factors that might prevent a couple from providing effective guarantees of fault-free behavior counsels hesitation. It is interesting to consider, for example, what security a wife might demand as a precondition to giving up a well-paying job to care for the children. Becker, *Treatise on the Family* (2d ed.), 331. *See, more generally,* Robert C. Ellickson, *Order without Law: How Neighbors Settle Disputes* (Cambridge: Harvard University Press, 1991).

18. Becker, *Treatise on the Family,* 245, 248.

19. Ira Ellman, "The Theory of Alimony," *California Law Review* 77 (1989): 1. *See also* June Carbone, "Economics, Feminism, and the Reinvention of Alimony: A Reply to Ira Ellman," *Vanderbilt Law Review* 43 (1990): 1463.

20. *See, e.g.,* Susan Faludi, *Backlash: The Undeclared War against American Women* (New York: Crown, 1991), 26 (national surveys indicate that "less than a third of divorced men say they were the spouse who wanted the divorce, while women report they were the ones actively seeking divorce 55 to 66% of the time); Sanford L. Braver, Marnie Whitley, and Christine Ng, "Who Divorced Whom: Methodological and Legal Issues," *Journal of Divorce and Remarriage* 20 (1993): 1 (in a sample of 378 families, interviewer found that in two out of three cases the parties identified the wife as the first party to want out of the marriage); National Center for Health Statistics, *Monthly Vital Statistics Report,* 38 (May 21, 1991): 2 (in 1,988 divorces involving families with children, 64.9% were filed by women); *Healthpoint: Mills-Peninsula Hospital,* Jan.-Feb. 1992 (reporting on a study by Joan Kelly, which found that women under age forty-five were significantly more likely to initiate divorce than their husbands, whereas the rates for men and women above age forty-five were even). For a more recent review of this issue, *see* Margaret F.

Brinig and Douglas W. Allen, " 'These Boots Are Made for Walking': Why Mostly Wives File for Divorce," *American Law and Economics Review* 2 (2000): 126.

21. Quoted from the back cover of Susan Moller Okin, *Justice, Gender, and the Family* (New York: Basic Books, 1989). *The Oxford Dictionary of Philosophy* provides the following definition of distributive justice: "Justice, distributive. The problem is to lay down principles specifying the just distribution of benefits and burdens: the outcome in which everyone receives their due. A common basis is that persons should be treated equally unless reasons for inequality exist; after that the problems include the kind of reasons that justify departing from equality, the role of the state in rectifying inequality, and the link between a distributive system and the maximization of well-being." Simon Blackburn, *The Oxford Dictionary of Philosophy* (New York: Oxford University Press, 1994).

22. Okin, *Justice, Gender, and the Family,* 7–8.

23. John Rawls, *A Theory of Justice* (Cambridge: Harvard University Press, 1971). Okin, *Justice, Gender, and the Family,* 89.

24. Okin, *Justice, Gender, and the Family,* 90.

25. Ibid., 93. *See also* John Rawls, *Political Liberalism* (New York: Columbia University Press, 1993), which moves away from Rawls's emphasis on the original position.

26. Cited in Okin, *Justice, Gender, and the Family,* 94.

27. Albert O. Hirschman, *Exit, Voice, and Loyalty: Response to Decline in Firms, Organizations, and States* (Cambridge: Harvard University Press, 1970).

28. Okin, *Justice, Gender, and the Family,* 157–59. Okin bases her conclusions on power within the family on two studies: Robert O. Blood Jr. and Donald M. Wolfe, *Husbands and Wives: The Dynamics of Married Living* (New York: Free Press, 1960); and Philip Blumstein and Pepper Schwartz, *American Couples* (New York: Morrow, 1983). Okin notes that the Blood and Wolfe study, "though informative, is now outdated and unreliable in the way it interprets its own findings." She protests that "the authors' biases are apparent throughout, from their labeling of the less powerful husband "Caspar Milquetoast" to their pronouncement that families ranging from husband-dominance to "extreme egalitarianism" are "appropriate" but that wife-dominance is a "deviant" and "not normal" reversal of marital roles (156–57). Of course, Blood and Wolfe may have been using the term *deviant* in the same sense that Becker did, as a statistical rather than a normative statement.

29. Okin, *Justice, Gender, and the Family,* 160–67.

30. Ibid., 171.

31. Rhona Mahony, *Kidding Ourselves: Breadwinning, Babies, and Bargaining Power* (New York: Basic Books, 1995).

32. Ibid., 227.

33. Nigel Hamilton, *JFK: Reckless Youth* (New York: Random House, 1992), 41.

34. James B. Stewart, *Blood Sport: The President and His Adversaries* (New York: Simon and Schuster, 1996).

35. The story, however, may be apocryphal. "The story about the school nurse is not true, but it is a good one," Hillary Clinton is reported to have said. "Family File: Hillary's a Busy Lady, but She's Not That Busy," *Los Angeles Times,* June 15, 1994.

36. Becker, *Treatise on the Family* (2d ed.), 37.

37. Okin, *Justice, Gender, and the Family,* 172.

38. Becker, *Treatise on the Family,* 350.

39. Ibid.

40. Friedman, *Price Theory,* 596–97. Peg Brinig and I have also argued that women's labor market participation has resulted in more, rather than less, specialization. *See, e.g.,* June Carbone and Margaret F. Brinig, "Rethinking Marriage: Feminist Ideology, Economic Change and Divorce Reform," *Tulane Law Review* 65 (1991): 953.

41. Okin, *Justice, Gender, and the Family,* 153, citing Bergman. *See also* Barbara R. Bergman, *The Economic Emergence of Women* (New York: Basic Books, 1986), 263. Men have assumed somewhat greater responsibility in the last decade, but even fatherhood advocates acknowledge

that women still perform twice as much child care as men, it's just that twenty years ago they were performing three times as much. For a summary of the data, *see* Nancy Levitt, *The Gender Line: Men, Women, and the Law* (New York: New York University Press, 1998), 44.

42. Faludi, *Backlash*, 15, 17, 36–39, summarizes the data.

43. Okin, *Justice, Gender, and the Family*, 157.

44. Becker, *Treatise on the Family*, 331. I thank Bill Sundstrom for reminding me of this point.

45. Shoshana Grossbard-Shechtman, *On the Economics of Marriage: A Theory of Marriage, Labor, and Divorce* (Boulder, CO: Westview Press, 1993). Grossbard-Shechtman, who uses even more equations and opaque language than Becker, develops her theory over the course of two chapters that defy succinct summarization. Nonetheless, she describes the model's principal insights as the following: the hypotheses that labor force participation of married women varies with the sex ratio of those eligible for marriage, that income changes influence wives' labor supply more than husbands,' that group differences in patterns of division of spousal labor influence the elasticity of female labor supply, and that a positive correlation between achievement in markets for labor and spousal labor can provide an additional explanation for the backward-bending supply of labor. The theory also offers interesting insights regarding consumption, fertility, and marriage (51). The starting point for Grossbard-Shechtman's observations is that the conventional labor market and the marriage market are interrelated and that, for example, increased income affects both the supply and demand of household labor, marriage, and divorce.

46. Lenore J. Weitzman, *The Divorce Revolution: The Unexpected Social and Economic Consequences for Women and Children in America* (New York: Free Press, 1985), 346.

47. *See generally* Michael S. Kimmel, ed., *Changing Men* (Newbury Park, CA: Sage Publications, 1987).

48. The literature on race and gender roles is complex. Popular accounts report a gulf between black men and women. *See, e.g.,* Ellis Cose, "Black Men and Black Women," *Newsweek,* June 5, 1995, 66; Michelle Wallace, *Black Macho and the Myth of the Superwoman* (New York: Dial Press, 1979); Ellis Cose, *A Man's World* (New York: Harper Collins, 1995), 64. Cose cites surveys as finding that 42 percent of black men, compared with 32 percent of white men, held a primarily "recreational" view of sex, whereas fewer than 9 percent of black women, compared with more than 21 percent of white women, saw pleasure as the primary purpose of sex. More rigorous studies confirm the existence of gender differences among blacks that follow different patterns from those among whites. *See, e.g.,* Orlando Patterson, *Rituals of Blood: Consequences of Slavery in Two American Centuries* (Washington, DC: Civitas/Counterpoint, 1998); Noel A. Cazenave and George H. Leon, "Men's Work and Family Roles and Characteristics," in *Changing Men,* Michael S. Kimmel, ed. (Newbury Park, CA: Sage Publications, 1987). Cazenave and Leon summarize the literature as finding that "social class and SES operate differently for black and white respondents. For white respondents, being middle class and of a high SES are associated with less sex typing and more liberal gender roles. For black respondents these factors are correlated with greater sex typing and conservatism on gender-role items than they are for either white middle-class respondents or black working-class respondents ("Men's Work and Family Roles," 245).

49. It is interesting, in this respect, to consider the case of Japan. A recent newspaper account summarizes the trends:

> Between the skyhigh cost of living and an oppressive, male-dominated society, Japanese women seem to have seized upon their own form of revenge: They have stopped having babies.
>
> Figures released over the weekend by the Health and Welfare Ministry showed that a mere 1.18 million babies were born in Japan last year, the lowest figure since the government began calculating the statistics in 1899. The ministry calculated that the average Japanese woman now produces an average of 1.43 babies in her lifetime, compared with 2.05 babies per American woman.
>
> Any figure below 2.08, demographers say, mean an inevitable decline in a country's population. . . .

[Critical to the falling birth rates, explained Haruo Sagaza, who teaches population studies at Waseda University's department of human science,] are the male-centered values of Japanese society, which assumes that it is the responsibility of the woman alone to raise children. As long as Japanese women work, they have freedom and their own money; once they become pregnant, their career choices diminish and they are forced to stay at home.

After knowing freedom, today's women prefer not to step into a marriage that will make them give up a lot of what they have, Sagaza said, calling the trend the "single-iza-tion" of women. (Michael Zielenziger, "Japanese Women Having Fewer Babies," *San Jose Mercury News,* July 9, 1996, 8A)

50. Victor R. Fuchs, *Women's Quest for Economic Equality* (Cambridge: Harvard University Press, 1988), 8.

51. Portions of this chapter appeared in June Carbone, *From Partners to Parents: The Second Revolution in Family Law* (Columbia University Press, 2000) and is reprinted with permission.

CHAPTER 18

Can Families Be Efficient?

A Feminist Appraisal

Ann Laquer Estin

Both feminist legal theory and Law and Economics analysis have come to occupy a significant place in the American legal academy, as demonstrated by
growing numbers of conferences, journals, casebooks and monographs, and
electronic mail lists in each area.[1] Not surprisingly, as the two fields have
grown, they have begun to touch, to overlap, and occasionally to come into
conflict. This process has been evident in the extensive literature on sex discrimination in employment and is increasingly apparent in writing on family
law issues. This article examines the convergence of feminist and Law and
Economics theory on family law questions, particularly issues of marriage and
divorce.

Laws governing financial aspects of divorce, including alimony and property
division rules, have been subjected to both types of theorizing; in some cases,
the policy recommendations of feminist and economics theorists have con-
verged. But the two frameworks are also remarkably different in their goals,
their methods, and their values. These differences emerge in both the prescriptions for legal change and the descriptive methodology of each approach.

Economists, and many of those in Law and Economics, have drawn a sharp
distinction between positive and normative economic theory. Feminist analysis, however, suggests that the boundary between positive and normative approaches is not easily drawn, or easily maintained, particularly when focusing
on nonmarket behavior, such as occurs in family relationships. In this essay I
put these methodological issues into sharper relief and suggest some conclusions about the potential and limits of economic approaches to family law in
light of the feminist critique.

Frameworks

As many writers have noted, economics as an academic discipline has been re-
sistant to feminist theory.[2] The primary reason is historical: for most of its life
span, economics as a discipline was not interested in women. Classical and
neoclassical models of economic activity constructed the market as the sphere

of production, the sphere of exchange, the sphere of economic life. The family was seen as entirely distinct from the market, and women's work in the family sphere was invisible and not valued.[3]

More recent generations of economists revised this view using economic methods to develop a theory addressing household production and family behavior.[4] Their "new home economics" has been primarily descriptive, developing explanations for patterns of family behavior from birth and education through courtship, marriage, divorce, and bequests. Some aspects of these new models, particularly the recognition that work in the home has real, productive value, are extraordinarily important.

There are many examples of the large gaps in traditional legal and economic thought where women's work is concerned: household labor is excluded from such statistical measures as the Gross National Product (GNP); it is ignored in the comparison of household living standards; it is not fully recognized by public benefits and tax laws; and it is treated differently than market labor in a wide range of tort, contract, and family law doctrines. In each of these areas, the new home economics provides a vocabulary and analytic framework that can be usefully employed to begin filling the gaps. This means that economic theories can help to remedy legal practices that have been consistently harmful to women's interests.[5]

At the same time, feminist theorists in law and in economics have challenged the descriptive model of the new home economics on a number of grounds. Although the model can be useful, it leaves out a great deal. Using the highly abstract approach and streamlined assumptions that are typical of economic proof, the new theory describes courtship, marriage, fertility, divorce, and making gifts and bequests to family members as rational, utility-maximizing behavior. Economists describe the gender-based division of labor in the household as efficient, in the sense that it allows a family to generate a maximum level of utility with a given set of resources.[6] But because these models omit much of the context and complexity of family life, the conclusions they yield have often seemed inadequate.

For feminists, the problem with these economic models is not only that they are so abstract but that the analysis often assumes precisely those points that we would most like to explore. Writing in 1977, Isabel Sawhill suggested that we should ask whether economists "have done anything more that describe the status quo in a society where sex roles are 'givens'—defined by culture, biology, or other factors not specified in the economic model."[7] As many writers have noted, the economists' conclusion that the traditional, gender-structured household is efficient depends to a great extent on factors the model does not examine, particularly women's comparative disadvantage in the labor force.[8]

There is a methodological distance between economic analysis and feminist legal theory that makes the two difficult to assimilate to each other. This has been elaborated in writing by a number of feminist economists, who advocate broadening the recognized methods of economic inquiry to include a variety of less quantitative methods. For example, Julie Nelson has called for a process of "imaginative rationality."[9] Along the same lines, Donald Mc-Closkey described the need for metaphor and story to supplement fact and logic, for questionnaires and interviews as well as numerical data sets, and for observation and conversation in addition to mathematical proofs.[10]

Some of the feminist objections to economic theories and methods are familiar from other literature that critiques neoclassical economic theory and the uses to which it has been put in law. Thus, many writers have argued that economists' premise that interpersonal utility comparisons are impossible serves to conceal distributive concerns and to defeat the possibility for larger "value" judgments.[11] There are also numerous critics of neoclassical theory who call for greater attention to issues of power, inequality, and other social factors.[12]

Although these types of criticism are repeated throughout the legal academy, they seem particularly sharp whenever economic analysis is brought beyond the sphere of explicit market activities.[13] In the context of family law, economic models are less readily tested or falsified than models used to analyze market behavior, because in the family there is no common currency for measuring value. Models based on self-interest also seem less adequate to explain family behavior, because of the broad spectrum of motivations we recognize in "private" life,[14] and the many competing normative visions of the family as a social institution. All of the standard criticisms of the economic approach take on added intensity when economic theory is employed not simply to describe and explain family behavior but to provide a normative base for a variety of specific family policy recommendations.[15]

Positive and Normative Economics

Neoclassical economics is staunchly positivist. Milton Friedman, in his classic essay on economic methods, explains the point this way:

> Positive economics is in principle independent of any particular ethical position or normative judgments. As Keynes says, it deals with "what is," not with "what ought to be." Its task is to provide a system of generalizations that can be used to make correct predictions about the consequences of any change in circumstances. Its performance is to be judged by the precision, scope, and conformity with experience of the predictions it yields. In short, positive economics is, or can be, an "objective" science, in precisely the same sense as any of the physical sciences.[16]

In order to predict various types of behavior, economists utilize abstract mathematical models. To those who object that these models omit too many variables, the customary response is that economic science is descriptive, not prescriptive, and these are not normative findings in any event.[17] Economic theorists argue that it is necessary to reduce the number of variables under consideration in order to develop testable hypotheses. Thus, these greatly simplified models of behavior are a prerequisite for rigorous scientific analysis. Again, in the words of Friedman:

> A hypothesis is important if it "explains" much by little, that is, if it abstracts the common and crucial elements from the mass of complex and detailed circumstances surrounding the phenomena to be explained and permits valid predictions on the basis of them alone. To be important, therefore, a hypothesis must be descriptively false in its assumptions; it takes account of, and accounts for, none of the many other attendant circumstances, since its very success shows them to be irrelevant for the phenomena to be explained.[18]

Economists relegate normative work to a second arena of economic inquiry, known as welfare economics. This type of analysis deploys notions of efficiency to determine whether a "particular proposed policy or legal change will make individuals affected by it better off in terms of how they perceive their own welfare." In general, the norms used in welfare economics assume and predict that "private ordering," based on individual rather than collective decisions, will lead to better outcomes across society.[19]

Economists recognize that their normative arguments depend heavily on the underlying positive analysis. According to Friedman: "Normative economics and the art of economics, on the other hand, cannot be independent of positive economics. Any policy conclusion necessarily rests . . . on a prediction that must be based—implicitly or explicitly—on positive economics." Friedman is not suggesting that normative economics can be reduced to a positive analysis; rather, his view is that an accurate descriptive account must precede the attempt to make policy prescriptions.[20]

Law and Economics has also laid claim to a positivist methodology. Most of the important early work generated accounts that explained legal aspects of economic regulation, beginning with subjects such as antitrust. Over time, Law and Economics began spreading to a wide range of other fields,[21] and it is now much more difficult to discern the traditional boundary between positive and normative analysis.[22] Thus, although Richard Posner defends his theory on the basis that it is intended as descriptive rather than prescriptive, his critics have noted that he has a tendency to mix normative judgments liberally in his positive analysis.[23] As Judge Posner himself suggests, the normative bent of Law and Economics analysis may be inevitable, given the highly normative character of our legal traditions.[24]

One reason that the separation between positive and normative analysis is difficult to maintain is that the language of "efficiency" figures prominently in both. In positive analysis, *efficient* is a descriptive term, denoting a utility-maximizing event or state of affairs.[25] As a normative guideline, *efficiency* is the economist's criterion for socially desirable legal rules in a wide range of spheres.[26] Frank Michelman suggests that although positive economics applies pure efficiency norms, normative analysis or "economic policy studies" are based on modified efficiency criteria.[27]

In Law and Economics writing on family law, the confusion between positive and normative theories is also apparent. Positive analysis, describing the perceived productive efficiencies of a traditional marital division of labor based on gender, has generated a spate of normative work, prescribing policy changes intended to protect and restore this type of household.[28] Other work, based on the descriptive premise that private agreements are value maximizing for the parties to the agreements, has generated policy recommendations intended to remove courts from the divorce process.[29] Throughout, although the touchstone of this writing is the idea of efficiency, it is often difficult to discern which meaning of the term is operating.

Further evidence, however, suggests that the two modalities of economic reasoning have in fact been distinguished. Descriptive economic accounts of family life have had significant influence on law, but work that reflects the shift to a normative economic framework has not been as warmly received.[30] Prescriptive theories seem to be a tougher sell, most likely because law responds to many competing normative visions of the family.[31] Ultimately, it appears that the claim to normative authority draws the most fire from critics and keeps many legal theorists at a cautious and skeptical distance from economic analysis.

Feminist Theory and Family Economics

Among feminist theorists, the responses to economic analysis seem to range from moderate discomfort to deep hostility. At one end of the spectrum there are a few writers who argue that feminist and economic theories, properly understood, often converge.[32] As Jana Singer points out, economic analysis "seems to cohere with notions of formal gender equality and the rejection of rigid gender roles."[33] At the other end of the spectrum, some feminist writers are deeply pessimistic, criticizing the entire enterprise of economic research as presently constituted as unavoidably tainted by the broader system of gender oppression.[34]

Between these two poles, a number of feminist scholars are interested in the insights and arguments that economic analysis can offer, while remaining troubled by many of the assumptions and methods of neoclassical economics. Writers in this group have pointed to a number of variables that are normally omitted from economic investigation but that seem centrally important for understanding women's experiences and concerns.[35] At a minimum, feminist theorists agree that the subjects of economic inquiry must be expanded to include the specific concerns of women and the effects of gender on experience.[36] Beyond this, some feminist economists have begun to challenge the predominance of choice theory, the paradigm of the rational, utility-maximizing individual agent, and the heavily mathematical nature of contemporary economic theory.[37] For these writers, a feminist economics would require entirely new models that do not dichotomize public and private life, that take issues of gender and power into account, and that recognize empathy and connection as well as self-interest and autonomy.

We are still discovering how a feminist economics would work: what new theoretical models it might employ; what empirical methodologies it might develop; and what new information and insights it could generate.[38] Most feminist economists work within existing methods, exploring a range of important new questions and also challenging the conclusions and policy implications of other economic research.[39] Their work has led to valuable contributions on important issues, including women's wages and labor force participation,[40] the economics of housework, child care, and nonmarket production,[41] the control and distribution of income within households,[42] divorce,[43] and poverty.[44] This work has encouraged the development of new mainstream economic theories addressing household production and family organization and bargaining.[45]

Feminist analysis has led many writers to conclude that even positive economic theory requires a new vision of the relationship between family life and market behavior, and an elaboration of the interdependent effects of gender in these two spheres.[46] This implies new modes of description that can more adequately model the complexity of women's experience. Thus, although mainstream theory depicts traditional gender-based family roles (and the split between public and private life) as efficient, feminist theorists have raised significant challenges to this view.[47] For example, Marianne Ferber and Bonnie Birnbaum have proposed a model that addresses the present and future well-being of both husband and wife rather than the total production of the household.[48] Julie Nelson has suggested a theory that considers family members not as independent individuals (or passive nonpersons) but as persons embedded in relationships, and that understands family decision making as a social process.[49]

Alimony and Divorce

At a normative level, there are points at which the feminist and economic understandings of family life converge, both pointing toward the same policy goals. Although some legal commentators have sought to abolish alimony, some feminist and economic theorists have sought to expand it.[50] Their agreement is clearest with the paradigm alimony case: a long-term marriage, children, an older housewife with no recent employment experience, and a husband with a good career and substantial earnings.[51] Beyond this core, although both frameworks can be utilized to advocate spousal support remedies in divorce, the analysis begins to diverge.

Early discussions of alimony in the Law and Economics literature were positivist, describing an economic rationale for alimony orders under traditional, fault-based divorce regimes.[52] More recent projects have led to a normative argument for alimony awards and against no-fault divorce regimes, based on a description of marriage and family life that emphasizes the benefits of specialization of labor in the family and the costs in "human capital" terms that these arrangements often entail.[53]

As the economic accounts recognize, specialization within the family has traditionally assumed clearly divided gender roles. Although these roles appear to be efficient during a marriage, they have put wives at significantly greater risk in the event of divorce. Economists, in order to protect the potential for gains from specialization in traditional marital roles, have recommended that both alimony and property division be structured to compensate for the greater investment that wives make in such marriages, or that divorce should be restricted in order to protect homemakers.[54]

Although feminist theorists do not generally share the goal of propping up traditional marital roles, many feminists have supported the goal of better financial remedies for women facing divorce. The economists' policy recommendations have therefore posed something of a dilemma. Feminists recognize the ways in which the arguments behind these proposals may be helpful to women who are now impoverished by divorce. At the same time, they recoil at the heavily gendered nature of the efficiency norms applied by economists.[55] As Jana Singer describes the problem, "the economic efficiency justification for alimony rests on assumptions that are extremely troubling from the perspective of feminist theory."[56]

There is also less agreement between feminist and economic theorists on the goal of making divorce more difficult. Elimination of no-fault divorce laws, to force spouses to bargain over the terms of divorce, has been advocated by economists including Nobel laureate Gary S. Becker.[57] There have not been economic voices raised loudly in support of the current regime. Among feminists, views of divorce law are more divided, with a number of writers pointing out that fault-based divorce was also a problem for women, or taking the view that restraining women's access to divorce may be more problematic than the harms that come from present divorce practices.[58]

These differences are closely tied to the criticisms that feminists have made more generally concerning the "new home economics." To the extent that the efficiency of traditional roles is a function of gender norms that remain unexamined, or worse, of factors such as discrimination against women in the marketplace, the analysis is circular and unpersuasive.[59] Moreover, even without considering the effects of discrimination against women, it is not clear that traditional gender-based household roles are "efficient." As a number of feminist writers have pointed out, the "economic approach" to the family has ignored empirical evidence suggesting that wives often bear much heavier loads of work and family responsibility than their husbands.[60] Conversely, as Gillian Hadfield has argued, economists' failure to question the structure of gender roles in the family has led to models of labor markets that ignore serious efficiency problems.[61]

Jana Singer, in an analysis of the "efficiency" arguments for alimony, points out that even if household specialization were efficient, feminists would be concerned about the link between specialization and gender inequality both within the family and in the larger society. She points out that traditional household roles have also been the source of significant problems for women. These include the perpetuation of gender-based inequality and power differentials in the wider society, and the problems generated in divorce when a wife bears a disproportionate share of the costs that may have made these roles "efficient" in the pre-divorce family.[62] Although the economic approach suggests that alimony should compensate some of these costs, the particular remedies these writers have suggested are clearly less than complete.[63] Given the potential harm to women in our society from household specialization, Singer asks whether it is sensible to "encourage women to abandon their careers . . . in exchange for a promise to 'hold them harmless' financially in the event of divorce."[64]

Picking up on several of these themes, Margaret Brinig explores in more detail the assumptions on which the economic theory is based, identifying a number of these that give feminist theorists reason to be cautious. Brinig emphasizes a number of ways in which family life is more complex than the economic models allow: marital decisions generate substantial externalities because they affect children, and these decisions are not easily reversed at the time of divorce.[65] Brinig also questions the assumption in the mainstream theory that the division of labor must occur only between husband and wife, because this ignores the possibility that other individuals may perform household work. Furthermore, she challenges the assumption that there are always increasing returns to scale from additional hours of home or market production.[66]

Feminist writers have proposed different rationales for alimony that would recognize the economic effects of household specialization on women without fostering sharply delineated gender roles. June Carbone describes a restitution-based system that she believes would both "encourage women to look to their own earnings rather than to marriage for their financial security" and "encourage women to continue to bear the primary responsibility for childrearing and to make sacrifices that will enhance their husbands' careers."[67] Singer proposes an income-sharing approach that would "combine the equal partnership ideal that underlies current equitable division schemes with the economist's recognition of enhancements in human capital as the most valuable asset produced during most marriages." She argues that this approach could help "to diminish existing power disparities during marriage" and would "encourage husbands to increase their investment in family care."[68] Joan Williams, who also recommends income equalization after divorce, would go further. She argues for new entitlements in property so that both husband and wife would have equal claims to wages that either earns during the time their children are dependent and for a considerable period after divorce.[69]

The differences between feminist and economic approaches to alimony are subtle but significant. If the goal of divorce remedies is to foster "efficiency" within marriage, alimony is important only in those cases in which a significant economic event has occurred. These would include the case in which one partner has increased his or her "human capital" by acquiring a diploma or professional license,[70] and the case in which one partner has suffered a decrease in market-based human capital by devoting time to child rearing.[71] Although these cases can be stated in gender-neutral terms, many economists presume that traditional gender roles are more efficient because of women's "comparative advantage" in reproductive activities.[72] These are also relatively easy cases, in which arguments for compensation could be made on a wide range of grounds.[73]

The economic approach does not seem to support alimony in a number of other situations, such as the case in which parties have a premarital or separation agreement excluding alimony,[74] the case of a relatively short marriage or one in which there had not been much specialization of labor,[75] the case in which there was a specialization of labor but no significant human capital changes during the marriage,[76] or the case in which the partner who would have an alimony claim is the one seeking a divorce.[77] Indeed, these present much more difficult normative problems on which our current practice is often divided.

Although the specific recommendations of feminist legal theorists are often similar to those of their Law and Economics counterparts, their approach to these alimony cases is quite different. Feminist analysis has devoted much greater attention to the pool of income and property interests of a married couple and has sought to redefine these as shared rather than separate.[78] It has also been less concerned with the project of measuring the contributions or losses of each partner, or specifying the particular form that families should take.[79] Feminists have emphasized support for ongoing care for children and their caregivers in marriage, after divorce, and in nonmarital families, rather than seeking compensation for the "lost opportunities" that caring for children may represent.[80] They are also more likely to look for solutions to the public sector rather than conceptualizing family matters as a purely private affair.[81]

The economic and feminist approaches to divorce are also divergent. Economists have argued for an end to unilateral no-fault divorce laws,[82] and for greater privatization of the divorce process.[83] The theoretical basis for these policy recommendations is that no-fault divorce laws allow inefficient divorces, defined in this literature as divorces in which although one individual may gain from the divorce, the parties' combined gain from divorce is less than their combined gain from remaining married. To address this problem, economists have advocated mutual consent rules, which would force the spouse seeking a divorce to bargain with the other over compensation for his or her anticipated losses.[84]

Although feminist writers have criticized the effects of no-fault divorce, they have not sought to abolish it. Some have argued that women did not fare appreciably better under the former laws.[85] Others have focused on the need for divorce in a number of specific situations that many women confront, for example, if a woman is subject to spousal abuse, or if a woman undergoes fundamental personal changes after her marriage that lead her to question or reject more traditional marital roles.[86]

Some economists have claimed common ground with feminist theorists on the question of divorce policy, highlighting the points at which the two approaches converge.[87] These accounts do not acknowledge that in many contexts, economics appears to lead to significantly different answers than a feminist analysis would suggest. The divergence begins with the radically different positive frameworks and methods on which the two approaches depend.

Methodology: Three Problems

The process of describing household labor in economic terms requires "valuing" it based on comparisons between labor in the household and in the market. Accurate valuations are impossible, however, because work in the home is structured entirely differently from work in the market, and because gender-based disparities affect the meaning and value accorded to work in both contexts. Moreover, in applying their descriptive methods to the family, economists have proceeded from the assumption that exchange and market metaphors and the concepts of rational choice and utility maximization are a sufficient language for speaking about the family. Feminist theories suggest that a wider range of conceptions is required. A third problem results from the first two: when the descriptive theory is used as a basis for prescriptive, normative pronouncements about what is "efficient" in family life, it requires that every aspect of family life be subject to this dual process of valuation and exchange. This prospect raises troubling commodification concerns and tests severely the premises of economic analysis in this setting.

Making Comparisons

Because most household work takes place outside the market, it is largely ignored in economic theory and policymaking. Feminist scholars in a number of disciplines have written about this problem, pointing out that the traditional exclusion of nonmarket work from economic analysis creates substantial policy distortions, many of which are heavily gendered.[88] For mainstream economists, an activity is not productive where no profits are produced. Marilyn Waring gives a wonderful example: a woman who supplies the labor of childbirth is not thought to be performing work or engaging in production, unless she is a paid surrogate. At the same time, a midwife, nurse, doctor, or anesthetist in attendance at the birth is engaged in work. By the same token, argues Waring, "growing and processing food, nurturing, educating, and running a household—all part of the complex process of reproduction—are unacknowledged as part of the production system."[89]

As economists have sought to include household production in their models, they have faced an obvious and immediate problem. Because the economic value of work is defined by the wages paid for it in the market, work that is not performed for a price has no measurable value. There are a number of solutions to this problem, all of which are based on comparisons between work in the home and work in established labor markets.[90] This type of comparison is made regularly in tort litigation involving injury or death to a homemaker. In this setting, an expert economist testifies as to what it would cost to purchase various household services on the market ("replacement cost") or as to what the homemaker's time was worth in the market place ("opportunity cost").[91]

In order to value household services or a homemaker's time, an economist must find an appropriate point of comparison in the market. Can a homemaker's services be "replaced" with a minimum-wage domestic worker, or should the comparison be to a teacher, chef, or nurse? Should the computation include the costs of fringe benefits, such as worker's compensation insurance, that would be paid for a market employee? If the homemaker works more than forty hours in a week, should the figures include overtime pay? And if she performs several tasks simultaneously, should the computation give credit for them separately? In practice, when these valuations are performed in tort actions, the comparisons are typically limited to a few basic services, those performed by individuals with wages among the lowest in the marketplace.[92]

Similar issues arise with the alternative method of computation, which asks what the homemaker would be paid if she sold her labor in the market. Here as well, forensic experts often conclude that a homemaker could only find a relatively unskilled or low-paid position in the labor force, which suggests an equally low value for her household work. More sophisticated economic theory goes a few steps beyond this analysis, pointing out that the market price reflects the lowest possible value for her time, and arguing that it would be more accurate to look at what the homemaker would be earning if she had had the opportunity to invest in the types of skills, training, and experience that are more highly valued in the job market.[93] This approach has been resisted in forensic circles, however, perhaps because it seems almost impossibly speculative, beyond what our personal injury damages rules can tolerate.

Both of these models incorporate into their valuation methods the lower values accorded by the market to women as workers and to the work of women. As feminist economists have elaborated in some detail, gender issues permeate the labor market.[94] If we use the market as a point of comparison, we bring all of these problems into the economic description of the household. Not surprisingly, tort recoveries for housewives who are injured or killed are typically far lower than those for wage earners.[95]

This is a real dilemma. Any approach that uses the market prices of women's work and women workers to set the value of household labor does not move us very far beyond the view that women's work does not really count. The feminist literature in economics suggests that the problem of value in the market and value in the home is the same problem: a large portion of the "gender gap" between men's and women's wages relates directly to the greater burdens of family work and caregiving borne by women.[96] As Gillian Hadfield points out, there is a close relationship between the structure of labor in the market and the household. To the extent that differences between men and women in labor markets are based on women's different burdens of family responsibility, most economists see no normative problem, and no lack of efficiency. Hadfield argues that this is because they have not explored very fully either the positive or normative aspects of the typical household division of labor:

> Although we have numerous theories of how the labor market contributes to the gender gap, economists have essentially only one theory of why the household is organized as it is. And because this theory concludes that the organization of the household is efficient, there has been no stimulus for economists, wedded to efficiency as a normative criterion, to explore with positive theory the impact that policies aimed at restructuring the traditional household might have on the wage gap.[97]

Although recognizing that the mainstream theory has led to valuable insights, Hadfield argues that there is a need to devise richer alternative theories and recommends that positive economic theory should begin to investigate "what creates and sustains the traditional division of labor in the household."[98]

Exchange Metaphors

The "economic model" of family behavior begins with the assertion that individuals decide whether to marry, have children, or divorce based on a comparison of the direct and indirect benefits and costs of different actions. It conceives of people in family relations as rational, utility-maximizing actors, facing a range of choices with limited supplies of time, energy, wealth, and other resources. It imagines that for most goods there are substitutes, although recognizing that these may not be perfect, and postulates that individual actors have an ability to choose freely.

As theorists seek to analyze behavior in families by using the models developed to explore behavior of individuals in the market, some scholars have decided to treat each "family" as if it were an individual, that is, an economic actor with a single utility function. Viewed historically, this approach suggests the common law spousal unity doctrine, which treated husband and wife as one legal person. It is problematic for many reasons, not least of which is that it excludes from analysis all of the interactions that occur within households and between family members. Another approach is to ignore the family entity and direct the analysis toward the behavior of individuals. Yet treating each family member as an independent utility-maximizer misses something as well, because it does not help us to understand how individuals in relationships with other individuals make decisions.

This problem has been explored by Gary Becker in a theory concerning altruism and its effects on allocations of resources within families.[99] His model describes how an altruistic head of a household can allocate resources in a manner to ensure cooperation and maximize the preferences of all family members. Some economists criticize this model because it also effectively ignores what occurs within families, and it has been particularly objectionable for feminists. Diana Strassman calls this model "The Story of the Benevolent Patriarch" and points out that the model ignores the effects of power: the household head is assumed to be the husband and father, who is in a position of control because he owns the financial resources entering the household.[100] Feminists point out that male household heads do not always behave altruistically, and in addition, that the model ignores the altruistic behavior of relatively powerless family members.[101] Another strand of economic theory treats the family as a type of "firm" and concentrates on understanding and elaborating the process and structure of family economic decision making. This model recognizes that family members have different access to financial and other resources, which translates into different abilities to bargain within marriage and in the event of divorce.[102] Bargaining models envision marriage as a cooperative process that is always influenced by the parties' awareness of what their opportunities would be outside of the marriage if the marriage were to fail. Where one spouse has relatively more attractive opportunities in the event of divorce, this fact will translate into greater power within marriage. Thus, this analysis leads us directly to questions of real concern for feminist legal theory. It permits us to investigate how women's social and economic opportunities and their legal entitlements affect their power within marriage. Once again, it leads us to consider the question Hadfield poses: what is it that creates and sustains the traditional division of labor in the household?

Market metaphors and exchange rhetoric have some significant precedents in family law, which has long used a contract metaphor to describe marriage. One reason that family law has proved to be a successful location for economic analysis is that our understandings of marriage, divorce, and child rearing are increasingly exchange based.[103] The scope for operation of contract principles has broadened substantially, and family law doctrines are increasingly inclined to view most aspects of family life as purely private.[104] At the same time, this revolution is not complete, and there is still significant discomfort evident in judicial opinions and academic literature, which resist treating marriage "as a business arrangement."[105]

The exchange approach to family life is problematic for a number of reasons. The first, and most traditional, concerns the protective function of family law. Historically, this was implemented with rules based on family status rather than contract principles.[106] Status relationships were not an unmitigated good for women, but they have certain advantages. Along with any contract-based regime comes a variety of problems that economists describe as contracting failures, including fraud, duress, and overreaching, or problems that result from the more subtle effects of unequal bargaining power and close family relationships. For feminist theorists, these power issues are at the core of the objection to contractual regulation of intimate relations.[107]

A second related question is whether the economists' contract models, based on rational maximizing behavior, adequately describe or explain relations in the family. Feminist critics often emphasize the harsher aspects of family behavior and the presence of many types of force or coercion directed at women both inside and outside the family.[108] To the extent that gender roles are the result of physical force or social coercion, it is not plausible to conclude that relations in the family are the product of contract or exchange within the terms of these models.

A third problem is that if we accept the bargaining view of family relations, we encounter the same valuation problems just discussed. Barbara Bergmann points out that bargaining within a marriage reflects a "market ethic" in which time "trades" at its market price. If a husband's household time is valued at his higher market rate, his lesser contribution to housework counts for more than his wife's more substantial efforts.[109] Similarly, Marianne Ferber and Bonnie Birnbaum argue that the relative financial contributions that husband and wife make to the family determine how status and power are allocated within the household.[110]

Finally, the exchange models of family interaction are especially problematic when we wish to consider children's interests. An analysis that assumes that family behaviors are motivated by altruism is clearly inadequate to help explain and address the failures of altruism in families.[111] Also, models based on exchange must take into account the powerlessness of most children. Some of the economic literature, including writing by Gary Becker, explores the barriers that prevent children from contracting directly with their parents.[112] Because of these difficulties, economists commonly treat children's interests as a type of "external effect" of parental bargaining and describe the law as regulating these effects through rules governing abuse and neglect, custody and support, and historically, the availability of divorce.[113] Much of the bargaining analysis is based on an assumption that at least one parent, usually the mother, will incorporate the children's best interests into that parent's own bargaining position. So far, however, the literature has not explored in much detail what effects this has on that parent's ability to negotiate.[114]

An alternative approach in the economic literature conceives of children not as participants but as one of the goods produced by marriage and bargained over in divorce.[115] This writing often focuses on money–custody trades or explores the connections between child support and visitation. But the children-as-goods approach risks treating them as merely an expensive commodity, and it raises serious concerns analogous to the concerns of many feminists with surrogacy and prostitution. That is, economic writing on the family, which alternates between models that define children as either members of a family or as goods produced by a family, demonstrates the inadequacy of these models.

Children are central to the economic description of the family. Economists describe the purpose of marriage as the rearing of children, the type of household production that seems to require a gender-based specialization of labor is child rearing, and the harms identified in economic writing on divorce concern women with children who are left with inadequate financial support. In most of the analysis, however, children are externalized or commodified, or their interests are simply collapsed together with the interests of mothers.[116]

Commodification

One risk of the use of market rhetoric is that it will be taken literally rather than metaphorically. What matters most about family life is not commodified: it cannot be bought and sold, and cannot be valued in money. This social reality creates problems for all but the most theoretical economic analysis, for although most family economists speak in terms of "utility" rather than money, the models they have used have depended on the universal "measuring rod of money."[117]

This is difficult enough if we are only concerned with housework, but when we understand *household labor* to include the entire spectrum of human reproduction and family life, the market paradigm raises troubling issues of its commodification. Feminists have been concerned with the commodification of women's reproductive capacities (surrogacy)[118] and sexual capacities (rape, prostitution, and pornography).[119] Much of the current Law and Economics analysis of the family treats children explicitly as commodities "produced" by the family from a variety of monetary and nonmonetary inputs,[120] or treats children implicitly as commodities in the context of divorce bargaining.[121]

Economic models that treat family choices as if various goods were commensurable have allowed testing of hypotheses, which produce interesting insights. It is not clear, however, that economic theory can move from these descriptive and explanatory contributions to policy proposals without creating serious problems of commodification. Once economists begin to prescribe certain policies on efficiency grounds, the analysis no longer simply treats various goods as if they could be substituted or exchanged in implicit, marketlike transactions. To base family policy on efficiency norms is actually to promote exchange relations within the family, requiring the explicit commodification of whatever goods are subject to the policies.

In divorce law, the prospect of "money for custody" bargains, as well as aspects of property division and alimony, raises this concern. Although various divorce statutes about property division speak of taking into account the contributions of both husband and wife to a marriage, the prospect of actually trying to list and measure them all has been steadfastly resisted. Judges deciding these cases typically presume that the wife's and husband's contributions have in fact been equal. In those cases in which a court feels compelled to notice a significant inequality, there is often a disclaimer attached: marriage is just not about keeping track of each party's debits and credits.[122]

These trends have contradicted the economic theories addressing divorce that have urged much greater use of remedies that would compensate for gains and losses in human capital. Despite the scholarly attention that has been brought to this question, it is not apparent that such measurements are possible, and it is even less clear that such a process would be worth the commodification risks it would entail.[123] There are certainly other possibilities: looking to the tort analogy, we could explore the possibility of social insurance schemes rather than direct financial remedies.[124] Or we might prefer rules that seek to recognize wrongs done and provide redress without attempting to rectify them. This might involve defining formulas for payments in the event of divorce, such as child support guidelines or income-splitting spousal support awards, which do not require us to "value" individuals in dollars and cents.

These three problems—of making comparisons between production in the family and the market, of using exchange metaphors to model family relationships, and of commodifying family life—all complicate the positive economic analysis of families, and prevent it from generating the sort of testable hypotheses and solid data that are the hallmark of economic analysis in other contexts. Here, the effort to reduce the complexity of social life to the elegant abstractions of theory requires eliminating too much. The project can succeed only if a set of normative judgments is admitted into the analysis at a very early stage. Thus, the descriptive analysis only succeeds if it begins with a framework of traditional gender norms. This is not the pure, positive analysis depicted in the theory of economic methods.

Can Families Be Efficient?

Economists writing about the family make both positive and normative efficiency claims: the positive claim that family life is (or can be) productively efficient, and the normative claim that law should promote efficiencies in the family. The positive analysis begins with the postulate that households are productively efficient, and then "explains" this efficiency with a model of specialization and division of labor by gender. In the normative analysis, policies that appear to undermine the traditional gender-based division of labor in the family, such as the advent of no-fault divorce, are then subject to criticism on efficiency grounds. Nowhere in this cycle, however, is the initial postulate closely examined.

Feminist economists, of course, have pointed out this mistake. Their more traditional colleagues regularly miss this point for two important reasons. First, in most economic analysis, social facts are simply taken as given, treated as exogenous or outside the scope of analysis. This is particularly true of social facts based on gender, which writers including Becker regularly render in biological terms, suggesting that they are inevitable and immutable.[125] If, as feminists argue, gender roles are a more complex phenomenon, socially constructed and subject to challenge, debate, and reformulation, then any analysis based on assumed gender facts is subject to question as well.

Second, the economic analysis understands the family based on the model of the market as an arena in which rational behavior prevails and in which individuals are well informed and able to make free choices. As discussed earlier, this analysis tends to suppress the reality of serious conflicts over wealth, power, and other goods in the family, substituting an assumption that behavior is not only rational but benevolent and altruistic. For feminists, who have been particularly concerned with the constrained opportunities women face and with the role that force and violence play in controlling women, both in the family and in the larger society, this is an impossibly idealized view of how family relationships are constituted.

With the narrow language economists have employed to describe the family, the issues most central to feminist concerns are defined out of the project. At best, we can say that the understanding proposed in this work is interesting, and occasionally useful, but too narrow to encompass all of the concerns and values we hold with family life. At worst, we may be suspicious that economic efficiency arguments serve to further reinforce and justify a social reality that is often systematically harmful to women. Because economic theory has been oblivious to so many of these conflicts, it is still hard to imagine what a different economics could tell us.

Feminist theory suggests that the terms of a descriptive system are heavily influenced by the normative commitments of its practitioners. This interdependence of descriptive and prescriptive accounts is an important reason why the boundary between positive and normative economic theory is so difficult to maintain. The limitations of the current descriptive theories in family economics are the reason for much of the present difficulty with its prescriptive judgments.

The problem is deeper than a question of whether a certain set of practices is efficient. We cannot determine whether resources are allocated efficiently until we know what resources to consider, what types of uses count, and what values we wish to maximize. When different claims or interests conflict, we cannot resolve which should prevail unless we have a means for comparison. In the market, the metric for such a comparison is money; in the family, there is no comparable scale. Without a common denominator, there is no basis for testing the assertion that one arrangement is more efficient than another.[126]

The validity of any normative analysis depends on the validity of the descriptive system on which it is based. To the extent that the current economic descriptions of the family are flawed, these models cannot be the basis for useful policy recommendations. Feminist theorists cannot use or accept efficiency-based arguments for family policy, because they are based on a descriptive theory premised on the continuation of the traditional gender system in marriage and in the world outside the family sphere. Gender is one of the inputs into the family production function. Until the existing positive theory can be restructured, feminist normative economic analysis is not possible.

Feminist theorists have devoted a great deal of attention to the forces that create and sustain the specialization of labor in the family. To a large extent, specialization has been based on the subordination of women, through labor markets that do not value women or women's work, cultural norms that channel women into domestic roles, and a system of divorce that often results in a "family" with no specialization of labor at all. Traditional economic theory does not take these factors into account, nor does it recognize problems of violence against women and discrimination in the workplace. It also fails to acknowledge the importance of reproductive freedom and the need for both high-quality, affordable child care and dependable public financial support for women with children. Efficiency arguments that ignore these issues are not neutral, nor can they be as long as the problems that many women face inside their families and in the world beyond remain unresolved.

Notes

1. This essay appeared in the *Michigan Journal of Gender and Law*, vol. 4, no. 1 (1996) (reprinted with permission), and an early version was presented at the Feminism and Legal Theory Workshop at Columbia Law School, on Feb. 25, 1995.

I use *feminist* to denote theory that centers on women's experiences and the diverse social, economic, and historical contexts of women's lives. For a useful introduction, *see Theoretical Perspectives on Sexual Difference* (Deborah L. Rhode ed., 1990). *See also* Gary Lawson, *Feminist Legal Theories*, 18 Harv. J.L. & Pub. Pol'y 325 (1995) (elaborating a number of possible definitions of feminist legal theory). For an introduction to Law and Economics, *see* Robert Cooter & Thomas Ulen, *Law and Economics* (1988); Richard A. Posner, *Economic Analysis of Law* (4th ed. 1992). *See also* Joyce P. Jacobsen, *The Economics of Gender* (1994).

2. *See generally* Julie A. Nelson, *Feminism, Objectivity, and Economics* (1996) [hereinafter Nelson, *Feminism, Objectivity, and Economics*]; *Beyond Economic Man: Feminist Theory and Economics* (Marianne A. Ferber & Julie A. Nelson eds., 1993); Marianne A. Ferber, *The Study of Economics: A Feminist Critique*, 107 Am. Econ. Ass'n Proc. 357 (1995).

3. I have described this more fully in Ann Laquer Estin, *Love and Obligation: Family Law and the Romance of Economics*, 36 Wm. & Mary L. Rev. 989, 991–99 (1995) [hereinafter Estin, *Love and Obligation*].

4. *See, e.g.*, Gary S. Becker, *A Treatise on the Family* (enlarged ed. 1991)[hereinafter Becker, *Treatise*]. For an early analysis of this work, *see* Isabel V. Sawhill, *Economic Perspectives on the Family*, Daedalus 115 (Spring 1977); and Marianne A. Ferber & Bonnie G. Birnbaum, *The New Home Economics: Retrospects and Prospects*, 4 J. Consumer Res. 19 (1977).

5. One important example is the growing use of opportunity cost and human capital concepts in the debate over alimony and property division in divorce. *See, e.g.*, E. Raedene Combs, *The Human Capital Concept as a Basis for Property Settlement at Divorce*, 2 J. Divorce 329 (1979); Joan M. Krauskopf, *Recompense for Financing Spouse's Education: Legal Protection for the Marital Investor in Human Capital*, 28 U. Kan. L. Rev. 379 (1980). *But see* Joan Williams, *Is Coverture Dead? Beyond a New Theory of Alimony*, 82 Geo. L.J. 2227, 2276 (1994) (criticizing the use that has been made of human capital analysis).

6. *See* Becker, *Treatise*, *supra* note 4, at 30–53.

7. Sawhill, *supra* note 4, at 120; *see also* Ferber & Birnbaum, *supra* note 4, at 21 ("Clearly tradition is the dominant factor in determining the division of tasks within the family."). Other feminist theorists have been far blunter. *See, e.g.*, Barbara R. Bergmann, *The Economic Emergence of Women* 266–73 (1986) (arguing in response to Becker that men's economic power is the basis for inequality between men and women within households); Marilyn Waring, *If Women Counted* 37–39 (1988) (referring to Becker as "the new high priest of patriarchal economics"); Marianne A. Ferber & Julie A. Nelson, *Introduction: The Social Construction of Economics and the Social Construction of Gender*, in *Beyond Economic Man*, *supra* note 2, at 1, 6 (describing feminist criticisms of Becker's work); *see also* Paula England, *The Separative Self: Androcentric Bias in Neoclassical Assumptions*, in *Beyond Economic Man*, *supra* note 2, at 37, 41–49 [hereinafter England, *Separative Self*]; Diana Strassman, *Not a Free Market: The Rhetoric of Disciplinary Authority in Economics*, in *Beyond Economic Man*, *supra* note 2, at 54, 58–63.

8. *See* Ferber & Birnbaum, *supra* note 4, at 20–21; Gillian K. Hadfield, *Households at Work: Beyond Labor Market Policies to Remedy the Gender Gap*, 82 Geo. L.J. 89, 97 (1993); *see also* Jana B. Singer, *Alimony and Efficiency: The Gendered Costs and Benefits of the Economic Justification for Alimony*, 82 Geo. L.J. 2423, 2437–47 [hereinafter Singer, *Alimony and Efficiency*].

9. Julie A. Nelson, *The Study of Choice or the Study of Provisioning? Gender and the Definition of Economics*, in *Beyond Economic Man*, *supra* note 2, at 23, 29–31; *see also* Ferber, *supra* note 2, at 359; Myra H. Strober, *Rethinking Economics through a Feminist Lens*, 106 Am. Econ. Ass'n Proc. 143 (1994).

10. *See* Donald N. McCloskey, *Some Consequences of a Conjective Economics*, in *Beyond Economic Man*, *supra* note 2, at 69.

11. *See, e.g.,* C. Edwin Baker, *The Ideology of the Economic Analysis of Law,* 5 Phil. & Pub. Aff. 3 (1975); James Boyd White, *Economics and Law: Two Cultures in Tension,* 54 Tenn. L. Rev. 161, 172–75 (1986).

12. *See, e.g.,* Ferber & Nelson, *supra* note 7, at 12–13 (citing these scholars as examples: Kenneth E. Boulding, *Three Faces of Power* (1989); Robert Frank, *Choosing the Right Pond* (1985); Robert M. Solow, *The Labor Market as Social Institution* (1990)). Related points are made in the legal literature. *See, e.g.,* Baker, *supra* note 11, at 37–41; White, *supra* note 11, at 185–93.

13. On the question of "economic imperialism," *see generally* Robert D. Cooter, *Law and the Imperialism of Economics: An Introduction to the Economic Analysis of Law and a Review of the Major Books,* 29 UCLA L. Rev. 1260 (1982). For a discussion of the advantages of economics beyond its sphere, *see* Ronald H. Coase, *Economics and Contiguous Disciplines,* 7 J. Legal Stud. 201, 209–10 (1978).

14. This is a particularly strong theme in feminist criticisms of economics, which have stressed the importance of factors beyond self-interest, such as empathy, connection, and altruism. *See* England, *Separative Self, supra* note 7, at 45–48.

15. Despite the controversies over economic "imperialism," there are a number of "true believers" prepared to enact family legislation based purely on efficiency criteria. Gary Becker writes regularly in *Business Week* magazine, offering proposals on a wide range of policy matters, including prenuptial agreements, no-fault divorce, and child support enforcement. *See* Gary S. Becker, *Why Every Married Couple Should Sign a Contract,* Bus. Wk. 30 (Dec. 29, 1997); Gary S. Becker, *Finding Fault with No-Fault Divorce,* Bus. Wk. 22 (Dec. 7, 1992) [hereinafter Becker, *Finding Fault*]; Gary S. Becker, *Unleash the Bill Collectors on Deadbeat Dads,* Bus. Wk. 18 (July 18, 1994) [hereinafter *Deadbeat Dads*]. *See also* Ann Laquer Estin, *Economics and the Problem of Divorce,* 2 U. Chi. L. Sch. Roundtable 517, 524–29 (1995) [hereinafter *Economics and Divorce*].

16. Milton Friedman, *The Methodology of Positive Economics,* in *Essays in Positive Economics* 3, 4 (1953) (citing John Neville Keynes, *The Scope and Method of Political Economy* 34–35, 46 (1891)).

17. *See, e.g.,* Posner, *Economic Analysis, supra* note 1, at 16–17.

18. Friedman, *supra* note 16, at 14–15; *see* Posner, *Economic Analysis, supra* note 1, at 16–18; *see also* Michael J. Trebilcock, *The Limits of Freedom of Contract* 3–6 (1993).

19. *See* Trebilcock, *supra* note 18, at 7–8; Posner, *Economic Analysis, supra* note 1, at 13–16.

20. *See* Friedman, *supra* note 16, at 5 (suggesting that many but not all policy disagreements trace to different predictions about the effects of a given policy change, and therefore "the progress of positive economics" could help resolve differences about economic policy).

21. Judge Richard Posner, in his textbook, describes this as "the economic theory of law." Posner, *Economic Analysis, supra* note 1, at 23–25 (noting that this larger inquiry includes what he calls "the efficiency theory of the common law," which is based on the hypothesis that some legal rules serve economic efficiency goals). *See also* Richard A. Posner, *Some Uses and Abuses of Economics in Law,* 46 U. Chi. L. Rev. 281 (1979) [hereinafter Posner, *Uses and Abuses*].

The arenas for economic analysis of law now range from antitrust, tax, and corporate law to laws governing a variety of nonmarket behaviors, including criminal law, civil rights, divorce, and adoption. A few examples serve to illustrate the point. For positive and normative economic arguments in criminal law, *see* Daryl A. Hellman & Neil O. Alper, *Economics of Crime: Theory and Practice* (2d ed. 1990); and Gary S. Becker, *Crime and Punishment: An Economic Approach,* 76 J. Pol. Econ. 169 (1968). For examples in civil rights, *see* Gary S. Becker, *The Economics of Discrimination* (2d ed. 1971); and John J. Donohue III, *Is Title VII Efficient?* 134 U. Pa. L. Rev. 1411 (1986). For arguments in family law, *see* Becker, *Treatise, supra* note 4; and Richard A. Posner, *Sex and Reason* 3, 33–36, 85–88 (1992) [hereinafter Posner, *Sex and Reason*].

In this move away from behavior in explicit markets, Law and Economics has followed the lead of economic theorists such as Gary Becker. *See* Gary S. Becker, *Nobel Lecture: The Economic Way of Looking at Behavior,* 101 J. Pol. Econ. 385 (1993). Posner notes that this work has precedent in the work of Jeremy Bentham. *See* Posner, *Uses and Abuses, supra* note 21, at 281–82.

22. *See* generally Frank I. Michelman, *Norms and Normativity in the Economic Theory of Law,* 62 Minn. L. Rev. 1015 (1978) [hereinafter Michelman, *Norms*]. I share the view that economics is generally more useful to law in its descriptive role than in its normative manifestations. *See* Estin, *Love and Obligation, supra* note 3, at 1082–86.

23. *See, e.g.,* Posner, *Economic Analysis, supra* note 1, at 16–18; Posner, *Uses and Abuses, supra* note 21, at 284–87. *See* Michelman, *Norms, supra* note 22, at 1038–40 ("we can carelessly slip from an approximate empirical Is to a definite ideal Must or Ought to Be"); Baker, *supra* note 11, at 4–6 (arguing that Posner uses efficiency "as a normative, and not merely as a technical standard").

Other Law and Economics theorists place themselves more explicitly in the welfare economics tradition; *see, e.g.,* Trebilcock, *supra* note 18, at 21–22; *see also* Werner Z. Hirsch, *Law and Economics: An Introductory Analysis* 4–10 (2d ed. 1988).

24. *See* Posner, *Uses and Abuses, supra* note 21, at 285; *see also* Michelman, *Norms, supra* note 22, at 1032.

25. *See, e.g.,* Frank I. Michelman, *A Comment on Some Uses and Abuses of Economics in Law,* 46 U. Chi. L. Rev. 307, 309 (1979); *see also* Cooter, *supra* note 13, at 1263 ("A process is efficient when it yields the maximum output from given input, or equivalently, when it yields a given output with the minimum input.").

26. *See* Posner, *Economic Analysis, supra* note 1, at 13–16.

27. *See* Michelman, *Norms, supra* note 22, at 1032–35; *see also* Estin, *Economics and Divorce, supra* note 15, at 526–29 (arguing that different economic approaches to divorce reflect different efficiency norms).

28. *See, e.g.,* Allen M. Parkman, *No Fault Divorce: What Went Wrong?* (1992) [hereinafter Parkman, *No Fault Divorce*]; Severin Borenstein & Paul N. Courant, *How to Carve a Medical Degree: Human Capital Assets in Divorce Settlements,* 79 Am. Econ. Rev. 992 (1989); Ira M. Ellman, *The Theory of Alimony,* 77 Cal. L. Rev. 1 (1989); *see also* Becker, *Finding Fault, supra* note 15. *See* generally Estin, *Love and Obligation, supra* note 3, at 1001–13.

29. *See, e.g.,* Martin Zelder, *Inefficient Dissolutions as a Consequence of Public Goods: The Case of No-Fault Divorce,* 22 J. Legal Stud. 503 (1993) [hereinafter Zelder, *Inefficient Dissolutions*]; *see also* Becker, *Finding Fault, supra* note 15.

30. The influence of positive economic models is described in Milton C. Regan Jr., *Market Discourse and Moral Neutrality in Divorce Law,* 1994 Utah L. Rev. 605, 626–59. For doubts as to the normative sufficiency of economic theory, *see, e.g.,* Carl E. Schneider, *Rethinking Alimony: Marital Decisions and Moral Discourse,* 1991 BYU L. Rev. 197, 217–27. My own work also falls into this category. *See* Estin, *Economics and Divorce, supra* note 15.

31. Judge Posner has repeated in many settings his view that efficiency is not a sufficient normative foundation for law. *See, e.g.,* Posner, *Economic Analysis, supra* note 1, at 27 ("[T]here is more to justice than economics."). *See also* Kenneth E. Boulding, *Economics as a Moral Science,* 59 Am. Econ. Rev. 1 (1969).

32. *See, e.g.,* Trebilcock, *supra* note 18, at 43–48; Richard A. Posner, *Conservative Feminism,* 1989 U. Chi. Legal F. 191, 191–92 (" '[C]onservative feminism' . . . is . . . the idea that women are entitled to political, legal, social, and economic equality to men, in the framework of a lightly regulated market economy."); Michael J. Trebilcock & Rosemin Keshvani, *The Role of Private Ordering in Family Law: A Law and Economics Perspective,* 41 U. Toronto L.J. 533, 553 (1991).

33. Singer, *Alimony and Efficiency, supra* note 8, at 2427.

34. *See* Wanda A. Wiegers, *Economic Analysis of Law and "Private Ordering": A Feminist Critique,* 42 U. Toronto L.J. 170 (1992). As a number of writers have noted, many of the differences between these poles echo the long-standing debate over "sameness" and "difference" issues within feminism. *See* Marcia Neave, *Resolving the Dilemma of Difference: A Critique of "The Role of Private Ordering in Family Law,"* 44 U. Toronto L.J. 97, 130–31 (1994); Trebilcock & Keshvani, *supra* note 32, at 535–37.

35. *See, e.g.,* England, *Separative Self, supra* note 7, at 41–49; Singer, *Alimony and Efficiency, supra* note 8, at 2434–37, 2443–51; Strassman, *supra* note 7, at 56–63; and Sawhill, *supra* note 4, at 120–24.

36. *See generally* Ferber & Nelson, *supra* note 7, at 2–7.

37. *See generally Beyond Economic Man*, *supra* note 2.

38. *See* Rebecca M. Blank, *What Should Mainstream Economists Learn from Feminist Theory?* in *Beyond Economic Man*, *supra* note 2, at 133, 136–38. In her book, Julie Nelson develops a feminist economic theory and then applies it to a series of specific topics in economics, including economics of the family, household equivalence scales, individual income tax, and macroeconomic methodology. Nelson, *Feminism, Objectivity, and Economics*, *supra* note 2.

39. Ferber and Nelson refer to this group as "feminist empiricists." *See* Ferber & Nelson, *supra* note 7, at 8; *see also* Blank, *supra* note 38, at 134.

40. *See* Bergmann, *supra* note 7; *see also Symposium, The Gender Gap in Compensation*, 82 Geo. L.J. 27 (1993); Francine D. Blau & Marianne A. Ferber, *The Economics of Women, Men, and Work* (1986); Paula England & George Farkas, *Households, Employment, and Gender* (1986); Paula England, *The Failure of Human Capital Theory to Explain Occupational Sex Segregation*, 17 J. Hum. Resources 358 (1982).

41. *See* Bergmann, *supra* note 7; Waring, *supra* note 7.

42. *See* Marjorie B. McElroy & Mary Jean Horney, *Nash-Bargained Household Decisions: Toward a Generalization of the Theory of Demand*, 22 Int'l Econ. Rev. 333 (1981); Marilyn Manser & Murray Brown, *Marriage and Household Decision-Making: A Bargaining Analysis*, 21 Int'l Econ. Rev. 31 (1980).

43. *See* Elisabeth M. Landes, *Economics of Alimony*, 7 J. Legal Stud. 35 (1978); H. Elizabeth Peters et al., *Enforcing Divorce Settlements: Evidence from Child Support Compliance and Award Modifications*, 30 Demography 719 (1993); H. Elizabeth Peters, *Marriage and Divorce: Informational Constraints and Private Contracting*, 76 Am. Econ. Rev. 437 (1986).

44. *See generally* Jacobsen, *supra* note 1, at 59–61, 201–2.

45. Diana Strassman calls this a "mainstream fix." Strassman, *supra* note 7, at 63–64. For a defense of the uses of traditional economic models in some settings, *see* Blank, *supra* note 38, at 138–40.

46. *See* Hadfield, *supra* note 8, at 96–97; Neave, *supra* note 34, at 99, 109.

47. *See, e.g.*, Hadfield, *supra* note 8; Singer, *Alimony and Efficiency*, *supra* note 8, at 2440. Efforts have been made to correct for these problems within the theory, but as Diana Strassman notes, the likelihood of achieving a "mainstream fix" depends on whether the problems identified lie at the core or the periphery of mainstream economic theory. Strassman, *supra* note 7, at 63–65. Despite the advances of the new home economics, the conceptual dichotomy between the public and private spheres remains deeply embedded in economic thinking. Revising this aspect of economic theory is a far more radical project because it calls into question the dominant economic paradigm of the market itself.

48. Ferber & Birnbaum, *supra* note 4, at 26–27.

49. Nelson, *Feminism, Objectivity, and Economics*, *supra* note 2, at 67–74.

50. Economic theorists advocating alimony remedies include Parkman, *No Fault Divorce*, *supra* note 28; Posner, *Economic Analysis*, *supra* note 1, at 147–48; Landes, *supra* note 43. For feminist approaches, *see infra* notes 55–56.

51. *See, e.g.*, Ellman, *supra* note 28, at 17; Ann Laquer Estin, *Maintenance, Alimony, and the Rehabilitation of Family Care*, 71 N.C. L. Rev. 721, 745 n. 84 (1993) [hereinafter Estin, *Maintenance*].

52. *See, e.g.*, Posner, *Economic Analysis*, *supra* note 1, at 147–48; Landes, *supra* note 43.

53. *See, e.g.*, Lloyd Cohen, *Marriage, Divorce and Quasi Rents; or, "I Gave Him the Best Years of My Life*," 16 J. Legal Stud. 267 (1987); Ellman, *supra* note 28.

54. *See, e.g.*, Cohen, *supra* note 53; Ellman, *supra* note 28; Trebilcock & Keshvani, *supra* note 32, at 549–58. The original positive economic explanation for alimony awards is in Landes, *supra* note 43.

55. *See* Margaret F. Brinig, *Comment on Jana Singer's "Alimony and Efficiency*," 82 Geo. L.J. 2461 (1994); June Carbone, *Economics, Feminism, and the Reinvention of Alimony: A Reply to*

Ira Ellman, 43 Vand. L. Rev. 1463 (1990); Singer, *Alimony and Efficiency, supra* note 8, at 2434–37.

56. Singer, *Alimony and Efficiency, supra* note 8, at 2424. There are also feminist theorists who oppose the institution of alimony. *See, e.g.,* Herma Hill Kay, *Equality and Difference: A Perspective on No-Fault Divorce and Its Aftermath,* 56 U. Cin. L. Rev. 1, 80–89 (1987) [hereinafter Kay, *Equality and Difference*]; but *see* Herma Hill Kay, *Commentary: Toward a Theory of Fair Distribution,* 57 Brook. L. Rev. 755, 763–65 (1991).

57. *See* Becker, *Finding Fault, supra* note 15; *see also* Parkman, *No Fault Divorce, supra* note 28; Zelder, *Inefficient Dissolutions, supra* note 29.

58. *See, e.g.,* Kay, *Equality and Difference, supra* note 56; Linda J. Lacey, *Mandatory Marriage "For the Sake of the Children": A Feminist Reply to Elizabeth Scott,* 66 Tul. L. Rev. 1435 (1992); Jana B. Singer, *Divorce Reform and Gender Justice,* 67 N.C. L. Rev. 1103 (1989) [hereinafter Singer, *Divorce Reform*].

59. *See* Carbone, *supra* note 55, at 1490–91. As Gillian Hadfield argues, to the extent that economists explain the "gender gap" in wages as a result of women's greater responsibilities at home, the analysis has not established that this organization of work is efficient. *See* Hadfield, *supra* note 8, at 96.

60. *See, e.g.,* Brinig, *supra* note 55, at 2469–73; Carbone, *supra* note 55, at 1485–88; Hadfield, *supra* note 8, at 97–98; Singer, *Alimony and Efficiency, supra* note 8, at 2440. This suggests the possibility that the division of labor is achieved by the male household head by exploitation rather than altruism. *See* Hadfield, *supra* note 8, at 98. At the very least, the data suggest that household heads do not act altruistically in the allocation of the more unpleasant aspects of household work. *See* Bergmann, *supra* note 7; *see also* Mary Ann Case, *Of Richard Epstein and Other Radical Feminists,* 18 Harv. J.L. & Pub. Pol'y 369, 390–92 (1995).

61. *See* Hadfield, *supra* note 8, at 97 (calling for more attention to the interconnections between family and market life). The interaction of gender roles in the family and in the work place works in both directions; *see, e.g.,* Cynthia L. Estlund, *Work and Family: How Women's Progress at Work (and Employment Discrimination Law) May be Transforming the Family,* 21 Comp. Lab. L. & Pol'y J. 467 (2000)(contending that women's greater equality in the work place has served to erode traditional gender roles and relations in the family).

62. *See* Singer, *Alimony and Efficiency, supra* note 8, at 2440–42; *see also* Estin, *Maintenance, supra* note 51, at 780–81.

63. As Singer notes, the theory attempts to specify both a justification for alimony in general and a method for computing particular awards. *See* Singer, *Alimony and Efficiency, supra* note 8, at 2441. *See also* Cohen, *supra* note 53, at 303; Ellman, *supra* note 28. In these formulas, however, factors such as the wife's "loss in marriageability" or emotional distress are typically excluded. *See* Estin, *Economics and Divorce, supra* note 15, at 567.

64. Singer, *Alimony and Efficiency, supra* note 8, at 2442 (quoting Carbone, *supra* note 55). This is a theme many others have sounded. *See, e.g.,* Kay, *Equality and Difference, supra* note 56, at 1, 80; *see also* Estin, *Maintenance, supra* note 51, at 778 n. 215, 800 n. 314 (noting a shift in position by Kay and others who have addressed this point).

65. *See* Brinig, *supra* note 55. As she points out, there is more than one "deal" to be considered in any marriage, and alimony makes much greater sense in some settings than others. *See also* Carbone, *supra* note 55, at 1488–89.

66. *See* Margaret F. Brinig, *The Law and Economics of No-Fault Divorce—A Review of No-Fault Divorce: What Went Wrong?* 26 Fam. L.Q. 453, 456–57 (1993) (book review). In addition, she notes that the analysis may fail to take into account various psychic costs for women and men that result from specialization. Ferber and Birnbaum also develop this point. *See* Ferber & Birnbaum, *supra* note 4, at 23. Along the same lines, June Carbone has argued that a model based on maximizing household income neglects other goods, such as the "psychic satisfaction" of employment or parenthood, and the prestige and security of economic independence. *See* Carbone, *supra* note 55, at 1488–89.

67. Carbone, *supra* note 55, at 1493. Carbone describes Ellman's alimony theory as a restitutionary system consistent with her own approach. She argues, however, that if the objective of alimony is to foster traditional household labor division, paying alimony as a form of expectation damages to wives would be most appropriate. *See id.* at 1495.

68. Singer, *Alimony and Efficiency, supra* note 8, at 2454–55.

69. *See* Williams, *supra* note 5, at 2257–66.

70. *See, e.g.,* Ellman, *supra* note 28, at 68–71, although he would limit alimony in this case to the amount of the other spouse's lost earning capacity. Many economists prefer property division remedies in this situation. *See, e.g.,* Parkman, *No Fault Divorce, supra* note 28, at 130–32; Borenstein & Courant, *supra* note 28.

71. *See* Ellman, *supra* note 28, at 71–73.

72. On comparative advantage in reproductive activities, *see* Becker, *Treatise, supra* note 4, at 38–41. Ellman designs his theory to address "economically rational marital sharing behavior" rather than traditional gender roles. *See* Ellman, *supra* note 28, at 48–49. He notes, however, that because of social mores, wives' noneconomic losses from divorce are generally more severe than husbands.' *See id.* at 43–44, 80–81. Amy Wax argues that women's specialization in household labor is not "natural" but rather has been coerced by social norms that prevent women from participation in the labor market on terms of equality with men. Recognizing that this appears to be inefficient in neoclassical economic terms, she suggests that this less-than-perfectly-competitive market is explained by society's need for the positive externalities of traditionally female tasks, which would not otherwise be adequately supplied. *See* Amy L. Wax, *Caring Enough: Sex Roles, Work and Taxing Women,* 44 Vill. L. Rev. 495 (1999).

73. *See generally* Schneider, *supra* note 30, at 246–47 ("The force of the paradigm case largely arises from the personal and moral relationship between the husband and wife.").

74. *See* Trebilcock & Keshvani, *supra* note 32, at 542–45. But *see* Parkman, *No Fault Divorce, supra* note 28, at 97–98.

75. For Ellman, this includes most childless marriages. *See* Ellman, *supra* note 28, at 63–66.

76. *See, e.g.,* Parkman, *No Fault Divorce, supra* note 28, at 133–34, 137; Ellman, *supra* note 28, at 66–71.

77. Ellman would recognize an alimony claim in this situation. *See* Ellman, *supra* note 28, at 56. The economists who advocate mutual consent divorce rules would require the spouse seeking a divorce to bargain with the other over terms. *See* Parkman, *No Fault Divorce, supra* note 28, at 137–40; Becker, *Finding Fault, supra* note 15. For a housewife who wants a divorce, this would often mean forfeiting any potential alimony award. *See generally* Estin, *Economics and Divorce, supra* note 15, at 533–50.

78. *See* Singer, *Divorce Reform, supra* note 58, at 1113–21; Williams, *supra* note 5.

79. *See* Estin, *Maintenance, supra* note 51, at 781–91.

80. *See* Martha Albertson Fineman, *The Neutered Mother, the Sexual Family, and Other Twentieth Century Tragedies* (1995); Nancy E. Dowd, *Stigmatizing Single Parents,* 18 Harv. Women's L.J. 19 (1995); Estin, *Maintenance, supra* note 51, at 781–802.

81. Deborah L. Rhode & Martha Minow, *Reforming the Questions, Questioning the Reforms: Feminist Perspectives on Divorce Law,* in *Divorce Reform at the Crossroads* 191 (Stephen D. Sugarman & Herma Hill Kay eds., 1990).

82. *See, e.g.,* Parkman, *No Fault Divorce, supra* note 28; Becker, *Finding Fault, supra* note 15, at 22; Zelder, *Inefficient Dissolutions, supra* note 29.

83. *See, e.g.,* Becker, *Deadbeat Dads, supra* note 15, at 18. *See generally* Jana B. Singer, *The Privatization of Family Law,* 1992 Wis. L. Rev. 1443 [hereinafter Singer, *Privatization*].

84. *See, e.g.,* Parkman, *No Fault Divorce, supra* note 28; Becker, *Finding Fault, supra* note 15, at 22; Zelder, *Inefficient Dissolutions, supra* note 29. *See generally* Estin, *Economics and Divorce, supra* note 15, at 533–50.

85. *See, e.g.,* Singer, *Divorce Reform, supra* note 58.

86. *See* Lacey, *supra* note 58, at 1443–48.

87. *See, e.g.*, Parkman, *No Fault Divorce, supra* note 28, at 116–20; Martin Zelder, *The Economic Analysis of the Effect of No-Fault Divorce Law on the Divorce Rate*, 16 Harv. J.L. & Pub. Pol'y 241, 260–62 (1993).

88. *See* Susan Moller Okin, *Justice, Gender, and the Family* 204 n. 48 (1989); Waring, *supra* note 7, at 36–43; *see also* Margaret G. Reid, *Economics of Household Production* (1934).

89. Waring, *supra* note 7, at 27–28.

90. This is not done as a general matter in computing various economic indicators, although there have been efforts to change the practice. *See* the Unremunerated Work Act, H.R. 966, 103rd Cong. § 3 (1993), and the Economic Equality Act, H.R. 2790, 103rd Cong. § 803 (1993), sponsored by Rep. Barbara Rose-Collins (D. Mich.), which would have required that gross national product be computed to include the value of unremunerated work, including household work and child care. Gary Becker has supported this type of change. *See* Gary S. Becker, *Housework: The Missing Piece of the Economic Pie*, Bus. Wk. 30 (Oct. 16, 1995).

91. *See generally* Posner, *Economic Analysis, supra* note 1, at 192–93.

92. *See* Neil K. Komesar, *Toward a General Theory of Personal Injury Loss*, 3 J. Legal Stud. 457, 480–83 (1974).

93. *See* Posner, *Economic Analysis, supra* note 1, at 193.

94. For an outstanding elaboration of these issues, *see* Bergmann, *supra* note 7.

95. *See* Estin, *Love and Obligation, supra* note 3, at 1023–35.

96. Victor Fuchs, in his book *Women's Quest for Economic Equality*, notes that white married women in their forties earn only 85 percent of what their unmarried counterparts earn per hour of work. Victor R. Fuchs, *Women's Quest for Economic Equality* 59 (1988). He emphasizes that there are many reasons why married women with family responsibilities receive lower wages, including the following: time taken out of the labor market for pregnancy, childbirth, and child rearing; constrained job choices in order to achieve flexibility required for child care; more absences from work; and a reduced investment in their own "human capital," starting even before marriage and child rearing began. *See* Fuchs, *supra*, at 60–64.

97. Hadfield, *supra* note 8, at 89. On this question, *see also* Wax, *supra* note 72.

98. Hadfield, *supra* note 8, at 96–98, 103. As Hadfield notes, this is an area in which feminist legal theory may be useful to economists.

99. *See* Becker, *Treatise, supra* note 4, at 277–306.

100. Strassman, *supra* note 7, at 58–59; *see also* England, *Separative Self, supra* note 7, at 47–48.

101. This type of contribution has always been difficult to capture in legal and economic norms. *See* Estin, *Love and Obligation, supra* note 3, at 1013–22.

102. *See* Ferber & Birnbaum, *supra* note 4, at 26–27. The pioneering work in this area was done by Manser & Brown, *supra* note 42, and McElroy & Horney, *supra* note 42. Viewing the family as a firm, some economists have described the gains that occur from cooperative behavior among family members, especially over the long term. *See, e.g.*, Douglas W. Allen, *An Inquiry into the State's Role in Marriage*, 13 J. Econ. Behav. & Org. 171 (1990); Yoram Ben-Porath, *The F-Connection: Families, Friends, and Firms and the Organization of Exchange*, 6 Population & Dev. Rev. 1 (1980); Arthur B. Cornell Jr., *When Two Become One, and Then Come Undone: An Organizational Approach to Marriage and Its Implications for Divorce Law*, 26 Fam. L.Q. 103 (1992). Others have theorized about how the coordination process occurs and how different bargaining endowments lead to different results. *See, e.g.*, Margaret F. Brinig & Michael V. Alexeev, *Trading at Divorce: Preferences, Legal Rules, and Transactions Costs*, 8 Ohio St. J. on Disp. Resol. 279 (1993); Shelly Lundberg & Robert A. Pollak, *Separate Spheres Bargaining and the Marriage Market*, 101 J. Pol. Econ. 988 (1993).

103. *See generally* Regan, *supra* note 30 (discussing, in part, why the economic model of the family resonates with modern experience).

104. *See generally* Singer, *Privatization, supra* note 83 (arguing that, within family law, private norms and private decisions have replaced rules and structures imposed by the state).

105. Estin, *Maintenance, supra* note 51, at 764–67 (citing *Mahoney v. Mahoney*, 453 A.2d 527, 533 (N.J. 1982)).

106. *See* Milton C. Regan Jr., *Family Law and the Pursuit of Intimacy* 34–35 (1993); *see also* Estin, *Love and Obligation, supra* note 3, at 1046–52.

107. *See, e.g.,* Neave, *supra* note 34; Weigers, *supra* note 34.

108. There is a large feminist literature on violence directed at women within families. *See* Linda Gordon, *Heroes of Their Own Lives* 250–88 (1988); Lenore E. Walker, *The Battered Woman* (1979); Elizabeth M. Schneider, *The Violence of Privacy*, 23 Conn. L. Rev. 973 (1991); *see also* sources cited *infra* note 119.

109. *See* Bergmann, *supra* note 7, at 266–73. In economic logic, this seems to "explain" the anomaly of the efficient household in which women work more hours than men. *See supra* note 59.

110. *See* Ferber & Birnbaum, *supra* note 4, at 22–23. Historically, there has been a strong appeal for some feminists in the idea of remaking the family on market terms. This has led to arguments for the reinvention of housework on an "industrial" model or for the integration of women's household labor into the market economy. In the last century, proposals for the "industrialization of housework" referred to the new science of home economics. *See* Susan Strasser, *Never Done* 202–23 (1982). Today, the phrase is more likely to refer to purchasing prepared food, day care, or housecleaning services in the market. *See, e.g.,* Bergmann, *supra* note 7, at 275–98. At times, an argument has been made to require wages for housework; *see* Bergmann, *supra* note 7, at 209–12; Frances E. Olsen, *The Family and the Market: A Study of Ideology and Legal Reform*, 96 Harv. L. Rev. 1497, 1539 (1983). A different proposal would define both partners in a marriage as equal owners of all wages earned by either partner. *See* Williams, *supra* note 5 (arguing that a single income in a traditional household represents the labor of two people and proposing that women who provide a household with domestic labor receive a portion of their husbands' salaries as an entitlement). Other feminist writers have argued that the structure of the family and market spheres make it impossible to bring the two together in this way; *see generally* Carole Pateman, *The Sexual Contract* (1988); Okin, *supra* note 88, at 181; Olsen, *supra*.

111. *See* Estin, *Love and Obligation, supra* note 3, at 1074–81.

112. *See* Gary S. Becker & Kevin M. Murphy, *The Family and the State*, 31 J.L. & Econ. 1 (1988).

113. *See id.; see also* Posner, *Economic Analysis, supra* note 1, at 149–57.

114. For a rare example, *see* Brinig & Alexeev, *supra* note 102. *See also* Eleanor E. Maccoby & Robert H. Mnookin, *Dividing the Child: Social and Legal Dilemmas of Custody* (1992).

115. *See, e.g.,* Yoram Weiss & Robert J. Willis, *Children as Collective Goods and Divorce Settlements*, 3 J. Lab. Econ. 268 (1985); Zelder, *Inefficient Dissolutions, supra* note 29, at 505.

116. *See, e.g.,* Becker, *Treatise, supra* note 4, at 37–38 and 375–76; Posner, *Economic Analysis, supra* note 1, at 143–44; Allen M. Parkman, *Reform of the Divorce Provisions of the Marriage Contract*, 8 BYU J. Pub. L. 91, 104 (1994). This practice also has some currency in feminist writing, but its usefulness for women may be questioned: to what extent does it operate to justify the increasingly tenuous relationships between divorced fathers and their children, and the unequal burdens mothers are expected to assume after divorce?

117. Coase, *supra* note 13, at 209. As Margaret Radin argues, our legal discourse reflects this problem in the conflict over tort remedies for nonpecuniary harms. Economic theories of corrective justice depict the process as one in which harms to persons are compensated by the payment of money damages, suggesting that harms and dollars can be ranked on a single scale. *See* Margaret Jane Radin, *Compensation and Commensurability*, 43 Duke L.J. 56 (1993); *see also* Margaret Jane Radin, *Market-Inalienability*, 100 Harv. L. Rev. 1849 (1987) [hereinafter Radin, *Market-Inalienability*].

118. *See, e.g.,* Martha A. Field, *Surrogate Motherhood* (1988); Pateman, *supra* note 110, at 209–18; Radin, *Market-Inalienability, supra* note 117, at 1925–26; Debra Satz, *Markets in Women's Reproductive Labor*, 21 Phil. & Pub. Affairs 107 (1992).

119. On rape, *see, e.g.,* Catharine A. MacKinnon, *Toward a Feminist Theory of the State* 171–83 (1989); Radin, *Market-Inalienability, supra* note 117, at 1879–81. On pornography, *see,*

e.g., MacKinnon, *supra*, at 195–214. On prostitution, *see*, *e.g.*, Pateman, *supra* note 110, at 189–209; Radin, *Market-Inalienability, supra* note 117, at 1921–25.

120. *See, e.g.*, Posner, *Economic Analysis, supra* note 1.

121. *See, e.g.*, Zelder, *Inefficient Dissolutions, supra* note 29.

122. *See Pyeatte v. Pyeatte*, 661 P.2d 196, 207 (Ariz. Ct. App. 1982); *Mahoney v. Mahoney,* 453 A.2d 527, 533 (N.J. 1982). Judges have also resisted, in most jurisdictions outside New York, the argument for defining and valuing a marital property interest in one spouse's professional degree or license. *See In re the Marriage of Olar,* 747 P.2d 676, 682 (Colo. 1987) (collecting cases in other jurisdictions); *Graham v. Graham,* 574 P.2d 75 (Colo. 1978). But *see O'Brien v. O'Brien,* 489 N.E.2d 712, 713 (N.Y. 1985).

123. For examples of these proposals, *see* Parkman, *No Fault Divorce, supra* note 28; Borenstein & Courant, *supra* note 28. *See also* Kristian Bolin, *The Marriage Contract and Efficient Rules for Spousal Support,* 14 Int'l Rev. L. & Econ. 493 (1994).

124. *See, e.g.*, Rhode & Minow, *supra* note 81.

125. *See, e.g.*, Becker, *Treatise, supra* note 4, at 37–40, 44–48; *see also* Posner, *Sex and Reason, supra* note 21, at 85–110; Richard A. Epstein, *Two Challenges for Feminist Thought,* 18 Harv. J.L. & Pub. Pol'y 331, 333–43 (1995). Epstein, for example, is willing to make both positive and normative arguments from biology. He asserts that societies can increase their overall social welfare if biological sex differences are exploited through a specialization of labor. This leads to the conclusion that traditional, gender-structured social roles will be more efficient. *See* Epstein, *supra*, at 339–43. The assumption of these roles is described by Epstein in terms of "voluntary transactions between the sexes," a phrase that masks the deterministic nature of his model. Epstein, *supra*, at 343. For a persuasive critique of how biology is used in Epstein's writing, *see* Case, *supra* note 60.

126. This statement assumes that a financial metric is not a satisfactory basis for measuring or comparing different family arrangements, for the reasons discussed in the section titled "Methodology: Three Problems." As Cass Sunstein argues, wealth maximization is too narrow a normative grounding for law because it does not enable consideration of various incommensurable goods at stake in a given situation and the risks of harm to those goods from a proposed decision. He suggests that part of the normative project of law is determining which kinds of valuation are appropriate in which contexts. *See* Cass R. Sunstein, *Incommensurability and Valuation in Law,* 92 Mich. L. Rev. 779, 818–19 (1994).

CHAPTER 19

Some Concerns about Applying Economics to Family Law

Margaret F. Brinig

In this essay I hope to point out some of the strengths and weakness of proceeding in the particularly oxymoronic path of mingling family law, feminism, and economics. I admit from the start that this is a task I particularly enjoy performing and one on which I've staked a good part of my academic career.[1] I begin with two criticisms of Law and Economics and conclude with a suggestion for how feminist thought can enhance both fields.

To start, I'd like to address the issue of whether it's appropriate to consider economics at all when we talk about choices people make about and within families. My introduction to the question was rather abrupt. One of the articles that many students of family law, Law and Economics, and dispute resolution all read is Mnookin and Kornhauser's *Bargaining in the Shadow of the Law.*[2] The first time I tried to analyze this article in class (in the mid-1980s), I was met with an amazingly hostile reaction from some of my students.[3] They asked how these authors could possibly imply that children could be traded for money.[4] The idea that such bargains might take place made them feel rather sick. A subset of that question is whether contract—private deals—should be a *primary* descriptor of family life,[5] or whether contract destroys intimacy and spontaneity.[6]

A second topic I will briefly explore involves the concept of externalities, or third-party effects. In the Mnookin and Kornhauser transaction, for example, even assuming parents ought to be making these bargains, how appropriate is it for them to be making decisions that will significantly affect their children's lives?

A final concern, and, I believe, a particularly feminist one, has to do with black letters and bright lines. Both law and economics are imperialistic in the sense that they claim to have all the answers. Feminism, particularly as applied to the family, dwells on subtleties and contexts.[7] Here I think the contributions of feminist thought can enrich not just economics but also law. Economists like to simplify, occasionally leaving out issues and parties. Lawmakers like to feel that their rules make a meaningful difference. For example, they expect that declaring a marriage over[8] means that the relationship is over. They expect that declaring a child emancipated means that she is no longer dependent on her parents.[9] They expect that declaring that one woman is no longer the legal mother of a child while another assumes that role means that the original maternal bond no longer exists (and perhaps that it never existed).[10] I propose instead that families are at once more complex and more permanent than these fields claim.

For purposes of this discussion, I would like to distinguish families from other relationships not on the usual legal basis of "consanguinity or affinity,"[11] which we could translate into "genetics or legally recognized relationship" such as marriage or adoption. Although some families have these characteristics, this legal description is at once too broad and too narrow. Some people are "blood relatives" but have never had any connection with their children. Sperm donors[12] or some biological fathers who beget children by forcible intercourse with mothers[13] come to mind. Some people, such as same-sex partners,[14] have never had legal relationships but do have the characteristics that for me set them apart from nonfamilies: a permanent commitment, unconditional love, and attachment to community.[15] The most famous example of such a family is the extended one recognized by *Moore v. City of East Cleveland.*[16]

Can Economics, or Contracts, Provide a Meaningful Framework for Discussions about Families?

One thing that economics doesn't explain very well is love, the most wonderful thing about families. I am not sure how any model, legal or economic, could pretend to.[17] What we can aspire to do is to see which conditions make love thrive and which stifle it. We may be able to think about what makes families successful ones, where love and intimacy can flow freely.[18] However, as students of the family, we are preoccupied with divorce. We write about families in crisis, and use the fabric of those lives worn thin and stretched to breaking to develop our ideas about what families are, and even what they ought to be.[19] In a way, of course, law teaching and the Socratic method drive us toward such family autopsies. Happily, most of us live most of our lives in families that are much healthier. We grow, we develop trust, we dare to share ourselves with these special people in our inner circle.[20] Much of the law that is in the broadest sense family law—frequently the unexplored law—protects us and encourages us and sometimes pushes us to live in families in particular ways.[21]

A closely related idea is normative: like Milton Regan[22] and Carl Schneider,[23] I believe that both family law and families have suffered from an overemphasis on the individual.[24] Rights have become a focus stronger than loyalty, giving, and commitment.[25] In much of my earlier theoretical work on families, I have argued that many of the workings of a family can be described in terms of two models: the market or contract model[26] and the firm or covenant paradigm.[27] The idea of contract is particularly useful in describing the law and relationships that govern parties about to enter into family relationships, for example, courtship and adoption.[28] Even here, the analogy isn't perfect. Family law beginnings involve people making decisions about lifetime partners (if children can be called partners). Courting couples and birth and adoptive parents necessarily know less about what will occur over the course of a lifetime than one can know about the market (price and technology changes), and usually they know less about each other than one knows about repeatedly purchased consumer items. And, obviously, people are already much more emotionally invested before they pursue these family-related transactions than before they purchase consumer goods or services.

To some extent, and with the qualifications I'll make later on involving the continuing nature of the family and the frequent effects on third parties, contract may also be appropriate for framing the context of dissolving families: those disrupted by separation, divorce,[29] or termination of parental rights.[30] However, contract law dragged out of its usual commercial context and into family law has serious drawbacks. The most obvious of these is that it is virtually useless for treating love, trust, faithfulness, and sympathy, which more than any other terms describe the essence of family.[31] As an aside, I read again an e-mail correspondence I received from Allen Parkman, another economist-lawyer who had read my then unpublished book on the law and economics of the family. He asked me whether covenant and franchise weren't also species of contracts, merely with different remedies.[32] Perhaps men, however well-meaning and educated, just can't get it.

The second problem (which Parkman did identify) is that contract law implies the possibility of breach. When a better deal comes along, it may be most appropriate to breach, pay damages, and recontract with the inviting third party.[33] When people are involved, particularly if some of these are children, paying damages doesn't really compensate. As I've noted before, treating children as "goods" in the context of divorce or surrogacy "commodifies" them.[34] One's affections are not, and, normatively speaking, should not be, readily transferable.[35] Moreover, the idea of continually being on the lookout for better family "deals"—better spouses, children, or parents—itself destroys family life.[36]

Covenant, as opposed to *contract,* is preferable for describing families that are well under way: for illuminating the relationship between husband and wife or parent and child.[37] Covenant implies a particularly serious agreement that has characteristics of permanence, unconditional love, and community involvement. Covenants aren't particularly efficient. They aren't meant to be efficient, just important. They aren't meant for commodity production but rather to provide environments in which growth—emotional and moral growth—can take place.

The current Law and Economics literature about the family concentrates on working together as a couple or family because it is better for us individually. Economists say it is more efficient or satisfactory to our "interdependent utility functions." Patricia Bradford urges us to rearrange compensation so as to encourage the development of self-identities for women.[38] My view is that we should encourage commitments because the family (or firm) has a value in itself. This contrast in emphasis frequently appears in family law. One example that readily comes to mind is the thread that runs through the child custody and adoption cases: the "best interests of the child." The focus on individuals (who are, after all, the parties in custody cases) leads almost inevitably to the primacy of parents' interests.[39] This occurs because the market and contract paradigms can't comfortably accommodate the fact that the "good" to be bargained over or litigated for is a person too. Nor can the individual-based models deal well with parental love. We love our children despite the fact that it's not "efficient"[40] and despite the fact that they have some traits, whether disabilities or personality quirks, that annoy us.

Efficiency, as we have heard it used in the economics literature, is reached when the highest amount of utility can be derived from the lowest expenditure.[41] More than some other terms, efficiency almost always means either more wealth or greater production, that is, more of some material good. We've already seen how emotional or spiritual satisfaction is not part of the efficiency test, and how not taking a wider view affects our study of families. Further, efficiency usually is calculated by the parties directly involved in the transaction, not outsiders, such as children, who might be affected by it.

The Concept of Externalities as It Applies to Families

Perhaps the new institutional economics concept that is the most helpful in our discussion of families is the idea of the *externality.*[42] Economists, including Coase, usually describe an externality as an effect on people who were not direct parties to a transaction. Two people are, for example, parties to a contract involving the making of cement. The cement plant is located in a neighborhood that suffers from the noise, dust, wear, tear, and danger presented by the cement trucks. The ill effects suffered by the neighbors are externalities, and much of the Law and Economics (and economics) literature involves making the parties to such a contract internalize these ill effects. Sometimes this is done through government regulation, sometimes by giving people in the position of the neighbors the right to sue. Thus the contract may become less than fully enforceable where there are substantial negative third-party effects.[43] Although most contracts affect third parties, at least indirectly, sometimes the contracting parties, like those involved in the cement factory transaction, must buy off the affected outsiders.[44] So long as the compensation takes place,[45] the contract remains efficient and enforceable. When the costs to the third party or parties are too high, the contract may be prohibited criminally,[46] enjoined,[47] or just not enforced.

There are two primary kinds of externalities in family transactions. The first, and perhaps most obvious, occurs when there are minor children. In fact the market analogy itself breaks down in adoption and surrogacy situations because the "goods" are themselves people who will be affected by the grownups' activities. Whenever couples have children at home, their actions must be taken with the children in mind. This includes creating "second-hand smoke" or displaying sexually explicit materials. Investing in a career may have positive externalities by giving the children a better parental role model or creating more financial security, and negative externalities by taking the student or employed parent out of the home.[48] The presence of children for divorcing parents presents a huge externality problem because children are almost always worse off in a divorced rather than intact family.[49] A custodial parent's moving out of state causes an external effect because it makes visitation more difficult for the noncustodial parent.

Thus, children of divorce suffer substantial negative externalities,[50] so much so that we may make it more difficult for the parents to divorce.[51] We try to make things easier for these children by allowing child support to the standard of living they would have enjoyed if their parents had remained together.[52] In some states, the court may order the divorcing parents to provide the children a college education that children with married parents cannot claim.[53]

In a surrogacy situation, there may be externalities as well.[54] Although any negatives flowing to the contracted-for child are probably outweighed by the benefits of existence,[55] what are the benefits of the contracted-for child's existence to the surrogate's other children?[56] Less directly, what about the "hard to place" children who may languish in institutions because people who otherwise might be candidates to adopt them choose to "buy" surrogate services? Jane Cohen and I have worried about these problems in print;[57] I don't see much concern from our male colleagues.

As another example of what I mean by the problem of third-party externalities, consider the minor who becomes pregnant. Regardless of what one feels about her personal right to choose whether or not to terminate the pregnancy, her decision will have consequences to numerous other people.[58] The most obvious is the man involved, although the Supreme Court's decisions since *Roe v. Wade* have consistently maintained that he need not be consulted by the pregnant woman. (Because in many teenaged pregnancies, statutory rape is apparently involved, there would seem even less reason to notify him.) Nevertheless, if the minor does elect to carry the pregnancy to term, the father will be responsible for the child's support. Another group of people who are clearly interested are the minor's parents. They may have the responsibility of supporting not only her but also their grandchild, at least until the child reaches minority.[59] According to the Personal Responsibility Act, their daughter must reside with them in order to receive public assistance for herself and the baby she chooses to keep.[60] They may have to readjust to having a baby or a toddler in their home and being the only experienced parents. On a nonfinancial note, but one that is more important to me (as the mother of four young, unmarried women), the parents of this young woman will want to be able to support her emotionally as she makes her decision, and to help her as she adjusts to abortion, adoption, or parenthood. Finally, there are the siblings of the pregnant woman. They may well be financially affected if she keeps the child. They will have to deal with the extra attention their sister gets, and perhaps the attention given to—and occasional annoyance caused by—their new niece or nephew. I'm not advocating a change in Supreme Court doctrine but merely illustrating how many people are affected by the young people's act.

There is another kind of externality we encounter with families that is more diffuse. Because families are critically important to the way society functions, any change in family life has a much wider impact—an effect on the community. Although allowing free contracting for divorce grounds, sexual or childbearing services, or the division of labor in the household may well promote individual autonomy, it also affects the quality of what is sometimes called social capital.[61] Allowing these agreements arguably changes the quality of life for the rest of society, the community.

My point here is simply that many legal decisions are treated as though the decision makers (those given the legal power to make the choices) are the only ones affected. When we live in families, everything we do has consequences for others. We aren't islands.

The very earliest work on the economics of the family completely ignored any third-party effects and basically theorized that the family operated as a single unit[62]—perhaps like the "unities" that made up the marriage in the (nearly obsolete) tenancy by the entireties,[63] perhaps like the "one" who was the husband in Blackstone's jurisprudence.[64] The family was like a "black box" that supplied labor to the market economy, purchased goods, and consumed them. Even with the additions of Gary Becker's household, the head of household—the altruist who allocated wealth among family members—is the only real economic actor.[65] More recently, even if economists described bargaining by couples (at least at the time they were courting[66] and breaking up), standard contract models were used (so, for example, children were treated as "goods"[67] or "hostages" but not actors) and the third-party effects largely ignored. The last few years have seen a resurgence of interest in norms and norm formation among both pure economists and legal scholars and especially in the Law and Economics field.[68] The focus on norms appears to be a rebellion against the Chicago school's stress of efficiency, although some of the writers in the field treat norm formation as merely another shortcut toward efficient transactions.[69] A more feminist economics of the family begins where these models stop their explanations.

Externalities are not only a heuristic for the complex of problems we find in family law. When they are present, and they almost always are, their presence suggests a legal treatment that is distinctive, that may be different from the way the same sort of issue would be dealt with in other contexts. Take the antenuptial agreement, obviously a species of contract. Because there are externalities involved (for example, the spouse may go on welfare if the agreement is strictly followed, or spouses may contract in ways that will harm children they don't yet have), law may simply forbid contracting about some issues.[70] At other times, the scrutiny the agreements require may be heightened compared with other contracts.[71] Thus, for example, Katherine Silbaugh writes that both women's household labor and men's reciprocal labor force activities are done "out of love" and are not properly the subject of enforceable contracts between them.[72]

In families, we are constantly not only interacting with each other but with and for the wider community. This feminist emphasis on community and relationship comes to mind not only when we think about externalities but also about the fallacies that come from assuming that policymakers can always draw "bright lines."

Black-Letter Law and Bright-Line Rules

My personal odyssey as an adult and my forays into family law are coextensive, and perhaps unsurprisingly, each path has led to similar insights. Perhaps the most important things I have learned are that family commitments are permanent and that children are central to families. Thus, even when we say they are legally over, parts of the relationships continue.[73] Further, most family practices in law and life promote and protect our progeny. Nor do we escape the centrality of children by remaining childless, for we live as children so long as we have parents and perhaps while we have living siblings. Finally, the small communities that are families ripple outward into the larger society, just as the breakwater of society's rule (law) binds and influences them. Because of these ramifications, or wider externalities, the relationships persist to a certain degree in spite of divorce or emancipation or adoption. To the extent such a relationship persists, it is what I call the franchise.

In her celebrated *The Joy Luck Club*, Amy Tan describes a mother[74] who leaves infant twin daughters beside the road in despair that she will die and in the hope that they will be found and raised in a better life.[75] She spends the rest of her life looking for them, and it is only after her death that they are found. Although she married again and formed another family, she never forgot her little girls whose loss cost her so much. The tie did not break. In a case-law parallel, a Vietnamese woman places her children in a Saigon orphanage after a harrowing journey through the wartime Central Highlands.[76] Both she and they end up in the United States, where by the time she finds them, several of the children have been placed for adoption in an American home. Not surprisingly, the court looks beyond time and class and culture and returns the children to the mother. Again, although legal events had ostensibly severed the ties, the court recognized they still bound mother and children.

Someone who acted in good faith will clearly be unhappy with any outcome in a court case involving such children. When a family has been disrupted by war, or hardship, or death,[77] need the ties be cut as clearly as we sever them in adoption? From the perspective of the mothers, placement of the child clearly was the appropriate action at the time.[78] From the perspective of the child, should he or she know his heritage and how much the mother (or father) loved him?[79]

The quest for each other by birth parents and children defies easy characterization.[80] The law protects the birth parents by hiding their identities from all who seek them,[81] except in some palpable cases of emergency. This is clearly what adoptive parents want as well, for the protection allows them to determine when their children should be told of their adoptive status. But increasingly states are responding to lobbying efforts on the part of both birth parents and adoptive children and enacting statutes permitting parents to leave identifying information with adoption agencies.[82] Although the provisions differ, they usually allow the adopted child, at his or her option, to discover the birth parent's identity at majority.

Does this appropriately satisfy the longing felt on both sides of what seems to be a franchise?[83] Or should we, as a society, move toward a more open adoptive process, as some are urging?[84] One commentator has suggested that this might be a "middle ground" for cases in which father's rights have been cut off without proper notice, allowing children to remain in their current placement.[85] On the other side of the story, it might give more "market" power to birth parents, who seem to have the upper hand in this time of relative scarcity of adoptable children. My own view, consistent with the themes I have been developing here, is that on balance, permitting continued contact between parents and children (so long as the birth parents wish it) is a good thing.[86]

In some ways, this idea of the continuing family reflects a "difference" feminist approach.[87] Patriarchal men, more than women, think bimodally and in terms of absolutes: right and wrong, victor and vanquished, self versus other.[88] To these dualities, I would add married versus unmarried, child versus adult, parent versus stranger. I maintain that family, and therefore family law, is continuous, not discrete. One does not just turn a family off and on like an electric switch. To the extent we have built laws that deny the oceanlike expanse and eternity of family life, we create regret and hurt, moral malaise and longing. When we see these negative emotions in large categories of people encountering family laws, we must be alert to a need for change. Some of our current laws seemingly encourage pathological behavior—elder abuse, will contests, deadbeat attitudes, surrogacy suits, and other ugly custody battles. If we legislatively choose outcomes that promote continuing family relationships, we should see more positive family outcomes.[89]

It may be that as more women make laws, the laws themselves will reflect the texture of relationships. For example, an opponent of same-sex marriage reported his observations of the oral arguments in the *Baker v. Vermont* litigation.[90] He began by noting that the plaintiffs, their lawyer, and the judge who decided the case were all women. With some astonishment he pointed out that the argument didn't seem to be about equal protection as much as it seemed to be about belonging to a community and feeling welcomed by the community.[91]

All of the things I've talked about—what we might call commodification, externalities, and the oversimplification of law and economics—don't mean that economics has nothing to say to a feminist study of the family. At the very least, because we are revolted by the application of economics to certain concepts, we've identified things that are really important. When we see ways in which adult-centered laws are deeply affecting children, we can pause at least long enough to consider what we are doing. When we see that either lawyers or economists are treating the world as though portions of lives can be amputated, we can be at the same time more sensitive and sensible.

Notes

1. My recent book, *From Contracts to Covenant: Beyond the Law and Economics of the Family* (2000) [hereinafter Brinig, *Covenant*], purports to do exactly this. Other recent work that concentrates on matters of gender and critiques Law and Economics includes Steven L. Nock & Margaret F. Brinig, *Weak Men and Disorderly Women: Divorce and the Division of Labor*, in *Marriage and Divorce: An Economic Perspective* (Robert Rowthorn & Anthony W. Dnes eds., Cambridge U. Press 2000). *Contracts to Covenant* is extended to the relationship between family and community, in Margaret F. Brinig, *Troxel and the Limits of Community*, 32 Rutgers L.J. 733 (2001) [hereinafter Brinig, *Limits of Community*].

2. Robert H. Mnookin & Lewis Kornhauser, *Bargaining in the Shadow of the Law: The Case of Divorce*, 88 Yale L.J. 969 (1979). Robert Mnookin, a lawyer, is the director of the Center for Negotiation at Harvard Law School. Lewis Kornhauser, an economist, teaches on the N.Y.U. law faculty. *Bargaining in the Shadow*, which can be read by students without formal training in either discipline, supposes that as they make separation agreements, husbands and wives "trade" between time with children (custody) and money (alimony, property division, and child support). The article also establishes a critical role for law in such bargaining because it sets what the authors call an "endowment point," a threshold below which neither, acting rationally, will accept

a proposed settlement. The alternative to settling is what each spouse thinks he or she will get in court. Women are disadvantaged, according to *Bargaining in the Shadow,* because the "endowment point" moved when custody rules became less determinate. In addition, mothers lost bargaining ability because they fear loss of their children more than their husbands do and would settle for less money just to avoid the possibility of losing custody.

3. Perhaps the reaction would not have been amazing at most law schools. George Mason, my former academic home, is Law and Economics heaven, however.

4. I explore whether this trading actually occurs, in Margaret F. Brinig & Michael V. Alexeev, *Trading at Divorce: Preferences, Legal Rules, and Transaction Costs,* 8 Ohio St. J. on Disp. Resol. 279 (1993). My conclusion, shared by Marsha Garrison and Mnookin himself, is that we can't find explicit trading between children and financial assets. Marsha Garrison, *How Do Judges Decide Divorce Cases: An Empirical Analysis of Discretionary Decisionmaking,* 74 NC L. Rev. 401 (1996); Eleanor E. Maccoby & Robert H. Mnookin, *Dividing the Child: Social and Legal Dilemmas of Custody* (Harvard U. Press 1992).

5. A related problem is explored in Jana B. Singer, *The Privatization of Family Law,* Wis. L. Rev. 1443 (1992). Carl Schneider and I discuss the use of contract in family law at some length in our casebook. Carl E. Schneider & Margaret F. Brinig, *An Invitation to Family Law: Principles, Process, and Possibilities* ch. 5 (2d ed., West Publishing 2000). Contract can be thought of as one way the concept of autonomy translates into family law. For a look from the contracts perspective, *see* Steven L. Burton, *Principles of Contract Law* (Foundation Press 1995), especially the introduction and chapter titles.

The Supreme Court case of *Troxel v. Glanville,* 530 U.S. 57 (2000), can be read as constitutionalizing autonomy. *See* Brinig, *Limits of Community, supra* note 1.

6. The issue is explored in Milton C. Regan, *Family Law and the Pursuit of Intimacy* 35–42 (NYU Press 1992) [hereinafter Regan, *Law and Intimacy*]. *See also* Nock & Brinig, *supra* note 1.

7. For one example of what I mean, consider the final lines of the famous article by Frances E. Olsen, *The Family and the Market: A Study of Ideology and Legal Reform,* 96 Harv. L. Rev. 1497, 1578 (1983): "This does not mean making women more like men, or men more like women. Rather, it means radically increasing the options available to each individual, and more importantly, allowing the human personality to break out of the present dichotomized system. We have all experienced occasional glimpses of what this might mean—moments of power, sensitivity, and connectedness. We should recognize these fleeting experiences as a source of hope, a foreshadow of the human beings we can become. In some ways women will be less like present men, and men will be less like present women. Rather than shades of grey as an alternative to all black and all white, I envision reds and greens and blues."

8. The technical term *divorce a vinculo* means divorce from the bonds or chains of matrimony.

9. *See* Margaret F. Brinig, *The Family Franchise: Elderly Parents and Adult Siblings,* 1996 Utah L. Rev. 393 (families and family dynamics continue after emancipation) [hereinafter Brinig, *Family Franchise*]; Margaret F. Brinig, *Finite Horizons: The American Family,* 2 Int'l J. Children's Rts. 293 (1994) (the attitude adults have toward their own parents interacts with their relationship with their children).

10. On a yet more subtle level, law tends to assume that adoption severs the ties to a child's cultural heritage. For recent Canadian proof that this is not so, *see N.H. and D.H. v. H.M., M.H,* 169 DLR (4th) 604 (Supreme Court of Canada 1999). The case involves a couple from the Swan Lake Nation who gave up a daughter for adoption by some Caucasian people in the United States. When she was still a minor, this daughter herself had a child with an African American father. Because the teenager did not want to care for the child, the two sets of grandparents and an aboriginal group sought custody.

11. Legal scholars may recognize these terms from marriage law. Because two people are already in a family, they are unable to marry. *See* Homer Clark, *Law of Domestic Relations in the United States* § 2.1, at 23 (2d ed., West 1987). For statutory examples of this concept or including the terms, *see, e.g.,* Ga. Code § 19.5-3 (ground for divorce); Ala. Code § 11-44-102 (nepotism); Ariz. Rev. Stat. Ann. § 21-211(3) (disqualification of jurors); Cal. Civ. Code § 1708.7

(stalking; definition of "immediate family"); Fla. Stat. Ann. § 794.027(5) (disqualification from need to report sexual battery); Haw. Rev. Stat. § 707-741(1) (incest).

12. *See, e.g.,* Ohio Rev. Code § 3111-37(b): "If a woman is the subject of a nonspousal artificial insemination, the donor shall not be treated in law or regarded as the natural child of the donor." Of course, this may be varied by agreement between the parties. For some cases in which the mothers agreed to let the sperm donors have visitation rights, *see Shepherd v. Clemens,* 752 A.2d 533 (Del. 2000); *La Chapelle v. Mitten,* 607 N.W. 2d 151 (Minn. 2000); and *C.O. v. W.S.,* 64 Ohio Misc. 2d 9, 639 N.E. 2d 523 (1994). *See generally* Marsha Garrison, *Law Making for Baby Making: An Interpretive Approach to the Determination of Legal Parentage,* 113 Harv. L. Rev. 835 (2000).

13. *See, e.g.,* 13 Del. Code § 728(d); Ind. Code § 31-3-6g(2)(B); Ohio Rev. Code 3111–371(b); *cf. Michael H. v. Gerald D.,* 491 U.S. 110, 124 & n. 4 (1989)(opinion of Justice Scalia). Cases in which the mothers have agreed to let statutory rapists have visitation rights include *Shepherd v. Clemens,* 752 A.2d 533 (Del. 2000); *Mulles v. Kinder,* 568 N.E. 1081 (Ind. 1991)

14. *See, e.g., In re Custody of H.S.H.-K.,* 533 N.W. 2d 419 (Wis. 1995); *J.A.L. v. E.P.H.,* 682 A.2d 1314 (Pa. Super. 1996); and *LaChapelle v. Mitten,* 607 N.W. 2d 151 (Minn. 2000) (all allowing access to biological child of same-sex partners).

15. As Ore. Rev. Stat. § 109.119 provides, people with standing to seek custody demonstrate "emotional ties creating the child–parent relationship are based on having had physical custody of a child or residing in the same household within six months except unrelated foster parents." These three elements are discussed at length in Brinig, *Covenant, supra* note 1. *Cf.* Elizabeth S. Scott & Robert E. Scott, *Parents as Fiduciaries,* 81 Va. L. Rev. 2401, 2433 (1995) ("Most parents are influenced to a greater or lesser degree by biological, psychological and social forces which, in combination, generate a norm of parental obligation.").

16. 431 U.S. 494, 503–4 (1977)("our decisions establish that the Constitution protects the sanctity of the family precisely because the institution of the family is deeply rooted in this Nation's history and tradition. It is through the family that we inculcate and pass down many of our most cherished values, moral and cultural.").

17. For related discussions on inalienability, *see* Margaret Jane Radin, *Market-Inalienability,* 100 Harv. L. Rev. 1845 (1987); Guido Calabresi & Douglas Melamed, *Property Rules, Liability Rules, and Inability: One View from the Cathedral,* 100 Harv. L. Rev. 1089 (1972). On incommensurability, *see* Cass Sunstein, *Incommensurability and Valuation in Law,* 92 Mich. L. Rev. 779 (1994). I use these ideas as reasons why surrogacy cannot be considered like a commercial contract, in Margaret F. Brinig, *A Maternalistic Approach to Surrogacy,* 81 Va. L. Rev. 2377 (1995) [hereinafter Brinig, *Maternalistic Approach*].

I attended a talk given by Gillian Hadfield at the University of Toronto at which she explained her frustration with a male economist trying to discuss family relationships in terms of symbolic representations of "interdependent utility functions." The idea was something like $U_A'f(c_A + U_B(Hw_A - c_A))$. No wonder economics gets a bad name in feminist circles!

18. For better ideas, *see* Judith S. Wallerstein & Sandra Blakeslee, *The Good Marriage: How and Why Love Lasts* (Houghton Mifflin 1995); and Milton C. Regan, *Alone Together: Love and the Meaning of Marriage* (Oxford U. Press 1999).

19. For more on these points, *see* Brinig, *Family Franchise, supra* note 9; and the preface to Schneider & Brinig, *supra* note 5.

20. For descriptions of the creation of intimacy, *see* Regan, *Law and Intimacy, supra* note 6; and Jennifer Roback Morse, *The Development of the Child,* prepared for The Family, the Person, and the State, Liberty Fund Colloquium, Arlington, Va. (July 14, 1995) (parent and child).

21. Carl E. Schneider, *The Channeling Function of Family Law,* 20 Hofstra L. Rev. 495, 498 (1992).

22. Regan, *Law and Intimacy, supra* note 6.

23. *Moral Discourse and the Transformation of Family Law,* 83 Mich. L. Rev. 1803 (1985).

24. For a recent example, based on concerns that state involvement with "family values" might jeopardize the values hard won through the Civil War and Reconstruction, *see* Peggy

Cooper Davis, *Changing Images of the State: Contested Images of Family Values: The Role of the State*, 107 Harv. L. Rev. 1348 (1994). I address this in Margaret F. Brinig, *The Supreme Court's Impact on Marriage, 1967–90*, 41 Howard L.J. 271 (1998).

25. For a recent example, *see* the Supreme Court case of *Troxel v. Glanville*, 120 S. Ct. 2054 (2000), in which the Court found that the fundamental right of legal parents to make decisions about the care, custody, and control of their children trumped the rights of nonparents to visit the child in the child's best interests. (The plurality opinion did not even consider any relevant constitutional protection children might have "against the arbitrary exercise of parental authority that is not in fact motivated by an interest in the welfare of the child," as Justice Stevens suggested in his dissent.)

26. *See, e.g.,* Margaret F. Brinig & Michael V. Alexeev, *Fraud in Courtship: Annulment and Divorce*, 2 European J. L. & Econ. 45 (1995); Margaret F. Brinig, *The Effect of Transactions Costs on the Market for Babies*, 18 Seton Hall Legis. J. 553 (1994); Margaret F. Brinig & Steven M. Crafton, *Marriage and Opportunism*, 23 J. Legal Stud. 869 (1994); and Margaret F. Brinig, *Rings and Promises*, 6 J.L. Econ. & Org. 203 (1990).

27. *See* Brinig, *Covenant, supra* note 1; Margaret F. Brinig, *Status, Contract and Covenant*, 79 Cornell L. Rev. 1573 (1994) [hereinafter Brinig, *Status*]; Brinig, *Family Franchise, supra* note 9.

28. In addition to the articles cited *supra* note 26, *see* Marjorie Macguire Schultz, *Contractual Ordering of Marriage: A New Model for State Policy*, 70 Cal. L. Rev. 204 (1982)(discussing, among other contracts, prenuptial agreements).

29. *See, e.g.,* Margaret F. Brinig & June Carbone, *The Reliance Interest in Marriage and Divorce*, 62 Tulane L. Rev. 855 (1988); June Carbone, *Economics, Feminism, and the Reinvention of Alimony or Why the Desire to Remove Distorting Incentives Does Not a Theory Make*, 43 Vand. L. Rev. 1463 (1990); Arthur Cornell, *When Two Become One and Then Come Undone: An Organizational Approach to Marriage and Its Importance for Divorce Law*, 26 Fam. L.Q. 103 (1992); Brinig & Crafton, *supra* note 26.

30. *See* Margaret F. Brinig, *The Nature of the Contract between Parent and Child*, prepared for The Family, the Person, and the State, the Liberty Fund Colloquium, Arlington, Va. (July 14, 1995).

31. *See, e.g.,* Regan, *Law and Intimacy, supra* note 6, at 4; Brinig, *Status, supra* note 27, at 1573; Schneider, *supra* note 21, at 498.

32. As used here, *contract* leans almost exclusively on the legal meaning of the terms of a legally enforceable agreement. Covenants reflect those agreements enforced not by law as much as by individuals and their social organizations. Although rich in religious provenance, *covenant* means the solemn vows that create and characterize the family. Enforcement stems from the solemnity and the values held by the family members. Thus, although some covenants draw power from religious values, today we find families whose covenants draw most power from the mutual commitment to each other and to preservation and protection of the family itself.

33. Brinig, *Maternalistic Approach, supra* note 17, at 1586 & n. 79.

34. Radin, *supra* note 17, at 1853, argues that some things should be permitted as gifts but not sold, so that they are placed outside of the marketplace but not outside the realm of social intercourse. *Id.* at 1853 n. 14. The market-inalienable things are those that are important to personhood, *id.* at 1903, and these include one's politics, work, religion, family, love, sexuality, friendships, altruism, experiences, wisdom, moral commitments, character, and personal attributes, all of which are integral to the self. *Id.* at 1905. *See also* Cass R. Sunstein, *Incommensurability and Valuation in Law*, 92 Mich. L. Rev. 779, 850 (1994)("Certainly the desire of infertile couples for children would be better satisfied through a market system. But part of the objection to free markets in babies is not quite engaged by Judge Posner. Instead the objection is that a system of purchase and sale would value children in the wrong way. This system would treat human beings as commodities, a view that is itself wrong."); Joan Mahoney, *An Essay on Surrogacy and Feminist Thought*, 16 Law Med. & Health Care 81, 82 (1988) ("Either [usual form of surrogacy or one in which surrogate becomes pregnant by anonymous sperm donor] would seem to result in the 'commodification of babies.' "). Perhaps society is channeling couples away from the

institution, as Carl Schneider suggests, *supra* note 21, at 503–4, 520; *see also* Elizabeth S. Scott, *Pluralism, Parental Preference, and Child Custody,* 80 Cal. L. Rev. 615, 667–69 (1992)(noting the power of informal social norms in regulating behavior).

35. In a way, this is like the difference between endorsing a check as "pay Martha Fineman" (nontransferable) as opposed to "pay to the order of Martha Fineman" (transferable). In the first instance, only Martha gets the money. In the second, she may delegate to whomever she wishes. Although after divorce you are free to love another and begin a new life (and a hypothetical new contract) with someone else, as anyone dealing with divorced or divorcing people knows, not only financial resources but emotions are enmeshed.

36. Brinig, *Status, supra* note 27, at 1601. I think of this continuing search as "hedging."

37. *See id.;* for a lengthy discussion using the terminology of status rather than covenant, *see* Regan, *Law and Intimacy, supra* note 6; *see also* William Everett, *Contract and Covenant in Human Community,* 35 Emory L.J. 557 (1987) (covenants between parents regarding parenthood); for discussions of partnership in the context of dissolution, *see* Bea Smith, *The Partnership Theory of Marriage: A Borrowed Solution Fails,* 68 Tex. L. Rev. 689 (1990); Cynthia Starnes, *Playing with Paper Dolls: Partnership Buyouts and the Law of the Displaced Homemaker,* 60 U. Chi. L. Rev. 67 (1993).

38. Patricia C. Bradford, *Intrafamily Bargaining and Taxing Women,* 6 S. Cal. Rev. L. & Women's Stud. 397 (1991).

39. Ira Lupu has noticed, and regretted, this phenomenon. Lupu, *Mediating Institutions—Beyond the Public/Private Distinction: The Separation of Powers and the Protection of Children,* 61 U. Chi. L. Rev. 1315 (1994). But his solution of protecting children through separation of parental powers reinforces the individual rather than the family unit, and to that extent, I believe, leads us down the wrong track. A thoughtful attempt to finesse this problem is the American Law Institute, *Principles of Marital Dissolution* ch. 2 (Preliminary Draft No. 6, 1996). In this chapter, the prevailing concepts are agreement about custody, continuity of existing parent–child relationships, and as a minimum, meaningful contact with each parent. *Id.* at § 2.02.

40. This contrast appears in Ira Ellman, *The Theory of Alimony,* 77 Cal. L. Rev. 3 (1989). Ellman is arguing for compensation for efficiency-based losses in the labor market. To accommodate children at all, he adds sacrifices made for childbearing and child rearing as a separate category.

41. Hal Varian, *Microeconomic Analysis* 15 (2d ed., Norton 1984).

42. *Id.* at 545–46; D. McCloskey, *The Applied Theory of Price* 331 (2d ed., Macmillan 1985).

43. For example, Epstein has written that the only sound justification for inalienability is "the practical control of externalities," externalities that are usually present when resources must be shared. Richard A. Epstein, *Why Restrain Alienation,* 85 Colum. L. Rev. 970, 990 (1985). In *Surrogacy: The Case for Full Contractual Enforcement,* 81 Va. L. Rev. 2305, 2315 (1995), Epstein writes that "the legal response should be to ban or restructure those transactions whose negative third-party consequences outweigh the gains to the transacting parties, . . . [when] gains and losses are measured by a compensation criterion." *See also* June Carbone, *The Role of Contract Principles in Determining the Validity of Surrogacy Contracts,* 28 Santa Clara L. Rev. 581, 582 (1988)(arguing in favor of enforcement so that genetic fathers can enter the agreements with confidence in the certainty of the outcome).

44. In situations where they do, the contract becomes Pareto-optimal. For discussions of Pareto optimality, *see* Jack Hirschleifer, *Price Theory and Applications* 496–97 (4th ed., Prentice Hall 1988); Varian, *supra* note 41, at 262–63.

45. At least the compensation occurs theoretically, according to Kaldor-Hicks optimality. *See, e.g.,* P. R. G. Layard & A. A. Walters, *Microeconomic Theory* 32 (McGraw Hill 1978); Varian, *supra* note 41, at 218. The original articles are Nicholas Kaldor, *Welfare Properties of Economics and Interpersonal Comparisons of Utility,* 49 Econ. J. 549–51 (1939); J. R. Hicks, *The Valuation of Social Income,* 7 Economica 105–24 (1940).

46. This would include such conduct as drag racing, popularly called "chicken." *See, e.g., In re Fox, Alleged Delinquent Child,* 395 N.E. 2d 918 (Ohio Ct. Com. Pleas 1979). For a game theoretic explanation, *see* Charles Goetz, *Law and Economics* 15–17 (West 1984).

47. This is the case in nuisance situations. *See, e.g., Hart v. Wagner,* 184 Md. 40, 40 A.2d 47 (1944).

48. How much of a problem this is is hotly contested. For two recent and contrasting views, *see* Joe Armstrong, *The Mad Myths of Parenthood,* Irish Times (Sept. 15, 2000); and Manci Hellmich, *Stay Home with the Kids if You Can: 2 Experts Say Parents Must Weigh Their Careers,* USA Today (Sept. 28, 2000) ("Brazelton says he doesn't want to make working parents or single parents feel guilty if they have no control over how much time their children are in day care, but he'd like all parents to think about the needs of their children when planning their own lives. 'We're not in the Dark Ages anymore. We know some parents have to work. But if there is a choice, we certainly prefer parents being with their own children.'")

49. *See, e.g.,* John H. Johnson IV & Christopher J. Mazingo, *The Impact of Divorce on Child Outcomes: Evidence from Variation in Unilateral Divorce Laws,* Department of Economics, Massachusetts Institute of Technology (April 2000); Judith A. Seltzer, *Consequences of Marital Dissolution for Children,* 20 Ann. Rev. Soc. 235–66 (1994); Frank Furstenberg Jr. & Andrew J. Cherlin, *Divided Families: What Happens to Children When Parents Part* (Harvard U. Press 1991); Carol Bruce & Greer Litton Fox, *Accounting for Patterns of Father Involvement: Age of Child, Father-Coresidence, and Father Role Salience,* 69 Soc. Inq. 458–76 (1999).

50. Judith S. Wallerstein, *Second Chances: What Happens to Men, Women, and Children a Decade after Divorce* (Ticknor & Fields 1989); Mavis Hetherington, Martha Cox, & Roger Cox, *Effects of Divorce on Parents and Children,* in *Nontraditional Families: Parenting and Child Development* (M. E. Lamb ed., Erlbaum 1982); Mavis Hetherington, Martha Cox, & Roger Cox, *Long-Term Effects of Divorce and Remarriage on the Adjustment of Children,* 24 J. Am. Acad. Child Psych. 518 (1985); Judith S. Wallerstein, *The Long-Term Effects of Divorce on Children: A Review,* 30 J. Am. Acad. Child & Adolescent Psych. 349 (1991). A less formal account is presented in Barbara Dafoe Whitehead, *Dan Quayle Was Right: Harmful Effects of Divorce on Children,* 271 Atlantic 47 (Apr. 1993).

51. Va. Code Ann. § 20-91. *See also* Elizabeth S. Scott, *Rational Decisionmaking in Marriage and Divorce,* 76 Va. L. Rev. 9 (1990); Barbara Defoe Whitehead, *A New Familism,* Fam. Aff. 1, 5 (1992).

52. *Cole v. Cole,* 44 Md. App. 435, 409 A.2d 734 (1979); *Conway v. Conway,* 10 Va. App. 653, 397 S.E. 2d 464 (1990).

53. *See, e.g., Crocker v. Crocker,* 971 P.2d 469 (Ore. App. 1998); *Rohn v. Thuma,* 408 N.E. 2d 578 (Ind. 1980). Of course, money (and even higher education) does not buy happiness. The requirement that the noncustodial parent pay for college might palliate the pain of divorce somewhat.

54. These are explored at some length in Brinig, *Maternalistic Approach, supra* note 17.

55. *Cf. Berman v. Allen,* 80 N.J. 421, 404 A.2d 8 (1979); *Zepeda v. Zepeda,* 41 Ill. App. 2d 240, 190 N.E. 2d 849 (1963). But *see generally Baby M. Reconsidered,* 76 Geo. L.J. 1741, 1746–48 (1988). Richard Epstein has written that "[t]he current view sees externalities everywhere. In effect it isolates one negative consequence of any action on third parties and uses it to justify the prohibition of that action, no matter how large the gains for others." I agree with him that the "full range of consequences has to be grasped and evaluated, comprehensively and not selectively, not case by case, but by broad categories of cases." Richard A. Epstein, The Harm Principle—And How It Grew 35, address given at the Canadian Law and Economics Association Annual Meeting, Toronto (Sept. 30, 1994).

56. There is a kind of double bind here. If the surrogate has never had children, there is a greater information problem. *See, e.g.,* Mark Strasser, *Parental Rights Terminations: On Surrogate Reasons and Surrogacy Policies,* 60 Tenn. L. Rev. 135, 143–33 (1992). If she has them, the children may be deeply and permanently injured by the surrogacy contract. The compensation paid the surrogate is surely not enough to justify this harm. Virginia, for example, requires a prior live birth. Va. Code Ann. § 20-160B(6), as does New Hampshire, N.H. Rev. Stat. Ann. § 168-B:17(V).

57. Brinig, *Maternalistic Approach, supra* note 17; Jane Maslow Cohen, *Posnerism, Pessimism, Pluralism,* 67 B.U. L. Rev. 105 (1988).

58. Some of these are listed in Justice O'Connor's opinion in *Planned Parenthood of S.E. Pennsylvania v. Casey*, 505 U.S. 833 (II)(1992): "Abortion is a unique act. It is an act fraught with consequences for others: for the woman who must live with the implications of her decision; for the persons who perform and assist in the procedure; for the spouse, family, and society which must confront the knowledge that these procedures exist, procedures some deem nothing short of an act of violence against innocent human life; and, depending on one's beliefs, for the life or potential life that is aborted."

59. *See, e.g.*, Wis. Stat. § 49.90(2).

60. Personal Responsibility and Work Opportunity Reconciliation Act of 1996, P.L. 104-193, 110 Stat. 2105.

61. *See generally* James S. Coleman, *Foundations of Social Theory* (Harvard U. Press, 1990); and James S. Coleman, *Social Capital in the Creation of Human Capital*, 94 Am. J. Soc. S95 (1988).

62. *See, e.g.*, Yoram Ben-Porath, *The F Connection: Families, Friends, and Firms and the Organization of Exchange*, 6 Pop. & Dev. Rev. 1 (1980).

63. But *see Fazekas v. Fazekas*, 1999 Pa. Super. 223; 737 A.2d 1262; *Sundin v. Klein*, 221 Va. 232, 269 S.E. 2d 787 (1980).

64. *Vasilon v. Vasilon*, 192 Va. 735, 743; 66 S.E. 2d 599, 604 (1951) ("pour tout et non pour my"). According to Blackstone, "By marriage, the husband and wife are one person in law: that is, the very being or legal existence of the woman is suspended during the marriage, or at least is incorporated and consolidated into that of the husband; under whose wing, protection and cover, she performs everything; . . . and her condition during the marriage is called her coverture." William Blackstone, *Commentaries on the Law of England* vol. 1 at 442.

65. Gary S. Becker, *A Treatise on the Family* ch. 8 (Harvard U. Press 1991).

66. Paula England & Gary S. Farkas, *Households, Employment and Gender* ch. 2 (Aldine 1986); Brinig & Alexeev, *supra* note 26.

67. Martin Zelder, *Inefficient Dissolutions as a Consequence of Public Goods: The Case of No-Fault Divorce*, 22 J. Legal Stud. 503 (1994). *See also* Nancy Golbre, *Children as Public Goods*, 84 Am. Econ. Rev. 86, 86 (1994).

68. *See, e.g.*, Robert C. Ellickson, *Order without Law: How Neighbors Settle Disputes* (Harvard U. Press, 1991); Richard H. McAdams, *The Origin, Development and Regulation of Norms*, 96 Mich. L. Rev. 338, 339 & nn. 19–38 (1997); Lawrence Lessig, *Social Meaning and Social Norms*, 144 U. Pa. L. Rev. 2181 (1996); Cass R. Sunstein, *On the Expressive Function of Law*, 144 U. Pa. L. Rev. 2021 (1996); Anita Bernstein, *Better Living through Crime and Tort*, 76 B.U. L. Rev. 169, 177–80 (1996); Herbert Jacob, *The Elusive Shadow of the Law*, 26 Law & Soc. Rev. 565 (1992); William K. Jones, *A Theory of Social Norms*, 1994 U. Ill. L. Rev. 545; Paul Robinson & John M. Darley, *The Utility of Desert*, 91 Nw. U. L. Rev. 453 (1997); Walter Otto Weyrauch & Maureen Anne Bell, *Autonomous Lawmaking: The Case of the "Gypsies,"* 103 Yale L.J. 323 (1993). Perhaps the leading example of the success of this phenomenon is the use of "business norms" in the U.C.C. *See, e.g.*, Uniform Commercial Code 1–102(1)(b); Lisa Bernstein, *Merchant Law in a Merchant Court: Rethinking the Code's Search for Immanent Business Norms*, 144 U. Pa. L. Rev. 1765 (1996); Robert Scott, *Conflict and Cooperation in Long-Term Contracts*, 75 Cal. L. Rev. 2005 (1987).

69. Thus Eric Posner, for example, views much "norm creation" as a signaling device designed to make your opposite number in a transaction believe that you are trustworthy, or, in his terminology, that you have a low discount rate. *See, e.g.*, Eric A. Posner, *Symbols, Signals, and Social Norms in Politics and the Law*, 27 J. Legal Stud. 765 (1998); and Eric A. Posner, *Efficient Norms*, in *The New Palgrave Dictionary of Economics and the Law* (Peter Newman ed., Macmillan 1998).

70. A number of states refuse to honor provisions that waive spousal support after marriage. *See, e.g.*, Iowa Code 596.5(2) (1996). None of them will strictly enforce child custody or child support provisions but will require a judicial look at the "best interests of the child." *See, e.g.*,

Smith v. Saxon, 186 Ariz. 70, 918 P.2d 1088 (1996); *Huckaby v. Huckaby,* 74 Ill. App. 3d 195, 393 N.E. 2d 1256 (1979); *Kelley v. Kelley,* 17 Va. App. 93, 435 S.E. 2d 421 (1993).

71. This is less true of the antenuptial agreement than it was twenty years ago, partly because courts are loathe to treat women as being unable to bargain effectively for themselves. But a place where the sensitivity, or heightened concern with procedural protections, seems undiminished is in voluntary placement for adoption.

72. Katharine Silbaugh, *Marriage Contracts and the Family Economy,* 93 Nw. U. L. Rev. 65, 138–39 (1998).

73. The concepts discussed in this section form the basis of my (substantially lengthier) argument in Brinig, *Family Franchise, supra* note 9. In it, I also discuss post-divorce parenting and particularly the relationship between adult siblings as "family franchises."

74. Clearly fathers are hurt by such circumstances as well. *See* Gilbert A. Holmes, *The Tie That Binds: The Constitutional Right of Children to Maintain Relationships with Parent-Like Individuals,* 53 Md. L. Rev. 358 (1994); Gregory A. Locken, *Gratitude and the Map of Moral Duties toward Children,* 31 Ariz. St. L.J. 1121 (1999); David Meyer, *Family Ties: Solving the Constitutional Dilemma of the Faultless Father,* 41 Ariz. L. Rev. 753 (1999); and Mary Shanely, *Unwed Father's Rights and Adoption and Sex Equality: Gender-Neutrality and the Perpetuation of Patriarchy,* 95 Colum. L. Rev. 60 (1995).

75. Amy Tan, *Queen Mother of the Western Skies,* in *The Joy Luck Club* (Ivy Books 1989).

76. *Doan Thi Guong An v. Nelson,* 245 N.W. 2d 511 (Iowa 1976).

77. In *Sarah, Plain and Tall* (Harper & Row, 1985), Patricia Maclachlan tells us of one family's experience coping with the death of a young mother and how important acknowledging the tangible and intangible memories of her were to its rebuilding.

78. Another familiar case comes from Exodus 2. Fearing that her son would be drowned on Pharaoh's order, Moses' mother places him in a basket, where he is soon found by Pharaoh's daughter. The mother, who has been watching nearby, is recruited to nurse him.

79. One of the issues in the contemporary film *Losing Isaiah* is the transracial question we discuss at some length in Schneider & Brinig, *supra* note 5, at 1258–82. The movie ends ambiguously, with the possibility, however, of a franchise-like solution. *See also* Zanita E. Fenton, *In a World Not Their Own: The Adoption of Black Children,* 10 Harv. Blackletter L.J. 39, 63 (1993)(suggesting alternatives to "traditional adoption," such as parenting with grandparents and great-grandparents).

80. For a recent fictional account of the process written for teenagers, *see* Lois Lowry, *Find a Stranger, Say Goodbye* (1977), in which a seventeen-year-old girl ready to leave for college is given permission by her adoptive parents to search for her natural mother. Once she finds and speaks with her, she is able to put aside her quest forever.

81. *See, e.g., Alma Society v. Mellon,* 601 F.2d 1225 (2d Cir. 1979); *see also In re Roger B.,* 418 N.E. 2d 751 (Ill. App. 1981), *app. dism'd,* 454 U.S. 806 (1981). A moving article written by a birth mother highlights the problems and suggests a paradigm switch in the way we conceptualize the adoption process. Maureen A. Sweeney, *Between Sorrow and Happy Endings,* 2 Yale J. L. & Feminism, 329, 353–55 (1990).

82. *See, e.g.,* Conn. Gen. Stat. § 45-68e; Ind. Code Ann. §§ 31-3-4-27-31; N.D. Cent. Code §§ 14-15.1-0-14-15.1-07; Va. Code Ann. §§ 63.1-126.

83. For psychological evidence of this phenomenon, *see* Leverett Millen & Samuel Roll, *Solomon's Mothers: A Special Case of Pathological Bereavement,* 55 Am. J. Orthopsychiatry 411, 412–13 (1985); *see also* Arthur D. Sorosky, Annette Baran, & Reuben Pannor, *The Adoption Triangle: The Effects of the Sealed Record on Adoptees, Birth Parents and Adoptive Parents* 55–72 (Corona 1989). For an account of her own experience, *see* Sweeney, *supra* note 81, at 530–33. Sweeney begins her article with the lyrics from the Joni Mitchell song "Little Green" (from the album *Blue,* Sigomb Music, 1967).

84. *See, e.g.,* Naomi Cahn & Jana Singer, *Adoption Identity and the Constitution: The Case for Opening Closed Records,* 2 U. Pa. J. Const. L. 150 (1999); Holmes, *supra* note 74;; Laurie A.

Ames, *Open Adoptions: Truth and Consequences,* 16 Law & Psych. Rev. 137 (1992); Nancy E. Dowd, *A Feminist Analysis of Adoption,* 107 Harv. L. Rev. 913, 931 (1994).

85. Annette Haselhoff, *Survey of New York Practice,* 67 St. John's L. Rev. 169 (1993); Meyer, *supra* note 74.

86. *See, e.g.,* Ind. Code § 31-19-9-6 (1994); *In re Francisco A.,* 866 P.2d 1175 (N.M. 1993) (foster mother who had sought to adopt children was permitted visitation with them when the children requested it, after her husband died and the adoption was finalized with another couple).

87. *See, e.g.,* Carol Gilligan, *In a Different Voice* 25 (Harvard U. Press 1982); Carrie Menkel-Meadow, *Portia in a Different Voice: Speculating on a Woman's Lawyering Process,* 1 Berkeley Women's L.J. 39, 42 (1988).

88. In addition to Gilligan, *supra* note 87, *see* Katharine T. Bartlett, *Feminism and Family Law,* 33 Fam. L.Q. 475 (199) ("They have challenged the inevitability or naturalness of family privacy, arguing that where the line is drawn between private and public is itself a highly discretionary, political act"); Tina Grillo, *The Mediation Alternative: Process Dangers for Women,* 100 Yale L.J. 1545, 1547 (1991) ("The western concept of law is based on a patriarchal paradigm characterized by hierarchy, linear reasoning, the resolution of disputes through the application of abstract principles, and the ideal of the reasonable person"); and Kenneth Karst, *Woman's Constitution,* 1984 Duke L.J. 447, 462 (law relies on rights and adopts an abstract hierarchy of rules regulating the interaction of individuals); Olsen, *supra* note 7.

89. For suggestions for improving legislation, *see* Brinig, *Covenant, supra* note 1, at 216–20.

90. David Organ Coolidge, *Marriage and Belonging: Reflections on* Baker v. Vermont, in *Revitalizing the Institution of Marriage for the Twenty-First Century* 145 (Alan J. Hawkins et al. eds., 2002).

91. Note the ultimate result of the litigation: there is no same-sex marriage in Vermont, but there is a status that has the same legal benefits and obligations as does heterosexual marriage. The Vermont Civil Union legislation, 2000 Acts 21.

CHAPTER 20

The Business of Intimacy

Bridging the Private–Private Distinction

Martha M. Ertman

---

econ·o·my: . . . 2. Household management.
The New Shorter Oxford English Dictionary vol. 1 (1993)

The law governing intimate relationships would benefit from exploring the metaphorical and doctrinal analogies between business and intimate affiliations.[1] These analogies bridge the private–private distinction by drawing connections between private business law and private family law.[2] They also improve on conventional family law's understanding of family, remedying long-standing inequities within current family law that are fossilized artifacts of the naturalized construction of intimate relationships.

The naturalized model of family is a socially constructed norm that defines what families should be. This model is often inadequate because it cannot respond to changing forms of intimate relationships. The percentage of households considered "nonfamily," those in which people live alone or with non-relatives, doubled from 15 percent in 1960 to 30 percent in 1995.[3] As a result, greater numbers of Americans are living in relationships that do not fit within the naturalized model; these include same-sex affiliations, polyamorous affiliations,[4] nonsexual unions, and new parenting relations.[5] Because these relationships lie outside the bounds of conventional family law, a patchwork of legal doctrines has emerged to regulate them. In various jurisdictions, nonmarital affiliations are called reciprocal beneficiary relationships, domestic partnerships, meretricious relationships, and civil unions. Each affiliation is defined differently and accorded different rights and duties.[6] The diversity of policies among states, municipalities, companies, and educational institutions indicates that a new model of intimacy is needed to account for the growing number of legally recognized forms of intimate relationships.

In addition to being descriptively inadequate, the naturalized model of family contributes to inequalities both within relationships and among various types of relationships.[7] In its various forms, the naturalized model of intimate affiliations contributes to race, sex, gender, sexual orientation, and class hierarchies. Due to these hierarchies, those deemed naturally inferior are economically and socially marginalized within intimate relationships.[8] Coverture, for example, deemed women naturally inferior to men and accordingly limited married women's right to contract, hold property, or otherwise participate in public life. Similarly, miscegenation laws deprived women of color who were intimately or sexually involved with white men of the benefits afforded by marriage doctrines such as intestate succession rules.[9] The naturalized model of family also constitutes and reinforces hierarchies of purportedly natural relationships over supposedly unnatural ones. For example, miscegenation laws marginalized interracial couples by construing these affiliations as unnatural, and the contemporary ban on same-sex marriage rests on the purportedly natural superiority of heterosexual couplings.[10]

This chapter explores private law's potential to provide a metaphor that accounts for the range of intimate affiliations and counteracts the inequalities of the natural model. Three justifications exist for considering the commonalities between business models and intimate affiliations. First, judges and legislators will be open to business models because family law is already progressing toward privatization.[11] Family law doctrine increasingly favors private ordering in matters such as entry into marriage, contractual ordering of marriage, nonmarital relationships, divorce, adoption, the use of reproductive technologies, and the privatization of domestic relations dispute resolution.

Second, business law's flexibility is compatible both with the various ways that people order their intimate lives and the range of legal and institutional responses to those arrangements. Much as the Uniform Commercial Code (U.C.C.) allows for changes in the ways businesspeople conduct their commercial transactions,[12] business models offer a repertoire of tools to address both extant and future problems in private relationships. Business law dynamically responds to demand; as the demand for legal rules to regulate an expanding array of intimate relationships increases, business law supplies new ways to understand those relationships.

Third, because much of the legal intervention in intimate relationships is related to financial issues, such as dividing debts, assets, and income when a relationship ends, models tailored to solve financial problems are well suited to address family law problems. Given the benefits of importing business models to remedy the inadequacies of traditional, naturalized models of domestic relations law, it is not surprising that both statutory schemes and scholarly proposals have begun to do so.[13]

In addition to remedying the naturalized model's inadequacies, business models have the potential to disrupt its inequalities. Business models are relatively free of the antiquated notions of status, morality, and biological relation that have hampered family law's ability to adapt with the times.[14] A major problem with this focus is that it often is expressed in a view of marriage as the foundation of modern society,[15] so that any threat to marriage seems to threaten society as a whole. Unlike family law, business models are largely un-hampered by this moral, biological baggage, allowing for consideration of important contractual elements of intimate relationships.

Because family includes both status and contractual elements, approaches that focus on contract are often criticized for ignoring status-based elements of intimate affiliation.[16] Yet the business models discussed in this chapter (business partnerships, corporations, and limited liability companies) are similar to intimate relationships in that they have significant status elements that complement their contractual character. The status hierarchies in business models, however, are fundamentally different from those in the natural model. Status differences in family law reflect and perpetuate inequality, grounding that inequality in purportedly natural differences. Business analogies, in contrast, substitute functionalist reasoning for moral judgment.[17]

The business model suggests that differences among relationships are equivalent to differences among business entities, making those differences morally neutral and thereby undermining hierarchies among them. An understanding of marriage as akin to corporations, cohabitation as akin to partnerships, and polyamory as akin to limited liability companies would enable us to avoid attaching moral judgments to the differences among those relationships. Regulation would turn on the functional needs of particular arrangements rather than moralistic reasoning and ideas about naturalistic hierarchy.

Moreover, making the analogy between business models and intimate relationships would alleviate the hierarchy that is created by affording legal benefits to those who already have a private safety net, sexual and affectionate ties, and an extended family. Legally recognizing alternative affiliations intervenes in the pernicious pattern in law and life that those with more get more, thus alleviating the inequality that results from the "haves" coming out ahead.[18] Bridging the private–private split allows us to combine elements of status and contract to craft doctrines that counteract the systemic inequality in the current naturalized model of family.

This chapter explores how the partnership model, the corporate model, and the limited liability company (LLC) model are similar in some ways to cohabitation, marriage, and polyamory and suggests that this insight justifies importing elements of business law to improve domestic relations law. First I critique the naturalized model of family and suggest private ordering as a remedy for its defects. Then I analogize business models to intimate relationships. Departing from the conventional approach that analogizes marriage to business partnerships, I suggest that marriage might be more similar to close corporations, and that opposite-sex cohabitation and same-sex relationships may be more analogous to business partnerships. Finally, most speculatively, I explore whether polyamorous relationships, often overlooked or pathologized in family law literature, might be analogous to limited liability companies or other hybrid business forms that combine elements of partnerships and corporations. For each analogy, I explore similarities between the business form and the intimate affiliation, detailing the manner in which the analogy could alleviate inequality not only within relationships but also among various types of relationships.

Of course, private law is not a silver bullet that can eradicate all inequalities. Private ordering often imposes contractual norms of autonomy and consent on marginalized people for whom these ideals are illusory. Moreover, the reality is that only a few people, mostly those who have both sophistication and assets (and the bargaining power that accompanies these advantages), will enter into contractual arrangements that counteract rather than contribute to hierarchies within and among relationships. Although importing business models (metaphorically and doctrinally) to the regulation of intimate relationships may not solve all problems, this approach does hold the unique promise of providing new ways of understanding basic financial issues that family law, hampered by outdated notions of status, has failed to resolve.

Comparing the Naturalized Model with a Contractual Approach

In this section I critique the naturalized model of intimate affiliations and contend that the functionalism of a contractarian approach remedies the inadequacy and inequality of the naturalized model.

The Natural Model and Its Deficiencies

Nature is a slippery term, with different meanings in different contexts.[19] Legal designations of some groups or intimate affiliations as natural have three distinct but overlapping meanings. First, nature usually implies biological imperatives that are dictated by forces independent of human intervention. Second, nature often includes a moral dimension, referring to divine or other sources of authority rather than human authority. Finally, something designated as natural is taken for granted, as not needing explanation, or as intuitively obvious. Under all three meanings of *nature,* the natural is also universal.[20] I argue here that naturalized arguments suffer from two major defects.

THE NATURAL MODEL RESTS ON IRRATIONAL BIASES

Naturalized arguments support and reinforce judgments that some people or arrangements are inferior to others. These arguments contend, for example, that African Americans tend to be less intelligent than whites, that women are morally inferior to men, and that gay people are inferior to heterosexuals by divine mandate.[21] Thus, naturalized rhetoric both masks and underlies biases that cannot be justified rationally.[22] It is said that nature abhors a vacuum.

Apparently nature so abhors a vacuum in legal reasoning that it fills the void with nature itself.

The naturalized model takes various forms, most typically understanding the family as biologically, morally, or divinely based. The most common model constructs the family as a married man and woman living with their biological offspring and dictates a gendered division of labor in which the woman is the primary homemaker and the man is the primary wage earner. John Finnis has opposed legal recognition of same-sex relationships on the grounds that heterosexual sexuality, particularly penile–vaginal penetration, is morally superior to same-sex sexuality because the former can result in procreation.[23]

Progressive scholars have revealed the vacuity of this logic. Mary Becker has demonstrated that Finnis's own arguments show that heterosexual sexuality is actually morally inferior to same-sex coupling because same-sex coupling is grounded in the moral values of consent and other-regarding behavior.[24] Similarly, Andrew Koppelman has revealed that the purported defense of marriage is actually a defense of race, sex, and gender subordination.[25] He explores the manner in which the miscegenation ban designated interracial unions as unnatural and linked race, sex, and gender hierarchy with biology, morals, and divine will.[26]

THE NATURAL MODEL MASKS AND REINFORCES SUBORDINATION

Beyond being analytically flawed, naturalized rhetoric masks and reinforces existing hierarchies. For instance, statutory prohibitions have denominated a wide range of nonreproductive sexuality (between opposite-sex or same-sex partners) as crimes against nature.[27] Doctrinal silence on what precisely is a criminally unnatural act or status allowed courts to strategically ignore the fact that (purportedly natural) heterosexuals routinely engage in crimes against nature.[28] Similarly, southern courts in the nineteenth century referred to incest as "an outrage upon nature,"[29] but imposed few penalties on men who abused their female relatives absent a showing of force. Peter Bardaglio suggests that judicial reluctance to punish defendants, despite the strong rhetoric condemning sexual abuse of women and girls, was due to the jurists' desire to uphold what they deemed to be legitimate patriarchal authority in the family while loudly condemning excessive exercises of that authority.[30] In this way, naturalized rhetoric can both mask and justify hierarchy.

A recent Texas case illustrates that naturalized models are alive and well, actively contributing to inadequacy and inequality in legal doctrine. In a remarkably candid opinion asserting that sex is biologically or divinely mandated, the Texas Court of Appeals refused to recognize a marriage between a transsexual woman and a man.[31]

Christie Littleton underwent surgical and hormonal treatments associated with sex reassignment in the late 1970s. She married Jonathan Mark Littleton in 1989 and lived with him until he died in 1996. When Littleton filed a wrongful death action against her husband's doctor, the doctor moved for summary judgment on the grounds that Littleton lacked standing because she was really a man, making her marriage legally invalid.[32]

Framing the question as whether Littleton's sex was "immutably fixed by our Creator at birth," the court concluded that Littleton "was created and born a male."[33] The final words of the decision succinctly articulate naturalized approaches to the world: "There are some things we cannot will into being. They just are."[34]

Only an irrational resort to naturalized understandings can support this result. A New Jersey court, faced with facts similar to those in *Littleton*, recognized the marriage.[35] The New Jersey court's reliance on the transsexual plaintiff's "full capacity to function sexually as . . . female," however, is equally problematic in that it implies there is only one way for males to function sexually and another, complementary, way for females to function sexually.[36] This assertion is demonstrably false.[37]

The treatment of transsexual marriage in both New Jersey and Texas remains firmly grounded in a naturalized understanding of sex, gender, and sexual orientation. Both cases assume that only natural men and natural women can marry each other. The inadequacy of this reasoning demonstrates the natural model's inability to recognize emerging forms of intimate affiliation, as well as its collusion with inequality both within and among various types of relationships.

Contractualization as a Solution to the Weaknesses of the Natural Model

Business models offer an attractive alternative to naturalized constructions of intimate relations for at least two reasons. First, market rhetoric is rarely naturalized. Second, contracts do not require public or majoritarian approval to be enforced and could therefore disrupt the hierarchical structure that naturalized understandings impose on marginalized groups. In short, contract provides a way around majoritarian morality.

Markets are not biological, evolutionary, or divinely ordained. They are social creations, functioning through arm's-length transactions that theoretically benefit all participants. This conception is admittedly idealized. Market forces presume rather than create equality, commercial contracts are often relational rather than arm's length, and many contracts disadvantage the participant with the weaker bargaining position. Premarital and marital contracting, for example, raises the issue of the limited bargaining power of economically vulnerable spouses.[38] However, contractarian business models also have the potential to remedy existing inequality by providing innovative ways to compensate primary homemakers for their contributions to family wealth.

Moral rhetoric has certainly been central to progressive reform in some historical contexts.[39] In the current political climate, however, moral arguments are more likely to buttress than contest subordination. The antigay movement charges that same-sex sexuality is morally wrong, and the gay rights movement counters with liberal arguments about entitlement to equal treatment based on principles of autonomy, individualism, and choice.[40] Much of the moral rhetoric used to justify the traditional conceptions of family is rooted in a religious commitment to hierarchy.

Seemingly moral considerations do underlie elements of contract law, such as the doctrines of unconscionability and nonenforceability for violating public policy.[41] These doctrines, however, are exceptions to the general rule of a morally neutral stance toward contracts. Generally courts will enforce private agreements even when moral considerations argue against doing so.[42] Thus, when a majority expresses hostility toward a marginalized group, private ordering is sometimes the only remedy for a bad situation. Just as the classical liberalism of contract enables parties to skirt moral rhetoric, private ordering offers a way around majoritarian rules that harm marginalized people.

The following doctrinal examples illustrate how private law enables marginalized people to use contract law's moral neutrality to circumvent hostile public rules. Some nineteenth-century wills skirted constructions of family as naturally monoracial by including African American women as beneficiaries of white decedents. Such inclusion, which gave rise to legal claims by those women, disrupted existing race, sex, gender, and class hierarchies. Similarly, a 1997 Florida case enforced a same-sex cohabitation contract, skirting constructions of marriage as naturally heterosexual and intervening in sexual orientation hierarchies. Both instances of private ordering improved on family law doctrine by expanding the range of recognized relationships and counteracting hierarchy within and among relationships.

NINETEENTH-CENTURY TRUST AND ESTATE LAW

Adrienne Davis documents the way in which some women of color in the nineteenth-century South obtained some benefits, through the wills of their white paramours, that miscegenation laws otherwise would have prevented.[43] The Georgia Supreme Court observed in 1887 that "[e]very man in this State has a right to will property to whom he pleases. There is no policy of the State which would make it unlawful or contrary to such policy for a man to will his property to a colored person, to any bastard or to his own bastard, and such considerations as these alone would not authorize a will to be set aside."[44] Davis points out the broad significance of the morally neutral enforceability of wills. As individuals, African American beneficiaries obtained some measure of economic independence. As a group, these beneficiaries—African Americans, formerly enslaved, and illegitimate—were invested with a measure of economic personality and market rights. Economic personality was extraordinarily valuable to those who had been defined as objects of commerce themselves: "emancipated blacks rejected their denomination by law as solely commodities, seeking instead to establish relationships to property, and thereby to enter the market sphere."[45] Decisions that allowed these women and their children to inherit intervened in the naturalized hierarchy by recognizing the economic personality of African American concubines, who were typically marginalized on the basis of their race, sex, and gender.[46]

A recent case in Washington illuminates the continued significance of naturalized understandings of family in trust and estate law. Robert Schwerzler died intestate after living with Frank Vasquez for eighteen years.[47] Although Washington recognizes marriagelike rights of opposite-sex cohabitants, the court, paradoxically calling this affiliation a "meretricious relationship,"[48] refused to apply this rule to same-sex partners.[49] Of course Schwerzler could have skirted this hostile rule by making a will. However, because he failed to do so, his partner of nearly two decades is situated similarly to nineteenth century African American women not mentioned in their white lovers' wills.

COHABITATION CONTRACTS

Washington's failure to recognize the long-term relationship between two men for intestacy purposes contrasts with Florida's willingness to recognize the relationship of two women formalized in a contract.[50] The presence of private ordering explains the difference. Dr. Nancy Layton convinced nurse Emma Posik to move in with her, and to give up her job and home. In return for Posik's agreement to move in and care for their home, Layton promised to support them, leave her estate to Posik in her will, and pay $2,500 a month for the remainder of Posik's life as liquidated damages for breach of the agreement. The agreement further provided that Posik could move out if Layton failed to provide adequate support or brought a third person into the home for more than four weeks without Posik's consent.[51] When Layton got involved with another woman and wanted her to move into the house, Posik sued to enforce the agreement. Remarkably, given Florida's explicit ban on same-sex marriage and adoption, Posik won. Echoing the nineteenth-century southern courts that prioritized morally neutral, liberal, freedom of contract notions over naturalized status-based understandings of intimate relationships, the court reasoned that "the State has not denied these individuals their right to either will their property as they see fit nor to privately commit by contract to spend their money as they choose."[52]

The Georgia Supreme Court similarly enforced a cohabitation contract between two women despite the state's then-valid sodomy statute.[53] The court found that the agreement in question included a merger clause that prohibited the court from considering parol evidence relating to the "illegal and immoral" nature of the relationship.[54] The court also held that even if parol evidence were permissible, any "alleged illegal activity was at most incidental to the contract rather than required by it."[55]

Taken together, these two cases stand for the proposition that private law offers unique opportunities for same-sex partners to contract around a majoritarian morality that ignores or vilifies their relationships. Every time a court enforces a same-sex cohabitation contract, it intervenes in the understanding that the only legally recognizable relationships are those that cohere with naturalized notions of intimacy as biologically, morally, or divinely dictated. Not surprisingly, contractual analysis has a rich history in antisubordination discourse.

Feminists have long agreed that the marriage contract as traditionally construed disfavors women.[56] Some feminists contend that contractualization offers the possibility of altering outdated status-based understandings of marriage.[57] But in this matter as in others, feminists disagree. Margaret Jane Radin compellingly challenges legal economists' universal commodification approach.[58] However, as she acknowledges, we might contractualize aspects of intimate relationships that already have value on the market, such as homemaking services.

This chapter highlights similarities between businesses and intimate affiliations, thereby suggesting a new conception of intimate relationships that could disrupt subordination.[59] This comparison is not an equation; not every intimate interaction is akin to a business transaction, nor are all business relationships solely financial in character. I seek simply to open discursive space to bridge the private–private divide, making room for new ways to think about the old problems rooted in naturalized understandings of intimacy.

Analogizing Particular Intimate Relationships to Particular Business Models to Alleviate Inequality within and among Relationships

Once the law departs from naturalized models of family, it is free to recognize a range of legitimate affiliations. Having explored what business models can offer the law regulating intimate relationships generally, we are left with the specific question of which business forms should regulate which relationships. One might claim that all intimate relationships between consenting adults are functionally equivalent and as a normative matter should be governed by the same rules. Current legal regimes, however, distinguish among different kinds of intimate relationships. A wide variety of legal doctrines regulate marriages, same-sex partnerships, opposite-sex partnerships, and affiliations that include more than two adults. Yet perhaps treating different relationships differently is not, as a normative matter, a good thing.

The next question is which business models are most analogous to particular intimate affiliations. Generally, the literature points to partnership, focusing on the marriage analogy and only occasionally considering same-sex couples and polyamory.[60] In this section I fill the void by exploring a range of doctrines governing partnerships, close corporations, and limited liability companies. Recognizing this range of business models as viable analogies for intimate relationships would alleviate the inequality that results from the naturalized model's designation of some relationships as natural and others as unnatural.

I focus on two important points of state intervention in the relationship—formation and dissolution—occasionally referring to other state interventions such as dispute resolution and the imposition of fiduciary duties. Markedly absent from this discussion are the myriad ways in which state nonintervention in business and family life determines the course of events during the relationship.[61] The law is most involved in a business or intimate affiliation at entry and exit, however, and these moments determine which law governs. Accordingly, it makes sense to focus on parallels in formation and dissolution.

Partnership and Cohabitation

The literature that describes importing business models to domestic relations law implicitly assumes that the model being imported is a general partnership.[62] A review of doctrines governing partnership formation and dissolution reveals that partnership may, however, be more analogous to cohabiting relationships than to marriages. Critiques of the partnership model of marriage—contending that it erroneously assumes equality between spouses and lacks doctrinal bite—further support this conclusion. This very equality, paired with the informality of the general partnership, make it analogous to cohabitation.

A well-developed literature explores analogies between partnership and intimate relationships, suggesting that partnership doctrine offers a way to remedy inequalities within marriage. Partnership has thus provided a new metaphor, replacing ideas such as coverture. Model statutes such as the Uniform Marriage and Divorce Act (UMDA)[63] and the Uniform Probate Code[64] apply partnership models to domestic relations law. Scholarly proposals use partnership models to alleviate homemaker indigency upon divorce by applying partnership buyout rules at dissolution,[65] justifying the payment of spousal debts in bankruptcy,[66] holding spouses to fiduciary duties,[67] and recognizing same-sex relationships through domestic partnership legislation.[68]

At the heart of the partnership analogy of marriage is an idealized image of marriage as "equal partnerships between spouses who share resources, responsibilities, and risks,"[69] a norm that "encourages commitments between spouses, promotes gender equality, and supports caretaking of children and elderly dependents."[70] The appeal of these norms is reinforced by factual similarities between intimate relationships and partnerships:

[B]oth relationships typically commence with the exchange of commitments and without express agreement or advice of counsel . . . seek profits
though profit in the case of marriage may be emotional, sexual, and perhaps spiritual as well as financial . . . [and] often involve a specialization
of labor. Commonly, one partner contributes capital primarily or exclusively, while another contributes services primarily or exclusively—a specialization that resembles a traditional marriage, as well as many
contemporary ones, in which the husband contributes income through
outside employment and the wife contributes caretaking services.[71]

Certain commentators reject the partnership analogy. Some of them claim that
it cannot justify spousal support or other important aspects of family law.[72]
Others contest the applicability of such an idealized model to actual marriages,
in which gender hierarchy and inequality are likely to exist.

The suggestion that marriages are more like close corporations than partnerships seems to fly in the face of doctrines that already apply partnership
models to marriage. However, thinking about marriage as akin to a close corporation and cohabitation as akin to general partnership makes sense for a
number of reasons.

THE SIMILARITY OF BUSINESS AND COHABITING PARTNERSHIPS

Cohabitation is remarkably analogous to a business partnership, particularly
with regard to formation, dissolution, and the presumption that the parties are
equal. A business partnership is formed whenever two or more persons operate a business for profit.[73] The partners need take no formal action, and the
agreement can be oral or written.[74] In business law, an equal partnership is the
default entity. Partnership doctrine incorporates the ideal that partners are
equal, enjoying equal rights to share in the profits and to control and manage
partnership property.[75] One of the reasons that business relationships and intimate relationships are described as private is the purported lack of state intervention in those relationships. The end of a partnership (romantic or
business) is one of the few instances in which the state can play an active role.
During the course of the relationship, the state generally allows the parties to
regulate their own affairs.[76] By contrast, the state is involved in both the formation and dissolution of corporations, just as it is involved in both the formation and dissolution of marriages. Thus partnership, like cohabitation, is
characterized by more private ordering than corporations or marriage.

In cohabitation, the formal relationship begins when the parties move in together. Similarly a general partnership is formed when two or more people operate a business for profit; presumably couples move in together expecting to
benefit from the arrangement personally and economically. Neither arrangement requires state action. In fact, unless the partners live in a jurisdiction that

permits domestic partners to register, no involvement of the state at this stage is even possible.[77]

Similarly, the division of power in the business partnership is closer to the division in an opposite-sex cohabiting relationship than that in a marriage.[78] Spouses tend to engage in gendered division of labor, whereas opposite-sex cohabitants are less likely to do so.[79] This gendered division of labor translates into power differences because the primary homemaking spouse has less time for wage labor, and wages are a significant source of power in the relationship. Wives tend to do more than 70 percent of homemaking and caretaking, whereas cohabiting women do considerably less.[80] Further, cohabiting women are more likely to engage in the same amount of wage labor as their male partners.[81] Of course, power in any relationship, including cohabitation, is heavily influenced by the funds that each person brings into the relationship. Men generally have more money than women,[82] and hence potentially have more power. Moreover, opposite-sex cohabitation generally does not create joint rights to property acquired during the relationship.[83] Women are much more likely than men to seek legal relief to obtain a return on their nonmonetary investments in a romantic partnership, suggesting that the title for property acquired during the partnership is more likely to rest with the male.[84] Thus, the general partnership rule of equal access to partnership property may not apply consistently to opposite-sex cohabitants. Overall, however, the comparisons outpace the contrasts.

Business partnerships are analogous to same-sex cohabiting relationships in many of the same ways they are analogous to opposite-sex cohabiting relationships. As with partnership and opposite-sex cohabiting relationships, same-sex cohabiting relationships have high levels of informality. Individuals create them not through state action but rather by moving in together. However, same-sex cohabiting relationships may be less prone to the gendered specialization of labor that both reflects and perpetuates inequality in opposite-sex relationships.[85] Although studies on organization of household and wage labor in same-sex relationships are rare because of the difficulties in identifying a random sample of a stigmatized minority, the results of these studies suggest that same-sex couples are more likely to participate equally in wage labor, and less likely to divide household labor along gendered lines.[86] This pattern makes sense, given that gendered specialization may be less likely in a relationship where the partners are both women or men.[87] Moreover, some same-sex partners structure some elements of their romantic partnerships to look like business partnerships in order to avoid judicial hostility to cohabitation agreements deemed to be based on meretricious consideration.[88]

A third similarity between business partnerships and cohabitation lies in the rules governing dissolution. The dissolution of a business partnership is more like the dissolution of a cohabiting relationship than the end of a marriage. A business partnership dissolves when one partner leaves, and no judicial action is required to formalize the dissolution.[89] This end is more like cohabitants breaking up than spouses divorcing.

In some ways, however, partnership dissolution is akin to divorce. Partnership dissolution is available at the will of the parties, at the end of a given term, or for the insolvency, insanity, exit, or death of a partner.[90] Partnership dissolution at will is akin to contemporary no-fault divorce, whereas other bases such as insolvency, insanity, or exit echo fault-based divorce (which is enjoying a renaissance as covenant marriage).[91] Similarly, marriage ends with the death of a spouse. However, unlike a marriage, a partnership need not be terminated by court decree,[92] and death or exit of one of the partners also ends a cohabiting partnership. Finally, one could argue that cohabitation, more than marriage, exists at the will of the parties because cohabitation ends when one party seeks to dissolve the affiliation, whereas divorce requires state action. In short, despite the similarities between divorce and partnership dissolution, business partnerships and cohabitation share a higher level of private ordering.

A fourth reason that the analogy of partnership to cohabitation makes sense turns on the proliferation of domestic partnership legislation and contractual arrangements. Domestic partnership law is based both in private contract and public regulation. Numerous private employers and universities make contractual promises to provide benefits to the same-sex partners of their employees or students. In addition, many municipalities and a few states offer benefits to the domestic partners of public employees.[93] California offers benefits to the same-sex domestic partners of state employees.[94] Hawaii provides inheritance and other benefits to pairs of people statutorily defined as reciprocal beneficiaries.[95] Similarly, the Oregon Court of Appeals has held that the state constitution requires a state university to provide benefits to the domestic partners of its employees.[96] The wide range of sources of domestic partnership law provides numerous definitions of a domestic partner. In California, for example, domestic partners must be of the same sex (unless they are over sixty-two) and cannot be closely related.[97] Vermont combines these models by recognizing civil unions between same-sex romantic partners and reciprocal beneficiary relationships between unmarried people who are closely related.[98]

Finally, the tax treatment of partnerships is similar to the tax treatment of cohabitants and dissimilar to the tax treatment of corporations and marriages. Partnerships, like cohabitants, are taxed as disaggregated groups, whereas corporations, like marriages, are generally taxed as separate entities.[99]

In sum, partnership is more analogous to cohabitation than to marriage because of the informality in formation and dissolution and the greater likelihood of equality among the partners. The next section operationalizes this insight, suggesting ways that partnership doctrine, in the cohabitation context, could alleviate inequality within and among relationships.

THE PARTNERSHIP MODEL COULD REMEDY INEQUALITY
WITHIN COHABITING RELATIONSHIPS

The partnership analogy could alleviate inequality within cohabiting relationships in several ways. First, it would relieve cohabitants of the burden of proving a contract (express or implied), constructive trust, or other legally cognizable claim to justify dividing assets when the relationship ends.[100] Current law, which requires an express or implied contract or equitable claim such as restitution or constructive trust, burdens economically vulnerable parties. The partner with the cash is most likely to have title to property such as a home or car, whereas the other partner may contribute sweat equity, such as maintaining the car or fixing up the house. Partnership law offers a way to recognize the sweat equity of the partner who contributes more labor than cash to the relationship. Upon dissolution, cohabitants would be required to show the domestic equivalent of operating a business for profit, which might be articulated as operating a household for mutual benefit. Once this burden is met, business partnership law could provide a model for distributing cohabiting partnership property. Under such a model, a rule that assets purchased or improved with partnership property are partnership property could remedy the difficulty of distinguishing individual property from partnership property.

Another way that partnership law might alleviate inequality within a cohabiting relationship is by providing a buyout remedy, which recognizes the contributions a cohabitant might make to her partner's increased earnings during the partnership. One of the major issues in family law scholarship of the last decade is how legal doctrine contributes to the indigency or near-indigency of many primary homemakers upon divorce, due to the law's traditional refusal to recognize homemakers' contributions to family wealth.[101] Prominent among this literature is Cynthia Starnes's proposal to give primary homemakers a buyout of their interest in the marital partnership. Starnes analogizes marriage to business partnership and contends that divorce should be structured to mirror partnership dissolution, so that a homemaker's contributions to the enterprise could be remunerated through a buyout.[102] She suggests that the homemaker be reimbursed at divorce for her contributions to the value of the marital enterprise, including investments in the household and the wage earner's career and the homemaker's own lost opportunity costs.[103]

Third and finally, partnership law would impose a fiduciary duty on partners to treat one another fairly.[104] Partners are not acting at arms length and are held to "something stricter than the morals of the marketplace. Not honesty alone, but the punctilio of an honor the most sensitive, is then the standard of behavior."[105] Specifically, a partner is held to a duty of loyalty (accounting to the partnership for benefits derived from partnership property, refraining from adversarial dealings with the partnership, or competing with the partnership) as well as a duty of care (refraining from grossly negligent or reckless conduct, intentional misconduct, or a knowing legal violation).[106] Without these duties, cohabiting partners could misrepresent facts or appropriate partnership property. With the duties in place, a socially or economically weak cohabitant could protect her interests.

THE PARTNERSHIP MODEL COULD REMEDY INEQUALITY
AMONG VARIOUS TYPES OF RELATIONSHIPS

Applying the partnership model to cohabitation also addresses inequality among various types of relationships by providing a morally neutral range of options, thus justifying state recognition of the relationship in a fashion that reflects the parties' needs and expectations rather than making a moral judgment that one form of intimate affiliation is natural while others are unnatural and immoral.

Many people see domestic partnership as an alternative to same-sex marriage. Paula Ettlebrick, for example, argues that achieving legal marriage for same-sex couples may reinforce, rather than undermine, subordination if marriage retains its normatively superior status.[107] Moreover, domestic partnership policies that include opposite-sex couples prevent the dual-status regime from being a separate-but-equal one in which same-sex partners are governed by different, less comprehensive rules than opposite-sex partners.

The ability of domestic partnership models to fill the vacuum created by the ban on same-sex marriage illustrates the strengths of the partnership model. The primary impediment to state recognition of same-sex relationships is majoritarian morality. Partnership and other contractarian models have the potential to get around this obstacle in three ways. First, private law is generally based on functionalist concerns about regulating existing relationships rather than a desire to express moral truths about the best or most superior relationships. Second, private law reasoning, focusing as it does on the intent of the parties rather than the public's view of what the terms of the arrangement should be, is independent of both moral and majoritarian concerns. Finally, because domestic partnerships are recognized at the local level (businesses, universities, municipalities, and some states), their proponents can convince smaller, more accessible groups of decision makers to implement the policies. In short, domestic partnerships illustrate one way that business models may avoid many of the problems posed by the naturalized model of intimate affiliation.

Finally, if government more regularly recognized cohabiting relationships, cohabitants might have some public safety net in the form of Social Security, wrongful death, intestacy, or other claims. Without these support systems, married people, who already have the most social and economic security, also have the strongest legal safety net. Recognizing the similarities between business partnerships and cohabitation thus counteracts the invidious pattern of the haves coming out ahead of the have-nots.

Close Corporations and Marriage

If cohabitation co-opts the partnership model, and if marriage is considered to be distinct from cohabitation, then marriage requires a distinct business model. Marriage has unexpected commonalities with the close corporation, especially regarding formation and dissolution. Moreover, analogizing marriage to a close corporation could alleviate inequality within marriage by providing weak economic partners the opportunity to bring claims such as oppression and breach of fiduciary duty. The corporate analogy also could alleviate inequality between marriage and other intimate affiliations by making it only one in a whole range of legally recognized relationships, with functionalist—rather than morally charged—distinctions between those various forms.

THE SIMILARITY OF CLOSE CORPORATIONS AND MARRIAGES

Both close corporations and marriages are intended to be "long-term, ongoing entities" that require "stability and predictability to function properly."[108] Like marriages, corporations are formed and dissolved through state action.[109] Publicly traded corporations are markedly different from marriages, of course, by virtue of their size, their separation of ownership from control, and the free transferability of their shares.[110] However, close corporations are quite different from publicly held corporations. Close corporations are typically family businesses or small businesses run by close associates. They are smaller; they rarely separate ownership from control, because the majority shareholders often serve as officers and directors; and there is no market for their shares.[111] Moreover, close corporations enjoy the special rights of limited liability and perpetual life, much as spouses enjoy special rights such as inheritance and joint parenting. These parallels between close corporations and marriages accompany significant differences between the two forms.

Corporations are significantly different from marriages in a number of ways, complicating the analogy between the two institutions. Seeming impediments to comparing corporations and marriage include the size of corporations, the differences between spousal and corporate roles, and the status of corporations as fictitious persons with perpetual life and limited liability. On closer examination, however, many of these differences are less extreme.

The first complication in the analogy results from the potential difference in size between a corporation and a marriage. A corporation can be formed by one person or it can comprise thousands of shareholders and employees.[112] In contrast, marriage requires two (and only two) people. Of course, partnerships can include hundreds of partners, yet that fact has not prevented widespread acceptance of the partnership theory of marriage.

A second complication in analogizing marriages to corporations is the difficulty in identifying the rights and roles of spouses. In the partnership analogy, romantic partners correspond to business partners; in the corporate analogy, spouses may correspond to shareholders, incorporators, directors, or officers.[113] Similarly, it is difficult to find an analogy between shareholder rights and spousal rights. For example, shares in publicly traded corporations are freely transferable,[114] and a shareholder can exit the corporation by selling her shares without affecting the life of the corporation. These options are unavailable to spouses. Moreover, it is unclear what the marital equivalent to the shareholder right to elect new directors would be,[115] other than freely available divorce and remarriage.

The rights of spouses may be more similar to the rights of shareholders in close corporations than those in public corporations. Because close corporations are held by a few people who are shareholders and managers, minority shareholders often are unable to elect new managers, cannot freely transfer their shares, and generally cannot leave the corporation without affecting its life. Most significantly, a close corporation often is a hybrid of family and business that bridges the private–private divide by its very existence.[116] The special circumstances of management and control of family businesses require doctrinal recognition of shareholders' particular interests and vulnerabilities in such businesses.[117] Like a minority shareholder, a disadvantaged spouse (often a woman) takes a serious financial risk when exiting marriage. Applying the selected doctrines of close corporation law to marriage may reduce some of this risk.

A third complication in analogizing corporations to marriages is the fact that corporations are free-standing entities with perpetual life. Marriages, in contrast, end with the death of one spouse. According to conventional wisdom, a corporation is a legal fiction, sometimes even a person in the eyes of the law,[118] whereas a marriage is legally nothing more than the two individuals who create it.[119] However, neither one of these characterizations is entirely accurate. Both corporations and marriages involve individuals forming a new fictional legal entity and operating it for their mutual (and, presumably, society's) gain. Although individual spouses often act independently of one another, the marriage is, for some purposes, a separate entity. For example, the U.C.C. definition of *organization* includes "a corporation, government . . . partnership or association, *two or more persons having a joint or common interest,* or any other legal or commercial entity."[120] Under this definition, a husband and a wife qualify as an organization, as do corporations and partnerships.[121] Given this understanding of marriages as similar to business organizations, it is not surprising that legal doctrines prevent a spouse from disposing of or encumbering marital property without the other spouse's consent.[122]

Moreover, critics have challenged the assertion that a corporation can be conceived of as a person.[123] Many commentators have developed this insight more fully, suggesting that the corporation should be viewed as a nexus of contracts rather than as an entity itself.[124] Similarly, some commentators have suggested that marriage be understood as a set of contracts.[125] Clearly, both marriages and corporations contain elements of status and contract.

Further, although civil law provides that a marriage is not perpetual, this view is not universal. Some religious doctrines assert that marriages are perpetual and that spouses are reunited in heaven.[126] Thus, although civil marriage is often conceived of as temporary, ending when either spouse dies, other cultural understandings of marriage may perceive it as an institution with perpetual life, similar in that way to a corporation.

A final complication is that corporations have limited liability. Spouses generally are liable for debts incurred on behalf of the marriage,[127] although they enjoy some limited liability. Bankruptcy law, for example, does not require nonfiling spouses to help pay debts incurred by the filing spouse, in effect granting nondebtor spouses limited liability.[128]

In sum, many of the seemingly stark differences between marriages and corporations become less marked on closer examination. The similarities are sufficiently numerous to merit exploring how corporation law might parallel marriage law. Although corporations and marriages are not identical, marriages are more analogous to close corporations than to business partnerships.

Corporations are similar to marriages with regard to formation and dissolution. The purposes for which a corporation may be formed parallel the two major purposes of marriage cited in the legal literature. A corporation may be formed for any lawful purpose, usually either for profit maximization or for a charitable or educational purpose.[129] Legal economists view marriage, like other enterprises, as existing for profit maximization,[130] while romantics, moralists, and others see marriage as existing for social purposes that are often unprofitable, such as pursuing intimacy, caring for dependents, or controlling sexual conduct.[131] In reality, marriage is both economic and social, both for profit and for nonpecuniary purposes.

The formation of both types of relationships requires application to and certification from the state.[132] Incorporation occurs when the articles of incorporation are filed with the secretary of state.[133] Similarly, marriage is formed when the spouses file a marriage license with the state. Marriage generally requires a ceremony in addition to this filing. The ceremony itself, however, may be a perfunctory civil hearing as minimalist as the most skeletal articles of incorporation.[134]

Corporate dissolution, particularly for close corporations, parallels divorce.[135] Voluntary corporate dissolution, for example, is akin to no-fault divorce. Likewise, administrative corporate dissolution is analogous to annulment: it results from the corporation's failure to fulfill statutory requirements, such as filing an annual report.[136] Similarly, judicial corporate dissolution, pursuant to a motion by the attorney general, could also be analogous to annulment because it occurs when the corporation received its articles of incorporation by means of fraud. Another, perhaps better, corporate analogy to annulment is the ability of the incorporators or initial directors to file articles of dissolution when the corporation has neither conducted any business nor issued any shares.[137] This circumstance is akin to lack of consummation in marriage. Just as some states require a waiting period prior to divorce or impose additional requirements beyond the standard of irreconcilable differences,[138] some business organizations require a supermajority of the shareholders and the board to dissolve a corporation by vote.[139] Moreover, corporate dissolution requires the formality of filing articles of dissolution, just as divorce requires formal state action.[140] Finally, shareholders divide assets upon dissolution based on their percentage of ownership, just as spouses divide assets based on their ownership interest.[141]

The dissolutions of both close corporations and marriages can be judicial, as in the case of dissolution due to shareholder or spousal deadlock.[142] Courts also dissolve close corporations when minority shareholders are victims of oppression, or when minority shareholders' reasonable expectations of the enterprise are frustrated.[143] The marital version of dissolution due to the frustration of reasonable expectations is divorce either in a fault-based regime or in a regime entitling an economically vulnerable spouse to a share of family wealth.[144]

THE CORPORATE MODEL REMEDIES INEQUALITY WITHIN MARITAL RELATIONSHIPS

On a concrete level, three doctrinal elements of close corporation law demonstrate how the corporate metaphor might alleviate inequality within marriage: the minority shareholder cause of action for oppression and other breaches of fiduciary duty; annual shareholder meetings; and claims related to ultra vires action. Moreover, a corporate finance model can be used to craft an entitlement-based justification for postdivorce income sharing.

Shareholders can petition the court to dissolve a close corporation as a result of either oppression or deadlock. Oppression occurs when majority shareholders breach their fiduciary duty to minority shareholders by acting illegally, oppressively, or fraudulently.[145] Shareholder deadlock is also grounds for dissolution either if the directors are deadlocked and there is irreparable damage to the corporation, or if the corporation cannot be employed to the shareholders' advantage.[146] Fiduciary duties and the duty of good faith differ for close and publicly traded corporations.[147] Majority shareholders of close corporations often are held to fiduciary duties similar to those that business partners owe each other.[148] This heightened duty parallels the fiduciary duty that some jurisdictions have imposed on spouses.[149]

Applying the partnership fiduciary duty to spouses could benefit spouses who do not control assets during the marriage. Fiduciary duties include the duty to act for the beneficiary's benefit, the duty to forego profit accrued at the beneficiary's expense, and the duty to avoid self-dealing and self-preference.[150] Particularly relevant is the implication that the fiduciary duty remains intact despite strained relations between the partners.[151]

Historically, courts held that husbands owe their wives fiduciary duties stemming from the husbands' exclusive right to control and manage community property. Contemporary husbands and wives both have the right to manage community property, and each spouse is a fiduciary in relation to the other regarding property management.[152] This duty has been interpreted to require divorcing spouses to fully disclose information about the existence and value of property when they determine how to divide their assets.[153]

Corporate doctrine might also alleviate inequality within marriage by importing the idea of the annual shareholder meeting. These meetings would enable spouses to address distribution of assets and labor in their marriage, particularly when conditions change. For example, although spouses often marry thinking that each will participate fully in the wage labor force, this plan may falter once the couple has children.

Additionally, corporation law could help balance power in marriage by importing the shareholder's right to sue the corporation for acting ultra vires. This cause of action for exceeding one's authority could stem from misappropriation of marital assets. In a different context, Linda Hirshman and Jane Larson propose a cause of action for damages when one spouse commits adultery.[154] The action for damages as a result of one spouse's ultra vires actions provides a possible doctrinal framework to compensate both economic and nonpecuniary losses.   —

Models proposing buyout of one spouse's investment in the other spouse's career during the marriage, typically based on partnership law or corporate finance, are similar to the buyout remedy courts apply during the dissolution of close corporations.[155] Katherine Meighan proposes a corporate finance solution to the problem of reimbursing a nonstudent spouse for his or her investment in the other spouse's education or training. She conceives of this investment as a hybrid of debt and equity. Under Meighan's model, the nonstudent spouse therefore is entitled to a return on her investment.[156]

THE CORPORATE MODEL COULD REMEDY INEQUALITY
AMONG VARIOUS KINDS OF RELATIONSHIPS

Accepting the corporation analogy to marriage addresses the inequality among various types of relationships by providing a morally neutral range of options.

This analogy justifies state recognition of relationships tailored to the needs and expectations of the parties rather than a moral judgment that one form of intimate affiliation is natural whereas others are unnatural and immoral. One could argue that marriage (and married people) would suffer if marriage lost its preeminent status as the one natural affiliation. To the extent that this status is based on the demonization of competing affiliations, it is unjustifiable. Perhaps further discussion will at some point provide a better justification for marriage's preeminent status than the naturalized (and hierarchical) model of family. Until then, the law should recognize a range of intimate affiliations, one of which could be the close corporation/marriage.

Limited Liability Companies and Polyamory

A third business entity that shares commonalities with intimate relationships is the limited liability company. Like the partnership and corporation analogies, the LLC analogy is based on doctrinal similarities and has the potential to remedy inequality within relationships and among various types of relationships.

DEFINING POLYAMORY AND EXPLORING ITS LEGITIMACY

Although the polyamory/LLC analogy may be the most counterintuitive comparison, the surprise may be due partly to the relative infancy of the LLC and the rarity with which we discuss polyamory. Once we accept the feasibility of business analogies and recognize the existence of polyamory, however, it becomes clear that the LLC's legal structure might be particularly appropriate in providing a way to understand polyamorous relationships. Given the considerable flexibility in tailoring LLCs, the LLC model might fit best with Jeffrey Stake's proposal that intimate partners select from various options to determine the rules regarding dissolution and asset distribution.[157]

As used in this chapter, the term *polyamory* describes a wide variety of relationships that include more than one participant. For example, one man may affiliate with a number of women who are sexually involved with him but not with one another. Such an arrangement, polygamy, has been associated with Mormons and is still common in many nonindustrialized societies.[158] Polyamory also includes arrangements whereby one woman is involved with more than one man,[159] regardless of whether the men are sexually involved with one another. The term also includes arrangements with combinations of people who organize their intimate lives together, regardless of the extent of the arrangement's sexual elements. Thus, if a lesbian couple has a child by alternative insemination, using a gay man as a known donor to father the child, and the donor remains involved in the child's life, I see the arrangement as polyamorous. These three individuals love one another, or are bonded by the love for the child. The lesbian couple's relationship is romantic and sexual, and similar to marriage in that the couple lives together and jointly parents the child. The two biological parents, in contrast, are neither romantic partners nor even involved in the way that cohabitants and co-parents are.[160]

Polyamory could also include a group arrangement in which none of the participants is sexually involved with one another, but where there is some requisite level of intimacy associated with organizing lives together. For example, if Hawaii's reciprocal beneficiaries legislation (which covers any two single people barred from marrying) were expanded to cover relationships with more than two people, such arrangements could be seen as polyamorous.[161] Although *polyamory* literally means "many" and "love," the term does not impose additional conditions such as sexual relations.

The policy rationale behind family law justifies the recognition of polyamorous relationships. Family law recognizes that society and individuals benefit when individuals need not stand alone against emotional, physical, and financial challenges. I suggest that the law should encourage and reward intimate groupings, regardless of their form, penalizing such arrangements only when they are nonconsensual or subordinate their participants.[162]

One could argue that intimate arrangements involving more than two people differ from pairings and are therefore normatively inferior.[163] In fact, some forms of polyamory (such as polygamy) have been criminalized.[164] Despite polygamy's historical connection with the Church of Latter Day Saints, the practice is not protected under the Free Exercise Clause of the First Amendment.[165] However, legal hostility to polygamy is decreasing; antipolygamy statutes are rarely enforced.[166] Moreover, courts have held that participation in polygamous arrangements does not bar adoption or child custody.[167]

It is not surprising that opponents of gay rights often cite legal prohibitions on polygamy to justify legal prohibitions on same-sex relationships.[168] Despite ideological divides between gay people and polygamists, both groups are participants in tolerated, exoticized arrangements. Analogizing same-sex cohabitation and polyamorous arrangements to business models both accommodates common elements in these arrangements and morally neutralizes the differences between these affiliations and marriage. Doing so coheres with supportive toleration.[169] If particular arrangements cause harm, then criminal or tort law can intervene.

One difficulty in extending legal regulation to new affiliations lies in distinguishing legally recognized relationships from intimate relationships that do not lead to rights and obligations under civil law, such as the right to share in wealth accumulated during the course of the relationship. Yet this difficulty is not insurmountable as it exists in current law. Most states require some ceremony and state filing for a relationship to qualify as a marriage,[170] but there are exceptions to this seemingly bright line between spouses and nonspouses. For example, a de facto spouse can claim unemployment and wrongful death benefits.[171] Moreover, some jurisdictions recognize the rights of a same-sex partner with regard to children born during the relationship when the biological or legal parent refuses to allow the nonbiological parent to have contact with the child.[172] In addition, as discussed earlier, many jurisdictions recognize cohabitants' contractual and equity claims when the relationship ends. Thus, legal regulation already extends to intimate relationships other than marriage. Making this regulation more comprehensive will respond to the need for background rules to govern breakups and will also serve expressive functions.

THE SIMILARITY OF LLCS AND POLYAMOROUS ARRANGEMENTS

The flexibility of the LLC model makes it particularly well suited for regulating polyamorous relationships. The wide variety of polyamorous relationships lends itself to the tremendous contractual tailoring available with LLCs. Moreover, the hybrid nature of LLCs (part corporation, part partnership) mirrors the hybrid nature of many polyamorous affiliations (which may include a marriage or other primary relationship alongside relationships with more peripheral individuals). Some people have already formed what they call "relationship LLCs."[173]

LLCs are a hybrid of corporations and partnerships that allow their members to tailor the organization contractually to be more like a partnership or a corporation.[174] Because a primary characteristic of LLCs is their flexibility, they may take many different forms. The following comparison of LLCs is based on default rules in most LLC statutes. However, because members can vary the terms by agreement, these default examples do not hold true for every LLC. Such an alteration of the agreement would be equivalent to a prenuptial or cohabitation contract, both of which are generally enforceable.[175]

The characteristics that LLCs share with corporations include relative formality, limited liability, perpetual life, and free transferability of ownership interests.[176] Unlike general partnerships, LLCs are formed by filing Articles of Organization with the secretary of state or equivalent agency.[177] Members also enjoy limited liability unless a court pierces the corporate veil.[178] LLCs, like corporations, often enjoy perpetual life.[179] Finally, most LLC statutes provide that ownership interests are freely transferable.[180]

LLCs resemble partnerships more than corporations with regard to the number of members and management. Most LLC statutes require at least two members. In this way, the LLC more closely resembles an intimate relationship than a corporation in that one person can form a corporation.[181] Absent contrary agreement, LLCs are managed by their owners, unlike corporations, in which ownership and control are often separated.[182] Moreover, like partnerships, LLCs are relatively free of mandatory statutory provisions, leaving members to order their affairs by contract.[183] Many states allow oral LLC operating agreements, and members may require unanimous agreement to allow a member to transfer her interest.[184] As such, LLCs cohere more with contemporary contractual understandings of intimate relationships than with outdated status-based models. In short, LLCs can be almost as informal as general partnerships.

LLCs are analogous to polyamorous arrangements in that they take many different forms. The LLC model is particularly appropriate for closely held businesses,[185] and therefore could be analogous to the other types of intimate relationships. Furthermore, LLCs combine corporate and partnership elements in a way that mirrors the combination of marriage and cohabitation in many polyamorous arrangements. Where a woman is married to one man and a second man joins their relationship, it might make sense to have this new entity include elements of both corporate (marriage) doctrine and partnership (cohabitation) doctrine.

The LLC dissolution rules provide further support for a comparison to polyamory. As with partnerships, dissociation differs from dissolution. Dissociation marks the exit of a member, whereas dissolution marks the end of the entity.[186] A member dissociates from the LLC upon voluntary withdrawal, death, bankruptcy, or the figurative death of member business associations.[187] Members, like partners, have a default right to payment for their interests in the LLC. This buyout right empowers minority members against more powerful majority members because liquidation may ensue if the entity lacks the capital to buy out the dissociating member. As with partnerships, dissociation triggers dissolution unless the members elect to continue operating the firm. Dissolution of an LLC also can result when the firm's agreed-on duration expires, when a particular event occurs, when all members consent, or when a judge decrees. As with marriage, LLC statutes generally require state filings when the entity dissolves.[188]

THE LLC MODEL COULD REMEDY INEQUALITY
WITHIN POLYAMOROUS RELATIONSHIPS

Current doctrine tends to recognize only two people in an intimate affiliation. In a custody fight among a lesbian couple (one of whom is the biological mother) and the sperm donor of their child, the law generally recognizes only one of two relationships: the romantic/sexual partnership of the lesbians, or the biological parent partnership of the donor and the biological mother. Either determination excludes an important part of the family and permits abuses of power (either heterosexual privilege by the donor against the nonbiological mother, or couple privilege by the nonbiological mother against a single donor). Contract helps to balance the power in these difficult situations in that the parties may allocate rights more fairly when drafting the agreement. As a practical matter these ex ante intentions should be relevant to an ex post judicial determination once the parties' relationship breaks down. In

LaChapelle v. Mitten,[189] the Minnesota Court of Appeals adopted this approach, recognizing the parental rights of the biological mother, her former partner, and the sperm donor of their child. The three had contractually agreed that the donor would be entitled to share legal custody of the child. The court reasoned that it was in the child's best interests to allow all parties to maintain a "significant relationship" with the child.[190]

People leave polyamorous arrangements just as they leave marriage or cohabiting relationships. Although many polyamorous relationships end, it is hard to determine whether these relationships are less stable than monogamous arrangements because the relationships are socially and legally stigmatized.[191] Just as criminalizing prostitution facilitates abuse of prostitutes by keeping their working conditions out of the public eye (and depriving them of other social benefits such as Social Security or unemployment insurance), social and legal marginalization of polyamorous affiliations may exacerbate inequality within these relationships. If people oppose polyamory because they fear abuse within the relationships, the LLC model and the accompanying legitimacy of polyamory could expose any power abuses, improve the minority members' bargaining power, and further provide exit strategies for weak participants through the forced buyout.

THE LLC MODEL COULD REMEDY INEQUALITY
AMONG VARIOUS TYPES OF RELATIONSHIPS

The LLC analogy to polyamory also could address the inequality among various types of relationships by virtue of being one affiliation in a morally neutral range of options. This reasoning justifies state recognition of the relationship to the extent that recognition reflects the needs and expectations of the parties rather than a moral judgment that one form of intimate affiliation is natural whereas others are unnatural and immoral. Current law ignores, criminalizes, or tolerates polyamorous arrangements to various degrees. The LLC model would elevate polyamorous relationships to the level of legally recognized intimate affiliations, thereby justifying claims for division of assets, intestacy, or wrongful death that currently are recognized for marriage. If the law retains its general refusal to recognize these affiliations, it should do so for functional reasons (such as the difficulty of determining membership, or determining the extent of intended rights and liabilities) rather than moralistic objections to nonmarital affiliations.

Conclusion

I contend that business models are analogous to various intimate affiliations. In particular, partnership is akin to cohabitation (especially same-sex arrangements), and close corporations are akin to marriages. Perhaps most speculatively, this chapter seeks to expand conventional analysis to include polyamorous affiliations, suggesting that such affiliations are most analogous to limited liability companies.

Recognizing the analogies between business models and intimate affiliations has the potential to improve family law by remedying the inadequacy and inequality of current doctrine, both of which are by-products of reliance on the naturalized model of family. Business models could remedy the naturalized model's failure to account for nonmarital alliances and could alleviate inequality within relationships and among various kinds of intimate affiliation. For instance, business models can counter inequality within relationships by providing an appropriate set of default rules to govern affiliations, such as the fifty–fifty distribution of assets upon dissolution. In marriage, business models offer an entitlement-based theory of postdivorce income sharing. Entitlement, based on homemaker contributions to family wealth, alleviates the economic subordination of primary homemakers. The naturalized model of family, in contrast, suggests that homemakers contribute to their family because of moral obligation, biological destiny, or divine mandate, none of which presupposes the agency to leave the affiliation or addresses the inequality within the relationship.

Recognizing the metaphorical connections between business forms and intimate affiliations also remedies inequality among types of relationships by intervening in naturalized understandings of family that view some affiliations (such as marriage and heterosexuality) as natural and others as unnatural. In contrast to the naturalized model, business law recognizes a range of equally valid arrangements, such as corporations, general partnerships, and limited liability companies. Just as these various business forms respond to the needs of particular arrangements, domestic relations law could account for the needs of particular intimate affiliations without designating one as superior to others. Thus, differences among intimate affiliations would be morally neutral. Choosing marriage over cohabitation would have the same social meaning as choosing to incorporate rather than form a general partnership.

Business models also could remedy inequalities among relationships that result from current law's provision of a public safety net to those who need it least. People in legally recognized families often enjoy a public safety net in addition to the emotional, physical, financial, and social benefits of a relationship. In contrast, those in legally marginalized relationships stand largely alone in the world; if a financial, health-related, or other type of disaster strikes, there may be neither a public nor a private safety net to catch them. Legal recognition should extend beyond those who are in marriage or marriagelike relationships to include those in a range of affiliations that may be neither sexual nor romantic.

Although I do not attempt to propose an ideal domestic relations law based on business law, neither do I foreclose the possibility of such a project.[192] This chapter does suggest underlying justifications for undertaking such an endeavor or for altering domestic relations law to remedy the inadequacies and inequalities inherent in naturalized models of family. If domestic relations law were to recognize a range of intimate affiliations, this change alone would provide the coherence and consistency currently lacking in family law doctrines that recognize marriage as the only fully legitimate affiliation and simply cobble together regulations for the vast array of other intimate affiliations.

Importing business models to family law would counteract inequality in at least two ways. First, business analogies would make differences among relationships morally neutral—the equivalent of the differences among partnerships, corporations, and LLCs. Second, they would alleviate the inequity of the haves coming out ahead of the have-nots[193] by expanding the definition of family to include, for instance, same-sex cohabitation and polyamory.

In this chapter I have attempted to bridge the traditional gap between the private/domestic world and the private/business world. The purpose of this exercise is not to collapse the distinctions between these two realms, but rather to consider new approaches to old problems and reconsider the nature and purposes of legal regulation of intimate affiliation generally.

Notes

1. This chapter is adapted from my article *Marriage as a Trade: Bridging the Private/Private Distinction*, 36 Harv. Civ. R. & Civ. Lib. L. Rev. 79 (2001) (© 2001 by the Presidents and Fellows of Harvard College and the Harvard Civil Rights-Civil Liberties Law Review) (reprinted with permission).

2. Commentators frequently discuss the split between the market and the family in public–private terms, constructing them as separate, dichotomous realms. *See* Elizabeth Anderson, *Value in Ethics and Economics* xiii (1993); Frances E. Olsen, *The Family and the Market: A Study of Ideology and Legal Reform*, 96 Harv. L. Rev. 1497 (1983). This chapter uses the conventional categories but reconfigures the public–private split between market and family as a private–private split. This reconfiguration reveals that both the market and the family rely on elements of private ordering and concern financial arrangements.

3. *A Statistical Portrait of the United States* 24 (Mark S. Littman ed., 1998).

4. *Polyamory*, as used in this chapter, refers to any intimate affiliation between more than two adults, regardless of whether it has a sexual component. *See infra*, the section titled "Limited Liability Companies and Polyamory."

5. *See, e.g.*, Unif. Parentage Act § 5(b) (1973), 9B U.L.A. 301 (1987).

6. *See, e.g.*, Haw. Rev. Stat. §§ 572C-1 to 572C-7 (1997); Vt. Stat. Ann. tit. 15, §§ 1201–1207, 1301–1306 (2000); *Vasquez v. Hawthorne*, 994 P.2d 240, 243 (Wash. Ct. App.), *review granted*, 11 P.3d 825 (Wash. 2000).

7. This chapter builds on, but is distinct from, Martha Fineman's influential reconceptualization of family as a unit of dependency and caretaking. It seeks to fill the gaps in Fineman's analysis by suggesting default rules to govern various forms of intimate relationships. It also expands

the definition of family to include affiliations of more than two adults and nonsexual dyads. *See, e.g.,* Martha A. Fineman, *The Illusion of Equality: The Rhetoric and Reality of Divorce Reform* (1991) [hereinafter Fineman, *Illusion of Equality*]; Martha A. Fineman, *The Neutered Mother, the Sexual Family, and Other Twentieth-Century Tragedies* (1995).

8. *See generally* Peter W. Bardaglio, *Reconstructing the Household: Families, Sex, and the Law in the Nineteenth-Century South* 54–55 (1995); Linda R. Hirshman & Jane E. Larson, *Hard Bargains: The Politics of Sex* 33–36, 43–44, 53 (1998); Norma Basch, *In the Eyes of the Law: Women, Marriage, and Property in Nineteenth-Century New York* (1982).

9. *See* Bardaglio, *supra* note 8, at 62; Adrienne D. Davis, *The Private Law of Race and Sex: An Antebellum Perspective,* 51 Stan. L. Rev. 221 (1999).

10. *See* Bardaglio, *supra* note 8, at 185; *Defense of Marriage Act, May 15, 1996: Hearings on H.R. 3396 before the Subcommittee on the Constitution of the House Committee on the Judiciary,* 104th Cong. 99–100 (1996). One state has lifted the ban. *Goodridge v. Dep't Pub. Health,* 798 N.E. 2d 941 (Mass. 2003).

11. *See* Jana B. Singer, *The Privatization of Family Law,* 1992 Wis. L. Rev. 1443, 1531–65.

12. *See, e.g.,* U.C.C. § 1-102(1)(b) (1990).

13. Partnership models include Uniform Marriage and Divorce Act, 9A U.L.A. 161 (1998); and the Uniform Probate Code, 8 U.L.A. 1 (Supp. 1997). *See* Jana B. Singer, *Alimony and Efficiency: The Gendered Costs and Benefits of the Economic Justification for Alimony,* 82 Geo. L.J. 2423 (1994) [hereinafter Singer, *Alimony and Efficiency*]; Cynthia Starnes, *Divorce and the Displaced Homemaker: A Discourse on Playing with Dolls, Partnership Buyouts, and Dissociation under No-Fault,* 60 U. Chi. L. Rev. 67 (1993). Corporate finance models include Katherine Wells Meighan, *For Better or for Worse: A Corporate Finance Approach to Valuing Educational Degrees at Divorce,* 5 Geo. Mason L. Rev. 193 (1997); and A. Mechele Dickerson, *To Love, Honor, and (Oh!) Pay: Should Spouses Be Forced to Pay Each Other's Debts?* 78 B.U. L. Rev. 961 (1998).

14. *See generally* Bardaglio, *supra* note 8, at 184.

15. *See, e.g.,* Maynard v. Hill, 125 U.S. 190, 205 (1888); Defense of Marriage Act, 1 U.S.C. § 7 (Supp. IV 1998), 28 U.S.C. § 1738C (Supp. IV 1998).

16. *See, e.g.,* Milton C. Regan Jr., *Alone Together: Law and the Meanings of Marriage* 33 (1999) [hereinafter Regan, *Alone Together*].

17. In the context of postdivorce income sharing, for example, business models offer rules based on entitlement. The naturalized model, in contrast, awards alimony based on a homemaker's need and a wage earner's ability to pay, which translates to charity rather than entitlement. *See, e.g.,* Unif. Marriage & Divorce Act §§ 307, 308 (amended 1973), 9A U.L.A. 288, 446 (1998).

18. *See* Marc Galanter, *Why the "Haves" Come out Ahead: Speculations on the Limits of Legal Change,* 9 Law & Soc'y Rev. 95 (1974).

19. One dictionary lists twenty-eight meanings of *natural. The New Shorter Oxford English Dictionary* Vol. II, 1888–1889 (1993).

20. These understandings can clash with each other. John Stuart Mill, *Nature* (1874), reprinted in *Three Essays on Religion* 3, 64–65 (1969).

21. *See, e.g.,* Richard J. Herrnstein & Charles Murray, *The Bell Curve: Intelligence and Class Structure in American Life* (1994); Lawrence Kohlberg, *The Philosophy of Moral Development* (1981); and Robert H. Bork, *Slouching toward Gomorrah: Modern Liberalism and American Decline* 286 (1996).

22. *See, e.g.,* Bardaglio, *supra* note 8, at 55.

23. John M. Finnis, *Law, Morality, and "Sexual Orientation,"* 69 Notre Dame L. Rev. 1049 (1994); *see also* Gerald Dworkin, *Devlin Was Right: Law and the Enforcement of Morality,* 40 Wm. & Mary L. Rev. 927 (1999); Robert P. George & Gerard V. Bradley, *Marriage and the Liberal Imagination,* 84 Geo. L.J. 301, 302 (1995).

24. Mary Becker, *Women, Morality, and Sexual Orientation,* 8 UCLA Women's L.J. 165, 185–91, 197–202 (1998) [hereinafter Becker, *Women, Morality, and Sexual Orientation*].

25. Andrew Koppelman, *Why Discrimination against Lesbians and Gay Men Is Sex Discrimination*, 69 N.Y.U. L. Rev. 197 (1994).

26. *Id.* at 224, 213, 226–27, 261, and 263.

27. *See, e.g.*, Okla. Stat. tit. 21, § 886 (1994); Model Penal Code § 213.2 cmt. 1 (1999). Such bans have recently been struck down as unconstitutional. *Lawrence v. Texas*, 539 U.S. 558 (2003).

28. Janet E. Halley, *Don't: A Reader's Guide to the Military's Anti-Gay Policy* 7–8 (1999).

29. Peter Bardaglio, *"An Outrage upon Nature": Incest and the Law in the Nineteenth-Century South*, in *In Joy and in Sorrow: Women, Family, and Marriage in the Victorian South, 1830–1900* 32, 33 (Carol Bleser ed., 1991).

30. *Id.* at 34.

31. *Littleton v. Prange*, 9 S.W. 3d 223 (Tex. App. 1999), *cert. denied*, 121 S. Ct. 174 (2000). I use the term *transsexual woman* to refer to a male-to-female transsexual.

32. Both the trial court and the court of appeals found for Dr. Prange on the ground that there was no genuine issue of material fact as to Littleton's sex. *Littleton* 9 S.W. 3d at 231.

33. *Id.* at 224, 231.

34. *Id.* at 231.

35. *M.T. v. J.T.*, 355 A.2d 204 (N.J. Super. Ct. App. Div. 1976), *cert. denied*, 364 A.2d 1076 (N.J. 1976).

36. *Id.* at 210.

37. Alfred C. Kinsey et al., *Sexual Behavior in the Human Female* (1953); Alfred C. Kinsey, et al., *Sexual Behavior in the Human Male* (1948).

38. *See* Barbara Ann Atwood, *Ten Years Later: Lingering Concerns about the Uniform Premarital Agreement Act*, 19 J. Legis. 127, 131 (1993); Mary Becker, *Problems with the Privatization of Heterosexuality*, 73 Denv. U. L. Rev. 1169 (1996).

39. The abolitionist movement and the Women's Christian Temperance Union's campaign to raise the age of consent are two examples. *See* Henry Mayer, *All on Fire: William Lloyd Garrison and the Abolition of Slavery* (1998); Jane E. Larson, *"Even a Worm Will Turn at Last": Rape Reform in Late Nineteenth Century America*, 9 Yale J.L. & Human. 1 (1997). For a contemporary example of progressive use of moral rhetoric, see Becker, *Women, Morality, and Sexual Orientation*, *supra* note 24.

40. Although liberalism relies on problematic assumptions of agency and an essentialized notion of self, it can also serve progressive ends. *See* Lisa Duggan, *Queering the State*, in *Sex Wars: Sexual Dissent and Political Culture* 179 (Lisa Duggan & Nan D. Hunter eds., 1995).

41. Restatement (Second) of Contracts § 208 (1981); *id.* at §§ 178–79.

42. Richard A. Posner, *Ask, Tell*, New Republic 52, 53 (Oct. 11, 1999) (reviewing William N. Eskridge Jr., *Gaylaw: Challenging the Apartheid of the Closet* (1999)).

43. Davis, *supra* note 9.

44. *Id.* at 285 (quoting *Smith v. DuBose*, 78 Ga. 413, 430 (1887) (internal quotations omitted)).

45. *Id.* at 284.

46. *See id.* at 261–63.

47. *Vasquez v. Hawthorne*, 994 P.2d 240 (Wash. Ct. App.), *review granted*, 11 P.3d 825 (Wash. 2000).

48. *Connell v. Francisco*, 898 P.2d 831 (Wash. 1995).

49. *Vasquez*, 994 P.2d at 243.

50. *Posik v. Layton*, 695 So. 2d 759 (Fla. Dist. Ct. App. 1997).

51. *Id.* at 760.

52. *Id.* at 761.

53. *Crooke v. Gilden*, 414 S.E. 2d 645 (Ga. 1992).

54. *Id.* at 646.

55. *Id.*

56. Cicely Hamilton, *Marriage as a Trade* (1912).

57. *See, e.g.,* Lenore J. Weitzman, *The Marriage Contract: Spouses, Lovers, and the Law* (1981); Marjorie Maguire Shultz, *Contractual Ordering of Marriage: A New Model for State Policy,* 70 Cal. L. Rev. 205, 280 (1982).

58. Margaret Jane Radin, *Contested Commodities* (1996).

59. Other commentators have observed or promoted importation in the opposite direction. *See* Milton C. Regan Jr., *Spouses and Strangers: Divorce Obligations and Property Rhetoric,* 82 Geo. L.J. 2303 (1994); Martha Minow, *"Forming under Everything That Grows": Toward a History of Family Law,* Wis. L. Rev. 819 (1985).

60. *See, e.g.,* Shultz, *supra* note 57, at 239–40; Weitzman, *supra* note 57, at xxi; Lawrence W. Waggoner, *Marital Property Rights in Transition,* 59 Mo. L. Rev. 21, 43 (1994).

61. *See* Frances Olsen, *The Myth of State Intervention in the Family,* 18 U. Mich. J.L. Reform 835 (1985).

62. Limited partnerships are less analogous to contemporary marriage in that limited partnerships involve limited liability of the limited partner as well as passivity in corporate affairs.

63. The UMDA adopted the partnership theory of marriage to justify its alteration of the rules governing asset distribution upon divorce. Unif. Marriage & Divorce Act, prefatory note, 9A U.L.A 161 (1998). The act refers to termination of a marriage as dissolution, a term borrowed from partnership law.

64. Unif. Probate Code, 8 U.L.A. 1 (Supp. 1997). Eight states have adopted the 1990 revisions of the Uniform Probate Code. *Id.*

65. Singer, *Alimony and Efficiency, supra* note 13; Starnes, *supra* note 13.

66. Dickerson, *supra* note 13, at 964.

67. Alexandria Streich, *Spousal Fiduciaries in the Marital Partnership: Marriage Means Business but the Sharks Do Not Have a Code of Conduct,* 34 Idaho L. Rev. 367 (1997).

68. *See, e.g.,* Charles R. P. Pouncy, *Marriage and Domestic Partnership: Rationality and Inequality,* 7 Temp. Pol. & Civ. Rts. L. Rev. 363 (1998); Craig A. Sloane, *A Rose by Any Other Name: Marriage and the Danish Registered Partnership Act,* 5 Cardozo J. Int'l. & Comp. L. 189 (1997).

69. Deborah L. Rhode & Martha Minow, *Reforming the Questions, Questioning the Reforms,* in *Divorce Reform at the Crossroads* 191, 198 (Steven D. Sugarman & Herma Hill Kay eds., 1990).

70. Starnes, *supra* note 13, at 119.

71. *Id.* at 119–20.

72. *See, e.g.,* Fineman, *Illusion of Equality, supra* note 7, at 4–5; Marjorie E. Kornhauser, *Theory versus Reality: The Partnership Model of Marriage in Family and Income Tax Law,* 69 Temp. L. Rev. 1413 (1996); Bea Ann Smith, *The Partnership Theory of Marriage: A Borrowed Solution Fails,* 68 Tex. L. Rev. 689, 706–7 (1990).

73. Unif. P'ship Act § 6(1) (1914), 6 U.L.A. 256 (1995); Revised Unif. P'ship Act § 202(a) (1997), 6 U.L.A. 53 (Supp. 2000); *see also* Unif. P'ship Act § 7(4) (1914), 6 U.L.A. 280 (1995); Revised Unif. P'ship Act § 202(c)(3) (1997), 6 U.L.A. 54 (Supp. 2000). This chapter refers both to the Uniform Partnership Act and the Revised Uniform Partnership Act, the latter of which has been adopted by twenty-eight states. 6 U.L.A. 1 (Supp. 2000).

74. Larry E. Ribstein, *Unincorporated Business Entities* 50–51 (1996).

75. Unif. P'ship Act § 18 (1914), 6 U.L.A. 526 (1995); Revised Unif. P'ship Act § 401 (1997), 6 U.L.A. 74 (Supp. 2000). Partners can, of course, contract around this default rule in their partnership agreement. *See* Revised Unif. P'ship Act § 103 (1997), 6 U.L.A. 42 (Supp. 2000).

76. Shultz, *supra* note 57, at 205. For a discussion of courts' willingness to enforce agreements between partners but not spouses, *see* Sanford N. Katz, *Propter Honoris Respectum: Marriage as Partnership,* 73 Notre Dame L. Rev. 1251, 1261 (1998).

77. An exception is criminal prosecution for violating fornication laws. Richard A. Posner & Katharine B. Silbaugh, *A Guide to America's Sex Laws* 98–99 (1996).

78. *See* Julie Brines & Karla Joyner, *The Ties That Bind: Principles of Cohesion in Cohabitation and Marriage,* 64 Am. Soc. Rev. 333, 348–49 (1999).

79. *Id.* at 334–36.

80. Scott J. South & Glenna Spitze, *Housework in Marital and Nonmarital Households,* 59 Am. Soc. Rev. 327, 332 (1994).

81. Brines & Joyner, *supra* note 78, at 341; *see also* U.S. Census Bureau, *Statistical Abstract of the United States* 60, at 416 (1999) [hereinafter *Statistical Abstract*].

82. *Statistical Abstract, supra* note 81, at 481. This general trend does not apply to the same degree in communities of color. *Id.*

83. A notable exception to this general rule is Washington's recognition of nonmarital "meretricious relationships" between men and women.

84. Atwood, *supra* note 38.

85. Michelle Huston & Pepper Schwartz, *The Relationships of Lesbians and of Gay Men,* in *Under-Studied Relationships: Off the Beaten Track* 89, 108–11 (Julie T. Wood & Steve Duck eds., 1995). *But see* Christopher Carrington, *No Place Like Home: Relationships and Family Life among Lesbians and Gay Men* 12–14, 17 (1999).

86. Virginia Rutter & Pepper Schwartz, *Same-Sex Couples: Courtship, Commitment, Context,* in *The Diversity in Human Relationships* 197, 209 (Ann Elizabeth Auhagen & Maria von Salisch eds., 1996).

87. Philip Blumsten & Pepper Schwartz, *American Couples: Money, Work, Sex* 148 (1983).

88. *See, e.g., Crooke v. Gilden,* 414 S.E. 2d 645 (Ga. 1992). *But see Jones v. Daly,* 176 Cal. Rptr. 130, 134 (Cal. Ct. App. 1981).

89. Unif. P'ship Act §§ 29, 31 (1914), 6 U.L.A. 752, 771 (1995); Revised Unif. P'ship Act § 801 (1997), 6 U.L.A. 103 (Supp. 2000).

90. Unif. P'ship Act § 31 (1914), 6 U.L.A. 771 (1995); Revised Unif. P'ship Act § 801 (1997), 6 U.L.A. 103 (Supp. 2000).

91. La. Civ. Code Ann. art. 102 (West Supp. 1998); Ariz. Rev. Stat. § 25-901 (1999). For extended discussion of covenant marriage, *see* Katherine Shaw Spaht, *Marriage: Why a Second Tier Called Covenant Marriage?* 12 Regent U. L. Rev. 1 (1999).

92. Unif. P'ship Act §§ 29, 31 (1914), 6 U.L.A. 752, 771 (1995); Revised Unif. P'ship Act § 801 (1997), 6 U.L.A. 103 (Supp. 2000).

93. Lambda Legal Defense and Education Fund, *State-by-State,* http://www.lambdalegal.org/cgi-bin/pages/states (last visited Dec. 3, 2000).

94. Cal. Gov't Code § 22867 (West Supp. 2000).

95. Haw. Rev. Stat. § 572C-4 (1998). The Hawaii definition is broad enough to include, for example, a widowed mother and her son.

96. *Tanner v. Oregon Health Scis. Univ.,* 971 P.2d 435 (Or. App. 1998).

97. Cal. Fam. Code § 297 (West Supp. 2000).

98. Vt. Stat. Ann. tit. 15, §§ 1201–1207, 1301–1306 (2000).

99. Boris I. Bittker & James S. Eustice, *Federal Income Taxation of Corporations and Shareholders* para. 2.01[2] (6th ed. 1994).

100. For an example of a statutory scheme that would switch the current burden of proof in establishing a contract regarding property sharing in a nonmarital relationship, see American Law Institute, *Principles of the Law of Family Dissolution: Analysis and Recommendations* (2000).

101. *See, e.g.,* Margaret F. Brinig & June Carbone, *The Reliance Interest in Marriage and Divorce,* 62 Tul. L. Rev. 855 (1998); Martha M. Ertman, *Commercializing Marriage: A Proposal for Valuing Women's Work through Premarital Security Agreements,* 77 Tex. L. Rev. 17 (1998).

102. Starnes, *supra* note 13, at 71–72.

103. *Id.* at 130–37.

104. Ribstein, *supra* note 74, at 143.

105. *Meinhard v. Salmon,* 164 N.E. 545, 546 (N.Y. 1928).

106. Revised Unif. P'ship Act § 404 (1997); 6 U.L.A. 79 (Supp. 2000); *see also* Unif. P'ship Act § 21 (1914), 6 U.L.A. 608 (1995).

107. Paula L. Ettlebrick, *Legal Marriage Is Not the Answer,* Harv. Gay & Lesbian Rev. 34 (Fall 1997).

108. Note, *In Sickness and in Health, in Hawaii and Where Else? Conflict of Laws and Recognition of Same-Sex Marriages*, 109 Harv. L. Rev. 2038, 2053 (1996). Of course, cohabitation also can be a stable, long-term project.

109. *See* Robert W. Hamilton, *Business Organizations* § 8.13, at 207 (1996); F. Hodge O'Neal & Robert B. Thompson, *O'Neal's Close Corporations* § 9.27 (3d ed. 1998).

110. Hamilton, *supra* note 109, at § 1.4.

111. *Id.* at §§ 1.02, 1.14; Terry A. O'Neill, *Reasonable Expectations in Families, Businesses, and Family Businesses: A Comment on Rollock*, 73 Ind. L.J. 589, 590 (1998).

112. O'Neal & Thompson, *supra* note 109, at § 1.03.

113. Children could be analogized to nonvoting shareholders or beneficiaries of a fiduciary relationship. Elizabeth Scott & Robert E. Scott, *Parents as Fiduciaries*, 81 Va. L. Rev. 2401 (1995).

114. O'Neal & Thompson, *supra* note 109, at § 1.4.

115. *See* Model Bus. Corp. Act § 8.03 (1999).

116. *See id.* at § 14.30 cmt. 2.

117. *See id.* at § 8.01 cmt.; *see also Donahue v. Rodd Electrotype Co.*, 328 N.E. 2d 505, 517 (Mass. 1975) (noting the "particularly scrupulous fidelity" owed by majority shareholders to minority shareholders in a family-owned close corporation).

118. O'Neal & Thompson, *supra* note 109, at § 8.4.

119. *See* Lee E. Teitelbaum, *The Family as a System: A Preliminary Sketch*, 1996 Utah L. Rev. 537, 542–43.

120. U.C.C. § 1-201(28) (1990) (emphasis added).

121. U.C.C. § 3-403 cmt. 4 (1990).

122. *See, e.g.*, Colo. Rev. Stat. § 4-9-203(2) (2000).

123. Daniel J. H. Greenwood, *Fictional Shareholders: For Whom Are Corporate Managers Trustees, Revisited*, 69 S. Cal. L. Rev. 1021 (1996).

124. Hamilton, *supra* note 109, at § 8.6, 193.

125. Brinig & Carbone, *supra* note 101, at 877–82.

126. Mark Oppenheimer, *Mormon's New England Temple a Symbol of Arrival*, Hartford Courant A5 (Sept. 20, 2000).

127. Homer Clark, *Domestic Relations* at § 15.4 (2d ed. 1988).

128. Dickerson, *supra* note 13, at 964.

129. Model Bus. Corp. Act § 3.01 (1999).

130. *See, e.g.*, Richard A. Posner, *Economic Analysis of Law* 155–56 (5th ed. 1998).

131. *See* Regan, *Alone Together, supra* note 16; Jack Hitt, *Marriage à la Market*, N.Y. Times Magazine 17 (Mar. 19, 2000).

132. *See* Model Bus. Corp. Act §§ 2.02, 2.10 (1999).

133. *Id.* at § 2.03.

134. *See, e.g.*, Unif. Marriage & Divorce Act §§ 203, 206, 9A U.L.A. 179 (1998).

135. *See* Model Bus. Corp. Act § 14.05 (1999). As with partnership law, corporate dissolution precedes winding up. *Id.* at § 14.03.

136. *Id.* at § 14.20.

137. *Id.* at § 14.01.

138. Louisiana, for example, allows spouses to agree at the formation of their marriage that they will be governed by a fault-based regime. La. Civ. Code Ann. art. 102 (West Supp. 1998).

139. Model Bus. Corp. Act § 14.02 (1999).

140. *Cf.* Model Bus. Corp. Act § 14.03 (1999), *with* Unif. Marriage & Divorce Act § 303, 9A U.L.A. 216 (1998).

141. *Cf.* Model Bus. Corp. Act § 14.05 (1999), *with* Unif. Marriage & Divorce Act § 307, 9A U.L.A. 288 (1998).

142. *See* O'Neal & Thompson, *supra* note 109, at § 9.26.

143. *Donahue v. Rodd Electrotype Co.*, 328 N.E. 2d 505 (Mass. 1975). As an alternative to dissolution, the majority shareholder can, and often does, buy out the minority shareholder. Model Bus. Corp. Act § 14.34, official cmt. (1999).

144. Fault can be grounds for divorce and can also be relevant to the distribution of assets upon divorce. Barbara Bennett Woodhouse, *Sex, Lies, and Dissipation: The Discourse of Fault in a No-Fault Era,* 82 Geo. L.J. 2525, 2528–29 (1994); Unif. Marriage & Divorce Act § 307, 9A U.L.A. 288 (1998).

145. Model Bus. Corp. Act § 14.30(2)(ii) (1999).

146. *Id.* at § 14.30(2)(i). A third ground for dissolution exists when shareholders are deadlocked in voting power and have failed, for a period that includes two annual meeting dates, to elect successors to directors whose terms have expired. *Id.* at § 14.30(2)(iii). This action is similar to covenant marriage in Louisiana, which imposes a two-year waiting period for divorce. La. Civ. Code Ann. art. 102 (West Supp. 1998). A fourth ground for dissolution is waste or misallocation of corporate assets. Model Bus. Corp. Act § 14.30(2)(iv) (1999).

147. Model Bus. Corp. Act §§ 8.30, 8.42 (1999). Fiduciary duties and the duty of good faith are separate but related obligations that close corporation shareholders owe each other.

148. *Donahue v. Rodd Electrotype Co.,* 328 N.E. 2d 505, 515 (Mass. 1975).

149. Streich, *supra* note 67, at 367–68.

150. *Id.* at 373 (quoting *Bakalis v. Bressler,* 115 N.E. 2d 323, 327 (Ill. 1953)).

151. *Id.* at 379.

152. *Id.* at 376.

153. *See Compton v. Compton,* 612 P.2d 1175, 1183 (Idaho 1980); *see also* California's Family Code provision imposing "the highest good faith and fair dealing on each spouse, and neither shall take any unfair advantage of the other." Cal. Fam. Code §§ 1100(e), 1101 (West 1994).

154. Hirshman & Larson, *supra* note 8, at 285.

155. Starnes, *supra* note 13, at 130–31; Meighan, *supra* note 13. When a shareholder seeks dissolution of a close corporation under Model Bus. Corp. Act § 14.30(2) (1999), the corporation or another shareholder may elect to purchase the minority shareholder's share for fair market value. *Id.* at § 14.34(a). If the parties cannot agree on a fair price, the court will determine the fair value of the shares. *Id.* at § 14.34(d).

156. Debt is fixed and is repaid in set installments (principal with interest), whereas equity varies and depends on the return on the investment. Meighan, *supra* note 13, at 214.

157. Jeffrey Evans Stake, *Mandatory Planning for Divorce,* 45 Vand. L. Rev. 397 (1992).

158. David L. Chambers, *Polygamy and Same-Sex Marriage,* 26 Hofstra L. Rev. 53, 61 (1997) [hereinafter Chambers, *Polygamy*].

159. John Cloud, *Henry & Mary & Janet & . . . ,* Time 90 (Nov. 15, 1999)(describing an arrangement among a woman, her husband, and another man).

160. Although not using the term *polyamory,* the Minnesota Court of Appeals recognized the parental rights of a biological mother, her lesbian partner, and the sperm donor of their child. *LaChapelle v. Mitten,* 607 N.W. 2d 151 (Minn. Ct. App. 2000).

161. Such a change in the law is not inconceivable. *See, e.g.,* Jan Battles, *Cork Opens Door to Gay Couples,* Sun. Times (London), Home News Section (Feb. 6, 2000).

162. *See* Shultz, *supra* note 57, at 298. *See also* David L. Chambers, *The "Legalization" of the Family: Toward a Policy of Supportive Neutrality,* 18 U. Mich. J.L. Reform 805, 813–27 (1985) [hereinafter Chambers, *Legalization of the Family*].

163. *See* William N. Eskridge, *The Case for Same-Sex Marriage* (1996), at 148–49; Maura I. Strassberg, *Distinctions of Form or Substance: Monogamy, Polygamy, and Same-Sex Marriage,* 75 N.C. L. Rev. 1501, 1531–37 (1997).

164. Posner & Silbaugh, *supra* note 77, at 143–54.

165. *Reynolds v. United States,* 98 U.S. 145 (1878).

166. *See* Chambers, *Polygamy, supra* note 158, at 71–72. *But see* Michael Janofsky, *Trial Opens in Rare Case of a Utahan Charged with Polygamy,* N.Y. Times A12 (May 15, 2001); *A Utah Man with 5 Wives Is Convicted of Bigamy,* N.Y. Times A19 (May 20, 2001).

167. *See, e.g., Johanson v. Fischer (In re W.A.T.),* 808 P.2d 1083 (Utah 1991); *Sanders v. Tryon,* 739 P.2d 623 (Utah 1987).

168. *Romer v. Evans*, 517 U.S. 620, 644 (1996) (Scalia, J., dissenting) (using criminalization of polygamy to justify Colorado's Amendment 2, which deprived gay people in Colorado of the right to seek legal protection from discrimination). *See* Chambers, *Polygamy, supra* note 158, at 53–60, 77–81.

169. Chambers, *Legalization of the Family, supra* note 162.

170. Clark, *supra* note 127, at § 2.4.

171. *See, e.g., Reep v. Comm'r of Dep't of Employment & Training*, 593 N.E. 2d 1297 (Mass. 1992).

172. *E.N.O. v. L.M.M.*, 711 N.E. 2d 886 (Mass. 1999).

173. *What Is a Relationship LLC?* at http://www.relationshipllc.com/main.htm (1999) ("Now there is a new way to tie the knot. . . . 'LLCs' may prove to be the new marriage model. . . . LLCs are available to everyone, couples . . . a single parent family and groups of friends.").

174. Hamilton, *supra* note 109, at § 6.1, p. 123.

175. Unif. Premarital Agreement Act, 9B U.L.A. 369 (1987).

176. Ribstein, *supra* note 74, at 286–309.

177. *Id.* at 288; Hamilton, *supra* note 109, at § 6.6, p. 126.

178. Ribstein, *supra* note 74, at 289.

179. Hamilton, *supra* note 109, at 133 ("[LLC] statutes make the period of existence of LLCs a matter for determination by the individual LLC. Many of the earlier statutes, however, provided an outside term of 30 years. Some statutes provide for 'perpetual' existence, as in modern corporation statutes.").

180. Ribstein, *supra* note 74, at 308–9.

181. *See id.* at 289.

182. *Id.* at 304. Close corporations, however, do not separate ownership and control. In this sense, LLCs are similar to close corporations.

183. Hamilton, *supra* note 109, at § 6.3, p. 128.

184. *Id.* at § 6.3, p. 129 ("An LLC, in short, is, or may elect to become, quite 'partnership-like' without sacrificing the benefits of limited liability.").

185. *Id.* at § 6.10, p. 137.

186. Ribstein, *supra* note 74, at 313, 316.

187. *Id.* at 313.

188. *Id.* at 316–17.

189. 607 N.W. 2d 151 (Minn. Ct. App. 2000).

190. *Id.* at 157.

191. Chambers, *Polygamy, supra* note 158, at 74; Cloud, *supra* note 159, at 90.

192. For a discussion of importing business law to better understand domestic relations law, see Carol Weisbrod, *The Way We Live Now: A Discussion of Contracts and Family Arrangements*, Utah L. Rev. 777 (1994).

193. For instance, couples in legally recognized relationships generally earn higher incomes than those in legally marginalized relationships. *See Statistical Abstract, supra* note 81, at 479.

CONTRIBUTORS

Regina Austin, William A. Schnader Professor of Law, University of Pennsylvania

Margaret F. Brinig, William G. Hammond Distinguished Professor of Law, University of Iowa

Neil H. Buchanan, Assistant Professor of Law, Rutgers University–Newark

June Carbone, Professor of Law, Santa Clara University

Terence Dougherty, Patterson, Belknap, Webb & Tyler LLP, New York

Paula England, Professor of Sociology, Stanford University

Martha M. Ertman, Professor of Law, University of Utah College of Law

Ann Laquer Estin, Professor of Law, University of Iowa

Martha Albertson Fineman, Director of the Feminism and Legal Theory Project and Robert W. Woodruff Professor of Law, Emory University

Laura T. Kessler, Associate Professor of Law, University of Utah

Douglas A. Kysar, Associate Professor of Law, Cornell University

Risa L. Lieberwitz, Associate Professor of Labor Law, School of Industrial and Labor Relations, Cornell University

Elizabeth Mayes, independent scholar

Linda C. McClain, Rivkin Radler Distinguished Professor of Law, Hofstra University

Deirdre McCloskey, UIC Distinguished Professor of Economics, History, English and Communication, University of Illinois at Chicago and Tinbergen Visiting Professor of Philosophy, Economics, and Art and Cultural Studies, Erasmus University of Rotterdam

Martha T. McCluskey, Professor of Law, State University of New York at Buffalo

Katharine B. Silbaugh, Professor of Law and Associate Dean for Academic Affairs, Boston University

Katherine V. W. Stone, Professor of Law, UCLA School of Law

Myra H. Strober, labor economist and Professor of Education, Stanford University

INDEX